EQUAL JUSTICE UNDER THE LAW: AN INTRODUCTION TO AMERICAN LAW AND THE LEGAL SYSTEM

THOMAS R. VAN DERVORT

Professor of Political Science

Middle Tennessee State University

WEST PUBLISHING COMPANY

Minneapolis/Saint Paul • New York • Los Angeles • San Francisco

Cover image:
Cecile Gray Bazelon
WINTERSET
1990, oil/canvas, 38" x 28"
West Art and the Law 1991
copyright 1991 West Publishing Corp.
Eagan, Minnesota

Copyeditor: Linda J. Ireland Falk
Cover and Text Design: Lois Stanfield, LightSource Images
Composition: Northwestern Printcrafters
Index: Pat Lewis
Production, Prepress, Printing and Binding by West Publishing Company

WEST'S COMMITMENT TO THE ENVIRONMENT

In 1906, West Publishing Company began recycling materials left over from the production of books. This began a tradition of efficient and responsible use of resources. Today, up to 95 percent of our legal books and 70 percent of our college and school texts are printed on recycled, acid-free stock. West also recycles nearly 22 million pounds of scrap paper annually—the equivalent of 181,717 trees. Since the 1960s, West has devised ways to capture and recycle waste inks, solvents, oils, and vapors created in the printing process. We also recycle plastics of all kinds, wood, glass, corrugated cardboard, and batteries, and have eliminated the use of styrofoam book packaging. We at West are proud of the longevity and the scope of our commitment to the environment.

Copyright © 1994 by West Publishing Company
610 Opperman Drive
Eagan, MN 55123

All rights reserved

Printed in the United States of America

01 00 99 98 97 96 95 94   8 7 6 5 4 3 2 1 0

Library of Congress Cataloging-in-Publication Data

Van Dervort, Thomas R.
   Equal justice under the law : an introduction to American law and the legal system / Thomas R. Van Dervort
     p. cm.
   Includes index.
   ISBN 0-314-02530-8 (hard : acid-free paper)
    1. Law—United States. 2. Justice, Administration of—United States. 3. Procedure (Law)—United States. I. Title.
KF385.V36   1994
349.73—dc20
[347.3]

93-30594
CIP

*This book is dedicated to my wife, Elsa;
my daughter, Nadine; and my son, Shawn.
My family's support and encouragement
has been invaluable to me.*

CONTENTS

About the Author   *xi*
Preface   *xiii*

PART ONE

GAINING FAMILIARITY WITH BASIC LEGAL CONCEPTS

Chapter 1   The Basic Meaning and Importance of Law in Society   **3**

Fundamental Purposes and Functions of Law   3
What Is Law? • *The Function of Law* • *The Rule of Law* • *Law and Politics* • *Methods of Changing the Law*
Pre-Historical Developments   8
Western Legal Traditions   8
The Roman Legal Heritage • *The English Legal Heritage* • *United States Constitutional Developments*
Chapter Summary   25
Key Terms   26
Discussion Questions   27
Sources and Suggested Reading   27

Chapter 2   The Expanding Legal Professions   **29**

The Litigious Society   30
The Citizen and the Law   30
Cultural Factors • *Social Responsibility* • *Law-related Education*
The Law Enforcement Officer and Public Administrator   33
State Agencies • *Federal Agencies*
The Paralegal and Law Office Manager   34
Paralegal Training and Education • *Paralegals in Other Countries*
Lawyers and Judges   36
The Demand for Lawyers • *Judges*
Ethical Standards in Law-Related Professions   42

Ethical Standards for Judges • Ethical Standards for Lawyers • Ethical Standards for Law Enforcement Officers

Chapter Summary	45
Key Terms	47
Discussion Questions	47
Sources and Suggested Reading	47

Chapter 3 Judicial Process and Legal Reasoning — 49

The Dual Hierarchies of Our Court Systems — 50
The State Court Systems • The Federal Court System
An Introduction to Legal Reasoning — 56
Different Forms of Legal Reasoning • The Case Method of Legal Training
Basic Forms of Law — 67
The Hierarchy of Laws • Equity • Substantive and Procedural Law
Introduction to Procedural Due Process — 69
Due Process of Law
Chapter Summary — 71
Key Terms — 72
Discussion Questions — 73
Sources and Suggested Reading — 73

PART TWO

UNDERSTANDING CIVIL LAW PROCEDURE

Chapter 4 Initiating Legal Process in an Illustrative Civil Case — 77

Finding a Lawyer — 78
Types of Civil Legal Action — 80
Equity in Practice • Money Damages • Workers' Compensation • General Elements of Tort and Contract Law
Preliminary Investigation — 82
A Contractual Agreement
Legal Research — 85
Federal Jurisdiction • State Jurisdiction • Choice of Law and Court
Request to Settle Out of Court — 90
Defense Considerations
Chapter Summary — 92
Key Terms — 93
Discussion Questions — 93
Sources and Suggested Reading — 94

Chapter 5 Pretrial Process in Civil Cases — 95

The Pleadings — 95
The Complaint • Service of Process • Defendant's Response • The Answer
Discovery — 104
Interrogatories • Depositions • Production of Documents

	Pretrial Conferences	110
	Attorneys' Conference • Judge's Conference	
	Chapter Summary	113
	Key Terms	114
	Discussion Questions	115
	Sources and Suggested Reading	115

Chapter 6 Trial: Argument and Adjudication — 117

The Jury Selection Process — 117
Voir Dire Challenges
Trial Arguments — 120
Preliminary Jury Instructions • Opening Statements • Examination of Witnesses • Closing Arguments • Judge's Charge to the Jury
The Verdict and Judgment of the Court — 145
Chapter Summary — 145
Key Terms — 147
Discussion Questions — 147
Sources and Suggested Reading — 147

Chapter 7 Evaluation of the Civil Process — 149

The Appeals Process — 150
The Right of Appeal • Appeals Court Actions • An Actual Case of Appeal • Ending Civil Legal Actions
Problems of Civil Litigation — 159
The Major Issues • The Case Load Problem • The Liability Problem • Tort Differences in Other Countries • German Civil Procedures
Chapter Summary — 171
Key Terms — 172
Discussion Questions — 172
Sources and Suggested Reading — 173

Chapter 8 Legal Research: Dimensions of the Law — 175

How to Use State and Federal Annotated Codes — 176
State Annotated Codes • Federal Codes • Administrative Codes
How to Find the Common Law — 186
Secondary Sources • Primary Sources • Reporters • Digests
How to "Shepardize" (Update) Particular Cases — 192
Other Resources — 196
Chapter Summary — 199
Key Terms — 200
Common Abbreviations — 200
Sources and Suggested Reading — 200

PART THREE

UNDERSTANDING CRIMINAL LEGAL PROCEDURES

Chapter 9	**Introduction to Criminal Legal Process**	**203**
	Initial Investigation and Arrest	204
	Basic Criminal Concepts	206
	Crimes	
	Criminal Due Process	208
	The Fourteenth Amendment • Basic Court Decisions	
	The Pretrial Process	214
	Arrest • Initial Appearance • Preliminary Hearing	
	Chapter Summary	228
	Key Terms	229
	Discussion Questions	229
	Sources and Suggested Reading	230
Chapter 10	**Pretrial Process in Criminal Cases**	**231**
	The Prosecutor	231
	The Grand Jury Function	234
	Right to a Speedy Trial	237
	Defense Considerations	239
	Sentencing Alternatives • Plea Bargaining Illustrated	
	The Arraignment	246
	Plea Alternatives	
	Sentencing	248
	Chapter Summary	249
	Key Terms	249
	Discussion Questions	250
	Sources and Suggested Reading	251
Chapter 11	**A Murder Trial**	**253**
	Defense Investigation	254
	Prosecutor's Decision	255
	The Death Penalty	256
	Criminal Discovery Process	258
	The Murder Indictment	
	Pretrial Planning	259
	Defense Strategy • Prosecution Strategy	
	The Trial	261
	Bifurcated Trial Procedure • Criminal Voir Dire • Opponents' Opening Statements • Prosecutor's Case in Chief • Defense Case in Chief • Closing Arguments • Judge's Charge to the Jury • Verdict and Sentencing	
	Chapter Summary	279
	Key Terms	280
	Discussion Questions	280
	Sources and Suggested Reading	281

Chapter 12 Evaluating The Criminal Process — 283
    Appellate Review in Criminal Cases — 283
    Plea Bargaining Issues — 284
    Arguments Against Plea Bargaining • Arguments for Plea Bargaining • Constitutional Issues
    Prison Conditions and Overcrowding — 292
    Prisoners' Rights • Community-Based Programs • Juvenile Justice Systems
    Criminal Procedures in Other Countries — 296
    Plea Bargaining Differences • Victims' Rights • Comparison of German and American Procedures
    Chapter Summary — 301
    Key Terms — 303
    Discussion Questions — 303
    Sources and Suggested Reading — 303

Chapter 13 Understanding Administrative Due Process — 305
    State and Federal Regulatory Agencies — 306
    Federal Regulation • State Regulation • The Rule-making Function • The Investigative Function • The Adjudicative Function • Judicial Review
    Other Specialized Courts — 317
    Administrative Procedure in Other Countries — 318
    The Scandinavian Ombudsman • French and German Administrative Courts
    Chapter Summary — 322
    Key Terms — 324
    Discussion Questions — 324
    Sources and Suggested Reading — 324

Conclusion — 327

Appendixes A: The Constitution of the United States of America — 329
    B: Illustrative Cases in Law — 339
    C: Witness Statements — 355

    Glossary of Key Terms — 365

    Index — 379

ABOUT THE AUTHOR

The author of this textbook is a professor of political science at Middle Tennessee State University where he has taught courses in law and the legal system for the past ten years. He holds a doctorate degree from the University of Tennessee and has a background in international law. The author obtained a masters degree from the Fletcher School of International Law and Diplomacy as a Woodrow Wilson Scholar, and he studied at the University of Cologne in West Germany as a Fulbright Scholar. He maintains regular contact with German scholars and academicians. The author has achieved a broad grasp of the relationship between law and society through a varied teaching career that began with teaching international relations and has also included courses in comparative government, American government, state and local government, and research methods.

The author, who has a long-standing interest in law-related education, serves as a member of the board of directors of the American Mock Trial Association and as chair of the Tennessee Political Science Association's Committee on Education. He also has served in state government as research director for the Tennessee Advisory Commission on Intergovernmental Relations.

PREFACE

This textbook is designed for students at all levels who seek an introduction to American law and judicial processes. Our law is complex and not easily understood by the average person; however, modern society increasingly demands greater knowledge of the law and how its functions affect individuals and society as a whole.

My experience as a professional educator with more than thirty years of interaction with students in both graduate and undergraduate courses has demonstrated the need for an introductory text to help students understand the origins of basic legal concepts, sources of the law, and fundamental procedures of the law. A firm foundation in the language of the law is necessary to the development of citizen competence and professional education in the areas of teaching, law enforcement, paralegal studies, and the practice of law.

Why This Book Is Needed

Law is the central function of the political system, and every informed citizen needs to understand its basic principles. For the average American citizen, however, law is a mystery that can be understood only by the trained legal professional. Law-related education, sponsored by the American Bar Association, is beginning to take hold in some communities, aided by the acitivities associated with the two hundredth anniversary of the United States Constitution, but for the most part, fundamental understanding of the American legal system is not widespread, even among teachers of social studies classes.

This introduction to the basic concepts of the American legal system is designed to provide the conceptual tools needed to prepare individuals for their roles as citizens, teachers, law enforcement agents, government employees, paralegals, future lawyers, and judges. An introductory text cannot provide specialized training in the legal professions but can provide the basis for further study in more specialized courses.

Traditionally, American undergraduate education programs have provided no clearly defined departmental locus for the student interested in the study of law. The increase in general interest in the study of law and the enormous expansion of educational programs to train legal assistants (paralegals), however, have caused an expansion of undergraduate offerings in law courses. Law courses are now taught in various uncoordinated fields such as criminal justice, sociology, political science, business, journalism, and education departments.

Although it is important to study law from these various perspectives, a holistic approach to a fundamental understanding of law and its function in society is essential to the development of an educated citizen and to the systematic education of legal professionals.

This introduction attempts to transcend the narrow disciplinary approach to the study of law. It provides the beginning student with an overview of the field of law and promotes general understanding of the law. It is hoped that this introduction will stimulate students to pursue higher education goals related to the expanding legal professions.

General Features

This textbook provides basic instruction in how to read and understand case law; do legal research; and understand fundamental civil, criminal, and administrative legal procedures. The text is designed to prepare students who are considering careers in law-related fields for advanced courses in more specialized fields such as business law, media law, education law, torts, criminal evidence, or constitutional law.

The text is divided into three parts and thirteen chapters plus a conclusion to facilitate planning for the typical semester course of fourteen weeks. It is designed for sophomore-level students and can be taught in several areas of discipline. Substantive law material is illustrated throughout the text, and Chapter Eight provides a general summary of the sources that contain our substantive and procedural laws.

Methodology

The methodology employed in this introduction is eclectic, utilizing a variety of approaches to stimulate student involvement and understanding. The book focuses upon the most fundamental concepts of law and demonstrates how legal terms and concepts are used in practice. Such terms as natural law, common law, and federalism are especially difficult for beginning students to understand and require some historical background in order to be fully comprehended.

Illustrative case opinions from various jurisdictions are used to demonstrate the ways in which modern judges use the fundamental concepts of law to decide specific disputes. Legal reasoning and practical decision making are emphasized to stimulate the student's analytical skills. Students need considerable assistance in applying what has been introduced in the abstract.

Special Features

A major purpose of this textbook is to promote clear understanding of basic terms and concepts as they are used in law. Such terms and concepts, therefore, are defined in the margins, and an extensive glossary of expanded definitions is included at the end of the book. These aids, along with chapter summaries, discussion questions, and suggested readings, provide useful review mechanisms for students who will be required to become familiar with hundreds of terms that are new to them.

The principal focus of this introduction to law is on the procedures of the American legal system. Federal and state jurisdictional procedures are illustrated, and the interaction between the dual hierarchies of state and federal courts is demonstrated. Law is not a static set of rules but is a dynamic process of continuous adjustment to changing circumstances and conditions. The spirit of the law, therefore, is emphasized, and the central functions of law in society are explained. Comparative analysis of the differences in decision-making approaches between the adversarial system characteristic of the United States and the non-adversarial systems of civil law countries is used where contrast is needed.

Chapter Eight provides a basic introduction to legal research that exposes the beginning student to the extensive sources of the law as practiced in various jurisdictions. The chapter illustrates the use of statutory codes, digests, reporters, and case updating services so the student can learn how to find detailed provisions of the law.

A particularly important feature of this textbook is the use of an expanded case study approach to explain the more detailed terms and concepts associated with civil, criminal, and administrative due process. Basic terms and concepts are explained in Part I, a single civil legal action is followed through the chapters in Part II to help the student develop an understanding of civil procedure, and a criminal legal action is followed through most of the chapters in Part III to explain the stages of criminal procedure. The administrative law process is explained in Chapter Thirteen, which also provides examples of the application of fundamental administrative procedures.

ACKNOWLEDGMENTS

The author is indebted to many individuals who contributed to the development of this textbook. I must first of all thank my students who have taught me much over the years about the kind of educational marerials that would best meet their needs and assist them in achieving their goals. I am expecially indebted to Dr. John R. Vile, chair of the Department of Political Science at Middle Tennessee State University, who encouraged me to undertake this project. He graciously read and commented on all the chapters and provided helpful suggestions and corrections.

Federal District Judge Thomas A. Wiseman also read a substantial portion of the original manuscript and made important contributions to my understanding of specific procedural matters of practical importance in the administration of the law. Administrative Law Judge David Torbett of the United States Department of Interior reviewed the chapter on administrative procedure and made helpful suggestions that improved my understanding of administrative law. My son-in-law, Jeffrey G. Jones, a practicing attorney in Cookeville, Tennessee, provided additional valuable insight into the practice of law.

To Middle Tennessee State University, and the Dean of Liberal Arts, Dr. John McDaniel, I wish to acknowledge the assistance given to me in the preparation of this manuscript. The university's noninstructional assignment program allowed me to devote my full efforts to this project during the spring of 1992. Without this noninstructional assignment, it would not have been possible for me to complete this task.

I also wish to thank Professor Herman Avenarius of the German Institute for International Educational Research, located in Frankfurt am Main, Germany, for his assistance in reviewing those aspects of the manuscript dealing with the German legal system. My friend Uwe Lauterbach, also of the German Institute for International Educational Research, rendered valuable assistance to me over the years by helping me understand the comparative differences between Germany and the United States.

My editor, Joan Gill, and her assistant, Becky Stovall, at West Publishing were extremely helpful in their support and guidance throughout this project. They were instrumental in finding an excellent group of reviewers who offered extensive comments on the original manuscript. These comments greatly enhanced the final version of the text, and I am deeply indebted to them for their helpful suggestions. The reviewers are Michael Connelly (Southwestern Oklahoma State University), Brenda Rice (Johnson County Community College, Kansas), Rebecca Parker (Arapahoe Community College, Colorado), Elizabeth Sullivan (Phillips Junior College, Alabama), Richard Goldman (Santa Barbara School of Law, California), Ray Canals (Bronx Community College, New York), Williard Overgaard (Boise State University, Indiana), Reggie Shehan (Michigan State University), Stephen B. Wall-Smith (University of Missouri—Lincoln), Ellen Van Valkenburgh (Jamestown Community College, New York), William McLauchlin (Purdue University), Doran Hunter (Mankato State University, Minnesota), George D. Schrader (Auburn University at Montgomery, Alabama), Jeffrey B. Robb (Texas Women's University—Denton), Dominic Latorraca (Arapahoe Community College, Colorado), and Chris Albright of Chattanooga State Technical Community College. Production editors, Debra A. Meyer and Stacy Lenzen, at West Publishing provided valuable assistance in smoothing out the final text and making this material more presentable to the reader.

Finally, I must take responsibility for the remaining errors in this text. I wish to invite any reader to communicate with me about errors or suggestions for future revisions of this introduction to American law.

Thomas R. Van Dervort
February 21, 1993

EQUAL JUSTICE UNDER THE LAW: AN INTRODUCTION TO AMERICAN LAW AND THE LEGAL SYSTEM

PART ONE

GAINING FAMILIARITY WITH BASIC LEGAL CONCEPTS

Part I of this textbook on American law and legal procedure defines the scope of this inquiry into the vast field of law by examining the basic meaning and importance of law in society. Historical background is given to explain how the basic concepts of American law have evolved from historical antecedents and to provide comparative analytical references.

In many respects, law involves the definition of rules in an authoritative way. The first three chapters deal with questions such as: "What is law?" "How is law distinguished from other rules in our society?" "What are the sources of law?" "What basic types of law exist and how are they distinguished from each other?" "What practical rules apply when different types of law are in conflict?" "Who decides these issues?"

Key terms and concepts that are fundamental to an understanding of American law are identified by boldface type in the body of the text, briefly explained in the margin, and defined more extensively in the Glossary at the end of the text. A review of the list of key terms at the end of each chapter will help the reader understand how they are used in American legal practice. The basic distinctions mentioned in the first three chapters are explored in greater depth in later chapters.

The first two chapters in Part I introduce some of the most fundamental concepts of law and demonstrate how they developed historically. Chapter Two deals with the importance of the study of law, provides an overview of the expanding legal professions in the United States, and explores the basic ethical and legal responsibilities of citizens and legal professionals, such as police officers, paralegals, lawyers, and judges.

Chapter Three introduces jurisdictional aspects of the state and federal court systems and explains how to read and understand case law opinions of the courts. Legal reasoning and case law interpretation are useful not only for the introduction to law, but also for advanced study in history, political science, and economics, and for specialized courses that prepare for advanced study of the law. The illustrative cases provided in the appendix show how the key terms and concepts are applied in practice by judges who deal with issues of law in dispute on a daily basis.

Parts II and III of this text explore, in greater depth, the procedures and practices used by legal professionals in regard to civil, criminal, and administrative legal actions.

CHAPTER ONE

THE BASIC MEANING AND IMPORTANCE OF LAW IN SOCIETY

> "[T]he Law is a magic mirror [wherein] we see reflected, not only our own lives, but the lives of all men that have been!"
> — Justice Oliver Wendell Holmes, Jr.
>
> "True law is right reason in agreement with nature."
> — Marcus Tullius Cicero
>
> "The end of law is not to abolish or restrain, but to preserve and enlarge freedom."
> — John Locke

Law is an essential element of civilized society. Wherever human beings have formed communities of more than passing existence, they have found that some set of *normative rules* of behavior are necessary to settle disputes without mortal combat. Even animals that have developed communal bonds observe relatively complex behavior patterns that order their social relationships.

The formalization of these rules of social behavior in human communities has been universally recognized as the essential attribute that marks the emergence of the great civilizations of ancient history. Modern secular law derives from these ancient origins, but its content is different in each society.

FUNDAMENTAL PURPOSES AND FUNCTIONS OF LAW

Many definitions of law in introductory textbooks create confusion for beginning students. Part of this confusion results from failure to distinguish the concept of jurisprudence from that of law. **Jurisprudence** refers to the philosophy of law, or to the basic principles of a particular school of thought about the origin, development, and application of the law. Learned jurists assert that jurisprudence, properly defined, is the science that ascertains the principles upon which legal rules are based and allows us to proceed by logical deduction to proper application of these rules in new or doubtful cases. Since different legal systems proceed from different assumptions, there are many schools of jurisprudence.

jurisprudence: philosophy or study of the law.

What Is Law?

The typical student, when asked to define law, is immediately drawn to the associations of the word *law* with "order," "social control," and "crime and punishment." These aspects of law occupy our immediate recall because they are the subjects of current debate and concern. The study of the subject of law must begin with a definition that is more precise; a basic definition of law should enable us to distinguish that which is law from that which is *not* law.

Law refers to rules (norms or standards) of behavior. But are all rules law? Is law merely a set of rules, or does it also include the process of making and applying the rules? What is the fundamental purpose of law? Is it order, power, justice, control, and punishment? Or is there a more fundamental reason for the existence of legal principles? Should the definition be concerned with what law *is*, or what it *ought* to be?

These questions have perplexed scholars for centuries, and answers depend upon one's particular point of view and area of focus. For practical purposes, law may be defined simply as *that set of rules and procedures recognized by governmental authority as obligatory (binding)*.

law: rules and procedures recognized by governmental authority as binding.

Government is properly defined today as the body that has the fundamental control function in society. Governmental agencies may define the law, but their function in doing so is to establish standards (norms) for dispute settlement. In this sense, law is a function of government, but not synonymous with government. Today it is widely accepted that even the government must follow the norms established by constitutional principles of law. The use of sanctions by governmental authority to bring about compliance often is considered essential to a definition of law. A law that is not enforced, however, because of either governmental neglect or judicial interpretation, may be revitalized through subsequent decisions and regain its legitimacy.

The Function of Law

Law provides standards for judging human behavior and thus promotes social stability and protection of basic human rights. Obedience to these standards depends on the degree of society's acceptance of their legitimacy and the perceived fairness of their application. Reliance on the use of force alone to compel compliance ultimately will fail.

The development of widely accepted norms of human conduct not only enables us to resolve conflicts peaceably but also prevents conflict from arising by structuring interactions and options in potentially conflicting situations so as to preclude consideration of conflicting alternatives. As society becomes more complex and interdependent, a greater variety of conflicting situations arise. Primitive societies, therefore, required less complex legal systems. Religious belief systems provided some of the earliest forms of values that could be used to achieve the degree of acceptance of legitimate norms needed to provide social stability. Today, all societies recognize the need for a set of rules and procedures to make human relationships tolerably stable and predictable, at least within broad limits.

These rules, recognized in modern societies as obligatory, were developed through the centuries in an evolutionary process that was heavily influenced by historical circumstance. Much of what is law in the United States today has its origin in Western Europe—particularly the concepts of law associated with the early Greek and Roman civilizations, and the more directly related British common law heritage. As Justice Oliver Wendell Holmes, Jr., once observed, "This abstraction called the Law is a magic mirror [wherein] we see reflected, not only our own lives, but the lives of all men that have been!"

The Rule of Law

The framers of the United States Constitution used language that many students find difficult to understand. James Madison, considered the intellectual father of the Constitution, frequently referred to the goal of the constitutional framers as that of producing a government characterized by the "rule of law," and not merely rule by persons in governmental authority. Students often question what is meant by the rule of law.

The **rule of law** refers to limitations upon governmental authority by reference to established legal principles. These legal principles are referred to as "due process of law," and they are expressly stated or implied in the United States Constitution. The framers of our Constitution did not rely upon the words of the Constitution alone to limit governmental authority. They used the principle of separation of powers to construct a political system that would protect the rule of law through competing institutions. Political ambition would be used to control ambition through the independent exercise of legislative, executive, and judicial authorities.

rule of law: limitations upon governmental authority by reference to established principles referred to as due process of law.

The idea of rule of law, a noble goal, is constantly challenged. Human beings are imperfect, and so is the law. Much of history consists of the struggle to determine who guards the guards. How can the law be made "ruler" when human beings make the law and enforce it? This textbook strives to answer that question, and it is this issue that makes the study of law and society so interesting and challenging.

The most extreme example of what happens when the rule of law breaks down is open warfare and social chaos. Thomas Hobbes (1588–1679) observed that life in the state of nature was "solitary, poor, nasty, brutish and short." The chaotic periods in the history of civilization have taught us that law is essential to our survival. Respect for law and orderly procedures for changing the law are essential elements in a stable society.

Law and Politics

Aristotle once defined human beings as "political animals." If humans were above politics, they would be called gods, and if they were beneath politics, they would be called animals. What distinguishes human beings from other animal forms, according to Aristotle, is their ability to make reasoned decisions through compromise and the weighing of conflicting interests. As human beings, therefore, judges are political animals.

In modern legal practice, **political questions** are defined as those issues that are clearly within the discretionary authority of the political institutions (legislative and executive branches). For example, if Congress has given the president authority to impose emergency price controls and the president acts within that constitutional authority, the courts will refuse to decide whether the president acted appropriately, since their intervention in the situation would involve an encroachment upon the executive or legislative authority. If the issue in-

political questions: those issues subject to discretionary authority of legislative or executive branches of government.

volved a constitutional question, however, the courts would be able to decide the issue because it would then become a legal question.

Judges apply the law and make distinctions concerning issues that are legal in nature and those involving the discretionary authority of legislative and executive institutions. However, some issues arguably mix the legal and political areas of authority and are highly controversial. Court decisions often are regarded as political in nature and criticized as such, but courts are the most limited of the governmental institutions in their ability to make political decisions.

Courts may be viewed as both legal and political institutions. Many political scientists insist that understanding the legal and political context within which courts operate is important in studying the role of courts within American society. Courts provide a forum for resolving disputes through the application of legal rules. However, they do not apply these rules in a vacuum, and are subject to nonlegal influences in exercising their discretionary authority. Courts also form a part of the political process involved in the formulation of the rules.

American courts are limited in the exercise of their creation of law function. In Medieval England, the source of our legal tradition, the courts were the center of the creation of law function. Today, however, the concept of separation of powers in government exists. But separation of powers is not absolute in any political system, and courts still exercise a significant area of discretionary authority.

The function of the courts is to apply the law in specific cases that come before them. In cases of conflict of laws, and where the law is vague, the courts must decide what the law is. In doing so, they exercise a limited political discretionary authority, but this authority is not the wholesale power to create law that is given to the other "political" branches. In general, the courts do not control their agendas, as do the other branches. Courts depend upon issues raised by the parties to disputes, and they do not have the discretion to refuse to deal with an issue. Once a lawsuit is filed, the courts cannot refuse to decide the legal issue, although they may refuse to hear the case altogether if they decide there is no legal basis, or jurisdiction, for the court to decide the issue. Political institutions often take advantage of the courts by refusing to deal with a significant issue, hoping to avoid controversy, and then criticize the courts when they make a "political" decision on the issue.

Courts differ from political institutions in their decision-making methodology. Courts are more insulated from popular pressure than political institutions and are supposed to make decisions on the basis of principle and clearly established law. In most cases, the courts do act as the "rule of law" would require. However, with regard to a small number of controversial issues, the established legal principles are unclear and the area of judicial discretion great. Here the courts may be said to exercise political powers, but the political institutions may override the decisions of the courts by enacting positive laws or constitutional changes that are clearly intended to supersede judicial authority.

Methods of Changing the Law

Total obedience to the law has never been an observable characteristic of the members of known societies. Indeed, one of the most important requirements of any law is that it be flexible enough to accommodate changing circumstances. The law is not a static set of rules and procedures; it involves a dynamic process by which rules are constantly being adapted and changed to fit the complex situations of a developing society. Although modern interdependent society is made possible in large part by the successful development of legal institutions that provide a measure of consistency and predictability to the settlement of disputes, the rapidly changing nature of modern society requires an equally flexible and dynamic legal system to preserve social stability.

Our society is undergoing the most rapid and profound changes that have ever been witnessed in human history. The technological revolution has profoundly affected all areas of society, including some of our most basic attitudes and values. The law is a stabilizing influence in this period of rapid change, but even the law must change to meet the needs of society. These twin needs for *consistency* and *flexibility* in law are the key elements in the maintenance of social stability and the successful functioning of the legal system. In the sections that follow, we will explore these two central themes in order to understand how those societies from which we have drawn our most significant ideas about law have attempted to cope with the dilemma these needs pose.

Natural Law

Ancient thinking about the law was greatly influenced by the idea that there must be an ideal source of law that could be discovered by humans through right reasoning and logical deduction. This idea was developed by the ancient Greek school of philosophy known as Stoicism, founded by Zeno of Citium in Athens during the third century B.C. The concept is known as **natural law** and can be traced through the contributions of great political thinkers such as Aristotle, Cicero (pre-Christian Rome), Justinian (post-Christian Rome), St. Thomas Aquinas (Middle Ages), Blackstone (England prior to the American Revolution), and Thomas Jefferson (American revolutionary period).

natural law: ideal law in conformity with nature.

The concept of natural law is certainly alive and vigorous today and continues to provide inspiration and motivation for all who seek justice and desire to change the law to bring it into conformity with principles of human value considered to be timeless and immutable. Martin Luther King, Jr., found that he would have to break the secular law to demonstrate its injustice and lack of conformity with the ancient principles of natural law.

Positive Law

Modern societies have developed legislative institutions to cope with the need for changing the law. Law that is enacted by these institutions is called **positive law**. These law-making institutions, however, are of fairly recent origin; most have existed for less than two hundred years. Prior to the existence of legislative, or positive, law-making bodies, political organizations had to cope with the dilemma of meeting the basic needs for consistency and flexibility in the law.

positive law: enacted by modern legislative authority.

These fundamental concepts of what law ought to be (natural law) and what law is (positive law) should occupy our interest throughout this introduction to basic legal concepts. We will emphasize what law is, rather than what law ought to be, because it is essential first to understand the basic rules and procedures that are recognized by governmental authority as legally binding and that citizens have a responsibility to obey. To the extent that what we learn conforms to our reasoned analysis of what law ought to be and do in society, we should support these principles. To the extent that we find these rules in conflict with our conception of what law ought to be, we should do our part to change what the law is to what we think it ought to be.

PRE-HISTORICAL DEVELOPMENTS

The law is an accumulation of diverse influences that have historically shaped the character of modern legal institutions and practices. Tribal customs and religious influences are the sources that predate the development of secular law and modern governmental authority. Tribal customs are extremely diverse and are the subject of anthropology of the law, which is beyond the scope of this introductory text.

Theocracies are forms of government in which a supernatural being is conceived to exercise direct law-making (sovereign) power or in which divine power is believed to be wielded through human intermediaries. These forms of government were more prevalent in ancient times than in recent history. Examples include the Oriental monarchies (Near East and Far East), the papal states, Calvinist Geneva, Puritan Massachusetts, and Mormon Utah.

The modern Jewish state of Israel and the Muslim countries of the Middle East still display many of the characteristic features of theocratic states, but even in these societies modern Western ideas of secular (nonreligious) principles of law tend to dominate commercial and criminal law. Many of the Muslim countries continue to use family and land law of local origin and even accept special religious courts that administer the law of distinct religious communities within the secular state.

Religious influences are observable in all political cultures today. The Judeo-Christian ethic is particularly strong in the United States. The working laws of most nations, however, are not considered sacred or as having the quality of divine intervention. The issue of state religion was bitterly contested in the religious wars of the Reformation period in Europe (sixteenth and seventeenth centuries). The secularization of the state has been dealt with in the First Amendment of the United States Constitution, which prohibits laws "respecting an establishment of religion, or prohibiting the free exercise thereof."

The recognition of freedom of individual thought and belief is fundamental in our modern legal systems but remains a continual source of unresolved conflict. The concept of natural law provides a unifying secular (or nonreligious) concept of ideal law that incorporates many of the universal ideas associated with the basic principles of the world's great religions.

WESTERN LEGAL TRADITIONS

Many of the principles in modern legal systems are of ancient origin. The prevalence of Latin terms indicates that these concepts date back to the contributions of the Roman secular law tradition. Many of our ideas about law originated with the ancient Greek philosophers, but the practical development of Roman jurisprudence provided the world with the "longest known history of any set of human institutions" (Maine 1861,18). The modern civil law countries of western Europe have a more direct link to the Roman law tradition than do common law countries, which were more influenced by English law development, but both owe much to the jurisprudence of ancient Greece and Rome.

In the past two hundred years Western legal concepts and institutional practices have spread throughout the world. Even Japan and China have recognized legal principles that clearly are of western European origin. In practice, however, all national legal systems show some degree of blending with ideas of native origin. In the following historical sections, we will trace the Roman legal heritage and its absorption of ancient Greek ideas. The Roman conquest of most of western Europe and areas surrounding the Mediterranean Sea in the period from about 450 B.C. to 565 A.D. produced an enduring legacy of legal jurisprudence that can be traced to the modern **civil law countries** of the world today. The English legal heritage, which emerged from the time of the Norman Conquest in A.D. 1066, is more directly related to modern American jurisprudence. The development of English common law is described in the section that follows. The **common law countries** of today owe their basic concepts of jurisprudence to this distinctive English legal heritage. The English assumptions about the origin, development, and logical extension of law are different from those found in the civil law tradition of continental Europe.

The historical sections that follow also describe the way in which the American legal system has incorporated ideas from both Roman and English legal heritage but added some unique contributions to the accumulation of legal concepts. These brief historical descriptions will help us gain an understanding of the origin of concepts that are fundamental to our legal system today.

civil law countries: continental European countries that trace their legal heritage to Roman law (*e.g.*, Italy, France, Spain, and Germany).

common law countries: those that trace their legal heritage primarily to English law (*e.g.*, United States).

civil law (or code law): refers to the Roman legal heritage that recognizes only statutory or written law.

common law: refers to the English legal heritage that accepts judicial decisions as a source of law.

The Roman Legal Heritage

The oldest known codification of written law is the Code of Hammurabi, king of Babylonia (1945–1902 B.C.). This code was an ancient form of detailed rules and regulations that attempted to provide the basis for settlement of all possible disputes. The Code of Hammurabi became known to the early Romans through their trade with the Phoenicians and influenced Roman thinking about law. This simple, fundamental idea of a universal code ultimately became the distinguishing feature of the Roman legal heritage. This idea also became the basis of the division of the two great influences on modern legal institutions—the Roman **civil law** and the English **common law**.

Early Roman Law

Roman jurisprudence descends from the Twelve Tables (circa 450 B.C.), which also was a written code. Although the content of Roman **code** law would undergo many subsequent revisions, the secular (nonreligious) character of the law and the use of a single document that attempted to provide the basis for settling all possible disputes were fundamental to the success of the Roman law. The major advantage of the code was simplicity and consistency.

code: written formulation of detailed rules and principles of law.

The early adoption by the Romans of the Twelve Tables was an attempt to simplify and clarify the law so that every Roman citizen could understand it. It was such a simple code that it could be inscribed on the walls outside the court for everyone to read and understand. (see Twelve Tables illustrated on next page)

The Roman city-state expanded into the Roman Empire with a series of conquests over the centuries that eventually encompassed much of the known world. Although many of the conquered territories of the Roman Empire found that this new legal order provided comparative advantage over more complicated and uncertain native legal systems, the Romans themselves began to realize that without elasticity of application, a formal code, rigidly interpreted, could not fully meet the needs of new circumstances and changing conditions. The Ro-

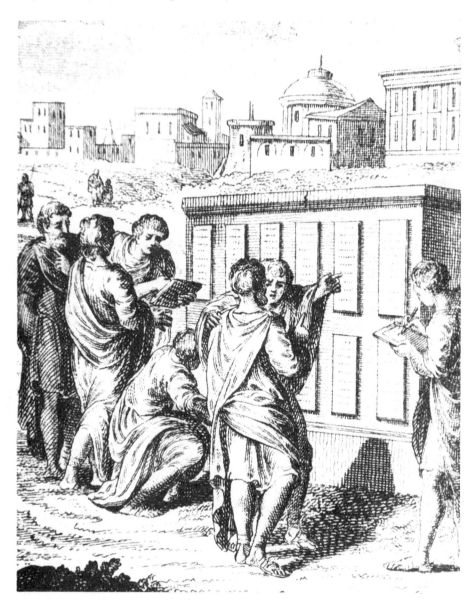

The Twelve Tables were the first codification of Roman law. They were posted in the Roman Forum in 449 B.C.

man College of Pontiffs provided the interpretive process that enabled the law to meet the changing needs of Roman society.

Absorption of Greek Ideas

Socrates, Plato, and Aristotle, along with a host of other Greek philosophers, are the source of many of our ideas about government, law, and politics. Plato was founder of the Academy, a center for the study of philosophy and the sciences, which flourished around the third century B.C. These philosophers' ideas were absorbed into Roman culture, particularly after the conquest of Greece and Macedon in 146 B.C. The expansion of the Roman Empire and its civilizing influence on most of western Europe and northern Africa brought these ideas into practice through the legal institutions developed by Roman authority.

After nearly a thousand years of Roman legal experience and development, the Emperor Justinian I (483–565 B.C.), in Constantinople, appointed a team of scholars to systematize Roman law. Excessive supplements in the form of commentaries and treatises written by legal scholars, known as juris consultants, had accumulated through the interpretive process. Justinian sought to restore the simplicity and consistency of Roman law by abolishing the authority of all but the greatest of the juris consultants of the classical period. The resulting *Corpus Juris Civilis*, or Code of Justinian, was promulgated (put into force) in 533 B.C., and the emperor forbade any further reference to the works of the juris consultants as well as any commentaries on the code itself (Merryman 1985,7).

The Influence of Natural Law

Marcus Tullius Cicero (106–43 B.C.) was one of the most famous of the juris consultants whose ideas were retained in the Justinian Code, and perhaps the most famous Roman lawyer and orator. Cicero was sent to Greece for his education at the Academy, where he was able to overcome a speech defect and absorb the philosophy of the classical Greeks. Cicero is best known for his expression of the idea of natural law. He maintained that "[t]rue law is right reason in agreement with nature," and since it comes from God, it is universal, unchanging, and ever-

A Roman hall of justice.

Cicero addresses a group of Romans

lasting. Attempts to alter it are futile and sinful. One who violates it is attempting to flee from oneself because the law is part of nature, and for this reason the violator will suffer the worst penalties even if he or she escapes what is commonly called punishment.

The Decline of the Roman Empire

The Roman Empire declined over a period of nearly five hundred years, and the Justinian code was one of its final legal achievements. The Justinian code preserved the experience of a thousand years of Roman legal development. The gradual decline of the Roman Empire left remnants of Roman legal principles that were later revived in various parts of continental Europe.

The medieval period, or "Dark Ages," was characterized by the loss of the unifying force of Roman law. The feudal systems that developed involved various bodies of tribal law, many of which relied upon custom and royal decrees. In the later medieval period, territorial states began to emerge, but the revival of Roman legal traditions occurred only after many centuries of feudal law development.

The law of the Anglo-Saxons (present-day England), the law of the Alemanni (present-day Switzerland), and that associated with the empire of Charles the Great (768–814) were examples of the medieval legal traditions. In Germany, the

Germanic tribes used rules of law that were developed in the course of legal practice and handed down primarily by word of mouth. These developments produced similar results in that the systems were based upon local customs and featured courts with lay assessors (or jurors). The use of judicial precedent and bodies of local common law were typical throughout Europe during this period. The revival of the Roman code law tradition did not take place until after the rise of modern nation-states.

The Roman Catholic Church was particularly influential throughout the medieval period, and feudal society included both secular and ecclesiastical law. The Church administered marriage and family law all over Europe and was the center of learning and preservation of knowledge of ancient Roman law.

The founding of the great universities of Italy and France in the twelfth and thirteenth centuries revived the study of Roman law, but the law survived only in the form of academic texts and commentaries rather than as a set of statutory enactments.

Revival of Roman Law in Continental Europe

As continental European nations began to emerge out of the feudal societies that characterized the Middle Ages, they began to restore the idea of a comprehensive code influenced by the Code of Justinian. In Spain, revival of a comprehensive legal code was associated with the rise of Spanish power. This civil code was extended to the Spanish colonies in the New World and initiated the code law tradition of colonial Louisiana, where it was further modified by French influence. This basic code remained in force in Texas until 1840, and in California until a decade later (Edmunds 1959).

The idea of the possibility of devising a universal code of comprehensive law discoverable by right reason and logic became a major element of the Enlightenment period in western Europe. This central idea became associated with natural law and ultimately became the basis for modern legal systems in civil law countries throughout the world. The Justinian civil code consisted of the Institutes, Code, Digest, and Novels, which were collectively titled *Corpus Juris Civilis*. This civil law, or code law, tradition is distinguished from the common law tradition of England and the canon law tradition of the Roman Catholic Church—hence, the term *civil law countries*. The term *civil law* is often confused with civil legal actions in the Anglo-American legal tradition, in which the same term refers to all noncriminal legal actions before the courts. Civil law countries, however, are those countries that follow the civil code of ancient Rome.

The Modern French Code

The French Revolution (1789) was the powerful political influence that was needed to restore the central ideas of the Roman civil code. The *Civil Code des Frances* was initiated by Napoleon (the consolidator of the French Empire) in 1807. Though hardly a democrat, Napoleon's ideas were influenced by the spirit of the French Revolution. He insisted that legislators focus on the realities of life rather than on the technicalities of law. The style of drafting he insisted upon was to be "transparently clear and comprehensible to a non-lawyer like himself" (Zweigert, Konrad, and Koetz 1987,195). The initial provision of the code prohibited judges from making any general rule of law (Edmunds 1959,181).

Although elements of flexibility have allowed these codes to be adjusted to changing economic and social conditions, the civil law systems of modern nation-states are principally direct descendants of Roman ideas. In civil law systems, statutory law is considered the one and only source of law to which all others are subordinate. Opinions of judges are considered merely evidence of what the law is, not a source of law. The function of the judges is to discover the applicable provisions of the code and to apply them to the specific facts of the cases before them (Murphy and Pritchett 1986; Damaska 1986).

The English Legal Heritage

The British Isles were barely touched by the far-flung Roman Empire, which established only outposts in that distant land. The influences of Roman law took an indirect route to England through the accumulation of foreign influences beginning with the French (Norman) conquest in 1066. Prior to the Norman Conquest, there was no "law of England." There were three general groups of traditional law: the law of the West Saxons, the law of the Mercians, and the law of the Danes (the Danelaw). Within and outside these larger groups, there were innumerable local customs as well as privileged boroughs and crafts, all of which had their own law and courts.

The Norman Influence

The French invaders, led by William (the Conqueror) in 1066, gradually began to fashion the variety of local customs of England into a single body of general principles. This process began in 1086 when William sent commissioners throughout the realm to make a record of the names of towns and numbers of persons, cattle, and houses as well as the customs and norms of the population. The Norman Conquest made French the language of the royal household and the royal courts. Anglo-French, or "law French," was used in pleading before the emergent courts. Lawyers of the period had to become multilingual, since they were required to draft all formal records in Latin, the language employed in the Middle Ages for formal written records. Anglo-French was a dialect from which the English legal profession first developed a precise vocabulary for the expression of legal concepts. Words such as *tort*, *plaintiff*, and *defendant* are of French origin (Hogue 1966,7).

Judge-made law

judicial precedent: judicial decisions regarded as controlling in future cases.

stare decisis: the doctrine of following judicial precedent.

In the early Anglo-French courts, judges placed great reliance on previous judgments given in similar cases. This practice gave rise to the doctrine of following **judicial precedent** that is now known as the doctrine of **stare decisis** (stand by the previous decision). Even under powerful and vigorous kings like Henry I (1100–1135) and his grandson Henry II (1154–1189), feudal courts of traditional origin continued to exist, although they were subordinate to the king's justice in several ways. At first the king's justice focused upon taxes through the royal courts of the Exchequer. The extent of royal jurisdiction later increased through the growth of royal manors (estates) and the interventions of a peculiar legal institution known as the *curia*, or later as the *Curia Regis*. Henry I appointed this group of judges to ride circuit throughout the realm and do the king's justice.

Chapter One The Basic Meaning and Importance of Law in Society

The Norman "trial by battle" was used as a method for settling disputes between feudal lords.

The king's justice was based on the concept of the "king's peace," which was a limited jurisdiction that related to the protection the king offered directly to his immediate vassals as well as to all persons found in places where his jurisdiction was paramount, such as the king's highway and the seacoast. The king's peace could also be invoked by persons who failed to get justice in the feudal courts to which they belonged. This interference with the local forms of justice eventually led to bitter struggles between the crown and the great feudal lords. However, the king's justices sitting in the *curia* were controlled by no definite body of customary law, as the other courts were. They were merely directed to decide *secundum acquitatem*, that is, by general consideration of fairness and equity.

Early Methods of Dispute Settlement

Several interesting methods of decision making were used during this early period of court evolution. One of these methods was the Norman "trial by battle," a procedure used in the royal courts for some purposes for a considerable period after the Norman Conquest. Trial by "ordeal" was also used during this early period of common law development. The use of inquest-juries was the beginning of the modern jury method of deciding questions of fact at trial. In these jury proceedings, the lay jurors were actually witnesses and were called upon to establish the facts in the case before the court. Gradually, by the end of the thirteenth century, the inquest-juries (witness juries) were converted to a disinterested body of laypersons who were to draw their own conclusions based solely on testimony provided by witnesses.

Limiting the Monarchy

Henry II aggressively asserted his authority but never thought of himself as an absolute monarch, or even as being outside the feudal framework. The Great Council of the Realm was an early consultative body. It consisted of the tenants-in-chief of the king, especially the great barons and magnates of the feudal estates. This council was the early forerunner of the British Parliament. Early statutory instruments called "assizes" appeared gradually beginning in 1166 and 1176 (the assizes of Clarendon and Northampton). In these documents, the royal authority gave new protection to the king's subjects by clarifying what was an early form of penal law.

The Emergence of the Common Law of England

Gradually a body of law began to emerge from these historical developments. The mounting numbers of writs (or cases) made it possible to collect them into a "law book." The first of these collections was made in 1227. Toward the middle of the thirteenth century, Henry Bracton prepared a huge treatise on the law as administered by writs in the king's curia, which Bracton embellished with large amounts of rather irrelevant Roman law.

The struggle between feudal barons and the king was a characteristic feature of the period and may be considered the basic reality of the evolving nation-state, later to become known as Great Britain. The Magna Charta, signed in 1215, was produced out of the barons' dissatisfaction with the king. Its most important accomplishment was to establish that the king must obey the law, because it is the law that makes him king. Later documents, culminating in the Great Charter of 1225, resulted in the codification of feudal rights, chiefly the rights of great vassals against the king. The charter was, however, deliberately drafted in general terms, and its most famous section included every free person.

By 1297 the law of the king's courts had acquired the special name of "common law." This body of law was now recognized by a literature and a professional group of pleaders. "Year Books" that recorded actual cases argued before the courts were produced, and a Court of Common Pleas had been added. By the end of the thirteenth century, the process of legislation had made great strides. General regulations intended to change or abrogate customary law and to be valid for the entire realm became recognized as statutes. Thus statutory authority to create positive law emerged along with the common law of the realm. During the fourteenth century, it became established that a statute, in order to be valid, needed the formal agreement of the Great Council of the Magistrates. The Latin term for this conference, *parliamentum*, ultimately gave rise to the name of the British legislative body known today as Parliament.

Even at the end of the fourteenth century, the common law was far from being the law of all England. The use of the king's courts increased rapidly, but the feudal courts retained a great deal of their importance. Ecclesiastical (church) courts maintained control over such matters as marriage and divorce and other family matters including the distribution of personal property upon death.

King John signs the Magna Charta.

The Origin of Equity and the Chancery Court

A new court developed out of the king's curia in the fifteenth century called the **Chancery Court**. The king's chancellor had been the closest adviser of the king and the head of the Curia Regis in his absence. During this period petitions to the king asking that justice be done—not as a matter of right (or law), but by grace to be extended to those who could not get justice in the other courts—began to multiply. The Chancery thus evolved into a real court with a procedure of its own. The language of this court of equity was English (not Latin or "law French"). Decisions of the court were called decrees (not judgments) and contained commands that were enforced through contempt charges.

The Chancery Court and the concept of **equity** (or use of principles of fairness) provided flexibility to the emerging system of law. The concept of equity is

Chancery Court: court of equity that may grant relief in the form of injunction or specific performance.

equity: remedy based upon principles of fairness as opposed to strict application of law.

still a significant part of Anglo-American jurisprudence. The four basic courts of the British legal system had now been established, and over the next three hundred years they grew and developed into a legal system that spread to the American colonies and beyond.

The English Bill of Rights

During the time of the Stuart monarchs, in the seventeenth century, English government went through a period of turmoil in which one king was beheaded and another abdicated. This turbulent period involved experiments in royal rule without Parliament and parliamentary rule without a monarch; both a civil war and a military dictatorship were involved.

Parliament's principal solution to this confusion was an invitation to William of Orange to succeed to the throne in 1689 and the enactments of the Bill of Rights in 1689 and of the Act of Settlement in 1701. The English Bill of Rights of 1689 was more like the American Declaration of Independence than the American Bill of Rights in that it spoke of "inalienable rights" and restoration of ancient rights rather than of legal innovation. The Crown was forbidden to suspend the laws, or to levy money without the approval of Parliament. The Act of Settlement of 1701 ensured that monarchs must bow to the rule of Parliament and established an independent judiciary that could not be dismissed by the Crown.

Understanding the Common Law

Thomas Littleton provided an early guide to the complex legal system in 1470. Edward Coke's *Institutes* in the sixteenth century replaced Littleton as a guide and became the major source for understanding English law for many generations. It was Sir William Blackstone, however, a lecturer in Oxford on the "Laws of England," who produced the most influential treatise on the common law called *Commentaries* and published in four volumes in 1756. For the first time, the common law was set forth in a classification that seemed to have a rational basis. Blackstone argued that there was a natural law character to the body of common law and asserted that any human law contrary to natural law had no validity (Abadinsky 1991,5).

Blackstone's treatise was enormously successful not only in England but also in the American colonies. The first book of *Commentaries* in particular, which set out the fundamental rights of individuals, provided American revolutionary publicists with many of their principal arguments.

The common law of England took root in the American colonies. After gaining independence, the individual colonies became nation-states in which their own brands of common law charted separate courses of development. One of the most significant attributes of the common law concept initiated in Great Britain is that it provides a method by which the body of the law (corpus juris) can be built upon and extended. A **case of first impression** (where no previous precedent exists) is decided by the judges, and this decision creates a new precedent that adds to the body of the law.

In England the common law lost many of the characteristics that made it different from the law of the continent during the nineteenth century. Procedural reforms in England culminated in the Judicature Act of 1873, in which the ancient common law forms of action were abolished and reduced to three types of pleadings, at most, and the courts were fused into one Supreme Court with three

case of first impression: a new set of facts never previously adjudicated that adds new precedent.

divisions: King's (Queen's) Bench, Chancery, and a court of probate and admiralty.

Common and civil law countries have grown more alike in recent years. From their separate developments, these divisions of modern legal systems have portrayed obvious advantages in terms of the inherent need for consistency (civil law) and flexibility (common law). Modern jurisprudence acknowledges the important contributions of both. In addition, both systems have moved to compensate for their deficiencies by borrowing from each other. Modern legislative authorities in common law countries, for example, have enacted statutory codifications of the law in various areas to clarify and simplify the law. Civil law countries increasingly have engaged in the drafting and publication of opinions by judicial authorities that serve as a guide to legal interpretation, although these decisions are considered not to be sources of law but rather evidence of what the law is. The recognition of judicial decisions as a source of law is not as vocally proclaimed in common law countries now as in the past, and there is considerable opposition to this practice among the public at large.

Major distinctions continue to exist in procedural and substantive matters of law between these divisions of modern jurisprudence. This introduction emphasizes American legal practices, but a comparative analysis of the contrast between the American *adversarial* system and the *inquisatorial* system of trial court procedure in contemporary civil law countries is presented later. One major distinction is the prevalence of the jury system in common law countries. Civil law countries use a group of judges and some laypersons in modern court proceedings, but there is no real parallel to the jury system, which has been elevated to constitutional status in the United States.

United States Constitutional Developments

Beginning in 1607–1620, British colonization in America came at a time when the common law of England was quite formal and strict—equity and the Chancery Court were still in their developmental stages. According to Roscoe Pound (1953), a great American jurist, the common law of that period was heavily laced with Latin and French legal language developed in the Middle Ages and was unfit for a wilderness society that stressed individualism.

Application of Common Law in the Colonial Period

During the early period of colonization, there was little opportunity for legal development. Some of the original colonies were corporations chartered by the Crown, called Charter Colonies (Massachusetts); others were termed Royal Colonies (Virginia); and in a third group, called Proprietary Colonies (Maryland), a single owner or corporation exercised control. These distinctions represented some initial differences that later became quite obscure. All the colonies ultimately looked to England for legal guidance.

Local ordinances and bylaws were developed that were of American origin, but they related more to survival in a harsh environment than anything that could be considered a body of law. Colonial law was subordinate to English law in much the same way that city and county ordinances are subordinate to state and federal law today. Colonial charters required legislation to conform to the common law, and those deemed contrary could be reversed by an appeal to the Privy Council in England.

In practice, this distant attachment to English law was of little importance because it was not clear which acts of Parliament and which court decisions were binding on the colonists. Groups of settlers brought with them an English legal heritage, but the colonies were established at different times in the evolution of British development. For example, Massachusetts and Georgia were founded one hundred years apart. The colonies also differed in geography, immigration, religion, and economic and political development. Many of the settlers were from different legal cultures of continental European countries.

These early colonies were characterized by a commercial center on the eastern seaboard of the American continent and a rugged hinterland of wilderness. The harsh conditions of the frontier fostered a sense of individualism and independence that led to the scrapping of important common law practices incompatible with life in these new agrarian communities. These conditions were radically different from those in England and required major changes in the law to enable the colonies to survive and develop. English law itself had developed great flexibility through a practical method of accumulating legal principles, and this pragmatic character of the law proved useful in the New World.

The incredibly complex land laws of England were ill suited to the needs of the colonies. Over the centuries land had become scarce in England, while in colonial America, there was a shortage of people, not land. In England there were few landowners. In the American colonies, nearly everyone could become a landowner. A shortage of labor supply in the colonies produced a relaxation of the harsh penalties that were characteristic of English justice.

Bradley Chapin (1983) notes that "in the colonies, the need for labor urged the use of penalties that might bring redemption." Colonial crimes against persons remained basically English law, but the law of crimes against property became increasingly indigenous in character. Penalties were adjusted to the scarce labor conditions of the colonies, and the death penalty (often given for property crimes in England) was practically eliminated and replaced with corrective methods such as branding, whipping, terms in the workhouse, and restitution.

In individual communities, such as New Amsterdam (first settled by the Dutch and later to become metropolitan New York City), the system of law had a civil law character because of its citizens' origins in continental European countries, in this case, Holland. The Puritans in New England and the Quakers in Pennsylvania sought to establish societies based on religious precepts. French communities also had their own identity during the early period of settlement. By the time of the American Revolution, however, the variations began to diminish and a distinctive American approach to law and justice began to emerge.

Distinctive American Legal Concepts

The American Revolution (1776–1780) and the development of the United States Constitution (1787–1789) brought pervasive changes that are still affecting America as well as the rest of the world. The Declaration of Independence was drafted by a committee headed by Thomas Jefferson and was the result of long-standing grievances between the colonies and the Crown. The United States Constitution was not the immediate result of the Revolution, but the culminating event in a process of change that lasted for more than a decade.

The Declaration of Independence essentially was an act of high treason against the British Crown that, under English law of the period, was punishable by death. The Continental Congress that ordered its drafting agonized over the decision for many months. Jefferson and his committee drew upon their collective knowledge of law and history to draft a document that purported to justify the Revolution and the act of treason against duly constituted authority.

The actual words of the document are a classic example of the natural law philosophy that originated in ancient Greece two thousand years earlier.

> *The Declaration of Independence*
>
> We hold these truths to be self-evident, that all men are created equal, that they are endowed by their Creator with certain unalienable Rights, that among these rights are Life, Liberty and the pursuit of Happiness—That to secure these Rights, Governments are instituted among Men, deriving their just Powers from the consent of the governed—That whenever any Form of Government becomes destructive of these ends, it is the Right of the People to alter or to abolish it, and to institute new Government, laying its foundation on such principles and organizing its powers in such form, as to them shall seem most likely to effect their Safety and Happiness. . . .
>
> (July 4, 1776)

Although these words did not convince the British authorities to relinquish their control over the American colonies, they illustrate the kind of spirit that, after four long and bitter years of war, ultimately resulted in the defeat of the most powerful military nation in the world at that time.

The Revolution was merely the beginning of a much longer struggle to devise a system of government that, in Jefferson's words (about the American colonies), would "effect their Safety and Happiness." The individual American colonies had fully developed hierarchical court systems that were served by a professional bar operating under rather sophisticated procedural rules. Colonial governments had established popularly elected Assemblies and had achieved considerable administrative authority and competence, independent of the mother country. In many areas, the Declaration of Independence had little immediate effect on government, although the war disrupted conditions throughout the eastern seaboard communities.

The legal effect of the Declaration, for the colonies, was to signal the creation of thirteen independent nation-states, each of which established constitutional conventions to draft fundamental legislation for the organization of their new governments. The popularly elected Assemblies appointed patriotic judges, who continued to conduct business using the only law they knew—English law, much of which was based on common law. Although British statutes were set aside, common law was respected. Blackstone had unintentionally provided much of the inspiration for the Revolution, and American courts of this period cited Blackstone frequently as authority for their decisions. The new American state constitutions generally weakened the governors' powers (a reaction against oppressive Crown-appointed predecessors) even though governors could now be elected by the citizens of the former colony.

Attempted Alteration of the Common Law

The support of the French government and Lafayette's army led to a brief flirtation with things French after the Revolution, and some even proposed basing the American legal system on that of the French codes. The complexity of reading and comprehending law books written in a foreign language proved prohibitive and the British common law prevailed, but not without the vigorous opposition of those who favored codification. "In general, the common law was favored by Federalists and later, Whigs, who were aligned with commercial and business interests. Codification was supported by Jacksonian Democrats" (Abadinsky 1991,45).

The tendency for power to gravitate toward the Assemblies during this revolutionary period led to abuses of authority and ineffective government; economic problems and debt foreclosures soon plagued the former colonial communities. Lawyers and courts became despised as tools of the monied interests. Trade with other nations was disrupted because of the inability of these new nation-states to fulfill their treaty obligations, and a general decay in the relations between the various states took the form of border disputes, internal tariffs, and lack of common currency.

The national government under the Articles of Confederation was inadequate to cope with these problems, and the Constitutional Convention of 1787 was convened in an attempt to find a solution. The document produced by the convention proposed a wholly new form of government, never before attempted. Its basic innovative feature was the concept of American federalism.

Federalism

sovereignty: ultimate, supreme authority to govern; having authority and responsibility to settle disputes and capacity to carry out obligations.

The concept of federalism grew out of the impasse at the convention over the principle of sovereignty. The concept of **sovereignty** was considered the essential element of the nation-state, which required some ultimate governing authority. European theorists had asserted that in order to have a nation-state, there must be some ultimate dispute-settling authority.

Under the Articles of Confederation, each state retained its sovereignty and independence. The states would have to be persuaded to give up this authority voluntarily in order to form a "more perfect union," which the framers of the Constitution concluded was the only solution to the host of problems that beset the former colonies. If the states would not give up sovereignty to the collective government totally, perhaps they could be persuaded to give up those elements of sovereignty that would give the national government functional powers that would be most effectively exercised in a collective manner (national defense, treaty power, interstate commerce, regulation of money, and so on).

federalism: constitutional division of authority between national and state governments.

The concept of **federalism** can best be described as "divided sovereignty." The states would retain their own court systems, including authority over the administration of justice, and a significant power collectively referred to today as the state police power. The federal government, soon to be located in Washington, D.C., would be given the authority to create a nationwide court system that would have jurisdiction over all disputes arising out of the federal Constitution, the laws passed by Congress, and all treaties. The compromise was truly an American invention—inspired, perhaps, by what Madison and Franklin had observed in the centuries-old tradition of the six-nation Iroquois Federation.

The "supremacy clause" in article VI of the United States Constitution provides:

> This Constitution, and the Laws of the United States which shall be made in Pursuance thereof; and all Treaties made, or which shall be made, under the Authority of the United States, shall be the supreme Law of the Land; and the Judges in every State shall be bound thereby, any Thing in the Constitution or Laws of any State to the Contrary notwithstanding.

Federalism thus provides for a dual system of national and state courts, judges, and laws, separated only by the constitutional and statutory principles of jurisdiction under which they operate. This concept in law is confusing and is the source of many conflicts and much misunderstanding.

During the ratification struggle that ensued, several of the states extracted promises, sometimes in the form of reservations, that a Bill of Rights would be added to the Constitution through the amending process as soon as the new government was established. This promise was kept in 1791, and the first ten amendments form the federal Bill of Rights, designed initially to protect individuals from a potentially abusive national government. The Bill of Rights is an example of a practical consequence of the idea of natural law. The provisions in the Bill of Rights prohibit the national government from invading a sphere of individual sovereignty. (Part III of this text deals more extensively with the Bill of Rights as it relates to criminal procedure.)

Thus sovereignty was divided into three basic spheres: a state sphere, a federal (or national) sphere, and a sphere reserved to the individual. The Constitution attempted to define and protect each of these separate spheres of authority.

Separation of Powers

The concept of separation of powers, with checks and balances, was central to the ideal of fostering the rule of law that gained universal acceptance among the framers of the Constitution. The framers were warned by John Adams (then ambassador to Great Britain) that an attempt to create a purely democratic form of government was doomed to failure and that such a government would end up destroying itself. James Madison argued, in *Federalist Number 10*, that the system of government proposed by the Constitution was actually a *republic*, rather than a *democracy*, because of the constitutional checks on, and limitations of, power that prohibited simple majority popular will from violating the principles of rule of law. The framers drew upon ideas of Greek and Roman legal philosophy, including Aristotle's concept of "mixed government," upon Roman experience, as well as upon the newer ideas of Montesquieu and John Locke.

Madison and the other framers of the Constitution argued that the proposed constitution would set up separate legislative, executive, and judicial institutions that would have balanced powers and authority in their separate functional spheres. "Ambition must be made to control ambition" in this new government characterized by separation of powers. If one branch got too far out of line, the independent powers of the others would be able to check abuses of power.

Alexander Hamilton, in *Federalist Number 78*, asserted that the judiciary would be given life tenure (good behavior) because it must have independence in this system of separation of powers. It would be given the power to negate violations of the other branches of government, he argued, because it was the "least dangerous branch" and would be adequately checked by the "power of the purse" given to Congress and the "power of the sword" given to the presidency (Vile 1967).

Judicial Review

Another unique American contribution to the development of legal concepts is not so obvious from the specific wording of the Constitution. The framers of the Constitution, however, knew that conflict would arise over these complex pro-

The Constitutional Convention

visions and devoted considerable thought to how such conflicts would be resolved. They clearly intended for the federal courts to have the power to nullify any state law or state constitutional provision that is contrary to the United States Constitution, but what would happen if the national Congress violates the provisions of the Constitution?

The words of the supremacy clause are reasonably clear on the subject, for the language prohibits state violations of the United States Constitution, and the words that qualify congressional acts "in pursuance" of the Constitution are clear enough. When the court used the power of judicial review for the first time against an act of Congress in 1803, however, the decision created considerable opposition.

Alexander Hamilton, one of the influential framers of the Constitution, clearly understood the framers' intent to provide the federal judicial system with authority to enforce the Constitution against all forms of governmental abuse, and he attempted to justify that authority during the ratification struggle.

judicial review: the power of the courts to hold acts of all governmental agencies nonenforceable when they are in conflict with the Constitution.

The power of **judicial review** is a logical extension of the traditional powers of the court to interpret the law (say what the law is); when the court finds laws in conflict with one another, the court is obliged to resolve the conflict. A more fundamental law takes precedence over a less fundamental law; hence, any act of governmental authority—legislative, executive, or judicial—can be rendered "null and void" and "nonenforceable" under this principle.

State and Federal Legal Institutions

Both the state courts and the federal courts continued the common law practices of their British heritage. Statutory enactment by legislative authority was used to eliminate those principles of common law found to be objectionable to independent American authorities. Each state now had its own common law that would be allowed to be extended by judicial decisions alone as long as these principles did not conflict with any higher form of law. The common law had progressed to a point where it was understood that statutory and constitutional interpretations in case law were not considered part of the common law proper, but the practice of writing opinions and later following them as precedents (stare decisis) now pervaded the entire system of laws and continued to provide extensive flexibility in the law.

The United States Constitution gives federal judges authority to decide all cases in **law and equity** arising out of the Constitution or laws of the United States, and Congress was given authority to extend that jurisdiction. More complicated questions of original and appellate jurisdiction are dealt with later, but these basic provisions led to the merging of principles of law and equity and did away with the need for a separate Chancery Court as had existed in England. Several state court systems have, in contrast, preserved the Chancery Court as a separate institution.

The Merger of Common and Code Law Traditions

The development of the United States Constitution was a monumental achievement that merged the principles of law characteristic of the two divisions of the world's legal systems into one system. The basic principles of the concept of natural law that motivated the civil law heritage were incorporated clearly in the federal Bill of Rights and in the Constitution itself, which is an instrument of simplicity and consistency. The common law heritage was retained but basically relegated to state law practice. The idea of case law development and flexible interpretation of statutory and constitutional law was a by-product of this grand merger of the two leading systems of modern law. It is perhaps this merger to which we owe the success and endurance of the American legal system over the two hundred years of its existence.

CHAPTER SUMMARY

1. Law is that set of rules and procedures recognized by governmental authority as legally binding which are used to resolve disputes between human beings and legal entities.

2. "Rule of law" refers to dispute settlement by reference to established legal principles. Decision making in conformity with "due process of law" requires specialization of governmental institutions and distinction between legal and political issues. "Political questions" are issues that are within the discretionary authority of the political branches of government as defined in law.

3. Social stability requires that successful legal systems provide both consistency and flexibility to meet the basic needs of the law, which are predictability and accommodation to change.

4. Our Roman and English legal heritage provide illustrations of two types of legal traditions that stressed either consistency (Roman civil law tradition) or flexibility (English common law tradition).

5. Roman jurisprudence was influenced by the ancient Greek notion of "natural law" and by the development of a written code of universal laws. This code law tradition was secular in nature and provided the major advantages of simplicity and consistency.

6. The Roman code law has been revised many times throughout its nearly two and one-half thousand years of existence, but each revision has attempted to return to the basic advantages of simplicity and consistency.

7. Modern civil law countries have maintained the ancient code law tradition in which written law in statutory form is the only source of law. Opinions of judges are considered merely evidence of what the law is, not a source of law.

8. The origin and development of English jurisprudence were different from those of Roman law. The Norman conquerors of England attempted to build a common body of legal rules and procedures in a diverse, uncoordinated feudal society by gradually creating judicial precedents in the king's courts that were later applied to like cases through the doctrine of "stare decisis."

9. The development of the common law of England provided a system for the building of law through judicial experience, which allowed great flexibility and creativity, enabling the law to accommodate changing circumstances.

10. The British common law tradition was transferred to the American colonies where it grew and developed over a period of nearly one hundred and fifty years before it was substantially altered by the Constitution of the United States.

11. The federal structure of the Constitution allowed the states freedom to continue the common law tradition but added a national legal system. The result is the existence of the fifty-one separate, distinct legal systems that operate simultaneously in the United States today.

12. The Constitution provides a rational system of order of authority for the many legal systems, but the complexity of its provisions leave considerable room for court interpretation. The common law ability to extend the law by judicial precedent now pervades the system and is applied to the interpretation of all forms of law, written and unwritten.

13. The power of judicial review obligates the courts in our legal system to uphold the Constitution against any violation by the legislative, executive, or judicial branches of government, and to preserve the supremacy of federal law.

KEY TERMS

jurisprudence	common law countries	Chancery Court
law	civil law (code law)	equity
rule of law	common law	case of first impression
political questions	code	sovereignty
positive law	judicial precedent	federalism
natural law	stare decisis	judicial review
civil law countries		

DISCUSSION QUESTIONS

1. How is law distinguished from other rules of behavior and moral conduct?
2. How is law distinguished from jurisprudence?
3. What is the basic function of law in society?
4. What is meant by the rule of law?
5. What are the basic methods of changing the law?
6. How do courts distinguish political questions from legal ones in deciding the basis for settlement of disputes?
7. How does legal procedure differ from decision-making procedures of political institutions?
8. What is meant by natural law?
9. What is meant by common law?
10. What are the major differences in the legal heritage of civil law countries and common law countries?
11. How does American law combine major features of the Roman and English legal traditions?
12. What are the unique American contributions to law and the development of legal institutions?

SOURCES AND SUGGESTED READING

Abadinsky, Howard. 1991. *Law and Justice: An Introduction to the American Legal System*. 2d ed. Chicago: Nelson-Hall Publishers.

Abraham, Henry J. 1986. *The Judicial Process*. 2d ed. New York: Oxford University Press.

Chapin, Bradley. 1983. *Criminal Justice in Colonial America: 1606–1660*. Athens: University of Georgia Press.

Damaska, Mirjan R. 1986. *The Faces of Justice and State Authority: A Comparative Approach to the Legal Process*. New Haven: Yale University Press.

Edmunds, Palmer D. 1959. *Law and Civilization*. Washington, D.C.: Public Affairs Press.

Hall, Kermit L. 1989. *The Magic Mirror: Law in American History*. New York: Oxford University Press.

Hart, H.L.A. 1961. *The Concept of Law*. Oxford: Clarendon Press.

Hogue, Arthur R. 1966. *Origins of the Common Law*. Bloomington: Indiana University Press.

Hyman, Harold M., and William M. Weicek. 1982. *Equal Justice Under Law: Constitutional Development 1835–1875*. New York: Harper & Row.

Kelsen, Hans. 1957. *What Is Justice?: Justice, Law, and Politics in the Mirror of Science*. Berkeley: University of California Press.

Maine, Henry S. 1961. *Ancient Law: Its Connection with the Early History of Society, and Its Relation to Modern Ideas*. New York: Cockcroft & Co.

Merryman, John H. 1985. *The Civil Law Tradition: An Introduction to the Legal Systems of Western Europe and Latin America*. 2d ed. Stanford: Stanford University Press.

Miller, Henry G. 1962. *The Legal Mind in America: From Independence to the Civil War*. Garden City, N.Y.: Anchor Press.

Murphy, Walter F., and C. Herman Pritchett. 1986. *Courts, Judges, and Politics*. New York: Random House.

Patterson, Edwin W. 1953. *Men and Ideas of the Law*. Brooklyn, N.Y.: Foundation Press.

Pound, Roscoe. 1942. *Social Control Through Law*. New Haven: Yale University Press.

———. 1953. *The Lawyer from Antiquity to Modern Times*. St. Paul: West Publishing Co.

Vile, John R. 1993. *A Companion to the United States Constitution and Its Amendments*. Westport, Conn.: Praeger Publishers.

Vile, M.J.C. 1967. *Constitutionalism and the Separation of Powers*. Oxford: Clarendon Press.

Zweigert, Konrad, and Hein Koetz. 1987. *Introduction to Comparative Law*. Vol. I, *The Framework*. Oxford: Oxford University Press.

CHAPTER TWO

THE EXPANDING LEGAL PROFESSIONS

> "Thousands of students just graduated all over the country in law. Going to take an awful lot of crime to support that bunch. A man naturally pulls for the business that brings him in his living. That's human nature, so look what a new gang we got to assist devilment. All trained to get a guilty man out on a technicality, and an innocent one in on their opposing lawyer's mistake."
>
> Will Rogers

After our brief introduction in the last chapter to the concept of law and how it developed, it is appropriate to address the question—why study law?

Many students become interested in law when they realize that law profoundly affects their daily lives and well-being. Some students are from broken families wrenched apart by divorce proceedings that they did not understand. Others have experienced civil litigation that has affected them or their families. Still others have had personal contact with the criminal justice system as juveniles. Many students become concerned about the legal system when they or their families or friends have been victims of crime.

This book cannot answer all the questions that arise from such experiences, but it can help put them into perspective and contribute to an understanding of how our system works, or fails to work, to perform the important functions of law in society. It is hoped that this understanding will lead to the realization that law does profoundly affect our daily lives and that we, as individual citizens, have important rights, duties, and responsibilities in a society governed by the rule of law.

The study of law has a more specific relevance for those considering careers in law-related professions. The general expansion of litigation in modern society and the societal concerns generated by the current crisis in law enforcement have created new opportunities for meaningful careers in law. Many students who have become interested in law for one reason or another are concerned about the job market for lawyers and wonder whether there is a need for more lawyers in a society that already has more lawyers than it has medical doctors.

A better understanding of the characteristic features of the American legal system may help to explain why there is a great need for legal professionals in our society. A brief summary of the characteristic trends in the litigious nature of modern society may serve to encourage those who are thinking about legal careers, but law-related careers are not confined to the traditional practice of law. Legal professionals include teachers, law enforcement officers, court and law firm managers, paralegals, lawyers, and judges.

THE LITIGIOUS SOCIETY

Various statistical sources indicate that our society may be the most litigious society in the world. More and more of our disputes are finding their way into the courts. Since 1960 there has been an astounding threefold increase in the filing of suits in state and federal trial courts. In 1991 more than 33 million new cases were filed in state courts. Each year there are more than 300,000 additional new cases filed in federal courts.

These figures were compiled by the National Center for State Courts, which has been attempting to provide statistics for court systems over the past fifteen years. The effort, however, suffers from lack of comparability and the difficulty of classification of litigious activity in the United States. The general trends and magnitude of litigious activity nonetheless are quite clear. The overwhelming majority of the 33 million court cases (which exclude minor traffic violations) were filed in state courts. About 57% of these cases were civil litigation, 38% were criminal cases, and 5% represent juvenile cases filed in the state courts. (National Center for State Courts 1991)

Professor Earl W. Johnson of UCLA's Law School asserts that "the United States is 25 percent more litigious than West Germany, and some 30 to 40 percent more so than Sweden." We may be only slightly more litigious, however, than the country of our legal heritage, England (Lieberman 1981,6).

Research by the American Bar Foundation reveals that "almost two-thirds of the adult population have consulted a lawyer at least once about a personal nonbusiness legal problem" (Zemans and Rosenbloom 1981,2). Uniform crime reporting statistics compiled by the Federal Bureau of Investigation indicate that reported crime has more than trebled in the three decades since 1960. Current figures indicate that one out of every six of us will be victims of crime this year. There is some indication, however, of a slowing in the general trend of doubling of litigation every ten years.

These figures are astounding evidence of the extent to which law has grown to affect our daily lives and sense of well-being in society. However, they do not reflect the enormous growth of governmental regulatory activity, bankruptcies, and administrative legal proceedings; nor do they include the enormous cost in terms of wasted lives and money (an annual estimated four to five hundred billion dollars) caused by illegal activity in this country.

THE CITIZEN AND THE LAW

The efficacy of any legal system depends in large part upon the willingness of citizens to obey the law. There can be no effective law enforcement without the cooperation and understanding of the overwhelming majority of the people in the society. Law enforcement cannot depend upon the threat of punishment alone as a deterrent to illegal activity. The ultimate answer to the problem must begin with citizen attitudes.

Most people obey the law because they believe it is the right thing to do; that is, it is consistent with what they believe to be just and fair. When this consistency is not present, they are more likely to violate the law, and in these situations threat of punishment may act as a deterrent. If the punishment is not credible (that is, not very likely to be carried out), the threat of punishment will not work as a deterrent. Likewise, lack of knowledge or understanding of the societal norms (laws) in question will produce ineffective results.

People begin to acquire a basic knowledge of right and wrong behavior in the home environment, where parents have an obligation to help their children understand and respect societal norms and behavioral expectations. Churches and other social groups add to this accumulation of moral values, as do peer groups and playmates, in what sociologists call the socialization process. Today, the educational system, the most universal socializing agent in modern society, shares a primary responsibility with parents to help children develop an understanding of law and the legal expectations required for individual behavior.

Cultural Factors

Our society demonstrates many deficiencies in regard to the general socialization process, and these deficiencies account for much of the breakdown in effective adherence to legal norms. Other societies are more effective primarily because they do a better job in the normative socialization process than we do. Japan and Germany, for example, have crime rates that are less than five percent of ours, and their cultures are noted for their heavy stress on rules and obedience to social norms. These societies also have the advantage of being culturally homogeneous nations.

The United States, on the other hand, is extremely heterogeneous—a "melting pot" of diverse races, cultures, and national origins. We stress liberty and individuality. Our heroes are often those who break the law. Even our most sacred expression of societal values in the Declaration of Independence is a philosophical justification for the ultimate act of legal disobedience—revolution against governmental authority. The state constitutions and the United States Constitution are attempts to reconcile this apparent dilemma by providing stable and reasonably orderly processes for changing the law to bring it into conformity with our beliefs of what is just and fair.

Social Responsibility

The society we have developed places heavy demands and responsibilities upon its citizens. The extent and complexity of these demands may mean they are too much to expect of the average citizen. We are expected to know and understand an increasingly complex set of laws emanating from fifty-one separate and independent law-making authorities and augmented by fifty-one different court systems. As adults, we are expected to keep track of as many as fifty different elected officials and to oversee their functions by intelligently exercising our right to vote. We are supposed to participate in the identification of community problems and to petition government for redress of grievances. We are called upon to serve on juries (both investigative grand juries and trial juries, called petit juries). And we have a legal obligation to report crimes and to be witnesses in trials involving matters of which we have personal knowledge. Above all, we have an obligation to obey the law.

This summary of the citizen's obligations under law makes it clear that our society needs competent teachers who can find ways to engage students in the important process of developing knowledge and skills that will improve the efficacy of our legal system. An introduction to American law and the legal process helps us gain a better understanding of the characteristic features of our legal system and contributes to our abilities to know what focus we need in our teaching careers. Knowing what to teach and how to teach are the particular skills of the teaching profession that cannot be dealt with effectively in an introductory course, but the following discussion may be of general interest.

Law-related Education

The widespread recognition of our deficiencies in law-related education has produced some notable developments that have been given additional emphasis through a nationwide effort to inform teachers and citizens about educational programs that work. The American Bar Association and other interested groups are promoting **law-related education** and have developed significant new curriculum materials that are being integrated into schools across the nation. Former Chief Justice Warren Burger resigned from his position as chief justice in part because of his commitment to educational reform. He became the Chair of the Commission on the Bicentennial of the United States Constitution, a celebration of a five-year period (from the drafting of the Constitution in 1787 to the ratification of the Bill of Rights in 1791) that has produced some exceptional teaching materials.

A study conducted with the support of the federal Office of Juvenile Justice and Delinquency Prevention has demonstrated that law-related education, when taught properly, results in a significant reduction in delinquent activities by students. This two-year study, which involved a comparison of control and experimental classes of senior high school students in six communities across the nation, has important implications concerning what the schools can do to help reduce delinquency and crime among youth.

The experimental classes in the study used curriculum materials developed by the Constitutional Rights Foundation, Law in a Free Society, and the National Street Law institute—organizations that have been instrumental in developing teaching materials and techniques for teachers in the general area of citizenship and law-related education. These techniques are designed to foster civic competence, responsibility, and commitment to the fundamental values of a free society. The methods do not attempt to impose a particular course or curriculum on the schools, and they do not attempt to teach people to become lawyers. They are designed for use in a variety of courses and at all levels of the educational process.

The findings of the study confirm the belief expressed by more than two thousand professionals surveyed in 1980 and 1981 that law-related education can improve the behavior of young persons and that the schools can teach moral development. In the 1960s this issue was thoroughly debated in the educational community where some contended that the schools could not teach moral education. The late Professor Lawrence Kohlberg of Harvard University devoted a lifetime of research to demonstrate how wrong we were to think that moral development cannot be taught. Although there are still skeptics, Professor Kohlberg made a major contribution to our understanding of moral development

law-related education: programs developed to promote integration of legal concepts into the K–12 curriculum.

and the educational processes necessary for achieving progressive moral development (Kohlberg 1987).

Teaching opportunities in higher education are expected to increase considerably in the next decade, since a great number of the professors employed in the expansion of the profession in the 1960s are reaching retirement age. The number of positions in law-related fields also is increasing; professorships in law and the related fields of political science, criminal justice, and business are expanding.

THE LAW ENFORCEMENT OFFICER AND PUBLIC ADMINISTRATOR

Because of increased recognition of the problems of law enforcement in today's society, careers in law enforcement have become an area of major growth in terms of employment opportunity. No longer is this profession confined to the traditional "cop on the beat." Increased specialization and professionalization of law enforcement has expanded the range of career opportunities to include some 1,400 job classifications. Many employees are now required to meet stringent entrance requirements and have college degrees.

Expanding opportunities for meaningful careers in law enforcement fields exist at the local, state, and national levels. These fields are the most racially and sexually integrated areas of employment today. The overwhelming majority of employees work at local levels in traditional patrol and traffic officer positions. Modernization of local law enforcement agencies has been extensive, and new standards are being imposed to require college degrees for law enforcement officers who must become involved in solving community problems, preventing crime, and reducing delinquent behavior. Many of these modern police officers are public relations and educational specialists. Detectives and criminal investigators are other positions of local specialization that offer challenging opportunities for young people with motivation to serve the public in one of the most essential, though often least appreciated, areas of service.

State Agencies

At the state level, the traditional highway patrol officer is generally more highly trained and more adequately rewarded than local officers. This agency is supported by highly trained and educated investigative bureaus (similar to the Federal Bureau of Investigation) that employ many career officers in law-related fields. The current crisis in corrections departments of state governments has resulted in a tremendous expansion of employment opportunities in this area. More than half of the states are under federal court orders to reform their correctional systems. State legislatures also are being forced to develop modern systematic procedures. The result of these efforts has been a great increase in the need for probation officers who can work closely with criminal judges to conduct background studies and sentencing recommendations as well as administer alternative sentencing programs.

Federal Agencies

Law enforcement opportunities at the federal level are also expanding tremendously, and many of the fields involved are generally unknown to the student thinking about career decisions. The Department of Justice employs some 72,000 persons throughout the world who perform many law enforcement functions as well as legal services to the government. The department also employs summer law interns and work-study students. The Office of Justice Programs coordinates five major bureaus that assist law enforcement programs across the country with statistical information and exemplary programs: the Office for Victims of Crime, the Bureau of Justice Assistance, the Bureau of Justice Statistics, the National Institute of Justice, and the Office of Juvenile Justice and Delinquency Prevention.

The Federal Bureau of Investigation has jurisdiction over two hundred types of cases, including white-collar crime, organized crime, foreign counterintelligence, public corruption, civil rights violations, terrorism, federal drug violations, kidnapping, bank robbery, and interstate criminal activity. The bureau works with other federal, state, and local law enforcement agencies to investigate matters of joint concern. Special agents, lawyers, accountants, language specialists, and computer specialists are growing areas of opportunity within the bureau.

Another area of employment opportunity is the Federal Bureau of Prisons. The Drug Enforcement Administration is one of the most rapidly expanding agencies actively seeking young people from a variety of college disciplines to help conduct the government's "war on drugs." The Immigration and Naturalization Service is both a law enforcement and service-oriented agency with responsibilities ranging from admitting, excluding, investigating, and deporting aliens to guiding and assisting them in gaining entry to the United States, receiving benefits, and becoming naturalized citizens.

Finally, there is the United States Marshal's Service, which is the nation's oldest federal law enforcement agency. This agency is responsible for protection of federal courts, judges, jurors, and witnesses; apprehension of federal fugitives; custody and transportation of federal prisoners; execution of court orders; custody, management, and sale of property seized from criminals; administration of the National Asset Seizure and Forfeiture Program; and operation of the Witness Security Program.

We do not have a national police force in the United States. Our federal system places the primary responsibility for law enforcement and maintenance of domestic order with the states and local communities. As the nation has grown more interdependent in modern times, the need for interagency cooperation in law enforcement has increased. Multiple and overlapping jurisdictions of local, state, and federal agencies often produce conflicts that impede effective law enforcement, but they also extend our system of checks and balances and ultimately produce pressure to resolve these conflicts.

THE PARALEGAL AND LAW OFFICE MANAGER

paralegal (or legal assistant): a person authorized by law to perform many legal tasks independently or under a lawyer's direction.

The rapid expansion of litigation in our society over the past three decades has produced a new career opportunity in law—the paralegal profession. This area of employment opportunity is rapidly becoming a more defined profession, with emerging standards and competencies that are widely recognized by the legal and academic community (Statsky 1992).

The **paralegal**, or legal assistant, is a person with legal skills who works under the supervision of a lawyer, or who is otherwise authorized by law to use these skills. Most larger law firms, corporations, and government agencies employ an increasingly large number of these legal assistants to perform many of the tasks formerly entrusted to lawyers. Drafting legal documents and discovery instruments; doing legal research, investigation, and title searches; preparing briefs; and closing real estate transactions are tasks that require considerable legal competence and ability but can be performed by trained individuals who are neither lawyers nor legal secretaries.

In the 1960s larger law firms began to realize that they could earn more money and provide better client services at lower cost by employing legal assistants to perform many of the tasks that more highly trained and skilled courtroom lawyers performed. Lawyers generally work on a billing system at an hourly rate that may be four or five times the rate a client may be billed for a paralegal doing the same task. This economic discovery by law firms and clients has been the principal motivating factor contributing to the rise of this profession.

Paralegal Training and Education

In the early 1970s the American Bar Association (ABA) not only recognized paralegals but also took steps to encourage the development and creation of more adequate training programs in this field by establishing an ABA approval procedure. Textbooks began to be published for the training of paralegals, and many institutions of higher education began to introduce educational programs specifically for paralegals. In the early 1980s there were some three hundred public and private educational programs for paralegals across the country, and by 1992 the number of such programs increased to over six hundred. Practicing paralegals, who display an increasing sense of pride in their profession, have taken steps toward the development of certification, which is usually required in a recognized profession. Most major cities now have local chapters and there are two major national associations—the National Federation of Paralegal Associations (NFPA) and the National Association of Legal Assistants (NALA).

In the 1980s major law firms and corporations had become so convinced that management skills were needed to coordinate the activities of firms employing as many as one hundred lawyers and twenty to thirty paralegals that they created a new position—the paralegal administrator. These individuals are hired for their management skills and are frequently involved in the recruitment, training, and management of the office paralegals.

The NALA has developed a certification program that is gaining recognition and will ultimately lead to more clearly defined professional standards for paralegals. Some have estimated that the number of paralegals may eventually exceed the number of lawyers in law offices, although today many rural and small law practices have yet to recognize the need for paralegals.

Paralegals in Other Countries

Many other countries have long recognized an official division of labor in the practice of law. Our most closely related legal system—that of England—divides lawyers into solicitors and barristers. The **solicitor** handles the everyday problems of legal practice and has only limited rights to represent clients in certain lower courts. The **barrister** is necessary for representation of clients in the higher courts in contested cases. When the case gets to this stage of trial process, the solicitor arranges for the barrister to enter the case. Both of these branches

solicitor: a lawyer in England who handles most legal matters until they go to trial.

barrister: a lawyer in England who is authorized to argue at trial for litigants in contested cases.

legal executives: legal assistants in England who are more established as paralegal professionals than their counterparts in the United States.

of the legal profession require law degrees and compliance with bar admission standards. In modern practice even solicitors employ **legal executives** and delegate many responsibilities to them. These paralegal professionals are required to undergo extensive training and pass a rigorous examination for certification by the Institute of Legal Executives (Statsky 1986,25).

Law office administrators in the United States are becoming more prevalent as firms recognize the need for effective management of large offices. This trend also can be observed within governmental agencies, corporations, and courts. State attorneys general offices and other agencies at both the state and federal level employ paralegals and office administrators to manage activities. Court administrators are now commonplace, and a special school has been established to train persons for careers in this field—the Institute for Court Management in Denver, Colorado (Meador 1991,67).

LAWYERS AND JUDGES

Many students are considering their potential for successful entry into law schools. The lure of the law is great, and many are attracted to this profession: "Even though the profession suffers from something of a bad image (created probably by a few), lawyers usually gain respect, are thought to be bright, are secure, are positioned to exert power, and often become rich" (Moll 1990,21).

The astounding increase in the number of lawyers, now estimated to be more than 850,000 nationwide, and the enormous rise in the number of those taking the law school entrance examination (LSAT) in recent years indicate that competition for law schools and legal careers will increase. Fears that the profession is overloaded, however, are unfounded. The rate of increase in new law school graduates from the one hundred and seventy-five ABA-accredited programs, and especially new admissions to the Bar, has kept pace with the expansion of litigation since 1960.

The Demand for Lawyers

Peter Pashigian has traced the increases in the number of lawyers and in their income over the past fifty years. He concluded that the legal profession has followed the general rise in real income in the nation as a whole and that it experienced parallel periods of economic prosperity in the 1920s and 1960s. He was surprised, however, to discover that law school enrollments lagged behind the increase in demand for lawyers. (Pashigian 1978,51)

Law offers challenging professional careers for those who are willing and able to undertake the rigors of professional education and acquire the skills needed to become successful lawyers and judges in today's highly competitive society. Law continues to attract so many students, according to a report sponsored by the ABA because of:

1. prestige and high earnings;
2. intellectual interest in the study of law and legal work;
3. the traditional image of the lawyer as a professional dedicated to ideals of service, high ethical standards, and problem solving;
4. the function of law as a mechanism for distributing rights, power, and influence among different social groups; and

5. external reasons such as the advancement of a nonlegal career, influence of significant others, and lack of opportunity to pursue a field of first choice. (American Bar Association 1980,17)

"What does it take to become a lawyer?" "Do I have the 'right stuff' to make it in this demanding profession?" These are questions most students ask. Interest in and fascination with the subject of law is an important prerequisite; however, "many are called, but few are chosen!" If law school is not an option, there are still many law-related career areas that offer challenging occupations.

College guidance and counseling offices can usually provide self-scoring interest inventories. These materials help students assess their interest compatibility with those who have found successful careers in the law. Once a student has concluded that the field of law is where the student's interests lie, the long process of assessment and development of the student's abilities and skills begins.

Law schools do not require any particular undergraduate major, but they expect the student to have a broad liberal arts background and a transcript that indicates the student has taken courses that involved reading, writing, and thinking. A large number of majors in political science, history, and English are admitted to law schools, but almost as many come from other academic disciplines. Law is an extremely versatile field, and backgrounds in business, engineering, and medicine are assets because they provide the kinds of knowledge needed to deal with the increasingly technical aspects of the law. Law school is the place where the student specializes in the law itself.

Law School Admission

Admission to law schools is based primarily upon two criteria: a student's undergraduate grade point average, and a student's score on the **Law School Admission Test** (LSAT). These two criteria often determine the initial screening process, but other factors are involved in later screening. The LSAT attempts to measure a student's potential for success in law school by testing verbal skills and reasoning abilities. Grade point averages are better indicators of success than the LSAT, but the two factors combined are considered the best predictor and is relied on by most law schools across the country.

The increasing competition for a limited number of seats in law schools means that the student who has innate ability and begins early in undergraduate school to develop those abilities and skills associated with successful entrance will be more likely to enter his or her law school of choice. Courses that make the student read, write, and think enhance reading comprehension and logical thinking skills. Mastery of the English language, basic understanding of history (both world and American), and knowledge of how governmental institutions function broaden a student's vocabulary and make the student a cultured and literate person. An understanding of logic and practice in critical thinking skills along with general understanding of economics and business practices are other important areas a student should stress.

Those entering law school must be confident enough in themselves, and personally committed to the pursuit of a professional career in the law, to undergo the intensive and rigorous training required in law school. A minimum of three years of full-time exacting course work is required, and upon completion of law school, there is no assurance that the student will pass the **Bar Examination**,

Law School Admission Test (LSAT): almost universally used in the United States as a criterion for admission to law schools; an aptitude test of logic and critical thinking.

Bar Examination: required proficiency to obtain license to practice law, give legal advice, and represent clients.

which is administered by individual state agencies and must be passed before the individual can practice law in that state.

Professional Legal Education

The evolution of American legal education has been gradual and prone to resist change. Legal education initially was based on the English model and continued as a type of apprenticeship system until after the Civil War. An aspiring lawyer in the 1800s would apply with an established lawyer with whom the apprentice would "read the law," which meant observing the mentor, drafting documents, assisting in case preparation, and reading assigned cases and commentaries until the apprentice was able to open a private practice with a letter of recommendation from the mentor.

It was not until the 1870s that law schools began to emerge as formalized educational programs, although some lawyers attended the Inns of Court in England, some gained their education in law-office-schools like the one established by Tapping Reeve in Litchfield, Connecticut, in 1784, and some worked with individuals who had obtained the few law professorships at various universities (Abadinsky 1991,78–79). Robert Stevens attributes the rise in formal professional law schools, in the period from the 1870s to the close of the nineteenth century, to the prevalent "middle class urge to get ahead through structured education" and the growing dissatisfaction with the apprenticeship model (Stevens 1983,22). The legal profession also became a booming industry during this period of industrial revolution in the United States, and the emerging model of legal education became associated with Christopher Columbus Langdell of Harvard University. Langdell perfected the dreaded "Socratic method" and case study approaches that have been so prominent in American legal education. These methods still characterized formal legal education in the 1970s when Scott Turow's best-selling autobiography *One L*, about first-year law students at Harvard University, critically described the formal legal education process (Turow 1977). These methods later were popularized by Professor Kingsfield in the television series "The Paperchase."

Debate over whether law schools have erred by overemphasis on scholarship and deemphasis on practical skills continues. Paul Wice quotes Associate Supreme Court Justice Robert Jackson as epitomizing this debate in a speech at Stanford University Law School some forty years ago: "If the weakness of the apprenticeship system was to produce advocates without scholarship, the weakness of the law school system is to turn out scholars without skills of advocacy" (Wice 1991,9).

Law schools have made minor adjustments in recent years by adding practical requirements in moot court, advocacy skills, negotiations, and ethics, but the curriculum has remained surprisingly stable and uniform across the country. Jerome Kramer (1989) has concluded that the American system could profit by returning to a more practical, tutorial type of instruction. He finds that "our typical law schools are still using the same methodology, and except for frills at the expense of substance, the curriculum has not changed much since the turn of the century. This in the face of a revolution in the way law is practiced and the virtual abandonment of formerly classic areas of practice to lay persons and agencies" (Kramer 1989,15).

The typical first-year law student has no electives and is required to take two semesters of courses in torts, property, civil procedure, and contracts, along with one-semester courses in constitutional law, criminal law, and legal research. The case study approach predominates, and the student is expected to come to class prepared, having read and briefed several cases, to discuss the cases in class recitation. Typically, only one essay examination is given each semester upon which the student's future prospects hinge. There is fierce competition for grades, and the student's class rank at the end of the year determines status and awards, such as being nominated to serve on the "law review," an honor given to only the highest-ranking students.

In the second and third years of law school, there are more electives and opportunities to specialize, but students generally are required to take courses in the ethics of the legal profession, income tax, corporations, and evidence. They also are encouraged or required to participate in a clinical law program, which provides some practical experience. The remainder of the second- and third-year curriculum comprises a wide variety of elective course offerings, including courses in administrative law, wills, trusts, estate law, labor law, family law, environmental law, and international law.

Specialization in Legal Practice

Specialization may begin in law school but often awaits a more significant aspect of the legal education process—practical experience with the law firm. Most lawyers claim that, in spite of formal law school education, they really learned the practice of law from experience, and many became specialized through recognition of client needs. Students may intern with law firms even before graduation, and some of the highest-ranking students are selected to be law clerks at the federal and state supreme court levels.

The most prestigious law firms today have national reputations, and the attorneys in these firms generally are described as "Wall Street lawyers." About fifty of these firms have more than two hundred lawyers (one has over a thousand). They hire the highest-ranking graduates from the most prestigious law schools at very high starting salaries; the "Craveth" system is the prevalent model, involving a kind of practical postgraduate induction into the world of corporate law and lawyering (Smigel 1964). New lawyers work as lawyer interns for several years, usually for a number of the firm's partners. After ten years, the intern is considered for a partnership or leaves the firm. These elite law firms handle big corporate clients and practice preventive law—litigation generally represents failure, and "much of what these lawyers do involves planning a client's activities so that disputes are not likely to arise" (Burton 1985,19). Such firms are no longer confined to New York but have branched out into nearly every major metropolitan area, especially Washington, D.C. Many Washington law firms practice influence and lobbying rather than law. An increasing number of these firms are expanding into global concerns with offices in major cities throughout the world.

Large corporations have their own in-house counsel, with major legal divisions headed by the general counsel. Beneath the general counsel are deputy, or associate, administrators who supervise staff attorneys. Staff attorneys may be distributed throughout the different divisions of a corporation, but all are responsible to their superiors in the law department. These in-house law departments, like elite firms, actively recruit the highest-ranking law students with high starting salaries. Corporate law departments do not have the prestige of the national law firm, but a position in such a department has considerably more prestige than that of the typical lawyer in a small firm. Corporate law departments also practice preventive law, or dispute anticipatory law, and are more heavily involved in corporate planning.

The typical lawyer falls into a third category of lawyers who do not work for national law firms or in corporate law departments. About half of practicing attorneys-at-law are in solo practice or in a two-lawyer firm. The typical attorney may not "hang out a shingle" immediately after law school but may do so after substantial experience with a large law firm or a government agency (such as a prosecutor's office). Lawyers in firms of four to ten lawyers account for about twenty percent of practicing attorneys, and lawyers who are employed by government agencies for about ten percent. A study by the ABA found that the typical lawyer is male; is thirty-nine years of age; specializes in personal injury, products liability, and business law; and earns between $75,000 and $100,000 per year (Blodgett 1986).

Although eighty-five percent of practicing lawyers are men, more than half the students currently enrolled in law schools are female. Racial and ethnic minorities also are underrepresented among practicing lawyers, but law schools are actively encouraging minority applicants and their numbers are increasing across the nation.

Judges

The judicial profession in the United States is not a field in which one sets out to develop a starting career. It is generally necessary to become a lawyer first and then consider opportunities for seeking a position on the bench. American judges sit on courts of widely different types, come from an assortment of backgrounds and experiences, and are selected by a variety of methods; therefore, it is difficult to generalize about them.

Judges in Other Countries

In other countries judges are appointed and advance through the hierarchy of the courts as they prove their competence. In the civil law systems of Western Europe, judges qualify to enter judicial service after completing university law study (usually at the top of their classes). They go through a practical training process and are appointed to the bench, then are promoted to sit on higher courts after they prove their competence at lower levels. In England, barristers who have shown competence in litigation are recruited for appointments on the bench at lower levels and then work their way through the hierarchy. The American system is unique in that (1) judges initially come to the bench from other lines of legal work after a substantial number of years of professional service, and (2) once on the bench, they do not, in general, follow a promotional pattern through the ranks of the judiciary (Meador 1991, 54).

American Judges

Our federal system has fifty-one separate and independent court systems, and hence, fifty-one different methods of recruiting, selecting, and removing judges. There are four basic methods of selection, however, although some states combine two or more of them.

1. The federal model of nomination by the chief executive, with confirmation by a legislative body, is used in only a handful of states; and only Rhode Island extends life terms to their judges, as is the federal practice.

2. The so-called "merit plan," or **Missouri Plan**, involves appointment by the chief executive from a short list of persons certified by an independent commission to be qualified for the position. This method has been promoted as a reform measure to provide a buffer against pure partisan politics and gives some assurance of professional quality. A majority of states now use this method in some form and apply it at least to the selection of the intermediate appeals court judges.

3. Direct popular election of judges for fixed terms of office (usually longer than the terms for legislators) is the predominant method of state judicial selection. The overwhelming majority of judges are selected in this manner.

4. Judicial selection by election in the legislature is the fourth method of selection and is now used in only two states—Virginia and South Carolina.

Missouri Plan (or "merit plan"): appointment of judges by the governor from a list of qualified applicants. The appointee must be accepted by the voters and is subject to periodic retention approval by the voters.

The dominant method of direct popular election of judges makes our system unique among the world's judicial systems. We are the only country that allows politics to enter the judicial function to this degree. It was not the predominant method of selection during the period of formation of the union, when selection by state legislatures was used in a majority of the states. Popular election was introduced during the period of "Jacksonian Democracy" after 1830, and many state constitutions still reflect the impact of this era by requiring popular election of judges. Modern reform movements have had to deal with this reality. Removing constitutional provisions is a very difficult process in most states, and it is almost impossible when the process involves removing a popularly elected office.

Modern Reform Movements

The "Missouri Plan" coupled with the governor's selection being placed on the ballot at the next general election for approval or rejection by the voters will meet constitutional requirements in most states; and in many states, the majority of judges are initially appointed by the governor to fill vacancies that occur between elections. Judges appointed under this plan must face a retention vote after each term of appointed office. Long terms strengthen the appearance of judicial independence, and in some states, the reelection of judges is by retention elections in which the judges run on their own records without opponents. Nevertheless, our state systems suffer from considerable ambivalence concerning the goals of judicial independence and professional quality.

The highest degree of judicial independence is found in the federal system. All judges hold office "during good behavior" (for life) and can be removed only through impeachment by the House of Representatives and removal from office by the Senate. The Senate exercises a significant check on the president's appointment power and must approve all initial appointments. The variety of methods used in the states compromise judicial independence. However, many techniques are being tried to increase judicial independence while ensuring professional quality. Longer terms, innovative removal processes (such as independent commission review and recommendation to the state supreme court for removal), protection against salary reductions, retention elections, governor's appointments, voluntary (and in some cases mandatory) training programs for judges once selected, and the judicial ethics enforced through the hierarchy of courts are some of the methods employed.

Characteristics of Judges

magistrates: lower court judicial authorities including justices of the peace.

With the relatively minor exception of some lay **magistrates** who serve in judicial capacities on state courts of limited jurisdiction, all American judges have studied law and been licensed to practice law. The majority of trial judges have come directly from private practices, with a broad range of legal specialties being represented. The overwhelming majority are white Anglo-Saxon male Protestants. Women and minorities have been graduating from law schools in greater numbers, and some have been selected as state and federal judges. The number of female judges on the state courts nearly doubled in the decade of the 1970s, although the number remains small. According to recent studies, the few blacks that have become state and federal judges have career patterns and personal credentials that are very similar to those of white judges. The courts are becoming integrated, but they are still dominated by white, middle-class, politically experienced, former lawyers.

According to Lawrence Baum, trial court judges come from a broader cross-section of less successful practitioners than appeals court judges, who are drawn from more successful practices and are more likely to have worked in larger law firms (Baum 1986,126). State supreme court judges tend to follow a predictable route, and the existence of previous judicial experience is increasing (up from fifty-eight percent in 1961–1968 to sixty-three percent in 1980–1981) (Wice 1991,53). Two-thirds of state supreme court judges begin work in a moderate-sized firm, enter public life as either a prosecutor or legislator, and serve briefly as a trial court judge. Many also have experience at the intermediate appellate level (Strumpf 1988,182). About one-third of state supreme court judges have experience in the prosecutor's office.

Political involvement seems to be a primary characteristic of American judges, with some studies showing as much as seventy percent of the state's judiciary describing themselves as having been politically active. Paul Wice concludes that "gaining the favorable attention of the public officials who choose judges . . . is the most common characteristic shared by all members of the bench" (Wice 1991,57).

Judges are viewed as members of a highly respected profession in terms of occupational prestige, in spite of the public's growing dissatisfaction with the judicial system. Most judges are positive about their positions and enjoy the responsibilities and challenges inherent in their profession, although an increasing number of them are criticizing the working conditions, relatively low pay (in comparison to private law practice), administrative tedium, and irritating political involvements.

ETHICAL STANDARDS IN LAW-RELATED PROFESSIONS

All law-related professions perform day-to-day functions that require a high degree of responsibility to the community interest they serve. Law enforcement officers, paralegals, administrators, lawyers, prosecutors, and judges occupy positions of public trust that impose upon them ethical standards that are higher than those for persons employed in non–law-related areas. Any person may be sued for negligence (failure to exercise due care), but in these professions, violations of the more stringent ethical standards of personal behavior may result in loss of the privilege to engage in that profession.

Professional **ethical standards**, particularly in the area of law and government, are not merely desirable virtues or expectations but, in many respects, have been elevated to the status of legally binding rules imposed by the courts of law. The ABA standards for lawyers and those for judges are very different. Since most judges are drawn from the ranks of practicing attorneys, especially prosecutors, they may have difficulty making the ethical transition from lawyer to judge. Some critics assert that this is an example of the general bias inherent in our system as opposed to those of most countries in the world where judges are not drawn from the ranks of lawyers. An individual's likelihood of obtaining justice in our system may depend upon scrupulous adherence to the canons of ethics by the judge and the lawyers involved.

ethical standards: professional standards, usually set by state bar associations, that often are legally binding and can result in suspension or loss of license to practice law.

Lawyers are regulated by their state bar association, which in turn operates under the authority and supervision of the state's highest court. These regulations are known as the **canons of ethics**, and violation of these regulations can lead to sanctions such as suspension and disbarment. In cases of disciplinary action, a committee of the bar association usually conducts a hearing and makes a preliminary decision. This action can be appealed to a designated state court, which will make the final decision on whether sanctions should be imposed.

canons of ethics: usually refers to model statements of ethical standards drafted by the American Bar Association.

One of these canons covers the lawyer's use of paralegals. This canon requires, in essence, that the lawyer must supervise the paralegal and ensure that the paralegal does not engage in the unauthorized practice of law. A lawyer can be disciplined for what the paralegal (or other nonlawyer) does within the employ of the lawyer. Paralegals can be prosecuted under criminal statutes for the unauthorized practice of law or legally held responsible for negligence, but Bar sanctions apply only to lawyers (Statsky 1986,244).

The **American Bar Association** (ABA) has the major role of proposing model ethical standards and issuing opinions interpreting these rules, but the standards are not binding until state and local bar associations officially adopt them. Most state and local bar associations have adopted some or all of the ABA ethical positions. For example, a judicial candidate for elective office who publicly takes a position on a political issue or on a pending case, in violation of Canon 7 of the *Model Code of Judicial Conduct,* can lose the office to another candidate, and may even face disbarment in forty-seven states (Abadinsky 1990,177).

American Bar Association: voluntary national association of lawyers and judges that represents the legal profession in the United States.

Ethical Standards for Judges

The **judge's role** in legal proceedings requires that the judge exercise responsibility for enforcing the rules that govern criminal and civil cases. The judge must have no personal interest in the outcome of the case. A judge is responsible for ensuring impartial justice under law and must avoid any impropriety, or appearance of impropriety, in the discharge of this function. When a jury is used, the judge determines issues of law, and the jury determines issues of fact in dispute. When there is no jury, the judge determines issues of both law and fact. A judge's failure to conform to the principles of ethics and law may lead to reversal of the decision by an appellate court—a blow to the professional standing of any trial judge. Other forms of disciplinary action include being voted out of office,

judge's role: one of impartiality and neutrality toward the parties.

denial of confirmation when appointed, and impeachment followed by removal from office.

The basic canons of the ABA *Model Code of Judicial Conduct* cover the following topics:

1. A judge should uphold the integrity and independence of the judiciary;
2. A judge should avoid impropriety and the appearance of impropriety in all activities;
3. A judge should perform the duties of office impartially and diligently;
4. A judge may engage in activities to improve the law, the legal system, and the administration of justice as long as they do not cast doubt on the judge's capacity to decide impartially;
5. A judge should regulate extrajudicial activities to minimize the risk of conflict with judicial duties;
6. A judge should regularly file reports of compensation received for quasi-judicial and extrajudicial activities; and
7. A judge should refrain from political activity inappropriate to the judge's office.

Ethical Standards for Lawyers

lawyer's role: that of advocate for the client, who is entitled to vigorous and competent representation.

The **lawyer's role** is that of advocate for the client, and the standards of ethics require that the lawyer must serve the client to the best of his or her ability without violating the law or the lawyer's code of ethics. The essential standards imposed by the ABA *Model Rules of Professional Conduct* include:

1. to provide competent representation to a client;
2. to refrain from counseling a client, or assisting a client, to engage in conduct that the lawyer knows is criminal or fraudulent;
3. to refrain from knowingly making false statements or unlawfully obstructing another party's access to evidence, and to use candor and honesty in the practice of law;
4. to keep the client informed and to conform to certain standards concerning reasonable fees;
5. to refrain from revealing confidential client information without the client's consent, except in cases where criminal acts are likely to result from such confidentiality;
6. to avoid conflict of interest concerning the adverse effect to another client;
7. to withdraw from a case if (a) the client demands that the lawyer engage in illegal or unethical activities, (b) the lawyer is physically or mentally unable to represent the client, or (c) the client fires the lawyer;
8. to avoid even the appearance of professional impropriety; and
9. to conform to other standards concerning prohibitions against knowingly filing frivolous claims, communication with the opposing party without the consent of that party's lawyer, false or misleading advertisement, unethical solicitation of legal business, and reporting of professional misconduct.

Ethical Standards for Paralegals

The ABA standards require that lawyers give their paralegals "appropriate instruction" on the "ethical aspects" of the practice of law. The paralegal must be careful to avoid misrepresenting himself or herself as a lawyer and may not give legal advice or represent a client in court (Statsky 1986, ch. 4).

Ethical Standards for Law Enforcement Officers

Administrative action against law enforcement officers is generally subject to civil service rules that emanate from state authority and are applied locally. Disciplinary actions may include temporary or permanent suspension from the force, and criminal sanctions may be applied in extreme cases. Law enforcement officers are guaranteed a "fair hearing," and they can appeal decisions they think are unfair. Civil suits against law enforcement officers are extensive and represent an increasing occupational hazard in this area of employment.

The law enforcement officer has a fundamental duty to safeguard the lives and property of all people in the society; to respect every person's legal rights; and to maintain personal honesty, self-control, and exemplary conduct. The officer must set an example through personal adherence not only to the general law but also to the department's regulations and the community's expectations. The officer must refrain from abuse of authority, enforce the law courteously and appropriately, never employ unnecessary force or violence, and never accept gifts for services.

These standards are difficult to interpret and enforce under the extremely varied conditions of modern life, but the underlying assumption of our legal system is that justice can be done in the individual case only if ethical standards and due process of law are followed.

CHAPTER SUMMMARY

1. The expansion of legal activity in the United States over the past three decades has produced expanding opportunities for meaningful careers in law-related areas. We are perhaps the world's most litigious society. The number of disputes taken to court has been doubling every ten years.

2. The efficacy of our legal system depends upon the willingness of citizens to obey the law. This willingness is conditioned on the socialization process by which citizens are taught the moral and legal values of society.

3. Citizens are expected to have a general understanding of law and know the difference between right and wrong behavior, participate in selecting officials, identify community problems, serve on juries, report crimes, serve as witnesses, and obey the law.

4. Teachers who are adequately prepared to teach law-related education are needed in greater numbers to improve our educational and socialization processes. Studies demonstrate that law-related education reduces crime and promotes moral development.

5. Increased recognition of the problems of law enforcement has led to increased specialization and professionalization of law enforcement agencies at local, state, and national levels. More emphasis is being placed upon crime prevention and corrections institutions.

6. Most of the new positions in law enforcement require college degrees and knowledge of basic concepts of law. The complex nature of our federal system places primary responsibility for law enforcement with the states and local communities.

7. The expansion of litigation has created a new career field for specialists called paralegals, who are neither lawyers nor legal secretaries. The paralegal is a person with legal skills who works under the supervision of a lawyer or who is otherwise authorized by law to use these skills.

8. The number of persons who aspire to be lawyers and judges is increasing, and the competition for entry into law school has become more difficult. The production of new lawyers, however, has kept pace with the expansion of litigation.

9. A student who plans an undergraduate education properly can increase the chances of successful entry into law school, and can choose a more prestigious law school than one who does not plan ahead.

10. Entering the profession of law requires a personal commitment, rigorous training, three years of postgraduate course work, and ability to pass the state bar examination.

11. The most prestigious law firms are large organizations, located in major metropolitan centers, that practice corporate law. Large corporations also have law departments in which a staff of lawyers practice corporate planning and preventive law. However, fifty percent of practicing attorneys are in small practices of one or two lawyers, twenty percent are in firms of four to ten lawyers, and ten percent work for government agencies.

12. Each state government and the federal government employ different methods of recruiting, selecting, and removing judges. Although there are four basic methods of selection, the dominant method in the states is popular election for fixed terms, while in the federal government, judges are selected for life terms by presidential nomination and confirmation by the Senate.

13. Judicial independence and professional quality are important goals, but our system contains much ambiguity in regard to achieving them, particularly at the state level. Compared with other legal systems, the United States is unique in that (a) judges come to the bench from the ranks of practicing lawyers, and (b) once on the bench, they usually do not follow a promotion pattern through the ranks of the judiciary.

14. All positions in law-related professions are positions of public trust that impose upon those holding them ethical standards that are higher than those for persons employed in other professions.

15. Judges are regulated by the American Bar Association's *Model Code of Judicial Conduct* and lawyers by the ABA's *Model Rules of Professional Conduct*. These standards impose ethical and legal obligations on judges and lawyers to avoid any impropriety or appearance of impropriety. The function of judges is different from that of lawyers. They must be impartial, neutral, and fair, while lawyers are obligated to represent clients to the best of their ability, carefully avoiding any illegal or unethical activity.

16. The paralegal must not misrepresent himself or herself as a lawyer and may not give legal advice or represent a client in court.

17. Law enforcement officers must respect every person's legal rights while protecting lives and property. Officers must obey departmental regulations, refrain from abuse of authority, never employ unnecessary force, and never accept gifts for services.

KEY TERMS

law-related education	Law School Admission Test	canons of ethics
paralegal (or legal assistant)	Bar Examination	American Bar Association
solicitor	Missouri Plan (or "merit plan")	judge's role
barrister	magistrates	lawyer's role
legal executives	ethical standards	

DISCUSSION QUESTIONS

1. How has the expansion of legal activity in the United States resulted in the expansion of law-related career opportunities?

2. Does the complexity of our society and legal system generate unnecessary conflict?

3. What are the basic responsibilities of citizenship in our society?

4. What role do teachers and law-related education play in the process of political socialization?

5. How have the problems of our society in the areas of law enforcement and corrections expanded opportunities for law-related careers?

6. How has the expansion of the amount and cost of litigation contributed to the rise of the paralegal (or legal assistant) in the United States and other countries?

7. What qualifications are needed to enter law school and to become a lawyer?

8. What are the major characteristics of professional legal education in the United States, and how does the process differ from that in other countries?

9. How are judges selected in the United States, and how does this process differ from that of other countries?

10. What are the basic ethical standards for judges, lawyers, paralegals, and law enforcement officers?

SOURCES AND SUGGESTED READING

American Bar Association. 1980. *Law Schools and Professional Education*. Chicago: American Bar Association.

Abadinsky, Howard. 1991. *Law and Justice: An Introduction to the American Legal System*. 2d ed. Chicago: Nelson-Hall Publishers.

Baum, Lawrence. 1986. *American Courts: Process and Policy*. Boston: Houghton Mifflin.

Blodgett, Nancy. 1986. "A Look at Today's Lawyer." *ABA Journal* (Sept. 1).

Burton, Steven L. 1985. *An Introduction to Law and Legal Reasoning*. Boston: Little, Brown.

International Association of Legal Assistants, Inc. 1992. *Manual for Legal Assistants*. 2d ed. St. Paul: West Publishing Co.

Kohlberg, Lawrence. 1987. *Child Psychology and Childhood Education: A Cognitive-Developmental View*. New York: Longman. (See also entire issue of *Social Education*, April 1976, devoted to practical application of Kohlberg's stages of moral development for teachers.)

Kramer, Jerome. 1989. "Scholarship and Skills." *National Law Journal* (January 9).

Lieberman, Jethro K. 1981. *The Litigious Society*. New York: Basic Books.

MacKenzie, John P. 1974. *The Appearance of Justice*. New York: Charles Scribner's Sons.

Meador, Daniel John. 1991. *American Courts*. St. Paul: West Publishing Co.

Moll, Richard W. 1990. *The Lure of the Law*. New York: Penguin Books, Inc.

National Center for State Courts. 1991. *State Court Case-*

load Statistics: Annual Report 1991. Williamsburg, Va.: National Center for State Courts.

Pashigian, A. Peter. 1978. "The Number and Earnings of Lawyers—Some Recent Findings." *American Bar Foundation Research Journal* (Winter).

Siegel, Brian. 1974. *How to Succeed in Law School*. Woodbury, N.Y.: Barron's Educational Series, Inc.

Smigel, Erwin O. 1964. *The Wall Street Lawyer: Professional Organization Man*. Glencoe, Ill.: Free Press.

Statsky, William. 1992. *Introduction to Paralegalism: Perspectives Problems, Skills*. 4th ed. St. Paul: West Publishing Co. (See also 3d ed., 1986.)

———. 1993. *Paralegal Employment: Facts and Strategies for the 1990s*. 2d ed. St. Paul: West Publishing Co.

Stevens, Robert. 1983. *Law School: Legal Education in America from the 1850s to the 1980s*. Chapel Hill: University of North Carolina Press.

Stinchcomb, James D. 1976. *Opportunities in Law Enforcement and Related Careers*. Louisville, Ky.: Vocational Guidance Manuals.

Strumpf, Harry. 1988. *American Judicial Politics*. New York: Harcourt Brace Jovanovich.

Turow, Scott. 1977. *One-L*. New York: Penguin Books, Inc.

Wice, Paul. 1991. *Judges and Lawyers: The Human Side of Justice*. New York: Harper Collins.

Zemans, Francis, and Victor Rosenbloom. 1981. *The Making of a Public Profession*. Chicago: American Bar Foundation.

CHAPTER THREE

JUDICIAL PROCESS AND LEGAL REASONING

> "Law is what the judges say it is."
>
> Anonymous
>
> "We are under a Constitution, but the Constitution is what the Court says it is."
>
> Justice Charles Evans Hughes
>
> "The life of the law, has not been logic: it has been experience. The felt necessities of the time, the prevalent moral and political theories, institutions of public policy, avowed or unconscious, even the prejudices which judges share with their fellow-men have had a good deal more to do than the syllogism in determining the rules by which men should be governed."
>
> Justice Oliver Wendell Holmes, Jr.

This chapter will demonstrate how many of the concepts introduced in the first two chapters are used in current practice by judges to decide legal issues. A general understanding of how courts are organized, of questions of jurisdiction (or access to the courts), and of the hierarchy of laws are essential prerequisites for case law analysis.

The common law origin of our legal system and the extension of the doctrine of following precedent require reference to the law in its most precise form. Case law is the foundation of the legal system we inherited from English jurisprudence. As Oliver Wendell Holmes observed, "[T]he life of the law has not been logic: it has been experience." Case law is the accumulated experience of attempts by legal institutions to define and clarify the law. Case law analysis is a practical and pragmatic method of studying the law because each case deals with a specific set of facts and demonstrates how the courts apply the law to that set of facts.

This chapter will provide experience in reading case law. The illustrative cases demonstrate how judges use the basic concepts of law in practice. Much of the chapter explains how to read and "brief" cases in law. Legal reasoning is based upon logic and proceeds from known premises to logically consistent conclusions. As Holmes indicates, this logic is not always scientific or precise.

The case precedent becomes a part of the law until it is specifically overruled. This experience is recorded in the history of case law.

THE DUAL HIERARCHIES OF OUR COURT SYSTEMS

The basic character of our federal system of government, as explained in chapter one, involves a division of sovereignty between the states and the national government. Each of these sovereign elements retains the power and authority to create and alter their own court systems. This basic fact causes much confusion about law and judicial process in the United States.

Many people believe that we have only one legal system and that the federal courts are simply higher judicial authorities that review cases on appeal from state courts. In issues of a federal constitutional nature, which are the ones we hear about the most often, this unitary idea has some validity. This area of unitary authority, however, applies only to issues involving federal law, including the United States Constitution. Most legal issues do not involve federal law and are adjudicated in state courts, which have the final authority over state laws.

In comparison with the state court systems taken collectively, the federal court system is quite small. The overwhelming majority of the enormous volume of legal actions filed in the United States each year are filed in state courts. As explained in chapter two, the federal system handled less than 1% of the more than 33 million civil and criminal cases filed in our courts annually. (National Center for State Courts 1991)

jurisdiction: authority of a court to hear and determine a judicial action.

Federal courts have **jurisdiction** over all matters involving the United States Constitution, "federal questions" related to acts of Congress, and all treaties. All other matters are subject to the jurisdiction of the state courts. Issues of court jurisdiction are perhaps the most complex of legal issues and are frequently the subject of legal actions that become part of the body of case law.

diversity jurisdiction: authority in civil legal actions that is shared by the state and federal courts when there is diversity of citizenship of the parties and the sum in question is more than $50,000.

There is an area of overlapping jurisdiction that exists between federal and state courts known as **diversity jurisdiction**. This concept is important because it constitutes a major exception to the dual hierarchy of our state and federal court systems. It applies only in civil (noncriminal) cases where the parties are citizens of different states. The party bringing the legal action may elect to file the case in federal or state court.

The State Court Systems

Each of the fifty states has its own written constitution that creates the entire court system in some states and authorizes the state legislature to establish the judicial structure in others. Thus, the state court systems are defined by state constitutional and legislative authority. They differ in detail, but resemble each other in broad outline. The key components of state court systems, which provide a general pattern, are described below. The reader may wish to supplement this discussion with details that are current and applicable in the reader's own state.

Trial Courts

trial courts: courts of original jurisdiction.

The **trial courts** are the lower courts that form the base of the state's judicial pyramid. They are extremely varied, even within any particular state, and they serve many different jurisdictional functions. They extend throughout the cities and counties of the state and are referred to as courts of "first instance" or "original jurisdiction." When parties commence **civil legal actions**, or the state commences **criminal legal actions**, often called prosecutions, they do so in the trial courts.

In most states this base of trial courts is subdivided into two levels. The major trial courts at the upper level are referred to as courts of "general jurisdiction" because they have authority to hear and decide numerous types of cases. These general jurisdiction courts may be called "circuit courts," "superior courts," "chancery courts," "courts of common pleas," or other names. Many states have several of these named courts that divide jurisdiction by subject matter. This lack of uniformity is one of the many factors contributing to confusion concerning American courts.

The lower level trial courts, below the courts of general jurisdiction, are called courts of "limited jurisdiction." In contrast to courts of general jurisdiction, these courts have relatively restricted authority and often handle only one specific type of case; for example, traffic courts are vested with jurisdiction over relatively minor motor vehicle offenses. In some states there are probate courts, with authority over the administration of deceased persons' estates, and small claims courts with jurisdiction defined in monetary terms. Other courts have limited jurisdiction to try misdemeanors (less serious crimes) and to conduct preliminary hearings for more serious offenses. Here again, there is considerable variation among the states.

A major twentieth century movement has been aimed at unifying state trial courts. The states that have attempted such reforms have produced varied results, but grouping trials courts into one tier, even nominally, permits more effective management of trial level business. According to Professor Daniel J. Meador of the University of Virginia Law School, "Under a single administrative authority, judges can be assigned from one division to another as work requires. It is thought that a unified trial court also serves to avoid the appearance of second-class justice for cases that would otherwise be handled by courts of limited jurisdiction" (Meador 1991,12–13).

The trial courts are the forums in which cases are initially heard and decided. Trial courts of general jurisdiction often conduct jury trials in which witnesses are called to testify and contested facts are resolved. A trial is a fact-finding procedure in which issues of both fact and law are adjudicated (authoritatively decided). However, the judgments of trial courts are subject to review and possible reversal by courts above them in the judicial hierarchy. For some courts of limited jurisdiction, the first review is in the upper level trial court of general jurisdiction. For the trial courts of general jurisdiction, and sometimes for lower trial courts, review is in the **appellate courts**.

civil legal action: a suit initiated by private parties, corporations, or agencies seeking recovery or redress of private and civil rights in law or equity.

criminal legal action: an action prosecuted by the state or federal government as a party, against a person charged with a public offense.

appellate courts: courts having jurisdiction of appeal and review from the trial courts.

Appellate Courts

At the top of the judicial pyramid in every state is the court of last resort, usually called the supreme court. However, in New York and Maryland, the highest tribunal is called the court of appeals; in Massachusetts and Maine, it is called the supreme judicial court; and in Texas and Oklahoma, there are two courts of last resort: the supreme court (for civil cases) and the court of criminal appeals (for criminal cases). Most state courts of last resort have seven judges called "justices." The smallest court has three justices, and the largest nine. In a few states these courts function in panels of fewer than all their members; however, in most states, all justices sit together so that the court functions as a unit when hearing and deciding appeals (Meador 1991,13–14).

Prior to the twentieth century, most states had only one appellate court. There has been a major expansion of appeals courts in modern times. Thirty-eight states had created intermediate appellate courts by 1991. The major purpose of creating this extra tier of appeals courts was to increase the capacity for hearing litigants' appeals while reserving the state supreme court of last resort for more important cases related to law development and administration of justice.

Some states have a single intermediate appellate court, while others have multiple courts organized into geographical districts or divided by subject matter jurisdiction. Regardless of how they are divided, these intermediate level courts sit in three-judge panels for purposes of hearing and deciding appeals. Many of these courts have more than three judges, but at least three judges are involved in the appeals process in a particular case.

The intermediate appeals courts are primarily involved in error correction functions, and the appeals courts of last resort are primarily involved in the law development role inherited from the English common law tradition. However, roles of the appeals courts are not clearly separable, and both levels are involved with the two basic functions of error correction and law development. The appeals courts are not fact-finding bodies and do not conduct trials. If a further fact-finding process is deemed necessary, the appeals courts will remand (refer) the case back to the courts of original jurisdiction.

court hierarchy: ranking of courts in their order of superiority.

The outline of the typical state **court hierarchy** is depicted in Figure 3.1. This diagram provides a visual image of the dual hierarchies that characterize our judicial system. The diagram illustrates the pattern of relationships between the bewildering array of courts in the United States. The dual hierarchies in the diagram show the relationships between state and federal judicial hierarchies.

The Federal Court System

Article III of the United States Constitution (see Appendix A) provides: "The judicial Power of the United States, shall be vested in one supreme Court, and in such inferior Courts as the Congress may from time to time ordain and establish." The Constitution designates the existence of "one supreme Court" and defines its original and appellate jurisdiction. It has original jurisdiction in "all Cases affecting Ambassadors, other public Ministers and Consuls, and those in which a State shall be a Party. . . ." In all other cases, the Supreme Court has appellate jurisdiction.

The vague and general language used in the Constitution left the composition of the Supreme Court and nearly the entire structure of the federal court system to be defined by acts of Congress. That body moved promptly to enact the Judiciary Act of 1789, setting up the federal judicial system with trial courts in every state. In 1891 Congress created the first set of intermediate courts with purely appellate jurisdiction. These acts put in place the federal court structure that essentially exists today.

federal district courts: the basic trial courts in the federal system.

District Courts

The basic trial courts in the federal judicial system are called **federal district courts**. Congress has created ninety-four districts that serve as the base of the federal judicial structure. There is at least one district in each state and in all territories of the United States. Because each district covers either an entire state or a large part of a state, the court typically holds sessions in several cities in the district.

Each case in a United States district court is usually presided over by a single judge who handles both civil and criminal cases. The fact-finding procedures are substantially the same as those in state trial courts. In a case involving diversity jurisdiction, the district court applies the substantive law of the state in which that particular court sits. These federal courts, however, always apply federal procedural rules.

The federal judiciary has a position similar to that of a judge in a court of limited jurisdiction in the state systems. These judges are called "federal magistrate judges" and are subordinate to the federal district court judges. Any judgments entered by federal magistrate judges are considered judgments of the district courts.

Courts of Appeal

Congress has established thirteen federal judicial circuits that provide the federal intermediate court structure. In each circuit there is a court of appeals, officially designated the United States Court of Appeals for that circuit. Eleven of these circuits are numbered (first to eleventh) and are organized on a territorial basis, each embracing several states and territories of the United States (see map, Figure 3.2). The remaining two circuit courts are officially named the United

FIGURE 3.1 The Dual Hierarchies of State and Federal Courts in the United States

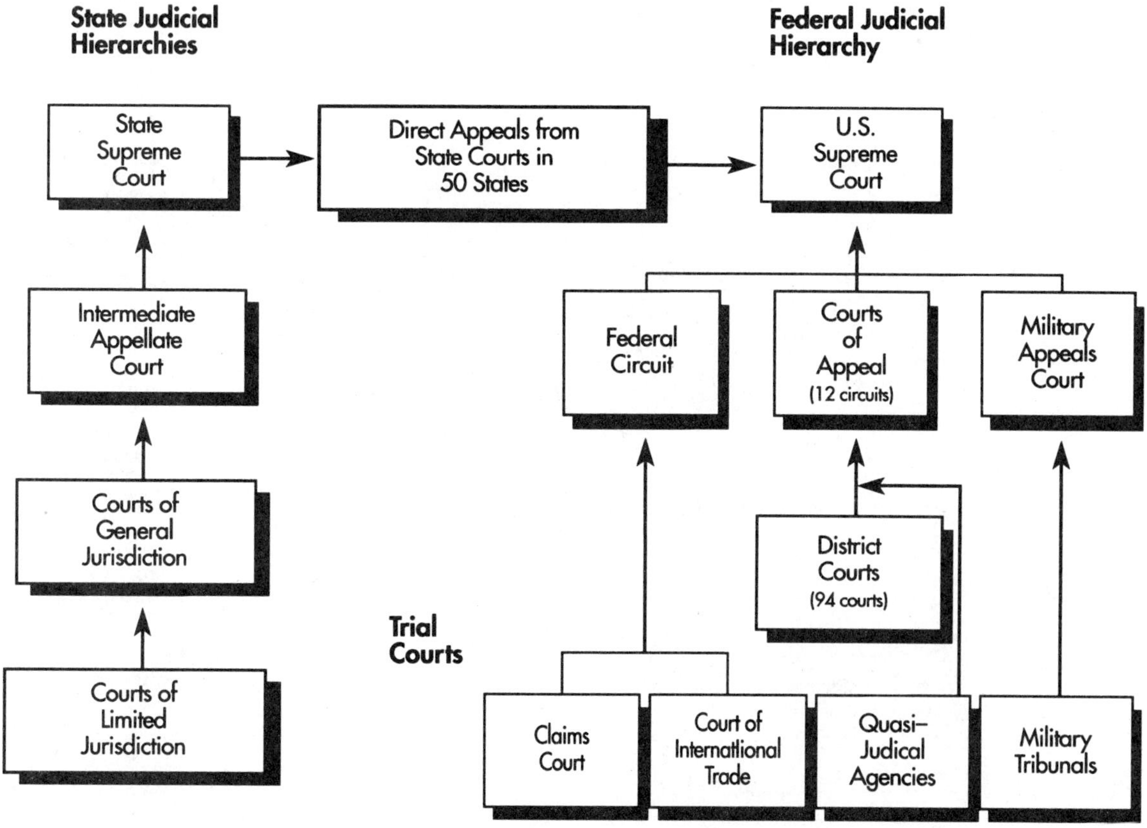

States Court of Appeals for the District of Columbia Circuit and the United States Court of Appeals for the Federal Circuit. Both are located in Washington, D.C.

Some confusion exists about why there are two appellate courts located in the nation's capital. The reason is that the D.C. circuit court serves the territory of the District of Columbia and the federal circuit court serves the entire nation. The federal circuit court has jurisdiction over appeals from all ninety-four district courts in cases arising under the patent laws and in certain damage suits against the federal government. It also has jurisdiction over appeals from several administrative agencies and from decisions of two special trial courts: the claims court and the court of international trade.

The number of judges serving on each of the thirteen appellate courts varies considerably, but the average circuit has between ten and fifteen. Each court of appeals usually hears and decides cases in panels of three judges. Some unusual cases may be heard, or reheard, by the entire court.

Since the federal government has the constitutional authority to govern the military forces in service of the United States, Congress has created the Military Court of Appeals, which serves as the appellate court in cases arising from judgments of military tribunals. In 1983 Congress enacted the Military Justice Act, which conferred jurisdiction on the Supreme Court to review designated categories of appeals from the Military Court of Appeals. This marked the first time in the history of the United States that any court established under article III of the

FIGURE 3.2 The Federal Judicial Circuits

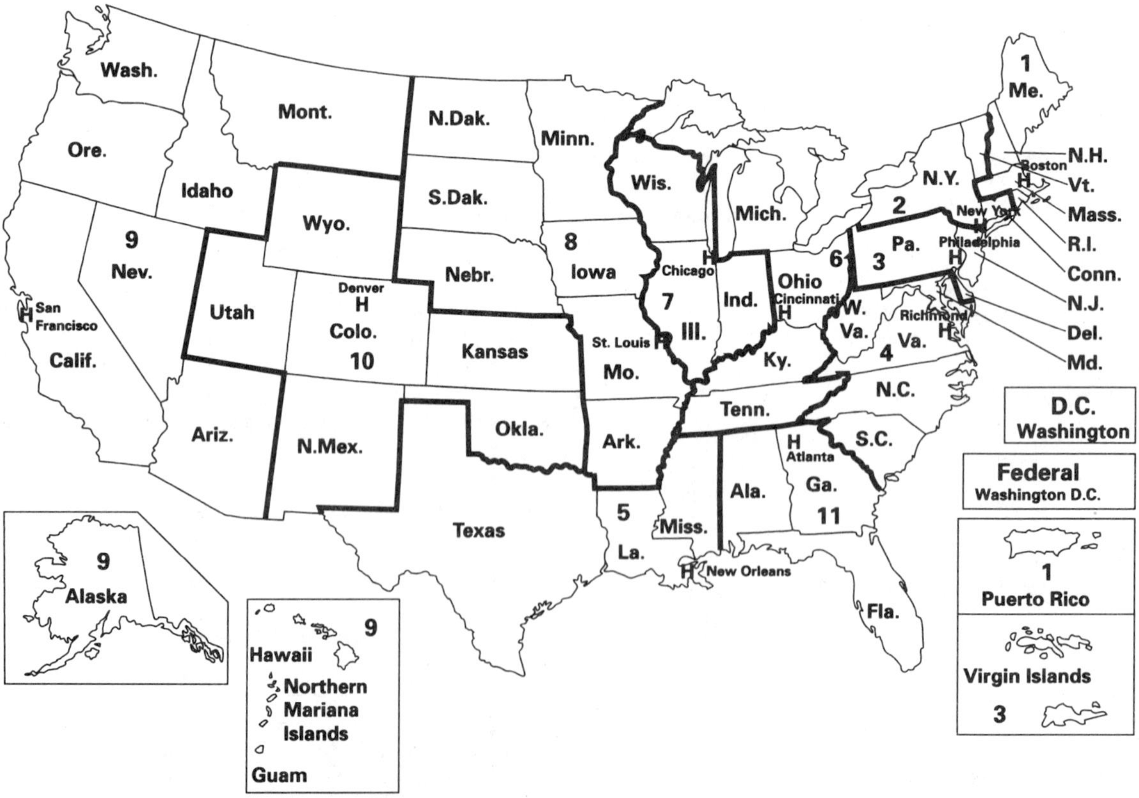

Source: *Federal Reporter*, 2d series (West Publishing Co.).

Constitution was authorized to review the decisions of military courts (Grilliot and Schubert 1992,92).

The Supreme Court

The United States Supreme Court occupies a unique position in the American judicial system because it has jurisdiction to review all decisions of the federal appellate courts and also has jurisdiction over decisions of the highest state courts when those courts have decided a question of federal law.

With minor exceptions, the Supreme Court's jurisdiction is discretionary. Litigants must petition the Court for a **writ of certiorari**—in effect, they ask the Court to hear and decide a legal issue. A decision on the petition is made by the "rule of four." If any four of the nine justices decide to grant the writ of certiorari, the case will be taken up for decision; otherwise, certiorari is denied and the decision of the court below stands.

The Supreme Court always acts through all nine justices (when it has a full court) and never functions in panels when rendering judgments of cases it reviews. Whether the case comes to the Court from the federal hierarchy or from a final decision of the state courts, the litigants must apply for certiorari. The only circumstance in which the Supreme Court can review a district court judgment directly, bypassing the intermediate appeals court, is when the district court sits with three judges, as it is authorized to do in certain instances. In this situation, an appeal can be taken directly to the Supreme Court.

The two exceptions to the Supreme Court's discretionary right to refuse appeal are by "right of appeal" and by "certification." These exceptions are very rare and barely alter the generalization that the Supreme Court's jurisdiction is discretionary.

The Supreme Court's jurisdiction over state courts is confined to reviewing decisions of the highest state court that involve a controlling question of federal law. The federal law may be either statutory or constitutional in nature, but the federal question is controlling only if the Supreme Court's reversal of the state court's determination of that question would necessarily reverse the entire judgment. "The Supreme Court has no jurisdiction to decide state law questions in cases coming from the state courts; in each state the state supreme court is the final and authoritative expositor of that state's law" (Meador 1991,29). This rule is true even if the federal courts have ruled on state law under their diversity jurisdiction.

writ of certiorari: an order, dependent on higher court's discretion, to have lower court records sent to higher court for review.

Federal Court Jurisdiction

State trial courts of general jurisdiction can entertain all types of legal disputes regardless of the law under which they arise or the identity of the parties, unless the trial courts are specifically prohibited from doing so. Federal district courts, in contrast, are not courts of general jurisdiction. They have authority to adjudicate only those types of cases specified in acts of Congress, and Congress can authorize them to entertain only the nine categories of cases and controversies listed in article III of the Constitution.

The most important area of federal jurisdiction is cases arising under federal law, i.e., based on the Constitution, an act of Congress, or a treaty. Most of the claims based on the Constitution rely on the Fourteenth Amendment's due process and equal protection clauses. These claims may be brought against state officials, state agencies, or city and county officials; and the claimants may seek damages, injunctions, or both.

Suits arising under federal regulatory statutes form an increasingly significant portion of federal judicial actions. The statutes govern a wide range of concerns including labor conditions, public accommodations, voting, safety, health, financial transactions, broadcasting, transportation, and environmental protection. The statutes vary in the relief authorized; under some statutes the court can award only damages, under others it can award only injunctions, while in still others both types of relief can be obtained.

Diversity cases, as opposed to federal question cases, are the second major category of civil litigation adjudicated in federal district courts. There must be complete diversity of citizenship; in multiparty cases, if citizens of the same state are found on both sides, federal jurisdiction will be denied. The sum in question must exceed $50,000 and the federal courts cannot hear domestic relations cases (e.g., divorce, child custody disputes) or cases involving administration of deceased persons' estates (Meador 1991,32).

Admiralty cases, involving all kinds of maritime claims relevant to navigable waters and shipping, are subject to federal jurisdiction. They are quite important but have declined in relative volume in more recent times. They are handled by the federal district courts in original jurisdiction.

Finally, all federal crimes must be prosecuted in federal district courts. Only a small fraction of the total criminal prosecutions is based on federal crimes. Federal crimes are those related to areas of special federal concern such as interstate commerce, national security, and federal agencies. Congress has expanded these areas in recent times to include bank robbery, kidnapping, various drug-related activities, and fraud. However, the basic protection of persons and property is a matter for state criminal law.

This list of areas of federal jurisdiction seems more inclusive than it really is. The states are still the major providers of judicial services in the United States and handle the overwhelming majority of all court cases.

AN INTRODUCTION TO LEGAL REASONING

black letter law: written law in statutory or constitutional form.

case law: aggregate of reported cases forming a body of jurisprudence.

The basic forms of law recognized by governmental authority in the United States may be divided into two categories: (1) written law, or what law school students call **black letter law**, and (2) **case law**. The basic forms of written law include constitutions, statutes, and official administrative rules and regulations. Case law refers to the authoritative decisions of courts that not only give specific life and meaning to the written law but also define substantive and procedural law in areas left to the court's discretion—the common law proper.

The most important aspect of traditional legal education in the United States, as practiced in law schools across the nation, involves the development of legal reasoning skills. Most undergraduates find it extremely difficult to grasp the basic concepts involved in legal reasoning. They typically enter the area of law with the idea that rules of law are to be memorized, and rarely do they think about the problems of rule application in the extremely diverse factual situations of real life.

Both black letter law and case law make imperfect statements of the detailed rules of law. Whoever states a rule necessarily must do so in imperfect language. This is true because no one can anticipate all future circumstances that might be described plausibly in the language of the rule. We are human beings with imperfect knowledge; even if a person stating a rule had perfect knowledge at the time, circumstances change and the future brings new factual situations into awareness.

The English common law tradition has been preserved, and even extended, because of the realization of the imperfect nature of our rule-making capacity. Lawyers and judges must analyze and interpret established rules in light of possible cases, and the specific factual situation in question may present new possibilities.

"Thinking like a lawyer" involves understanding this concept of flexibility in the law, and the student wishing to achieve the skills of a lawyer must understand the developmental nature of the law. The "spirit" of the law is more important than the "letter" in achieving this state of awareness. Consequently, a lawyer must go beyond the rules themselves to predict what a court would rule, or could be persuaded to rule, in a case involving a particular set of facts.

Different Forms of Legal Reasoning

The two basic forms of legal reasoning are deductive reasoning and inductive reasoning. They are not much different from commonsense reasoning; however, they have been given more formal, and consequently more self-conscious, rigorous, and uniform expressions in law than in everyday life. As Justice Oliver Wendell Holmes indicated, the formalism must be tempered with the understanding that the life of the law is experience, not logic.

Deductive Reasoning

Logicians call the form of reasoning involved in deductive logic a **syllogism**. The conclusion of a valid syllogism follows necessarily from the premises. The classical syllogism was used by the ancient Greeks to develop an understanding of deductive reasoning. Its simplest form is illustrated below.

syllogism: the full logical form of a single argument.

> Major premise: All men are mortal;
> Minor premise: Socrates is a man;
> Conclusion: Socrates is mortal.

The syllogism is valid only if all the premises are true and if the conclusion must necessarily follow. This form of reasoning is very powerful and is used extensively in legal reasoning. It is not infallible, and an argument is not correct simply because it takes the form of a syllogism. It can be demonstrated to be in error. See how many errors you can find in the following syllogism.

> Major premise: A foot has 39 inches;
> Minor premise: Susan has a foot;
> Conclusion: Susan has 39 inches.

(See Steven J. Burton, *An Introduction to Law and Legal Reasoning*, for a more thorough discussion of legal reasoning.)

Inductive Reasoning (by Analogy)

Inductive logic in the scientific community refers to reasoning by reference to empirical facts, *i.e.*, the formulation of conclusions to explain the observed facts through a systematic analysis. This method is not quite the one the legal com-

analogistical form: reasoning by analogy; analysis of likeness.

munity uses in inductive reasoning. This form of legal reasoning is more properly called the **analogistical form**, since it basically proceeds by analogy. The common law tradition of stare decisis means that like cases should be decided alike. It is often expressed as the doctrine of following precedent, or the principle of equal treatment under the law. The Latin phrase from which the term is derived is *stare decisis et non quieta movere*: "stand by the decision and do not disturb what is settled." The spirit of this doctrine is that it would be unfair to change rules that have been previously applied to others. An even more fundamental principle, however, is that the rules must be essentially fair, and a previously applied rule that does injustice in light of changed circumstances must be altered. Thus a more essential principle than stare decisis is that experience must teach us to do justice in the individual case.

One method of altering the previous rule is to distinguish the facts of a particular case as different from those of the precedent-setting case by applying a new rule or a different rule. A judge may not in good conscience ignore a relevant authoritative precedent without incurring much criticism. The principle that like cases should be decided alike implies that unalike cases should be decided differently, if the differences are more important than the similarities under the circumstances.

A more drastic method of dealing with problem cases is for the highest court to overrule its own precedents. A case that overrules earlier case law becomes the proper base point for future cases and properly represents a change in the law. Courts do not often make such decisions because they tend to undermine the credibility and authority of the court. Courts will take great pains to construe the law, if at all possible, in a manner that will not overturn precedent.

Legitimacy

Finally, all the factors mentioned by Holmes—"necessities of the times," "prevalent moral and political theories," "institutions of public policy," "even the prejudice of judges"—influence judicial decision making. In the final analysis, the "law is what the judges say it is." The legitimacy of the court, however, is determined by the court's ability to exercise its function within the general parameters of reason and fairness. The court ultimately will fail if it cannot explain its decisions on these grounds. Courts neither command armies nor appropriate funds to enforce their decisions. They depend upon the moral conscience and sense of legitimacy that reason and logic dictate.

The Case Method of Legal Training

The skills of legal reasoning involve habits of mind that develop over a person's lifetime. No one is born with these skills; however, the propensity to acquire them may be innate. Legal training involves exposure to the written forms of legal reasoning illustrated in court opinions. These opinions form a record of the legal reasoning of the courts and are relied upon as evidence of what the law is, as applied to specific factual situations.

What Is a Case in Law?

Steven J. Burton describes a case in law as "a short story of an incident in which the state acted or may act to settle a particular dispute. Decided cases tell a story with a beginning, a middle, and an end—a story that occurred once and resulted in the settlement of a particular dispute by the coercive dispute settlement machinery of the state" (Burton 1985,21). These specific sets of factual situations press lawyers and judges to think hard about justice, the limits of proper governmental power, and the scope of individual freedom.

Very few legal matters that are adjudicated involve problems of rule development. Most legal issues fall into clearly defined categories of established law. These typical fact situations are settled by reference to already recorded norms of judicial behavior and allow lawyers to give clients reasonably accurate legal advice about what the "law will allow." However, in those court cases where the rules are unclear, or doubtful in their application to a particular set of facts, the courts may find it necessary to render a written opinion that expresses the court's reasoning in applying a new rule or clarifying an older rule. These court opinions, in problem cases, accumulate and provide the voluminous body of case law that is characteristic of the common law tradition.

How to Analyze a Case in Law

Legal training usually begins by learning how to read a case in law. The student must develop the ability to identify the most significant elements of the opinion because some cases get quite complicated. Following a careful procedure will help the student focus on the essential legal issues. Understanding the legal issues, as opposed to the litigant's interest, will help to identify the narrow kernel of law being developed in the opinion. Case law is not a record of individual litigation; its central purpose is to explain the rules of law.

Judges differ in the way they formulate written opinions. They often discuss material that helps to clarify the ruling, but which is not necessary in deciding the fact situation that is a part of the kernel of law being defined. The beginning student who is used to underlining the most important statements in a text may be confused by this approach, but the list of basic elements provided below will help the student find the significant elements of the case in law and avoid this confusion. Once the advice given has been practiced and applied to the cases illustrated in Appendix B, the student will know what to look for in reading other cases. Noting the important elements of a case becomes easier with practice.

The method of note taking, often referred to as the "case brief," is simply reformulating the written opinion to conform with a systematic scheme of analysis. The most difficult task for beginning students is formulating the **holding**, which represents the narrow kernel of law that may be used as precedent in future cases. "The holding is a statement that captures in a sentence or two the probable significance of a single precedent as a base point for reasoning by analogy in future cases" (Burton 1985,37). It is said that Anglo-American jurisprudence grinds out law (the mill analogy): "It grinds ever so slowly, but it grinds exceedingly fine."

Many opinions make statements that are not **on point**, that is, relevant directly to the specific facts of the case. These statements are often confused with the holding. They are called **dicta** (or **obiter dicta**) and cannot be used as precedent in future cases. The student must avoid confusing such statements with the specific holdings in the case. These extraneous statements are useful and help the reader understand the essential spirit of the underlying concepts of law that are being expounded in the case. The legal reasoning behind the rule laid

holding: legal principle drawn from the opinion of the court.

on point: the distinct proposition of law propounded in the case in agreement with the basic facts.

dicta (or obiter dicta): opinions that go beyond the facts before the court.

ratio decedendi: the grounds for or reasoning behind the decision; point in the case that determines the judgment.

down in the case is called the ***ratio decedendi*** and should be noted in the element referred to as "the court's reasoning."

The end of the opinion is always signaled by the court's disposition of the case. This end statement lets the reader know what specific action the court took in the case, but it should not be confused with the holding, which refers to the precedent the case establishes for future cases.

Basic Elements of a Case in Law

The illustrative cases that follow this section will help the student learn to identify basic elements. After the first case, *Marbury v. Madison*, we will discuss how that case might be summarized using the following list of elements.

1. *Title and citation*: Note who the parties are, whether the case is civil or criminal, which court is deciding the case (trial or appeals), and where to find the case in the law books. It is important to note the date the opinion was issued.

2. *Background*: Note what type and form of litigation is involved. Is it a trial court judgment, an appeal from a preliminary trial court decision, or an appeal from a final trial court judgment? What basic facts are relevant to the decision?

3. *Sources of law*: Note relevant constitutional, statutory, or common law sources and whether a question of conflict of law is involved.

4. *Legal issues*: Note the specific legal issues, as framed by the judge, in terms that can be answered with a yes or no.

5. *Holdings*: Note the answer to each of the legal issues (see above) and follow the yes or no answer with a clear, concise statement that includes the basic facts that will identify this holding as a precedent in future cases. (Draft a clear statement of the rule of law created by the decision.)

6. *Reasoning*: Note how the court supported its decision; identify the most important statutory and case citations as well as the logical argument used to apply these rules.

7. *Questions*: The student should note comments he or she has about dissenting or concurring opinions, anything that is disturbing about the case, and whether the student agrees with the decision and why or why not.

Judicial Review

Perhaps the most famous case in American jurisprudence is the celebrated opinion in *Marbury v. Madison*, 5 U.S. (1 Cranch) 137, 2 L. Ed. 60 (1803). This opinion is noted for its clear formulation of the basic power and authority of the courts in the United States under constitutional law. The Supreme Court's decision was drafted by Chief Justice John Marshall in the early years of the republic when the Court had not yet achieved the prestige it holds today.

The problem facing the Court was a very delicate matter involving appointments to a number of new judicial posts created by the Federalist-controlled "lame duck" Congress in 1801. Thomas Jefferson, representing the first opposition party to the Federalists, had been chosen president in 1801. This was the nation's first change of parties in power, and the transition took some time because it was complicated by the failure of the electoral college to decide who was to become president, which raised problems that had to be resolved in the House of Representatives.

The positions of justice of the peace authorized by the outgoing Federalist-controlled Congress were quickly filled by President Adams and approved by the Senate. In the midnight rush to deliver these confirmed appointments, four of them were left on the desk of the outgoing secretary of state. The new president, Jefferson, ordered his secretary of state, James Madison, to refuse to deliver them. William Marbury and the other three appointees hired the former attorney general, Charles Lee, to sue Madison to force him to deliver the confirmed appointments. They filed suit directly in the Supreme Court, seeking a court order to compel the performance of an official duty, called a **writ of mandamus**. Section 13 of the Judiciary Act of 1789 provided in part that the Supreme Court had the authority to issue writs of mandamus in original jurisdiction.

Marshall was a master of the syllogism. Note the method of development of the arguments in this case. The Court's decision affirmed Marbury's right to the commission, but it did not grant the writ of mandamus because it held the operative part of section 13 of the Judiciary Act of Congress unconstitutional.

writ of mandamus: order issuing from a court of competent jurisdiction commanding a public official to perform a purely ministerial duty imposed by law.

Marbury v. Madison

United States Supreme Court 1803
5 U.S. (1 Cranch) 137, 2 L. Ed. 60.

Mr. Justice Marshall delivered the opinion of the Court.

AT THE LAST TERM on the affidavits then read and filed with the clerk, a rule was granted in this case, requiring the secretary of state to show cause why a mandamus should not issue, directing him to deliver to William Marbury his commission as a justice of the peace for the county of Washington, in the District of Columbia.

No cause has been shown, and the present motion is for a mandamus. The peculiar delicacy of this case, the novelty of some of its circumstances, and the real difficulty attending the points which occur in it, require a complete exposition of the principles on which the opinion to be given by the court is founded.

These principles have been, on the side of the applicant very ably argued at the bar. In rendering the opinion of the court, there will be some departure in form, though not in substance, from the points stated in that argument.

In the order in which the court has viewed this subject, the following questions have been considered and decided.

1st. Has the applicant a right to the commission he demands?

2d. If he has a right, and that right has been violated, do the laws of his country afford him a remedy?

3d. If they do afford him a remedy, is it a mandamus issuing from this court?

The first object of inquiry is,

1st. Has the applicant a right to the commission he demands? . . .

Mr. Marbury, then, since his commission was signed by the President, and sealed by the Secretary of State, was appointed; and as the law creating the office, gave the officer a right to hold for five years, independent of the executive, the appointment was not revocable, but vested in the officer legal rights, which are protected by the laws of his country.

To withhold his commission, therefore, is an act deemed by the court not warranted by law, but violative of a vested legal right.

This brings us to the second inquiry; which is,

2d. If he has a right, and that right has been violated, do the laws of this country afford him a remedy? . . .

The government of the United States has been emphatically termed a government of laws, and not of men. It will certainly cease to deserve this high appellation, if the laws furnish no remedy for the violation of a vested legal right. . . .

It remains to be inquired whether,

3d. He is entitled to the remedy for which he applies. . . .

With respect to the officer to whom it would be directed. The intimate political relation subsisting between the President of the United States and the heads of departments, necessarily renders any legal investigation of the acts of one of those high officers peculiarly irksome, as well as delicate; and excites some hesitation with respect to the propriety of entering into such investigation. . . . [T]he assertion, by an individual, of his legal claims in a court of justice, to which claims it is the duty of that court to attend, should at first view be considered by some, as an attempt to intrude into the cabinet, and to intermeddle with the prerogatives of the executive.

It is scarcely necessary for the court to disclaim all pretensions to such jurisdiction. An extravagance, so absurd and excessive, could not have been entertained for a moment. The province of the court is, solely, to decide on the rights of individuals, not to inquire how the executive, or executive officers, perform duties in which they have a discretion. Questions in their nature political, or which are, by the constitution and laws, submitted to the executive, can never be made in this court.

But, if this be not such a question; if, so far from being an intrusion into the secrets of the cabinet, it respects a paper which, according to law, is upon record, and to a copy of which the law gives a right, on the payment of ten cents; if it be no intermeddling with a subject over which the executive can be considered as having exercised any control; what is there in the exalted station of the officer, which shall bar a citizen from asserting, in a court of justice, his legal rights? . . .

This, then, is a plain case for a mandamus, either to deliver the commission, or a copy of it from the record; and it only remains to be inquired,

Whether it can issue from this court.

The act to establish the judicial courts of the United States authorizes the Supreme Court "to issue writs of mandamus in cases warranted by the principles and usages of law, to any courts appointed, or persons holding office, under the authority of the United States."

The Secretary of State, being a person holding an office under the authority of the United States, is precisely within the letter of the description, and if this court is not authorized to issue a writ of mandamus to such an officer, it must be because the law is unconstitutional, and therefore absolutely incapable of conferring the authority, and assigning the duties which its words purport to confer and assign.

The constitution vests the whole judicial power of the United States in one Supreme Court, and such inferior courts as congress shall, from time to time, ordain and establish. This power is expressly extended to all cases arising under the laws of the United States; and, consequently, in some form, may be exercised over the present case; because the right claimed is given by a law of the United States.

In the distribution of this power it is declared that "the Supreme Court shall have original jurisdiction in all cases affecting ambassadors, other public ministers and consuls, and those in which a state shall be a party. In all other cases, the Supreme Court shall have appellate jurisdiction."

It has been insisted, at the bar, that as the original grant of jurisdiction, to the Supreme and inferior courts, in general, and the clause, assigning original jurisdiction to the Supreme Court, contains no negative or restrictive words, the power remains to the legislature, to assign original jurisdiction to that court in other cases than those specified in the article which has been recited; provided those cases belong to the judicial power of the United States.

If it had been intended to leave it in the discretion of the legislature to apportion the judicial power between the Supreme and inferior courts according to the will of that body, it would certainly have been useless to have proceeded further than to have defined the judicial power, and the tribunals in which it should be vested. The subsequent part of the section is mere surplusage, is entirely without meaning, if such is to be the construction. If congress remains at liberty to give this court appellate jurisdiction, where the constitution has declared their jurisdiction shall be original; and original jurisdiction where the constitution has declared it shall be appellate; the distribution of jurisdiction, made in the constitution, is form without substance.

Affirmative words are often, in their operation, negative of other objects than those affirmed; and in this case, a negative or exclusive sense must be given to them, or they have no operation at all. It cannot be presumed that any clause in the constitution is intended to be without effect; and, therefore, such a construction is inadmissible, unless the words require it. . . .

The authority, therefore, given to the Supreme Court, by the act establishing the judicial courts of the United States, it issue writs of mandamus to public officers, appears not to be warranted by the constitution; and it becomes necessary to inquire whether a jurisdiction so conferred can be exercised.

The question, whether an act, repugnant to the constitution, can become the law of the land, is a question deeply interesting to the United States; but, happily, not of an intricacy proportioned to its interest. It seems only necessary to recognize certain principles, supposed to have been long and well established, to decide it.

That the people have an original right to establish, for their future government, such principles, as, in their opinion, shall most conduce to their own happiness is the basis on which the whole American fabric has been erected. The exercise of this original right is a very great exertion; nor can it, nor ought it, to be frequently repeated. The principles, therefore, so established, are deemed fundamental. And as the authority from which they proceed is supreme, and can seldom act, they are designed to be permanent.

This original and supreme will organizes the government, and assigns to different departments their respective powers. It may either stop here, or establish certain limits not to be transcended by those departments.

The government of the United States is of the latter description. The powers of the legislature are defined and limited; and that those limits may not be mistaken, or forgotten, the constitution is written. To what purpose are powers limited, and to what purpose is that limitation committed to writing, if these limits may, at any time, be passed by those intended to be restrained? The distinction between a government with limited and unlimited powers is abolished, if those limits do not confine the persons on whom they are imposed, and if acts prohibited and acts allowed, are of equal obligation. It is a proposition too plain to be contested, that the constitution controls any legislative act repugnant to it; or, that the legislature may alter the constitution by an ordinary act.

Between these alternatives there is no middle ground. The constitution is either a superior paramount law, unchangeable by ordinary means, or it is on a level with ordinary legislative acts, and, like other acts, is alterable when the legislature shall please to alter it.

If the former part of the alternative be true, then a legislative act contrary to the constitution is not law: if the latter part be true, then written constitutions are absurd attempts, on the part of the people, to limit a power in its own nature illimitable.

Certainly all those who have framed written constitutions contemplate them as forming the fundamental and paramount law of the nation, and, consequently, the theory of every such government must be, that an act of the legislature, repugnant to the constitution, is void.

This theory is essentially attached to a written constitution, and, is consequently, to be considered, by this court, as one of the fundamental principles of our society. It is not therefore to be lost sight of in the further consideration of this subject.

If an act of the legislature, repugnant to the constitution, is void, does it, notwithstanding its invalidity, bind the courts, and oblige them to give it effect? Or, in other words, though it be not law, does it constitute a rule as operative as if it was a law? This would be to overthrow in fact what was established in theory; and would seem, at first view, an absurdity too gross to be insisted on. It shall, however, receive a more attentive consideration.

It is emphatically the province and duty of the judicial department to say what the law is. Those who apply the rule to particular cases, must of necessity expound and interpret that rule. If two laws conflict with each other, the courts must decide on the operation of each.

So if the law be in opposition to the constitution; if both the law and the constitution apply to a particular case, so that the court must either decide that case conformably to the law, disregarding the constitution; or conformably to the constitution, disregarding the law; the court must determine which of these conflicting rules governs the case. This is of the very essence of judicial duty.

If, then, the courts are to regard the constitution, and the constitution is superior to any ordinary act of the legislature, the constitution, and not such ordinary act, must govern the case to which they both apply.

Those, then, who controvert the principle that the constitution is to be considered, in court, as a paramount law, are reduced to the necessity of maintaining that courts must close their eyes on the constitution, and see only the law.

This doctrine would subvert the very foundation of all written constitutions. It would declare that an act which, according to the principles and theory of our government, is entirely void, is yet, in practice, completely obligatory. It would declare that if the legislature shall do what is expressly forbidden, such act, notwithstanding the express prohibition, is in reality effectual. It would be giving the legislature a practical and real omnipotence, with the same breath which professes to restrict their powers within narrow limits. It is prescribing limits, and declaring that those limits may be passed at pleasure.

That it thus reduces to nothing what we have deemed the greatest improvement on political institutions, a written constitution, would of itself be sufficient, in America, where written constitutions have been viewed with so much reverence, for rejecting the construction. But the peculiar expressions of the constitution of the United States furnish additional arguments in favour of its rejection.

The judicial power of the United States is extended to all cases arising under the constitution.

Could it be the intention of those who gave this power, to say that in using it the constitution should not be looked into? That a case arising under the constitution should be decided without examining the instrument under which it arises?

This is too extravagant to be maintained.

In some cases, then, the constitution must be looked into by the judges. And if they can open it at all, what part of it are they forbidden to read or to obey?

There are many other parts of the constitution which serve to illustrate this subject.

It is declared that "no tax or duty shall be laid on articles exported from any state." Suppose a duty on the export of cotton, of tobacco, or of flour; and a suit instituted to recover it. Ought judgment to be rendered in such a case? Ought the judges to close their eyes on the constitution, and only see the law?

The constitution declares "that no bill of attainder or ex post facto law shall be passed."

If, however, such a bill should be passed, and a person should be prosecuted under it; must the court condemn to death those victims whom the constitution endeavors to preserve?

"No person," says the constitution, "shall be convicted of treason unless on the testimony of two witnesses to the same overt act, or on confession in open court."

Here the language of the constitution is addressed especially to the courts. It prescribes, directly for them, a rule of evidence not to be departed from. If the legislature should change that rule, and declare one witness, or a confession out of court, sufficient for conviction, must the constitutional principle yield to the legislative act?

From these, and many other selections which might be made, it is apparent, that the framers of the constitution contemplated that instrument as a rule for the government of courts, as well as of the legislature.

Why otherwise does it direct the judges to take an oath to support it? This oath certainly applies in an especial manner, to their conduct in their official character. How immoral to impose it on them, if they were to be used as the instruments, and the knowing instruments, for violating what they swear to support!

The oath of office, too, imposed by the legislature, is completely demonstrative of the legislative opinion on this subject. It is in these words: "I do solemnly swear that I will administer justice without respect to persons, and do equal right to the poor and to the rich; and that I will faithfully and impartially discharge all the duties incumbent on me as_____, according to the best of my abilities and understanding agreeably to the constitution and laws of the United States."

Why does a judge swear to discharge his duties agreeably to the constitution of the United States, if that constitution forms no rule for his government? If it is closed upon him, and cannot be inspected by him?

If such be the real state of things, this is worse than solemn mockery. To prescribe, or to take this oath, becomes equally a crime.

It is also not entirely unworthy of observation, that in declaring what shall be the supreme law of the land, the constitution itself is first mentioned; and not the laws of the United States generally, but those only which shall be made in pursuance of the constitution, have that rank.

Thus, the particular phraseology of the constitution of the United States confirms and strengthens the principle, supposed to be essential to all written constitutions, that a law repugnant to the constitution is void; and that courts, as well as other departments, are bound by that instrument.

The rule must be discharged.

Notes

Title and citation: Marbury v. Madison was a civil legal action decided by the United States Supreme Court in 1803. It can be found in the case reporter known as the *United States Reports* in volume 5 on page 137. (Cranch is an older reporter used at the time.)

Background: Plaintiffs sought a writ of mandamus ordering the secretary of state to deliver previously authorized commissions. They claimed that the Judiciary Act of 1789 gave the Supreme Court original jurisdiction in such matters and filed directly in the Supreme Court. Their commissions had been properly approved by the previous president and confirmed by the Senate.

Sources of law: The laws involved were section 13 of the Judiciary Act of 1789, authorizing writs of mandamus to be issued by the Supreme Court in original jurisdiction, and article III of the Constitution of the United States, defining the original jurisdiction of the Supreme Court.

Legal issues: Was section 13 of the Judiciary Act of 1789 altering the original jurisdiction of the Supreme Court in conflict with the Constitution?

Holdings: Yes. The Court held that section 13 of the Judiciary Act of 1789 was unconstitutional insofar as it purported to change the original jurisdiction of the Supreme Court and therefore could not be enforced by the Court.

Reasoning: Marshall reasoned that the Constitution defined the original jurisdiction of the Supreme Court, which could not be changed by an act of Congress. The opinion relied upon the wording of the Constitution to show intent so to define the original jurisdiction of the Supreme Court, as opposed to the appellate jurisdiction of the Court. If the framers of the Constitution had intended to give Congress discretionary authority to change the Court's original jurisdiction, they would not have needed to define it. Marshall used logical syllogisms throughout the opinion to show that Marbury was entitled to his commission, but that the writ of mandamus demanded could not be granted by the Supreme Court because the Court had no legal authority (jurisdiction) to grant it.

Questions: There are no dissenting opinions in this case, but one might wonder why the Court acted in this manner. This is a question for class discussion. Was this purely a political decision? Has the decision in law been upheld by future court decisions? Could the legal issue have been decided differently?

BASIC FORMS OF LAW

The United States Supreme Court decision in *Marbury v. Madison* concerns an issue of conflict of laws. This issue arises in all political systems, even unitary ones. However, it arises more frequently in the United States because of our federal structure, which recognizes so many different lawmaking authorities. John Marshall's opinion established the initial precedent for holding an act of Congress unconstitutional. However, the principle of judicial review is a much more general principle asserting that acts of all governmental agencies deemed contrary to the fundamental law are void and nonenforceable in the courts. Such general rules are often referred to as principles or **axioms**.

As Marshall explains, the power of judicial review rests on a basic principle applied to situations of conflict of laws that was understood in English jurisprudence. The axiom is that in situations of conflict of laws, when there is no opportunity to interpret the rules in question not to be in conflict, *the more fundamental law prevails over the less fundamental law.*

In English jurisprudence, even today when there is no written constitution, this principle provides a system of rational legal order and a body of constitutional law. In the United States, this principle applies within each state jurisdiction concerning state laws. The federal laws are ordered according to this same principle, including the United States Constitution. Problems of conflict of laws are further clarified by the supremacy clause of the federal Constitution.

axiom: a fundamental rule.

The Hierarchy of Laws

The principle of fundamentality of laws creates a **hierarchy of laws** that enables us to understand how all the various forms of law discussed in the evolution of law can be rationally ordered. The basic hierarchy in order of priority is:

1. constitutional law,
2. statutory law,
3. common law, and
4. contracts.

hierarchy of laws: order of priority of various sources of law.

Constitutional Law

This form of law is the most fundamental because it deals with the organization and framework of government. The branch of law known as **constitutional law** defines and limits the power and authority of government. Thus, constitutions are the highest forms of law in their respective jurisdictions. Constitutional law includes both the expressed words of the constitution and all court interpretations of expressed or implied provisions, often called constitutional case law.

constitutional law: body of law that deals with fundamental principles of governmental authority.

Statutory Law

This form of law includes both statutes that have been made by legislative authority and all court interpretations of their meaning in specific cases (statutory case law). This body of law takes priority over all lower forms of law, including common law. However, when **statutory law** comes into conflict with a constitutional principle, the statutory law is considered invalid.

statutory law: body of law created by acts of the legislature.

Common Law

common law: body of law that is not based upon any expressed, positive act of legislative authority.

This form of law is properly defined as that body of law that has no source other than judicial decision to support its authority. Common law has been relegated to a limited role in our modern legal system and can be changed by legislative authority. Common law retains its vigor, however, because the legislative authorities, and the popular will acting through constitutional law, have left certain discretionary authority to the courts.

All common law today is case law, but not all case law is common law; that is, case law that explains the meaning of a statute or constitutional provision is not considered common law in this hierarchy. Constitutional case law cannot be changed by legislative enactment.

The subordinate nature of the English common law gave John Marshall another occasion to assert the independence of the courts in 1807. President Thomas Jefferson accused his former vice-president, Aaron Burr, of treason and wanted him tried under the common law precedents of the English courts. Marshall was the presiding judge at this trial and ruled that the United States Constitution defined the crime of treason. Under this ruling, the jury acquitted Aaron Burr, and the rule of law was upheld contrary to the expressed wishes of a popularly elected president.

Contracts

contracts: agreements between two or more parties creating legal obligations that can be enforced in court.

This form of creation of legal obligations is not general law, but a form of private law. **Contracts** create legal obligations between the parties as long as the parties do not violate any of the higher forms of law listed in the hierarchy of law. Thus, not only do legislatures and judges have certain lawmaking powers, but so, in a limited sense, do individuals. All forms of legally enforceable agreements are considered contracts.

Equity

equity: justice administered by fairness as contrasted with strictly formulated laws.

This concept is not included in the hierarchy of law because it can be used as a remedy at all levels in the hierarchy. **Equity** is not a law, but rather a principle of fairness used to provide a solution to problems when strict application of the law would do an obvious injustice.

Equity is designed to provide justice where damages may come too late to be meaningful. In an equity case, the court may order that something be done (specific performance) or forbid certain actions (injunction). This concept provides a remedy in situations in which the common law does not apply. It is frequently used in child custody cases and decrees stipulating parental visitation rights. The federal Constitution gives the courts the authority to decide disputes in both law and equity. Many significant disputes that have resulted in fundamental changes in our society were essentially equity suits seeking specific performance orders, such as writs of mandamus.

Substantive and Procedural Law

procedural law: that which prescribes the method of enforcing rights or obtaining redress for violation of rules.

These two aspects of law are often difficult for beginning students to distinguish but can be easily grasped if specific examples are given. **Procedural law** refers to the rules of law that have been developed to govern the actions of governmental authorities in the administration of justice. They may be of constitutional, statutory, or common law origin, but they all provide regulated procedure for the proper conduct of governmental authority. The concept of due process of law is a central feature of the procedural rules, which protect our most cherished liberties from governmental abuse. The entire body of these rules is quite large and includes criminal, civil, and administrative procedural rules. The constitutional right to trial by jury is a good example of procedural law.

Substantive law refers to the rules of law that have been developed to govern the behavior of individuals in our society. These rules may be criminal, civil, or regulatory rules of individual behavior. Examples are rules regarding crimes, torts, and governmental regulations. The area of substantive law known as **tort** is defined as a private or civil wrong (or injury), other than breach of contract, for which the court will provide a remedy in the form of an action for damages.

substantive law: the basic law of rights and duties, as opposed to procedural law.

tort: civil wrong for which the law provides a remedy in the form of an action for damages exclusive of contract.

Illustrative Cases (see Appendix B)

This chapter has provided some preliminary definitions and distinctions that will enable the student to read case law. In Appendix B, six illustrative cases are provided to allow students to gain more experience in reading and briefing cases in law. They are taken from a variety of state jurisdictions and include examples of issues relevant to torts, crimes, fundamental due process, and contracts.

INTRODUCTION TO PROCEDURAL DUE PROCESS

The rest of this textbook, which demonstrates how basic legal concepts are applied in specific factual situations, is divided into two parts that separate the two fundamental forms of legal procedure—civil and criminal. These traditional divisions of procedural law differ substantially from each other, but both are administered by the courts of law. A third form of procedural rules, discussed in chapter thirteen, deals with administrative due process.

Due Process of Law

The United States Constitution uses the term *due process of law* in both the Fifth and Fourteenth amendments. These amendments are designed specifically to limit governmental authority. The Fifth Amendment prohibits the federal government from depriving any person of life, liberty, or property without due process of law. After the Civil War, the adoption of the Fourteenth Amendment applied this concept to the states as well.

American jurisprudence places great emphasis on procedural fairness. The meaning of the constitutional phrase **due process of law** is vague, and there is no comprehensive definition of due process that applies to all situations. However, the central core of the idea centers on fundamental fairness. "A person should always have notice and a real chance to present his or her side in a legal dispute, and no law or governmental procedure should be arbitrary or unfair" (Neubauer 1991,40).

due process of law: according to appropriate procedures of law.

Although all legal actions must be essentially fair and are limited by procedural rules recognized by law, they differ considerably in form and substance. Civil, criminal, and administrative procedures require separate legal actions, although a real life situation may involve all these dimensions. Each legal action has to conform to the rules of procedure in a specific area and must be filed with the appropriate court (or agency) having jurisdiction in such matters.

The following overview of the three basic divisions of legal procedure (see Figure 3.3) will provide an initial orientation to the fundamental differences among civil, criminal, and administrative actions. Parts II and III of this text contain extended hypothetical examples of the various stages involved in these forms of legal actions.

Civil Legal Actions

Private (or civil) law is the area of legal process that allows individuals to bring their disputes into the courts for authoritative settlement. **Civil legal actions** enable individuals to file suit before the courts against another individual, group of individuals, or corporation. Corporations generally have the right to sue and be sued in civil jurisdiction, and even governmental agencies can be sued (or bring suit) where governmental authority has been granted to do so. The funda-

FIGURE 3.3 The Three Grand Divisions of Legal Procedure

I. Civil Actions in Law and Equity
Substantive duties owned by one individual to another which include torts, contracts, property, or other constitutional or statutory rights.

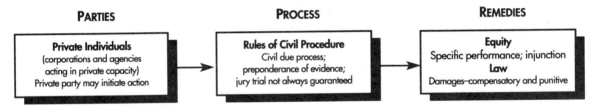

II. Criminal Actions
Substantive duty involves conduct that is offensive to society as generally defined by legislative authority.

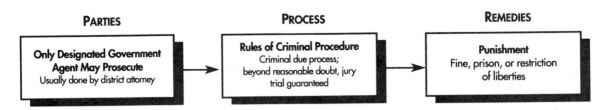

III. Administrative Actions
Substantive duty involves conduct regulated by government in its capacity to enforce administrative rules and regulations authorized by legislative authority.

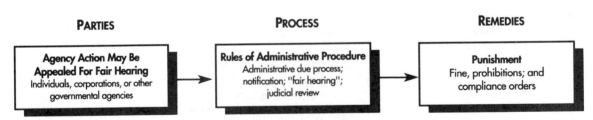

mental principle of sovereign immunity prevents government from being sued without its consent; however, in modern times, such authority has been extensively granted by legislative enactment.

The **plaintiff** is the party bringing suit and the **defendant** is the party being sued. These parties are called litigants in all noncriminal actions before the courts.

plaintiff: party bringing suit.

defendant: party being sued.

Civil actions may be taken in both law and equity in areas involving substantive duties owed by one individual to another, including torts, contracts, property, and other constitutional or statutory rights. Civil due process involves a less stringent standard of proof than criminal due process; the standard is known as "preponderance of evidence." A jury trial is not always guaranteed in civil actions.

Criminal Legal Actions

Crimes are defined as conduct deemed offensive to society. **Criminal legal actions** are brought only by a designated agent of either the state or federal government, known as a **prosecutor**. A crime is defined by the legislative authority as a wrong against society, so the governmental entity that has been wronged must bring suit.

prosecutor: agent of state or federal government authorized to prosecute persons in criminal actions.

The rules of criminal procedure are quite extensive and subject to all the constitutional guarantees because they involve the most severe penalties. Criminal due process involves the more stringent standard of proof "beyond a reasonable doubt," and a trial by jury is guaranteed.

Administrative Legal Actions

Administrative law may cover all the procedural areas of legal action; however, governmental agencies must exercise their authority within the limits of fundamental rules of fairness. **Administrative legal actions** fall into a very extensive area involving legal matters that do not fit into the traditional civil and criminal rules of procedure. All governmental actions must follow fundamental concepts of fairness, but not the extensive procedural rules of civil and criminal legal actions. They must not be arbitrary or capricious, and they must follow rudimentary due process of law. These concepts have been applied even to private entities, as illustrated in the *Ryan* case included in Appendix B.

administrative legal action: an adjudication within an administrative agency, which must comply with fundamental concepts of fairness.

Administrative standards vary considerably and, in many instances, depend upon statutory authority as well as common law court decision. Due notification of an action, the right to a fair hearing, and the right to confront witnesses are considered minimal guarantees to ensure that the fundamental principles of fairness are met.

CHAPTER SUMMARY

1. The American legal system is characterized by the dual hierarchies of its court systems. This complexity results from our peculiar federal governmental structure. Each state has a complete court hierarchy that defines court jurisdiction, and the federal government has a separate court hierarchy.

2. The United States Supreme Court occupies a unique position in the American judicial system because it has jurisdiction to review all decisions of the federal appellate courts and also has jurisdiction over decisions of the highest state courts when those courts have decided questions of federal law, including alleged violations of the United States Constitution.

3. The state court of last resort has final authority in all cases involving issues of that state's laws, even if the federal courts have ruled on state law under their diversity jurisdiction. However, the states are also limited by the United States Constitution insofar as that body of law applies to the specific case.

4. Legal reasoning involves both deductive logic and a form of inductive logic called analogistic reasoning. Deductive logic proceeds from accepted premises to logically consistent conclusions, while analogistic reasoning involves analysis of likeness or similarity—reasoning by analogy. The underlying concept of stare decisis requires consistency with past decisions that adhere to fundamental principles of fairness.

5. Reading case law effectively requires careful attention to the basic elements of written court opinions. The holding of the court and its reasoning are the most significant elements. The holding must be stated in clear, concise terms that can be used as precedent in future cases, and the reasoning is an explanation of why the court has made this decision.

6. A basic axiom of Anglo-American jurisprudence is that when an unavoidable conflict of laws occurs, the more fundamental law prevails over the less fundamental law. This axiom creates a basic hierarchy of laws in the following order of priority: constitutional law, statutory law, common law, and contracts. Federal law and state law each has its own hierarchy. However, the United States Constitution, constitutional acts of Congress, and treaties are the supreme law of the land and take priority over any state law.

7. Equity is not included in the hierarchy of laws because it is essentially a remedial concept that may be used at all levels to effect a remedy. It takes the form of specific performance or injunction and refers to the principles of fairness used to decide these questions.

KEY TERMS

jurisdiction	syllogism	common law
diversity jurisdiction	analogistic reasoning	contracts
trial courts	holding	equity
civil legal action	on point	procedural law
criminal legal action	dicta (or obiter dicta)	substantive law
appellate courts	*ratio decedendi*	tort
court hierarchy	writ of mandamus	due process of law
federal district courts	axiom	plaintiff
writ of certiorari	hierarchy of laws	defendant
black letter law	constitutional law	prosecutor
case law	statutory law	administrative legal action

DISCUSSION QUESTIONS

1. Why do we have dual hierarchies of court systems in the United States?

2. What basic principle distinguishes federal from state court jurisdiction?

3. What are the essential differences between trial courts and appeals courts?

4. How do cases reach the United States Supreme Court? Why does this Court occupy a unique position in the American judicial system?

5. What courts have final jurisdiction over issues of state law that do not raise a "federal question"? How does this system preserve an area of state sovereignty?

6. How are both deductive logic and inductive logic involved in legal reasoning?

7. What are the most significant elements of the court's opinion in a case in law?

8. Why must the holding be stated in terms that include the salient facts of the case?

9. Why must the court use the underlying "spirit" of the law to decide issues of law in dispute?

10. Must the principle of stare decisis always prevail, or is there an even more fundamental standard of fairness?

11. What is the basic hierarchy of laws, and why should a more fundamental law prevail over a less fundamental law in cases of conflict of laws?

SOURCES AND SUGGESTED READING

Abraham, Henry J. 1986. *The Judicial Process*. 5th ed. New York: Oxford University Press. (See also 6th ed., 1993.)

Aldisert, Ruggero J. 1989. *Logic for Lawyers: A Guide to Clear Legal Thinking*. New York: Clark Boardman.

Burton, Steven J. 1985. *An Introduction to Law and Legal Reasoning*. Boston: Little, Brown.

Calvi, James V., and Susan Coleman. 1989. *American Law and Legal Systems*. Englewood Cliffs, N.J.: Prentice Hall.

Carp, Robert A., and Ronald Stidham. 1990. *Judicial Process in America*. Washington, D.C.: Congressional Quarterly Press.

Garraty, John A., ed. 1987. *Quarrels That Have Shaped the Constitution*. New York: Harper & Row.

Grilliot, Harold J., and Frank A. Schubert. 1992. *Introduction to Law and the Legal System*. 5th ed. Boston: Houghton Mifflin.

Levi, Edward H. 1948. *An Introduction to Legal Reasoning*. Chicago: University of Chicago Press. (This is a classic and concise explanation of the evolution of law through the process of legal reasoning.)

Lewis, Alfred J. 1985. *Using American Law Books*. 2d ed. Dubuque, Iowa: Kendall/Hunt.

Meador, Daniel John. 1991. *American Courts*. St. Paul: West Publishing Co.

Murphy, Walter F., and C. Herman Pritchett. 1986. *Courts, Judges, and Politics: An Introduction to the Judicial Process*. 4th ed. New York: Random House.

National Center for State Courts. 1991. *State Court Caseload Statistics: Annual Report 1991*. Williamsburg, Va.: National Center for State Courts.

Siegel, Brian. 1974. *How to Succeed in Law School*. Woodbury, N.Y.: Barron's Educational Series, Inc.

van Geel, T.R. 1991. *Understanding Supreme Court Opinions*. New York: Longman Publishing Group.

PART TWO

UNDERSTANDING CIVIL LAW PROCEDURE

Part Two of this text is designed to help the student understand civil procedure in the United States by describing the development of a dispute in products liability tort law. This hypothetical situation contains discussion of various types of civil legal problems that introduce a number of new terms and concepts associated with civil legal actions. The entire development of the dispute, from its inception through trial, is examined, and the basic elements of the case and of the decisions involved are explained.

The basic elements of the civil law process that are presented in the hypothetical case are typical of most jurisdictions. Basic variations in state practice are discussed, but the focus is on the elements that are common to all or most states. Federal procedure is illustrated, as well as ways in which state and federal procedure interact.

Chapter Four establishes the events leading to legal action: finding a lawyer, the preliminary investigation, and the legal research necessary to arrive at a decision to bring civil action. Chapter Five describes the official formulation of a civil legal action and the instruments used in the discovery process to gain access to the facts needed by both sides to prepare for an adversarial trial. Chapter Six presents the elements of the adversarial trial process, including the roles of the principal actors: the parties to the suit, the judge, the opposing lawyers, the witnesses, and the jurors. Chapter Seven analyzes the characteristic features of the adversarial process by comparing it with some of the features typical of the nonadversarial process in civil law countries. This chapter also raises significant issues regarding the tort system and reform proposals.

CHAPTER FOUR

INITIATING LEGAL PROCESS IN AN ILLUSTRATIVE CIVIL CASE

> **THE CENTERVILLE NEWS JOURNAL**
> September 9, 1991
> **LOCAL RAINSTORM CAUSES ACCIDENTS, DEATH**
>
> The Centerville area witnessed a severe rainstorm last night. Power lines were reported out of operation for as long as two hours in some areas of Rural County. Seven accidents were reported in the area ranging from minor fender benders to a severe accident on Interstate 24 about three miles from Centerville.
>
> William P. Consumer, a professor at Middle State University, was reported dead on arrival at the hospital after his automobile collided with a tractor-trailer. He is survived by his wife, Jane Consumer, who was also injured in the accident. Jane Consumer was reported in serious condition by the Mid-State Medical Center this morning.
>
> Details of the accident are not known at this time, but it appears that the Consumer vehicle was traveling south on I-24 and crossed over the median, hitting a tractor-trailer traveling north on the opposite side of the highway.
>
> The storm lasted only about 30 minutes and began around 10:30 P.M. The *News Journal* rain gauge recorded 1.5 inches of precipitation. Heavy flooding was reported in some low-lying areas, which caused damage to homes and automobiles.
>
> There has not yet been an assessment of the damage caused by the storm in the area.

Automobile accidents are one type of personal and property damage that frequently lead to disputes of a civil nature involving private parties. The accident described above may seem somewhat unusual, but such events appear in newspapers quite often. In the example, Bill Consumer was killed and his wife, Jane Consumer, was severely injured in an accident that occurred during a rainstorm. Such a personal tragedy has several important legal implications, and this example will be used to illustrate many aspects of private, or civil, law.

Jane Consumer found that her life had been drastically altered by a sudden and completely unexpected event. She suffered a broken back in the accident and the loss of her husband. Bill Consumer was an associate professor of psychology at Middle State University. He was the sole support for the Consumer family, which included three children. The oldest child was a sophomore in college, and there were two younger children aged fifteen and eleven. The Consumers were a typical middle-class family that considered themselves fortunate to enjoy a decent standard of living and thought they would be able to provide for the education of their children and a secure future.

After the accident, Jane Consumer realized she was confronted with a number of significant problems that required the assistance of a lawyer. Bill Consumer's employer was helpful in providing information about the benefits Jane would receive from an insurance policy carried by the university, but after a few months, she would no longer have the benefit of group health insurance rates. The automobile insurance company indicated that the family car could not be repaired and offered to settle Jane's claims under the family's liability and casualty insurance policies; Jane was not sure whether the insurance company was offering a fair value to compensate for the "totaled" automobile. Jane also know she would have to file legal papers concerning her husband's estate but knew nothing about the process.

Above all, Jane Consumer was concerned about why the accident happened in the first place. The car just suddenly went out of control on the way home from a shopping trip. Bill was trying to pass a van on the interstate highway when he looked at her in panic and said, "The wheel won't turn." The car went out of control and crossed the median, hitting a truck on the other side of the interstate highway. Jane had heard a strange noise just before the car went out of control and thought there was something wrong with the vehicle. Bill had complained about the car leaning to the left for some time and had even taken it to the dealer to be fixed, but they said they found nothing wrong with it. After going through Bill's papers, Jane found a letter from the manufacturer of their car that indicated the car should be taken to the dealer for repairs.

Jane began to suspect that she might have cause for legal action against the manufacturer or the dealer for failing to repair the car. At any rate, she needed legal advice about the probate matters concerning her husband's estate. She was uncertain and confused about her financial affairs and thought it would be helpful to have professional advice about them.

FINDING A LAWYER

There is no simple answer to the question of how to choose a good lawyer. Complaints against lawyers, stories of malpractice suits and of lawyers who have taken advantage of their clients are common, but the majority of lawyers are honest professionals dedicated to client service. The Rules of Professional Conduct for lawyers require high ethical standards, and attorneys can be disbarred for violations of these professional ethics. Nonetheless, most people are reluctant to seek legal advice because of the fear that a lawyer's services will be very expensive and the feeling that even though a lawyer is needed, it is difficult to know whom to trust.

Choosing a lawyer is a lot like choosing a doctor. Professional services such as legal aid societies, local bar associations, better business bureaus, and even private lawyer referral services can be contacted for advice. The best lawyers achieve reputations for various types of practice within their communities, so asking friends and relatives is another method of locating a lawyer.

In many communities, reputable lawyers do not charge for initial consultation, or charge only a nominal fee. Jane Consumer knew that her husband had employed a lawyer to draft their separate wills. His name was John Gaither. Jane did not know him very well and had met him only once when she and Bill signed the wills. It was logical for her to contact Mr. Gaither for initial consultation concerning her problems. The secretary indicated that since Mr. Gaither had drafted wills for the Consumers, he would not charge for initial consultation. Jane and the secretary agreed on an appointment date.

Jane brought Bill's will, her auto insurance policy, the letter from the manufacturer, and other papers to the appointment. At the law firm, she anxiously waited for the secretary to show her into Mr. Gaither's office. Mr. Gaither greeted her with a friendly handshake and expressed his regrets about Bill's death. She told him what she knew concerning Bill's **estate** and **probate** matters. Mr. Gaither also had a copy of the will and proceeded to explain that the simple will he had drawn up made her the "executrix" of the estate of her late husband, William P. Consumer; that is, she would be responsible for seeing that the provisions of the will were effectively executed.

Jane would have to file the petition she had received from the clerk's office to open the estate, and then appear before the probate judge to open the estate and admit the will to probate. The assets of the estate would be frozen for six months to allow creditors to file claims. She would have to announce the opening of the estate in the newspaper and prepare an accounting of the assets and liabilities. At the end of the six-month probate period, the estate would be placed on the probate court docket, and Jane would have to show that the estate was free and clear of all obligations, including inheritance taxes due to the state. She would then receive an order from the judge closing the estate.

Mr. Gaither said Bill wisely had drafted the will three years before the accident. He explained to Jane, "Most people your age don't think its important to have a will, but when someone dies 'intestate'—that is, without a will—it can be a very complex matter to close an estate. Even a self-drafted, handwritten document, witnessed properly, can prevent many costly problems. But in your case, the matter is quite simple; you don't have any complex problems."

Jane told the attorney how concerned she was about her finances and that she wondered how she would keep her daughter Kim in college. She asked Mr. Gaither how much he would charge for his services. He indicated that his normal fee for probate work, when a will existed, was $150 an hour. However, the testate procedure involving a simple will would require very little of his time, and his legal assistant, Chris Martin, would be able to do most of the work. The firm would bill only $40 an hour for Mr. Martin's services. "I will, of course, oversee his work and make sure it is complete," said Mr. Gaither, "but as long as we don't run into any complications, a minimal fee of $350 would be a reasonable estimate from what you have told me."

Jane was relieved. She thought lawyers charged more for their services. She then told Mr. Gaither that she had a number of other questions that troubled her. The first had to do with the car they were driving—a 1990 Supreme Brougham Executive. The insurance company said it was totaled and wanted to settle for a $10,000 payment on the collision insurance. Jane pointed out "We paid $15,000 for it, and it's only two years old."

The attorney looked up the "book" value in a small paperback on his desk and asked a few questions about extras on the vehicle. He concluded that the agent had quoted the correct amount according to the information normally used to calculate replacement value. "It would be difficult to get more from them under your contract," he replied.

---

estate: the degree, quantity, nature, and extent of interest a person has in real and personal property.

probate: court procedure by which a will is proved. The term includes all matters and proceedings concerning administration of estates of deceased persons.

Jane then explained her suspicion that there may have been something wrong with the car that could have caused the accident. The attorney listened attentively as she explained about the noise she heard just before the car went out of control, and he asked questions as she told her story. He said he would have to investigate to determine whether she had a legal cause of action against the dealer or manufacturer of the automobile. He asked where the car was located and whether her husband had any receipts for the inspection of the car by the dealer. Jane thought they might still be in the glove compartment of the car, which was located at a local wrecker service impoundment lot. Mr. Gaither also was very interested in the factory "recall" letter that Jane gave him during their conversation.

After giving Jane a list of various documents and records of assets and liabilities that could be attributed to Bill Consumer's estate, which Mr. Gaither explained he needed to probate the will, the attorney said he would start investigating the possible cause of the accident and would let Jane know what he found.

TYPES OF CIVIL LEGAL ACTION

Civil legal actions cover a vast array of issues and include all noncriminal actions within the jurisdiction of the courts. The overwhelming majority of legal actions filed in court are included in this general classification. Civil actions include actions in both law and equity. The distinction between "law" and "equity" here relates primarily to the remedy sought. Suits for money damages must be brought in law, as opposed to equity actions that are sought to secure specific performance orders, such as injunctions.

Equity in Practice

The Anglo-American legal system owes much of its flexibility to the concept of equity, which began as a special court to grant exceptions to the stiff requirements of the common law in Medieval England. In most state jurisdictions, and in the federal courts, the concepts of law and equity have been merged and are remedies administered by the courts having civil law jurisdiction. In some states, a Chancery Court still exists as a separate court having jurisdiction over equity cases. One of the basic principles of equity is that "equity suffers not a right without a remedy." The limited nature of equity remedies makes it possible for relief to be granted in a wide variety of cases where an abatement of the wrong is sought, such as nuisance abatement.

Some of the most significant legal actions of a constitutional nature were brought as civil actions to secure specific performance orders. This type of civil action allows private parties to initiate suit to enforce constitutional provisions. Examples of such cases are *Brown v. Board of Education of Topeka*, 347 U.S. 483, 74 S. Ct. 686, 98 L. Ed. 873 (1954) to secure racial integration of public schools, *Baker v. Carr* 369 U.S. 186, 82 S. Ct. 691, 7 L. Ed. 2d 663 (1962) to secure reapportionment of election districts, and *Gideon v. Wainwright* (1963) to secure the right of indigents to counsel in criminal cases. These cases are exceptional cases that have received much publicity because they represent the acceptance of new legal avenues for civil action by private parties seeking to redress grievances.

Money Damages

In general, the typical lawsuit involves civil legal action to recover money damages in the areas of tort or contract. These areas of law were originally developed through the common law, as described in Chapter One. Modern legislative enactments have codified much of the common law today; however, the common law still plays a significant role.

Modern statutory enactments have added a host of new areas of authorized civil legal actions that include such important issues as civil rights, employment discrimination, sexual harassment, and worker's compensation.

The law strives to afford a suitable remedy to every person who has suffered an actual loss caused by the unlawful conduct of another. The key word "unlawful" is used to describe conduct that is in violation of statutory or common law standards. The fact that Jane Consumer has suffered an actual loss does not mean that she has a legal remedy for that loss. Attorney Gaither needs to conduct a preliminary investigation to determine the potential for establishing a **cause of action** in law.

cause of action: the fact for facts that give a person a right to judicial relief.

Workers' Compensation

If the accident in question had been directly related to Bill Consumer's employment, there would have been a possibility of recovering through workers' compensation legislation. **Workers' compensation laws** are basically "no fault" in character and provide "limited liability" for injuries suffered as a result of employment-related accidents. The "no fault" character refers to the concept that a cause of legal action exists, regardless of fault, if the injury occurs as a result of the worker's employment. Generally, these laws have exceptions for injuries that are deliberate and self-inflicted or a result of the worker's use of drugs and alcohol. The "limited liability" character of this legislation means that the amounts for damages are limited by the specific wording of the statutes, which have provisions for maximum amounts that are legally recoverable.

workers' compensation laws: laws that make the employer strictly liable to an employee for injuries sustained by the employee that arise out of and in the course of employment.

Much of a lawyer's education is devoted to obtaining an understanding of causes of action—their elements and their application. Since the accident occurred during a private shopping trip, Mr. Gaither was quite certain the workers' compensation avenue of potential cause of action would be closed to his client. He knew he would need to explore the areas of tort and contract law for an appropriate cause of action that would enable his client to recover for damages sustained.

General Elements of Tort and Contract Law

Tort law is the area of civil law concerning personal injury or property damages excluding those recoverable under the area of law known as contracts. Some common torts are assault, battery, trespass, negligence, products liability, libel, and slander. There are both intentional and nonintentional torts as well as personal and property torts. Each of these types of torts have specific elements that must be proved by the party bringing the legal action.

tort law: the area of civil law involving personal injury or property damages excluding contracts.

General Elements of Torts (Negligence)

The following general elements are required in most tort actions. The plaintiff must prove that:

contract law: the area of civil law involving agreements between two or more parties that create, modify or destroy a legal relationship.

breach of contract: failure, without legal excuse, to perform any promise that forms the whole or part of a contract.

affirmative defense: a matter constituting a defense that relieves the defendant of liability.

1. the defendant breached a legal duty owed to the plaintiff;
2. the plaintiff sustained an injury to person or loss of property recognized by law; and
3. the defendant's breach of duty was the proximate cause of the plaintiff's injury or property loss.

General Elements of Contracts

Contracts is the area of civil law involving claims based on **breach of contract**. The plaintiff's lawyer must obtain evidence to prove that:

1. the parties were legally competent to enter into a contractual relationship;
2. a contract was made through a valid offer and acceptance;
3. legal consideration was exchanged between the parties;
4. formalities were met if the alleged contract is of the type that must be in writing and signed; and
5. the defendant's alleged breach of contract caused the plaintiff to suffer an actual loss.

Affirmative Defense

The defendant can defeat the claim, whether in tort or in contract, by disproving any one of the elements necessary to the plaintiff's cause of action. For each cause of action, certain affirmative defenses may be available. Each **affirmative defense** has certain elements that the defendant must prove. Proof of the affirmative defense either totally defeats the plaintiff's cause of action or reduces the amount of money damages recovered. In addition to the recovery of money damages, certain claims may include specific performance remedies, such as injunctions or court orders.

PRELIMINARY INVESTIGATION

John Gaither had another appointment that afternoon and could not begin research into Jane's questions, but he kept thinking about the accident and the recall letter. At the end of the day, he gave his legal assistant, Chris Martin, instructions to begin work on Jane Consumer's petition to open the estate. He asked Chris to meet with him in the morning at 9:00 to discuss the questions raised by Jane about the cause of the accident that killed her husband.

Chris Martin had been employed by Smith and Gaither for about two years as a paralegal and had worked with Attorney Gaither on several cases, doing a lot of title searches and preliminary investigations. At their meeting the next morning, Attorney Gaither explained the situation concerning Mrs. Consumer's case. "The letter from the factory concerning the recall on Bill's car needs to be checked out with the factory and dealer," he told Chris. "And go down to the garage and see if you can find any maintenance receipts in the glove compartment of Bill's car. We are looking for some comment on checking the suspension (left side) or coils."

That afternoon Chris had some interesting facts to report. The factory confirmed that there was a problem with the coil spring suspension on the left side of that particular model automobile with serial numbers within the range of

Bill's car. Chris also found two maintenance receipts that indicated an order to check the rear suspension, because the "car leans to the left." Both receipts had dealer's notations that said, "Checked, o.k." The receipts were dated 7 March 1991, and 15 August 1990. "The factory wouldn't tell me what was wrong with the coil spring," Chris explained.

"Who's the best mechanic in town, Chris?" asked Gaither. Chris had no answer, but the attorney said, "Mack Racer, he owns the Speed Shop in town and works on championship race cars—everybody knows he's the best. I'll call him and see if we can get him to look at Bill's car."

Mack Racer took a couple of days to get to it, but he reported to Attorney Gaither that he had removed the rear coils from Bill's car and found the left coil broken in half. He also found that the right coil was obviously made of thicker stronger material and was undamaged. "Why would they be different?" asked the attorney. "Could this difference have caused the accident?"

Mack responded, "I'll stake my reputation on it. These coils are made for two different cars, and the left coil was too weak to support that heavy car. If it broke when Bill was passing that van, it would have caused the accident. I'll testify to that in court."

In order to verify this report, John Gaither had an engineer from the National Safety Research Institute examine the coils. The engineer's report to the firm was consistent with that of the expert mechanic who had removed the coils from the accident vehicle. He stated that the coils were definitely not matched and that the right coil was of a different gauge and thickness from that of the left coil. He could not say that this caused the accident, but he verified that the coils should not have been used on the same vehicle.

The attorney then decided to discuss the matter with the manager of the City Auto Company that had sold the vehicle to the Consumers and whose service department had reportedly done regular maintenance on the car. He explained the situation to the manager over the phone and asked if he could retrieve the service records on the Consumers' car. The manager indicated that he would examine the service records and check on the manufacturer's recall concerning the vehicle in question. They agreed to meet in the manager's office.

This meeting confirmed that the Consumer vehicle had been serviced properly at regular intervals. The attorney was convinced that even a reasonable mechanic could not have detected the fact that the rear suspension coils were not matched and it was clear that the City Auto Company had not replaced any of the original equipment on the vehicle. The service manager, Jody Courteous, met with them and agreed to sign an **affidavit** (see Form 4.1), which is a sworn statement regarding factual evidence from a potential witness.

affidavit: written statement of facts made voluntarily under oath.

John Gaither was now convinced that he had a good products liability action against the Factory Motor Company, the manufacturer of the accident vehicle. He concluded that he had enough preliminary evidence to discuss the terms of a contractual agreement with his client, Jane Consumer.

A Contractual Agreement

Attorney Gaither had his secretary set up an appointment with Jane Consumer the next day. After telling her what he had discovered in his preliminary investigation, he indicated that he thought she had a case worth pursuing. "If all this checks out, I believe we have grounds to sue the Factory Motor Company for damages caused in the accident. Since you are the executrix of your husband's

Form 4.1
AFFIDAVIT

This affidavit was given by Jody Courteous, Service Manager of City Auto Company, Centerville, Middle State, on December 2, 1991, before a Notary Public in the presence of Attorney William Green.

1   My name is Jody Courteous. I am forty-two years old, and I have been employed by
2   the City Auto Company as service manager for the past three years. I was employed by
3   the same company as a mechanic for five years before being promoted to service man-
4   ager. I was certified by the Factory Motor Company as a qualified mechanic in 1985 and
5   attended more recent training sessions in Lake State.
6   We try to keep thorough records on the vehicles we sell, and I can confirm that the
7   vehicle owned by William P. Consumer was purchased from us on October 20, 1989, and
8   that regular service maintenance was done on the car. I recall when Mr. Consumer
9   brought the car in for the last maintenance check, he asked me to examine the suspension
10 and complained of the car leaning to the left. My mechanic asked me to look at the car
11 after he had it jacked up in the shop. I looked at both coils and checked their attachment,
12 making sure they were secure. Neither the mechanic nor I could conclude from this visual
13 inspection that there was anything wrong with the coils. We did not remove the coils or al-
14 ter them in any way. I made a note on the work order that the coils checked out o.k.
15 We did get a factory recall on this vehicle, which I discovered when Mr. Sellers, the
16 owner of City Auto Company, asked me to check on it. The recall instructed us to replace
17 the left coil on 1990 models that matched Mr. Consumer's vehicle serial number. This order
18 to us was dated September 1, 1991, and was received six months after our inspection of
19 the car in March. Had we been given any indication from the factory that these coils were
20 a problem, we might have been able to detect the differences in the coils. But when we
21 inspected Mr. Consumer's vehicle in March, it was impossible to detect the differences
22 without pulling both coils and looking at them side by side.

THE UNDERSIGNED HEREBY CERTIFIES THAT THIS IS A TRUE AND ACCURATE STATEMENT:

Sworn to and subscribed before on this
____ day of _____, _____.

_____
Jody Courteous, Service Manager
City Auto Company

SEAL OF NOTARY PUBLIC

estate, you may be able to recover damages both for your injuries and for those suffered by his estate."

Jane wanted to know if a lawsuit would be very costly to pursue and what the risks were if the court did not award her damages. John explained that he would work on her case on a "contingency fee" basis and that she would not owe him anything for his services if he was unable to recover damages on her behalf. She would, however, be required to pay court costs if the case got that far. He would keep track of the expenses in the case, and if an award were made, the expenses and court costs would be deducted from the award.

"If we do recover damages, my fee would be a percentage of the award after court costs and expenses are deducted—twenty-five percent if settled out of court, one-third if we have to file suit, and forty percent if we have to go to appeal with the case," explained the attorney. "I'll give you my standard **contingency fee contract** that explains this in writing so you can think it over."

"Can I get out of this contract if I'm dissatisfied with your progress?" asked Jane.

"Yes, all you have to do is tell me I'm fired. Lawyers are employed by the clients and represent them only on their request. You would owe me only for the court costs and expenses in the case, including a reasonable hourly fee for my services up to that point."

Jane took the contract (see Form 4-2) home and consulted her daughter and father-in-law about it. They agreed that she should sign the contract and proceed with the case. Bill's father indicated that Attorney Gaither had a good reputation. He asked some of his friends if the contract was a good one and was told that other lawyers charge more for settlement out of court, which might induce the lawyer to bargain for a lower settlement, so Mr. Gaither's offer appeared satisfactory. Jane was gratified with Attorney Gaither's interest in the case. Maybe there was a chance that she could recover some of the monetary loss she knew would adversely affect the family, and she hoped the recovery would allow her to keep Kim in school.

contingency fee contract: agreement to pay for attorney services contingent upon recovery in damage suit.

LEGAL RESEARCH

After receiving the contract from Jane Consumer, Attorney Gaither began his legal research in the firm's law library. He knew from his legal training and experience in Middle State that he had a potential cause of action in three areas of law. These areas are known as negligence, products liability, and contract. He also knew that he could bring suit in either federal district court or in state court because of the diversity of citizenship of the two parties involved.

This area of overlapping, federal and state, jurisdiction in civil cases exists because of the complicated structure of our federal government. Historically, diversity jurisdiction has served an important purpose by enabling disputes that might not be admitted in state court jurisdiction to enter the courts through the federal structure.

diversity jurisdiction: jurisdiction of the federal courts when the two parties are citizens of different states or foreign countries and the sum in question exceeds a set amount.

Federal Jurisdiction

Civil cases involving diversity of citizenship of the parties to the dispute were first granted federal jurisdiction in the Judiciary Act of 1789. Thus, **diversity jurisdiction** has been a significant feature of the federal courts for over two hundred years, and has been the subject of debate over that entire period. It was first

Form 4.2

AGREEMENT WITH LAWYER

The Law Firm of
Smith and Gaither, Attorneys
57 Courthouse Square
Centerville, Middle State

John Gaither
Attorney-at-Law

    I, the undersigned client, hereby retain and employ John Gaither as my attorney to represent me in my claim for damages against the seller and/or manufacturer of the 1990 Supreme Brougham Executive, involved in an accident that occurred on September 8, 1991, in which William P. Consumer, my late husband, was killed and I was severely injured.

    As compensation for said services, I agree to pay for the court costs, if necessary, and to pay my attorney from the proceeds of recovery, after the deduction of court costs and expenses the following fees:

25% if settled without suit;
33⅓% if suit is filed;
40% if an appeal is taken by either side.

    It is agreed that this employment is on a contingent fee basis, so that if no recovery is made, I will not owe my attorney any amount for attorneys' fees.

Dated this ____ day of _____ 19____.

_____
Client

I hereby accept the above employment.

_____
John Gaither, Attorney

granted because of the fear that state courts would be biased against out-of-state litigants. However, modern state courts are improved, and many argue that parochial state prejudices have been altered to the point where diversity jurisdiction is no longer needed. This area of overlapping jurisdiction could be eliminated without changing the Constitution, and jurisdiction could be left to the states only; however, many lawyers remain concerned about local favoritism in state courts and fight to retain the option of filing their cases in either state or federal court.

Since 1938 the United States Supreme Court has tried to reduce the potential for conflict of law arising out of this situation of overlapping jurisdiction by adopting a curious rule known as the **Erie Doctrine**. In the case of *Erie Railroad Co. v. Thompkins*, 304 U.S. 64, 58 S. Ct. 817, 82 L. Ed. 1188 (1938), the Court held that the substantive law of the state where the case is filed will be applied in federal diversity cases when no federal question is involved. This decision means that whether the case is filed in the state or federal court, the law of the state where the court sits will be applied; however, the procedural rules of the federal courts will be applied when the case is filed in federal court.

Erie doctrine: federal practice in civil diversity cases applying the substantive law of the state where the case is filed.

Diversity of citizenship of the opposing parties must be complete; no two parties on opposing sides may be citizens of the same state. As mentioned in Chapter Three, the sum in question must be greater than $50,000 to meet federal diversity jurisdiction requirements. Federal case law has also established that the parties must have "minimum contact" with the state where jurisdiction is sought. In *World-Wide Volkswagon Corp. v. Woodson*, 444 U.S. 286, 100 S. Ct. 559, 62 L. Ed. 2d 490 (1980), the United States Supreme Court held that a corporation that conducts no business in the state and has no "contacts, ties, or relations" with the state cannot be expected to answer to legal action in that state under diversity jurisdiction.

John Gaither was confident that Jane Consumer's case met all the qualifications for diversity jurisdiction, since the Factory Motor Company was incorporated in Lake State and had its headquarters in that state. Thus, the attorney could prove that the defendant was a citizen of Lake State and that Jane Consumer, the plaintiff, was a citizen of Middle State. The Factory Motor Company had dealerships in Middle State and did business in the state on a regular basis, thus establishing the "minimum contacts" required by the federal courts.

State Jurisdiction

Both Middle State and Lake State had jurisdiction over civil matters as well; indeed, states have jurisdiction over all matters that are not specifically designated in the United States Constitution, in valid federal statutes, or in treaties. These "supreme laws of the land" confer exclusive federal jurisdiction over certain matters, and these matters are not a part of state court jurisdiction. This rule leaves a vast residual area of jurisdiction to the states, and much of it is shared between the state and federal governments, as in diversity cases.

John Gaither thus knew that he could file his legal action in either Middle State or Lake State's civil trial courts. He also could file his action in either Middle State or Lake State's federal district courts, since there is a federal court in every state and territory of the United States. The choices were fairly easy to make in this case, but these options can have important implications for the lawyer making such a decision. In some cases, the lawyer's choice may have an influence on the outcome of the case.

Choice of Law and Court

negligence: failure to exercise due care.

products liability: legal liability of manufacturers and sellers to compensate buyers, users, and even bystanders for damages or injuries suffered because of defects in goods purchased.

Attorney Gaither knew from his legal research that Middle State substantive law recognized the principle of products liability in tort law described in section 402A of the *Restatement (Second) of Torts*. This concept, often referred to as "strict liability," defines a special liability that deviates from the specific elements of **negligence**. Gaither's focus was on **products liability** law from the beginning because he knew that this special tort does not require proof of a duty of care, as is required in negligence actions. It requires proof of a "dangerously defective product" (see Table 4-1).

The strict liability concept was originally developed through the process of the common law but was elevated to statutory law in Middle State in 1978. Middle State's code specifically recognizes the elements of the law described in the *Restatement (Second) of Torts* below.

TOPIC 5. STRICT LIABILITY
402 A, Special Liability of Seller of Product for Physical Harm to User or Consumer
(1) One who sells any product in a defective condition unreasonably dangerous to the user or consumer or to his property is subject to liability for physical harm thereby caused to the ultimate user or consumer, or to his property, if
    (a) the seller is engaged in the business of selling such a product, and
    (b) it is expected to and does reach the user or consumer without substantial change in the condition in which it was sold.
(2) The rule stated in Subsection (1) applies although
    (a) the seller has exercised all possible care in the preparation and sale of his product, and
    (b) the user or consumer has not bought the product from or entered into any contractual relation with the seller.

contributory negligence: act or omission amounting to lack of ordinary care on the part of the complaining party that, along with defendant's negligence, is the proximate cause of injury.

comparative negligence: negligence measured in terms of percentages; any damages allowed are reduced in proportion to the amount of plaintiff's negligence.

voluntary assumption of known risk: where plaintiff voluntarily assumed a known risk.

Comparing Affirmative Defense Elements

The affirmative defense in regard to products liability (defective product) had more advantages in the *Consumer* case than that of the traditional law of negligence. The basic affirmative defense in negligence actions is **contributory negligence**, that is, a plaintiff's negligence with regard to the injuries sustained would negate recovery for damages in many jurisdictions. This rule was the law in Middle State at the time this case was conceived, although later Middle State followed the lead of many other jurisdictions and altered this concept to allow for what has become known as **comparative negligence**. Here, the plaintiff's claim may be reduced by the percentage of negligence attributable to the party bringing suit. For example, if the plaintiff's negligence is twenty percent of the fault, the court may reduce the damage claim by twenty percent. The claim is negated if the degree of fault reaches fifty percent.

John Gaither found the basic affirmative defense in the products liability law of Middle State more advantageous to his case than that of negligence law. The products liability law stipulated an affirmative defense of **voluntary assumption of a known risk**. This defense requires proof that the plaintiff knew the risk involved in use of a defective product and voluntarily assumed the risk. This defense is more difficult to prove than contributory negligence.

Statute of Limitations

Another question that concerned Attorney Gaither in his legal research was the time limitation provided in law for the initiation of a cause of legal action. This limitation is generally known as the **statute of limitations**. These statutes are provided by the state and federal governments. The time limitation for torts is generally one year, but the time limitation for contract is usually longer. In Middle State, contract actions had a time limitation of three years, but the time began to run at the time of consummation of the contract, in this case, when the automobile was purchased two years before the accident. Tort time limitations begin at the time the injury is detected. If Jane Consumer delayed filing suit beyond one year, she would have no cause of action that the courts would recognize. Jane had consulted her lawyer within three months of the accident, however, so John Gaither had ample time to file before the twelve-month deadline.

Standing to Sue

Another factor considered by the attorney was **standing to sue**. Jane Consumer had standing to sue for recovery of damages she sustained in the accident, but the larger amount of potential claim would be to the estate of William P. Consumer. Under ancient common law concepts, the right to legal action ended with an individual's death. However, modern legislative enactments known as **wrongful death and survival statutes** specifically provide for status to sue on behalf of the estate of the deceased person. These statutes may specify and limit recoverable damages on behalf of the estate.

Middle State statutes used the survival concept, limiting "pain and suffering" to the individual. The estate could not recover damages for the mental suffering of the family resulting from loss of spouse's affection or loss of spouse or parent. The estate could recover damages for lost earnings that would have benefited

statutes of limitations: statutes that prescribe the periods within which actions may be brought upon certain claims or within which certain rights may be enforced.

standing to sue: requirement that is satisfied if plaintiff has a legally protected and tangible interest in the litigation.

wrongful death and survival statutes: provide a cause of action in favor of the decedent's personal representative for the benefit of certain beneficiaries.

TABLE 4.1 Comparative Elements of Negligence and Products Liability

Negligence **Must Prove**:	Products Liability **Must Prove**:

1. Duty of care
2. Breach of duty
3. Proximate cause
4. Injury or damage
	1. Defective product
	   a. Unreasonably dangerous
	   b. Defective at time of sale
	   c. Substantially unchanged from condition at sale
	   d. Sold by seller engaged in business of selling
	2. Proximate cause
	3. Injury or damage

Affirmative Defense: Contributory or comparative negligence	**Affirmative Defense**: Voluntary assumption of known risk

the family and for necessary expenses to the estate resulting from the deceased's injuries, although the deceased's potential earnings had to be reduced by the probable living expenses for the deceased had he lived. These exceptions to the recovery of damages are in keeping with the theory of "survival" benefits, which are benefits that would have accrued to the deceased had he survived the injuries sustained.

Damages Estimated

John Gaither calculated the estimated damages that Jane Consumer could reasonably expect to recover at about $285,000. William P. Consumer was only 48 years of age when he died and could have earned much more than this amount during his lifetime. According to life expectancy tables, he would have twenty-seven years of reasonable life remaining had he not been killed in the accident. Middle State law required that William P. Consumer's potential earnings must be reduced by the amount he would have spent had he lived.

A more significant reduction would be the adjustment of his potential earnings to **present value**. This calculation involves a sort of reverse compounding of interest to arrive at a sum of money that could earn the expected amount over the twenty-seven years of life expectancy. There was no question about whether his case would meet the $50,000 limitation for filing a federal diversity action.

present value: adjustment to account for investment earnings of a specific sum of money over time.

Choice of Federal District Court

The attorney had given considerable thought to whether he should file his case in Middle State's circuit court or in the federal district court located in Capital City, only thirty miles away. Because of the *Erie* doctrine, he knew the both courts would apply the substantive law of Middle State. The Federal Rules of Civil Procedure would be used in the federal district court, however, and Gaither preferred them to those rules applied in Middle State. They were more flexible and gave him advantages in service of process and procedure that might make a difference in the outcome of the case. With so much at stake in the case, he also preferred the quality of the judges in federal court; he felt that both the quality and efficiency of the federal court were greater than those of the state court. He also checked the dockets in both courts and found that his case would be handled much faster in federal court.

John Gaither was now confident that he could report to his client that she had cause for legal action against the Factory Motor Company.

REQUEST TO SETTLE OUT OF COURT

Attorney Gaither mailed Jane Consumer a report of his preliminary investigation, outlining what he had uncovered so far in the case. He asked her to contact his secretary for an appointment so they could discuss the progress of her case against the Factory Motor Company and make some decisions about how to proceed. He included an estimate of the damages he could claim under the laws of Middle State.

At the meeting with his client, John Gaither reviewed his findings orally and explained that the facts indicated that she had a possibility of recovering damages through a products liability, or defective products, suit. There were a number of negative factors in the case, including the rainstorm and wet highway, that would undoubtedly be used by the Factory Motor Company in their defense. But the faulty manufacture of the vehicle with unsafe equipment was evident from the factory recall letter and had been confirmed by the City Auto Company. Gaither told Jane, "We have two experts, one an expert mechanic and the other an engineer, who will verify that the coil on the left side was broken and was not the proper coil for the vehicle. This indicates that we have reasonable grounds to proceed with the case. However, it is far from certain that you will be able to recover the amount of our initial estimate."

The law provides a standard for the private settlement of disputes, and well over ninety percent of civil cases are settled out of court based on the requirements of the law. "We can try for an out-of-court settlement at this point, but don't get your hopes up," the attorney warned Jane. "This is a complicated case, and the Factory Motor Company will more than likely want to take it at least through the discovery process, where we will both have the power of the court to compel evidence, which will enable us to conduct a much more thorough investigation of the precise facts in the case."

John informed his client that he would draft a letter to the Factory Motor Company informing them of the intent to file legal action and asking for a conference to negotiate settlement. Jane Consumer agreed and asked about the amount he would be requesting in the settlement.

"I will send them our initial estimate of the damages," said Gaither. "If they intend to settle we will set up a conference and you, the client, would have to approve any offer of settlement. I will let them know that you are intent upon filing suit for the amount in our estimate. If they do intend to settle, it will be for considerably less than the amount of our estimate. We will just have to consider the offer and the alternative consequences of going to court. My decision will depend upon your determination. My job is to provide competent legal advice."

Attorney Gaither sent a letter to the Factory Motor Company requesting damages in the amount of $285,000 for the injuries caused by the defective coil which he asserted was the proximate cause of the accident.

Defense Considerations

When the letter arrived at the Factory Motor Company, it was sent to the firm's general counsel, Herman Hardnose. Mr. Hardnose called in his staff attorney, Maria Farmer, who had eight years of experience dealing with defective products suits against the firm. Mr. Hardnose explained that this situation needed to be looked into and dealt with effectively—that the particular defect involved in the recall was not considered dangerous, and the company had not received any previous reports of accidents resulting from the problem. He wanted her to work closely with the City Auto Company and their legal counsel on the matter. He indicated that she should not settle out of court unless there was no possibility of winning the suit.

Maria Farmer understood her instructions and proceeded to check out the information in Attorney Gaither's letter. The Factory Motor Company contended that the coil in question was not dangerously defective and that it would have held up under normal use. There was a problem with a particular run on the assembly line that affected 250 vehicles; a mix-up had resulted in the installation of the wrong coil on the left side of these vehicles, and the mistake was not detected until after the automobiles were sold. The factory engineers tested the equipment and determined that the unmatched coils did not present a safety hazard. Factory simulation indicated that the equipment would take normal wear for at least 200,000 miles. The firm issued a recall order only because the coils in question affected the appearance of the car, not the safety of the vehicle. Maria Farmer, therefore, concluded that the Factory Motor Company would not attempt to settle out of court.

When Attorney Gaither received this reply, he again let the Factory Motor Company know that his client was resolute in filing a formal legal claim. Maria Farmer confirmed that she would not consider settling before the conclusion of the discovery process.

Attorney Gaither informed his client that the defendant had refused to settle out of court. He asked if she wished to proceed to file suit and indicated that she would risk only court costs and expenses if he were unsuccessful in winning an award. Jane Consumer agreed that he should file suit. John Gaither then asked his paralegal, Chris Martin, to prepare all the file documents relevant to the *Consumer* case for his review, as he would need to prepare a formal complaint. The various aspects of filing a complaint and discovery are discussed in the next chapter.

CHAPTER SUMMARY

1. The material described in this chapter illustrates several areas of law that are of concern to the average person. The subjects of wills and estates are those about which people most commonly contact lawyers. The basic elements of torts and contracts are important to the understanding of civil law.

2. Competent legal advice is needed in crisis situations, and it is a good idea for one to have a lawyer with which one feels comfortable before a crisis arises. Lawyers provide initial consultation at no cost or on a nominal fee basis. They will state their fee for a particular problem to the client, so the client usually can seek a second opinion and compare the differences easily.

3. Preliminary investigation is needed to determine if there is a legal cause of action based upon the specific facts in the case. Civil legal actions cover all non-criminal actions within the jurisdiction of the courts. They include actions in law and equity, with equity providing a remedy in the form of a specific court action, and law providing a means by which to seek money damages.

4. Some of the most significant civil legal actions of a constitutional nature are brought as actions to secure specific performance, but the typical civil lawsuit involves an action to recover money damages in the areas of torts and contracts.

5. The law strives to afford a suitable remedy when parties suffer actual loss caused by the unlawful conduct of another. However, there must be a cause of action in law to establish a legitimate claim.

6. Workers' compensation laws provide recovery for losses suffered as a result of employment. They have the characteristics of "no fault" and "limited liability," which set this area of cause of action apart from those involving the usual requirement of proof of wrongful action.

7. The general elements of tort law include breach of a legal duty, damage, and proof of proximate cause. Breach of contract requires competence to contract, offer and acceptance, exchange of legal consideration, breach of contract, and actual loss suffered because of the breach. Each specific area of tort and contract law may involve more detailed elements that must all be proved in order to recover damages. Each tort has certain affirmative defenses that may provide a means by which the defendant can negate a claim or reduce the amount of the award.

8. Clients enter into contractual relations with lawyers in both oral and written form. Contingency fee contracts are used frequently in tort cases. Hourly rates are used in other cases, and some lawyers can be kept on retainer to secure their services. These contracts do not bind the client to keep the lawyer if the client becomes dissatisfied, but they do require the client to provide reasonable compensation to the lawyer for services rendered.

9. Legal research in tort cases usually starts with a preliminary review of the areas of law that are relevant to the known facts in the case. Each type of tort has specific elements that must be proved. The specific elements of negligence and products liability law were examined in this chapter as the attorney in the example chose an appropriate legal basis for the action.

10. The basic means of dividing state and federal court jurisdiction involves the concept of federal question jurisdiction. If the issue is relevant to a provision of the United States Constitution, treaties, or federal statutes, it is a federal question and the federal courts have jurisdiction. The states have jurisdiction in all other areas including diversity cases. The diversity jurisdiction of the federal courts is shared with the states.

11. The *Erie* doctrine requires the federal courts in diversity cases to use the substantive law of the state in which the case is filed along with federal procedure. No two parties on opposing sides can be citizens of the same state, and the sum in question must be greater than $50,000.

12. Complicated issues of jurisdiction, time limitations, status to sue, recoverable damages, and choice of courts must be considered before an attorney can conclude that a party has a reasonable cause of legal action. Notification to the opposing party and some attempt to settle the matter informally is expected before the decision to file a formal legal action is made.

KEY TERMS

estate	contingency fee contract	voluntary assumption of known risk
probate	diversity jurisdiction	statutes of limitations
cause of action	*Erie* doctrine	standing to sue
workers' compensation laws	negligence	wrongful death and survival statutes
breach of contract	products liability	present value
affirmative defense	contributory negligence	
affidavit	comparative negligence	

DISCUSSION QUESTIONS

1. How would one go about finding a lawyer if one needed legal assistance?

2. What is meant by a legal cause of action, and why is it important to consult a lawyer as soon as possible after a legal question arises?

3. What are the major types of civil legal actions?

4. What are the general elements of tort and contract law?

5. How does products liability law differ from negligence law?

6. What are the basic affirmative defenses in negligence and products liability actions?

7. What choice of courts did Jane Consumer have in her case against the auto manufacturer, and why was the federal district court chosen?

SOURCES AND SUGGESTED READING

Ball, Howard. 1987. *Courts and Politics: The Federal Judicial System*. 2d ed. Englewood Cliffs, N.J.: Prentice Hall.

Blanchard, Roderick D. 1990. *Litigation and Trial Practice for the Legal Assistant*. 3d ed. St. Paul: West Publishing Co.

Bumiller, Kristin. 1980–81. "Choices of Forum in Diversity Cases: Analysis of a Survey and Implications for Reform." *Law and Society* 15:749–74.

Neubauer, David W. 1991. *Judicial Process*. Pacific Grove, Calif.: Brooks/Cole Publishing Co.

Restatement (Second) of Law: Torts. 1965. Vol. 2, 281–503. Washington, D.C.: American Law Institute.

Schuck, Peter H. (editor). 1991. *Tort Law and the Public Interest: Competition, Innovation, and Consumer Welfare*. New York: W.W. Norton & Co. (See particularly "The Evolution of Products Liability as a Federal Policy Issue" by Linda Lipsen.)

Tennessee Code Annotated (T.C.A.) (Each state has a similar code of statutory law arranged by topic for specific reference. These codes contain a wealth of information including case law citations, scholarly publications, cross-references, and tables to find life expectancy and compound accumulation for damage estimates.)

Uniform Commercial Code (U.C.C.) This uniform legislation has been enacted by most states and attempts to codify the general principles of common law to facilitate commercial transactions.

United States Code (U.S.C.) This series of volumes contains all federal law arranged by topic, like the state codes, for handy reference.

Weaver, Jefferson Hane. 1990. *The Compact Guide to Tort Law: A Civilized Approach to the Law*. St. Paul: West Publishing Co.

———. 1990. *The Compact Guide to Contract Law: A Civilized Approach to the Law*. St. Paul: West Publishing Co.

CHAPTER FIVE

PRE-TRIAL PROCESS IN CIVIL CASES

"A lawyer should represent a client zealously within the bounds of the law."
Canon Seven: ABA Model Rules of Professional Conduct

This chapter discusses the pleading and discovery process used in modern civil procedure to prepare the evidence for settlement or trial. During this process, parties have access to the power of the court to compel the production of evidence that is relevant to the legal action. John Gaither intended to file his case in federal district court and, therefore, was required to use the **Federal Rules of Civil Procedure (FRCP)**, which is a detailed set of rules that define the steps in legal procedure. The rules are somewhat complex because of the wide variety of circumstances that can arise, but they also are quite flexible. Great effort has been made to simplify the rules and remove the technicalities that once characterized Anglo-American common law practice.

Federal Rules of Civil Procedure: detailed rules of federal civil procedure that must be followed. Most states have similar statutory rules.

THE PLEADINGS

The English common law tradition initially provided the stiff, technical set of rules of pleading often referred to as **fact pleading**. "The common law courts placed great emphasis on pleadings which proceeded through a set of rigid stages and could continue almost indefinitely. The object was to reach a single issue of law or fact that would dispose of the case. The emphasis on developing the facts of the case through pleadings represented a perilous course for lawyers and litigants alike" (Neubauer 1991, 279). This practice was transferred to the United States during the colonial period where it took on a more relaxed, but still cumbersome, character.

fact pleading: common law emphasis on detail in pleadings which was rigid and cumbersome.

As was explained in Chapter One, the English common law was ill suited to the frontier conditions of the New World. Reformers who opposed the cumbersome methods of common law pleadings were first successful in New York in 1848 when statutory enactment of a complete code of civil procedure took place under the leadership of David Dudley Field. This reform movement spread to other states and has even influenced modern practices in England. However, the process of reform has been gradual, and many states have retained the old common law rules of pleading with certain modifications. The rules of pleading that resulted from this first wave of reform were called *code pleadings* because the statutory enactment of a set of written rules was an innovation.

Modern federal civil procedure began in 1938 with the adoption of the Federal Rules of Procedure in statutory form, abolishing fact pleading in favor of **notice pleading**. Notice pleading emphasizes the need for notification to the opposing party, and the court does not require verification of the allegations during the pleading stage of civil procedure. The rules initially adopted by statute in 1938 have not remained static, and the effort to remove technical barriers to the efficient development of evidence in preparation for a lawsuit has continued through a series of revisions.

The Judicial Conference of the United States and its extensive committee system composed of judges at all levels (including practicing attorneys) have proposed and secured adoption of numerous changes designed to improve the efficiency of the process of handling legal actions in the federal courts. The Judicial Conference is presided over by the Chief Justice of the United States. Committee recommendations are submitted to the Supreme Court membership and, when passed by a majority of the members, transmitted to Congress where they automatically become law in ninety days unless Congress acts adversely. Thus, not only are the rules themselves more flexible, but so also is the process by which these rules may be changed.

The states also have altered their cumbersome procedures and have tended to follow the federal leadership. About thirty-five states have adopted the basic federal rules for local use, and the remainder have revised their rules to reflect at least partially the federal innovations (Neubauer 1991,280).

Modern notice pleading is much more flexible and able to accommodate reasonable changes that do not inject a bias against one part or the other as the legal process develops. A **complaint** and **answer** are the basic pleadings. Under the common law, each type of case had a separate form for pleading. Modern pleadings do not attempt to prove facts, but merely provide a short, plain statement of the basic elements of the complaint or answer.

notice pleading: simplified rules of modern pleading that emphasize notification and response and leave the narrowing of facts to discovery.

complaint: initial pleading by which a legal action is commenced.

answer: formal written statement setting forth the grounds of defense.

The Complaint

Rule 8 (FRCP) defines the general rules of pleading to include a short and plain statement of the grounds upon which the court's jurisdiction depends, a claim showing that the pleader is entitled to relief, and a demand for judgment for the relief the pleader seeks.

Rule 10 (FRCP) outlines the form of pleadings. Every pleading must contain a caption setting forth the name of the court, title of the action, and file number (added by the clerk). The complaint must include the names of all parties, but other pleadings may name the first party on each side with appropriate indication of other parties. The basic elements must be asserted in separate numbered paragraphs, each limited, as far as practical, to a single set of circumstances.

The complaint must be signed by the lawyer preparing it or by the party entering the plea. This requirement carries penalties for violation of it because a responsible agent must be filing the complaint, and the signature certifies that the person who has signed the pleading has read it and believes there are grounds to support the allegations in the pleading. If the pleading has been filed for purposes of an ulterior or malicious motive, the court may award the opposing party retribution in the form of reasonable expenses and attorneys' fees caused by the action. Paralegals may prepare a pleading, but the signature certifies that it has been read by an attorney or by the party acting as his or her own attorney. The person who signs the pleading must assume responsibility for the legal action.

A complaint was prepared in the *Consumer* case by Chris Martin and presented to Attorney John Gaither for his approval (see Form 5-1). Gaither had Jane Consumer come into the office to discuss the complaint. He asked her if she had any questions about the complaint and whether she agreed with the statements in the complaint. Jane Consumer agreed with all the factual information in the complaint and thought it expressed the essential elements of the legal action. John then asked her if she agreed that a **jury trial** should be demanded.

Jane said she had not given it any thought. "What are the alternatives?" she asked.

"You have a choice, as the plaintiff in a civil suit of this nature, to demand a jury trial," replied the attorney. "If a jury trial is not demanded, the court will conduct what is known as a **bench trial**, without a jury. In a jury trial, the jury is the 'trier of fact' in the case and is called upon to answer questions of fact in dispute. In a bench trial, the judge decides all questions of fact and law in the case."

Failure to demand a jury trial in the manner prescribed by Rule 38(b) (FCRP) results in a waiver of the right to a jury trial, and all issues of fact and law are tried by a judge without a jury. The plaintiff can demand a jury trial by a statement in a conspicuous place on the complaint that "a jury trial is demanded." If the plaintiff waives this right, the defendant has an opportunity to demand a jury trial in the answer. The Seventh Amendment to the United States Constitution grants a fundamental right to a jury trial in federal civil cases "at common law," as opposed to equity. Some states restrict the use of jury trials in civil actions, in which case this federal amendment applies only to the federal courts.

Jane thought a jury was essential to what she considered a fair trial. "I would stand a better chance of winning with a jury, wouldn't I?" she asked.

"Yes, I think you would," John agreed, "although jurors can become confused about their instructions from the judge regarding the legal standards they must apply, particularly in strict liability cases. But jurors are likely to be more sympathetic with your situation and less sympathetic with that of the manufacturer in this case."

> **jury trial**: trial of issues of fact in dispute by an impartial and qualified jury.
>
> **bench trial**: trial conducted without a jury where the judge decides issues of both fact and law in dispute.

Service of Process

Attorney Gaither took two copies of the complaint to the office of the clerk of court for the United States District Court in Capital City. The court was located in the Federal Building only about thirty miles from Gaither's office, so the forum would be as convenient for witnesses as the state court located in Centerville.

The clerk received the complaint and demanded payment of the filing fee. She then assigned a case number (92-147) to the case and entered it on the court's **docket**. The first two numbers of the case number indicate the year, and the remaining numbers the order of filing during the year. The docket is the formal record of the court's activities; all action taken in each case must be recorded.

> **docket**: list of important acts done in court in the process of each case; sometimes used to refer to the calendar of cases set to be tried in a specific term.

Form 5.1
COMPLAINT

IN THE UNITED STATES DISTRICT COURT FOR THE
MIDDLE DISTRICT OF MIDDLE STATE

JANE CONSUMER)
   Executrix of the)
   ESTATE OF WILLIAM P. CONSUMER,)
   and JANE CONSUMER, individually)
)
        Plaintiffs)
)   Civil Action
        v.)   No. _____
)
FACTORY MOTOR COMPANY,)
   a manufacturing corporation)   JURY DEMAND
)
        Defendant)

COMPLAINT

Comes now Jane Consumer, executrix of the estate of William P. Consumer, deceased, on behalf of William P. Consumer and Jane Consumer, individually, and states unto the court the following:

1. The plaintiff Jane Consumer resides at 140 Consumer Lane, Centerville, Middle State. Jane Consumer is also the executrix of the estate of William P. Consumer, deceased, who was killed on September 8, 1991, in the accident referred to herein.
2. The defendant, Factory Motor Company, is a corporation organized under the laws of Lake State. Factory Motor Company is engaged in the manufacture of automobiles and does substantial business in Middle State.
3. On or about October 20, 1989, the plaintiffs purchased a 1990 model Supreme Brougham Executive (serial number: 1FMCB14T9KUA14073) from City Auto Company, Centerville, Middle State. This model was manufactured by the defendant, Factory Motor Company.
4. On or about September 8, 1991, around 10:30 p.m., the plaintiff and her decedent, William P. Consumer, were traveling south on Interstate 24 approximately three miles from Centerville, Middle State. Upon passing a van on this interstate highway, the aforementioned automobile, manufactured by the defendant, would not respond to the steering wheel, and the plaintiff's decedent was unable to maintain control of the automobile. William P. Consumer was killed and the plaintiff Jane Consumer was seriously injured when the automobile collided with a tractor-trailer on the opposite side of the interstate highway.
5. At the time of the accident, the plaintiff's decedent was a user of the automobile in question and was using it in the manner and for the purpose expected and intended by the defendant.
6. At the time of the accident, the automobile existed without substantial change from the condition in which it was manufactured and sold. The automobile was less than two years old and had been driven only 22,000 miles. It was in a defective condition in that the left rear coil was defectively manufactured and unreasonably dangerous to users. Defendant knew or should

have expected that the automobile would reach users without substantial change in the condition in which it was manufactured and sold.

7. Death of plaintiff's decedent and resulting injury to the plaintiff Jane Consumer, a passenger in the vehicle, were caused by the conduct of the defendant in defectively manufacturing such automobile and selling it in a defective or unreasonably dangerous condition to intended users as well as to persons reasonably expected to be within the orbit of such use. Defendant is strictly liable for the death and injuries set forth herein.

8. By reason of the aforesaid wrongful acts of the defendant that directly and proximately caused the death of William P. Consumer, and for bodily and mental injury to his spouse, plaintiff-executrix claims damages of the defendant on behalf of the wife and children of the deceased as follows:

    a. To the estate for loss of established earnings and earning power of the deceased for a period of time beginning September 8, 1991, and continuing to the termination of his natural life, which earnings and earning power would have continued but for his death on September 8, 1991; and for medical and funeral expenses under the Abatement and Survival Act (T.C.A. 20-5-106) in the amount of $222,000.

    b. To plaintiff for loss due to bodily and mental injuries sustained in the accident in the amount of $63,000.

    For further relief the plaintiff forever prays.

A JURY TRIAL IS DEMANDED.

JOHN GAITHER

By: _____
    Attorney for Plaintiffs
    57 Courthouse Square
    Centerville, Middle State

summons: instrument used as a means of acquiring jurisdiction over a party and to commence a civil action.

service of process: reasonable notice to the defendant of legal proceedings to afford the defendant an opportunity to appear and be heard.

Federal courts usually have several judges and use a rotation system of assigning cases. In state court, the lawyer filing the case may have some choice about and knowledge of the particular judge who will handle the case. In federal court, the clerk assigns a judge to the case at the time of filing. This system evens the case load among the judges and prevents "judge shopping." Judge Stern was assigned to the *Consumer* case.

Judge Stern would follow all aspects of the case through trial in accordance with the local procedure of that district court. Other district courts use a master calendar system by which different aspects of the same case are handled by different judges assigned to specific functions. The clerk's office is responsible for the record-keeping function. The case number and the judge's name were stamped on the *Consumer* case's file jacket, and notice of assignment was sent to Judge Stern. All actions and documents would be kept in the office of the clerk until needed by the judge.

The clerk then issued a **summons** to be served upon the defendant, Factory Motor Company (see Form 5-2). **Service of process** refers to the important task of notifying the defendant that a lawsuit has been filed against that individual or corporation. The consequences of failure to respond to a summons are severe; hence, assurance that proper notification has been received is important. The defendant must answer the complaint within a specified period of time (usually twenty days) or risk judgment by default.

Had Attorney Gaither filed his suit in state court, the process would have been more complicated. Most states have "long arm statutes" that enable them to exercise jurisdiction over nonresidents whose actions produce a wrong within the state, even if those actions take place out of state. Various forms of substitute service of process may be used that involve processing the complaint through the secretaries of state for the states involved. Local sheriff's offices usually serve state process—a method that is less flexible than the new methods provided in Rule 4 (FRCP).

The 1980 amendment to Rule 4 (FRCP) authorizes service of process to be made by any person who is not a party to the lawsuit and is at least eighteen years of age. The current provision of Rule 4(a) instructs the clerk to issue a summons and deliver the summons to the plaintiff or the plaintiff's attorney, who shall be responsible for proper service of the summons and a copy of the complaint.

Filing the complaint commences a civil lawsuit; however, the time limitation in the summons (twenty days) does not begin to run until the day after service of process. If the action is not perfected by service within 120 days after filing the complaint, the action is subject to dismissal.

The default provision in the summons (twenty days) is subject to the defendant's motion for reasonable delay, but if the defendant does not respond within the twenty-day period and has been verifiably served, the default may be executed, and the court will award reasonable uncontested damages to the plaintiff.

The summons and complaint may be served on an adult defendant by mailing copies to the defendant along with two copies of a notice and acknowledgment of service. The acknowledgment is to be returned if the defendant accepts service, and it is customary for the plaintiff to provide a self-addressed envelope with postage prepaid. If the defendant fails to acknowledge receipt of the summons and complaint, service is not perfected; the plaintiff then has to use the services of a United States marshal or process server to consummate service. The

Form 5.2
SUMMONS

IN THE UNITED STATES DISTRICT COURT FOR THE
MIDDLE DISTRICT OF MIDDLE STATE

JANE CONSUMER,
   Executrix of the
ESTATE OF WILLIAM P. CONSUMER,
and JANE CONSUMER, individually,

               Plaintiffs

                  v.

FACTORY MOTOR COMPANY,
   a manufacturing corporation

               Defendant

Civil Action
No. 92–147

SUMMONS

To the above-named defendant:

    You are hereby summoned and required to serve upon   John Gaither , plaintiff's, attorney, whose address is   57 Courthouse Square, Centerville, Middle State , an answer to the complaint that is herewith served upon you, within   20   days after service of this summons upon you, exclusive of the day of service. If you fail to do so, judgment by default will be taken against you for the relief demanded in the complaint.

SEAL OF THE COURT

                                                                          Clerk of Court

Dated: February 20, 1992

Note: This summons is issued pursuant to Rule 4 of the Federal Rules of Civil Procedure.

cost of the service of process may be charged to the defendant if the defendant loses the case.

Defendant's Response

In the *Consumer* case, service of the summons and complaint was made by regular mail; they were delivered to Factory Motor Company's general legal counsel, Herman Hardnose. Mr. Hardnose called Maria Farmer into his office to discuss the complaint and again indicated that she should prepare to go to trial with the case.

Maria told Hardnose that she would need local assistance in Middle State. She had been in contact with Bill Green of the Capital City law firm of Green, Wagnor, and Johns. He represented the City Auto Company that sold and serviced the vehicle in question and was familiar with local court rules. His office would be needed during the discovery process and trial. Mr. Hardnose approved, stating, "You will have whatever resources you need to prepare our defense in this case."

Maria then contacted Bill Green in Capital City and asked if he would assist in Factory Motor Company's defense of the lawsuit filed in federal district court in Capital City. Bill was concerned about the interests of his client City Auto Company, and he wanted assurance that he would not be placing himself in a **conflict of interest** situation. He asked Maria, "Is there any chance that my client will be drawn in as a party to the suit that has been filed?"

Maria assured Bill that the complaint named Factory Motor Company as the sole defendant. Bill again emphasized, "I can accept your offer only under the condition that my first obligation is to defend my existing client as required by professional ethics."

Maria understood this professional obligation and agreed that Bill should withdraw from the case if a conflict of interest became evident. She asked him to begin immediately gathering preliminary information from local sources that would be needed in the case. Maria said she would work on gathering information relevant to the case from sources in Lake State. The complaint and summons would be FAXed to Bill's law firm so he could get started right away. Maria indicated that they would stay in touch by telephone and coordinate their activities.

Maria then called the research department of Factory Motor Company and set up a meeting with the chief engineer in charge of testing, Mr. Superior Tester. She had a written report on the assembly line mix-up concerning the original coils on the cars manufactured in 1989, and the serial number in the complaint matched the range of serial numbers involved in this incident. The report indicated that the coils mounted on the left side of these vehicles were tested to see if they would hold up. Mr. Tester brought his lab report on the testing of the coils in question to their meeting.

"Did the coils that were installed on the left side of these vehicles," asked Maria, "violate any of the governmental standards prescribed by the Department of Transportation's safety specifications?"

"No," replied Mr. Tester. "There are no particular safety standards for these coils. They are installed primarily for comfort to guarantee a smooth ride for the passengers."

"What were the results of your tests in the lab on these coils?" Maria queried.

---

conflict of interest: ethical conflict involving violation of trust in matters of private interest and gain. A lawyer may not serve two clients with opposing interests.

Mr. Tester explained, "We put three of these coils on a simulation machine and let them run under stress until they broke. They all broke after 1700 hours on the machine. The first one broke at 1726 hours, and the other two at 1824 and 1891 hours. The 1700 hours of testing simulated 204,000 miles of normal wear. We, therefore, concluded that the coils would be safe for the normal life of the vehicle."

Maria kept copies of the report for her files. She explained that a lawsuit had been filed concerning these coils and that an allegation had been made that one of the coils caused an accident. "Do you think this is possible, Mr. Tester?"

Mr. Tester said he could not say for certain, but he doubted that even a broken coil could affect the safety of the vehicle. "It would most likely cause some noise, and perhaps discomfort," he noted. "It might tip the vehicle to the left, but it would not cause it to go out of control."

"We may have to prove that in court," Maria responded.

After the meeting with Mr. Tester, Maria called an independent expert, Professor Drivesafe from Lake State University. She explained the complaint and the factory testing done on the coils to the professor and asked if driving conditions could be a potential cause of the accident. He had no details concerning the accident with which to work, but he agreed to look into the matter once the case was far enough along that detailed information about the accident would be available. He had served as consultant concerning the cause of accidents in many cases and would be willing to so serve in this case.

Maria examined fifty complaints that had been forwarded to the factory from owners of the two hundred and fifty vehicles involved in the production mix-up. All the owners had complained of the vehicles leaning to the left. The decision to recall these automobiles was made on the basis that the problem was a cosmetic one that should be eliminated. The records indicated that two hundred of these cars had received coil replacements since the recall notice was mailed and that no other accidents had been reported.

The Answer

The defendant may appear in the case by serving a motion to challenge jurisdiction, a motion for an order to strike the complaint, a motion for a **judgment on the pleadings**, or a motion for an order to compel a more definite statement of the allegations in the complaint (Rule 12(a) [FRCP]). The defendant does not need to serve an answer while a Rule 12 motion is pending, since such a motion suspends the twenty-day time period for the answer. After the court rules on the motion, an answer is due within ten days of the ruling, unless the court dismisses the complaint or sets a different time limit within which to answer (Rule 12(a) [FRCP]).

judgment on the pleadings: motion after the pleadings are closed by which any party may seek summary judgment by challenging the pleadings.

Maria Farmer concluded that no reasonable grounds for Rule 12 motions existed at the time, although a motion to rule on the pleadings can be made at any time after the answer is filed and before the trial (but may not be used to delay the trial).

The defendant's answer must admit the truth of those allegations in the complaint that are known to be true. Formal admissions in the answer remove these allegations from controversy, and the plaintiff does not have to prove these admitted facts. Since the jury ultimately will be informed about the admissions, it is advantageous to the plaintiff to frame the complaint in such a way as to encourage the defendant to admit as many facts as possible.

The defendant's answer must specifically deny those allegations in the complaint that are not true. Any allegation in the complaint that is not denied is presumed to be admitted (Rule 8(d) [FRCP]). If the defendant does not have sufficient knowledge upon which to form a belief concerning an allegation, a statement to that effect is interpreted as a denial.

The defendant's answer uses numbered paragraphs, as does the complaint, to separate each set of circumstances and each admission or denial. The answer must allege all of the defendant's affirmative defenses (Rule 8(c) [FRCP]), since any affirmative defense not asserted in the answer is waived. An affirmative defense is a fact or set of circumstances that defeats the plaintiff's claim even though the plaintiff is able to prove a cause of action.

Maria Farmer mailed the answer to the complaint in the *Consumer* case to the court, and she sent copies of the answer to the plaintiff's attorney, John Gaither (see Form 5-3).

DISCOVERY

The stage in the legal process during which each party has access to the court's power to compel testimony and factual materials relevant to the case is known as **discovery**. This period can be quite lengthy and generally exists from the time the complaint is filed until the time of trial. Power to compel information may be granted even before the complaint is filed if warranted by the circumstances.

discovery: pretrial devices used to obtain information relevant to the case in preparation for trial.

In civil cases, the discovery process is relatively unlimited and allows each party to gain access to information relevant to the legal action. The concept of "relevancy" is interpreted broadly by the courts, and even material that might not be admitted as evidence at trial can be within the definition of relevant information. The parties generally have access to any information if it is even remotely relevant to the subject matter of the action or if there is a possibility that the information will lead to other evidence that will be admissible at trial.

Nonetheless, there is some information that is privileged and immune from the court's power to compel testimony and materials. The most important privilege is the individual's protection from being compelled to testify against himself or herself in a criminal matter. In civil cases, this privilege may operate when there is a potential for criminal action. Protective orders may be obtained from the judge that limit or bar discovery of material in privileged areas. Other privileges include the lawyer-client privilege, protection of the attorney's work product, and protection from unreasonable use of the discovery process as a means of harassment.

The discovery rules are enforced by the judge who can hold an unresponsive party in contempt of court. In extreme cases, the contempt may involve incarceration. The purpose of discovery is to prevent surprises at trial, to encourage settlement, and to facilitate a just result. Competent attorneys use the discovery process to reveal all the knowable facts in the case and do not conclude the process until that objective has been reached.

The rules of discovery, which are found in Rules 26 through 37 (FRCP), are extensive. There also may be local rules that need to be followed. The instruments of discovery include interrogatories, depositions, and requests to produce documents or material evidence. Other forms include requests for admissions (specific questions requiring answers) and requests for mental or physical examinations. The date by which discovery must be concluded is usually estab-

Form 5.3
ANSWER FROM FACTORY MOTOR COMPANY

IN THE UNITED STATES DISTRICT COURT FOR THE
MIDDLE DISTRICT OF MIDDLE STATE

JANE CONSUMER)
   Executrix of the)
ESTATE OF WILLIAM P. CONSUMER,)
and JANE CONSUMER, individually)
                Plaintiffs)
                            Civil Action
            v.)   No. 92–147

FACTORY MOTOR COMPANY)
   a manufacturing corporation)   ANSWER
                Defendant)

Now comes the defendant FACTORY MOTOR COMPANY, U.S.A., a corporation, and by its attorneys files the following answer to the plaintiff's complaint:

FIRST DEFENSE
1. Defendant admits the averments in paragraphs 1, 2, and 3 of plaintiff's complaint.
2. Defendant is presently without sufficient information to form a belief as to the truth of the averments in paragraphs 4, 5, 6, and 7 of plaintiff's complaint.
3. Defendant denies the averments in paragraph 8 of plaintiff's complaint.

SECOND DEFENSE
4. Plaintiff's complaint fails to state a cause of action upon which recovery can be had by the plaintiff against the defendant.

THIRD DEFENSE
5. If William P. Consumer's death was caused by defendant's acts as alleged in plaintiffs' complaint, William P. Consumer voluntarily assumed the risk.

MARIA FARMER

_____
Attorney for Defendant

lished in federal court by agreement, and a formal discovery schedule must be filed with the court fairly early in the process.

Interrogatories

The plaintiff's attorney and the two attorneys for the defendant in the *Consumer* case wanted more specific information in order to be prepared for trial. They knew that much of the information was already known to the opposing attorneys. Bill Green and Maria Farmer communicated frequently about what information they would need. Bill understood that his law firm would be called upon to provide much of the legal work because of their location in Middle State and that it would be unproductive to have both lawyers for the defense duplicating their efforts.

Bill Green's paralegal, Jan Professional, received a briefing on the *Consumer* case. Bill gave her access to his file on the case and outlined her responsibilities. He told her that she could get a copy of the accident report from the highway safety department down the street from the law office and that this document would give them valuable information and identify the patrol officer who filed the accident report. "In addition, we will need to construct interrogatories to John Gaither to find out what witnesses he has identified," Bill instructed.

Jan had prepared many interrogatories in similar cases and knew that they represented an inexpensive method by which to gain preliminary information about potential witnesses. **Interrogatories**, which are sent by mail and contain written questions that must be answered under oath by the party served, may be sent only to the parties to the lawsuit. Local rules often stipulate that the court clerk receive copies as well as all parties concerned. Jan was familiar with these rules. She was instructed to send copies of the accident report to Maria Farmer in Lake State.

While Bill Green and Jan Professional were discussing the case and preparing their interrogatories (see Form 5-4) in Capital City, John Gaither and Chris Martin were engaged in similar discussions concerning the information they needed to prepare for trial. Chris also was instructed to prepare interrogatories for service upon the defendant. John wanted to make sure the following items were included in these interrogatories:

1. existence of any documents explaining the cause of the recall of automobiles relevant to the plaintiff's recall letter;
2. existence of any documents involving testing of the coils in question; and
3. names and addresses of any expert witnesses that have been or are likely to be called in regard to this case.

Once the interrogatories were answered, the lawyers on both sides of the *Consumer* case would be able to assess the need for the use of more precise methods of discovery. The answers to the interrogatories would identify the witnesses to be called in the more expensive face-to-face questioning process known as a deposition.

Depositions

The **deposition** is a formal stage in the discovery process that amounts to a rehearsal of what will more than likely take place at trial. Potential witnesses are

interrogatories: written questions about the case submitted by one party to the other party or witness.

deposition: testimony of a witness taken outside of court, where both parties may question the witness and a transcript of the statement is made.

Form 5.4
INTERROGATORIES

IN THE UNITED STATES DISTRICT COURT FOR THE
MIDDLE DISTRICT OF MIDDLE STATE

JANE CONSUMER,)
   Plaintiff)
)
                        Civil Action
          v.)   No. 92-147
)
FACTORY MOTOR COMPANY,)   INTERROGATORIES
   Defendant)

Defendants respectfully submit to the plaintiffs for answer by them under oath as provided for by the Federal Rules of Civil Procedure the following interrogatories:

1. State decedent's date and place of birth.

2. Describe fully the extent of decedent's formal education, including the schools attended, degrees obtained, and dates of completions.

3. State the amount decedent reported as income in the United States federal tax returns for each of the years 1988, 1989, and 1990 respectively.

4. Describe decedent's employments during the five years preceding his death, including the name of each employer, period of time for each employment, his job title, and a description of the work he performed in each job.

5. As to each personal injury accident the decedent had, state:

    a. the date of the accident;

    b. the location of the accident;

    c. the type of accident;

    d. the nature and extent of the injuries sustained;

    e. the names and addresses of physicians who attended him;

    f. the names and addresses of hospitals at which he received treatment;

    g. the nature and extent of any consequential disability; and

    h. the name and address of all persons against whom claims were made due to the accident.

6. State the name, address, age, and relationship to decedent of each next of kin for whom claim is being made in this action.

7. Describe in detail the occurrence of the accident referred to in the complaint.

8. State the medical cause of decedent's death.

9. If decedent was ever convicted of a crime, identify the court where judgment was entered and the date of conviction and describe the nature of the offense for which he was convicted.

10. State the names and addresses of all witnesses who have any knowledge or information about the alleged accident.

11. Identify by name, address, and occupation each person who has custody of photographs relevant to the alleged accident.

12. State the names and addresses of all persons from whom statements have been obtained and indicate the date on which each statement was made.

13. State the names and addresses of all other persons who have any knowledge or information about the accident referred to in the complaint, including expert witnesses.

[Note: Adequate space should be allowed where appropriate answers can be typed in spaces provided.]

June 1, 1992

_____
Attorney for Defendant

called to an appropriate location (usually within forty miles of the place of service) to answer questions under oath. A court reporter records every question and answer, and a transcript of the entire session is prepared.

The deponents are allowed to read the transcript before signing it and attesting that it is a true and accurate copy of the facts known to the deponent. There is no judge present at these sessions, but the answers given are important. Depositions can be introduced at the trial and used for such purposes as contradicting testimony, known as impeaching the witness. Or these statements can be read into the trial record if the witness cannot be present at the trial.

Notice to all parties is required prior to deposition and is served upon the parties' attorneys as well as the parties themselves. The direct parties to the lawsuit do not require subpoenas but must be notified. Potential witnesses that are not parties must be served in person by **subpoena** requested through the court clerk's office. The subpoena commands the person to whom it is directed to appear and give testimony at the time and place specified, and a *subpoena duces tecum* commands that the person bring along relevant documents or materials in his or her possession.

subpoena: a command to appear at a certain time and place to give testimony upon a certain matter.

After several months of difficulties with scheduling and notifications, the potential witnesses were all questioned by the attorneys involved in the case. John Gaither had to travel to Lake State to participate in the deposition session held there. Maria Farmer and Bill Green also had to travel to meet in places that were convenient for the witnesses. Ambulance driver, Jackie Lifesaver, was identified and subpoenaed for a deposition session. Professor Drivesafe was sent to Middle State to investigate the site of the accident and the condition of the vehicle that was still located at the garage. The professor's deposition was taken in Lake State during the same week as that of Superior Tester. The transcripts resulting from these sessions were quite lengthy, since they included direct and cross-examination of witnesses and follow-up questions by all attorneys.

Depositions were taken for some of the potential witnesses at trial, but some potential witnesses were not subjected to this process, since they would not be principal witnesses. The defense deposed Jane Consumer, Jim Trucker (an eyewitness whose tractor-trailer was hit by the Consumer vehicle), George Goodcop (the patrol officer who responded to the scene of the accident), and Mack Racer (the expert mechanic who discovered the broken coil)—all of whom were considered principal witnesses for the plaintiff and would be likely to testify for the plaintiff's side at the trial. The plaintiffs deposed Dr. Jan Intern (the attending physician at the hospital), Superior Tester (the Factory Motor Company laboratory technician), Jackie Lifesaver (the attending paramedic at the scene of the accident), and Professor Drivesafe (an engineer whose special field was accident research).

The full transcripts from these deposition sessions were made available to all parties, and copies were placed in the court's record by the court clerk. For purposes of convenience, the transcripts were reduced to short summaries containing the essential facts revealed during these sessions. (See Appendix C of this text for these summary statements. They illustrate what was discovered through the deposition process.) The lawyers would base their decisions during the next stages on what they learned, and the statements made at deposition helped to define the issues of controversy in the case.

Production of Documents

Another discovery method used by both sides in the *Consumer* case was a **request to produce**. This request may be served on any party having relevant

request to produce: discovery method used to secure relevant documents or material evidence.

documents or material evidence and can be used to gain entry to the premises of the other party for purposes of inspection, photographing, sampling, copying, and other means of obtaining relevant evidence. The request is backed by the court's authority to order compliance and can be executed by law enforcement officers if necessary.

This type of request was used in the discovery process to enable Professor Drivesafe to conduct his investigation and to enable John Gaither to obtain information from the factory concerning their decision to recall the passenger car involved in the accident (see Form 5-5). The Factory Motor Company allowed John to make copies of the relevant documents when he attended Superior Tester's deposition session in Big City, Lake State.

PRETRIAL CONFERENCES

The attorneys on both sides of the *Consumer* case gradually worked through their lists of leads to be followed and information to be obtained through discovery. John Gaither and Chris Martin sat down to review the information they had obtained. Cora Smith, the senior partner in the firm, was asked to review all the materials in the *Consumer* file, which had now grown to fill a small file cabinet. They were aware that their opponents had every fact that they had obtained in the case and began to grow confident that there were no surprises to be uncovered.

John Gaither said, "What the case really boils down to is a contest between expert witnesses."

Chris Martin commented that the defense had two witnesses that they would attempt to qualify as experts. "Does this hurt our chances?" he asked.

Cora Smith cautioned, "It depends on the jury. We have material evidence on our side, but we'll have to make some convincing arguments at trial."

"Are we agreed then that we are ready to talk with the defense attorneys?" asked John. Cora agreed but thought they should consult with the client first.

When they consulted with Jane Consumer about what they had discovered during the months of fact-finding in the case, Jane agreed that she could think of no further questions, but she was concerned about what would be discussed at the lawyers' conference.

John explained that the attorneys for both sides would be involved in a complicated process of negotiations concerning the strength of their respective cases. This process is often crucial to successful settlement out of court. "Cora and I will attempt to convince the Factory Motor Company lawyers that our case is so strong that they should settle," explained the attorney. Both sides would assess the probability of the trial outcome. If they agreed on all the issues of fact, the law would decide the outcome. The lawyers would assess the results of the discovery process and determine what facts are agreed to as stipulated and what facts remain in contention. This process narrows the issues that will be argued at trial and enables the parties to decide what witnesses to call and to plan the trial. Any issues of law in dispute also would be discussed to alert the opponent that the issues will be raised at trial.

Jane was puzzled. "This sounds like you will be trying to make a deal and I'm not involved." she commented.

John indicated that if the defendant made an offer, Jane would be informed of it and could make the decision at that time. Both John and Jane agreed that a settlement would be preferable to trial, since the trial outcome was uncertain.

Form 5.5

REQUEST TO PRODUCE

IN THE UNITED STATES DISTRICT COURT FOR THE
MIDDLE DISTRICT OF MIDDLE STATE

JANE CONSUMER,
Plaintiff

v.

FACTORY MOTOR COMPANY,
Defendant

Civil Action
No. 92–147

REQUEST TO PRODUCE

Plaintiff above named hereby requests pursuant to Rule 34 of the Federal Rules of Civil Procedure that defendant, Factory Motor Company, Inc., a corporation, produce and permit plaintiff to inspect and to copy each of the following documents:

a. reports of tests conducted by defendant on the coils installed in 1990 Supreme Brougham Executive sold to plaintiff, serial number 1FMCB14T9KUA14073; and
b. reports of causes for recall of such automobiles within the serial number range of plaintiff's vehicle.

It is requested that the aforesaid production be made on the day of August 6, 1992, when plaintiff's attorney will be present for a deposition session at the Law Department of the Factory Motor Company, Big City, Lake State.

By _____
Attorney for Plaintiff
57 Courthouse Square
Centerville, Middle State

John then called Bill Green and asked if the defense was ready for a pre-trial conference. Bill said he would get in touch with Maria Farmer and let him know.

Bill and Maria agreed to review their notes and files on the case and to set up a telephone conference with the general counsel for the law department of Factory Motor Company and Jan Professional, Bill's paralegal. During this conversation, everyone agreed that the files were complete and that there would be no surprises. They also agreed that a conference should be set up with John Gaither and that Maria would attend. Jan Professional asked about stipulations and whether there was agreement on what witnesses to call. Maria and Bill agreed to work on this matter before the conference with the plaintiff's attorney.

Attorneys' Conference

attorneys' conference: meeting of lawyers for both sides in a civil legal action to discuss the results of the discovery process and reach settlement or prepare for trial.

After checking with his client, Bill Green set up the **attorneys' conference** with John Gaither. John indicated that he wanted his senior partner at the meeting, which would be held at the law firm of Smith and Gaither in Centerville in two weeks.

At the meeting it quickly became evident that the defendant was not interested in an out-of-court settlement, and the business turned to the construction of a pretrial memorandum that must be submitted to the court by each side in preparation for the pretrial conference with the judge. The discussion followed the format that would be needed to prepare the memoranda: questions of jurisdiction, contentions of liability, discussion of damages, witnesses to be called by each side and identification of those who would serve as experts, review of pleadings to determine if amendments were in order, matters to be stipulated, and estimated length of trial. Issues concerning exhibits were explored, with each side letting the other know about any exhibits they intended to bring to trial.

stipulation: agreement, admission, or confession made in a judicial proceeding by the parties or their attorneys.

A **stipulation** is an agreement to admit the truth of those matters no longer at issue. The following lists illustrate the matters that were stipulated and the matters that would be contested at trial before the jury in the *Consumer* case:

Matters Stipulated:

1. questions of jurisdiction;
2. defendant manufactured automobile in question;
3. City Auto Company did not replace coil in question;
4. coil reached user in substantially unaltered condition;
5. left coil was not identical to right coil;
6. no federal standards existed for suspension coils; and
7. automobile was properly serviced and maintained.

Matters Still at Issue:

1. whether coil was dangerously defective;
2. whether accident was caused by coil breaking;
3. whether accident was caused by wet road conditions;
4. whether driver was under influence of intoxicants;
5. whether coil was broken before or after the accident; and
6. whether damages were fairly assessed.

Judge's Conference

A final conference with Judge Stern was scheduled in three weeks. The attorneys would meet briefly with the judge to submit their drafted pretrial order that would include all of the matters discussed at the attorneys' conference. Most judges are very active in their efforts to try to settle cases out of court because of the case load, but Judge Stern was favorably impressed with the thorough preparation of the parties' attorneys and agreed that the lists of witnesses were not excessive. He did not even attempt to convince them to settle out of court. He asked, "I suppose you have considered settlement of this case, haven't you?" Both parties indicated agreement. The judge then asked each party's attorney to prepare and submit to him a brief of the legal issues involved in the case, copies of which would have to be sent to the opposing parties as well as the judge before the trial date.

The judge can render a **summary judgment** at this stage if there is no dispute on relevant questions of fact and if the only questions in dispute are issues of law. Either party can file a motion for summary judgment. Since there were plenty of facts in dispute in this case, the issue was not raised.

The two parties in the *Consumer* case were notified in February that their trial date would be August 9, 1993. Although it was almost two years after the accident, Jane Consumer would finally get her "day in court." The next chapter discusses preparation for the trial process.

summary judgment: any party may make such a motion and the judge may agree that there is no genuine issue of material fact and that the party is entitled to prevail as a matter of law.

CHAPTER SUMMARY

1. This chapter illustrates the initiation of a civil legal action involving the filing of a complaint, service of process, and answer. Successful completion of this process subjects both parties to the court's jurisdiction. The discovery process enables both sides to gain access to the court's power to compel relevant evidence in preparation for trial.

2. The complaint serves to initiate legal action and to inform the court and defendants of the nature of the allegations and the basis in law for settlement. It need not present proof of these allegations, but it must include enough information to assert a claim that a legally protected interest of the plaintiff has been violated by the parties named as defendants.

3. The complaint and summons must be served upon the defendants in a legally acceptable manner to allow them to answer the complaint within a reasonable period of time (usually twenty days). Failure to answer the complaint can result in an award to the plaintiff by default; therefore, proper service of these documents is important to a fair process.

4. An answer to the complaint by the defendant informs the plaintiff and the court whether facts will be contested and whether other forms of relief will be sought. A motion to dismiss for lack of jurisdiction indicates a contention that the plaintiff failed to meet the court's jurisdictional requirements. Agreement to the allegations indicates no contest and allows the judge to rule on issues of law. An answer that poses questions of fact in dispute indicates the beginning of the discovery process.

5. The discovery process generally exists from the time the complaint is filed until trial. The discovery period allows both parties access to the court's power to compel evidence and witness testimony. This power covers all relevant information in civil actions and is applied broadly by the courts. The courts have power to issue compliance orders and to impose contempt penalties for noncompliance with these orders.

6. Interrogatories are mailed requests for specific information that can be served on the opposing parties to the complaint. The questions in the interrogatories must be answered under oath, but there is no opportunity for cross-examination. This method of discovery is used to obtain general information in an inexpensive manner.

7. Depositions, which are also part of the fact-gathering process, are more formal than interrogatories. Subpoenas may be issued through the court to compel the presence of potential witnesses. Both parties' attorneys must be notified and given ample opportunity to question potential witnesses. A transcript of all statements made is prepared by a court reporter, and the potential witnesses must verify the accuracy of the transcript. These transcripts may be used to impeach witnesses at trial or may be read into the trial record if witnesses are unable to attend the trial.

8. Requests to produce relevant documents or material evidence are another form of discovery. These requests are backed by the court's power to compel evidence, which includes the power to gain entrance to premises where such evidence may be located. Admissions and medical examinations (physical and mental) are additional forms of discovery backed by the court's authority.

9. The discovery process is supervised by the judge and usually ends once both parties have concluded that all available evidence and testimony concerning the facts of the case have been revealed. Discovery ensures that there will be no surprises at trial and, thus, that the process is fair. If the parties are unable to come to agreement on termination of discovery, the judge may be asked to rule on the issue.

10. An attorneys' conference is usually required in order for the attorneys for both sides to discuss the findings of the discovery process and to explore the possibility of out-of-court settlement on the basis of these findings. When factual issues remain in contention, the attorneys must prepare pretrial memoranda describing the factual issues still in contention, the witnesses they will call, and the estimated length of trial time needed.

11. A pretrial conference with the judge has become common practice to facilitate more efficient use of the court's time. The judge becomes more familiar with the case, and the parties are encouraged to refrain from calling an excessive number of witnesses. At this time, settlement out of court may be achieved by agreement of the parties, or a summary judgment is possible if the only questions in dispute are issues of law.

12. The calendaring of the case on the court's docket is a problem because both state and federal courts are overloaded. The difficulty of scheduling cases has produced pressures on the courts to improve their efficiency, but the problem is far from being solved.

KEY TERMS

Federal Rules of Civil Procedure (FRCP)

fact pleading

notice pleading

complaint

answer

jury trial

bench trial

docket

summons	interrogatories	attorneys' conference
service of process	deposition	stipulation
conflict of interest	subpoena	summary judgment
judgment on the pleadings	request to produce	
discovery		

DISCUSSION QUESTIONS

1. How is a civil legal action initiated through the formal process of filing the complaint and answer?

2. Why are these pleadings necessary in order for the court to have jurisdiction over the parties involved in a lawsuit?

3. What is meant by a ruling on the pleadings?

4. What are the basic purposes of discovery?

5. How could the discovery process be abused by those filing frivolous or malicious complaints?

6. Is settlement more likely to occur before or after discovery? Why?

7. Are the lawyers' conference and the conference with the judge necessary stages in the pretrial process?

8. If more than ninety percent of the cases filed are settled out of court, what types of cases proceed to trial?

SOURCES AND SUGGESTED READING

Blanchard, Rodrick D. 1990. *Litigation and Trial Practice for the Legal Assistant*. 3d ed. St. Paul: West Publishing Co.

Kane, Mary Kay. 1991. *Civil Procedure in a Nutshell*, 3d ed. St. Paul: West Publishing Co.

Neubauer, David W. 1991. *Judicial Process*. Pacific Grove, Calif.: Brooks/Cole Publishing Co.

Federal Rules of Civil Procedure can be found in various publications:

United States Code (U.S. Government Printing Office)

United States Code Annotated (West Publishing Company)

Federal Civil Judicial Procedure and Rules (West Publishing Company)

(State rules of civil procedure can be found in the state's annotated code or in paperbacks published by West Publishing Company that have the state's name and *Rules of Court*. These publications contain both federal rules of court and those of the particular state. It is important to check the most recent edition of these publications.)

CHAPTER SIX

TRIAL: ARGUMENT AND ADJUDICATION

> "A judge should perform the duties of his office impartially and diligently."
> Canon Three: ABA Model Rules of Judicial Conduct

On the morning of August 9, 1993, the date set by Judge Stern for the *Consumer* trial to begin, Jane Consumer was very nervous. She did not know what to expect, as she had never been involved in a trial before. She met John Gaither and Cora Smith at their office, and together they drove to Capital City in Attorney Gaither's car.

The two lawyers reassured Jane on the trip to the federal courthouse that they were well prepared to handle her case effectively. They explained that the jury selection process would allow all the participants at trial to become familiar with each other. This process would last through at least the first day of the trial and might last longer, depending upon the complexity of the problems involved.

They arrived at the courthouse early and found their way to the assigned courtroom before anyone else had arrived. This gave the lawyers a chance to explain the physical arrangements. The judge's bench, in the center of the room, occupied the immediate focus of attention in the courtroom. From this lofty perch, the judge would have a clear view of all participants and would immediately symbolize the authority in the court proceedings. The witness stand was to the judge's right and was boxed to protect the witness. The jury box was located somewhat further to the judge's right beyond the witness box but within clear view of the judge, which meant the jury box was somewhat tilted toward the judge's bench and the witness box. The bailiff (or tipstaff), who maintains order in the courtroom, would be seated to the right of the judge, and the court reporter, who makes a complete transcript of the court's proceedings, would be seated in the same area. Modern courtroom arrangements form a semicircular design to facilitate closeness, permitting the major participants to hear and see each other.

THE JURY SELECTION PROCESS

The jury selection process is known as **voir dire**, which is a Law French term meaning "to speak the truth." This phrase denotes the preliminary examination

voir dire: preliminary examination of jurors, or witnesses, to challenge their qualifications to serve in such capacities.

of potential jurors during which their competence and objectivity to serve as jurors in a specific case may be questioned. The trial court clerk generally uses the voter registration lists in the judicial district to select a jury "venire," or panel of potential jurors, large enough to serve the needs of the court. These potential jurors are notified for jury duty well in advance of the court date and are warned that failure to appear can result in contempt of court charges against them.

Usually there is some form of screening device used, such as a questionnaire, to eliminate those who are obviously incompetent, who may belong to certain occupational groups considered vital to the community, or whose governmental employment may present a conflict of interest. This practice excludes a large number of persons on a systematic basis. Physically or mentally handicapped persons, those who have been convicted of a felony, and law enforcement officers, doctors, teachers, nurses, and members of the clergy are frequently excused or not even considered in the pool of potential jurors.

The court clerk had assembled the potential jurors in the *Consumer* case in an adjoining room. A jury wheel was used to select twenty persons for the trial panel designated for Judge Stern's courtroom. These individuals were then escorted into the courtroom and asked to be seated in the audience section.

As Judge Stern entered the courtroom, the bailiff announced the court in session with, "All rise! Oyez, Oyez the Federal District Court for the Middle State District is now open to oral statement, the Honorable Judge Stern presiding, all persons having business before this Honorable Court draw near, give attention, and you shall be heard. God save the United States and this Honorable Court."

Judge Stern took his place at the bench and invited the audience to be seated. He called the case of *Consumer v. Factory Motor Company* and checked to see that the lawyers for both sides were present and ready for trial. He then addressed the jury panel and explained the purposes and procedures of the voir dire process.

Voir Dire Challenges

There is considerable variation in local practice regarding the conduct of the jury selection process. The judge has to explain the manner in which he or she will proceed. The judge is aware that he or she is responsible for conducting a fair process and that the lawyers on both sides may ultimately challenge the manner in which the process was conducted on appeal. Therefore, the judge generally seeks to establish the concerns of the opposing lawyers and to identify the potential issues.

Challenges for Cause

The judge may ask the questions or may also allow the lawyers to address the jury panel and pose their own questions. The lawyers are allowed to move that the court disqualify a juror "for cause," but the decision to remove that juror must be made by the judge. The judge will allow both parties to present opposing arguments concerning **challenges for cause**.

Peremptory Challenges

When arguments concerning elimination of potential jurors for cause have been exhausted, the judge allows both parties an opportunity to exercise their

challenges for cause: requests from parties to the judge to remove potential jurors for specified reasons.

peremptory challenges. The number of these challenges is fixed by the rules of civil procedure for that jurisdiction and may vary from state to state. Three peremptory challenges per party in the selection of a jury of six would be typical. Parties do not have to use all their peremptory challenges.

It is good strategy for the lawyer to approach potential jurors in a courteous manner, taking care not to arouse their animosity. Many lawyers try to ingratiate themselves to the jurors and win their sympathy from the start. One strategy is to display confidence by not asking too many questions and being very cooperative with all jurors, making them feel good about themselves and sympathetic toward the lawyer. For this reason, the judges in federal courts usually conduct the voir dire themselves, and the lawyers are required to formulate questions through them. This practice attempts to reduce the skillful attorney's ability to win the jury before the facts are established.

The voir dire process is quite diverse in American courts, and the procedures used in practice are about as varied as the number of judges who hold trials. In the *Consumer* case, Judge Stern used a combination of methods in conducting the voir dire. He first asked the trial panel to stand and raise their right hands. "Do you solemnly swear to make true answers to all questions that shall be asked of you touching your competency as jurors?" he asked. The entire trial panel responded affirmatively.

The judge then identified the parties to the lawsuit, their respective legal counsel, and the witnesses who would appear in the case. He asked the jurors if any of them were related to or had any personal dealings with any of these persons, or if the jurors knew of any reason that they might be disqualified from serving on the jury in this case. A secretary employed at Middle State University knew the deceased plaintiff, a nephew of Jim Trucker had talked with him about the accident, a salesman was employed at City Auto Company, and one potential juror was a former client of Bill Green's law firm. The judge asked several questions of these potential jurors and allowed the opposing lawyers to comment or pose questions of their own, then thanked them and asked them to rejoin the general jury panel in the assembly room.

Both parties to the dispute made use of their peremptory challenges. The judge allowed each party to name any three potential jurors for elimination without cause. John Gaither and Cora Smith agreed to eliminate the owner of a small factory, the manager of a small airport, and a salesperson for an auto parts firm. Bill Green and Maria Farmer chose a college student, a union steward, and a widowed housewife for their arbitrary eliminations.

Once Judge Stern was satisfied that an impartial jury had been selected, he thanked the remaining members of the jury panel who had not been selected as trial jurors or alternates in the *Consumer* case, and they were escorted back to the jury assembly room to await consideration for selection on other juries.

Federal practice now uses six jurors in civil cases, but several states still use twelve jurors. Most states at least have the option of using six jurors in civil trials today. The jury finally selected by Judge Stern for the *Consumer* trial included six jurors and one alternate, who would replace any of the original six jurors if circumstances arose during the trial to make it impossible for an original juror to continue. The principal jurors were Tina Spencer, age 24, married to a construction worker, two children; John Hollis, age 35, a computer programer employed by an advertising firm, married, no children; Nancy Blast, age 26, secretary for a real estate firm, single; William Johnson, age 54, salesman for a local department store, married with two children in college; Mary Janowitz, age 40, bank teller,

peremptory challenges: requests from parties to remove jurors without cause. Each party is allowed a fixed number of these challenges.

single (divorced) with one child; and Bobby Stans, age 39, service manager at a local supermarket, married with two children. The alternate juror was Betty Moore, age 42, factory worker, single parent of one child.

When the selection process had been completed, the judge asked the jury to take a second oath, "to judge this case fairly, according to law." The jurors all agreed to the oath.

TRIAL ARGUMENTS

The next day, Judge Stern opened the session with the following preliminary instructions to the jury.

Preliminary Jury Instructions

"Ladies and gentlemen of the jury:

"Now that you have been sworn as jurors in this case, I will briefly tell you something about your duties as jurors and give you some instructions. At the end of the trial, I will give you more detailed instructions, and those instructions will control your deliberations.

"It will be your duty to decide from the evidence what the facts are. You, and you alone, are the judges of the facts. You will hear the evidence, decide what the facts are, and then apply those facts to the law that I will give to you. That is how you will reach your verdict. In doing so, you must follow the law whether you agree with it or not.

"You must not take anything I say or do during the trial as an indication of what your verdict should be. Don't be influenced by my taking notes at times. What I write down may have nothing to do with what you will be concerned with at this trial.

"You will not be allowed to take notes so that you can devote your full attention to the witnesses and evidence presented. You will be given written evidence and exhibits that have been admitted during the trial to assist you in your deliberations, but you will need to listen carefully to the personal testimony of the witnesses.

"The **opening statements** and **closing arguments** of the attorneys are not evidence, but are provided to the court for the purpose of clarification and understanding of the facts that will be presented through the witnesses and material evidence. In like manner, the lawyers' questions are not evidence.

"We will begin with opening statements for the plaintiff. Is counsel ready to begin?" (Adapted from Devitt et al. *Federal Jury Practice and Instructions* (Civil). Vol. 3, 4th ed., 1987.)

Opening Statements

John Gaither took the lawyer's position at the podium in front of the judge's bench and looked at the judge as he asked, "May it please the court, your honor?" Getting a nod from the judge, Attorney Gaither began his opening statement.

Plaintiff's Opening Statement

"Ladies and gentlemen of the jury, I am John Gaither, and this is my co-counsel Cora Smith [pointing toward plaintiff's table]. We will be representing Jane Consumer at this trial against the Factory Motor Company.

---

opening statements: opposing lawyers' formulations of the nature of the case and anticipated proof to be presented.

closing arguments: opposing lawyers' summaries of the evidence they think has been established or refutations of opposing evidence.

"Ladies and gentlemen, this is a case involving a tragic accident caused by an inferior and defective part installed in the Consumer's automobile at the factory by mistake.

"Bill Consumer and his wife had been shopping and had dinner in Capital City. They were driving home at about ten-thirty in the evening of September 8, 1991. About halfway home, it began to rain, and Bill slowed down to about sixty miles per hour. They were traveling on Interstate 24 and were almost home—just three miles from the Centerville turnoff. The car approached a van from the rear that was traveling at a slower speed, and Bill pulled into the left passing lane in a normal passing maneuver. Jane Consumer, who was sitting beside Bill in the passenger seat, will tell you she heard a loud 'popping noise' coming from the rear of the car. She looked at Bill, whose face revealed sheer panic as he shouted, 'The wheel won't turn!'

"He was pumping the brakes as the car sped across the grassy median separating the two lanes of directional traffic. The car collided with a tractor-trailer headed in the opposite direction, spun around, and ended up on the far side of the interstate. Bill was killed and Jane severely injured in the accident.

"An expert mechanic will testify that upon examination of the wrecked automobile, after the accident, he found a broken suspension coil on the left side of the vehicle that did not match the coil on the right side. A factory mix-up on the assembly line resulted in the improper installation of this defective coil in the Consumer's car. The defective coil was shorter and weaker than the coil on the right side. It broke at the moment when Jane Consumer will testify it made a loud 'popping noise' just before the accident.

"The broken coil dropped the left rear side of the vehicle down at least three inches, causing the weight of the car to shift to the left rear axle. This shift of weight lifted the front of the car, causing the tires to hydroplane on the wet pavement and resulting in Bill's inability to control the vehicle.

"The Factory Motor Company, who manufactured this car, knew that it was improperly assembled and waited more than two years before issuing a letter. The letter they issued did not warn of the danger or even identify the defective condition of the coil in question but merely asked that the car be taken to a certified dealer for replacement repairs. Bill had received this letter the day before the accident and had intended to take the car to the dealer the next Monday morning. Unfortunately, Bill was killed in the accident on Friday night.

"The defendant's lawyers in this case will tell you that they tested the mistaken coils and concluded they were safe. But the coils they tested were only like the one mounted in the Consumer's car by mistake. They did not test the defective coil in the car that caused the accident. Their testing is a lame excuse for not doing what they should have done in the first place—immediately issue a factory recall when they discovered their mistake. Instead, they waited for testing and complaints, allowing Bill Consumer and his wife to drive an unsafe vehicle for two years and 22,000 miles before making any effort to contact them. The Factory Motor Company put money ahead of safety in their corporate philosophy, and it cost Bill Consumer his life!

"The Consumer family has suffered irreparable damage from this accident in the form of loss of a loved one who cannot be replaced. Jane Consumer has suffered needless physical and mental injuries, and their three children cannot be made to suffer further injury from the loss of the income their father would have provided.

"The witnesses and evidence we will present will prove these facts to you, the members of the jury. You will decide this matter on the legal basis of a special liability standard that requires merely the existence of a defective condition that was the proximate cause of the injuries sustained. The legal standard of proof is a preponderance of the evidence . . . and ladies and gentlemen, when you have heard all the evidence, I am confident you will conclude that the weight of the evidence supports the plaintiff's right to recover damages."

Defense Opening Statement

Judge Stern then asked the defense team if they were ready for their opening statement, and Maria Farmer approached the lawyers' podium. "May it please the court, your honor?" she asked. She then introduced her co-counsel, Bill Green, and began her statement.

"Ladies and gentlemen of the jury, the tragic accident involved in this case was caused by unavoidable weather conditions and driver error, not by any alleged defective condition of the automobile in question.

"On the night of the accident, the section of Interstate 24 where the car left the road was soaked by a drenching rainstorm—one and one-half inches of rain fell within half an hour. This sudden downpour caused water to stream down the gentle slope there, collecting in a pocket at the bottom of the slope where Bill Consumer's car left the road.

"When the front tires of the car hit this pool of water at sixty miles an hour, they began to ski across the surface of the water, preventing the driver from controlling the vehicle because the tires were not in contact with the road surface. One of the foremost experts in the country on the causes of accidents has carefully examined these road conditions and the condition of the wrecked vehicle involved. He will testify that the weight of the scientific evidence proves vehicle hydroplaning to be the cause of this accident, and not an alleged faulty coil.

"Bill Consumer had been drinking beer on the night of the accident, and his reaction time had been affected. He also had failed to slow his vehicle to a speed appropriate for the heavy rain he encountered before the accident. These were factors contributing to the accident that would not have happened had he been more cautious.

"The suspension coil in question was not defective, unsafe, or dangerous, as we will demonstrate from the results of our extensive testing using 'state of the art' scientific equipment. The specific coil in question did not break before the accident, as the plaintiff alleges, but that damage was caused by the impact of the collision itself. The car hit a tractor-trailer on the opposite side of the interstate. Both vehicles were traveling in excess of sixty miles per hour, and the combined speed generated a force equivalent to that of hitting a stationary object at more than 120 miles an hour. The tremendous force of this collision caused the car to spin around. It made a complete circle, and ended up facing in the opposite direction from that of the initial impact. Needless to say, the coils on this vehicle were not designed to withstand that kind of impact.

"The testimony of expert witnesses and the evidence we will produce during the trial will prove these facts. The Factory Motor Company acted responsibly in manufacturing this vehicle to meet all governmental safety standards. This company is proud of the record it has achieved by using existing technology to prevent accidents caused by defective products—but the factory cannot be held responsible for the weather, for road conditions, or for driver error.

"Just because a tragic accident occurred, that fact does not prove that it was caused by a defective product; and it would be grossly unfair to assume so. I have faith in the good sense of this jury not to be fooled by sympathy or prejudice. I know you will listen carefully to the scientific facts in this case and arrive at a just verdict."

Examination of Witnesses

The examination of each witness called to testify at trial is conducted in accordance with the following steps.

1. **Direct examination** consists of questioning by the attorney for the party who calls the witness. The objective is to establish the facts or claim of that party.

2. **Cross-examination** involves questioning by opposing counsel and is optional. It offers counsel for the opposing party opportunity to attack both the credibility and the testimony of the witness. Cross-examination is generally limited to matters covered on direct examination.

3. Redirect examination, or requestioning by the attorney who conducted the direct examination, is optional and is generally used to "rehabilitate" a witness following cross-examination; that is, to recapture the witness's lost credibility. The subject matter is usually limited to that which was brought out on cross-examination.

4. Recross-examination, or requestioning by the opposing counsel, is an option following the redirect examination. The questioning is generally limited to new matters brought out on redirect examination.

Further exchange is limited by the recross-examination, if used, and the judge will not allow testimony to proceed beyond this point with this witness.

direct examination: initial questioning by the attorney who calls the witness.

cross-examination: questioning done by opposing counsel of the party who called the witness.

Rules of Evidence and Objections

The **rules of evidence** are a detailed set of standards governing the admissibility of evidence at trial and must be carefully followed by the lawyers. The opposing lawyer has the responsibility of raising objections to any infraction of these rules during the conduct of the trial. The judge will allow opposing lawyers to comment, but ultimately he or she will decide if the material in question is admissible or will instruct the lawyer to follow the rules.

The complexity of the rules of evidence prohibits full explanation of them in this chapter. However, a few of the basic topics that may cause concern are leading questions, relevancy, asked and answered, beyond the scope, excessive narration, hearsay, and best evidence.

rules of evidence: detailed rules that govern the admissibility of evidence at trials and hearings.

Leading Questions

In the direct examination of a witness, **leading questions** are not usually permitted. These are questions that instruct the witness how to answer or imply an answer, that is, put words into the mouth of the witness. They are not permitted because the attorney, rather than the witness, may actually be testifying by the way the lawyer frames the questions. The object on direct examination is to al-

leading questions: questions that instruct the witness how to answer or put words into the witness's mouth to be echoed back.

low the witnesses to testify to their firsthand knowledge that is relevant to the case, in their own words.

On cross-examination, the leading questions rule does not apply. The lawyer for the party who did not call the witness can ask leading questions to probe the credibility of the witness.

Hearsay and Best Evidence Rules

hearsay rule: testimony in court of a statement made out of court, offered to show the truth of matters asserted, is not permitted.

best evidence rule: prohibits introduction of copies of original documents unless the originals have been lost or destroyed.

One of the most complex rules of evidence is the **hearsay rule**, which excludes evidence that consists of what another person has said or written outside the court when that evidence is offered for purposes of establishing the truth of what was said or written. The very nature of hearsay evidence suggests its weakness, since the competency and credibility of the originator of the statement cannot be tested.

The purpose of the hearsay rule is related to that of the **best evidence rule**, which prevents secondhand information from being presented as evidence unless the court is satisfied that there is no better source from which the evidence can be obtained. Rules 803 and 804 of the Federal Rules of Evidence list at least twenty-nine specific exceptions to the hearsay rule, including statements of a deceased person who can no longer testify and statements made in a moment of excitement.

The Plaintiff's Case in Chief

Judge Stern asked if the plaintiff's attorneys were ready to call their first witness. Cora Smith called Jane Consumer as her first witness, and the bailiff administered the oath to "tell the truth, the whole truth, and nothing but the truth" before she was seated in the witness box.

Direct Examination

Jane was a little nervous being on the witness stand for the first time. Cora tried to put her at ease by asking questions that prompted her to explain her answers. After the preliminary questions dealing with identification were answered, Jane related her experiences on the night of the accident. She began by telling about the shopping trip and dinner that evening. Cora prompted her with pointed questions. "What did Bill have to drink with dinner?" Cora asked.

"He had one glass of beer with his meal," replied Jane.

Jane continued relating the events that occurred during the trip home that evening, with prompting from Cora's questions. When she reached the point of stating that she heard a loud "popping noise" after Bill started his passing maneuver, Cora asked, "What did this noise sound like, to you?"

"It sounded metallic—like a 'poing'—as though a spring snapped under pressure," Jane replied.

"What did you do then," Cora continued to prompt Jane, "after you heard the noise?"

"I looked at Bill and he was frantic," Jane said. "He shouted, 'My God, the wheel won't turn.'"

"What do you think he meant by that statement?" Cora queried.

"He must have meant that the steering wheel would not turn the car, because he was turning the steering wheel in panic at the time," answered Jane.

Cora asked, "What else did you observe him doing at this time?"

"He was pumping the brakes," related Jane. "I could see his knee going up and down."

Cora introduced the bill of sale for the car and the affidavit from the service manager at City Auto Company attesting to the fact that the vehicle in question had not been altered by the dealer. These documents provided proof of purchase, date of purchase, that the car had been properly maintained, that complaints had been made concerning the leaning of the vehicle prior to the accident, and that the coil had not been altered by the dealer.

The procedure for introducing documents is first to show the document to the judge to mark as plaintiff's or defense's exhibit and give it an identifying number, then to show the document to the opposing counsel for their examination. At this point, the lawyer introducing the document asks the judge to admit it as evidence. The judge asks opposing counsel if there are any objections. The judge may consider any objections in making the ruling to admit the document as evidence or to exclude it.

No objections were raised regarding the bill of sale and the service manager's affidavit, and the documents were admitted as plaintiff's exhibits "A" and "B," which meant they could later be used during the trial and by the jurors in their deliberation.

A letter from the manufacturer (see Form 6-1) was then introduced in the manner described above and was accepted as evidence. "What is this document, Mrs. Consumer?" Cora asked.

"It is the letter I found on Bill's desk after the accident," explained Jane.

"What does is say?" Cora prompted.

"It asks Bill to bring the car in for recall repairs at the factory's expense," Jane said. "But," she noted, "it doesn't say anything about any danger involved, and it doesn't say anything about the coils being improperly installed."

Cora continued her questioning. "Did Bill mention this letter to you?"

"Yes, he said he thought it was important and that he would have our daughter take him down to have it done on Monday morning," replied Jane.

"What Monday morning was that?" Cora queried.

"The Monday following the accident on Friday," Jane stated.

Cora shifted the topic to damages and introduced the death certificate, the hospital bills, the doctor bills, and the funeral expenses. She asked Jane about her husband's employment and salary, including what she knew about his expectations for promotions and fringe benefits. Attorney Smith also asked a line of questions concerning Jane's personal injuries sustained from the accident. This exchange produced no new information but had to be entered for the record. Cora then indicated that she had finished her direct examination.

Cross-examination

Bill Green slowly approached the lawyers' podium after Cora had finished her direct examination. He was obviously thinking of some penetrating questions to ask Jane on cross-examination.

"I'd like to ask you a few questions about your shopping trip at that new mall, before you had dinner on the night of the accident," Bill began. "Were you with your husband all the time during this shopping period?"

"No," Jane replied. "We were separated for about an hour during this period."

Form 6.1

LETTER FROM FACTORY MOTOR COMPANY TO WILLIAM P. CONSUMER

(PLAINTIFF'S EXHIBIT C)

THE FACTORY MOTOR COMPANY, INC., U.S.A.
BIG CITY, LAKE STATE

September 1, 1991

Mr. William P. Consumer
140 Consumer Lane
Centerville, Middle State

Dear Mr. Consumer,

Our records indicate that you purchased a 1990 Supreme Brougham Executive manufactured by the Factory Motor Company with serial number <u>1FMCB14T9KUA14073</u>.

If you are still in possession of this vehicle, please bring it in to the dealer where you purchased it, or a certified Factory Motor Company dealer, as soon as possible for recall repairs at our expense.

Bring this letter with you to your preferred dealer and present it to the service manager.

We hope you are satisfied with the automobile you have purchased and want to assure you that our company is dedicated to consumer satisfaction. At the Factory Motor Company, quality is our most important priority.

Sincerely yours,

A. B. Johnson
Production Director

"Did your husband like to shop, Mrs. Consumer?" asked Bill.

"No, not very much," admitted Jane.

"Is there a place that sells beer at the mall, Mrs. Consumer?" Bill queried.

"I don't know. . . . I suppose so," Jane replied uncertainly.

"Did Bill often have a beer while you were shopping?" the attorney asked.

"Not to my knowledge," answered Jane.

"But he could have had a beer, or two, during that hour you were separated, couldn't he?" Bill persisted.

"Yes, I suppose so," Jane replied.

After several other questions, Attorney Green got to the point of asking Jane about the moments just prior to the accident. "When did it start raining on the trip back home, Mrs. Consumer?" He queried.

"I don't know exactly." Jane hesitated, then said, "About ten minutes before the accident, I guess."

"Was it raining hard enough to affect visibility?" Attorney Green asked.

"Yes, I suppose so, but Bill slowed down and had the windshield wipers on," replied Jane.

Bill then asked about the speed at which the vehicle was traveling. "You said that Bill slowed down from 65 to 60 miles per hour. How could you tell us that so precisely?"

"I looked at the speedometer," answered Jane.

"Wasn't it dark in the vehicle and hard to see the speedometer?" Bill wondered.

"No," Jane replied, "I could see from the dash lights and I was sitting close to Bill."

The defense attorney said pointedly, "I thought you said you had your seat belt on, Mrs. Consumer. Could you get close to your husband under these conditions?"

"I could see the speed indicator," Jane reiterated.

"Could you smell beer on Bill's breath?" the attorney asked.

"No," replied Jane.

Redirect Examination

Cora chose the option of redirect examination. "How much alcohol did your husband normally consume, Mrs. Consumer?"

"He only drank beer with his meals, sometimes," Jane replied. "He was not a heavy drinker."

"What is the condition of your eyesight and hearing?" Cora asked.

Jane answered, "I have never worn glasses. My vision is 20/20, and I have never had any trouble with my hearing. I could see the speedometer clearly, and I heard the 'popping noise' distinctly."

There was no recross-examination.

Direct Examination

Judge Stern called for the next witness, and John Gaither called Jim Trucker to the stand. John began with the same prompting questions that Cora had used to aid the witness through the known testimony without putting words in his mouth. Jim Trucker was a good witness who confirmed many aspects of the accident, but he had little to add to the facts that Jane had provided.

Cross-examination

The defense attorney, Maria Farmer, asked a few questions about the amount of rain on the night of the accident and the road conditions, but Jim Trucker's answers did not add any significant information. There was no redirect examination and, therefore, no recross-examination of this witness.

Direct Examination

Cora Smith called George Goodcop to the stand. After establishing the officer's identity and his relationship to the accident, the attorney introduced the officer's accident report and asked for permission to show the jury an enlarged version of the sketch in the officer's report (see Figure 6-1). The judge and the opposing party had no objections.

Cora asked the officer, "Where did you start your investigation of the path of the Consumer's vehicle?"

"I walked across the median, and my feet got pretty wet on the way, as I recall," George answered. "There were tire marks on the southbound traffic lane starting at the point I have indicated on my sketch [he went to the exhibit and pointed to the start of the skid marks]. This indicates that the driver had applied the brakes before he left the asphalt roadbed."

"How wet was the roadbed where you found the skid marks?" queried Cora.

"There was no standing water on the highway at that time," George replied. "But," he noted, "I made this investigation more than half an hour after the accident took place and it had stopped raining."

Cross-examination

Bill Green proceeded to cross-examine the witness. "Did you investigate the interior of the accident vehicle after the medics had removed the passengers?" he asked.

"Yes, I did," answered George.

"Did you find any evidence related to alcohol consumption in the vehicle?" the attorney asked.

"I did find an empty beer can in the floorboard," George said.

"You said the driver was not wearing a seat belt," Bill continued. "Does the law in Middle State require seat belts?"

"Yes, it does," confirmed George.

"Therefore, the driver was in violation of the law, wasn't he?" persisted Bill.

"Yes, sir," George replied.

"How many accidents have occurred at this location, to your knowledge?" questioned Bill.

"I have been patrolling this section of the highway for four years," answered George, "and to my knowledge, there have been two other accidents at this particular location. We have had several complaints about poor drainage in this area."

Redirect Examination

Cora Smith tried on redirect examination to reduce the impact of George's testimony. "Whose beer can did you find in the car, Officer?"

FIGURE 6.1 Officer's Accident Sketch

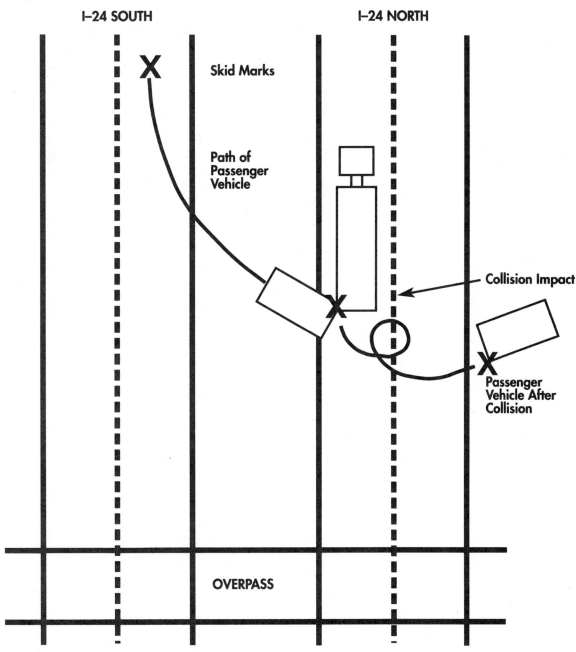

"I have no idea," George replied. "Single beer cans are often stored under seats and they fly out in accidents."

Following this exchange, there were no further questions for Officer Goodcop.

Direct Examination

John Gaither called Mack Racer as the next witness and began the final direct examination of the plaintiff's witnesses. John was careful to lay a foundation for qualifying this witness as an expert mechanic. He asked a number of detailed questions about Mack's qualifications and experience. Most witnesses cannot be asked hypothetical questions that call for opinions. But if a proper foundation is laid showing the witness is qualified by reason of special knowledge, skill, experience, training, or education to arrive at conclusions concerning a given set of facts, the rules of evidence allow an exception for such an **expert witness**.

expert witness: one who has specialized knowledge in a particular field, obtained from either education or personal experience, that qualifies the person to answer opinion questions.

After aiding the witness to explain his extensive experience and qualifications, John Gaither asked the judge to qualify Mack Racer as an expert mechanic who could be asked opinion questions in his area of expertise. Maria Farmer objected, stating that the witness lacked the proper educational and theoretical knowledge and training to be qualified as an expert. Judge Stern overruled the objection but cautioned that he might sustain an objection at the time the specific hypothetical questions were posed.

John focused on the coils that the mechanic removed from the vehicle and asked, "What was the condition of the shock absorbers when you removed the coils from the accident vehicle?"

"Both rear shock absorbers were broken loose from their mountings," answered Mack.

Attorney Gaither introduced as evidence, without objection by defense counsel, the actual coils that had been removed from the Consumer's car by the mechanic. "Are these the coils you removed?"

"Yes, they are. [Taking them in his hands, Mack held up the obviously thicker and longer coil.] This is the right coil that is undamaged, and the left coil, as you can see, is broken off at the base. The left coil is made of thinner and weaker material and is about one inch shorter than the right coil," explained Mack.

The coil parts were passed around to the jury members for their inspection, then John resumed questioning Mack. "In your opinion, would the shorter coil on the left side have caused any change in the vehicle's performance?"

Maria stood. "Objection, your honor. It is beyond the scope of witness qualifications to answer a hypothetical engineering question."

The judge looked at John. "Attorney Gaither, do you have a reply to this objection?"

"Yes, your honor," John answered. "As was established earlier, this witness has been an engineering consultant for several nationally prominent race car teams and is fully qualified to answer this question."

"Objection overruled," the judge declared. He told Mack, "You may answer the question."

"In my opinion," said Mack, "it would have caused the weight of the vehicle to be unevenly distributed. More specifically, it would have transferred the weight of the vehicle to the rear axle, thus reducing the weight on the right front axle. This weight shift would cause the vehicle to have reduced traction on the right front tires. This would, in turn, affect the steering capabilities under adverse conditions, such as driving through snow, ice, or water. We put heavy duty coils on our racing stock cars to increase the traction on the front tires specifically for the purpose of increasing handling capabilities."

"In your opinion," John continued his line of questioning, "what would be the effect if the coil broke under the conditions you have just described?"

"Objection, your honor," Maria interjected, "this witness is not an engineer and is not qualified to answer this question."

"Overruled," declared the judge, and turning to Mack, "You may answer."

"If the left coil had broken under wet driving conditions," Mack explained, "the weight of the vehicle would have dropped five or six inches to the axle. This sudden force would have caused the front end of the vehicle to be lifted in corresponding fashion. The reduced traction of the front tires would have caused the vehicle to hydroplane, even if there was only soaked pavement under the front tires."

Cross-examination

Maria Farmer was obviously irritated when she took the podium for cross-examination, but she regained her composure and managed a smile as she began, "You're a good mechanic aren't you, Mr. Racer?"

"I try to be," Mack agreed.

"Do you have an engineering degree, Mr. Racer?" Maria queried.

"No," he replied, "but I have more than twenty years of experience working on Factory Motor Company vehicles and advising race car drivers."

"Can you prove that the left coil broke before the accident?" Maria asked.

"No, I can't say for certain that the coil broke before, or after, the accident," replied Mack.

"Could the coil break from an impact at a speed equal to 120 miles per hour?" Maria asked, and added, "Just answer yes or no."

"Yes," answered Mack.

Redirect Examination

John Gaither used his opportunity to recover his witness on redirect by asking, "What area of the accident vehicle took the initial impact of the collision, Mr. Racer?"

Mack answered, "The left driver's side of the vehicle was collapsed, indicating that the hood of the car had passed underneath the tractor-trailer and the driver's cab had taken the initial impact on the corner where the driver sits."

"Where would the corresponding stress, or secondary impact, have taken place?" John asked.

"On the right coil," Mack said, "because the initial impact would have transferred the stress to that location. The right coil should have broken, not the left one."

Maria Farmer declined to recross-examine the witness.

Direct Examination

John Gaither called Professor Walter Rogers, an economist specializing in questions concerning economic values. The attorney was careful to establish how many times the witness had given expert testimony in the past and had the economist list his professional publications. Rogers was thus accepted as an expert in the field of economic value estimates. John asked that the professor's report (see Form 6-2) be read into the record and, as there were no objections, the judge so ordered. Then, after questioning the expert concerning his assumptions, Attorney Gaither indicated that he had finished his direct examination.

Form 6.2
Estimate of Damages Prepared by Professor Walter Rogers, Ph.D. Economics
(Plaintiff's Record)

FOR THE ESTATE: William P. Consumer held the rank of Associate Professor with tenure at Middle State University where he had been employed for five years. His annual salary was $35,000, and he normally earned another $2,500 for summer teaching. He could expect annual raises and promotion to the next higher rank at the university. The average salaries of Associate Professors is $43,000 and for full Professors it is $51,000.

Professor Consumer was 48 years of age, in remarkably good health, and could expect to continue in university employment. His life expectancy is estimated at 27.04 years. (T.C.A. Tables 1990 Supplement)

Assuming an average annual salary increase with promotions of 9%, fringe benefits of 27.5%, a present value discount rate of 8%, and an estimated savings rate of 30%, Professor Consumer's net economic value to the estate, according to Middle State law, would be:

Base: $37,500 X 27 Years Plus Expected Increases and Promotion
 Calculated At 9% Compounded = $3,852,117

Fringe benefits of university employment, including group medical insurance and other benefits, are estimated to amount to an additional 27.5%. This would increase the base amount to $4,911,500. This base amount must be discounted by 8% (the average earnings on U.S. Treasury certificates) to estimate what investment would produce this amount in 27 years.

Base Amount Plus Fringe Benefits Discounted For Present Value:

$614,900 (An Investment Of This Amount Of Money At Present Could Be Expected To Earn
 The Above Base Amount Of $4,911,500 In 27 Years At 8% Interest Compounded)

Middle State law allows an estimate of the decedent's contribution to the household services (14 hours per week at $5 per hour), and we must deduct probable living expenses for the deceased had he lived. *Wallace v. Couch*, 642 S.W.2d 141 (Tenn. 1982). Using an estimated savings rate of 30%, we arrive at the final amount of present economic value in legal damages, and then we add hospital and burial expenses to arrive at the final estate value of the claim.

Present Value Taken From Above ($614,900) Plus Household Services	=	$713,200
Minus Probable Living Expenses For the Deceased	=	$214,000
Plus Medical Expenses	=	$ 1,000
Plus Funeral Expenses	=	$ 7,000
Grand Total For Deceased	=	$222,000

FOR WIFE INJURED IN ACCIDENT: Medical expenses for Jane Consumer are evidenced by the hospital and doctor bills amounting to $10,500. Pain and suffering sustained by Jane Consumer from her injuries caused by the defendant is estimated to be five times that of the medical expenses for Jane amounting to $52,500.

Medical Expenses	=	$10,500
Plus Pain And Suffering	=	$52,500
Grand Total For Damage To Jane Consumer	=	$63,000

Total Damage To Both Deceased's Estate And Jane Consumer Is Equal To $222,000 Plus $63,000 = $285,000.

Cross-examination

Bill Green attempted to challenge the expert witness by implying that there was only one standard method for calculating present value and that the usual period for calculating earnings stops at age 65 when social security benefits begin. The professor took issue with these assumptions and denied Bill's inference.

There were no further questions for this witness, and John Gaither indicated that the plaintiff had no other witnesses to call at this time.

Conclusion of the Plaintiff's Case in Chief

Bill Green moved for a **directed verdict** in favor of the defense. The plaintiff has the initial **burden of proof** and must establish evidence that, if not refuted, will meet all of the required elements of the law. The judge could have ended the *Consumer* trial at this point if he believed that the plaintiffs had failed to meet their initial burden of proof of a prima facie case.

There was no question in this case that the plaintiffs had met their burden of demonstrating sufficient evidence for a **prima facie case**. Judge Stern overruled the motion for a directed verdict and declared a recess until the following Monday morning when the jury would begin hearing the defendant's case in chief. He cautioned the jurors not to discuss this case with anyone and not to seek any advice about matters involving this case. The jury would be required to make a decision solely on the basis of what they heard and observed in the courtroom.

The Defendant's Case in Chief

After Judge Stern reconvened the trial on Monday morning, Maria Farmer called Mr. Superior Tester as her first witness. Maria was careful to lay a proper foundation to qualify Mr. Tester as an expert witness. He had a master's degree from the Massachusetts Institute of Technology and eight years of experience as a laboratory technician. He also had been qualified as an expert witness on numerous occasions in federal court, and the plaintiffs raised no objections to his qualification as an expert.

Maria then introduced, without difficulty, the company report on the testing done by the factory (see Form 6-3). After handing the report to Mr. Tester, she asked, "Is this a true and accurate copy of your report?"

"Yes, it is," he replied.

"What equipment did you use for your testing?" asked Maria.

Mr. Tester answered, "The mechanical equipment used to test these coils are simulators made by Scientific Teck, Incorporated, the recognized leader in the field of mechanical simulators. This simulator was certified by the Board of Scientific Advisors to be 'state of the art' equipment using the most advanced technology available."

"How did you set up the equipment?" Maria queried.

"We were able to simulate the effect of these two dissimilar coils on an actual vehicle," Mr. Tester explained, "by mounting randomly selected coils from each type on the three available machines. This enabled us to test them under the condition of uneven distribution of the weight of the vehicle due to the shorter coil on the left side."

"And what was your conclusion?" Maria asked.

---

directed verdict: when party with the burden of proof has failed to present a prima facie case for jury consideration, the trial judge may enter a verdict as a matter of law.

burden of proof: obligation of a party to establish by evidence a requisite degree of belief concerning a fact in the mind of the court.

prima facie case: a case that will prevail until contradicted and overcome by other evidence.

Form 6.3

Factory Motor Company Memorandum Report on Testing of Coils Mistakenly Mounted on Vehicle Involved in the Accident

(DEFENSE EXHIBIT 1)

TESTING DIVISION
FACTORY MOTOR COMPANY, INC., U.S.A.

M E M O R A N D U M

TO: Mr. A. B. Johnson
Production Director

DATE: March 15, 1990

SUBJECT: REPORT ON TESTING OF SUSPENSION COILS SUPPLIED BY ACE SUPPLIERS, INC., BY MISTAKE AND USED IN THE PRODUCTION OF 250 SUPREME BROUGHAM EXECUTIVE PASSENGER VEHICLES IN THE 1990 PRODUCTION RUN (AUG. 20, 1989)

TESTING WORK ORDER: Simulate normal driving conditions using a random selection of suspension coils from those shipped by the supplier by mistake to determine if they will meet our standard 200,000-mile endurance test.

TEST RESULTS : We used our three simulators mounted with a normal coil on the right side and a randomly selected mistaken coil on the left side. The simulators ran for more than 1700 hours (or 200,000 miles) without any recorded damage to either types of coils. The first coil broke at 1726 hours, and it was one of the mistaken coils. The second coil to break was a normal coil, which broke at 1824 hours. The third simulator continued to run until another mistaken coil broke at 1891 hours. We then stopped our testing.

RECOMMENDATION: We conclude from this test that the mistaken coils will withstand normal wear at our 200,000-mile standard and do not pose a safety hazard.

Superior Tester
Director of Testing

Mr. Tester replied, "Based on this scientific evidence, we concluded that the mistakenly assembled coils did not pose a safety risk, and that they would hold up for the normal life of the vehicle. We based this decision on the fact that none of the coils broke before having simulated 200,000 miles of normal stress. The mistaken coils were only slightly lower in quality when compared to the originally designed equipment."

Maria then asked, "What are the governmental safety standards concerning suspension coils?"

"There are no specific governmental standards for these coils," Mr. Tester answered, "because the suspension coils are not considered essential to the safety of the vehicle. They are installed primarily for passenger comfort. Therefore these coils met governmental safety standards."

"Why did the factory decide to have these coils replaced?" Maria queried.

Mr. Tester explained, "Because there were complaints about the appearance of the vehicles in question, not because they posed a safety hazard. There have been no other complaints about safety or handling problems."

"What would happen if one of these coils broke under normal driving conditions, Mr. Tester?" questioned Maria.

"The vehicle would drop no more than three inches because the shock absorbers would prevent any further movement," Mr. Tester answered. "The displacement of the weight of the vehicle could cause some handling difficulty, but this automobile is equipped with power steering and the displacement of weight would not prevent the driver from maintaining control of the vehicle even under these adverse conditions."

Cross-examination

John Gaither assumed his position at the lawyer's podium and began his cross by saying, "Good morning, Mr. Tester. Did you have a good plane trip down here from Big City?"

"Yes, thank you," Mr. Tester replied.

"Does your simulator account for the amount of traction on the front tires?" John asked.

"Yes, it does," Mr. Tester confirmed. "The reduced traction was recorded and determined to be within limits set by industry standards."

"Who sets these industry standards?" queried John.

"The Automobile Manufacturer's Association," Mr. Tester replied.

"Is that a governmental agency?" John asked.

"No," answered Mr. Tester.

"In the absence of a governmental regulation concerning a particular part," John continued, "does that mean you are free to use anything you want to and say it meets governmental standards?"

"No," Mr. Tester said.

"The shock absorbers did not prevent the vehicle from dropping the length of the coil on Bill Consumer's car," John pointed out. "Can you explain that, Mr. Tester?"

"A collision with an impact equivalent to 120 miles an hour would account for that," said Mr. Tester.

"Who pays your salary, Mr. Tester?" John queried.

"The Factory Motor Company," replied the witness.

Maria saw no need for redirect examination of this witness.

Direct and Cross Examination

Bill Green then called Jackie Lifesaver, who added little to his deposition statement. The witness confirmed that Bill Consumer had not been wearing a seat belt; that Jackie had smelled alcohol on the driver's breath; and that Jackie had seen a beer can in the floorboard of the vehicle. Cora Smith declined to cross-examine the witness, and Judge Stern declared a recess for lunch.

After lunch the defense called Jan Intern to the stand. Bill Green carefully laid the foundation for the medical questions he would ask this witness by establishing her credentials and identifying the witness as the attendant emergency physician who had initially treated the Consumers at the hospital on the night of the accident. The defense attorney asked for the death certificate that had been introduced by the plaintiff earlier and handed it to the witness as he asked, "Who signed the death certificate?"

"I did, as the physician in charge of the patient," Jan replied.

"What was the specific cause of William P. Consumer's death?" Bill asked.

"Internal bleeding from severe chest wounds," answered the physician.

"Was the patient alive when he arrived at the hospital?" questioned Bill.

"That is a difficult question to answer," Jan said. "He had no pulse, which meant that his heart had stopped beating. However, we are able to revive many such patients today because of improvements in technology."

Bill asked, "Why were you unable to revive this patient?"

"We made every effort," Jan assured him, "but the chest wound and internal bleeding caused intense pressure on the heart, preventing it from responding."

"Would this patient have died if he had been wearing a seat belt?" Bill queried.

Cora rose to object. "Objection, your honor, leading question."

"Sustained, rephrase your question," the judge stated.

"What causes such massive chest wounds in automobile accidents?" Bill asked.

Jan answered, "This kind of chest wound could only have been caused by impact against the steering column and a seat belt or driver side airbag could have prevented it."

"What tests were made of the body during your examination?" the attorney asked.

"I smelled alcohol on the patient's breath," Jan replied. "The distinct odor of alcohol was present, but I took no blood sample for testing. The results would have been inconclusive because his blood had been supplemented by whole blood administered by the medics on the way to the hospital."

Bill Green asked several more questions that added little to the deposition statement, and then ended his direct examination. Cora Smith had no questions of this witness on cross-examination.

Direct and Cross Examination

Maria Farmer then called Professor Drivesafe to testify as the principal expert witness for the defense. At Maria's prompting, the professor carefully established his credentials as a nationally prominent expert on the causes of automobile accidents, and he recounted his extensive educational and professional standing as a leading publicist in the field of automotive safety engineering. Maria asked that he be accepted as an expert witness. The judge granted this request without an objection from the plaintiff. Maria's direct examination began with the question, "What did you find at the scene of the accident, Professor Drivesafe?"

"The accident report described the location of the accident," the professor responded, "and I was able to verify that location by the deep ruts in the median caused by the accident vehicle. I took measurements of the slope and elevation of the roadbed with surveying equipment. There was a one-inch depression in the roadbed at a point thirty yards from the point determined to be that where the car left the southbound asphalt roadbed. It extended for twenty yards to the north and would have resulted in standing water in the roadbed under heavy rain conditions."

"How deep would the water have been in this depression?" Maria asked.

"It would vary from half an inch to an inch and one-half in some spots," he replied, "but there would be some standing water along this poorly drained portion of the highway for twenty yards in the area where the driver lost control of his car."

Maria then introduced an official weather report from the United States government weather station at Capital City airport. There were no objections. She asked Professor Drivesafe, "Would you identify this document for us?"

"It is the official United States Weather Report for the Capital City area," the professor said.

"What amount of rainfall is recorded for September 8, 1991?" Maria queried.

"Almost one inch in the three-hour reporting period from nine P.M. to twelve midnight—ninety-eight hundredths of an inch," replied the witness.

"Where was this record made?" Maria asked.

"Thirty miles from the accident scene, at the Capital City airport," the professor stated.

"What conclusions can you draw from this evidence about weather conditions at the accident scene?" questioned the attorney.

"Rainfall can vary considerably," the professor answered, "particularly in thunder showers, as reported here, but this would be considered a heavy rain and would be sufficient to create the conditions conducive to hydroplaning under the poor drainage conditions I observed at the accident scene."

Maria then said, "Now let's go back to your inspection of the vehicle at the Garage after the accident. What did your investigation reveal about the cause of the broken coil?"

The witness stated, "Taking into consideration the diagram prepared by the officer, the speeds indicated in the deposition statements of the witnesses, and the condition of the vehicle after the accident, I concluded that the coil broke because of the impact and spinning of the vehicle after the crash. The tractor-trailer, traveling at a faster speed, pulled the passenger vehicle along with it, evidenced by the fact that it made a complete circle on the highway after the collision. This twisting force would be sufficient to cause the broken coil."

Cross Examination

John Gaither approached the podium and asked, "Professor, is it possible that the coil could have broken before the accident? Yes or no, please."

"Yes, it is possible, but unlikely," he replied.

"Would hydroplaning be more likely to occur if the weight of the vehicle was unevenly distributed?" John asked.

"Yes," confirmed the professor.

"How many times have you testified for the Factory Motor Company in court?" queried John.

"On many occasions. I have not kept count," the professor replied.

"What do you get paid for your services?" John asked.

"Objection, your honor, argumentative," Maria declared.

"Overruled," the judge stated. He told the professor, "You may answer."

The professor said, "Expenses and $200 per hour. What is your fee, counselor?"

Redirect Examination

Maria took the podium to rehabilitate her witness and asked, "How many times have you testified for the plaintiff in liability suits, Professor?"

"More frequently than for manufacturers," he replied. "Much of my work is done for consumers."

There were no further questions of this witness, and the defense called the next witness to the stand.

Direct Examination

Maria carefully established the credentials of Professor Alex Smith as an economist specializing in damage estimates. There was no objection to his testimony, since he had been called many times before to testify as an expert witness and his credentials were impressive. Maria asked that Professor Smith's report be read into the record (see Form 6-4), and the judge ordered that this be done. Maria asked the witness, "Is the method you used to calculate present value the standard method accepted by most economists?"

"Yes," confirmed Professor Smith, "damages in the future must be discounted by what they could be expected to yield at standard interest rates, and this is the method I have used."

"Why do you estimate that William P. Consumer would have worked to age 65?" Maria asked.

"This is the standard calculation in damages of this nature," replied the professor.

Cross Examination

John Gaither attempted to cast doubt on the expert's testimony by asking if there were other methods of estimating damages. However, the professor maintained that his estimate was the accepted standard in the professional field of damage estimates.

The defense did not redirect the witness, and Maria Farmer stated the defense rested its case.

Conclusion of the Defendant's Case in Chief

Now the plaintiff's attorney, John Gaither, moved for a directed verdict in favor of the plaintiff. Judge Stern could have stopped the trial at this point if he believed that a reasonable person could not rule any way other than for the plaintiff, which would mean that the defendant had failed to produce any admis-

Form 6.4

Estimate of Damages Prepared by Professor Alex Smith, Ph.D. Economics
(Defense Record)

FOR THE ESTATE: William P. Consumer held the rank of Associate Professor with tenure at Middle State University where he had been employed for five years. His annual salary was $35,000, and he normally earned another $2,500 for summer teaching. He could expect annual raises and promotion to the next higher rank at the university. The average salaries of Associate Professors is $43,000 and for full Professors it is $51,000.

Professor Consumer was 48 years of age, in remarkably good health, and could expect to continue in university employment. His work expectancy is estimated at 17 years. He could only have expected to work until age 65.

Assuming an average annual salary increase with promotions of 7%, fringe benefits of 27.5%, a present value discount rate of 8%, and an estimated savings rate of 30%, Professor Consumer's net economic value to the estate, according to Middle State law, would be:

Base: $37,500 X 17 Years Plus Expected Increases And Promotion
Calculated At 7% Compounded = $1,156,500

Fringe benefits of university employment, including group medical insurance and other benefits, are estimated to amount to an additional 27.5%. This would increase the base amount to $1,474,500. This base amount must be discounted by 8% (the average earnings on U.S. Treasury certificates) to estimate what investment would produce this amount in 17 years.

Base Amount Plus Fringe Benefits Discounted For Present Value:

$369,000 (An Investment Of This Amount Of Money At Present Could Be Expected To Earn The Above Base Amount Of $1,474,500 In 17 Years At 8% Interest Compounded)

Middle State law allows an estimate of the decedent's contribution to the household services (14 hours per week at $5 per hour), and we must deduct probable living expenses for the deceased had he lived. *Wallace v. Couch*, 642 S.W.2d 141 (Tenn. 1982). Using an estimated savings rate of 30%, we arrive at the final amount of present economic value in legal damages, and then we add hospital and burial expenses to arrive at the final estate value of the claim.

Present Value Taken From Above ($369,000) Plus Household Services	=	$430,900
Minus Probable Living Expenses For The Deceased	=	$129,300
Plus Medical Expenses	=	$ 1,000
Plus Funeral Expenses	=	$ 7,000
Grand Total For Deceased	=	$137,300

FOR WIFE INJURED IN ACCIDENT: Medical expenses for Jane Consumer are evidenced by the hospital and doctor bills amounting to $10,500. Pain and suffering sustained by Jane Consumer from her injuries caused by the defendant is estimated to be three times that of the medical expenses for Jane amounting to $31,500.

Medical Expenses	=	$10,500
Plus Pain And Suffering	=	$31,500
Grand Total For Damage To Jane Consumer	=	$42,000

Total Damage To Both Deceased's Estate And Jane Consumer Is Equal To $137,300 Plus $42,000 = $173,000.

sible evidence to refute the plaintiff's claim. Since this was obviously not the case here, the judge overruled the motion and declared a recess until the next day.

Closing Arguments

Judge Stern now called for **closing arguments** in the *Consumer* case. Each attorney is given an opportunity to review the important evidence and to restate the arguments and contentions in support of their client's case. Like opening statements, closing arguments do not constitute evidence and are offered for summary and clarification purposes. The plaintiff would go first, and then the defense, as in the opening statements. Cora Smith gave the closing statement for the plaintiff.

Plaintiff's Close

"Ladies and gentlemen of the jury:

"The defense asked you, in their opening statement, not to be fooled by sympathy or prejudice. We are confident that likewise you will not be fooled by so-called 'scientific evidence.'

"This fatal accident produced irreparable damage to the Consumer family, and it was caused by a defective set of coils installed in the Consumer's automobile by mistake. The Factory Motor Company could have, and should have, corrected this mistake by an immediate recall. Had they done so, Mr. Consumer would be alive today, and we would not have to be here trying this case.

"The factory recall letter came two years and 22,000 miles after the factory knew about the mistake. It did not warn of danger. It did not say the wrong coils were installed. It said merely that the car should be taken in for recall repairs. Bill Consumer got this letter the day before the accident, which took place on a Friday, and he fully intended to take the car in on the following Monday morning. A reasonable person could not have known from this letter that he ran the risk of an accident if he did not take the car in immediately.

"Jane Consumer testified, under oath, that her husband had only one glass of beer with his meal on the evening of the accident. That amount of alcohol could not have adversely affected his driving capabilities, nor was there any evidence that his driving was at fault. Jane heard a loud 'popping noise' that sounded like 'a spring breaking under tension' just before the car went out of control. Bill reacted by trying to right the vehicle, but the tires would not respond to the steering wheel because the weight of the vehicle had shifted to the rear when the coil broke. He applied the breaks in time to leave skid marks on the asphalt pavement, as Office Goodcop testified.

"The defense has produced highly paid experts to try to convince you that this accident was caused by an 'act of God—the weather did it!' Seriously folks, you can't believe that. This accident was caused by their mistakenly assembled coil that broke just before the accident on that fateful night. Had the vehicle been properly balanced by two identical coils, and had the left coil not broken, there would have been no accident.

"Mack Racer is an expert mechanic who does not get $200 an hour to say what his employers want to hear. He gets his normal mechanic's fee, and he told you the truth. The coil broke before the accident, causing the front tires to lose traction and this, in turn, caused the vehicle to hydroplane on the wet pavement.

"The legal standard in this case requires merely that you find that a defect existed that was not altered before it reached the user, and that the defect was a proximate cause of the damages sustained.

"Ladies and gentlemen, we have proved those elements by a preponderance of the evidence. Proximate cause does not require absolute proof, but merely that, in the chain of events, the accident would not have happened had the defect not existed. The reduced traction on the front tires caused by defectively mounted coils was a proximate cause of this accident. That condition existed, whether you conclude the coil broke before or after the accident, and the accident would not have occurred had the manufacturer installed the proper identical coils on both sides of the vehicle."

Defendant's Close

"Ladies and gentlemen of the jury:

"My able co-counsel, Maria Farmer, said in her opening statement, 'the tragic accident involved in this case was caused by unavoidable weather conditions and driver error, not by any alleged defective condition of the automobile in question.' The witnesses and evidence you have heard at this trial proved those facts. The suspension coils in question were not defective, unsafe, or dangerous. They were tested using 'state of the art' simulation techniques as testified to, under oath, by a highly qualified engineer. His report concerning this extensive testing concluded that the coils were safe and would hold up for the 200,000-mile potential life of the vehicle. Mr. Tester also testified that even if the coil broke under expected driving conditions, the power steering mechanism would prevent the vehicle from going out of control.

"The medic who attended the accident victims and the hospital physician testified to the presence of alcohol on the driver's breath. Ladies and gentlemen, we do not have to prove that Bill Consumer was drunk on the evening of the accident. We have proven, however, that he had been drinking and that this affected his driving capabilities, lowering his reaction time and causing him to be less cautious than he should have been under the adverse weather conditions he encountered.

"Bill Consumer had received a letter from the factory telling him to bring the car in for recall. This he failed to do, and he therefore voluntarily assumed the risk of driving that vehicle after he had been warned of the risk.

"Finally, Professor Drivesafe, a nationally recognized authority on the causes of accidents, has testified that there was a measurable depression in the roadbed that created a drainage problem at the particular spot where Bill Consumer lost control of his vehicle. Officer Goodcop confirmed this finding by documenting two previous accidents and complaints about poor drainage in that same area. All of the eyewitnesses to the scene of the accident testified to the heavy downpour that flooded the highway that night prior to the accident.

"The professor testified that the force of the crash and the twisting of the vehicle as it spun around in the highway caused the coil to break.

"Ladies and gentlemen of the jury, the defendant cannot be held liable for the damages resulting from this tragic accident, because is was caused by the weather, road conditions, and driver error. These are conditions that are beyond the control of the manufacturer."

Judge's Charge to the Jury

Judge Stern's instructions for the jury's deliberation were carefully prepared after the lawyers were given an opportunity to submit requested instructions to the judge in writing. Some courts have pattern instructions, which are model statements prepared by committees of judges and lawyers, and their use may be required in some jurisdictions.

Judge Stern took both of the lawyers' suggestions into consideration in preparing his **charge to the jury** in the *Consumer* case. He realized that the way he explained the law to the jury in his charge would be one of the most carefully reviewed aspects of the trial if an appeal were made. Therefore, he approached this task cautiously, taking care to explain the language of the law clearly so that the jury could understand the legal standards they would have to apply to the facts in this case.

He began by repeating his initial jury instructions given before the facts were presented. Reminding them that they would be the sole judges of the facts, the judge explained that the jury must consider the credibility of the witnesses, that they should not be influenced by any sympathy or prejudice they might feel regarding the parties, and that they must base their verdict entirely on the evidence presented in the form of testimony of witnesses, documents, and exhibits admitted into testimony.

The judge then reviewed some of the facts in the case. He said there was no dispute about the fact that the manufacturer had assembled the automobile in question with rear suspension coils that varied in size and quality, that the vehicle was properly serviced and maintained, and that an accident had occurred involving this same vehicle that had been manufactured and sold by the defendant and was in substantially the same condition as when sold. Judge Stern then explained the law to be applied to the facts in dispute in the following words:

"Under the law of this state, one who sells a product in a defective condition is subject to liability for physical harm thereby caused to the ultimate user or consumer if: (a) the seller is engaged in the business of selling such a product, (b) it is expected to and does reach the user or consumer without substantial change in the condition in which it was sold, and (c) the defective condition was the proximate cause of the injury to the plaintiff.

"All of these elements must be present for you to find in favor of the plaintiff. Therefore, the elements in dispute in this case relate primarily to (1) whether or not the varied size and quality of the suspension coils constituted a defective product, and (2) whether or not the condition of the coils was a proximate cause of the injuries sustained.

"An absolute defense in law is known as 'voluntary assumption of the risk.' That means that the plaintiff knew of the defective condition and assumed the risk with knowledge of the consequences. If you find that under the particular circumstances a reasonable person of ordinary prudence would have used the product despite knowledge of the defect or condition, you may still find for the plaintiff.

"The words 'defective condition' mean a condition of a product that renders it unsafe for normal or reasonably anticipated handling and consumption.

---

charge to the jury: final address by the judge to the jury before the verdict; instructs the jury on the rules of law it must apply.

"A defective condition proximately causes an injury if the defect directly and in natural and continuous sequence produces or contributes substantially to producing the injury, so that it reasonably can be said that except for the defective condition, the injury complained of would not have occurred.

"This does not mean that the law recognizes only one proximate cause of an injury or damage, consisting of only one factor or thing, or the conduct of only one person. On the contrary, many factors or things, or the conduct of two or more persons, may operate at the same time, either independently or together, to cause injury or damage; and in such a case, each may be a proximate cause.

"The burden is on the plaintiff in a civil case, such as this, to prove every essential element of his claim by a preponderance of the evidence. If the proof should fail to establish any essential element of the plaintiff's claim by a preponderance of the evidence in the case, the jury should find for the defendant as to that claim.

"To 'establish by a preponderance of the evidence' means to prove that something is more likely so than not so. In other words, a preponderance of the evidence in this case means such evidence as, when considered and compared with that opposed to it, has more convincing force, and produces in your minds belief that what is sought to be proved is more likely true than not true. This rule does not, of course, require proof to an absolute certainty, since proof to an absolute certainty is seldom possible in any case.

"In determining whether any fact in issue has been proved by a preponderance of the evidence in the case, the jury may, unless otherwise instructed, consider the testimony of all witnesses, regardless of who may have called them, and all exhibits received and admitted into evidence, regardless of who may have produced them.

"I am charging you with a special verdict that you must all agree to before your deliberation is complete. You will first elect your own chairperson to aid you in organizing your deliberation. Then you must answer the questions submitted to you *unanimously*. [See Form 6-5.] You are not finished until you all agree. Only if you find for the plaintiff will you proceed to answer the final questions concerning damages."

The judge then dismissed the alternate juror, and he told the remaining official jurors that he had concluded his charge and that it was time for them to assume their deliberation.

Verdicts

Judge Stern gave the jury a combined special and general **verdict** charge in this case. In federal courts, the judge has discretion to request either a general or special verdict. A general verdict would require the jury to decide simply for one of the parties and, if damages were sought, to indicate the sum to be awarded. The judge also has the discretion under the federal rules to request a combined special and general verdict, as Judge Stern did in this case. This type of verdict gives the judge more information about the jury's reasoning and understanding of the law involved. If inconsistency is evident, the judge may recharge the jury or order a new trial.

The federal rules provide that the parties may stipulate that the finding of a stated majority shall be taken as the verdict. Maria Farmer stated in her written request for suggested jury charge, however, that she demanded a unanimous

verdict: formal decision or finding made by a jury concerning the matters of fact submitted to them.

Form 6.5
Questions Submitted to the Jury

1. Was the condition of the two rear coils at the time of the accident a "defective condition" as defined in law?

   Answer YES or NO _____

2. Was that defective condition a "proximate cause" of the injuries sustained in the accident?

   Answer YES or NO _____

3. Did William P. Consumer use the automobile in question knowing the risks involved and voluntarily assume those risks?

   Answer YES or NO _____

4. Do you find in favor of the plaintiff or the defendant?

   In favor of _____

5. What were the damages sustained by the estate of William P. Consumer?

   $_____

6. What were the damages sustained by Jane Consumer?

   $_____

verdict, and Judge Stern was required to honor that request. Some states provide for less than a unanimous verdict in their rules of procedure.

THE VERDICT AND JUDGMENT OF THE COURT

The jury deliberated for about two and one-half hours in this case and finally arrived at a verdict in favor of the plaintiff in the amount of $285,000. The reader should decide whether he or she agrees with their determination and why or why not.

Judge Stern asked the jury to make sure the decision was unanimous, and then asked the attorneys if they wished to enter motions or objections. The judge found that the jury had discharged its function properly, and he entered **judgment** consistent with the jury finding.

Objections could have been raised about the procedure followed in this case, and they would have been entered into the record before the judge's decision. The judge could have ordered a **judgment as a matter of law** (n.o.v.), which would have allowed the final judgment to differ from the jury's verdict, if he had agreed that a prejudicial (as opposed to harmless) error had taken place at trial. He also could have ordered a new trial or altered the jury's finding, but he would have needed to state a reason founded in law for such a decision.

Either party in a case may appeal the final judgment of the trial court (generally within thirty days). The next chapter discusses the appeal process and provides an illustrative case in law involving the area of products liability.

judgment: the official decision of the court upon the respective rights and claims of the parties.

judgment as a matter of law: This term, used in the Federal Rules of Civil Procedure, refers to a judgment in favor of one party notwithstanding a jury verdict in favor of the opposing party. (State courts may still use the older term, judgment n.o.v.)

CHAPTER SUMMARY

1. This chapter illustrates the trial procedure that begins with the voir dire (or jury selection) process. This process is an important aspect of the jury trial, since who is selected to serve on the jury may affect the outcome. Opposing lawyers are careful to take advantage of every opportunity to prevent a potentially biased juror from being selected. It is the judge's responsibility to see that jury bias is eliminated to the extent possible.

2. The judge has wide discretionary authority to conduct either the voir dire alone or allow the lawyers to ask questions of the jurors. Some jurisdictions allow extensive leeway to lawyers in conducting the process. The judge, however, must decide all challenges for cause and rule on the qualifications of potential jurors. The number of potential jurors who may be eliminated for cause is unlimited.

3. The lawyers for each party in the dispute have a limited number of peremptory challenges that do not require a showing of cause to disqualify a potential juror. In civil cases, the number of such challenges for each party is usually limited by statute to three, but this number may vary by jurisdiction and the particular circumstances of the case.

4. Trial arguments begin after the judge is satisfied that an impartial jury has been selected. The judge may provide preliminary jury instructions before the opening statements, but the detailed jury charge cannot be given properly until the evidence has been presented and the jury is ready for deliberation. The opening statements, first by the plaintiff and then by the defendant, are not evidence, but provide the court with a brief overview of the subject matter of the case and the major areas of contention.

5. The plaintiff's case in chief follows the opening statements. It includes testimony of all witnesses for the plaintiff and presentation of material or documentary evidence. The opposing attorney may cross-examine each witness after the direct examination by the plaintiff's lawyer. There may be a second examination by the plaintiff's attorney, called the redirect examination, and a second examination by the opposing attorney, called the recross-examination.

6. The rules of evidence are detailed procedural rules that regulate the admission of evidence at trial. They have been developed over centuries by the common law. The rule that prohibits the use of leading questions on direct examination but permits such questions on cross-examination is a good example. "Relevancy," "asked and answered," and "argumentative" are typical objections to attempts to elicit testimony or admit evidence at trial.

7. An expert witness is permitted to answer opinion questions within the expert's area of expertise if the expert has been qualified or a proper foundation has first been established for the expertise of that witness. Otherwise, witnesses are restricted to firsthand knowledge of events they have personally observed that are relevant to the case.

8. The best evidence rule and the hearsay rule restrict evidence to that which is clearly authenticated; that is, there must be an opportunity to question the validity of statements or documentary evidence. The rules are quite complex and have many exceptions, but their purpose is to prevent unfair testimony that cannot be verified.

9. After the plaintiff's case in chief, the defense has an opportunity to present its case in chief to refute the claims made against them. After the defense has rested (ended) its case in chief, the plaintiff can recall witnesses or produce new evidence in rebuttal, and the defense can offer new evidence in rejoinder. When the plaintiff rests its case, the judge calls for closing arguments.

10. The judge's charge to the jury is important; it instructs the jury about, and carefully explains, the principles of law the jurors are to use in arriving at their verdict. This charge will be carefully examined by the appeals court, if there is an appeal. The judge must explain the law clearly and make sure that the instructions are understood.

11. The jury is given documents and material evidence by the judge. The jurors also are allowed to take a copy of the judge's charge into the jury room, but they are sequestered (isolated) until they have reached a verdict.

12. A directed verdict may be handed down by the judge at the end of the plaintiff's case in chief if the judge believes that the plaintiff has failed to present admissible evidence to support a valid claim. After the defendant's case in chief, the judge, again, can stop the trial if the judge believes no evidence has been offered to refute the plaintiff's claim.

13. The jury's verdict is not the final judgment in the case. Judgment is made by the court. The judge may set aside the jury's verdict if the judge is convinced that there was prejudicial error in the trial procedure.

KEY TERMS

voir dire	rules of evidence	prima facie case
challenges for cause	leading questions (rule)	charge to the jury
peremptory challenges	hearsay rule	verdict
opening statements	best evidence rule	judgment
closing arguments	expert witness	judgment as a matter of law (n.o.v.)
direct examination	directed verdict	
cross-examination	burden of proof	

DISCUSSION QUESTIONS

1. What are the characteristic features of the jury selection process, and how can this process affect the outcome at trial?

2. How are challenges for cause and peremptory challenges decided during the voir dire process?

3. What is the basic procedure used for presentation of arguments and evidence at trial?

4. Why are the lawyer's arguments not considered evidence?

5. When and how is documentary and material evidence presented to the court and jury at trial?

6. What are the basic purposes and rules concerning direct examination and cross-examination of witnesses?

7. What are some of the basic rules of evidence that regulate the admission of evidence at trial?

8. What is the reason for excluding hearsay evidence, and why are there many exceptions to this rule?

9. What are the assumptions underlying the adversarial roles of the opposing lawyers?

10. Why is the charge to the jury one of the most carefully examined aspects of the trial by the appeals courts?

11. What is the function of the jury in the trial process, and how is it distinguished from the role of the judge?

12. What is the legal importance of the court's judgment as opposed to the jury's verdict?

SOURCES AND SUGGESTED READING

Blanchard, Roderick D. 1990. *Litigation and Trial Practice for the Legal Assistant*. 3d ed. St. Paul: West Publishing Co.

Devitt, Edward J., Charles B. Blackmar, and Michael A. Wolf. 1987. *Federal Jury Practice and Instructions* (Civil). Vol. 3. 4th ed. St. Paul: West Publishing Co.

Imwinkelried, Edward J. 1980. *Evidentiary Foundations*. Charlottesville, Va.: Michie Law Publishers.

Landsman, Stephan. 1988. *Readings on Adversarial Justice: The American Approach to Adjudication*. St. Paul: West Publishing Co.

Lewis, Alfred J. 1985. *Using American Law Books*. 2d ed. Dubuque, Iowa: Kendall Hunt.

Tennessee Practice Series. 1988. *Tennessee Pattern Jury Instructions* (Civil). Vol. 8. St. Paul: West Publishing Co. (The reader's state may have a similar series of practice volumes that should be consulted for local practice.)

CHAPTER SEVEN

EVALUATION OF THE CIVIL PROCESS

> "A Judge shall uphold the integrity and independence of the judiciary."
>
> Canon One: ABA Model Rules of Judicial Conduct
>
> "A judge shall not allow family, social, political or other relationships to influence the judge's conduct or judgment. A judge shall not lend the prestige of judicial office to advance the private interests of the judge or others; nor shall a judge convey or permit others to convey the impression that they are in a special position to influence the judge."
>
> Canon Two (B): ABA Model Rules of Judicial Conduct

The hypothetical *Consumer* case in products liability was developed in the last three chapters to illustrate what is involved behind the scenes in preparation for trial in contested cases. However, this fictitious case was simplified to make it a manageable demonstration of the stages of civil trial process. This chapter demonstrates how an actual case in products liability is evaluated by the appeals court.

The *Consumer* case assumed that the law of Middle State applied the traditional concept of strict liability defined in section 402A of the *Restatement (Second) of Torts*. However, many states have added new exceptions to this traditional concept, making actual cases more complex. Some of these modifications achieved by tort reform efforts are explained, and their effects are demonstrated, in the real case of *Abbott v. American Honda Motor Co.*, 682 S.W. 2d 206 (Tenn. App. 1984).

The general features of the appeals process are explained in this chapter, along with the manner in which civil legal actions are terminated. The court system is designed to provide a means of individual case evaluation for error correction as well as law development purposes. The intermediate appeals courts are primarily concerned with error correction and entertain issues of law in disputes arising from the trial courts.

This chapter also discusses some of the basic problems of our legal system in the area of civil litigation. Many critics argue that major reforms are needed to improve the system. The most critical problems relate to the extensive case load burden faced by the court system and the costs of modern civil litigation. These problems are explained, and some of the efforts being made to deal with them are discussed. The chapter concludes with a comparative analysis of the differences between the United States and other modern industrial societies regarding these problems.

THE APPEALS PROCESS

A century ago the only opportunity to reverse a final judgment was by "writ of error"; this reversal was difficult to accomplish and required an entirely new legal action. Since the 1950s, there has been an enormous expansion of the right of appeal granted through statutory and case law development.

Contrary to popular belief, there is no automatic right of appeal granted by the federal Constitution. In the early history of the United States, appeals were limited by stringent rules. The federal circuit court was not established as a true appellate court until 1891 when the Evarts Act created three-judge panels that included a circuit-riding Supreme Court justice to hear initial appeals from district courts.

In 1891, the basic structure of the federal appeals system was created, and in 1925, the jurisdiction of the Supreme Court was made almost entirely discretionary. The effect of this change was to make the decisions of the courts of appeal final in all but a very small percentage of appeals (Martineau 1985,13–14).

The Right of Appeal

final judgment: one that puts an end, generally on the merits of the case, to an action at law. Interlocutory appeals (before judgment on merits) may be allowed in exceptional cases.

Today, the federal appeals court has jurisdiction to review **final judgments** of the district courts as a matter of right in most cases. It also may hear certain interlocutory appeals from lower court judgments, such as injunctions or certifications of questions of law by trial judges to the appellate court.

There are only two states in which there is no right of at least one appeal from a final judgment (Virginia and West Virginia), even though the United States Supreme Court has refused to find that due process requires appellate review (Martineau 1985,9).

The expansion of the right of appeal has been one of the important contributing factors to the tremendous increase in the workload of the courts. Appeals Court Justice Richard A. Posner demonstrates that in the two decades of the 1960s and 1970s (1960–1983), the federal appeals courts increased their case load by nearly seven hundred (686) percent while the district court case load grew by only two hundred and fifty (250) percent (Posner 1985,82).

Appeals Court Actions

appellant: party bringing the appeal, who has the burden of proof on appeal.

prejudicial error: one that affects the final results of the trial, as opposed to harmless error.

The appeals court may affirm the lower court's decision, reverse that decision, or remand the case back to the trial court with directions for further action, such as a new trial. The appeals court does not try the case again, but a panel of at least three judges reviews the entire record, considering the arguments of both parties concerning the issues of law in dispute.

The **appellant** (party bringing the appeal, who now has the burden of proof) must convince a majority of the appeals court panel that **prejudicial** (as opposed to harmless) **error** resulted in miscarriage of justice. A review of facts established in the trial court record does take place, but the concern of the appeals court is with issues of law in dispute that are related to the facts (evidence) presented. New facts are not entertained by the appeals court and must be presented to the trial court either by reopening the case (which is very difficult) or securing an order from the appeals court requiring that a new fact-finding procedure be conducted.

Appealability

Although the right of appeal has been extended in modern times, the appellant must raise appropriate objections at the trial level and be able to demonstrate a cause of action founded in law for the appeal. Mere dissatisfaction with the trial outcome is not sufficient reason for appeal. The appellant must initiate action at the trial court level within the specified time period (thirty days in most court jurisdictions).

The appellant is required to pay for the cost of a complete transcript of the trial record taken by the court reporter and is responsible for ensuring that the entire record of the trial case is transmitted to the appeals court.

The Appellate Briefs

The appellant's brief (written arguments) must be filed and served within forty days after the trial record has been filed with the appeals court. The clerk usually notifies the parties of the date the record was filed, but failure of the clerk to give such notice does not excuse the late filing of the appellant's brief, which can result in dismissal of the appeal.

The **appellate brief** is a crucial part of the appeal process. Extreme care should be taken to prepare the brief in a manner that will be useful to the overloaded appeals court judges; in fact, successful appellate lawyers exercise extensive care in the preparation of this document. Specific form and organization are required, and simplicity in substance and style is considered an absolute necessity for any litigant who wishes to receive the full attention of either state or federal appellate courts.

Time elements vary for state appeals courts, but the majority of the state courts allow time periods similar to those of the federal courts. Strict requirements concerning length, for specific parts of the brief as well as for the overall brief, are imposed. For federal appellate courts, the initial brief of each party may not exceed fifty pages, and the reply brief may not exceed twenty-five pages. Length requirements vary for state appeals courts but average about the same as those for federal courts.

Rule 28 of the Federal Rules of Appellate Procedure (FRAP 28), which defines the contents of the appeals brief, is the model for most state as well as federal courts. It provides that the appellant's brief include:

1. a Table of Contents and Authorities;
2. a Statement of the Issues;
3. a Statement of the Case;
4. an Argument; and
5. a Conclusion.

The **appellee** is the party against whom the appeal is filed. This party must be notified. An appeal stays payment of the trial damage award, which must not be paid until all opportunities for appeal have been exhausted. The appellee is given an opportunity to respond in writing to the appellant's brief.

appellate brief: written argument that must be filed on appeal by the party bringing the appeal.

appellee: party against whom the appeal is filed. It may have been either the plaintiff or the defendant in the trial court.

The appellee's brief is due within thirty days after service of the appellant's brief. Within fourteen days after being served with the appellee's brief, and in any event, not less than three days before argument, the appellant must serve and file the reply brief, if any (FRAP 31a).

The appellee's brief is not required to contain a conclusion specifying relief sought, but otherwise has the same format requirements as the appellant's brief. The appellee may omit the statement of issues, the statement of the case, or both; but if the appellee is dissatisfied with statements in the appellant's brief, the appellee should restate them in his or her brief.

Appellate Court Functions

The appeals court has two basic functions—error correction and law development. The successful appellant must keep these functions in mind while preparing the brief. In jury trial cases, the general doctrine is that the jury finding must be upheld if there is sufficient evidence to support the verdict. Sufficiency of the evidence is defined to mean that there are in the record probative (testimony carrying quality of proof) facts from which the ultimate fact found by the jury can reasonably be inferred. The appellate court may not substitute its judgment for that of the jury. The appellant must show that the inferences drawn by the trial jury in favor of the appellee were unreasonable (Martineau 1985,137).

Oral Arguments

An important part of our Anglo-American heritage is the role played by oral arguments in the appeals process, but the increase in the case load has substantially reduced the opportunity for oral presentation.

In English practice, appellate argument was exclusively oral once the record had been filed. The decision was announced at the conclusion of oral argument, with each judge stating that judge's opinion and reasoning. This tradition was extended to the United States and continued until recent years. "Gradually as the courts became busier they began to impose limitations on the length of oral argument. At first each side was allowed several hours, then one hour, then 30 minutes or even less" (Martineau 1985,101).

The shortened time for oral argument has caused greater emphasis to be placed on the briefs. The general practice, in fact, is to allow oral arguments only when deemed necessary by the appeals panel. "Now only a few appellate courts provide for oral argument as a matter of course in every case" (Martineau 1985,102).

An Actual Case of Appeal

The following Tennessee Appeals Court case, *Abbott v. American Honda Motor Co.*, 682 S.W. 2d 206 (1984 Tenn. App.), illustrates the error correction function of appellate review of trial court judgments. This case was appealed and reviewed by a three-judge panel of the Court of Appeals of Tennessee sitting in the eastern district of the state.

The issues raised in this case demonstrate the basic characteristic of the appeals process—the appeals court focuses on the trial court judge's actions. The actions of the trial judge are carefully reviewed because it is the trial judge who is responsible for conducting a "fair trial" and for properly administering the laws of the state.

The intermediate appeals court in the *Abbott* case found no prejudicial error in the trial judge's conduct of the trial process and, therefore, affirmed the lower court decision. The appeals court also examined several alleged errors, all of which were concerned with the exact words the trial court judge used in his charge to the jury, and found that any errors that occurred did not affect the outcome of the jury's verdict. Thus, the lower court judgment, which was consistent with the jury's verdict, was sustained.

The Products Liability Act of 1978, a result of tort reform efforts in Tennessee, added a clear, positive law set of provisions to the previously developed common law of strict liability (402A *Restatement [Second] of Torts*). The act made two important concessions to the manufacturers and sellers of products. Business and insurance interests had contended that traditional strict liability was unfair to producers. The legislature provided new requirements that called for jury instructions concerning "compliance with governmental standards" and "state of the art testing." Similar concessions have been made in many states in recent years.

The following language defines these concepts in Tennessee law:

[Compliance with governmental standards]

Compliance by manufacturer or seller with any federal or state statute or administrative regulation existing at the time a product was manufactured and prescribing standards for design, inspection, testing, manufacture, labeling, warning or instructions for use of a product, shall raise a rebuttable presumption that the product is not in an unreasonably dangerous condition in regard to matters covered by these standards. [Acts 1978 (Adj. S.), ch. 703, § 4; T.C.A. § 23-3704.]

[State of the art testing]

(a) A manufacturer or seller of a product shall not be liable for any injury to person or property caused by the product unless the product is determined to be in a defective condition or unreasonably dangerous at the time it left the control of the manufacturer or seller. (b) In making this determination, the state of the scientific and technological knowledge available to the manufacturer or seller at the time the product was placed on the market, rather than at the time of injury, is applicable. Consideration is given also to the customary designs, methods, standards and techniques of manufacturing, inspecting and testing by other manufacturers or sellers of similar products. [Acts 1978 (Adj. S.), ch. 703, § 5, 8; T.C.A. § 23-3705.]

Abbott v. American Honda Motor Company

Court of Appeals of Tennessee, Eastern Section, 1984.
682 S.W.2d 206.
[Permission to appeal denied by the Tennessee Supreme Court, October 29, 1984.]
OPINION
SANDERS, Judge

IN THIS SUIT FOR personal injuries the Plaintiffs have appealed from a jury verdict in favor of the Defendants.

On June 12, 1981, Plaintiff-Appellant Scott Allan Abbott, aged 11, was riding a Honda ATC-70, three-wheeled, all-terrain motorcycle on his father's property near his home. As the Plaintiff was going up a hill, the vehicle lost its speed and power and Scott Abbott thereupon applied the brakes. Subsequently he released the brakes and began to ease the motorcycle backwards down the hill. The motorcycle then began to pick up speed, causing the Plaintiff to reapply the brakes. As a result of this action the front wheel came off of the ground, resulting in the Plaintiff's falling or being thrown over the back of the vehicle and onto the ground. The vehicle, in continuing its backwards and downhill movement, then passed over Abbott and seriously burned him when the unshielded underside of the exhaust pipe came into contact with him. The resulting burns are alleged to have caused permanent scarring and injuries, both physical and emotional.

Scott Abbott, by next friend Judith K. Abbott (his mother), sued Honda Motor Company, Ltd. (manufacturer), American Honda Motor Company, Inc. (distributor), and King of Sports, Inc. (seller) for damages arising from the injuries sustained in connection with the accident with the Honda ATC-70. Judith Abbott joined in the suit as a plaintiff, seeking to recover damages for various expenses, including her son's hospitalization and medical costs, and for the loss of her son's services, society, and companionship.

In their complaint, the Plaintiffs asserted that the Defendants were liable upon a variety of grounds, including strict liability, negligence and breach of implied warranties of merchantability and of fitness for a particular purpose. For their answer the Defendants completely denied any liability.

At trial the Plaintiffs proceeded solely upon the theory of strict liability. The jury returned a general verdict in favor of all of the Defendants and the trial court entered judgment in accordance with the verdict. Following the dismissal of their motion for a new trial, the Plaintiffs have appealed, assigning as error various instructions made by the court to the jury.

As their first assignment of error, the Appellants assert that the trial judge, at best, issued confusing instructions relative to the doctrine of contributory negligence and, at worst, issued incorrect instructions relative to the doctrine.

Toward the beginning of his charge to the jury the judge stated as follows: "Members of the jury, I charge you in this case that this is not a negligence case, but is based on Section 402A, Restatement of Torts, and I charge you that contributory negligence of this plaintiff, or plaintiffs, is not a defense to an action based upon strict liability for a defective product." Later in his charge the judge stated that "[t]he manufacturer of a product which involves a risk of injury to the user is liable to any person, whether a purchaser or third person, who without fault on his part sustains an injury caused by a defect in the design, the composition, or manufacture of the article, if the injury might reasonably have been anticipated or foreseen." The Appellants contend that, despite the original instruction that contributory negligence is not a defense in a strict liability action, the court's subsequent "references to 'fault' were so highly prejudicial and contrary to settled law that no cure could have undone the harm."

[1] Long ago, our Supreme Court established the rule that inconsistent or contradictory instructions can be the basis for reversal on appeal. In *Citizens' Street Railroad Co. v. Shepherd*, 107 Tenn. 444, 64 S.W. 710 (1901), the Court stated that it had "repeatedly held that inconsistent and contradictory statements do not neutralize or validate each other, but are vitally erroneous. . . . The parties are entitled to a clear and consistent charge, as well as a correct one, that justice may be reached." *Id.* at

449-50, 64 S.W. 710. *See also Employers Liability Assurance Corp. v. Farguharson*, 182 Tenn. 642, 188 S.W.2d 965 (1945).

It has been generally stated, in 75 Am. Jur.2d *Trial* § 628, 920 (1974), that:

"Instructions as a whole must be consistent and harmonious, not conflicting and contradictory. . . . Where instructions given to the jury for their guidance present contradictory and conflicting rules which are unexplained, and where following one would or might lead to a different result than would obtain by following the other, the instructions are inherently defective. This is true although one of the instructions correctly states the law as applicable to the facts of the case, since the correct instruction cannot cure the error in the contradictory erroneous instruction. . . . The fact that the court gave a correct charge at first will not avail to defeat an exception to a subsequent erroneous instruction."

See also 88 C.J.S. Trial § 338-39 (1955).

[2] Under Tennessee law, the jury charge will be "viewed in its entirety" or "considered as a whole" in order to determine whether the trial judge committed prejudicial error. *See Farguharson, supra; Cooper Paintings & Coatings, Inc. v. SCM Corp.*, 62 Tenn.App. 13, 457 S.W.2d 864 (1970); and *Hayes v. Schweikart's Upholstering Co.*, 55 Tenn.App. 442, 402 S.W.2d 472 (1965).

[3, 4] Considering the charge in question as a whole, we do not find that the trial judge committed prejudicial error relative to his instructions on contributory negligence. As heretofore mentioned, the trial judge originally stated unequivocally that contributory negligence will not serve as a defense in a strict liability action. His subsequent references to "fault," although perhaps a bit unqualified, do not serve to contradict or to confuse his original charge. "Fault," as used within the context of the trial court's charge, clearly connotes a form of improper conduct or omission. And although contributory negligence cannot be applied as a defense to strict liability, certain forms of improper conduct or omission by a plaintiff may serve to shield the defendant(s) from liability. In *Ellithorpe v. Ford Motor Co.*, 503 S.W.2d 516 (Tenn.1973), our Supreme Court stated:

"The courts do recognize, however, that plaintiffs can conduct themselves in such a way as to defeat recovery. Regardless of which label is used, 'contributory negligence' or 'assumption of risk,' the courts have generally held that ordinary lack of care is not a defense, while 'voluntarily and unreasonably proceeding to encounter a known danger' is a defense. *Williams v. Brown Manufacturing Co.*, supra [45 Ill.2d 418], 261 N.E.2d [305] at 309 [(1970)]; Prosser, The Law of Torts, Sec. 102 at 670; Restatement (Second) of Torts, Sec. 402A, comment n at 356. As the court said in *Carney v. Ford Motor Co.*:

"'We . . . conclude that when a plaintiff, with knowledge of the defect, uses the product in such a manner as to voluntarily and unreasonably encounter a known danger, the act may be plead as a defense to an action based on strict liability in tort. We do not deem it determinative of the availability of this defense whether it be called negligence, contributory negligence or assumption of risk. It is more a matter of unreasonableness of permitting a plaintiff to deliberately put in motion a known danger and attempt to profit thereby.' *Id*. at 9727.

"Likewise, the Restatement (Second) of Torts, Sec. 496A, comment d at 563, states that the *only* form of contributory negligence which can be used as a defense in strict products liability cases is that known as 'assumption of risk' as defined in *Carney v. Ford Motor Co.*, supra."

[5] We agree. Taking the court's charge as a whole, we do not believe the references to "fault" confused or contradicted the original and unequivocal instruction that contributory negligence is not a defense in a strict liability action.

The Appellants next contend that the trial court erred in its jury charge by failing to distinguish between "warnings" and "instructions." Pertinent to this matter, the trial judge stated:

"Where a manufacturer or seller of a product has reason to anticipate a danger may result from a particular use, then the manufacturer or the seller is required to give adequate warning of the danger, and a product sold without such warnings is in a defective condition.

"An adequate warning is one calculated to bring home to a reasonably prudent user of the product the nature and extent of the danger involved in using the product. . . . Where the warning is adequate to inform the minor child of the dangers incident to the use of the product, the parents are put on notice to take steps to avoid injury to the child through proper training, instruction, and supervision.

"A product is unreasonably dangerous if it is dangerous to a greater degree than the ordinary consumer would expect, having ordinary knowledge of the nature of the product. However, when the manufacturer is aware of the danger and gives the consumer warning adequately informing him of that danger, the product is not rendered defective and unreasonably dangerous, and no liability will attach to the manufacturer.

"If you find, therefore, that the danger inherent in the motorcycle in this case is not greater than an ordinary consumer would expect, or if you find that the warnings and instructions supplied by the manufacturer adequately apprise such consumer of said danger, the manufacturer cannot be subject to such liability.

"The warning should be such that if followed it would make the product safe for users. Where such a warning or instruction is given, the supplier may reasonably assume that it will be read and heeded. Furthermore, when a warning or instruction is given specifying a particular manner of use or caution, and that warning or instruction is not complied with, no liability will attach to the supplier.

"Therefore, if you find that the supplier knew or reasonably should have known of a danger in the use of the motorcycle, that the supplier warned of that danger in such a way that if the instructions were followed the injury would not have been sustained, and that the warnings or instructions were not in fact followed, the supplier is relieved from liability for said injury."

[6] The Appellants contend that the failure of the trial court to distinguish between "instructions" and "warnings" rendered its charge to the jury "confusing" and "misleading."

We disagree. First, the trial judge clearly focused his charge on "warnings," not "instructions." True, in a few instances, he spoke of the two concepts together. When reading the charge in its entirety, however, we do not find this charge to be either "confusing" or "misleading."

Additionally, it is not unusual for the two concepts to be spoken of together. In *Young v. Reliance Electric Co.*, 584 S.W.2d 663 (Tenn.App.1979), this court continuously refers to "instructions or warning" and concludes a portion of its opinion by stating that a "manufacturer is entitled to expect reasonable instructions or warnings to be heeded." *Id.* at 669.

Although "instructions" and "warnings" may be intended to serve different purposes, as the Appellants assert, obviously the two concepts are related in the fact that they both serve to lessen the potential for injury. It has been stated that "there should be adequate directions or instructions for the use of a product, as well as proper warning of foreseeable dangers in connection therewith." 63 Am.Jur.2d *Products Liability* § 339 (1984). In fact, as a practical matter, instructions, when followed, may prevent an improper use of a product—an improper use that might otherwise result in injury to the user.

With the above in mind, we believe the trial judge did not commit prejudicial error in his charge on "warning" and "instructions."

[7] The Appellants also say the court's charge on the state of the art was inadequate.

In determining whether or not a product is in a defective condition or unreasonably dangerous, a court will often give consideration to the state of the art. Addressing this concept, T.C.A. § 29-28-105(b) provides:

"In making this determination the state of scientific and technological knowledge available to the manufacturer or seller at the time the product was placed on the market, rather than at the time of injury, is applicable. Consideration is given also to the customary designs, methods, standards and techniques of manufacturing, inspecting and testing by other manufacturers or sellers of similar products."

In the present case, the trial judge charged the jury on the issue of the state of the art as follows:

"The defendants in this case have asserted that their liability is determined in the light of whether the product was reasonably suited for the purpose for which it was intended, in accordance with the general accepted standards of the industry, having due regard for the existent state of technology and the state of the art at the time the product was designed and manufactured.

"I charge you that industry standards are not conclusive as to ordinary care in design or manufacture, but rather are admissible evidence for your consideration. The manufacturer and seller of a product or products, such as that involved in this case, have the duty to design and manufacture such products so that the products would be safe for their intended uses or for their reasonable foreseeable uses.

"The manufacturer and seller have the further duties to design, test, and install whatever necessary safety devices and safety guards that were available to render such product safe for their intended uses or for their reasonable foreseeable uses.

"A manufacturer is entitled to rely upon the state of the art at the time the product is placed on the market rather than at the time of the injury. Scientific and technical knowledge available to the manufacturer, as well as customary design methods, standards and techniques of manufacturing, inspecting and testing by other manufacturers of similar products, are elements to consider in determining whether the product conformed to the state of the art at the time it was placed on the market.

"If you find, therefore, that the defendants' product conformed to the state of the art, that is that it was in conformance with the standard set by and customary design of similar products, and that the defendant used the same type of testing, inspecting, and manufacturing techniques as defendants' competitors used, then the product is not determined to be defective and unreasonably dangerous, and no liability will attach to the defendants."

Upon reading the state of the art charge in its entirety, we find absolutely no merit in the Appellants' contention that the charge was inadequate in any way. The language used by the trial judge closely followed that of the statute and was in conformity with our case law. *See Ellithorpe, supra*, at 519.

The Appellants also contend the jury charge on the issue of intervening negligence was in error. Pertinent to this matter, the judge charged:

"Ladies and gentlemen of the jury, in this case the defendants have interposed the plea of intervening cause or action. They say in this case that the parent, that is to say young Scott's father, failed to advise him and warn him of the instructions in that book, and therefore that was an intervening act and cause of this accident.

"The law is that the chain of causation is not broken by the occurrence of an intervening act or event if that act or event might reasonably have been anticipated. . . . Although there is an intervening act occurring after the defendant's act, nevertheless the defendant's act will be regarded as the proximate cause where the intervening act is a normal response to the stimulant of a situation created by the defendant's conduct.

"If a later, new, and independent act or event which would not reasonably have been foreseen by the original negligent party, or original party holding liability under 402A, intervenes in the sequence of events and itself causes an injury to another, the original party is relieved of liability for the injury. In order to breach the chain of causation, the intervening act or event must not have been reasonably foreseeable by the original wrongdoer and must not have been a normal consequence of the situation created by him.

"If you find, therefore, that the parent of the minor plaintiff did not properly instruct and supervise the minor plaintiff in the use of the motorcycle, and that such failure itself caused the injury sustained, then the acts and omissions of the parent are an intervening cause sufficient to relieve the defendants of liability."

[8] The Appellants first contend the trial court erred in giving the charge of intervening negligence since the charge "was not substantiated by the weight of the evidence."

We disagree. In this case, there was a question of whether or not the father of the injured minor plaintiff properly instructed the youngster as to the correct operation of the motorcycle, and was plead as an affirmative defense by the Defendants. As such, the issue of intervening negligence was properly submitted to the jury.

[9] The Appellants further appear to argue that the trial court erred by failing to distinguish between a foreseeable intervening cause (which will not serve to bar the Defendants' potential liability) and an unforeseeable intervening cause (which will serve to bar the Defendants' liability). From a plain reading of the court's charge, however, we find that the trial court clearly distinguished between the two. Therefore, the trial court did not commit error in his intervening negligence charge.

[10] As their final assignment of error, the Appellants claim that the trial judge erred in refusing to use five of their requested instructions.

We again disagree. Certain of the Appellants' proposed instructions were sufficiently covered by the court's actual charge. *See Lawing v. Johnson*, 49 Tenn.App. 403, 355 S.W.2d 465, 469 (1961). The rest were correctly refused by the trial court as being improper under the facts of this case.

The issues are found in favor of the Appellees. The judgment of the trial court is affirmed and the cost of this appeal is taxed to the Appellants.

GODDARD and FRANKS, JJ., concur.

Ending Civil Legal Actions

Note that the Tennessee Supreme Court denied further appeal in the *Abbott* case three months after the intermediate appeals court judgment. This action ended all further appeal in this case. There must be some point of finality in civil legal actions, and on issues of state law, the state supreme court is the court of last resort. At this point of finality, the case is referred to as res judicata.

Res judicata means that the case is finally decided and cannot be the subject of a future suit involving the same parties. At this point, **satisfaction of judgment** (payment of the award for damages) is required. Further court action can be taken to impose satisfaction by attaching property owned by the defendant if voluntary compliance does not take place.

When all opportunity for appeal has been exhausted and the case is said to be res judicata (ended), this closure of the case is a form of **estoppel** known as estoppel by judgment (further legal action is barred). Estoppel refers to a legal procedure barring a variety of evidence, testimony, or legal actions.

res judicata: finally decided; an action that is conclusive with regard to the same issues and parties.

satisfaction of judgment: payment of the court award for damages.

estoppel: legal procedure barring a variety of evidence, testimony, or legal actions.

PROBLEMS OF CIVIL LITIGATION

Many people believe that we have too many lawyers, that our laws are too complex, and that our procedures of adjudication are too cumbersome, causing excessive litigation and imposing excessive costs that benefit lawyers and litigants at the expense of society as a whole. These criticisms are serious and deserve consideration, even in an introductory text.

The Major Issues

In comparison with most modern democratic societies, there are about four to five times as many lawyers in the United States per 100,000 population. Our laws are complex and not easily understood by the general public. The litigation explosion of the past three decades is clearly evident in the enormous number of cases that have been filed, flooding our courts and trebling the case load. The amount of litigation in state and federal courts is clearly larger than that in other countries, and the costs of the American tort system are undoubtedly higher than those in comparable modern democracies.

The Litigation and Liability "Explosions"

Yale Law School Professor Peter H. Schuck refers to these enormous public policy issues as the litigation and liability "explosions." He explains that these issues should be carefully separated for analytical purposes. Although they are often lumped together in public discussion, they are quite different. One relates to the number of claims litigated in court, and the other refers to the amounts that defendants and their insurers are obligated to pay to plaintiffs as a result of court judgments and out-of-court settlements (Schuck 1991,22).

Causes of the Litigation and Liability Problems

In Chapter Three, the idea was expressed that the size of the legal profession in the United States may be attributed to the magnitude of litigation; that is, the legal professions have expanded to meet demand. However, the assumption that an overproduction of lawyers has caused the problems of litigation explosion also merits thorough and thoughtful examination. There is some truth to the idea that the supply of lawyers has created some of its own demand. Causal relationships are complex and involve many variables that make them difficult, if not impossible, to verify.

The causes of the litigation explosion are, frankly, unknown or so complex that they cannot be isolated. The extension of individuals' rights of access to the courts through the enactment of new legislation and the development of court decisions is certainly one of the more important causes of the litigation explosion. In the United States, the development and extensive use of the contingency fee contract has provided an inducement for lawyers to pursue lucrative individual claims in the courts and has extended the access of the poor to the courts, vastly increasing the case load, particularly in tort cases.

class action suit: legal action involving like situated parties who may collectively sue or be sued.

Class action suits, which have extended the concept of joint and several liability to include mass litigation involving hundreds (even thousands) of plaintiffs or defendants as "like situated parties," are blamed for the litigation explosion by many critics. However, these suits also have extended access to the courts for persons who otherwise would not have sought access to the courts. We know that liberalization of access to the appeals courts has vastly multiplied recourse to appellate review in the past two decades, making the rate of increase more than double that of complaints filed in trial courts.

All these developments can be viewed in different ways, depending on the point of view of the beholder. For the consumer and plaintiff lawyer, they have meant greater access to the courts and greater opportunity for compensation benefiting the average individual. For the producer, the insurer, and the defense lawyer in tort cases, they have meant greater costs of production and, some would assert, loss of competitive advantage in the world economy. For government, including the more than 80,000 units of state and local government in the United States, the costs of liability insurance and performing services has enormously increased because of rising litigation costs.

The Case Load Problem

The federal civil law case load is dwarfed by the enormous number of state cases filed each year. In 1991, the National Center for State Courts reported 18.9 million new state civil cases filed, as opposed to only 207,742 new civil cases filed in the federal courts (National Center for State Courts 1991, 3–4).

Whatever the causes of the litigation explosion and the liability insurance "crises," both problems have eased since 1987 by most accounts. It is very likely that the rate of increase in litigation over the last three decades will not continue into the future as society and the courts adjust to the current levels of litigation and appeals.

Out-of-Court Settlement

One basic conclusion reached by the National Center for State Courts in their 1988 report is that the overwhelming method of disposition of civil legal actions in state courts is by out-of-court settlement; only 9.2% of cases proceed to the trial stage. The percentage of dismissals and default terminations of civil cases varies widely from state to state, between 25% to 75% of total dispositions. If dismissal and default cases are excluded, the average number of civil cases settled out of court approaches 75%. Of the 9.2% of civil cases that go to trial, 87% are conducted as bench trials (National Center for State Courts 1990,61–62).

These figures demonstrate that the hypothetical *Consumer* case used in this textbook for illustrative purposes is the rare exception. Only in highly contested cases is there a need for the extensive trial procedure, and even when trials take place in civil cases, they are often bench trials. Most of the enormous number of cases filed are disposed of through negotiations and out-of-court settlement.

Evidence indicates that the appeals explosion has been subsiding. The 1988 report by the National Center for State Courts concludes, "The data appear to suggest . . . that appellate filings have assumed a more modest growth rate in the latter half of the 1980s relative to the experience of the 1970s and early 1980s. In addition, the growth in dispositions appear to be keeping pace with the growth in filings (National Center for State Courts 1990, 47 – 48). By and large, the court system excludes frivolous and unwarranted claims through the extensive pretrial opportunities for dismissal.

Jury Trials in Civil Cases

One of the arguments made by critics of the civil process is that jury trials are cumbersome, time-consuming, and expensive. The assumption is that this lengthy trial process causes a backlog of cases and creates the case load problem. The popular image of the American jury trial system, however, is grossly exaggerated. This image implies that every case is required to go through the extensive procedures described in the *Consumer* case illustration. The fact is that only 1.1% of the civil cases filed in state trial courts actually get to the stage of trial by jury. Our perceptions and educational orientations are misleading concerning the actual functioning of our legal system, since jury trials are the exception rather than the rule.

The 1988 report of the National Center for State Courts established that only 202,124 jury trials were held out of the 16.9 million civil cases filed in 1988. Federal courts may have a higher percentage of cases that utilize jury trials, but since the federal base of cases filed is so much smaller, the total percentage of state and federal cases with jury trials would not be appreciably altered. This percentage is still higher than that in any other country, but in the total scheme of dispute settlement, jury trials are rare.

The above figures show that 98.9% of the complaints filed are handled in a manner other than a trial by jury. About 1.4 million cases of a civil nature are handled by bench trials (about 8% of the total cases filed). The remaining cases are either settled out of court, dropped, or dismissed.

Settlements, Dismissals, and Defaults

Rising case loads have prompted a shift in resources away from formal trial proceedings and toward pretrial settlements in many civil courts. Data gathered by the National Center for State Courts indicate that dismissals and defaults constitute a large percentage of the civil dispositions in most states.

Negotiated settlements often occur at the end of the discovery process. The use of pretrial conferences to encourage settlement has become a principal tool of civil case management in many states and individual trial courts. The shift in emphasis from trial to settlement, however, may raise new questions about the importance of nontrial methods of disposition in civil cases. For example, some critics contend that many suits are initiated for minor damage claims that are settled out of court primarily because the defendant finds it less costly to pay the settlement than to incur the expense of litigation.

Alternative Dispute Settlement

James J. Alfini, editor of a special issue of *Judicature* in 1986, declares, "[T]he alternative dispute resolution (ADR) movement has taken hold in the United States and is now an established fact." Alfini describes the ADR movement as the second major wave of judicial reform in this country. The first wave emphasized the need for structural and administrative changes in the nation's judicial system, while this wave emphasizes the alternative dispute resolution techniques explained below (Alfini 1986, 252).

mediation: where third party assists in negotiation of a dispute.

conciliation: where third party proposes compromise solutions to a dispute.

arbitration: where parties agree in advance to abide by decision of third party to avoid litigation.

Alternative dispute resolution (ADR) enters a case after the two parties have been unable to realize an agreement through negotiations, thereby necessitating the assistance of a third "impartial" party to assist in the realization of agreement through mediation, conciliation, or arbitration. In **mediation**, the third party assists the disputing parties in identifying the points of agreement and disagreement and in finding bases of compromise and possible agreement. In **conciliation**, the third party finds possible solutions in the areas of disagreement and proposes these solutions to the disputants. **Arbitration** is a method by which the parties agree in advance to abide by the decision of the third party.

Court-Annexed Arbitration

One of the most important developments in the ADR movement has been the extensive degree to which mandatory court-annexed arbitration has been adopted by state and federal courts. In 1986 there were an estimated two hundred court-administered mandatory arbitration programs in the country's trial courts (Alfini 1986, 271). The first arbitration statute appeared in New York in 1920 and provided a basis for the Uniform Arbitration Act of 1955, a model law that was adopted by most states and the federal government. The federal government has long encouraged arbitration in labor-management disputes and more recently in the area of claims disputes. Court-mandated arbitration, however, is a new concept that is expanding rapidly as a means by which to efficiently handle many types of disputes.

Arbitration is distinguished from mediation by the parties' contract to abide by the arbitrator's decision. The parties select an arbitrator from a specified list of neutral third parties. A mediator, on the other hand, is essentially a third-party facilitator of a negotiated settlement between the disputing parties. Mediation has long been used in marriage counseling and other forms of personality conflicts where a disinterested third party can facilitate communication and amicable settlement of difficult issues more effectively than a court.

Court-annexed arbitration is a process in which judges refer civil suits to arbitrators to render prompt, nonbinding decisions. If a particular decision is not accepted by a losing party, a trial de novo may be held in the court system. Variations of arbitration methods are being experimented with widely, and some of these methods have been thoroughly institutionalized, such as the Philadelphia court-administered arbitration program initiated in 1952 that was the first of its kind.

Binding Arbitration Contracts

Labor-management contracts have commonly used binding arbitration clauses that provide particular rules of arbitration procedure and stipulate in advance the agreed-on method for settling various types of disputes. This method of providing for arbitration in advance has been extended to many business interests, and arbitration is becoming widely used to settle intercompany disputes. Many of these arbitration programs use retired judges as arbitrators, and costs are held to a minimum. Binding arbitration contracts are used in many industries including textile, construction, life and casualty insurance, caning, livestock, air transport, grain and feed, and securities.

The Liability Problem

Civil legal actions cover a wide range of types of disputes, including domestic relations, contract, and real property disputes as well as torts. The major areas of controversy in civil disputes, however, relate to torts. There are many types of torts including not only products liability, but also medical malpractice and other forms of professional malpractice. Workers' compensation is one major controversial issue. These controversial areas have received much publicity and are the subjects of heated debate. Insurance providers argue that huge increases in insurance premiums are caused by increased litigation and excessive awards in these areas.

Torts as a Percentage of Total Civil Cases Filed

The hypothetical *Consumer* case involving a products liability tort was used in this text because it illustrates a major area of controversy. The example demonstrates a number of legal issues including the full range of possible judicial procedures. Tort claims, however, represent only a small percentage of the total number of civil cases filed—less than ten percent in most states according to the National Center for State Courts.

Contract disputes are more numerous than tort claims and account for a larger portion of the court case load. Generally, two to three times as many contract cases are filed in the nation's courts than tort cases. Together contract, real property, and domestic relations disputes constitute the overwhelming majority of civil cases filed in the courts of general jurisdiction. There is insufficient data on the question of whether tort filings have been increasing or declining in relationship to contract and real property cases.

Tort Reform

The **tort reform** movement began as a general reaction on the part of insurance companies and producers who were forced to shoulder the burden of new liability risks. Peter Schuck (1991) refers to this development as the "politicization" of tort law. As illustrated in the *Abbott* case, many states have intervened in this traditional area of common law to enact statutory changes. As a consequence of the two general waves of tort reform activity, first in the late 1970s and then in the latter part of the 1980s, nearly every state legislature has enacted tort reform statutes.

tort reform: movement to modify tort concepts through legislative enactment.

Congress has been embroiled for more than a decade in disputes over new proposals designed to alter or supplant common law rules. The United States Congress has been reluctant to enter this traditional state sphere of authority, but the state changes have been quite far-reaching. "Almost all have been in the direction of limiting liability, most commonly by imposing caps on pain-and-suffering awards and by cutting back on doctrines such as joint liability and punitive damages that the courts had fashioned" (Schuck 1991, 27).

High Visibility Tort Actions

The sensationalism associated with actions like the Dalkon Shield (IUDs) and Bendectin (drug) cases have produced increased awareness of tort actions among the public at large. These cases are often based on what are referred to as "mass latent injury" torts. According to Peter Schuck, "Within this category, asbestos claims clearly drive the case load; asbestos cases accounted for half of the growth in all federal tort cases between 1974 and 1986 (apparently unadjusted for population growth); Bendectin and Dalkon Shield claims together comprised another 4 percent" (Source: U.S. General Accounting Office 1988a, 20–30).

Mass society has produced mass action lawsuits. A class action lawsuit is one in which one or more persons sue or are sued as representatives of a larger group similarly situated. Although class action suits have been possible for many years, their number has increased substantially since the 1940s as they have become vehicles for issues involving civil rights, legislative reapportionment, welfare, consumer protection, and environmental matters.

The courts generally have favored class actions because the suits consolidate litigation and reduce the case load when compared with numerous individual actions. Class action suits, however, reduce the chances of out-of-court settlement, since compromise has to involve all litigants and cannot be made without the court's permission. The class action suit also diminishes the possibility that a case will be dismissed as moot because the original plaintiff has died. A deceased plaintiff's counsel, to continue the suit, need only substitute another member of the class as the plaintiff.

Congress authorized state attorneys general to bring class action antitrust suits on behalf of state citizens in 1976. And in 1984, a federal judge in Philadelphia approved a suit against fifty-five asbestos manufacturers on behalf of the nation's primary and secondary schools, which was reportedly the first nationwide class action for property damage arising out of a products liability question. Federal courts have attempted to reduce the number of class action suits by ruling that each litigant in diversity cases must meet the $50,000 access limit and that all parties in some cases must be notified, but state courts are frequently involved in class action suits.

The Costs of the Tort System

Tort reform advocates point to the excessive economic costs of the American tort system, and frequently attempt to use comparative data from other modern democratic societies to bolster their argument that the excessive cost of our tort system already does, or will eventually, harm our ability to compete in the international economic arena. Domestically the insurance industry claimed record losses in 1984 of $21.5 billion compared with the previous record underwriting loss of $4.2 billion in 1975. Advocates of tort reform also claim that property and casualty losses exceed the country's economic growth as measured by the gross national product (GNP). They attribute the severe insurance crisis to the effect of the expanding tort system and the end of a period of artificially low insurance rates.

Opponents of tort reform claim there is scant evidence connecting the workings of the tort system and skyrocketing liability insurance premiums. "Insurance crises occur cyclically, indicating that these crises are a function of economic conditions rather than of the civil justice system" (Phillips 1986,690). Even though the insurance crisis has abated somewhat, the issues raised are serious. There is considerable disagreement concerning the costs of our tort system and no conclusive method of measuring them. There is also little evidence of an agreed-on classification scheme by which to ascertain how much of the cost is attributable to the peculiar characteristics of our tort system.

Nonetheless, economists have attempted to measure and compare the costs of the tort system in the United States with the costs of such systems in other modern democratic societies. A 1991 study by Tillinghast, a leading insurance industry consulting firm, provides estimates that are the most extreme of any published. The study may overstate the case, but the figures include comparative costs for other countries (see Figure 7-1). This study concludes that our tort system may be twice as expensive as the tort systems of other modern industrial societies. The Tillinghast study includes information about self-insurers in the data on the United States, but not in that on other countries, which may mean the United States figures are overstated; however, it also, in principle, understates the United States figures because it excludes costs of diverting corporate officials from their regular responsibilities and costs of risk avoidance measures.

This two percent "liability tax," as it is referred to by the tort reformers, is an alarming statistic, and the reasons for this apparent disparity should be examined. Conservatively estimated, the tort system costs $100 billion annually, including liability insurance costs and awards. Only about twenty-five percent of this total cost, according to Tillinghast, is paid to compensate victims' economic losses. According to tort reformers, any cost above this amount is without corresponding benefits.

Tort Differences in Other Countries

The litigious nature of American society produces a magnitude of legal actions that is not matched by any other society, with the possible exception of the United Kingdom. It is often assumed that the extreme number of lawyers in the United States causes this excessive amount of litigation.

It is true that the United States has proportionately more lawyers than other countries. There are roughly four times as many lawyers per 100,000 population in the United States than in Australia, Belgium, Canada, Denmark, France, Italy, Japan, Spain, Switzerland, the United Kingdom, or Germany. These countries are the most advanced industrial societies and our chief economic competitors. However, the premises of the above argument, that lawyers generate their own litigation, is contentious.

Do American Lawyers Generate Their Own Demand?

There are plenty of examples of unscrupulous lawyers who engage in ethically prohibited practices often referred to as "ambulance chasing." Accident victims

FIGURE 7.1 A Twelve-country Comparison of Tort Costs as a Percentage of Gross Domestic Product (GDP) 1991

Country	Tort Costs (% of GDP)
DENMARK	.4%
UNITED KINGDOM	.6%
JAPAN	.7%
AUSTRALIA	.9%
CANADA	.9%
FRANCE	.9%
SWITZERLAND	1.0%
SPAIN	1.0%
BELGIUM	1.2%
WEST GERMANY	1.2%
ITALY	1.3%
UNITED STATES	2.3%

Note: Gross tort costs for the U.S. include self-insured payments for liability claims. Gross tort costs for all other countries exclude self-insured payments (and include only liability insurance premiums).
Reprinted from: Robert Sturgis, *Tort Cost Trends 1992: An International Perspective*, a report by Tillinghast, the risk management and actuarial consulting arm of Towers Perrin.

are frequently contacted by lawyers and encouraged to at least discuss the possibility of taking legal action. There are also widespread reports of lawyers hiring unemployed persons to stand outside workers' compensation claims offices to pass out the lawyer's cards to existing claimants and encourage them to discuss their cases with the lawyer. Such unethical practices undoubtedly take place, in fact, many states have reported increasing numbers of complaints against lawyers, especially in times of economic recession.

On the other hand, there are several arguments that offset the idea that lawyers create their own demand for litigation. Most litigation that is frivolous or unwarranted is ultimately weeded out through dismissals. In addition, some evidence suggests that a relatively small percentage of potential tort victims actually file lawsuits. Two recent studies of the incidence of malpractice suggest that roughly one percent of patients admitted to hospitals incurred negligently caused injuries, but only a small fraction of these victims (ten percent in one study and less than three percent in the other) filed lawsuits. Moreover, most of the victims who did file tort claims received no payments through the system (Schuck 1991, 26).

Differences in Lawyers' Fees

Perhaps the most important difference affecting litigation rates between the United States and the other countries analyzed by the Tillinghast study is that none of these other countries allow the use of contingency fee contracts. The widespread practice of American lawyers offering their services contingent upon winning damage awards is a powerful inducement to potential plaintiffs to file lawsuits, especially when there is no penalty for failure. Other countries require the losing party in a civil legal action to pay the lawyer fees of both parties, which effectively eliminates any use of contingency fee contracts and restrains lawyers from filing frivolous or unsubstantiated claims.

In addition to contingency fee agreements, awards for **pain and suffering** are a widely accepted form of recovery in the United States. These awards may account for as much as twenty-five percent of total compensation paid to victims in tort cases. Such awards are generally not allowed in other countries. Lawyers in these countries are poorer than those in the United States, but most of them are adequately compensated through the method of assessment of lawyer fees by the court.

pain and suffering: term used to describe not only physical distress but also mental and emotional trauma that are recoverable as elements of damage in torts.

Access to the Courts

American lawyers counter that the use of the contingency fee contract provides legal services to poor and indigent victims, thus equalizing access to the courts. They argue that the American legal system affords greater access to the courts than do the systems in other industrial societies. Access to the courts is more restricted in most of the countries examined in the Tillinghast study than in the United States, although some of them have provisions that facilitate access by indigents to the courts.

Differences in Health, Hospital, and Medical Costs

A second major difference between the United States and other modern industrial societies is that we have the most expensive health care system in the world. Health care costs generally are considered to be as much as twice the comparable per capita health care costs in other countries. Health care costs in the United States are a major concern on the nation's political agenda. Our health care costs have been rising at more than double the inflation rate, while other major industrial nations have had some success in controlling these costs.

Other modern industrial societies have national health care schemes that include extensive governmental regulation of medical providers, drug prices, insurance companies, and safety standards. Most countries also have comprehensive national health insurance systems or some form of socialized medicine, and the bureaucracies that oversee the public interest in the insurance and health industries are more effective than those in the United States.

Cost differences in health care may account for a substantial amount of the difference in tort costs between the United States and other countries suggested by the Tillinghast study. Medical expenses are a major part of tort settlement and insurance costs.

Administrative Law Courts

Several modern industrial societies, such as France and Germany, have extensively developed administrative law courts that handle a significant part of the load carried by our civil courts. These court systems are discussed more fully in Chapter Thirteen in connection with the characteristics of American administrative legal procedures.

Strict Liability Differences

The United Kingdom, the source of our common law legal heritage, developed a concept of strict liability similar to that expressed in section 402A of the *Restatement (Second) of Torts* around the same time the concept was emerging in the United States. Other common law countries that share this legal development include Australia and Canada.

The other countries in our comparative sample, Belgium, Denmark, France, Italy, Spain, Switzerland, and West Germany, are traditionally civil law countries that share a Roman code law tradition. Even Japan has adopted significant aspects of the characteristic civil law tradition associated with the continental European countries.

Some tort reform advocates in the United States support legislative repeal of the concept of strict liability in the products liability area. The tort reform movement has had little success in changing this concept. The trend is in the opposite direction; many countries of the European Community are extending the strict liability concept.

Most of the civil law countries have maintained the older negligence standard of proof of failure to exercise due care, but West Germany has had considerable experience with a strict liability concept similar to our own. This indigenous standard requires a manufacturer who is sued for damages from a defective product to prove that it exercised due care in the manufacture or development of the products. This concept shifts the burden of proof to the defendant.

Giulio Ponzanelli, professor of comparative law at Pisa Law School in Italy, proclaims that the most interesting development in civil law in Europe during the last decade is the progressive adoption of the standard of strict liability by the member states of the European Community. In 1985, the Council of European Communities adopted a directive ordering each member state to adopt a statute providing for strict liability for product defects. The directive is based on the American model as illustrated in the *Restatement (Second) of Torts*, section 402A (Ponzanelli, in Schuck 1991, 238–39).

All United States trading partners, including Japan, are liable under our laws when injury occurs in this country because of a dangerously defective product. Modern industrial nations are coordinating their policies with regard to strict liability because they recognize that the principle of law involves a powerful inducement to manufacturers to produce and sell safe products.

Jury Trial Differences

Jury trials in civil cases are more available in the United States than in England and other common law countries in which only libel and slander cases are tried before juries. The civil law countries do not use juries in civil cases, and the **nonadversarial process** that characterizes the civil law concept differs substantially from the process used in common law countries.

Critics of our jury trial system and adversarial process argue that our court procedure places too much emphasis on the skills of the advocate. The **adversarial process**, which characterizes common law proceedings, requires competent lawyers to argue and develop the facts before a neutral and impartial jury. If the advocates are not equally competent and diligent in their pursuit of their clients' interests, the system may fail to produce a just result.

The British system of allowing only the most highly qualified lawyers (barristers) to argue cases at trial is the United Kingdom's attempt to solve the problem suggested by this criticism. The civil law countries use a different approach to trials that places far less emphasis on the skills of the opposing lawyers. Rather than being lawyer-centered, these proceedings are judge-centered in that panels of judges conduct the trial proceedings. In the nonadversarial process, the judges call the witnesses and question them to obtain factual evidence. This process assumes that the court decision makers, not merely the interested parties, should be allowed to ask the questions of the witnesses. American juries, in contrast, usually cannot ask questions of witnesses.

nonadversarial process: inquisitorial process associated with civil law countries in which judges play an active role in questioning witnesses.

adversarial process: descriptive of common law trial procedures in contested cases in which lawyers play the dominant role in questioning witnesses.

German Civil Procedures

The German trial process in civil cases offers an interesting contrast to the adversarial trial process in the American tradition. The German courts have institutionalized a court-administered mediation process in noncriminal cases that resembles some of the forms of alternative dispute resolution that have become widespread in the United States. The German civil trial process is divided into two basic stages: "the first instance," which is similar to a preliminary hearing, and the second "contested" phase, which is the more formal trial.

The First Instance

After a civil legal action is filed, the court sets a date for the first instance hearing. Both parties to the dispute are required to be represented (either by lawyers or in person), and the hearing is conducted informally by a panel of three judges. The judges hear an oral presentation of both sides in the dispute, then comment on the applicable law governing the subject matter of the dispute and seek to clarify factual issues in dispute. They also offer suggestions to encourage voluntary settlement of the issues. The judges' clarification of the law often encourages settlement.

The More Formal Trial

If settlement cannot be reached at the first instance hearing, a trial can be demanded by either party. The trial is conducted in a nonadversarial manner in which the judge plays a more active role than does a judge in our courts. Again the court consists of three judges who will ultimately decide the dispute. The lawyers petition the court concerning witnesses to be called and evidence to be presented; however, the judges do the basic questioning of the witnesses. The lawyers may be given an opportunity to pose questions to the witnesses after the judges have finished questioning them, but the procedure is definitely judge-dominated rather than lawyer-dominated, as in our adversarial process.

Since there are no juries, there is little opportunity to play to the sympathy of lay citizens. Trial procedures regarding presentation of evidence, consequently, are less cumbersome and greatly simplified in comparison with our complex rules of civil procedure. Costs are reduced by several methods that are not available, or seldom used, in American courts.

Cost Factors

In the German civil law process, the party against whom judgment is rendered—the losing party—is responsible for paying the court costs and the court-assessed lawyers' fees for the opposing party. Thus, if a plaintiff brings suit for damages and fails to prove the case, that person must pay all the costs of the legal process for both sides.

In American courts, a person can be sued in civil court and be forced to hire a lawyer, which can cost the defendant a substantial amount of money (thousands of dollars) that will not be recovered even if the plaintiff fails to prove the case. The plaintiff has to pay the court costs upon failure to prove the case, but this expense is often minor.

One of the greatest expenses in modern American civil trials is payment of expert witnesses. In Germany, the opposing parties petition the court to call experts, and the court selects the experts and exercises control over their competence in their fields of expertise The court determines the cost of these witnesses and assesses the cost to the losing party.

Since there are no juries in German civil trials, the three judges decide the dispute by majority vote. They decide all questions of fact and law in dispute. One factual question that is almost always given to the jury in American jury trials is that of determining monetary damages. In German courts, the judges make this determination based upon standards that show greater consistency and predictability in outcomes achieved—which, in turn, provides a strong basis for first instance settlement in future cases.

The argument that contingency fee contracts provide greater access of the poor to American courts is countered, in Germany, by a procedure that allows indigents to obtain judicial authority to litigate. A judge may authorize court-supported counsel if the judge determines that the indigent-plaintiff's case has legal merit. Plaintiffs are somewhat disadvantaged, however, because they risk being assessed for the entire cost of the legal procedure if they lose.

In German civil process, the concept of "private law" is less pronounced than in American courts. In the United States, the basic concept is that private parties are allowed access to the courts to settle a purely private matter that is in dispute. German courts recognize the community interest involved in civil disputes, and government takes an active part in defending that interest. Not only are the judges in Germany representative of the community interest, but the state prosecutor also is given a role in some civil cases in which a recognized public interest is involved.

Some civil law countries allow criminal prosecutions to include civil damage claims as well. The German courts do not allow such dual purpose trials;

however, they allow potential civil litigants to participate in and have access to the evidence of criminal trials that may be used in civil trials.

Appellate Differences

The German appeals process displays a typical difference between civil and common law procedures in that new trials can be conducted by the appellate courts. New facts can be considered in some cases, and the facts can be adjudicated again at a higher level.

Conclusion

The major differences between modern industrial societies that have been discussed in this chapter are extensive; however, any attempt to isolate single factors and attribute the tort cost differences to them would be in error. Cultural differences among the countries are, perhaps, the more significant variable in that they condition attitudes about dispute settlement and affect orientations toward adjudication of disputes. The strength of family ties and other forms of social stability in many of these countries contribute to the settlement of disputes without adjudication. In Japan, these factors are particularly pronounced, and there seems to be a cultural taboo against civil suits among average citizens. Negotiation, mediation, conciliation, and arbitration are used extensively in many countries as alternate dispute settlement techniques.

CHAPTER SUMMARY

1. The appeals process is characterized by a review of the entire record of the trial court proceeding and concerns the appellate court's error correction and law development functions. The intermediate appeals courts are primarily involved in error correction and are most concerned about the trial judge's conduct of the due process of law.

2. A finding of prejudicial error or legal error may result in reversal of the trial judgment or in remand of the case back to the trial court for further fact-finding procedures. These decisions are made by a majority of a panel of judges that includes at least three members.

3. The law development function is usually reserved to the court of last resort, which is the state supreme court in questions of state law. When all opportunity for appeal is exhausted, the case is res judicata or brought to a final conclusion.

4. The traditional concept of strict liability in tort has been altered by statutory exceptions that seek to accommodate new demands for change. Actual cases in modern times are complex and demand consideration of many legal issues related to the public interest.

5. Modern class action law suits have increased public awareness of a growing litigation and liability crisis in our legal system. Not only the number of cases but also the increased costs of our tort system are major problems affecting the civil process.

6. Recent trends indicate a slowing of the growth rate in numbers of cases filed and appealed. The overwhelming majority of cases filed are dropped, dismissed, or settled out of court; less than ten percent are contested, and most of these are handled in bench trials. Only about one percent of the total cases filed in civil courts are handled by jury trials.

7. Alternative dispute resolution (ADR) techniques involving mediation, conciliation, and arbitration are becoming widely used as a means of dispute settlement that does not involve the full range of judicial process.

8. The liability problem is related primarily to the area of civil law known as torts. However, torts are only a small percentage of the civil case load of the courts; cases concerning contracts, domestic relations, and real property far outweigh the tort cases. Tort disputes constitute only about ten percent of the civil cases filed.

9. The modern tort reform movement has raised major issues in the area of torts, and this area is the most controversial area involving the civil law process. Highly publicized class action law suits and press reports of problems associated with insurance premiums and tort damage awards have increased public awareness of the problems in this area of law.

10. The costs of the tort system in the United States have been estimated to be nearly twice the costs of comparable systems in other modern democratic societies.

11. Tort procedures in other countries demonstrate that several factors may account for the vast difference in tort costs between the United States and other modern industrial societies. The practice in other countries of assessing all litigation costs to the losing party, the differences in health care costs and health care systems, and cultural orientations are some of the significant factors.

12. Civil law countries use a nonadversarial trial procedure that is substantially different from the adversarial methods used in American courts. The German courts have several interesting features that may account for some of the differences in tort costs and litigation management.

KEY TERMS

final judgment	satisfaction of judgment	arbitration
appellant	estoppel	tort reform
prejudicial error	class action suit	pain and suffering
appellate brief	mediation	nonadversarial process
appellee	conciliation	adversarial process
res judicata		

DISCUSSION QUESTIONS

1. What are the most important functions of the appellate courts?

2. How are decisions made by the panel of appeals court judges, and how may the actions of these judges affect the trial court judgment?

3. How is a civil legal action finally terminated, and what are the consequences of this final termination?

4. How important was the law in determining the outcome in the hypothetical *Consumer* case? Would "governmental standards" and "state of the art testing" exceptions have made a difference?

5. What are some of the most important issues in the area of civil litigation in the United States?

6. Is there really a litigation crisis that threatens to overwhelm our courts?

7. What alternative dispute resolution (ADR) techniques are available to reduce the case load of the overloaded courts?

8. Is there a liability crisis concerning the costs and benefits of the American tort system?

9. Should we use juries to decide questions of fact in dispute (particularly monetary awards) in civil cases?

10. Should expert witnesses be designated by the court and the expenses billed to the losing party in the final judgment?

11. Should we develop a policy of awarding lawyer fees as part of the satisfaction of judgment required of losing parties in civil cases?

12. Should pain and suffering be eliminated from the damages that can be recovered in tort cases?

13. Do the practices in other countries suggest alternatives for court reform measures that might be introduced without drastically changing the character of our adversarial system?

SOURCES AND SUGGESTED READING

Alfini, James J., ed. 1986. "Alternative Dispute Resolution and the Courts: An Introduction." *Judicature* 69 (February–March).

Abadinsky, Howard. 1991. *Law and Justice: An Introduction to the American Legal System*. Chicago: Nelson-Hall Publishers.

Abraham, Henry J. 1986. *The Judicial Process*. 5th ed. New York: Oxford University Press.

Carp, Robert A., and Ronald Stidham. 1990. *Judicial Process in America*. Washington D.C.: Congressional Quarterly, Inc.

Glendon, Mary Ann, Michael W. Gordon, and Christopher Osakwe. 1982. *Comparative Legal Traditions*. St. Paul: West Publishing Co.

Litan, Robert E. 1991. "The Liability Explosion and American Trade Performance: Myths and Realities." In *Tort Law and the Public Interest*, edited by Peter H. Schuck. New York: W.W. Norton & Co.

Martineau, Robert J. 1985. *Fundamentals of Modern Appellate Advocacy*. Law student and moot court ed. Rochester, N.Y.: Lawyers Co-operative Publishing Co.

Murphy, Walter F., and C. Herman Pritchett. 1986. *Courts, Judges, and Politics: An Introduction to the Judicial Process*. 4th ed. New York: Random House.

National Center for State Courts. 1990. *State Court Caseload Statistics: Annual Report 1988*. Williamsburg, Va.: National Center for State Courts. (See also Annual Report 1991.)

Phillips, Jerry J. 1986. "Comments on the Report of the Governor's Commission on Tort and Liability Insurance Reform." *Tennessee Law Review* 53.

Ponzanelli, Guilio. 1991. "The European Community Directive on Products Liability." In *Tort Law and the Public Interest*, edited by Peter H. Schuck. New York: W.W. Norton & Co.

Posner, Richard A. 1985. *The Federal Courts: Crisis and Reform*. Cambridge, Mass.: Harvard University Press.

Schuck, Peter H. ed. 1991. *Tort Law and the Public Interest: Competition, Innovation and Consumer Welfare*. New York: W.W. Norton & Co.

Tillinghast, *Tort Cost Trends 1992: An International Perspective*. From a report authored by Robert Sturgis and published by Tillinghast, the risk management and actuarial consulting arm of Tower Perrin, 100 Summit Lake Drive, Valhalla, NY 10595.

CHAPTER EIGHT

LEGAL RESEARCH: DIMENSIONS OF THE LAW

> "There are no flat rules in legal research. But one that comes close is: check the statutes first."
>
> Alfred J. Lewis

By now the reader of this textbook has begun to realize the vast and complex nature of the modern legal system in the United States. No single individual or group of individuals can truthfully claim to command knowledge of all aspects of the law. It is said that "ignorance of the law is no excuse" for its violation. However, even the most law-abiding and well-meaning person must seek legal advice to avoid violating our complex laws.

Most legal professionals are involved in the process, not of dispute resolution, but of dispute prevention. Only a small fraction of lawyers today consider themselves to be trial advocates. The overwhelming majority of practicing attorneys are engaged in activities on a daily basis that attempt to provide competent legal advice to clients to prevent legal disputes from arising in the first place. These professionals are licensed by law to provide such advice and are ethically and legally bound to do so in a competent manner. Giving incompetent legal advice can result in a malpractice action against a lawyer or a charge of practicing law without a license against a nonlawyer.

The central function of professional law schools is to train competent individuals and equip them with the tools of research and conceptual knowledge that will enable them to provide client services that meet the high standards of the profession. In law school, the student is required to take an entire course in legal research, and all other courses are designed to contribute to a greater understanding of the proper use of legal research tools.

This chapter, in an introductory textbook designed for undergraduates, clearly is not intended to mislead students into believing that they can become lawyers overnight, or even that they can become competent to give themselves legal advice in most situations. As educated citizens, however, we need to know how to find the law and be able to read it with some degree of understanding. That degree of understanding may simply mean knowing enough to seek competent legal advice. Law enforcement officers, paralegals, and administrators must develop special skills in research and interpretation of the law.

An elementary overview of the vast field of legal research is provided in this chapter to give the reader an understanding of the dimensions of the substantive law areas and how to find information about them in the library. Since libraries vary considerably in their holdings, the focus is on the most basic of the extensive legal research tools available. A student who intends to continue education in a law-related profession will need additional courses in substantive law areas and legal research; this overview will be helpful to the beginner but is not intended to be comprehensive.

The historical evolution of our law and its varied sources and methods of application have already been examined. The remaining chapters continue to provide practical examples in discussing criminal and administrative substantive law, but examples are, of necessity, anecdotal and cannot cover the comprehensive dimensions of basic legal research tools. Knowledge of how to look up the specific rules of law and update this information with the most current sources is necessary if one is to stay abreast of our dynamic and ever-changing legal system.

HOW TO USE STATE AND FEDERAL ANNOTATED CODES

Alfred J. Lewis, one of the many authors of textbooks on how to use American law books, says, "There are no flat rules in legal research. But one that comes close is: *check the statutes first*" (Lewis 1985,59). This statement is good advice, because the legislatures at the state and national levels are recognized today as the primary agents of law-making authority. Their extraordinary activity in the last half century has resulted in massive expansion of statutory enactments and the codification of many areas of law that were previously governed exclusively by our common law tradition. As we have demonstrated in the illustrations associated with the hypothetical *Consumer* case, many aspects of the common law are no longer "private law" but have been elevated to "public law" by statutory enactment that takes precedence over the common law.

Statutes are enacted by the legislatures in each of the fifty states and the national Congress every year. They create new legal obligations and revise older ones. In order to understand the applicable law on a given subject, we must have some comprehensive tool that enables us to locate the current rule and be able to predict, with some degree of accuracy, the manner in which the courts will enforce the rule. This task is not simple. If we had to depend only on the publications produced by the legislatures, we would be lost.

Laws passed during the sessions of the legislative institutions in the United States are published in chronological order of their enactment and usually given the title of "Statutes at Large" or "Acts." These session laws are published in the form in which they are enacted into law, but using these publications to determine the current law on a given subject would be highly inefficient.

Fortunately, comprehensive codes break these statutes into subject elements, index them for easy reference, and supplement them with current enactments, revisions, and deletions. The annotated versions of these codes for each jurisdiction provide citations to key court interpretations and commentary to promote analytical understanding of the meaning of the "black letter law" of the statutes. Thus, the annotated codes provide citations to the three basic elements of the law: statutes, cases, and commentary.

State Annotated Codes

Where the researcher begins depends a great deal upon where he or she wants to go. The first rule is to frame the legal question as precisely as possible. The question must be narrowed to one for which an answer can be found that will resolve the issue at hand.

Problem No. 1

Look up the state statutory law on a particular subject that is of current interest, using the state's annotated code.

1. State the legal question precisely before starting and indicate why this subject would be governed by state law rather than federal law.
2. Explain what key descriptor terms are used to locate the referenced title and section of the code.
3. Explain the answer gained from the code in terms of specific statutory wording and citation to sources of interpretation and commentary. Be sure to check for updated information in the pocket part (or freestanding) supplement in the back jacket cover of the volume.

The reader may want to choose a researchable topic from the earlier discussions of the legal issues involved in the hypothetical *Consumer* case and look up the relevant state statutory provisions concerning "products liability" ("strict liability" may be the wrong term).

This assignment can be as simple or as complicated as the reader decides. The main goal is to become familiar with this basic legal research tool. Each state has its own annotated code that is an officially recognized source of the law currently in force. The code can be found in the reference sections of college libraries. Even the smallest law firm would consider this series of legal volumes essential for the practice of law in that jurisdiction. Libraries, however, even those of some law schools, find the cost of subscribing to the annotated codes of all fifty states prohibitive.

Most law books are designed for practicing lawyers, not for scholars. They are practical tools designed to answer specific questions pertaining to legal issues within a particular jurisdiction. Legal research is analytical, not mechanical, in nature. It differs from research in any other field, and it is rarely easy or straightforward because the law emanates from many sources and develops in complex ways. The law is not static, but is a dynamic, constantly evolving set of rules and procedures. The reader must use his or her mind and knowledge about the law to think of conflicts that may exist and analogous circumstances that may be covered by a general rule.

In selecting a research topic for problem no. 1, try to avoid topics that may be covered by local ordinances, such as "disturbing the peace." State laws relate to these topics in that "enabling legislation" has been passed to allow local units of government (cities and counties) to formulate their own local laws subject to state limitations. The organizational structures of local units of government are found in city charters and "private acts" of the legislature in most states. These local matters are not included in the state codes and would probably require local consultation or references. State constitutional provisions and public law statutes, however, are included in the code and will define the areas of local discretionary authority.

The annotated state code is a multivolume series that includes an annotated version of the United States Constitution, the state constitution, and all public acts. It is more authoritative than cases, administrative regulations, and other sources of the law; and it is the most efficient and complete of all legal research tools for the jurisdiction in question.

Once this set of volumes has been located in the library and an appropriate research topic has been chosen, the general index volume at the end of the series should be consulted to find the reference to the topic. This step may be difficult, since the descriptor terms the reader chooses may not be the terms used by the publishers to index the subject matter. The forward to the index will help by explaining how the index is organized and by providing some basic rules for using the index. It may surprise the reader to learn that there is no single index to the laws of all the states (Lewis 1985, 6).

The following general suggestions apply to the use of almost all legal tools:

1. Gain familiarity with the contents of the tool by consulting the publisher's explanations about use of the tool located in the first few pages of the volume.
2. Consult the principal subject, not the secondary subject. For example, look under MOTOR VEHICLES, not under REGISTRATION.
3. Look for the noun, not the adjective. Thus, for life insurance, look under INSURANCE, not under LIFE.
4. Consult the most pertinent subject. Thus, for depositions, look under DEPOSITIONS, not under EVIDENCE or TESTIMONY or WITNESSES.
5. Consult allied headings if the search under one heading is to no avail. Thus, if a search under the heading LARCENY is fruitless, try THEFT or EMBEZZLEMENT or STOLEN GOODS or other related headings.
6. Use cross-references.
7. Use reasoning capacity—continue the search until what reason implies must exist has been found.

The federal codes have fifty basic titles that provide the important divisions of the codes. All codes are arranged by subject, and all the statutory law for that jurisdiction is organized under such headings as Constitutions, Agriculture, Taxation, Vehicles, Civil Procedure, Education, and so on. An overview of a state's arrangement may be gained by glancing at the information on the spines as the set sits on the shelf. The subjects in the federal codes are given a title number (the first two numbers) and then divided into sections; some state codes are arranged in the same manner. Another common method of organization is the use of continuous section numbers from beginning to end of the entire set. In California, New York, and other states, the codes are labeled by name of subject matter and section (for example, Cal. Penal Code § 1243; N.Y. Educ. Law § 2585).

Once the research topic has been found in the appropriate bound volume of the code, the heading and contents at the beginning of that particular chapter (or section) should be read in order to gain an overview of the subject matter context for the particular rule (see Figure 8-1). Note that the correct citation to the statute is given in the "source note" (see "Short title" in Figure 8-1). Next, read the entire section of the "black letter law" and note particularly the definitions provided. Statutory language is very deliberate—each word counts. What does the statute say precisely about the topic? Does it answer the question or raise new questions?

| 29-28-101 | REMEDIES AND SPECIAL PROCEEDINGS | 498 |

CHAPTER 28
PRODUCTS LIABILITY ACTIONS

SECTION.
29-28-101. Short title.
29-28-102. Definitions.
29-28-103. Limitation of actions — Exception.
29-28-104. Compliance with government standards — Rebuttable presumption.
29-28-105. Determination of defective or dangerous condition.

SECTION.
29-28-106. Seller's liability.
29-28-107. Complaint — Statement of damages.
29-28-108. Product altered or abnormally used.

29-28-101. Short title. — This chapter shall be known and may be cited as the "Tennessee Products Liability Act of 1978." [Acts 1978 (Adj. S.), ch. 703, § 1; T.C.A., § 23-3701.]

Law Reviews. Statutes of Limitations — Personal Injury, Property Damage and Breach of Warranty, 8 Mem. St. U.L. Rev. 803.
The Tennessee Products Liability Act, 9 Mem. St. U.L. Rev. 105.
The Tennessee Products Liability Act of 1978 (Irvin L. Tankersley), 14-4 Tenn. B.J. 11.
Comparative Legislation. Products liability actions:
Ala. Code, tit. 6, §§ 6-5-500 — 6-5-525.
Ark. Stat. Ann. §§ 34-2801 — 34-2807.
Ky. Rev. Stat. Ann. §§ 411.300 — 411.350.
N.C. Gen. Stat. §§ 99B-1 — 99B-10.

Va. Code § 8.2-318.
Cited: Commercial Truck & Trailer Sales, Inc. v. McCampbell, 580 S.W.2d 765 (Tenn. 1979).
Collateral References. 63 Am. Jur. 2d Products Liability §§ 1-4.
77 C.J.S. Supplement Products Liability §§ 1-6.
Promotional efforts directed toward prescribing physician as affecting prescription drug manufacturer's liability for product-caused injury. 94 A.L.R.3d 1080.

29-28-102. Definitions. — As used in this chapter unless the context otherwise requires:

(1) "Anticipated life." The anticipated life of a product shall be determined by the expiration date placed on the product by the manufacturer when required by law but shall not commence until the date the product was first purchased for use or consumption.

(2) "Defective condition" means a condition of a product that renders it unsafe for normal or anticipatable handling and consumption.

(3) "Employer" means any person exercising legal supervisory control or guidance of users or consumers of products.

(4) "Manufacturer" means the designer, fabricator, producer, compounder, processor or assembler of any product or its component parts.

(5) "Product" means any tangible object or goods produced.

(6) "Product liability action" for purposes of this chapter shall include all actions brought for or on account of personal injury, death or property damage caused by or resulting from the manufacture, construction, design, formula, preparation, assembly, testing, service, warning, instruction, marketing, packaging or labeling of any product. It shall include, but not be limited to, all actions based upon the following theories: strict liability in tort; negligence;

[SEE TABLE IN FRONT OF THIS VOLUME FOR CHANGES IN SECTION NUMBERING]

Figure 8.1 State Annotated Code, Main Volume Page

Permission for the publication of sections of Tennessee Code Annotated was granted by the State of Tennessee.

There is a wealth of information surrounding the "black letter law" that is very valuable when one is thoroughly researching the law on a particular subject. The annotations refer to primary and secondary sources related to each section of the code. All leads need not be followed, but the major advantage of an annotated code is the provision of these citations.

Citation form is crucial. The reader's ability to follow the cryptic instructions in the citations and find the referenced material efficiently depends on citation form. Hence, there must be uniformity. The most widely recognized compilation of citation rules is *The Bluebook: A Uniform System of Citation* published by the Harvard Law Review Association. It is often referred to as simply the "bluebook." The reader should note the form of the citations in the state code in order to begin learning correct citation form. Use correct citations to identify the most authoritative sources of statements when taking notes or writing reports.

Read the annotations. Check the pocket part supplements, which include both changes to the statutes and updated citations to other sources (see Figure 8-2, note updated citations). Legal Encyclopedia and *American Law Reports* (A.L.R.) citations may be of particular importance in broadening the reader's understanding of particular concepts.

Corpus Juris Secundum (C.J.S.) and *American Jurisprudence 2d* (Am. Jur. 2d) are the two national encyclopedias with which the reader should be familiar. These publications are useful for gaining a quick overview in an unfamiliar area of the law. They provide pithy summaries and historical background notes along with copious case citations for jurisdictions throughout the United States. Many states also have encyclopedias and they are excellent sources as well.

American Law Reports (A.L.R.) is an annotated reporter. This publication is a powerful tool that selects cases from throughout the country that are particularly good illustrations of points of law (because of the facts, the opinion, or both). It is now in the fourth edition and includes a state (all states in one) and a federal series. The annotations focus on legal topics that are considerably more narrow than the topic headings in encyclopedias and are superseded by more up-to-date annotations later in the series. Many college libraries do not have these extensive annotated reports. Lawyers, however, find them very useful.

Law review articles, treatises, comparative legislation, and references to other publications are frequently cited in annotated codes (see annotation headings in Figures 8-1 and 8-2). The federal codes include historical notes and citations to administrative regulations.

Case references for a particular state jurisdiction are the most authoritative and significant annotations because they reveal how the wording of the statute has been interpreted (see "Notes to Decisions" in Figure 8-2). These annotations include brief statements explaining how the case affected the statute's interpretation. However, these statements are not authoritative themselves. The entire case must be read in the reporter to ascertain precisely how this case affects a particular problem. These statements are not official holdings, but they are useful in narrowing the search to those cases that relate specifically to the problem.

Federal Codes

There are three sets of parallel federal codes that are similar to the state codes but are organized differently because of the federal subject matter jurisdiction. These three federal statutory codes are:

CHAPTER 28
PRODUCTS LIABILITY ACTIONS

SECTION.
29-28-106. Seller's liability.

29-28-101. Short title.

Textbooks. Tennessee Jurisprudence, 18 Tenn. Juris., Limitations of Actions, § 45.

Law Reviews. Comments on the Report of the Governor's Commission on Tort and Liability Insurance Reform (Jerry J. Phillips), 53 Tenn. L. Rev. 679 (1986).

Constitutional Law — Limitation of Actions — Application of the Products Liability Statute of Repose, 52 Tenn. L. Rev. 97 (1984).

Constitutional Law — Limitation of Actions — Application of the Vested Rights Doctrine (David A. King), 51 Tenn. L. Rev. 129 (1983).

Economic Loss in Strict Liability — Beyond the Realm of 402 A (Joe E. Manuel and Gregory B. Richards), 16 Mem. St. U.L. Rev. 315 (1986).

Mass Tort Litigation in Tennessee (Paul Campbell, III and Hugh J. Moore, Jr.), 53 Tenn. L. Rev. 221 (1986).

Power of Sale Foreclosure in Tennessee: A Section 1983 Trap (Jack Jones and J. Michael Ivens), 51 Tenn. L. Rev. 279 (1984).

Products Liability — Lessors as Warrantors of Fitness in Tennessee, 16 Mem. St. U.L. Rev. 303 (1986).

Symposium: On Product "Design Defects" and Their Actionability (John W. Wade), 33 Vand. L. Rev. 551.

Symposium: Rethinking the Policies of Strict Products Liability (David G. Owen), 33 Vand. L. Rev. 681.

The Exclusiveness of an Employee's Workers' Compensation Remedy Against His Employer (Joseph H. King, Jr.), 55 Tenn. L. Rev. 405 (1988).

1985 Tennessee Survey: Selected Developments in Tennessee Law, 53 Tenn. L. Rev. 415 (1986).

Cited: Caldwell v. Ford Motor Co., 619 S.W.2d 534 (Tenn. Ct. App. 1981); Pemberton v. American Distilled Spirits Co., 664 S.W.2d 690 (Tenn. 1984); Harrison v. Celotex Corp., 583 F. Supp. 1497 (E.D. Tenn. 1984); Murphy v. Owens-Illinois, Inc., 779 F.2d 340 (6th Cir. 1985); Higgs v. GMC, 655 F. Supp. 22 (E.D. Tenn. 1985); Baker v. Promark Prods. W., Inc., 692 S.W.2d 844 (Tenn. 1985); Myers v. Hayes Int'l Corp., 701 F. Supp. 618 (M.D. Tenn. 1988); Goode v. Tamko Asphalt Prods., Inc., 783 S.W.2d 184 (Tenn. 1989); Brown v. McKinnon Bridge Co., 732 F. Supp. 1479 (E.D. Tenn. 1989).

NOTES TO DECISIONS

ANALYSIS

1. Constitutionality.
2. Punitive damages.

1. Constitutionality.

Tennessee Const., art. II, § 17 imposes two requirements: first, a bill is to embrace one subject that is expressed in the bill's title, second, any act repealing or amending another act must state as much in the caption or title of the repealing act. The Tennessee Products Liability Act of 1978 embraces the one subject mentioned in its title, that of products liability, and it would be unreasonable to require that every important particularity of an act be mentioned in its title. The Tennessee Constitution makes no such requirement. As for the second requirement of Tenn. Const., art. II, § 17, the act does not repeal, alter, or amend § 28-3-104. In § 29-28-103, the limitation of actions provision of the act, the general one-year statute of limitations (§ 28-3-104) is expressly mentioned as remaining in effect. The 10-year ceiling does not amend existing limitations but is superimposed upon them. Stutts v. Ford Motor Co., 574 F. Supp. 100 (M.D. Tenn. 1983).

2. Punitive Damages.

Under Tennessee law an asbestos product liability claimant can recover punitive damages if he meets the Tennessee standard for the awarding of punitive damages. Cathey v. Johns-Manville Sales Corp., 776 F.2d 1565 (6th Cir. 1985), cert. denied, 478 U.S. 1021, 106 S. Ct. 3335, 92 L. Ed. 2d 740 (1986).

Permission for the publication of sections of Tennessee Code Annotated was granted by the State of Tennessee.

Figure 8.2 State Annotated Code, Pocket Part Supplement Page

1. *United States Code* (U.S.C.): An official publication by the United States Government Printing Office. It is not annotated.
2. *United States Code Annotated* (U.S.C.A.): Includes everything in the official U.S.C. but adds annotations and citations to aid further research. Published by West Publishing Company.
3. *United States Code Service* (U.S.C.S.): Also includes everything in the official code but adds annotations and citations of an extensive nature (lawyer's edition). Published by Lawyers Co-operative/Bancroft Whitney Publishing Companies.

The two annotated codes are unofficial because they are not published by the government, but they are the most efficient sources for researching the statutory law for the federal jurisdiction. Most college libraries have both the official (nonannotated) U.S.C. and one of the annotated codes. All three sets of codes use the same statutory sections and the same organizational scheme of titles and chapter numbers.

Why are there so many different versions of the same statutory law? Many duplicative and overlapping tools exist for legal research because alternative approaches to research tasks are needed by the variety of users who have different research needs. If the reader is interested in reading only the text of an act in its current form, U.S.C. is considerably less bulky than the annotated versions, but updates are published less frequently and there are no extensive aids to further research. The private publishers of U.S.C.A. and U.S.C.S. are more timely in their publication and updating schedules and include both the text of the statutes and extensive references to other sources. The annotated versions contain the full text of the United States Code, provisions of the United States Constitution, Federal Rules of Civil and Criminal Procedure, Federal Rules of Evidence, the Internal Revenue Code, Court Rules for Federal Trial and Appellate Courts, and a wide range of administrative rules and regulations.

The differences between U.S.C.A. and U.S.C.S. are in part related to the services of competing publishers. One strength of the U.S.C.S. annotations is the "Research Guide" section that provides a range of resource citations not mentioned in U.S.C.A.

The comparable section of U.S.C.A. is called "Library References." It provides references to *Corpus Juris Secundum* (C.J.S.), which is also published by West. The West key numbers citations used in the U.S.C.A. (and explained later in this chapter) are a patented and unique cross-reference service provided only by West. Citations to research sources not published by West, such as A.L.R., Am. Jur., and law reviews, are included in U.S.C.S.; however, the citations to C.J.S. in the U.S.C.A. provide this same service.

Problem No. 2

Look up the federal statutory law on a particular subject that is of current interest using one of the available annotated codes (U.S.C.A. or U.S.C.S.).

1. State the legal questions precisely before beginning research and indicate why this subject would be governed by federal law rather than state law.
2. Explain what key descriptor terms are used to locate the referenced title and section of the code.

3. Explain the answer gained from the code in terms of specific statutory wording and citation to sources of interpretation and commentary. Be sure to check for updated information in the pocket part supplement to the volume.

Again, the assignment can be simple or complicated depending on the reader's orientation. The main goal is to examine this extensive legal research tool. Use the same basic procedures and tips provided in the instructions on researching state annotated codes. The reader may want to examine federal rules that may be in conflict with state rules to discover the manner in which our state and federal laws interact. Valid federal or United States constitutional laws and treaties are the supreme law of the land.

The fifty official federal titles are listed in Figure 8-3. Further instructions about the annotated set of the code can be found in the first few pages of the "General Index" to the series.

The reader may want to choose a topic for problem no. 2 by reviewing some of the federal legal issues in the hypothetical *Consumer* case. Look up "diversity jurisdiction" and find out the conditions necessary to meet federal court jurisdiction, or explore any other issues that were puzzling in that case.

A thorough index search using the annotated code will provide updated information to within three months of the latest changes, as well as an extensive set of references for follow-up on the particular research topic. The following checklist of steps illustrates all the bases that need to be covered in researching a topic:

Checklist of Steps in Using Annotated Codes
Step 1. State the issue.
Step 2. Find the annotated code for the jurisdiction in question.
Step 3. Go to the index.
Step 4. Go to the referenced title and section.
Step 5. Read the text of the law carefully.
Step 6. Read the annotations.
Step 7. Check the pocket part.
Step 8. Check the Annotations Supplementary Pamphlet.
Step 9. Check the Legislative Service volume.
Step 10. Further updating, if needed.

This list, however, may be too exhaustive for the introductory student, who may decide to stop once a satisfactory answer to the question has been obtained.

Steps 8 through 10 in the checklist go beyond the pocket part of the annotated code. The pocket part contains updated information only through the end of the prior year. During the current year, the publishers of most state codes issue softbound booklets called "Cumulative Pamphlets" or "Later Case Service" that update the statutes, cases, and annotations in the bound volumes and pocket parts. These federal legislative supplements to U.S.C.A. are called simply "Pamphlet number 1" (2, 3, and so on); those to U.S.C.S. are called "Cumulative Later Case and Statutory Service." The supplements are arranged by the same titles and sections as the main volumes of the set.

The legislative service provides the text of new sessions laws as they are passed by the legislature. It is published frequently while the legislature is in session, and each issue contains a table with titles such as "Table of Sections Amended" (Repealed, Added, and so on). Check the table to see if any changes

TITLES OF UNITED STATES CODE AND UNITED STATES CODE ANNOTATED

1. General Provisions.
2. The Congress.
3. The President.
4. Flag and Seal, Seat of Government, and the States.
5. Government Organization and Employees.
6. Surety Bonds (*See Title 31, Money and Finance*).
7. Agriculture.
8. Aliens and Nationality.
9. Arbitration.
10. Armed Forces.
11. Bankruptcy.
12. Banks and Banking.
13. Census.
14. Coast Guard.
15. Commerce and Trade.
16. Conservation.
17. Copyrights.
18. Crimes and Criminal Procedure.
19. Customs Duties.
20. Education.
21. Food and Drugs.
22. Foreign Relations and Intercourse.
23. Highways.
24. Hospitals and Asylums.
25. Indians.
26. Internal Revenue Code.
27. Intoxicating Liquors.
28. Judiciary and Judicial Procedure.
29. Labor.
30. Mineral Lands and Mining.
31. Money and Finance.
32. National Guard.
33. Navigation and Navigable Waters.
34. Navy (*See Title 10, Armed Forces*).
35. Patents.
36. Patriotic Societies and Observances.
37. Pay and Allowances of the Uniformed Services.
38. Veterans' Benefits.
39. Postal Service.
40. Public Buildings, Property, and Works.
41. Public Contracts.
42. The Public Health and Welfare.
43. Public Lands.
44. Public Printing and Documents.
45. Railroads.
46. Shipping.
47. Telegraphs, Telephones, and Radiotelegraphs.
48. Territories and Insular Possessions.
49. Transportation.
50. War and National Defense.

Figure 8.3
Titles of the United States Code

have been made in the section of the law that is being researched. The table is cumulative, so the latest issue for the current year will include information from the earlier issues as well.

The legislative service for U.S.C.A. is called *U.S. Code: Congressional and Administrative News*. The legislative service for U.S.C.S. is called simply "Advance." In addition to containing the current session laws, these services provide the text of certain documents that can be used for legislative history searches.

In extraordinary circumstances that require further updated information, consult a newsletter or other service that reports on legislative activities. A librarian can explain the sources that may be useful for this purpose.

Administrative Codes

Federal and state administrative agencies are authorized by law to exercise certain delegated rule-making powers within the limits of constitutional and legislative authority. This area of lawmaking, like that of judicial rule making, is the aspect of the law affecting our daily lives that is the least understood. This body of legal rules is technically not legislation but, if made pursuant to statutory authority, has the force of law.

Federal regulations that emanate from agencies such as the Environmental Protection Agency (EPA) and the Internal Revenue Service (IRS) are widely known and are good examples of administrative rules. On both the state and federal levels, however, a vast body of regulatory rules have been built that exceeds the volume of statutory law upon which it is based. Access to these detailed rules and regulations has become an essential element of knowledge of the law on any given subject. We cannot obey these rules if we cannot find them.

The problem of locating these rules led to a federal statute that requires publication of the *Federal Register* (the Federal Register Act of 1935, ch. 417, 49 Stat. 500). This act requires executive orders and administrative regulations of general legal applicability to be published in a daily official publication called the *Federal Register*. In the case of *Panama Refining Co. v. Ryan*, 293 U.S. 388, 55 S.Ct. 241, 79 L.Ed. 446 (1935), the United States Supreme Court had to admonish the government for not being aware of its own suspension of the "code of fair competition" that it was seeking to enforce. The code had been suspended by executive order (unpublished), and the government had to concede that there was no basis for prosecution for the time period in question. This discovery did not take place until the case had moved all the way through the appeals process to the Supreme Court. The public outcry over the fact that the government had been making law without telling anybody what the law was, resulted in the Federal Register Act of 1935 (Kunz et al. 1986,167–68).

The *Federal Register* consists of one hundred to four hundred pages of new rules and regulations and is published every work day. This publication of the mass of executive orders, promulgated rules, and potential rules that are about to be promulgated is the official source of these rules and regulations and, like session laws, should be used for citation purposes. However, the *Federal Register* is a poor research tool, since it is organized chronologically and must be supplemented by a comprehensive code to keep abreast of the ever-changing nature of these rules and regulations.

All the regulations in the *Federal Register* are codified in the *Code of Federal Regulations* (C.F.R.). More than half the states also publish their own administrative regulations, generally in codified form. All the larger (population) states have administrative codes; but in many smaller states, the appropriate state agency must be contacted for information about its rules and regulations, which are generally published in individual pamphlet form (Lewis 1985,107).

Problem No. 3

Look up a federal regulation on a subject of current interest using the *Code of Federal Regulations*.

1. State the legal question precisely before beginning, and indicate why this subject would be governed by a federal regulation.
2. Explain the key descriptor terms that are used to locate the referenced title and section of the code.
3. Explain the answer gained from the code in terms of specific wording of the regulation and citation to sources of interpretation and commentary.

The goal of this assignment is to gain some familiarity with the C.F.R. and some understanding of its basic contents. A college library should have C.F.R. on the shelves. It consists of about one hundred and fifty softbound volumes in two different colors, depending on the year of revision of that particular volume. It is arranged under the fifty basic titles of the U.S.C. (see Figure 8-3). This series is kept up-to-date by simply replacing individual volumes at least once a year, according to a quarterly schedule. Thus, there are no pocket part supplements as in the other codes.

Appropriate topics to research might be: "Who is qualified for food stamps?" or "Can college educational expenditures be deducted with the itemized deductions for income tax purposes?" Keep it simple, and ask a question that is of personal interest.

Follow the procedures learned in the research of other codes. Start with the C.F.R. index volume, which is usually located at the front of the series. The index refers to title, part, and section number in the main set. For example, 7 C.F.R. §55.160 is a typical citation: the title (7) is given first, followed by the part (55) and the section (160). Check the part headings to determine the statutory context of the regulation, then read the regulation carefully. The only source of updated information to check beyond C.F.R. is the most recent issues of the *Federal Register*.

HOW TO FIND THE COMMON LAW

Our common law heritage, which is discussed in Chapter One, is the reason for the prevalence of case law in our legal tradition. The assignments in this chapter have dealt with statutes and codes that contain copious references to cases that are based on statutes or constitutions and form a part of the most authoritative sources of American law. These constitutional and statutory case law decisions take precedence over the common law, which is that law that has no source other than judicial decision. Hence, the common law proper is not found in the codes.

The body of purely "judge-made" law continues to exist today. (The *du Pont* case in Appendix B illustrates the continuing growth of this law.) We must, therefore, have some means of understanding this body of law. The most precise method of determining the specific rules of common law for a particular jurisdiction is to examine individual case precedents. The cumbersome nature of this unique aspect of our legal heritage has been the subject of constant criticism and confusion. We have at least fifty sets of common law rules, and many local courts have their own rules that may vary within a state jurisdiction.

As a result of great national debate over the vague and cumbersome nature of our common law that occurred around the turn of the twentieth century, the now highly respected American Law Institute (ALI) was established. Founded in 1923, the ALI is an association of judges, law school teachers, and lawyers. The association's objective is to reduce the uncertainty and complexity of American common law principles by drafting model statements and creating one codelike reference that is more authoritative than existing treatises, often done by individuals. The ALI also drafts and promotes the adoption of model legislative codes and statutes, but its primary efforts are directed toward common law rule making by the courts.

Secondary Sources

The ALI's extraordinarily successful efforts have produced a *Restatement of the Law* series that exceeds the authority of ordinary treatises and, at times, is viewed as being on a par with persuasive case authority. However, the *Restatements* are not primary sources of the law—they are secondary references of exceptionally persuasive character (Kunz et al. 1986, 198–99).

The *Restatements* provide the student who wishes to gain a general understanding of the common law with an initial reference that is organized and stated in statutory language. The current *Restatement of the Law* sets, and their dates of publication by ALI are: *Agency (Second)* (1957), *Conflicts (Second)* (1969), *Contracts (Second)* (1979), *Foreign Relations Law of the United States (Third)* (1987), *Judgments (Second)* (1980), *Property* (1936–44) [*Landlord and Tenant (Second)* section completed in 1976], *Restitution* (1936), *Security* (1941), *Torts (Second)* (1964–77), and *Trusts (Second)* (1957).

Problem No. 4

Look up a general principle of common law in one of the sets of *Restatements* published by the American Law Institute (ALI).

1. State the legal question precisely before beginning and indicate why the subject would be governed by the common law rather than by statutory or constitutional law.
2. Explain how the particular set of *Restatements* were selected for the problem.
3. Explain the answer gained from the *Restatements* in terms of specific wording of the rule (section statement in bold print), the commentary, and illustrations.

The general area of the problem must first be selected. If the subjects the *Restatement* titles refer to are unfamiliar, look them up in a legal dictionary such as *Black's Law Dictionary* or *Ballentine's Law Dictionary*. A more extensive dictionarylike source is *Words and Phrases*, published by West, which can be very useful when a definition is needed.

The ALI *Restatements* are probably not all located on the same shelf in the library. They are usually located near other treatises, texts, reference materials, and other secondary sources on the subject matter covered. Look under *Restatement of the Law* in the card catalog or computerized locating service.

An appropriate research problem may be found by reviewing the discussion of *Restatements* in the hypothetical *Consumer* case in Chapter Four. Look up "strict liability" in the *Restatement (Second) of Torts* Section 402A or other related concepts.

The topic may be located in the *Restatements* through the index approach or the table of contents approach. Many of the *Restatements* are series of several volumes, but others are only single- or two-volume works. The index for a series is in the last volume (not the appendix), and a table of contents is in the front pages of every volume.

The *Restatements* and other treatises are used frequently as statements of general principles of common law when specific precedents are unavailable. Judges borrow from other jurisdictions, and the general acceptance of the highly respected ALI *Restatements* are persuasive when setting new precedents for a particular jurisdiction. For persons unfamiliar with the common law, these general statements are a good place to start your search. They provide the needed background to understand how a particular jurisdiction deviates from these general principles in detailed opinions.

The average practicing attorney would not think of the *Restatements* as a method of finding the case law of a particular jurisdiction. Even when interested in a practical guide to a common law area, such as Torts, the lawyer would probably prefer the widely used hornbooks, or treatises such as *Prosser on Torts*.

Primary Sources

The standard method of case law research starts with the most current set of digests for the particular jurisdiction in question. A digest is designed to assist the reader in finding relevant case law by topic. The text consists of a series of paragraphs, organized by topic, that provide brief abstracts (or digests) of opinions rendered by the courts.

Digests and *reporters* are closely related in that they are tools of cross-reference to each other. The reporters contain the full text of the opinions cited in the digests. West Publishing Company has developed the most commonly used digest system in modern times. Its patented Key Number System ties case headnotes in the reporters to the case abstracts in the digests. This key number indexing system consists of two items that must be noted: (1) the subject area, and (2) the number assigned to that particular concept. Every state in the United States is covered by West's American Digest System, either through individual state digests or through the regional digest and reporter system. Nevada and Delaware are the only two states that do not have individual digests, and they have access to West's multistate regional service.

The entire American Digest System, published by West, is quite extensive. Listing all of the services available would only confuse the beginning student. Methods of thorough case searches today include the extensive holdings of modern computer services—WESTLAW and LEXIS—and historical searches that go as far back as the 1600s. Discussion of these methods of research are covered in advanced courses for professionals; for introductory purposes, exposure to the state and federal digest and reporter services is sufficient.

The best state source is the individual state digest, which will refer to the state reporter and the state's regional reporter. Regional reporters are multistate reporters that provide the full text of the cases cited in the digests. They divide the United States into the reporting districts shown in Table 8-1.

Reporters

The regional reporters are the sources most widely used to find the full text of case law opinions. The library also may have a state reporter set that contains just the cases from that state's jurisdiction. These two sets are duplicative and overlapping; they provide alternate sources for identical services. Both the regional and the state sources report cases from all levels of the state courts and are complete reporters.

The federal reporting system is divided by court levels, and the reporter for the appropriate court level must be used to access the full text of the case law from that court jurisdiction. The official source of United States Supreme Court decisions, which should always be given first in case citations, is *United States Reports* (U.S.). *The Bluebook: A Uniform System of Citation* recommends that only this official citation be used; for example, *Gideon v. Wainwright*, 372 U.S. 335 (1963).

There are other reporters that provide additional headnote and cross-referencing services not available in the official *United States Reports*. Dearing, Lawyers Co-operative, and Equity publish case reporters. The one most frequently used by lawyers is *United States Supreme Court Reports—Lawyers' Edition*, which includes extensive research aids such as summaries of counsels' briefs and annotations related to secondary sources by the same publisher, Lawyers Co-operative.

As with the state reporters, the most uniform national reporting system is West's patented Key Number System that provides headnotes in the reporters with cross-references to the corresponding digests. The West *Supreme Court Reporter* (S. Ct.) integrates this system. In some references, parallel citations for all *United States Reports* citations are provided to enable the reader to select the

TABLE 8.1 The West National Reporter System: Regional Reporters

Regional Reporter	States Covered
Atlantic Reporter (A. or A.2d)	Connecticut, Delaware, Maine, Maryland, New Hampshire, New Jersey, Pennsylvania, Rhode Island, Vermont, and the D.C. Municipal Court of Appeals
North Eastern Reporter (N.E. or N.E.2d)	Illinois, Indiana, Massachusetts, New York, and Ohio
North Western Reporter (N.W. or N.W.2d)	Iowa, Michigan, Minnesota, Nebraska, South Dakota, and Wisconsin
Pacific Reporter (P. or P.2d)	Alaska, Arizona, California, Colorado, Hawaii, Idaho, Kansas, Montana, Nevada, New Mexico, Oklahoma, Oregon, Utah, Washington, and Wyoming
South Eastern Reporter (S.E. or S.E.2d)	Georgia, North Carolina, South Carolina, Virginia, and West Virginia
South Western Reporter (S.W. or S.W.2d)	Arkansas, Kentucky, Missouri, Indian Territories, Tennessee, and Texas
Southern Reporter (So. or So. 2d)	Alabama, Florida, Louisiana, and Mississippi

appropriate source; for example, *Gideon V. Wainwright*, 372 U.S. 335, 83 S. Ct. 792, 9 L. Ed. 2d 799 (1963).

Federal Reporter (F. or F.2d) is part of the West system and reports all cases decided by the federal appeals courts. The *Federal Supplement* (F. Supp.) reports cases decided by the federal district courts and other claims, customs, and international trade courts. There are also specialized reporters covering other federal matters such as bankruptcy (Bankr.), federal rules decisions (F.R.D.), military justice (M.J.), and claim's court decisions (Cl. Ct.). All these reporters include the key number citations of the West Publishing Company system and are part of the extensive West National Reporting System.

Problem No. 5

By now the reader should have notes with many citations to cases at all levels of federal and state jurisdiction relating to the reader's particular interests.

1. Look up one of these cases in a West case reporter.
2. Explain why this case was selected and which West reporter is used to access the court's opinion.
3. Note the publisher's headnotes and associated key numbering system; then read the case carefully.
4. Formulate statements of the holdings that are "on point" based on the specific facts of the case. Do not rely on the publisher's headnotes because they may not be acceptable as "on point" citations.

The headnotes, found before the official court opinion, include a summary of the case and a series of numbered statements (see Figure 8-4). These unofficial statements are constructed by the publisher to provide cross-references to points of law considered in the official opinion of the court that follows. Determination of the holdings of the court is a complex, time-consuming process, and one that is subject to varying interpretations. The editors make headnotes of every statement in the opinion that *might* be a holding. The case itself must be read to see if the stated rule was even at issue. Most of the headnotes would be considered dicta (the court's statements and opinions that are not "on point") and cannot be cited as precedent; do not cite them as if they were holdings.

There are also headnotes in the annotated codes that refer to case opinions; those statements cannot be considered as case precedent or holdings. The headnotes have functional utility as case finders, but legal research requires specific case analysis to determine the legal authority of any particular rule.

Note the numbered headnotes in Figure 8-4. They include (1) a term that identifies a subject heading in the corresponding digest, and (2) a key number that identifies the particular cross-referenced element found under that subject heading in the digest. Both the term and the number must be noted in order to use the cross-referencing service in West's national reporter and digest system.

Digests

The headnotes that are prepared by the editors for each case as it is published are grouped together and published as the corresponding digest for that jurisdiction. References to the annotated codes also may be found in headnotes (see Figure 8-1, headnote number 8). The headnotes provide cross-references to codes and digests, both of which provide cross-references back to reporters. Pro-

Figure 8.4 West Reporter Headnote Page

10 Tenn. **791 SOUTH WESTERN REPORTER, 2d SERIES**

STATE of Tennessee, Appellee,

v.

Pervis Tyrone PAYNE, Appellant.

Supreme Court of Tennessee, at Jackson.

April 16, 1990.

Defendant was convicted in the Shelby Criminal Court, Bernier Weinman, J., of first-degree murder, and was sentenced to death. On appeal, the Supreme Court, Fones, J., held that: (1) evidence was sufficient to support conviction; (2) evidence that defendant possessed drug paraphernalia at time of arrest was admissible; and (3) prosecutor's improper closing argument and conduct was harmless beyond reasonable doubt.

Affirmed.

1. Homicide ⚖=234(8, 11)

Murder conviction was sufficiently supported by evidence that defendant came out of victim's apartment building wearing blood soaked clothes and that he ran from arriving officer; jury was justified in rejecting as unbelievable and contrary to human conduct and experience defendant's claim that he entered apartment only to render aid to already stabbed victim.

2. Criminal Law ⚖=627.8(2)

Drug paraphernalia found on murder defendant at time of arrest was properly admitted, even if State did not learn of local police department's possession of evidence, or notify defendant of same, until a week and one-half before trial; there was no evidence that State was acting in bad faith or in intentional disregard of rules of discovery, or that defendant was prejudiced by a late discovery of such potentially inexculpatory evidence. Rules Crim.Proc., Rule 16.

3. Criminal Law ⚖=369.2(4)

Evidence that murder defendant possessed cocaine and drug paraphernalia at time of arrest was admissible as explanatory of circumstances of murders and relevant to defendant's mental state during commission of those crimes; considering inexplicable brutality with which crimes were committed, it was more probable than not that murderer was under influence of drugs or alcohol, and evidence that defendant had access to both drugs and alcohol was relevant and probative of his guilt. Fed.Rules Evid.Rule 401, 28 U.S.C.A.

4. Criminal Law ⚖=1169.1(10)

Admission of child's stuffed toy animal and pair of children's shoes found at scene of children's murder, though irrelevant, was harmless beyond reasonable doubt.

5. Homicide ⚖=343, 358(1)

Sentencing phase evidence, that four-year-old child of murder victim missed and cried for his mother, though technically irrelevant, did not create constitutionally unacceptable risk of arbitrary imposition of death penalty, and was harmless beyond reasonable doubt. U.S.C.A. Const.Amends. 5, 14.

6. Criminal Law ⚖=713

Prosecutor's closing argument in capital murder prosecution, referring to surviving three and one-half-year-old victim's physical and mental condition, was relevant in determining defendant's personal responsibility and moral guilt.

7. Homicide ⚖=358(1)

Videotape of crime scene was admissible, during sentencing phase of capital murder prosecution, as relevant to State's contention that murder was heinous, atrocious or cruel, and its probative value on that issue outweighed any prejudicial effect; videotape depicted number and severity of stab wounds, savagery of attack and struggle of victim to escape.

8. Criminal Law ⚖=768(1)

Jury, in capital murder prosecution, was properly instructed that they should not have any sympathy or prejudice or allow anything but law and evidence to have any influence upon them in determining their verdict. U.S.C.A. Const.Amend. 8.

fessionals use these cross-references to search for case law precedent that will be controlling or highly persuasive authority.

Problem No. 6

Find a headnote in a West reporter that expresses a rule of particular interest.

1. Note the subject term and the key number of the headnote.
2. Find the volume containing the subject heading in the appropriate digest for the jurisdiction in question.
3. Explain what additional headnotes are found in the digest indicating reporter citations to cases that may refine the initial understanding of the particular rule. Do not forget to check for updated information in the digest's pocket part supplement.

The digest subject heading also can serve as a place to begin a search for abstracts (headnotes) and case citations of interest. A key number can be found in the digest by going to the beginning of a subject heading and searching through the list of key numbers (see Figure 8-5). Note that there is also a Descriptive-Word Index volume at the beginning of the West digest set that may be used to look up topics and their relationships to the subject headings.

Most state digests are in the second (2d) edition. Readers may need to use the regional digest, particularly in Nevada and Delaware. For federal citations, the digests are in the third and fourth (3d and 4th) editions. *West's Federal Practice Digest 4th* responds to the continuing expansion of federal case law by directly supplementing *West's Federal Practice Digest 3d*. Key number classification has been expanded and refined to reflect recent developments in the law. New topics and key numbers have been provided for many areas including bankruptcy, civil rights, civil service, criminal law, double jeopardy, Employee Retirement Income Security Act (ERISA), farm labor, federal preemption, habeas corpus, intoxication tests, Racketeer Influenced and Corrupt Organizations (RICO), searches and seizures, and warranties. The reader should use *Federal Practice 4th* first, then work back to earlier editions if the search continues.

HOW TO "SHEPARDIZE" (UPDATE) PARTICULAR CASES

The term "shepardize" has become synonymous with the use of the extensive legal citator series known as *Shepard's Citations*, published by McGraw-Hill, Inc. There is a *Shepard's Citations* series for both statutes and cases for all state and federal jurisdictions. The case citator service for the reporters is the most extensively used of the various types of services provided in the *Shepard's Citations* system.

Once a case law precedent that is "on point" has been found and determined to be controlling authority concerning a particular point of law, there are two questions that must be answered:

1. What is the "history of the precedent"—that is, what has happened to the precedent since it was decided? Has it been appealed to a higher court? Have they reversed, affirmed, or modified the decision?
2. What is the "treatment of the precedent"—that is, how have later cases treated the precedent? Have they followed, overruled, criticized, or explained the decision?

25 Tenn D 2d—374

PRODUCTS LIABILITY

SUBJECTS INCLUDED

The liability of manufacturers, distributors, retailers, and others for damage caused by defects or dangers in their products whether the damage be suffered by those with whom they deal or by others

SUBJECTS EXCLUDED AND COVERED BY OTHER TOPICS

Bailor's liability, see AUTOMOBILES, BAILMENT

Particular products, liabilities relating to—

    Aircraft, see AVIATION

    Drugs or medicines, see DRUGS AND NARCOTICS

    Electricity, see ELECTRICITY

    Explosives, see EXPLOSIVES

    Firearms, see WEAPONS

    Food, see FOOD

    Gas, see GAS

    Poisons, see POISONS

Warranty, liability for breach of, see CONTRACTS, SALES

For detailed references to other topics, see Descriptive-Word Index

Analysis

I. SCOPE IN GENERAL, ⚛︎1–70.
    (A) PRODUCTS IN GENERAL, ⚛︎1–34.
    (B) PARTICULAR PRODUCTS, APPLICATION TO, ⚛︎35–70.

II. ACTIONS, ⚛︎71–98.

I. SCOPE IN GENERAL.
  (A) PRODUCTS IN GENERAL.
    ⚛︎1. Nature and elements in general.
      2. Constitutional and statutory provisions.
      3. What law governs.
      4. Liability as insurer.
      5. Strict liability.
      6. Negligence or fault.
      7. Representations or concealment.
      8. Nature of product and existence of defect or danger.
      9. Knowledge of defect or danger.
      10. Care required.
      11. Design.
      12. Precautions or safeguards.

Figure 8.5
West Digest Subject Heading Summary Page

The *Shepard's Citations* series provides information needed to answer these questions.

Problem No. 7

Select a case that has been read and analyzed in some detail and determine the reliability of that precedent.

1. Note the case citation: source, volume number, and page number.
2. Find the corresponding *Shepard's Citations* series in the library.
3. Explain the subsequent history and treatment of the precedent.

If the full case opinion has been found in a state or regional reporter, either the state or the regional *Shepard's Citations* series may be used. For federal cases, *Shepard's United States Citations* contains cases from the Supreme Court, and *Shepard's Federal Citations* contains cases from lower federal courts. Use the *Shepard's Citations* series that corresponds with the case source.

Once the appropriate *Shepard's Citations* series has been located in the library, find the volumes for case citations (not statutes, bankruptcy, claims, or names). There are several hardbound volumes with the source volume numbers (range of coverage) on the spines. Next to these basic volumes are a hardbound supplement, a softbound (gold-colored) annual supplement, and a softbound (red-colored) quarterly supplement.

Start with the softbound quarterly supplement, which is the latest update and will have a boxed-in statement of "what your library should contain" on the outside front jacket cover. For example, to "shepardize" *Abbott v. American Honda Motor Co.,* 682 S.W.2d 206, the *Shepard's Southwestern Citations* would be consulted. The red softbound supplement has the following note on the outside cover:

WHAT YOUR LIBRARY SHOULD CONTAIN
1985 Bound Vol. 1 (Parts 1–3)*
1985 Bound Vol. 2 (Parts 1–3)*
1985–1990 Bound Supplement*
Supplemented with:
—Feb. 1991 Annual Cumulative Supplement Vol. 83 No. 6 [gold]
—Dec. 1991 Cumulative Supplement Vol. 84 No. 4 [red]

This notation specifies the volumes that will be needed for the search. This information is updated with the latest volumes. If the red volume is more than three months old, notify the librarian that the set needs to be updated.

An example of a page in the *Shepard's Citations* series is shown in Figure 8-6. Each page provides the name and the volume of the case source at the top of the page. Once the correct volume number (in the *Abbott* case, 682) is located, scan the columns to find the page number (in this case, 206). This procedure locates the source citation (in the *Abbott* case, 682 S.W.2d 206). The reader will find a list of citations to related cases that will further research.

All the parts in the series listed on the cover of the quarterly supplement ("what your library should contain") must be checked before the search for citations to update the case will be complete. Of course, you will find no citations earlier than the date of the decision of the case, but you must go back through the supplements to the basic set of volumes to retrieve all the relevant citations. The sample page in Figure 8-6 is from the 1985–1990 supplement, and this is the

Figure 8.6 Sample Page from *Shepard's Citations*

SOUTHWESTERN REPORTER, 2d Series
Vol. 682

828SW[22]731	673FS[4]373	—53—	—86—	—118—	Wash	18A2d10s	—224—
829SW31	708FS[3]1546	714SW[2]833	s655SW752	712SW[5]75	819P2d374		733SW[4]118
830SW[23]894	2A2d27s	47A2d46n	e702SW511	d784SW[4]231	22A2d659s	—185—	763SW[4]762
833SW[22]435			710SW[5]479	d784SW[5]231	95A2d1229s	cc769SW841	
Cir. 8	—20—	—55—	717SW[3]545	809SW[1]42	55A2d342n	698SW[7]613	—227—
851F2d[13]1096	704SW[3]236	703SW[3]542	726SW[3]508	809SW[2]43	55A2d360n	725SW[5]70	e769SW[8]77
863F2d1393	707SW[4]457	745SW[1]670	56A2d107n	76A2d822n		729SW[3]593	j769SW[8]79
740FS1443	791SW[4]2			76A2d846n	—153—	731SW[8]857	797SW[9]642
39A3d550s		—56—	—88—	80A2d364n	s642SW378	j738SW476	797SW[7]646
47A2d1165n	—28—	f731SW[4]426	cc774SW559		cc727SW171	752SW[2]951	
63A2d536n	702SW952	835SW539	33A3d798s	—120—	694SW[7]811	752SW[3]951	—234—
64A2d783n	747SW[4]643			cc549SW906	698SW[6]544	759SW[3]389	696SW552
66A2d435n	768SW[4]135	—59—	—91—	cc585SW548	698SW[10]614	768SW624	731SW[1]705
74A2d340n	769SW[3]458	f702SW[2]547	12PST593§	cc771SW876	698SW[11]614	817SW[3]528	808SW112
74A2d342n	W Va	719SW[1]12	[30	732SW265	699SW[1]765		814SW[1]122
74A2d356n	357SE234	719SW[2]12		f783SW[6]437	705SW[1]586	—189—	e817SW[1]721
85A2d127n	EDP§ 6.13	719SW[1]17	—93—	22A2d621s	708SW[7]232	727SW[3]227	f822SW205
		d740SW[1]176	s706SW603		710SW[10]282	727SW[1]425	f822SW206
—948—	—31—	e776SW[1]42	734SW[5]913	—124—	710SW[11]282	744SW[1]471	824SW[1]743
712SW[2]411	683SW[2]289	24A3d1093s		s767SW69	710SW[10]461	781SW[3]561	Cir. 5
714SW[8]757	683SW[4]645		—96—	700SW[2]504	710SW[11]461	f788SW[3]771	672FS[1]961
718SW172	f684SW[2]452	—62—	708SW[4]277	702SW[1]905	714SW[13]587	d821SW[3]912	
718SW[8]173	713SW20	cc704FS978	708SW[2]277	798SW[2]731	732SW[8]537	EDP§ 8.03	—235—
	731SW[2]430		713SW[4]635		735SW[11]31		s682SW323
Vol. 682	762SW[1]453	—63—	713SW[6]635	—127—	738SW[7]512	—193—	696SW[1]415
	Me	d693SW890	717SW239	s657SW301	741SW[1]694	707SW[5]486	697SW[1]29
—1—	611A2d566	d693SW[3]891	718SW192	s720SW758	751SW[5]78	716SW[5]422	710SW105
d793SW[4]349		823SW[5]52	722SW[1]83	cc664SW605	761SW[1]709	716SW[4]826	724SW[1]937
Tenn	—33—		j738SW871	699SW[10]780	785SW[9]809	800SW[5]156	750SW[1]333
811SW[4]520	693SW324	—65—	h738SW[6]944	716SW[1]466	785SW[8]809		776SW[1]780
61A2d222n	Md	739SW[2]584	781SW[3]257	734SW[9]883		—196—	777SW[1]147
	499A2d952	740SW[1]674	783SW[6]444	734SW[10]883	—156—	725SW[2]955	801SW[1]25
—3—		740SW[2]674		742SW[11]620	823SW[4]949	731SW[2]922	j804SW515
723SW[1]614	—38—	f743SW[3]597	—103—	785SW[10]585		732SW[2]283	805SW[1]600
	764SW[2]485	760SW[2]620	US cert den	791SW[9]812	—160—	756SW[2]279	j822SW370
—12—	789SW[1]52	801SW[2]731	in105SC2120	9A3d203s	Case 2	756SW[5]279	826SW[1]695
754SW911		d801SW[5]735	cc693SW191	74A2d298n	51A2d573n	812SW[2]587	835SW[1]654
786SW[1]922	—42—	829SW[2]492	731SW[1]525		51A2d590n	813SW[1]44	835SW[1]659
800SW115	US cert den		f748SW[1]697	—132—		Cir. 8	
829SW44	in472US1008	—68—	751SW[1]391	731SW[3]317	—163—	c648FS[4]96	—236—
	in105SC2703	cc693SW175	f766SW[1]112		cc693SW137	N C	s672SW45
—16—		f691SW[6]474	778SW[1]664	—136—	729SW597	328SE247	682SW[1]239
Case 2	—44—	695SW[1]916	804SW[4]31	cc689SW809	j729SW602		693SW727
s640SW125	715SW[4]313	720SW[8]41		cc712SW442	j750SW637	—203—	694SW120
714SW[3]678	Cir. 7	731SW[9]22	—107—	703SW[1]589	768SW[3]121	d705SW[1]645	710SW615
714SW[3]836	930F2d1204	735SW[12]139	694SW509	716SW[1]435	779SW[1]281	710SW[3]517	j713SW724
f724SW[3]711	8COA163§ 36	750SW[2]678	714SW[4]922	716SW[15]436	796SW[2]95	717SW[3]874	739SW[1]611
724SW[4]713		779SW[2]606	747SW[3]758	721SW[1]596		750SW[3]744	778SW517
735SW[2]72	—47—	804SW767	747SW[3]758	723SW[13]504	—166—	780SW[3]735	
736SW[3]514	712SW[1]720	812SW[8]220	761SW717	747SW[7]770	s679SW294		—237—
736SW[4]514	712SW[2]720		763SW[4]276	793SW[7]879	720SW[1]414	—206—	s665SW836
738SW[2]582	758SW[2]731	—78—	j766SW689	825SW[13]365	727SW[3]413	738SW[2]174	728SW433
738SW[3]582	758SW[2]731	cc754SW43	809SW186	14A3d723s	735SW[2]38	817SW[2]685	728SW[2]434
748SW[2]72	758SW[3]731	704SW[9]272	f826SW[3]860	14A3d1297s	787SW750	836SW[2]111	736SW[2]834
e750SW[1]499	Cir. 3	704SW[8]693	f826SW[4]860			Cir. 1	739SW[2]949
750SW[3]621	706FS[6]1165	704SW[10]694		—146—	—173—	792F2d1235	739SW[5]949
752SW[3]328	Calif	708SW[9]290	—112—	f694SW[4]884	Case 2	Cir. 6	773SW640
758SW[3]134	282CaR764	714SW[9]716	728SW[5]230	699SW[7]137	d721SW80	779F2d[7]342	776SW646
759SW[1]313	286CaR431	714SW[10]717	730SW[5]579	d699SW[9]138	Cir. 8	826F2d[8]1511	778SW518
759SW[2]313	Iowa	716SW[10]371	752SW[9]888	724SW[1]614	137BRW774	925F2d[7]1005	794SW6
759SW[2]348	478NW640	755SW[9]245	752SW[1]889	733SW[1]465	72A2d445n	778FS1426	799SW[1]406
759SW[1]860	N J	791SW[9]877		733SW[2]465		784FS[4]497	e821SW[1]636
761SW[3]251	513A2d976	800SW[1]80	—116—	d733SW[8]467	—177—	SRI§ 7.16	822SW[3]363
762SW[2]487	Wash	d835SW435	685SW[5]576	d733SW[12]467	s654SW280	83A2d99n	
762SW[2]834	751P2d317	835SW[1]435	688SW[1]399	d733SW[13]467	704SW722		—240—
768SW[2]577	60A2d310s	d835SW[3]435	d688SW400	j735SW[1]359	717SW[3]536	—212—	e683SW[5]60
768SW[2]578		Cir. 8	779SW[5]584	754SW[1]33	24A2d350s	776SW[3]94	e683SW[6]60
779SW[3]337	—52—	779FS[9]1008	q779SW586	760SW131			705SW179
f791SW[2]840	738SW[1]578		j779SW588	770SW[16]391	—179—	—219—	711SW288
813SW[3]357	753SW657	—82—	785SW[2]593	710SW[4]444	776SW535		730SW[2]137
828SW[3]878	765SW[2]633	cc690SW839	786SW924	798SW477	735SW[2]390		730SW[4]137
Cir. 8	778SW[1]760	cc735SW133	57A2d994n	e798SW[13]478	742SW[4]248		j730SW853
q662FS[1]829		d714SW[2]588		d802SW[19]511	742SW[5]248		788SW[3]872
q662FS[2]829		719SW[7]232		805SW267	782SW[4]441		789SW[4]397
669FS[4]1504				806SW691	801SW[4]494		
				814SW690	825SW[4]323		Continued

Reproduced by permission of Shepard's/McGraw Hill, Inc. Further reproduction is strictly prohibited.

Shepard's Citations source that contains the largest number of citations relating to the *Abbott* case. Since the case was decided in 1984, the hardbound volumes from 1985 in the basic series were only one year old and, consequently, contained no citations for *Abbott*.

The cryptic citations in *Shepard's Citations* can be understood by examining the table of abbreviations in the first few pages of a bound volume in the citator series (see Figure 8-7). If no abbreviations appear before the citations, it is safe to assume the case has been merely cited, or referred to, in the cited sources. The case has not been overruled ("o"), questioned ("q"), criticized ("c"), or distinguished ("d"); and it has not been cited as controlling ("f," or to be followed) in any future case. This is sufficient information by which to conclude that the case has not been adversely affected by any subsequent decision and remains "good law."

The publisher's explanation (see Figure 8-8) is another resource to help the reader understand the cryptic citations used in *Shepard's Citations*. This page shows where to find various types of citations and explains how they are grouped in the columns. This page also illustrates the way in which the prefix abbreviations are used and describes how the raised numbers that follow the cited sources are to be used.

The sample page in Figure 8-6, found in the front of each volume, can now be better understood. The first citation refers to volume 738 of the *Southwestern Reporter 2d*, the second headnote, at page 174. Page 174 is not the page on which the case begins but is the page on which the case being shepardized is mentioned. This feature of *Shepard's Citations* leads the reader directly to the headnote that pertains to the case that is of interest, so the reader can select the appropriate cases for further analysis.

If a citation is prefixed by an "o" (overruled), the reader will want to know, "in what respect?" The case still may not be eliminated as having authority as precedent. The cited case must be read thoroughly to determine whether the case being shepardized still can be considered "good law."

This process is somewhat more difficult to explain than it is actually to accomplish. The *Shepard's Citations* series packs a lot of information into a very small space and, therefore, has great utility. As more familiarity is gained with the concept of shepardizing, the exceptional value of this tool for purposes of historical case analysis and treatment of the case will become apparent. The *Shepard's Citations* system also includes references to statutes, law reviews, federal agency materials, tax materials, *Restatements*, labor materials, and other sources. These additional research tools are explained in detail in advanced courses for professionals.

OTHER RESOURCES

The three basic elements of the law are statutes, cases, and commentary, but additional tools that augment the basic research materials containing these elements have been introduced in this chapter. These materials are all tied into the basic body of the law—"corpus juris." Citator services and finding tools are other resources for research, and different starting points and research methodologies can be used for various research problems.

This chapter has mentioned only some of the basic secondary source materials that are generally referred to as "commentary." These materials include encyclopedias, treatises, textbooks, law review articles, scholarly journals, and

ABBREVIATIONS—ANALYSIS

History of Case

a	(affirmed)	Same case affirmed on appeal.
cc	(connected case)	Different case from case cited but arising out of same subject matter or intimately connected therewith.
D	(dismissed)	Appeal from same case dismissed.
m	(modified)	Same case modified on appeal.
r	(reversed)	Same case reversed on appeal.
s	(same case)	Same case as case cited.
S	(superseded)	Substitution for former opinion.
v	(vacated)	Same case vacated.
US	cert den	Certiorari denied by U. S. Supreme Court.
US	cert dis	Certiorari dismissed by U. S. Supreme Court.
US	reh den	Rehearing denied by U. S. Supreme Court.
US	reh dis	Rehearing dismissed by U. S. Supreme Court.
(writ of error)		Writ of error adjudicated.
US	app pndg	Appeal pending before the U. S. Supreme Court.

Treatment of Case

c	(criticised)	Soundness of decision or reasoning in cited case criticised for reasons given.
d	(distinguished)	Case at bar different either in law or fact from case cited for reasons given.
e	(explained)	Statement of import of decision in cited case. Not merely a restatement of the facts.
f	(followed)	Cited as controlling.
h	(harmonized)	Apparent inconsistency explained and shown not to exist.
j	(dissenting opinion)	Citation in dissenting opinion.
L	(limited)	Refusal to extend decision of cited case beyond precise issues involved.
o	(overruled)	Ruling in cited case expressly overruled.
p	(parallel)	Citing case substantially alike or on all fours with cited case in its law or facts.
q	(questioned)	Soundness of decision or reasoning in cited case questioned.

Reproduced by permission of Shepard's/McGraw Hill, Inc. Further reproduction is strictly prohibited.

Figure 8.7
Shepard's Case Abbreviations—Analysis

other publications. There are also more detailed materials and sources such as practice guides, forms books, and collections of local rules. The full range of commentary and secondary source material on legal issues cannot be covered in an introductory textbook.

There are a number of looseleaf services that specialize in fast reporting of current legal documents. One of the most important of these is called *United States Law Week* (U.S.L.W.), which could be called a national legal newspaper. It

ILLUSTRATIVE CASE

Southwestern Reporter, Second Series
Vol. 233
–449–
(149Tex319)

s228SW960	1
258SW⁴790	
260SW³590	
278SW³581	
e290SW⁶266	
299SW173	
310SW⁷376	
333SW⁷411	
355SW³740	
355SW⁵741	
366SW²696	2
392SW⁴584	
498SW³516	
h598SW⁵723	
f701SW⁶60	
d762SW⁴213	
794SW¹775	
j794SW778	
e821SW⁵435	
e821SW⁷435	
Cir. 5 254F2d³683	3
Mo 305SW⁷102	4
NM 389P2d603	5
8A₃1254s	
16A₃80n	
16A₃82n	7
16A₃123n	
16A₃172n	

Citations to the case of *Massie v. Copeland* as reported in Volume 233 Southwestern Reporter, Second Series at page 449 are shown in the left margin of this page in the same form in which they appear in the Southwestern Reporter, Second Series division of this edition.

Cross references to a cited case as also reported in a series of state reports and the American Law Reports are shown enclosed in parentheses immediately following the page number of that case when first available and are not repeated in subsequent volumes. Thus the reference "(149 Tex 319)" immediately following the –449– page number of the *Massie* case indicates that that case is also reported in Volume 149 Texas Reports at page 319 and the absence of an American Law Reports reference enclosed in parentheses indicates that the *Massie* case is not also reported in the American Law Reports.

Citations to each cited case are grouped as follows:

1. citations by state and federal courts analyzed as to the history of the cited case;
2. other citations by courts of the state in which the cited case was decided analyzed as to the treatment accorded the cited case;
3. other citations by federal courts analyzed as to the treatment accorded the cited case;
4. citations, arranged alphabetically by states, by courts of states covered by the Southwestern Reporter other than the state in which the cited case was decided analyzed as to the treatment accorded the cited case;
5. citations, arranged alphabetically by states, by courts of states covered by any units of the National Reporter System other than Southwestern Reporter;
6. citations in articles in the American Bar Association Journal;
7. citations in annotations of Lawyers' Edition, United States Supreme Court Reports and the American Law Reports; and
8. citations in legal texts.

For the purpose of illustration only, this grouping has been indicated by bracketing the citations accordingly. It will be noted that as yet there are no citations in groups six or eight.

In indicating the history and treatment of a cited case, the letter-form abbreviations shown on page xvii are used.

An examination of the citations relating to the history of the cited case indicates that another phase of the same case "s" was reported in Volume 228 Southwestern Reporter, Second Series "SW" at page 960.

An examination of the treatment accorded the cited case indicates it has been explained "e" in 290 SW 266, harmonized "h" at 598 SW 723, followed "f" in 701 SW 60, distinguished "d" in 762 SW 213 and cited in a dissenting opinion "j" in 794 SW 778. The *Massie* case has also been referred to without particular comment in other Texas cases reported in the Southwestern Reporter, Second Series and in the Federal Reporter, Second Series. It should also be noted that this case has been referred to by a Missouri court as illustrated in group four by the citation 305 SW 102 and by the courts of New Mexico as cited in the Pacific Reporter, Second Series.

Citations by the various federal courts other than the United States Supreme Court appear under the headings indicating the federal courts or the judicial circuits from which the citations originated. Thus, federal courts cases decided in the Fifth Circuit appear under the heading "Cir 5".

Figure 8.8
Shepard's "Illustrative Case" Explanation

Reproduced by permission of Shepard's/McGraw Hill Inc. Further reproduction is strictly prohibited.

comes out in two volumes: "Supreme Court Sections" and "General Law Sections." *Law Week* covers mainly the United States Supreme Court, but it also may contain information about important federal statutes, federal or state cases, and federal administrative rulings that have not yet been reported elsewhere. It is the best place to find current decisions of the Supreme Court for the most recent cases that have not been bound into the various reporter volumes. *Law Week* reports the full text of the latest decisions of the Supreme Court with headnotes and commentary. The weekly issue is received by the libraries on Wednesday or Thursday of every week and contains the text of the Supreme Court decisions handed down on Monday (the usual "decision day" for the court). The current docket, journal, orders, and summary of oral arguments are included in *Law Week* coverage.

Finally, there is now extensive opportunity to conduct computer searches in legal research. Computer systems are particularly useful for researching specific names and fact patterns and narrow legal topics. The computer programs LEXIS and WESTLAW are not suited to the needs of beginners and nonprofessionals, nor are they particularly helpful in the research of broad legal concepts or in background research. They are very expensive to use; the cost of online time, even at commercial billing rates, exceeds thirty dollars per hour.

The coverage of library files and databases for these computerized systems is increasing, but these systems generally do not permit extended historical searches. For the period since the 1970s, however, they offer comprehensive indexing, speed, flexibility, and access to up-to-the-minute legal information. They may contain information that is not available in the library in printed form.

CHAPTER SUMMARY

1. Becoming acquainted with the basic legal research tools is an essential aspect of law-related education. Knowledge of the law requires knowing how to find the applicable law and assessing the practical application of the law to a specific set of factual circumstances.

2. Since legislative enactments are the primary means of lawmaking today, the annotated codes are the best sources with which to begin legal research. The state and federal codes are compilations of statutory and constitutional sources of law arranged by topic and indexed. Most of these codes have annotations that add significant cases and commentary to facilitate understanding of the interpretation of this "black letter" law.

3. The state and federal annotated codes are the most comprehensive reference sources; they provide updated information through pocket supplements located in the back jacket cover of each volume. Citations to cases and commentary allow the researcher to extend the search to original sources.

4. Federal and state administrative codes are compilations of governmental agency rules and regulations that have the force of law. The *Code of Federal Regulations* and state administrative codes are indexed sources of substantive administrative law.

5. Secondary sources of general principles of the common law are found in the *Restatements of the Law* and in other treatises. These sources are not the law itself, but they are secondary references of exceptionally persuasive character.

6. Primary sources of the common law may be found in digests and reporters. The digests for each jurisdiction are designed to assist the researcher in finding relevant case law indexed by topic. A digest consists of a series of brief abstracts (or digests) of cases decided by the courts concerning particular issues of law. The digests provide cross-references to the primary source, which is the full text of the court opinion found in the relevant reporter.

7. The case citator services provided in the *Shepard's Citations* system enable the researcher to update the history of a precedent to determine the reliability of that particular case as precedent. These volumes and their supplements refer the researcher to subsequent actions taken by the courts that might affect the legal precedent of the particular case. The *Shepard's Citations* series consulted must correspond with the reporter in which the opinion was originally found.

8. The basic elements of the law are statutes, cases, and commentary. This chapter has introduced the basic tools of research that identify these elements. Many other materials such as legal dictionaries, legal encyclopedias, practice guides, and forms books are valuable reference tools in legal research; and secondary source materials such as treatises, textbooks, law review articles, scholarly journals, and looseleaf legal news services provide commentary and explanation.

KEY TERMS: COMMON ABBREVIATIONS

(A. or A.2d) *Atlantic Reporter*

(A.L.I.) American Law Institute

(A.L.R.) *American Law Reports*

(Am. Jur. 2d) *American Jurisprudence 2d*

(C.F.R.) *Code of Federal Regulations*

(C.J.S.) *Corpus Juris Secundum*

(F. or F.2d) *Federal Reporter*

(F. Supp.) *Federal Supplement*

(L. Ed. 2d) *United States Supreme Court Reports—Lawyer's Edition*

(L.S.A.) *List of [C.F.R.] Sections Affected*

(N.E. or N.E.2d) *North Eastern Reporter*

(N.W. or N.W.2d) *North Western Reporter*

(P. or P.2d) *Pacific Reporter*

(S. Ct.) *Supreme Court Reporter*

(S.E. or S.E.2d) *South Eastern Reporter*

(So. or So. 2d) *Southern Reporter*

(S.W. or S.W.2d) *South Western Reporter*

(U.S.) *United States Reports*

(U.S.C.) *United States Code*

(U.S.C.A.) *United States Code Annotated*

(U.S.C.S.) *United States Code Service*

(U.S.L.W.) *United States Law Week*

SOURCES AND SUGGESTED READING

Kunz, Christina L., Deborah A. Schmedemann, C. Peter Erlinder, and Matthew P. Downs. 1986. *The Process of Legal Research*. Boston: Little, Brown.

Lewis, Alfred J. 1985. *Using American Law Books*. 2d ed. Dubuque, Iowa: Kendall/Hunt.

PART THREE

UNDERSTANDING CRIMINAL LEGAL PROCEDURES

The next four chapters of this textbook illustrate the major procedural stages in a felony (or serious) criminal case. In criminal cases, both state and federal governments must adhere to an extensive set of United States constitutional guarantees of "due process of law" in the exercise of the government's fundamental responsibility to see that the laws are faithfully executed.

The first chapter in this section introduces a hypothetical criminal case and provides an overview of the constitutional developments regarding criminal due process. The case is followed through the pretrial, trial, and appeal stages and illustrates the functional repsonsibilities of the control, court, and corrections subsystems of the criminal justice system.

CHAPTER NINE

INTRODUCTION TO CRIMINAL LEGAL PROCESS

CAPITAL CITY BANNER
August 12, 1992
CRITICAL SHOOTING IN MARKET ROBBERY

The Jiffy Stop convenience market (at State and Fifth streets) was the scene of an armed robbery last night. The owner, Samual J. Stone, is reported to be unconscious and in critical condition at Central Hospital after receiving a gunshot wound to the head.

Capital City police indicate the shooting occurred just before midnight. They were called to the scene by a customer who saw a car speed out of the service area of the market and who later discovered the victim and an empty cash register. Police were able to apprehend a prime suspect within hours because of the alert customer's observations.

The suspect is being held for questioning, and police are checking out his story before making official charges.

The above newspaper account of an armed robbery involving a convenience store describes an all too familiar occurrence in modern urban centers. This incident and subsequent events, however, as described in the next four chapters, demonstrate the basic concepts of criminal procedure. Note that citations for cases referred to by name and date in each chapter can be found in the Sources and Suggested Reading section at the end of each chapter.

Frank Builder had reported the robbery to the police shortly before midnight on August 11. He had seen two young men jump into their car and speed away as he drove into the convenience store parking lot. Suspecting that something was wrong, he made a note of the car's license plate number. Inside the store, Builder found the store owner unconscious behind the counter—blood was streaming from his face, and he was clutching a pistol in his right hand.

Frank Builder called 911 and reported the emergency situation, then assisted the officers and paramedics in their efforts to save the victim. Three plainclothes officers from the robbery detail arrived at the scene shortly thereafter to begin their investigation.

Initial Investigation and Arrest

The three officers from the robbery detail were briefed about what had been learned by the officers at the scene and were told the license number of the suspects' vehicle. One of the officers radioed in for a "make" on the license number. The detectives then asked Frank Builder to describe exactly what he saw when he arrived at the scene. The customer had calmed down, and the officers let him take his time to think of every detail.

He said he saw a young male with a dark complexion at a gas pump drop the hose and run to the passenger side of the car. He saw another figure run around the front of the car but did not get a good look at him. "He jumped into the driver's side, and the car shot out of there like they were in a big hurry," the witness explained.

He described the vehicle as a dark green passenger car, "pretty old, with several scrapes and dents in the fenders." He was unsure about the make of the car: "It wasn't an American car, some type of foreign compact, I think," he explained.

The police officers cordoned off the gas pump area of the filling station and store, directing all onlookers away. They found one of the pump hoses on the concrete pedestal beside the pump and dusted it for fingerprints. They also found an automobile gas cap on the asphalt area near the pump. In the store they found the cash register empty, and they took photographs of the crime scene. By this time the police dispatcher had been able to identify the owner of the vehicle. It was registered to one Jesse Williams, 467 Elm Street, apartment 4, in Capital City.

Initial Arrest

The robbery detail had a suspect; they wrapped up their preliminary investigation quickly in order to follow this significant lead. A cooperative and observant witness had provided them with something concrete to pursue. Two of the plainclothes officers from the robbery detail were dispatched to the suspect's address while the third remained at the scene to finish the investigation.

Officers Jim Cox and Mike Develon located Jesse Williams's address, which belonged to a small, four-unit apartment house on the west side of town. It was after 1:30 A.M.; there were no lights in the apartment, and there was no car in the front parking lot or on the street that matched the description of the vehicle they were seeking. They decided to "stake out" the place and wait for the occupant to return. As they watched from a convenient vantage point, they called for a records check on the suspect. The department reported that they had no prior arrest or conviction record on this individual.

At 2:21 A.M., a dark gray, four-door Toyota Corolla pulled into the parking lot. It had the suspect's license number. The police officers immediately stopped the individual as he got out of the car and placed him under arrest. They identified themselves as police officers and told the suspect to keep his hands raised and to place them on the top of the car. Mike patted down the suspect to search for concealed weapons, and Jim Cox placed the handcuffs on him. No weapon was found on his person, so they looked inside the vehicle for a weapon.

The officers opened the glove compartment, looked under the seats, and thoroughly examined the passenger area of the vehicle. They found no weapon or other evidence connected with the robbery in the vehicle. They then examined the outside of the vehicle and noted several scratches and dents that corroborated the witness's description of the car, and they also noted the absence of a cap on the vehicle's gasoline tank. The vehicle was locked and sealed with police tape.

The suspect, Jesse Williams, was placed in the officers' car, and while Jim drove to the police station, Mike explained to Jesse, "You have the right to remain silent, anything you say can and will be used against you in a court of law, and you have the right to an attorney to represent you." Jesse said that he understood his rights but that he did not know what this was all about.

Jail and Booking Procedure

At the police station, Jesse was strip-searched by the jailers while Jim and Mike consulted with their partner on the robbery detail. The officers learned that the convenience store victim was in critical condition and was not expected to live. "That means we have a potential murder charge on this one," said the partner. "Let's get the eyewitness down here to make a positive ID," Mike commented. The third partner thought that could wait until the next day. Frank Builder had been a very cooperative witness, and he had been up most of the night. Mr. Builder had been told to come to the police station at 1:00 P.M. the next day.

Jesse was being processed for "booking." This procedure involves fingerprints and "mug shots" to identify and secure the prisoner. These forms of identification enable the police to check their records and national FBI files for possible aliases or other identification the suspect might have used to commit crimes in other areas. The suspect's body cavities and clothing were thoroughly searched, but no concealed weapons, contraband, or further evidence concerning the crime were found. A wrecker was sent to Jesse's apartment to tow his vehicle into the police impoundment lot, since it was the most important evidence they had uncovered thus far.

Custodial Interrogation

The robbery squad called Jesse into an interrogation room for questioning. They again informed him of his right to remain silent and his right to a lawyer. He indicated that he understood his rights and wanted to know why he had been arrested. They asked him where he had been until 2:30 in the morning on a Tuesday night. He answered that he had been to see his girlfriend and gave them her name, address, and phone number. Jesse told the police he had been at his girlfriend's house all the time from 10:00 P.M. to 2:00 A.M. Mike asked, "Is that all you want to tell us?"

"Yes," Jesse replied, "but why are you holding me?"

They told him he was being detained on suspicion in connection with a robbery that took place at the Jiffy Stop convenience store. He denied any connection with the robbery.

Further Investigation

The police officers checked the suspect's story by going to his girlfriend's apartment. They checked the police records before they left and found that she had been convicted on charges of prostitution and drug possession. When they arrived, the sun was just coming up, and they were scheduled to go off duty in two hours. After knocking several times, they finally got her to the door. They asked if she knew Jesse Williams. She answered that she did and that he was with her until 2:00 last evening. They asked if she would let them come in, and she agreed.

The girlfriend said she had known Jesse for about six months and had gone out with him several times. They did not go out last night, but he came to her apartment.

"When did he arrive?" asked Mike Develon.

"I don't know exactly, but he left about 2:00," she replied.

"Could he have gotten here after 12:00?" Develon asked.

"I don't know exactly, it was late and I was asleep on the couch," she said.

"Did he leave anything in the apartment?" asked Jim Cox.

"I don't think so, he brought a six pack of beer with him, but that's all," she said.

The robbery squad found four beer cans in her trash and two full cans in the refrigerator. The girlfriend gave them permission to take them. The beer cans were carefully placed in plastic bags, and the officers left.

The robbery squad agreed to draft a report and leave a copy for the homicide department so a detective could continue the investigation when the officers went off duty. They put a "hold order" on Jesse to prevent any possible release on bail. The homicide detective assigned to the case would coordinate a lineup procedure for the witness who would arrive at 1:00. The detective would go over the facts of the case and follow up on a requested FBI check on the suspect.

BASIC CRIMINAL CONCEPTS

Our federal system places primary responsibility for the maintenance of public order and domestic crime control in the state and local units of government. The federal government has no expressly delegated constitutional mandate to make or enforce uniform criminal justice standards for the United States.

This legal concept of state responsibility for the maintenance of public order is generally referred to as the state "police power." The state police power, therefore, is a reserved power of the states to enact and enforce laws that protect the "health, safety, and morals of the people." The independent and decentralized police power is jealously guarded by the states. It is also interpreted by the courts to be one of the most fundamental characteristics of our form of federal government.

Crimes

What is a crime? The fundamental legal concept of crimes, as opposed to torts, is found in the public nature of this substantive area of the law. Crimes are acts or omissions prohibited by law that constitute wrongs against the state (or society as a whole) and must be prosecuted by a designated agent of the government. The concept of the "guilt" of the individual who is accused of having committed a crime is another fundamental characteristic that distinguishes crimes from torts.

An individual's guilt in connection with a crime becomes relevant only after it has first been established that a crime has been committed; that is, only after a prima facie case has been established. Those elements that the prosecutor must plead and prove to show that a particular crime has been committed are referred to as the **corpus delicti** (or body) of the crime. The two most fundamental elements of all serious crimes are:

1. **actus reus**, the commission of some prohibited act; and
2. **mens rea**, a criminal state of mind.

These concepts were introduced in Chapter Three and in the illustrative cases (*People v. Moore* and *People v. Braly*) in Appendix B. These ideas are expanded in the next few chapters to facilitate a deeper appreciation of how these basic principles affect the enforcement of criminal law. Each particular crime has its own distinctive elements; generally, the more serious the crime, the more elements it requires. If one or more of these elements is missing, the particular crime could not have been committed.

Development of Various Types of Crime

Our common law heritage still influences the criminal law even though most substantive criminal offenses now are defined by statute. As the common law of crimes emerged in England during the twelfth century, one of the primary distinctions was between offenses considered ***mala in se*** and those that were ***mala prohibita***. "Ordinary crimes" (murder, rape, theft, arson) were considered acts that were "bad in themselves" (*mala in se*). They were considered felonies that could be prosecuted in the central criminal courts. Crimes that were *mala prohibita*, on the other hand, were prohibited by legislation and were considered to be misdemeanors to be enforced by justices of the peace. These offenses (rioting, poaching, vagrancy, drunkenness) were crimes because they were prohibited by the positive law (*mala prohibita*).

The distinction between ordinary crimes and those that are prohibited provides a theoretical distinction between two major sociological theories—the "consensus model" and the "conflict model." The consensus model asserts that most western societies have agreed that murder, rape, robbery, arson, theft, and associated crimes of violence (*mala in se*) are crimes based on legal norms that emerged through the dynamics of cultural processes to meet certain functional needs and requirements essential for maintaining the social fabric. The conflict model, a relatively new sociological approach, asserts a contrasting view that the conflict of political power allows special interest groups to affect the content of modern criminal codes. Power, force, and constraint, rather than common values, are the fundamental sources of many crimes today. The emphasis is on crimes that are *mala prohibita*. "According to this approach, wrongful acts are characteristic of all classes in society, and the powerful not only shape the law to their own advantage but also are able to dictate the use of enforcement resources in such a way that certain groups are labeled and processed by the criminal justice system" (Cole 1993, 8).

Modern legislative authorities have become the dominant lawmakers, and almost all crimes are statutory in nature. The statutory elements of each crime can be found in modern criminal codes. However, these provisions are, in part, codifications of the ancient common law crimes, and in some states, common law crimes continue to be enforced. Common law definitions of the legal meanings of the words and phrases typically found in statutes continue our common law heritage. Many of the classifications of types of crimes are heavily laced with court interpretations based on the common law origin of these concepts.

corpus delicti: the body or substance of the crime, which ordinarily includes two basic elements: actus reus and mens rea.

actus reus: a wrongful act or deed that renders the actor criminally liable if combined with mens rea.

mens rea: a guilty mind or criminal intent; guilty knowledge and willfulness.

mala in se: acts normally wrong in themselves; offenses against conscience.

mala prohibita: prohibited wrongs or acts; acts made into offenses by positive law.

Basically, the types of crimes classified as *mala in se* have remained fairly static, and all are considered felonies today. But those crimes known as *mala prohibita* have been greatly expanded. Modern legislatures have added two major groups to the traditional offenses: so-called victimless crimes, and regulatory offenses. Victimless crimes (drug offenses, gambling, prostitution) and regulatory offenses are the most prevalent types of crime today.

Treason, Felonies, and Misdemeanors

The common law divided crimes into three major groups according to the gravity of the offense: treason, felonies, and misdemeanors. This division has important legal consequences. In most states, misdemeanors are processed in different court jurisdictions than are felonies, and convictions carry less severe punishments. Petty offenses (speeding, parking violations) are a fourth category of crimes that are treated as summary offenses: such petty offenses are usually left to the discretion of a local magistrate who has the authority to dispose of them summarily (without trial).

Treason

Treason is the only crime that is constitutionally defined. The nature of our federal system and the logical connection of this crime to the nation's conduct of foreign affairs makes it exclusively the subject of federal authority.

Felonies and Misdemeanors

The distinction between felonies and misdemeanors is the least understood concept in the classification of crimes. Both the state and the federal governments use this distinction, but each of the fifty-one jurisdictions has a somewhat different definition in statutory law of exactly what constitutes a felony and what constitutes a misdemeanor.

In general, a **misdemeanor** is a less serious crime. It usually is punishable by fines and short terms of incarceration in local jails or county workhouses. Misdemeanors are usually handled by somewhat different procedures than felony cases, and they are disposed of in the local courts. Federal misdemeanors are offenses for which the penalty is imprisonment for less than one year. In many states, however, a misdemeanor conviction can result in a maximum fine of $10,000 and imprisonment up to five years. The lack of a uniform standard has caused the United States Supreme Court to rule that in "right to counsel" issues, the accused has a right to counsel when the crime carries a potential jail sentence.

Felonies are the type of crimes discussed in the next four chapters. They are subject to the full range of "due process" procedures guaranteed by the United States Constitution. The states do not have uniform criminal justice procedures, but decisions of the United States Supreme Court in recent times have produced a uniform set of minimal standards that can be described as a "national criminal procedure" that is fairly uniform in character.

CRIMINAL DUE PROCESS

The Bill of Rights in the United States Constitution was ratified in 1791 as a result of state concerns over the potential abuse of authority by the national govern-

---

treason: defined by the United States Constitution, article III, section 3, as levying war against the United States by adhering to its enemies or giving them aid and comfort. Conviction requires two witnesses or confession in open court.

misdemeanors: offenses lower than felonies, generally punishable by fine or imprisonment in a facility other than a penitentiary.

felonies: crimes of a graver or more serious nature than misdemeanors.

ment. Many of these ten amendments (particularly the Fourth, Fifth, Sixth, and Eighth amendments) are directly concerned with criminal due process of law.

The amendments originally were interpreted to limit only the federal government in its exercise of the authority given to it by the Constitution. State criminal procedures were regulated only by state constitutions and were subject to the limitations of their own bills of rights. The various bills of rights were derived from our common law heritage and had many similarities, but there were substantial differences in both wording and interpretation.

The Fourteenth Amendment

The American Civil War (or War Between the States), from 1861 to 1865, produced substantial constitutional changes that ultimately led to a set of uniform standards of criminal justice procedure throughout the United States. The Fourteenth Amendment (ratified in 1868) specifically states:

> No State shall make or enforce any law which shall abridge the privileges or immunities of citizens of the United States; nor shall any State deprive any person of life, liberty, or property, without due process of law; nor deny to any person within its jurisdiction the equal protection of the laws.

The United States Supreme Court has struggled with the precise meaning of the "due process" clause of the Fourteenth Amendment since its ratification. Several individual Supreme Court justices have argued that the intended meaning of the framers of the Fourteenth Amendment was to incorporate the United States Bill of Rights and apply those amendments to state criminal actions. A majority of the Supreme Court has never expressed this total incorporation view of the meaning of the amendment's provisions. Instead, most Supreme Court justices have held the common law view that the Fourteenth Amendment protects "traditional notions" of due process. Justice Benjamin Cardozo's majority opinion in *Palko v. Connecticut* (1937), for example, expresses the philosophy that the Fourteenth Amendment refers to those principles "implicit in the concept of ordered liberty."

What Has Not Been Incorporated?

Several Supreme Court justices have insisted that the due process clause neither imposes on the states all the requirements of the Bill of Rights nor restricts the reach of the Fourteenth Amendment to only those rights enumerated in the first eight amendments. Fundamental fairness, not mere compliance with the Bill of Rights, is the touchstone. Consequently, under the fundamental rights interpretation, a state may violate due process even though its procedure is not contrary to any specific guarantee in the first eight amendments.

Nonetheless, the Supreme Court has adopted a **selective incorporation** doctrine that combines aspects of both the fundamental rights and the total incorporation theories. This contemporary theory incorporates nearly all the provisions of the Fourth, Fifth, Sixth, and Eighth amendments into the Fourteenth Amendment due process clause "whole and intact" and enforces them against the states in every case, according to the same standards applied to the federal government. Most of this development has occurred since the 1960s and is associated with the Warren Court era that seemed intent upon fashioning a clear set of minimal procedural guarantees in all criminal cases, whether prosecuted in the federal or the state courts.

selective incorporation: doctrine that combines the fundamental rights concept with selected provisions of the federal Bill of Rights to define criminal due process of law.

Of the Bill of Rights amendments that most clearly relate to criminal procedure, only the Fifth Amendment requirement of grand jury indictment has been specifically held *not* to be required by the due process clause of the Fourteenth Amendment (*Hurtado v. California*, 110 U.S. 516, 4 S.Ct. 111, 28 L.Ed. 232 [1884]). The Eighth Amendment prohibition against excessive fines and bails has, remarkably, never been ruled upon by the United States Supreme Court, since the issue has never been squarely presented in a specific case (Rossum and Tarr 1987,427–29).

The specific words of the United States Constitution in the Fourth, Fifth, Sixth, and Eighth amendments are of central concern to criminal justice procedure throughout the United States. See Appendix A at the end of the text for the specific wording of these amendments. The relevant clauses and the United States Supreme Court cases that have established precedent for the incorporation of those particular clauses into the interpretation of the Fourteenth Amendment due process clause are listed in Table 9-1.

Basic Court Decisions

Although there are numerous court decisions that must be consulted to appreciate fully the complexity of the constitutional limitations in the area of criminal due process, this textbook discusses only the most basic principles and the manner in which American courts have developed the philosophy currently employed to enforce these constitutional limitations.

The Exclusionary Rule

The United States Supreme Court has developed a unique remedy for implementing the constitutional guarantees in the area of criminal due process. That

TABLE 9.1 Selective Incorporation of Criminal Procedure Rights and Year of Application to the States

Rights	Case and Year
Fourth Amendment	
Unreasonable search and seizure	*Wolf v. Colorado* (1949)
Exclusionary rule (*Implied)	*Mapp v. Ohio* (1961)
Fifth Amendment	
Grand jury clause	Not incorporated
Double jeopardy clause	*Benton v. Maryland* (1969)
Self-incrimination clause	*Mallory v. Hogan* (1964)
Sixth Amendment	
Speedy trial clause	*Klopfer v. North Carolina* (1967)
Public trial clause	*In re Oliver* (1948)
Impartial jury clause	*Parker v. Gladden* (1966)
Jury trial clause	*Duncan v. Louisiana* (1968)
Notice clause	*Cole v. Arkansas* (1948)
Confrontation clause	*Pointer v. Texas* (1965)
Compulsory process clause	*Washington v. Texas* (1967)
Right to counsel clause	*Gideon v. Wainwright* (1963)
Eighth Amendment	
Excessive fines and bails clause	Not incorporated
Cruel and unusual punishment clause	*Robinson v. California* (1962)

remedy is often referred to as the "exclusionary rule" because it invokes a rule that prohibits the use of evidence obtained in violation of the Constitution. Most democratic societies, including England, allow evidence to be introduced that is relevant to the guilt or innocence of a person, no matter how it was obtained. After the case is settled in these countries, the police officers who have violated the constitutions may be punished for their own violations of the law in a separate tort action (Wilson 1989,505.)

The American evidence principle is sometimes referred to as the "poisoned fruit doctrine." The doctrine argues that if the tree is poisoned, so is its fruit; thus, even evidence that proves a defendant's guilt beyond a reasonable doubt cannot be entered into evidence at trial if it was secured in an unconstitutional manner.

The basic philosophy of the Supreme Court was clearly established with regard to federal criminal prosecutions in 1914, when the Court held for the first time that in federal prosecutions, the Fourth Amendment bars the use of evidence secured through an illegal search and seizure (*Weeks v. United States*, 232 U.S. 383, 34 S.Ct. 341, 58 L.Ed. 652 [1914]). The Court's interpretation of the Fourth Amendment meant, quite simply, that "conviction by means of unlawful seizures and enforced confessions ... should find no sanction in the judgments of the courts...."

However, in *Wolf v. Colorado*, 338 U.S. 25, 69 S.Ct. 1359, 93 L.Ed. 1782 (1949), the Court discussed for the first time the effect of the Fourth Amendment upon the states through the operation of the due process clause of the Fourteenth Amendment. Although the Court held "that in a prosecution in a State court for a State crime the Fourteenth Amendment does not forbid the admission of evidence obtained by an unreasonable search and seizure," it also concluded that only where "a State affirmativly sanction[ed] such police incursion into privacy [would] it ... run counter to the guaranty of the Fourteenth Amendment...." This decision created a situation of inconsistent application of a fundamental principle of justice that the Court ultimately attempted to rectify in its landmark decision unifying the exclusionary rule in 1961.

The Supreme Court, in *Mapp v. Ohio*, 367 U.S. 643, 81 S.Ct. 1684, 6 L.Ed.2d 1081 (1961), specifically overruled its previous decision in *Wolf v. Colorado* and created one universal standard by applying the principle expressed in *Weeks v. United States* to state as well as federal prosecutions. The majority opinion was to hold that "all evidence obtained by searches and seizures in violation of the Constitution is, by that same authority, inadmissible in a state court."

Justice Clark, in his majority opinion, explained the logical consistency of this decision by declaring that previous decisions had recognized the purpose of the exclusionary rule, which "is to deter—to compel respect for the constitutional guaranty in the only effectively available way—by removing the incentive to disregard it...." To hold otherwise would make the Constitution merely "a form of words," granting a right but in reality withholding its privilege and enjoyment. He noted the practice of federal officers who were invited by the previous rule to "step across the street to the State's attorney with their unconstitutionally seized evidence. Prosecution on the basis of that evidence was then had in state court in utter disregard of the enforceable Fourth Amendment."

This logic seems impeccable, but a great deal of criticism has been leveled at the exclusionary rule, particularly by persons in law enforcement and political conservatives. The critics have argued that the proper remedy for unconstitutional activity by the police is a tort action, not the suppression of evidence. Why should the criminal go free because the police blundered? Supporters of the exclusionary rule argue that a tort action is an awkward mechanism for controlling police behavior; a rule requiring such an action would be based on the assumption that victims of police misconduct would be able to secure adequate legal counsel, which is rarely the case.

The *Mapp* decision continues to be controlling precedent, but it has been under heavy attack since 1961. Chief Justice Warren Burger proposed an elaborate plan to eliminate the exclusionary rule in a dissenting opinion in *Bivens v. Six-Unknown Named Agents* 1971. The plan would have involved congressional legislation to establish a claims system for the punishment of constitutional offenders through civil tort actions. However, Congress has never passed such a law, and the Court has never accepted this argument.

Rehnquist Court Exceptions

The Supreme Court has modified the exclusionary rule somewhat through a number of exceptions. In *United States v. Leon*, 468 U.S. 897, 104 S.Ct. 3405, 82 L.Ed.2d 677 (1984) and *Massachusetts v. Sheppard*, 468 U.S. 981, 104 S.Ct. 3424, 82 L.Ed.2d 737 (1984), the Court held that the exclusionary rule should not be applied so as to suppress the introduction of evidence at a criminal trial obtained in the reasonable belief that the search and seizure at issue was consistent with the Fourth Amendment. This "good faith" exception has been supplemented with an "inevitable discovery" exception in *Nix v. Williams*, 467 U.S. 431, 104 S.Ct. 2501, 81 L.Ed.2d 377 (1984), in which the Court held that evidence obtained in violation of due process of law need not be suppressed if it would have been inevitably discovered by lawful means.

The Court also has recognized a "public safety exception" to the exclusionary rule that allows police officers to question suspects concerning the whereabouts of dangerous weapons concealed in public places. The Rehnquist Court, for example, held that school officials may search student belongings or lockers for prescribed articles, such as guns and drugs, on reasonable suspicion alone (*New Jersey v. T.L.O.*, 469 U.S. 325, 105 S.Ct. 733, 83 L.Ed.2d 720 [1985]).

The Court extended the good faith exception to the exclusionary rule by holding that the Fourth Amendment does not require the exclusion at trial of evidence found by police acting under a statute authorizing warrantless searches, although this holding was later struck down as unconstitutional according to dissenters in *Illinois v. Krull*, 480 U.S. 340, 107 S.Ct. 1160, 94 L.Ed.2d 364 (1987). In more recent decisions, the Court has held that introduction of evidence that was seized in violation of the Fourth Amendment is not sufficient ground for reversal of a conviction if there was enough lawfully seized evidence to uphold a conviction.

The Right to Counsel

The Sixth Amendment right to counsel was initially interpreted to mean that an individual accused of crime had the right to choose which lawyer to employ. It was not until the twentieth century that the Court began to examine the question of right to counsel for indigent persons accused of crimes who cannot afford to hire counsel to defend them.

In 1932, the Supreme Court began this process by examining the effect of poverty on persons accused of crimes that carried the death penalty. In *Powell v. Alabama*, 287 U.S. 45, 53 S.Ct. 55, 77 L.Ed. 158 (1932), the Court held that in capital felony cases, the right to appointed counsel at state expense was secured by the due process clause of the Fourteenth Amendment.

Then, in 1938, the right to appointed counsel was broadened to include counsel for indigent defendants in all federal criminal proceedings of a felony nature. In the case of *Johnson v. Zerbst*, 304 U.S. 458, 58 S.Ct. 1019, 82 L.Ed. 1461 (1938), the Court held: "The Sixth Amendment withholds from federal courts, in all criminal proceedings, the power and authority to deprive an accused of his life or liberty unless he has or waived the assistance of counsel."

With the exception of capital felony cases, the state courts were not required to provide counsel in cases where the defendant was unable to hire a lawyer. The Court considered the fundamental rights issue in *Betts v. Brady*, 316 U.S. 455, 62 S.Ct. 1252, 86 L.Ed. 1595 (1942) and concluded that the states had historically considered the appointment of counsel to be a matter of legislative policy, and "not a fundamental right essential to a fair trial." Justice Black dissented, stressing that "whether a man is innocent cannot be determined from a trial in which, as here, denial of counsel has made it impossible to conclude, with any satisfactory degree of certainty, that the defendant's case was adequately presented."

In the celebrated case of *Gideon v. Wainwright*, 372 U.S. 335, 83 S.Ct. 792, 9 L.Ed.2d 799 (1963), the Court specifically overruled *Betts* and unanimously concluded that an indigent defendant's right to court-appointed counsel is fundamental and essential to a fair trial in state as well as federal prosecutions. Justice Black drafted the majority opinion of the Court, declaring that precedent, reason, and reflection "require us to recognize that any person hauled into court, who is too poor to hire a lawyer, cannot be assured a fair trial unless counsel is provided for him."

This principle of the right to counsel was extended to all criminal cases carrying a potential jail sentence in *Argersinger v. Hamlin*, 407 U.S. 25, 92 S.Ct. 2006, 32 L.Ed.2d 530 (1972), and to all "critical stages" of the process, beginning with custodial interrogation by the police, in other decisions. These "critical stages" are explained more fully later in this and subsequent chapters.

Police Procedure

The Fifth Amendment provides that no person "shall be compelled in any criminal case to be a witness against himself." Although this right was applied in federal cases, it was not until *Mallory v. Hogan*, 378 U.S. 1, 84 S.Ct. 1489, 12 L.Ed.2d 653 (1964) that the Fifth Amendment right to remain silent was considered "a fundamental right necessary to a system of ordered liberty." The Court earlier, in *Brown v. Mississippi*, 297 U.S. 278, 56 S.Ct. 461, 80 L.Ed. 682 (1936), had overturned convictions of three defendants whom police had physically tortured in order to extort confessions. But the *Mallory* decision sought to establish uniform minimal standards by incorporating the Fifth Amendment right to remain silent—that is, by applying the federal rules and precedents to state criminal procedure through the Fourteenth Amendment due process clause.

The *Mallory* decision, however, did not provide adequate guidelines to law enforcement officers regarding the practices that would or would not pass constitutional muster. As a consequence, the Court was confronted with a barrage of "coerced confessions" cases. Practices by police such as attempts to coerce the defendant through a childhood friend on the police force, threats to bring a defendant's wife into custody for questioning, threats to place the defendant's children in the custody of welfare officials, and interrogations of wounded defendants under the influence of so-called truth serums were some of the issues confronting the courts (Rossum and Tarr 1987,435).

In 1966, the Supreme Court finally broke completely with past cases and established a set of administrative guidelines in *Miranda v. Arizona*. It announced specific procedures that would have to be followed by the police to ensure that confessions were knowingly, freely, and voluntarily given. Any statements elicited in violation of these procedures would be inadmissible. A person accused of crime must be informed of his or her basic right to remain silent, warned that any statements can and will be held against him or her in court, that the person has a right to counsel, and that counsel must be made available to the person at the time of custodial interrogation.

Miranda warning: requirement that the accused be informed of basic rights to ensure admissibility of evidence obtained by confessions.

Subsequent court decisions have upheld the ***Miranda* warnings**, but there have been modifications. For example, the prosecution has been allowed to use evidence suppressed as being in violation of *Miranda* to impeach the credibility of defendants who testify in their own behalf and, in so doing, contradict their earlier statements. In *Harris v. New York*, 401 U.S. 222, 91 S.Ct. 643, 28 L.Ed.2d 1 (1971), the Court declared that the privilege against self-incrimination does not include the right to commit perjury.

THE PRETRIAL PROCESS

In general, the police function is referred to as the control subsystem of the overall criminal justice system. The police officers in our illustrative criminal case acted swiftly and efficiently in pursuit of that function by arresting a potentially dangerous suspect when an eyewitness to an armed robbery and potential murder provided them with evidence. An **arrest** occurs when a person is taken into custody to answer for the commission of an offense.

arrest: to deprive a person of liberty by legal authority.

Arrest

Most arrests are made by law enforcement officers, but private individuals are also authorized, under certain conditions, to make interim arrests. Citizens have a duty to report crimes and to assist authorities in the process of law enforcement. Therefore, the **control subsystem** includes citizen participation and cooperation with law enforcement authorities. However, both private individuals and the police risk considerable danger in this process and can incur civil liability for false arrest or for the use of excessive force in making an arrest.

control subsystem: the police function of maintaining order shared with the general public.

An arrest without a warrant was made in our illustrative criminal case. Law enforcement officers are generally permitted to arrest any person without a warrant if the crime was committed in the officer's presence or for a felony committed out of the officer's presence when there are reasonable grounds to believe that the individual has committed the felony.

stop and frisk: the temporary seizure and pat-down search of a person who behaves suspiciously and appears to be armed.

Police officers are given considerable discretionary authority to issue citations for petty offenses, to "stop and frisk" persons suspected of criminal activity, and to make arrests. A **stop and frisk** refers to the use of police authority to stop individuals in public places and to "pat them down" for the possession of concealed weapons when the circumstances or actions of the individuals appear suspicious to the trained police officer. As the United States Supreme Court noted in a frequently quoted case upholding the validity of an arrest made after such a stop and frisk procedure: "[I]t would appear completely unreasonable to deny the officer power to take necessary measures to determine whether the person is in fact carrying a weapon and to neutralize the threat of physical harm . . ." (*Terry v. Ohio*, 392 U.S. 1, 88 S.Ct. 1868, 20 L.Ed.2d 889 [1968]).

This "reasonable" discretionary authority is limited, however, by the due process rules of both federal and state authorities. The arresting officer must file a complaint before a magistrate without unreasonable delay when a person is arrested without a warrant in most jurisdictions. The Federal Rules of Criminal Procedure, and the rules of most states, specifically require this "initial appearance" as a check upon police discretionary arrests.

An **arrest warrant** is a court order which commands that the individual named by it be taken into custody and brought before the court. A complaint must be filed as an application for an arrest warrant. The complaint must provide facts; mere conjecture or suspicion is not sufficient. The facts must be given under oath or by affirmation by a reliable and trustworthy source. Private persons as well as police officers are authorized to file such an application for an arrest warrant. It is the responsibility of the magistrate (usually a lower court judge) to determine if probable cause is sufficient to issue such a court order.

In many jurisdictions and various types of cases, the prosecutor (usually the district attorney) is authorized to seek indictment through a grand jury investigation of suspected criminal activity. If indictment is obtained, an arrest warrant is issued. Arrest is followed by the final pretrial stage generally known as the arraignment.

arrest warrant: a written order made on behalf of the state, based on a complaint issued pursuant to statute or court rule, commanding that the person be brought before a magistrate.

Probable Cause

The concept of "probable cause" is central to understanding of the entire pretrial process in criminal legal actions. The concept is necessarily vague to allow for reasonable discretionary authority, but it also provides limitations on that discretionary authority to protect individual rights against arbitrary and unreasonable use of authority. **Probable cause** is defined as more than mere suspicion. Some specific facts attested to by a trustworthy and reliable source are generally required, but probable cause does not require the degree of certainty that is necessary to justify a conviction.

This general definition must be tempered with the realization that different degrees of probable cause are required as the accused moves through the pretrial process, although all individuals accused of crime do not necessarily go through all of these stages. The basic stages in the pretrial process are:

1. arrest,
2. initial appearance,
3. preliminary hearing,
4. grand jury indictment (or information), and
5. arraignment.

probable cause: reasonable cause: more than mere suspicion; some evidence and reasonable grounds for belief in the existence of facts warranting the complaint.

A somewhat elevated form of probable cause is required at each stage to warrant movement of the accused to the next stage. The officer's discretionary authority to make an arrest is checked by the magistrate's review at the initial appearance stage. Another judge presides over the preliminary hearing, at which an elevated degree of probable cause is required to "bind the case over" to the grand jury. A grand jury indictment requires still more evidence to warrant putting the individual through the trial process. The final pretrial arraignment stage is where the accused is required to enter a plea. More than ninety percent of criminal cases end in sentencing decisions based upon guilty pleas.

Note that some states use the term "arraignment" to refer to the initial appearance stage. This textbook uses the term "arraignment" only for the final pretrial stage of criminal procedure.

Filing a Criminal Complaint

The day following the Jiffy Stop robbery (August 12), the eyewitness, Frank Builder, was asked to make an identification of the suspect from a lineup that included Jesse Williams and several other jail inmates. Frank was unable to make a positive identification of the suspect. He said he was uncertain because he did not get a good look at both suspects.

Frank was taken to the impoundment lot where several rows of cars were parked, including Jesse's. He was asked to identify the vehicle he had seen leaving the crime scene. Frank looked them over carefully from the rear and correctly identified the suspect's car. "That's the car I saw leaving the scene of the crime last night; I'm certain of it. It looks different in the daylight, but it has the same beat-up fenders and broken taillight. I thought it was dark green last night, but that must have been because of the yellow lights at the convenience store," he explained.

Frank Builder dictated a statement to the police legal secretary that was drafted as an affidavit, and he signed it under oath. The secretary was also a notary public and certified that the statement was made and affirmed under oath.

The police officers reviewed all the evidence they had assembled on the case. A check with the hospital revealed that the victim was still in critical condition. He had been identified as the owner of the convenience store in which he was shot. His family had authorized a delicate brain operation to remove the bullet lodged in his skull. A surgeon had removed the bullet, and a police officer was dispatched to retrieve it. The bullet and various sets of fingerprints were sent to the crime laboratory for identification. It would be several days before this information would be adequately processed. However, the police believed they had enough probable cause to charge the suspect, Jesse Williams.

Jesse's alibi was not conclusive. Even if he had been at his girlfriend's apartment, he could have arrived there after the robbery, which took place before midnight. The police were concerned about the accomplice, as the witness had seen two persons in the getaway car. No weapon or other evidence from the holdup had been found, but the eyewitness had placed Jesse's car at the scene of the crime, and Jesse had given no explanation for this. The police decided to charge Jesse with armed robbery involving serious injury to the victim.

Middle State Criminal Code defined robbery in two sections of the code as follows:

> Section 39-13-401. Robbery.—(a) Robbery is the intentional or knowing theft of property from the person of another by violence or putting the person in fear.
> Section 39-13-403. Especially Aggravated Robbery.—(a) Especially aggravated robbery is robbery as defined in § 39-13-401:
> (1) accomplished with a deadly weapon; and
> (2) where the victim suffers serious bodily injury.
> (b) Especially aggravated robbery is a Class A felony. [Acts 1989, ch. 591, § 1.]

The potential penalty for a Class A felony ranged from fifteen to sixty years in prison. If the victim were to die, the charge would be first-degree murder, which carried the death penalty in Middle State.

Initial Appearance

Jesse Williams was taken before the local magistrate authorized to handle preliminary matters such as **initial appearance**, bail, and issuance of search and

initial appearance: court proceeding where the judge advises the defendant of the charges against the defendant and of his or her rights, decides upon bail, and sets the date of the preliminary hearing.

arrest warrants. The magistrate's courtroom was located in another wing of the police headquarters where Jesse was being held. It is often referred to as "night court," but during the day, it is also occupied by a magistrate of limited jurisdiction authorized to handle preliminary matters.

Detective Mike Develon filed the complaint (Form 9-1) with the magistrate and took an oath regarding the truth of the contents of his statement. The "judge" turned to the defendant, handed him a copy of the charge, and informed him of his rights. Jesse said that he did not understand the charge; he was at his girlfriend's house last night. The judge asked the arresting officer whether this claim had been checked. The officer assured him that they had talked with Jesse's girlfriend and that she could not swear to his whereabouts at the exact time of the robbery. The judge informed Jesse that the initial appearance would not involve hearing evidence from the defendant and that he had a right to a preliminary hearing, which would be conducted by the general sessions judge on August 19, 1992, at 9:00 A.M. At that time, Jesse would have a right to have his lawyer present and could prepare evidence in his behalf.

"If you cannot obtain funds to hire a lawyer, you will need to make application for securing legal counsel," the magistrate told Jesse. "Do you want the court to appoint counsel for you?"

"Yes, I guess so," replied Jesse.."My mother is on welfare, and I don't have any money to hire a lawyer."

The judge gave Jesse an application form (see Form 9-2) and told him to complete it. "This is a very serious charge. If the victim dies, you may be charged under Middle State law with first-degree murder, which carries the death penalty," explained the magistrate.

The police officer appealed to the magistrate, asking that Jesse not be released on **bail** because of the potential first-degree murder charge. The magistrate asked if Jesse had any prior convictions or if he was wanted on any outstanding warrants. The officer indicated that they had found no such record, but they had requested a thorough records check through the FBI using Jesse's fingerprints and mug shot as identification.

The magistrate set the bail amount at $100,000. Magistrates are given considerable discretion in setting bail, but most states have general guidelines. In Middle State, the authorities could release the defendant on his own recognizance (ROR or OR) if the offense was minor and the defendant could assure the court that he would meet court appearances. A bail amount of $1,000 might be sufficient for a misdemeanor; $10,000 for a felony not involving a crime against a person; $50,000 for a felony involving a crime against a person; or $100,000 for some form of homicide.

The judge indicated that he could not deny bail until there was a charge of first-degree murder, but he agreed with the officer that the pending potential death of the victim was sufficient to warrant the maximum bail. Bail would be reviewed by the general sessions judge at the preliminary hearing.

Middle State law required that the magistrate notify the victim or the victim's family concerning the date of the preliminary hearing, which the magistrate had set for August 19. The magistrate thanked Officer Develon for providing the victim's address on the complaint and indicated that notification would be sent in the next day's mail.

Detective Develon then gave the judge an application for a **search warrant** (see Form 9-3), and the judge signed it (see Form 9-4).

bail: an amount of money paid to procure release of one charged with an offense; ensures accused's future attendance in court and compels accused to remain within jurisdiction of the court.

search warrant: written order issued by judicial authority directing law enforcement officers to search and seize any property that constitutes evidence of a crime.

Form 9.1
CRIMINAL COMPLAINT

STATE OF MIDDLE STATE v. __Jesse Williams__
                                        Defendant

Capital City, Middle State   Address:
Magisterial District _1_   467 Elm Street, Apt. 4

I, the undersigned, do hereby state under oath (affirmation):

(1) My name is __Detective Sgt. Michael Develon__ and I live at __Police Station #1__, Capital City, Middle State;

(2) I accuse __Jesse Williams__ who lives at 467 Elm Street, Apt. 4, Capital City, with violating the penal laws of the State of Middle State;

(3) The date when the accused committed the offense was on __Tuesday__, __August 11__, 1992; and __at about 11:50 p.m.__;

(4) The place where the offense was committed was in the County of __Local__;

(5) The acts committed by the accused were:
Especially Aggravated Robbery. On August 11, 1992, at about 11:50 p.m., defendant did intentionally take the contents from the cash register of the Jiffy Stop Market on the corner of State and Fifth Streets, Capital City, from the owner and operator of said filling station—convenience store at gun point and did cause serious bodily harm to the victim by inflicting a gunshot wound to the head of said victim. All of the above in violation of sections 39-13-401 and 39-13-403 of the Middle State Criminal Code.
The victim's name is Samual J. Stone. The victim is the owner of the Jiffy Stop Market. His residence is 1405 Main Street, Capital City. He remains in critical condition at Central Hospital at the time of filing this complaint.

(6) I ask that the accused be required to answer the charges I have made; and

(7) I swear to (or affirm) this complaint upon my knowledge, information, and belief, and sign it on __August 12, 1992,__ before _____, whose office is that of __magistrate__.

_____
Signature of Affiant

SEAL OF MIDDLE STATE   )
)
LOCAL COUNTY   )

Personally appeared before me on _____, 19___, the affiant above named who, being duly sworn (affirmed) according to law, signed the complaint in my presence and deposed and said that the facts set forth therein are true and correct to the best of ____ knowledge, information, and belief.

_____(SEAL)
Issuing Authority

Form 9.2
APPLICATION FOR APPOINTMENT OF LEGAL COUNSEL

THE PEOPLE OF MIDDLE STATE Charge_____
          V.
_____ No. _____ Term_____

APPLICATION FORM FOR THE ASSIGNMENT OF COUNSEL

The applicant _____ residing at _____ shows that:

1. I am a defendant in the above-entitled criminal cause of action alleging that I did commit the crime of _____ in the County of _____ and State of Middle State, on the _____ day of _____ , 19____.

2. I am unable to obtain funds from anyone, including my family and associates, by way of compensation for counsel and represent that the answers to the following questions are true to the best of my information and belief:

    (a) How much money do you have in your possession (on person, in bank, at home, in custody of warden, or elsewhere)?
State amount _____ location_____
    (b) Do you own an automobile?_____
State estimated value_____
Amount owed on automobile_____
Lien holder_____
    (c) Do you own any real estate? _____ If so, give location:_____
    (d) Do you own any other property or do you have any other assets? _____ If yes, furnish description thereof and specify its present location:_____
_____
    (e) What is your social security number?_____
Where did you last work?_____
What was the total amount of your income during the past 12 months?_____
What is your current employment status?_____

    WHEREFORE, petitioner prays:
    That this Honorable Court assign counsel to represent the defendant in the above-entitled criminal cause of action without fee or cost to the defendant.

_____

STATE OF MIDDLE STATE   )
) SS
County of_____   )

_____, being duly sworn according to law upon oath (or affirmation), deposes and says:

1. I am the petitioner in the above-entitled action.

2. I have read the foregoing petition and know the contents thereof and the same are true to my own knowledge, except regarding matters therein stated to be alleged as to persons other than myself, and as to those matters, I believe them to be true.

3. This affidavit is made to inform the court about my status of indigency and to induce the court to assign counsel to me as an indigent defendant for my defense against the criminal charges that have been made against me.

4. In making this affidavit, I am aware that perjury is a felony and that the punishment is a fine of not more than $3,000 or imprisonment for not more than seven years or both.

_____
Signature of Defendant

Form 9.3
APPLICATION FOR SEARCH WARRANT

STATE OF MIDDLE STATE   )
) SS
COUNTY OF Local   )

APPLICATION FOR SEARCH WARRANT

_____Michael Develon_____ OF _____Capital City Police Department_____
           Name   Police Department

being duly sworn (or affirmed) according to law, deposes and says that he has probable cause that certain property is evidence of or the fruit of a crime or is contraband or is unlawfully possessed or is otherwise subject to seizure, and is located at particular premises, as described below:

IDENTIFY ITEMS TO BE SEARCHED FOR AND SEIZED
(be as specific as possible)
gun and goods stolen from robbery of convenience store

DESCRIPTION OF PREMISES TO BE SEARCHED (e.g., street or other address, including apartment number, or specific description of vehicle, safe deposit box, etc.):
Apartment 4, at 467 Elm Street, Capital City, Middle State, and vehicle owned by defendant and identified as being involved in armed robbery

NAME OF OWNER, OCCUPANT, OR POSSESSOR OF SAID PREMISES (give alias or description if name is unknown):
Occupant of apartment is Jesse Williams, defendant in custody; defendant's automobile is impounded in police lot.

CRIME THAT HAS BEEN OR IS BEING COMMITTED (describe conduct of specify statute):
Especially aggravated robbery in violation of Middle State Criminal Code section 39-13-403

PROBABLE CAUSE BELIEF IS BASED ON THE FOLLOWING FACTS AND CIRCUMSTANCES.
Special instructions: (1) If information was obtained from another person, e.g., an informant, a private citizen, or a fellow officer, state specifically what information was received, and how and when such information was obtained. State also the factual basis for believing such other person to be reliable.
(2) If surveillance was made, state what information was obtained by such surveillance, by whom it was obtained, and date, time, and place of such surveillance.
(3) State other pertinent facts within personal knowledge of affiant.
(4) If nighttime search is requested (i.e., 11:00 p.m. to 6:00 a.m.), state reasonable cause for seeking permission to search in nighttime.
(5) State reasons for believing that the items are located at the premises specified above.
(6) State reasons for believing that the items are subject to seizure.
(7) State any additional information considered pertinent to justify this application:

On August 12, 1992, Capital City detectives James Cox and Michael Develon arrested Jesse Williams whose address is Apartment 4, at 467 Elm Street, Capital City, charging him with especially aggravated robbery. His automobile was identified by an eyewitness at the scene of the crime and was impounded in the police lot. The victim, convenience store owner and operator, was shot with a firearm in the head, and the contents of the cash register are missing. Both the weapon used and the goods stolen are likely to be in the locations specified in this application. Request thorough daytime search of the outside and inside of Jesse Williams's apartment and of his automobile.

_____
Signature of Affiant

SEAL:

_____
Badge Number   District/Unit

Magisterial District 1

Sworn to and subscribed before me this <u>12</u> day of <u>August, 1992</u>.

Office Address:
<u>1 State Street</u>
<u>Capital City, Middle State</u>

Date Commission Expires:
<u>December 31, 1994</u>

_____
Signature of Issuing Authority

Form 9.4
SEARCH WARRANT

STATE OF MIDDLE STATE   )
)   SS
COUNTY OF   Local   )

SEARCH WARRANT

TO LAW ENFORCEMENT OFFICER:

WHEREAS, facts have been sworn to or affirmed before me by written affidavit(s) attached hereto from which I have found probable cause, I do authorize you to search the following described premises or person:
Apartment house dwelling at 467 Elm Street, Apartment 4, Capital City, Middle State, including area surrounding said dwelling place and the vehicle belonging to Jesse Williams located in the police impoundment lot.

And to seize, secure, inventory, and make return according to the Middle State Rules of Criminal Procedure the following items:
firearms and goods missing in robbery

As soon as practicable but in any event no later than August 13, 1992, and only during the daytime hours of 6:00 a.m. to 11:00 p.m.

SEAL

Magisterial District 1

Office Address:
1 State Street
Capital City, Middle State

Date Commission Expires:
December 31, 1994

Issued under my authority on this
12 day of August, 1992,
at 2:00 p.m. (Time of issuance must be specified.)

_____
Signature of Issuing Authority

Jesse had completed the application for appointment of counsel by this time, and he handed it back to the judge. The judge checked it and told Jesse that a public defender would be appointed to serve as his legal counsel.

After returning Jesse to his cell, the police officers conducted a thorough search of Jesse's apartment and of the impounded automobile. They did not find a gun or any evidence of goods stolen during the robbery.

Defense Counsel

During the week of Jesse's incarceration, Jesse was told that his lawyer wanted to see him. He was taken into an interrogation room and introduced to his **public defender**, Jill Adams. Jill asked him how he was being treated in jail. He replied that nobody would talk to him: "They won't tell me anything. I didn't do nothing."

Attorney Jill Adams told him he was charged with a very serious crime and that she would need his full cooperation to help him as his defense counsel. Even though she was appointed by the judge, she had a legal obligation to defend him to the best of her ability. "You have to level with me, Jesse," Jill said. "If you tell me the truth, I can help you. But if you lie to me, it will only make things worse for you. The lawyer-client privilege is an aspect of the law that tries to ensure that what you tell me in confidence will not be used against you in court. Do you understand my role or have any questions about who I am?"

"Yeah, I understand that you're the lawyer they appointed for me," Jesse answered, "but the inmates tell me you got so many cases to handle you won't find out nothing."

"Give me a chance, Jesse. If you'll level with me, I can help, believe me!" Jill replied.

Jill asked a number of background questions, including requests for Jesse's parent's address, school record, and employment history, and particularly whether Jesse had any prior criminal record. Jesse said he was born in Florida but went to high school in Capital City. He dropped out of high school and joined the army at age 18. He served three years in the military and came back to Capital City two years ago. He had been employed at several fast food restaurants as a short order cook, but he had lost his last job because he could not get along with the boss. He said he had no prior arrest or conviction record with the police.

Jill said, "Now I want you to tell me everything you did on the night of August 11—I mean every person you met or talked with who could give us a positive time of your exact whereabouts."

Jesse said he was in his apartment until 10:00 P.M. watching television and then decided to go to his girlfriend's house. He said he stayed there until 2:00 A.M., and when he got home, the police arrested him.

"I'll talk to your girlfriend about this and get back to you. Is there anything else you want to tell me about your situation?" asked the attorney.

"Try to find out when this robbery was supposed to go down and what the police know about it. Why they tryin' to pin this on me," Jesse responded.

"Do you own a gun, Jesse?" asked the attorney.

"No, I don't have no gun," he said.

Jill Adams was not favorably impressed with her new client, but she had seen many like him. She would check his story and see if she could do anything

public defender: an attorney appointed by a court or employed by a government agency whose work consists primarily of defending indigent persons in criminal cases.

at the preliminary hearing set for next Wednesday. In the meantime, she had many other clients with whom to consult, and she had a big case to try the next day involving child abuse.

Monday morning Jill checked with the police department and found out that Jesse had a prior violent crime record with the military. The FBI check had found a conviction for aggravated assault involving Jesse who had stabbed another soldier in a barracks brawl in 1989. Jesse also had a dishonorable discharge. His girlfriend had prior convictions for prostitution and drug possession.

When Jill called the girlfriend to check Jesse's story, the girlfriend said she could not remember when Jesse arrived at her apartment. She knew only that it was late, maybe around midnight. She told Jill that the police had already asked her about this and that they had come into her apartment and had taken some beer cans Jesse brought in that night. Jill set up an interview with the girlfriend for the next day so they could be prepared for the preliminary hearing on Wednesday. She got a commitment from the girlfriend that she would attend the hearing at 9:00 A.M. in general sessions court.

Then the attorney met with Jesse again. She looked him straight in the eye and said, "You lied to me, Jesse. Why didn't you tell me about your conviction for aggravated assault in the military?"

"That was a long time ago, and in the military. I didn't think that counted," Jesse replied.

"You're in more trouble now. Your girlfriend will verify that you were there, but only from about midnight to 2:00 A.M. The police say the robbery occurred before that, and you don't have a real alibi," explained the attorney.

Peliminary Hearing

The purpose of the **preliminary hearing** is to determine if probable cause exists to believe that a crime has been committed and that the accused committed it. This determination is not the same as the determination of guilt beyond a reasonable doubt, which is the trial standard. The object of the preliminary hearing is to determine whether reasonable grounds exist for holding the accused and binding the defendant over to the grand jury. The grand jury is the next stage in most jurisdictions when a serious felony is involved. At the preliminary hearing, the judge has to decide to either dismiss the case or "bind it over."

Jesse's attorney explained what would be involved in the preliminary hearing, which was to be held the following morning. "This won't be a trial, Jesse," Jill said. "But you do have a right to have your lawyer present. I can cross-examine the witnesses they call, and we can call witnesses to refute their evidence. They probably have an eyewitness to the robbery. So you had better start telling me the truth," the attorney explained.

"My girlfriend'll help me out," replied Jesse.

"Don't count on it, Jesse," the attorney warned. "She's got a record, and they will get it out on cross. Besides, she won't even provide an alibi for the time of the robbery. The police say it took place around 11:50. Where were you at 11:50, Jesse?"

"I know I got to her apartment before that," Jesse answered, "Can't you talk to her about it?"

"If you mean that I should coach her to lie for you—no way, Jesse," declared Jill. "But I will let her know how important it is for her to tell the truth and

preliminary hearing: a hearing by a judge to determine whether a person charged with a crime should be held for trial or bound over to a grand jury; evidence may be presented by both parties, and the defendant has a right to counsel.

try to think of something that would fix the time of your arrival at her apartment."

Jill then asked whether anybody else could verify Jesse's alibi, but Jesse just shook his head and muttered something under his breath.

The next day at general sessions court, there were a number of cases, and Jesse's case was not called until 11:15. Most of the other matters were handled very quickly; charges of driving while intoxicated and bad check cases were predominant, and all of the defendants pleaded guilty and were sentenced. Felony cases are handled in the same court as misdemeanors but cannot be disposed of at this stage unless no probable cause is found.

When the clerk called the case of *People v. Jesse Williams*, the judge explained that this was a felony charge of especially aggravated robbery and checked to see that the defendant and his counsel were present. The judge then turned to the police officers that had been involved in the robbery investigation and Jesse's arrest. The police officer who first arrived at the scene of the crime was placed under oath and was asked to state his observations upon his arrival at the scene of the robbery. His testimony clearly established that a crime had taken place and that a witness had identified a vehicle leaving the scene of the crime. Detective Mike Develon was placed under oath and asked to explain how the arrest was made. He explained the eyewitness identification of the license number and description of the vehicle, the arrest, and the subsequent verification of the vehicle in the impoundment lot lineup.

Public Defender Jill Adams had an opportunity to cross-examine the officers but declined to do so. She had brought a tape recorder and recorded everything the officers said. This was her first opportunity to learn about the basic facts of the robbery and the eyewitness report. The officers did not produce the eyewitness at this hearing because they did not have to prove anything at the preliminary hearing. The testimony of the police officers was enough to demonstrate probable cause.

The magistrate recognized Jill Adams as counsel for the defense. She addressed the judge respectfully and requested that the police officers who had appeared as witnesses be excused from the courtroom to allow her to call a witness in behalf of the defendant. She explained that under Middle State case law, either party has the right to exclude opposing witnesses from the courtroom during testimony.

"You are quite right, Counselor," the judge agreed. The officers were dismissed from the courtroom. "Please wait outside until you are called," the judge told them.

The defendant's attorney then called Nancy Jones to the stand, and the judge placed her under oath. Attorney Adams established her identity, where she lived, and where she worked. She said she was a waitress at the City Cafe. The defense attorney asked if she knew the defendant and how long she had known the defendant. The attorney asked the witness if she had seen Jesse Williams on the night of August 11, 1992. She said that he was at her apartment until 2:00 in the morning on that night.

"Can you tell the court exactly when he arrived at your apartment?" asked the lawyer.

"It was before midnight; I'm sure because "Mash" was on the TV and it comes on at 11:00," replied the witness.

The judge proceeded to cross-examine the witness. He reminded her that she was under oath and explained the penalty for perjury. He asked her if she was certain of the time. She replied that she had fallen asleep on the couch while watching a "Mash" rerun that she had already seen. She said Jesse came in with a six pack of beer and woke her up, and they had several beers together.

The judge asked Nancy if she had ever been convicted of a crime. Nancy looked at the public defender and asked if she had to answer that question. The judge told her, "Yes, you do, Miss Jones, you are under oath and have sworn to tell the truth, the whole truth, and nothing but the truth." Nancy admitted that she had previous convictions for prostitution and drug possession. "But that was five years ago and I'm straight now." she added.

"Is this the only witness you have, Counselor?" asked the judge. Jill Adams answered affirmatively, and the judge called the officers back into the court.

The judge asked the officers if they were aware of the defendant's alibi. Mike Develon informed the judge that they had questioned Nancy Jones about that evening and she could not remember exactly when the defendant arrived at her apartment.

The judge then stated, "I'll have to bind this case over to the grand jury; the police officers' testimony and the eyewitness identification are sufficient to establish probable cause. We are not going to try this case here. The district attorney and the grand jury will have to deal with any conflicting testimony, and ultimately the case will be decided by a trial in criminal court."

The defense attorney asked that the bail be reduced, indicating that the defendant lived in the community and had no record of skipping bail and no outstanding warrants. The judge denied the request, stating that the potential for a first-degree murder charge was sufficient to warrant the $100,000 bail set by the initial appearance judge. He also asked if any relative of the victim was present in the audience. The wife of the victim identified herself. The judge asked her about her husband, and she said he was still in critical condition.

Under Middle State law, a person accused of a felony had a right to have the case presented to a grand jury for indictment. This stage is discussed in the next chapter. However, the United States Supreme Court does not consider this to be a fundamental right. The Fifth Amendment requirement of a grand jury in cases involving a "capital or otherwise infamous crime" allows an information procedure to be used as an alternative charging procedure in cases involving lesser federal offenses. Many states use the information method in criminal cases, particularly with regard to less serious crimes.

The **information process** differs from the procedure illustrated above in that the district attorney general reviews the charges made by the police at the initial appearance and makes a decision to draft a charging instrument known as an "information." The document is then heard before a judge at the preliminary hearing. The preliminary hearing is conducted in much the same manner as the one described above; however, an assistant district attorney usually is present to cross-examine defense witnesses. The judge then decides, in open court, whether the information demonstrates probable cause to warrant putting the accused through a trial process. When the information process is used, there is no grand jury review before the arraignment.

In both procedures, the criminal case moves out of the control subsystem after the preliminary hearing and into the court subsystem for adjudication, if probable cause is found. In many jurisdictions, the district attorney's office becomes involved in the case during the preliminary hearing stage. The police are still concerned about cases that have moved on into the court sub-

information process: accusation by public prosecutor made in open court before a magistrate in a preliminary hearing where accused may defend himself or herself, as opposed to grand jury indictment.

system, and they assist the district attorney's office; but decisions involving further progress of the cases are in the hands of state officers and out of local control.

CHAPTER SUMMARY

1. State and local governments have primary responsibility for maintenance of public order and domestic crime control. Although both federal and state governments may prosecute various forms of criminal activity, the basic "police power" is given to the states.

2. The fundamental elements of serious crimes include both an act prohibited by law (*actus reus*) and the required mental intent (*mens rea*). These elements constitute the body of the crime (*corpus delicti*) and are generally defined for each specific crime in modern state and federal criminal codes.

3. Crimes were originally classified in English common law as those that were bad in themselves (*mala in se*) and those that were legislatively prohibited (*mala prohibita*). The classification known as *mala in se* (murder, rape, theft, arson) has remained fairly consistent, and these crimes generally are considered felonies today. Modern legislatures, however, have added victimless crimes and regulatory offenses to the category of crimes that are *mala prohibita*.

4. Treason, felonies, and misdemeanors are the major classifications of crime today. The federal government alone has jurisdiction over the crime of treason, which is constitutionally defined. Felonies are serious crimes, as distinguished from misdemeanors. State and federal definitions of misdemeanors vary, but these crimes carry less severe penalties (usually less than one year of incarceration). Petty offenses (traffic violations) are the least serious violations; they involve only fines and are referred to as summary offenses.

5. Minimal uniform standards of criminal procedure in both state and federal jurisdictions have been established through selective incorporation of most of the rights expressed in the Fourth, Fifth, Sixth, and Eighth amendments to the Constitution and applied against the states through the Fourteenth Amendment due process clause.

6. The federal exclusionary rule was applied to the states in 1961 through the Supreme Court's decision in *Mapp v. Ohio*. This rule requires that evidence obtained in violation of the Constitution be declared inadmissible in criminal trials.

7. The federal right to counsel, including the right to appointed counsel in indigent cases, was applied to the states in *Gideon v. Wainwright* in 1963.

8. In the case of *Miranda v. Arizona* (1966), the Supreme Court established specific procedures that have to be followed by the police to ensure that confessions are knowingly, freely, and voluntarily given. The *Miranda* warning informs the defendant of his or her rights, and the police must refrain from using techniques that may coerce confessions in violation of the Fifth Amendment provision prohibiting such confessions.

9. Law enforcement officers have considerable discretionary authority to determine probable cause when making arrests—to "stop and frisk" and to conduct

"plain view" searches. This discretionary authority, however, is subject to constitutional limitations and is checked by independent judicial authorities.

10. Probable cause is defined as more than mere suspicion, but does not require the same degree of certainty necessary to convict a person of a crime. A police officer's determination of probable cause is checked by the local magistrate at initial appearance. Bail is set by this magistrate on the basis of factors involving risk to the community.

11. The accused has a right to a preliminary hearing at which defense counsel must be provided if demanded by the accused. At the preliminary hearing, the defendant may provide evidence to refute the charges. The judge determines whether there is sufficient reason to bind the case over to the grand jury or whether the case should be dismissed. In many states, the information process is used to determine probable cause to send the case to the arraignment stage, and the grand jury is not involved.

12. An individual accused of crime has a right to counsel when the crime involved carries a potential jail sentence. If the accused cannot afford counsel, the state must apppoint counsel to advise the defendant. The Supeme Court has held that counsel must be provided at the time of custodial interrogation and at all critical stages of the criminal process if demanded by the accused. Critical stages include the preliminary hearing, arraignment, trial, and appeal.

KEY TERMS

corpus delicti	felonies	probable cause
actus reus	Miranda warning	initial appearance
mens rea	selective incorporation (doctrine)	bail
mala in se	arrest	search warrant
mala prohibita	control subsystem	public defender
treason	stop and frisk	preliminary hearing
misdemeanors	arrest warrant	information process

DISCUSSION QUESTIONS

1. Where does the United States Constitution place primary responsibility for the maintenance of public order? Why?

2. What effect does federalism have on the ability of the national government to prevent crime?

3. What are the significant differences among felonies, misdemeanors, and petty offenses?

4. How important is citizen involvement in effective law enforcement and crime control?

5. Do you agree with the Supreme Court's selective incorporation doctrine? Why or why not?

6. Is the American exclusionary rule the only available way to compel effectively respect for constitutional guarantees?

7. Do you agree with the Supreme Court that the right of indigent persons to appointed counsel at public expense is necessary to protect fundamental rights in our adversarial system? Why or why not?

8. Does the prohibition against coerced confessions require the imposition of the *Miranda* guidelines for proper enforcement?

9. Are there any constitutional violations in the illustrative case involving Jesse Williams so far? If so, explain why they are violations.

SOURCES AND SUGGESTED READING

Abadinsky, Howard. 1991. *Law and Justice: An Introduction to the American Legal System*. 2d ed. Chicago: Nelson-Hall Publishers.

Cole, George F., ed. 1993. *Criminal Justice: Law and Politics*. 6th ed. Belmont, Calif.: Wadsworth Publishing Co.

Hall, Kermit L., ed. 1992. *The Oxford Companion to the Supreme Court of the United States*. New York: Oxford University Press.

O'Brien, David M. 1991. *Constitutional Law and Politics: Civil Rights and Civil Liberties*, Vol. 2. New York: W.W. Norton Co.

Rossum, Ralph A., and G. Alan Tarr. 1987. *American Constitutional Law*. 2d ed. New York: St. Martin's Press.

Wilson, James Q. 1989. *American Government*. 4th ed. Lexington, Mass.: D.C. Heath Company.

Court Cases

Argersinger v. Hamlin, 407 U.S. 25, 92 S.Ct. 2006, 32 L.Ed.2d 530 (1972)

Benton v. Maryland, 395 U.S. 784, 89 S.Ct. 2056, 23 L.Ed.2d 707 (1969)

Betts v. Brady, 316 U.S. 455, 62 S.Ct. 1252, 86 L.Ed. 1595 (1942)

Bivens v. Six-Unknown Named Agents, 403 U.S. 388, 91 S.Ct. 1999, 29 L.Ed.2d 619 (1971)

Brown v. Mississippi, 297 U.S. 278, 56 S.Ct. 461, 80 L.Ed. 682 (1936)

Cole v. Arkansas, 333 U.S. 196, 68 S.Ct. 514, 92 L.Ed. 644 (1948)

Duncan v. Louisiana, 391 U.S. 145, 88 S.Ct. 1444, 20 L.Ed.2d 491 (1968)

Gideon v. Wainwright, 372 U.S. 335, 83 S.Ct. 792, 9 L.Ed.2d 799 (1963)

Harris v. New York, 401 U.S. 222, 91 S.Ct. 643, 28 L.Ed.2d 1 (1971)

Hurtado v. California, 110 U.S. 516, 4 S.Ct. 111, 28 L.Ed. 232 (1884)

Illinois v. Krull, 480 U.S. 340, 107 S.Ct. 1160, 94 L.Ed.2d 364 (1987)

Johnson v. Zerbst, 304 U.S. 458, 58 S.Ct. 1019, 82 L.Ed. 1461 (1938)

Klopfer v. North Carolina, 386 U.S. 213, 87 S.Ct. 988, 18 L.Ed.2d 1 (1967)

Malloy v. Hogan, 378 U.S. 1, 84 S.Ct. 1489, 12 L.Ed.2d 653 (1964)

Mapp v. Ohio, 367 U.S. 643, 81 S.Ct. 1684, 6 L.Ed.2d 1081 (1961)

Massachusetts v. Sheppard, 468 U.S. 981, 104 S.Ct. 3424, 82 L.Ed.2d 737 (1984)

Miranda v. Arizona, 384 U.S. 436, 86 S.Ct. 1602, 16 L.Ed.2d 694 (1966)

New Jersey v. T.L.O., 469 U.S. 325, 105 S.Ct. 733, 83 L.Ed.2d 720 (1985)

Nix v. Williams, 467 U.S. 431, 104 S.Ct. 2501, 81 L.Ed.2d 377 (1984)

Oliver, In re, 333 U.S. 257, 68 S.Ct. 499, 92 L.Ed. 682 (1948)

Palko v. Connecticut, 302 U.S. 319, 58 S.Ct. 149, 82 L.Ed. 288 (1937)

Parker v. Gladden, 385 U.S. 363, 87 S.Ct. 468, 17 L.Ed.2d 420 (1966)

Pointer v. Texas, 380 U.S. 400, 85 S.Ct. 1065, 13 L.Ed.2d 923 (1965)

Powell v. Alabama, 287 U.S. 45, 53 S.Ct. 55, 77 L.Ed. 158 (1932)

Robinson v. California, 370 U.S. 660, 82 S.Ct. 1417, 8 L.Ed.2d 758 (1962)

Terry v. Ohio, 392 U.S. 1, 88 S.Ct. 1868, 20 L.Ed.2d 889 (1968)

United States v. Leon, 468 U.S. 897, 104 S.Ct. 3405, 82 L.Ed.2d 677 (1984)

Washington v. Texas, 388 U.S. 14, 87 S.Ct. 1920, 18 L.Ed.2d 1019 (1967)

Weeks v. United States, 232 U.S. 383, 34 S.Ct. 341, 58 L.Ed. 652 (1914)

Wolf v. Colorado, 338 U.S. 25, 69 S.Ct. 1359, 93 L.Ed. 1782 (1949)

CHAPTER TEN

THE PRE-TRIAL PROCESS IN CRIMINAL CASES

> "A lawyer shall provide competent representation to a client. Competent representation requires the legal knowledge, skill, thoroughness, and preparation reasonably necessary for the representation."
>
> Canon Six: ABA Model Rules of Professional Responsibility

This chapter explains the court subsystem phase of the pretrial process in criminal cases. The basic stages of the pretrial process and the roles played by the police in the control subsystem were discussed in the previous chapter. An important change takes place when the prosecutor becomes involved in the case. In our illustrative case, this transformation takes place in Middle State after the preliminary hearing; in many states, it takes place before the preliminary hearing, particularly when the information process is used. In all jurisdictions, the prosecutor may initiate criminal proceedings prior to arrest and may seek indictment by the grand jury prior to arrest.

Note that citations for cases referred to by name and date in this chapter can be found in the Sources and Suggested Reading section at the end of this chapter.

THE PROSECUTOR

The pretrial phase of the criminal justice system is largely controlled by the public **prosecutor**. The official prosecutor is either appointed or elected to manage the functions of the prosecutor's office for that particular jurisdiction. In rural areas, the official prosecutor may handle all of the cases, but in most jurisdictions, the official prosecutor manages a small bureaucracy. The district attorney (DA), who is the administrator in charge, hires assistant or deputy district attorneys to perform specific prosecutorial functions. Whether appointed, as in the federal system, or elected, as in most states, the lawyers who seek the office of district attorney frequently have higher political ambitions in mind.

In some jurisdictions, the district attorney's office files complaints in all felony cases and some misdemeanor cases and takes an active part in the preliminary hearing, especially when the information process is used. The district

prosecutor: one who, in the name of the government, prosecutes another for a crime.

attorney in Middle State is an elected public official selected by the voters from the local judicial district for an eight-year term. This elected official has the duty and responsibility to see that the laws are faithfully enforced. Although there is a statewide attorney general's office, the local district attorney is responsible for initiating prosecution in almost all cases. The statewide office mainly handles the state's cases on appeal and advises the governor and the legislature.

Nolle Prosequi

The most important discretionary power given to public prosecutors is the authority not to prosecute (nolle prosequi). The decision to prosecute an individual is ultimately checked by the courts, but the district attorney's decision not to prosecute is nearly absolute. There are few checks on the prosecutor's **nolle prosequi** (or, simply, nol-pros) decision. The decision takes the form of a formal entry on the record by the prosecutor that the state will not prosecute the case any further and is, in effect, a dismissal of the charges.

The police have discretion in deciding whether to arrest a suspect, but the prosecutor has the responsibility of determining if the cause of justice will be best served by continuing prosecution of that individual. As an officer of the court, the prosecutor must try to avoid prosecution of a person who is innocent or a person against whom the evidence is not sufficient to justify a verdict of guilty. The prosecutor needs a higher level of evidence to get a conviction than a police officer needs to make an arrest. The prosecutor's standard of evidence is "beyond a reasonable doubt."

nolle prosequi: a formal entry on the record by the prosecuting officer declaring that the officer will not prosecute the case further.

Plea Bargaining

The modern American practice of **plea bargaining**, which has become almost routine, is derived from the prosecutor's combined charging function and power not to prosecute. The prosecutor ultimately must fix the official charges brought against the individual and be prepared to go to trial and seek conviction on those charges.

The case load and political pressures of the district attorney's office have grown enormously in most districts in modern times, and these pressures have led to the procedures and practices that characterize the pretrial aspects of the **court subsystem**. The vast majority of cases never go to trial and are disposed of during the pretrial process. Of the criminal convictions obtained in the United States, more than ninety percent plead guilty and are sentenced at the arraignment stage.

The prosecutor is the dominant figure in this process. Although judges have a responsibility to check abuses of prosecutorial discretion, they depend upon the public prosecutor to screen cases and minimize court congestion. The prosecutor has become the most powerful figure in the criminal justice system, and in most state districts, that officer has to answer only to the electorate.

plea bargaining: process whereby the accused and the prosecutor in a criminal case work out a mutually satisfactory disposition of the case subject to court approval.

court subsystem: that part of the criminal process involving the courts directly. A case leaves the control subsystem under police discretion and progresses to the court subsystem when the case is transferred to the prosecutor.

Initial Screening and Case Assignment

The district attorney's office in Capital City had set up a screening system in the main office to receive incoming complaints and records. A young lawyer who just graduated from law school was one of those assigned to initially review the files coming into the office and assign them to appropriate units within the department. Bob Clark had been instructed to screen cases on the basis of designated criteria. The Capital City district attorney's office had a horizontally organized system for handling routine cases: misdemeanor, grand jury, and felony trial units existed. There was also a specialized crime unit that handled priority cases vertically after intake. Jesse Williams's case fit the criteria for assignment to the specialized unit. The charge involved a violent crime and a potential murder charge.

An experienced trial lawyer directed the specialized crime unit and generally assigned cases to one of six experienced trial lawyers who handled cases assigned to the six criminal court judges in Capital City. Jesse Williams's case had been assigned to Judge Otis Mann's court, which meant Rusty Kovaks would be the attorney on the case. This process of assignment and Rusty's review of the file took a couple of weeks.

Prosecutorial Investigation

When Assistant District Attorney Kovaks reviewed Jesse's file, he became concerned as he realized that the eyewitness had identified two individuals suspected of committing the armed robbery and shooting at the convenience store. He called the arresting officer, Mike Develon, to get a progress report on the police investigation. Mike assured him that the department was making every effort to follow all leads in the search for the second suspect, the weapon used in the crime, and the missing contents of the cash register.

"Jesse's alibi is no good," said Mike. "The beer cans we lifted from his girlfriend's apartment had a Jiffy Stop price label on one of them. Jesse was there alright. He must have picked up that six pack during the robbery. We haven't questioned him since right after the arrest. We were waiting for the case to be assigned to the DA's office."

Rusty asked what progress was being made in locating the other guy involved in the robbery. Mike explained that they had developed a list of all of Jesse's known friends and were checking on them. The eyewitness had looked at mug shots and had given the artist a description of the suspect's features. They had a "likeness," but no positive identification had been made.

"We have clear thumb and index fingerprints that were found on the gas hose nozzle and the gasoline cap. They did not match Jesse's prints, so we think they are the second suspect's. The lab has given us a positive match on the gasoline cap and Jesse's car," reported Mike.

"Where's the gun and the loot?" asked Rusty.

Mike said they were doing all they could. The lab had identified the bullet as one from a .38 "police special." Mike told Rusty, "We know what we're looking for—we just haven't found it yet."

"How much money was missing?" asked Rusty.

"Not more than $300 according to the normal evening's 'take' on that shift. We don't know if anything else was taken, except maybe that six pack that Jesse took to his girl's apartment," explained Mike.

Rusty also learned from Mike that the victim was still in a coma and on life support systems at the hospital. "The doctors don't know about his chances for recovery," said Mike.

Rusty told the police officer to keep him informed and to send over the laboratory reports. He would talk to the eyewitness and make an assessment about seeking grand jury indictment. "I don't think we'll get anything out of Jesse until he's ready—let him stew awhile, he'll come around," said Rusty.

After talking with the eyewitness and checking on his background, Rusty concluded that he was a good witness who could convince a grand jury. The laboratory reports added corroborating evidence, but he knew he would need more evidence to convince a trial jury to convict. Rusty thought to himself, "After a few more weeks and a grand jury indictment, Jesse will be looking for a deal." So he decided to proceed to the grand jury with Jesse's case.

THE GRAND JURY FUNCTION

grand jury: body of citizens whose duty it is to determine whether probable cause exists in a criminal case to warrant an indictment, as opposed to a petit (or trial) jury.

The **grand jury** was originally a part of our English common law heritage and has no counterpart on the continent of Europe or in the civil law systems. In England, it was designed as a charging (or accusatory) instrument before public prosecutors were used.

In the American colonies, both grand juries and petit (trial) juries achieved an enhanced reputation as protectors of the individual against abuses of British colonial authority. Sympathetic grand juries refused to indict opponents of the Stamp Act, and other local juries refused to convict persons accused of violation of laws they considered to be unjust. The United States constitutional provisions concerning grand juries and the right to jury trials in criminal cases are products of these developments.

England abolished the use of grand juries in 1933 and now confines the use of jury trials only to the most serious offenses. In America, this type of citizen involvement in the criminal justice process retains much of its vigor. The grand jury has been expanded to serve as an investigative body that is usually impaneled for a fixed term; however, there are special investigative grand juries that sit until the investigation is completed.

indictment: an accusation in writing, made and presented by a grand jury to a court in which it is impaneled, charging a person with a crime.

The grand jury has a function that is very different from that of the trial (or petit) jury. The grand jury does not determine guilt, but decides if there are enough facts to warrant putting the individual through the trial process. This is another form of the concept of probable cause and a further test of its existence.

In about half of the states, the grand jury **indictment** is optional, but an equal number of states still require the procedure, at least with regard to the most serious offenses. The defendant can waive a grand jury indictment, however, in those states where it is a right.

The Alternate Information Process

information: an accusation in writing made by a public prosecutor without the intervention of a grand jury, where the accused may demand a preliminary hearing.

The charging instrument that is an alternative to grand jury indictment is known as an **information**. United States Supreme Court decisions have established a right of the accused to demand a preliminary hearing at which the accused can present evidence in defense during the pretrial stage. This process is discussed in the previous chapter. Where the information is used, the prosecutor must file a "bill of information" with the court in which the trial will be held. The bill of information serves as the official charge that may be challenged in open court if a preliminary hearing is demanded.

In states in which both charging instruments—grand jury indictment and information—are allowed, the prosecutor has a choice. Prosecutors find the grand jury useful, even in states where it is optional. When the defendant cannot be located or when the statute of limitations is about to expire, the incentives for a prosecutor to seek an indictment are obvious. In addition, the secrecy of the grand jury allows the prosecutor to present all the evidence without fear that the defendant will use this evidence later at trial. Finally, "the need to protect undercover agents, the ability to test a witness before a jury, or the opportunity to involve the community in case screening may be contributing factors" (Emerson 1983, 13).

Federal Grand Juries

In the federal system, the grand jury consists of twenty-three citizens drawn from voter registration lists in the community served by the court. A quorum (number needed to conduct business) of sixteen is required, and twelve votes are needed for an indictment.

State Grand Juries

The states have no uniform grand jury practices. The state grand juries vary considerably in size from twelve to twenty-three members, and the number needed to indict ranges from four to nine in some states, although most states follow the federal standard and require twelve to indict.

In Middle State, the grand jury consists of thirteen members, and twelve are required to bring a "true bill" of indictment, which means that only two votes are needed to deliver a "no true bill." Middle State is one of the few states in which there was a right to both a preliminary hearing and grand jury indictment in all criminal cases.

Grand Jury Procedure Illustrated

In Capital City, each criminal court judge has a grand jury that sits throughout the year. Individual jurors served for three-month terms. The judge choses the foreperson, and that individual is responsible for selecting the grand jury members. These grand juries handle all cases assigned to that judge during the term. On September 7, 1992, they were scheduled to hear Jesse Williams's case as well as five other cases.

Rusty Kovaks requested that the foreperson issue subpoenas to ensure the appearance of Mr. Frank Builder, Officer Bill Sells (who first arrived at the crime scene), Detective Sgt. Michael Develon, and Mrs. Samuel J. Stone (the wife of the victim). The subpoenas used in criminal cases are essentially the same as those used in civil cases to require personal appearances and production of documents. Mike Develon was issued a *subpoena duces tecum* to bring the laboratory reports with him. All witnesses were required to appear on September 7 at 9:30, on the third floor of the Judicial Building in Capital City, for a grand jury hearing in the case of *People v. Jesse Williams*.

The foreperson sent Jesse Williams a notice of the grand jury hearing ten days prior to the scheduled meeting. Jesse talked to his public defender, Jill Adams, about the notice, and she informed him that it was not an invitation—he would not be called, and the defense attorney would not be allowed to be present.

"You mean I can't defend myself at this grand jury?" asked Jesse.

"About all we can do is to petition the foreperson to call your girlfriend and any other witnesses in your behalf," said Jill. "I'll call your girlfriend and see if she will testify, if you want me to."

Jesse agreed, and Jill Adams petitioned the foreperson to allow Nancy Jones to testify before the grand jury. The foreperson agreed to issue her an invitation, and she could appear on a voluntary basis.

On September 7, after the grand jury had completed deliberation on the previously scheduled case, the bailiff called the first witness in Jesse Williams's case, Frank Builder, into the jury room. Frank was ushered into a small room by the bailiff who administered the oath to tell the truth, the whole truth, and nothing but the truth.

Fourteen people were seated at one large table. Frank took a seat at the head of the table. The foreperson and assistant district attorney were seated at the far end of the table, and they introduced themselves to the witness.

The assistant district attorney, Rusty Kovaks, began questioning the witness by asking about his background and what he had done on the night of the robbery. Frank explained that he was a private building contractor and had been working late on a job. He was on his way home when he pulled into the Jiffy Stop Market to get some gas. He explained what he had observed at the market and the way in which he had identified the car he had seen leaving the scene of the crime at the police impoundment lot.

One of the grand jury members asked Frank how he could be so certain about the car, and he explained that the dented fenders and broken taillight convinced him that it was the same car, and besides he had written down the license number and it was the same.

After several other questions, Frank Builder was asked to wait outside the jury room so that other witnesses could be called. The foreperson called the officer who had arrived on the crime scene in response to the "911" call. The officer explained what he had observed and done at the scene: the condition of the victim, the open cash register, and his action in removing the gun from the victim's hand. This testimony did not take long, and Detective Mike Develon was then called to explain his observations at the crime scene, as well as the method of identification and arrest of the suspect. Rusty prompted Mike from time to time with additional questions, and several grand jury members asked questions about the lineup and vehicle identification of the witness.

The store owner's wife was called to provide testimony concerning the condition of the victim and the inventory of stolen property. The victim was still in a coma, and the doctors did not know the extent of the brain damage. She reported that about $300 was missing from the cash register.

Rusty asked that Sgt. Develon return to add testimony concerning his interview with Jesse's girlfriend, Nancy Jones. Mike Develon explained that Nancy did not know when Jesse arrived at her apartment that night, and he confirmed that the police had taken beer cans with Jiffy Stop price labels on them from her apartment as evidence.

Nancy Jones was then called into the jury room. She gave the grand jury the same testimony that she gave at the preliminary hearing—that she knew Jesse arrived before midnight because "Mash" was still on the television. Rusty reminded her that she was under oath and could be prosecuted for perjury if she was not telling the truth. "The truth is that you don't know for certain when Jesse arrived at your apartment. Isn't that right, Miss Jones?" asked Rusty.

Nancy repeated her testimony that she was certain that the television program "Mash" was still on at the time Jesse arrived.

"Could the program have been delayed on that evening, Miss Jones?" asked Rusty.

Nancy could not answer that question.

"Did Jesse have a gun, to your knowledge, Miss Jones?" asked Rusty.

"No," Nancy replied.

"Did he give you any money that night?" asked the attorney.

"No," she said.

After the witnesses were dismissed, the assistant district attorney was given an opportunity to address the grand jury. He summarized the evidence and challenged the credibility of the defense witness by adding the evidence of her past arrest and conviction records.

Grand Jury Deliberation

Middle State law required that the district attorney be removed from the grand jury while the jurors deliberated. This gave Rusty Kovaks an opportunity to talk informally with the witnesses who remained outside. Nancy Jones left immediately, but Mike Develon and the victim's wife were still there. This was a good opportunity for Rusty to get to know his witnesses and formulate a better idea of how to prepare his case for trial. Rusty knew he had a definite advantage over the defense at this stage. There were no rules of evidence and no judge to supervise the manner of questioning. It would be more difficult to convict on this evidence at trial.

In the jury room, one member said he agreed that the police had found the right car, but had they found the right man? Another member wanted to know about the missing gun and the missing money. The eyewitness had identified two persons who jumped into the car. "Where is the other suspect?" another member asked. The foreperson explained that the grand jury function was not to try the case on the standard of "beyond a reasonable doubt," but to decide if there was enough evidence to warrant putting the suspect through a trial. Most of the jurors agreed that there was enough evidence to send the case to trial. When they voted, only one member cast a "no" vote. The twelve "yes" votes were sufficient to allow the foreperson to sign the true bill of indictment (see Form 10-1).

RIGHT TO A SPEEDY TRIAL

The Sixth Amendment right to a **speedy trial** was incorporated and applied against state actions through the Fourteenth Amendment due process clause in the case of *Klopfer v. North Carolina*, 386 U.S. 213, 87 S.Ct. 988, 18 L.Ed.2d 1 (1967). However, the Supreme Court did not establish a "fixed time rule" for either federal or state criminal prosecutions. In *Barker v. Wingo*, 407 U.S. 514, 92 S.Ct. 2182, 33 L.Ed.2d 101 (1972), the Court identified the following factors to be considered in determining whether the speedy trial requirements have been met: (1) the length of delay, (2) the reason for the delay, (3) the defendant's claim of the right to a speedy trial, and (4) prejudice toward the defendant. In the *Barker* case, the Court held that the defendant was not deprived of his right to a speedy trial even though his trial was delayed for over five years. The defendant did not assert that his right to a speedy trial had been violated until three years after his arrest.

speedy trial: guaranteed in the Sixth Amendment and interpreted to mean without unreasonable delay. As applied to the states, it does not necessarily have fixed time elements.

Form 10.1

BILL OF INDICTMENT

MIDDLE STATE CRIMINAL COURT
LOCAL COUNTY

STATE OF MIDDLE STATE)
      v.)   Criminal Action No.
)
   Jesse Williams   1386 of 1992

    The Grand Jury of _Local_ County by this indictment charges that, on or about August 11, 1992, in said county, _Jesse Williams_ did _intentionally take the contents from the cash register of the Jiffy Stop Market on the corner of State and Fifth Streets, Capital City, from the owner and operator of said filling station—convenience store at gun point and did cause serious bodily harm to said victim by inflicting a gunshot wound to the head of said victim. All of the above in violation of sections 39-13-401 and 39-13-403 of the Middle State Criminal Code.

                                                                         Foreperson

by _____
      Attorney for the State

WITNESSES:
_____
_____
_____

Note: Notice of time, date, and place of arraignment on the reverse side.

Federal Speedy Trial Act

Congress passed the **Speedy Trial Act** in 1974 to add the statutory requirement of a "fixed time rule" in federal criminal prosecutions. This legislation sets the following time limits:

1. an information or indictment charging a person with a crime must be filed within thirty days from the time of arrest;
2. the arraignment must be held within ten days from the time of the information or indictment; and
3. the trial must be held within sixty days after the arraignment.

Speedy Trial Act: federal act of 1974 that added a statutory requirement of a fixed time rule that applies to federal criminal cases.

These time limits mean that the accused must be brought to trial within one hundred days after arrest in the federal system.

State Speedy Trial Acts

Although most states have enacted speedy trial statutes, their provisions vary considerably. Many states do not have specific time limitations, and some set limits only to prevent prosecution delay. In current practice, most states are taking some form of action to implement the American Bar Association's recommendations for effecting speedy trials and prompt dispositions of criminal cases. These standards include: "a) the trial of criminal cases should be given preference over civil cases; and b) the trial of defendants in custody and defendants whose pretrial liberty is reasonably believed to present unusual risks should be given preference over other criminal cases."

In Middle State, there was no speedy trial act setting time limitations, but the federal guidelines provided a good indication of the normal practice in most states. Jesse Williams was arrested on August 12 and was indicted on September 7. His arraignment was scheduled for September 17. At the arraignment, the prosecutor makes the formal and specific charges against the defendant, and the defendant is required to make a formal plea.

DEFENSE CONSIDERATIONS

Jill Adams, the defendant's attorney, met with Jesse after receiving notification of the grand jury indictment. Jesse was nervous and visibly shaken by the news that a grand jury had brought an indictment against him. He was told that he had ten days to decide how he would plead. Jill told him that if he pleaded "guilty," he would probably be able to make a deal with the prosecutor. However, if he pleaded "not guilty," he would face a trial and would risk a more severe penalty. She reviewed the potential penalties for the crime that had been brought in the indictment.

Sentencing Alternatives

Middle State had recently enacted comprehensive penal and sentencing reform legislation. These reform measures were enacted in 1989 when the entire criminal code was rewritten to create a unified approach to the relationship between the definition of an offense and the sentence for that offense. All felony offenses were divided into five classes based on the severity of the offense, with letter designations ranging from the most serious offenses, labeled class A, to the least serious offenses, labeled class E. The purpose of this classification system was to provide like punishment for the same offenses. All theft and theft-related offenses were graded according to the amount of the property taken.

A Modern Sentencing Grid

sentencing grid: modern sentencing plan that restricts judicial sentencing by classification of offenses and provides a narrow range of sentencing guidelines.

The classification of offenses permits construction of a **sentencing grid** so that the potential sentence for each offender can be rapidly ascertained. Each felony class carries a maximum and minimum sentence. In Middle State, a class A felony could be punished by incarceration for fifteen to sixty years. This span is divided into three ranges called range I, range II, and range III. The range determination is based upon the number of prior convictions, which in turn determines the potential span for the particular offender. Thus, for a class A felony, a range I sentence is fifteen to twenty-five years, a range II sentence is twenty-five to forty years, and a range III sentence is forty to sixty years.

The sample sentencing grid (see Figure 10-1) shows the five felony classes A, B, C, D, and E. The numbers below each classification letter indicate the absolute minimum sentence for that class. The RED percentages show the percentage of time that each offender must serve prior to parole eligibility or "release eligibility date." (RED). The RED years translate those percentages into numbers of years.

The second column displays the sentence spans for a defendant classified as an "especially mitigated offender." Where the judge finds mitigating factors but no enhancement factors, the judge may depart from the normal range determination and impose a sentence under the absolute minimum. The trial judge also has the option of decreasing the parole date.

The third column shows the sentence spans for offenders designated as "standard offenders" (range I). A standard offender is a defendant who does not fall into one of the other sentencing ranges (not more than one prior felony conviction).

The next column lists the sentence spans for "multiple offenders" (range II). A multiple offender is one who has several prior convictions (at least two but not more than four). The presence of these convictions enhances the potential length of sentence, depending on the felony class of the prior convictions.

The next column lists the ranges for "persistent offenders" (range III) who basically are defined as those who have any combination of five or more prior felony convictions.

The final column lists the ranges for the defendant who is designated as a "career offender." A career offender is one who has any combination of six or more class A, B, or C prior felony convictions. A defendant with such a designation must be sentenced to the maximum penalty imposed for range III with a substantially higher parole eligibility date.

Under Middle State's reform program, all sentences are determinate in nature, and the judge has to fix a specific length of sentence within the appropriate range for the particular offender. The presumptive sentence is the minimum in the range. The judge also has to consider the various mitigating and enhancing factors stipulated in the code when establishing the specific sentence. The judge fixes the specific length of the sentence and also determines how that sentence would be satisfied within the options depicted in the sentencing grid (Figure 10-1). Note that the blocks shaded the darkest represent higher felony classifications in which the person convicted must serve mandatory continuous confine-

FIGURE 10.1 Sentencing Grid

SENTENCE RANGES
RELEASE ELIGIBILITY DATES

FELONY CLASS	MITIGATED	STANDARD RANGE I	MULTIPLE RANGE II	PERSISTENT RANGE III	CAREER
A 15-60 yrs. RED % RED yrs.	(13.5 years) (20%) (2.7 years)	(15-25 years) (30%) (4.5-7.5 years)	(25-40 years) (35%) (8.8-14 years)	(40-60 years) (45%) (18-27 years)	(60 years) (60%) (36 years)
B 8-30 yrs. RED % RED yrs.	(7.2 years) (20%) (1.4 years)	(8-12 years) (30%) (2.4-3.6 years)	(12-20 years) (35%) (4.2-7 years)	(20-30 years) (45%) (9-13.5 years)	(30 years) (60%) (18 years)
C 3-15 yrs. RED % RED yrs.	(2.7 years) (20%) (.5 years)	(3-6 years) (30%) (9-1.8 years)	(6-10 years) (35%) (2.1-3.5 years)	(10-15 years) (45%) (4.5-6.8 years)	(15 years) (60%) (9 years)
D 2-12 yrs. RED % RED yrs.	(1.8 years) (20%) (.4 years)	(2-4 years) (30%) (.6-1.2 years)	(4-8 years) (35%) (1.4-2.8 years)	(8-12 years) (45%) (3.6-5.4 years)	(12 years) (60%) (7.2 years)
E 1-6 yrs. RED % RED yrs.	(.9 years) (20%) (.2 years)	(1-2 years) (30%) (.3-.6 years)	(2-4 years) (35%) (.7-1.4 years)	(4-6 years) (45%) (1.8-2.7 years)	(6 years) (60%) (3.6 years)

Presumptive Sentence minimum sentence in range.
R.E.D. Release Eligibility Date

■ Mandatory Continuous Confinement with the Department of Correction.

▨ Confinement with DOC available; alternative sentencing available if sentence 8 years or less.

▢ Alternative Forms of Punishment Encouraged.

□ Local Incarceration Required if County Contract.

Note: First Degree Murder excluded from classification for sentencing purposes and sentenced solely according to First Degree Murder statute.

Source: *Tennessee Code Annotated* § 40-35-101, Criminal Sentencing Reform Act of 1989.

ment with the Department of Corrections (state penitentiary). In other instances, the trial judge has the discretion to impose a wide range of sentencing alternatives.

Interpreting the Sentencing Grid

Jesse Williams had been indicted for a class A felony and had one prior felony conviction. He fell into the first sentencing block on the second column labeled "Standard Range I," so his sentence would be from fifteen to twenty-five years in the state penitentiary. After serving thirty percent of that time, he might be eligible for parole if he had a clean record and could convince the parole board that he was no longer a danger to the community.

Jill Adams explained that Jesse could expect a sentence of close to twenty-five years if he pleaded not guilty, went to trial, and was convicted. His record and the seriousness of the injury to the victim would be considered enhancement factors.

"Can't I 'cop-a-plea' and make a deal with the DA?" asked Jesse.

Plea Bargaining Illustrated

The defense attorney told Jesse, "I'm sure the DA wants to know who your accomplice is and where the gun and the stolen money are located. If you can provide this information, the DA will possibly reduce the charges. Assisting the authorities in locating or recovering any property or person involved in the crime is a mitigating factor. However, if the victim dies, they will charge you with first-degree murder and that carries the death penalty or life imprisonment."

"What if I didn't do the shootin'?" asked Jesse.

"In that case you may be able to get a substantially reduced sentence, but as an accomplice you are subject to the same criminal responsibility," explained Jill. "If you 'aided and abetted' and were ready to offer assistance, you are just as guilty as if you had pulled the trigger."

"What happens if I plead 'not guilty'?" asked Jesse.

"Then you will go to trial. We will have about sixty days to prepare for your defense. We will have the court's authority to subpoena witnesses and evidence in your behalf. The DA will have to prove that you are guilty beyond a reasonable doubt. You would have a right to demand a jury trial, and in this state you would get a jury of twelve," explained the attorney.

"How many did it take to pass that grand jury indictment?" asked Jesse.

"Twelve people had to agree that there was enough evidence to warrant putting you through a trial, Jesse. But they don't use the 'beyond a reasonable doubt' standard, and we did not have a chance to put up a defense," replied the public defender.

"I've been in here a month now and my girlfriend won't even talk to me no more. I thought she'd get me out of this, but now I don't know. Do you think they'll convict me?" asked Jesse.

"They have an eyewitness that puts you and your car at the scene of the crime, and they probably have a lot more we don't know about. You are in bad trouble, and you had better start telling me the truth, if you expect me to help you," answered Jill.

"I can't tell you no more," Jesse said.

"Do you want me to talk with the DA about a deal in exchange for your coming clean with everything that happened?" asked Jill.

"That means I'd have to plead guilty to some lesser charge, don't it?" Jesse queried.

"Yes, maybe the class B felony of aggravated robbery as an accomplice, if you did not do the shooting. That would reduce your sentence to from eight to twelve years and make you eligible for parole in about two and a half years," explained the attorney.

"Ok, see what kind of a deal you can make," said Jesse.

The Agreement

Jill Adams made an appointment with the assistant district attorney assigned to Jesse's case. Rusty Kovaks greeted Jill politely and asked, "What can I do for you, Counselor?"

"My client wants to make a deal. He'll tell you about the crime, if you will reduce the charge," Jill replied.

"We've got an eyewitness, Counselor, and the victim may die," said Rusty. "I don't think I can help your client with the reduced sentence."

"He might be able to identify the other suspect and enable you to recover the gun and the money taken," said the public defender. "He says he was not the one who fired the shot."

"Do you believe him, Counselor?" asked Rusty.

"I don't know, you can talk to him and see what you think," said Jill.

"Ok, if you think he's ready to talk, we could set up a meeting," replied Rusty.

The attorneys went to the jail and met with the defendant. Jesse looked scared but said he was ready to talk if he could get a good deal. Detective Sgt. Mike Develon set up an interrogation room that was wired for sound. Public Defender Jill Adams, District Attorney Rusty Kovaks, and Sgt. Develon entered the room with Jesse. First, Jesse was told his rights: that he had a right to remain silent, that what he told the district attorney would be held against him in court, that he had a right to an attorney, and that his attorney was present. "If you or your lawyer want this questioning to stop, all you have to do is to tell us, Jesse. Do you understand?" asked Sgt. Develon.

Jesse indicated that he understood and agreed. "What kind of a deal are you going to give me if I tell you what I know?" asked Jesse.

"If you give us information leading to an arrest and you were not the principal instigator or person doing the shooting, I will reduce the charge to aggravated robbery, which carries an eight- to twelve-year sentence," said Rusty.

"Ok, but how do I know I can trust you to keep your word?" asked Jesse.

"The Supreme Court has held that our promises must be fulfilled," said Rusty.

Jill added, "That's right, Jesse. We could get the confession excluded and get a new trial if they didn't live up to the agreement."

The Confession

Jesse decided to confess. "Robert Jackson was the one who did the shooting. He has the gun and the money," said Jesse.

"Where does he live, Jesse?" asked Rusty.

"He lives on Maple Street, on the west side of town," Jesse answered. "It's about three blocks from the Jiffy Stop Market. You turn right off State Street, and it's the third house on the right. I don't know the number."

Rusty asked Sgt. Develon to get a map from the police office in order to ascertain the house number. They confirmed the address on the map by checking the telephone book and identified the house as number 12 Maple Street.

"He lives there with his mother," commented Jesse.

"Now tell us everything you know about the robbery," said Rusty.

Jesse gave the following account of the events of that evening: "I met Robert at a bar, the 'Pub,' on the west side of town. There wasn't much going on there so we talked about doing some drugs. But neither one of us had any money to make a buy. So we drove around awhile, talking about how we could get some money. Robert had a gun and we decided to hold up the Jiffy Stop Market. It was late and there wasn't nobody around.

"Robert went in with me and I got a six pack of beer while he checked the place out. When I went up to the counter, Robert pulled his gun. Then the man behind the counter grabbed his gun from under the counter, and Robert shot him. Robert grabbed the money out of the cash register and we went out to the car. I told him somebody was coming, so we jumped in the car and left.

"We was both scared somebody had spotted us; so we went to his house first. He jumped out and went inside. All I got was a six pack of beer that I took to my girl's house. He's got the gun and the money."

They went over the story again, and Rusty asked more questions. Jesse stuck to his story, and the assistant district attorney asked the police department's secretary to type Jesse's confession as an affidavit for Jesse to sign. After Jesse read the typewritten confession, he signed it in front of the secretary who was also a Notary Public. The affidavit was witnessed by Jill Adams, Jesse's attorney, and by Rusty Kovaks, the assistant district attorney. Jesse was then escorted back to his cell.

Rusty immediately filled out a complaint and an arrest warrant application for Robert Jackson and delivered it to the city magistrate on duty along with the affidavit that Jesse had signed. The magistrate signed an arrest warrant, and Sgt. Develon was assigned to pick up the second suspect in the convenience store robbery.

Arrest of the Second Suspect

Sgt. Develon and two uniformed officers went to the address Jesse had given them to make the arrest. They expected the suspect to be armed and dangerous, so they planned their arrest procedure on the way. Mike had the artist's drawing of the suspect, which Jesse had identified as a good likeness of Robert Jackson, and he passed it around to the two uniformed officers.

Mike went to the door of the dwelling at 12 Maple Street with one of the uniformed officers. The other officer went around to the back of the house to block that avenue of escape. An older woman came to the door and Mike asked if Robert Jackson lived there.

"Yes, I'm his mother," the elderly woman replied.

Then the officers heard a door slam inside the dwelling and entered with their guns drawn. The officer outside also heard the noise and drew his weapon, shouting, "stop, police!" as he saw a person run out of the house. The suspect did not stop but kept running. The officer could see something in the suspect's hand that could have been a handgun. Should he shoot? The officer ran after the suspect as the suspect turned the corner of another building. When the pursuing officer rounded the corner, he saw the suspect drop something into a neighbor's trash can. The suspect then entered the neighbor's back door.

The other two officers had now caught up with the officer chasing the suspect, and they all barged into the neighbor's house and apprehended the suspect. He was forced to the floor where one of the officers put the handcuffs on him. He was frisked for weapons and identified as Robert Jackson. The occupant of the dwelling demanded an explanation, and Sgt. Develon showed the young woman the arrest warrant. Then Robert Jackson was told that he had a right to remain silent, that anything he told the officers would be used against him, that he had a right to a lawyer, and that a lawyer would be provided for him if he could not afford one.

The officer who had given chase and witnessed the suspect putting something into the neighbor's trash can opened the lid of the can and found a .38 "police special" on top of the garbage. "Is this what we're looking for, Mike?" he asked.

"It sure is," said Mike.

The suspect was taken to the police station, strip-searched and booked. His fingerprints were sent to the laboratory immediately to see if they matched the prints found at the scene of the crime. The .38 "police special" also was sent to the laboratory to be matched with the bullet recovered from the victim's head. Within two hours, the police had a laboratory report that provided a positive identification. The assistant district attorney, Rusty Kovaks, was notified of these developments, and he said he would come to the station to take Robert before the magistrate.

Robert Jackson was asked how old he was and given an application for appointment of counsel. He was only eighteen and said he could not afford a lawyer. He was so scared he could hardly talk. The officers tried to assure him that they were not going to harm him and helped him fill out the application. They gave him a copy of the arrest warrant, which contained the same information as the complaint filed earlier for Jesse Williams. Robert just hung his head and remained silent.

When Rusty Kovaks arrived, Sgt. Develon escorted the prisoner to the magistrate, who again informed Robert of his rights. Since Robert had already filled out an application for appointment of counsel, the judge accepted the application and said he would see that counsel was promptly appointed. After questioning the arresting officer and learning of the defendant's action to evade arrest, the magistrate decided to refuse to grant bail and ordered the defendant held without bail. He set the preliminary hearing for September 30 at 9:30.

After Robert had been returned to his cell, the magistrate recognized that the public defender's office was representing the other defendant, Jesse Williams, in the same robbery. Another lawyer from the public defender's office could not be appointed, since such an appointment would be a conflict of interest. The judge, therefore, would have to appoint counsel from a list of private criminal lawyers. The appointed attorney would be paid a fixed fee of about half what he or she would normally charge. The judge appointed the next lawyer on his list, who happened to be Attorney Alvin Sharp. Attorney Sharp's office was notified of the appointment.

THE ARRAIGNMENT

arraignment: procedure whereby the accused is brought before the court to plead to the criminal charges in the indictment or information.

The Assistant District Attorney, Rusty Kovaks, had promised Jesse Williams a reduction in the charge listed in the indictment handed down by the grand jury. Kovaks now had to prepare for the **arraignment** where he would be required to enter the formal charges against the defendant. He was able to promise Jesse a reduced charge because of the concept of **lesser included offenses**, which means that the crime stipulated in the indictment includes several other offenses. In a trial situation, the judge must charge the jury to consider lesser included offenses as alternate possible convictions.

lesser included offense: composed of some, but not all, of the elements of the greater crime.

Middle State criminal code listed two lesser included offenses within the crime of robbery. Robbery could be classified as (1) robbery, (2) aggravated robbery, or (3) extremely aggravated robbery. The basic offense of robbery was defined as "the intentional or knowing theft of property from the person of another by violence or putting the person in fear." In its least serious form, this crime was punishable as a class C felony. Aggravated robbery included one of the following elements: "1) accomplished with a deadly weapon or by display of any article used or fashioned to lead the victim to reasonably believe it to be a deadly weapon; or 2) where the victim suffers serious bodily injury." Aggravated robbery was a class B felony. Especially aggravated robbery required that both of the elements listed above be present; it was a class A felony.

If the prosecutor wanted to increase the charge to first-degree murder, he would have to go back to the grand jury and get an indictment for that offense. The lesser included offenses in the crime of murder would then be possibilities as arraignment charges or, in a trial situation, as convictions.

Victim's Rights

Middle State law required that the victim be informed of the developments in a felony case, including any plea bargain agreements. Rusty Kovaks called Mrs. Stone, the victim's wife, and asked her to come to his office so he could explain what was taking place.

confession: voluntary statement acknowledging guilt and disclosing circumstances of a criminal act.

After Mrs. Stone arrived and explained that there was no change in her husband's condition, Rusty told her that he had obtained a **confession** from Jesse Williams and that he had promised to charge Jesse with the lesser included offense of aggravated robbery. Rusty explained that if Jesse pleaded guilty at the arraignment, Jesse would receive a sentence of eight to twelve years in the penitentiary for his offense.

"The information he gave us has enabled us to apprehend the second suspect, Robert Jackson. We believe Jackson fired the shot. If I don't fulfill my end of the plea bargain with Jesse Williams, the evidence he has given us will be suppressed and we won't be able to use it at trial. But I want you to know that we are doing everything we can to make sure that these criminals are punished for what they did to your husband," said Rusty.

Mrs. Stone said she understood and thanked Rusty for the information. She was very worried about her husband. She told Rusty, "I don't think he'll recover. He's been in a coma for a month and a half now, and the doctors don't give him much of a chance. I'm afraid he's gone."

"Let's hope he pulls through, for everybody's sake," Rusty replied.

Mrs. Stone was told that she could come to the arraignment. Judge Otis Mann would be the criminal court judge responsible for hearing the arraignment and ultimately for pronouncing the sentence. There would be a presentence report prepared by the probation officer and a sentencing recommendation. Mrs. Stone would be given an opportunity to express her concerns to the judge during this process to make sure that her interests were considered.

Plea Day Illustrated

On September 21, Criminal Court Judge Otis Mann conducted what is often referred to as "plea day" in his court. Plea day is a day set aside on the court calendar to hear arraignments. The defendant, Jesse Williams, and his attorney, Jill Adams, were present, as was Assistant District Attorney Rusty Kovaks. The session was held in open court; interested parties, including the press, attended. The assistant district attorney was asked to read the charge against Jesse Williams, and Jesse was given a written copy of the charge, which was for aggravated robbery.

Jesse was told to rise, and the judge asked him, "How do you plead to this charge, Mr. Williams?"

Jesse answered, "Guilty, your honor."

"Do you understand the nature of the charge of aggravated robbery, Mr. Williams?" asked the judge.

"Yes, sir. It's armed robbery and a class B felony," Jesse replied.

"What in fact did you do that makes you guilty of this crime?" asked the judge.

"I participated in the robbery of the Jiffy Stop Market on August 11, 1992," said Jesse.

The judge asked Jesse to tell the court what happened, and Jesse repeated the same story he had given in his confession.

"Do you understand that you have a right to a jury trial?" continued the judge.

"Yes," said Jesse.

"Have you made a plea bargain with the district attorney's office?" asked the judge.

"Yes," Jesse answered. "The DA promised to reduce the charge if I would tell him all I knew about the crime. Robert Jackson was with me, and I told the DA where to find him and the gun used in the robbery."

The judge asked Jesse if he knew the range of the sentences for the offense of aggravated robbery to which he had pleaded guilty. Jesse said he understood the range was from eight to twelve years' imprisonment with a chance of parole after thirty percent of his time had been served. The judge then accepted the guilty plea as knowingly, willingly, and voluntarily given and that the defendant had waived his right to a jury trial.

"Have you anything further to say to this court about your crime before sentencing?" asked the judge.

"No, sir," replied Jesse.

Judge Otis Mann explained that the probation officer would conduct a presentence investigation and that the judge would be scheduled to pronounce sentence in two weeks, on October 5 at 2:00 in the afternoon. He asked the assistant district attorney if there would be any petition from the prosecutor concerning multiple prior offenses.

"No, Your Honor," answered Rusty Kovaks. "He has only one prior conviction, which is noted in the record, and it does not place him in any multiple offender classification. He is a standard range I offender."

The judge then called the next case, and Jesse was returned to his cell.

Plea Alternatives

guilty plea: formal admission in court as to guilt of a crime.

The basic pleas at the arraignment stage are **guilty** and not guilty but there are several variations in the plea process that need to be understood. In our example, Jesse pleaded guilty, and the judge had to be satisfied that the accused not only voluntarily, but also knowingly and willingly, waived his rights. In addition, the judge had to accept the conditions of any plea bargain agreement between the prosecutor and the accused. Failure to accept a plea bargain would allow the defendant to withdraw the plea and exercise his right to a jury trial. The evidence then would be suppressed and would not be given to the jury. This development obviously could destroy the likelihood of conviction; and for this reason, the prosecutor must be aware of the court's degree of tolerance in making plea bargain agreements.

nolo contendere: a plea in a criminal case that says "I will not contest it" and has a legal effect similar to a guilty plea. This plea may not be used in a civil action against the defendant.

Nolo contendere is another form of guilty plea that in effect says, "I will not contest it." This plea has the same effect as a guilty plea and results in a sentencing decision at the arraignment stage. The plea admits, for the purposes of the case, all facts that are well pleaded, but it is not to be used as an admission elsewhere. In a later civil action against the defendant, such a plea cannot be used as evidence.

not guilty plea: plea entered by the accused at arraignment that indicates desire to contest the charge at trial.

The plea of **not guilty** indicates a willingness to contest the charges against the defendant, and the judge is required either to dismiss the charges or set a trial date. The defendant has the right to demand a jury trial. A defendant who refuses to make a plea is said to "stand mute before the court." In this situation, the judge is required to send the case to trial, and the defendant is given a jury trial unless that right is waived.

Not guilty by reason of insanity is essentially the same as a not guilty plea, and the case goes to trial. The insanity defense is a trial consideration and generally the prosecutor has to prove sanity at trial. The defense must give notice that the insanity defense will be invoked. The prosecution must prove sanity in order to meet the general standards of mens rea (mental intent) required by law to convict.

SENTENCING

On October 5, Jesse Williams was sentenced to the determinate sentence of ten years in the state penitentiary. He could be released on parole in three years, but this action would be subject to review by the parole board in Middle State, which would take into consideration his behavior in prison during that period and the concerns of the community, including the victim, in making that decision.

Judge Otis Mann had agreed with the probation officer's recommendation that in light of the serious injury to the victim and the defendant's prior conviction for a violent crime, enhancement factors in this case outweighed the mitigating factors.

The sentencing grid system and determinate sentencing concepts used in Middle State are not used in all states. This system is relatively new; it is a result of a reform movement that is becoming more widespread. The federal system uses a similar grid system and requires federal judges to justify any deviation from it. Grid systems are discussed again in the next chapters.

The charges against the second suspect were in the formulation stages at the time Jesse was sentenced. The developments in that case will be followed in next chapter.

CHAPTER SUMMARY

1. This chapter explains the transition from the control subsystem to the court subsystem in the criminal justice process in American courts. The pretrial phase in the court subsystem is dominated by the public prosecutor who has extensive discretionary authority.

2. Most state prosecutors are elected by popular vote, while federal prosecutors are appointed. The position of prosecutor is a political office of high visibility. These posts are often used as stepping stones for persons seeking higher public office. The extraordinary discretionary power of those serving as prosecutors subjects them to a high degree of public trust and responsibility.

3. The official prosecutor (district attorney) in most urban jurisdictions heads a small bureaucracy that is responsible for managing large numbers of assistant prosecutors who handle the daily tasks of the office. Generally, these assistant prosecutors have wide individual discretionary authority; however, there is pressure to adhere to departmental policy concerning priorities, and the entire process is influenced by the case load and available resources.

4. The most important discretionary power given to prosecutors is the power not to prosecute (*nolle prosequi*). The decision to prosecute an individual is ultimately checked by the courts, but the district attorney's decision not to prosecute is nearly absolute.

5. Plea bargaining has become almost routine and is derived from the prosecutor's combined charging function and power not to prosecute. The heavy case load and pressures to handle cases more efficiently have made plea bargaining the characteristic feature of the American system of justice. More than ninety percent of the convictions obtained in the criminal justice system are obtained through guilty pleas, and these cases never go to trial.

6. Prosecutors frequently use their plea bargaining authority to get confessions from defendants, promising more lenient treatment for those who provide information about other criminal activities.

7. The grand jury indictment process involves a probable cause hearing at which a group of private citizens decide whether there is enough evidence to warrant putting the individual through a trial. Grand juries are used in almost all states, but they are discretionary in about half of the states. The number of members ranges from twelve to twenty-three, and it usually takes twelve votes to deliver a true bill of indictment. Grand juries are supposed to check the abuse of authority by prosecutors, but the prosecutor often dominates these lay bodies, since that officer is the most authoritative person present.

8. Grand juries have extensive latent power to initiate indictments, subpoena witnesses, and investigate local corruption. Most grand juries serve for fixed terms and are selected by the foreperson, who in turn is selected by the judge.

These juries consider all cases submitted to them by the local prosecutor. There are also special grand juries that sit until an investigation is completed.

9. The grand jury essentially hears the evidence against the accused. The proceeding is not adversarial, but investigative. The defendant frequently is not heard by the grand jury, and the defendant's attorney is not allowed to be present.

10. The courts have used several criteria to determine compliance with the Sixth Amendment right to a speedy trial. However, in 1974, the United States Congress enacted a "fixed time rule" for the federal jurisdiction that requires that the defendant be brought to trial within one hundred days from the time of arrest. Most states have instigated similar rules, often with longer time periods and more discretion. Priority is given to criminal cases over civil cases.

11. The sentencing grid system described in this chapter is similar to those of several states and the federal jurisdiction. This system is part of comprehensive reforms that are new to criminal justice practice, and the ultimate effect of these reforms is not known. The basic features of sentencing grid systems, however, facilitate certainty and predictability in a system that has been severely criticized as lacking in these qualities.

12. The overwhelming majority of cases exit the court subsystem at the arraignment stage of the pretrial process. These cases are moved into the corrections subsystem for the punishment phase of the criminal justice system. The arraignment proceeding is conducted by a superior (trial) judge, who calls upon the prosecutor to enter the formal charges and upon the defendant to enter a plea. The basic pleas are guilty and not guilty. A not guilty plea (or silence) sends the case to trial; a guilty plea (or nolo contendere) results in sentencing.

KEY TERMS

prosecutor
nolle prosequi (nol-pros)
plea bargaining
court subsystem
grand jury
indictment

information
speedy trial
Speedy Trial Act (federal)
sentencing grid
arraignment

lesser included offense
confession
guilty plea
nolo contendere
not guilty plea

DISCUSSION QUESTIONS

1. What are the most important duties and responsibilities of the public prosecutor?

2. Does the prosecutor have too much discretionary power?

3. Should prosecutors be elected or appointed?

4. What charging methods are used in the reader's state? How are the grand jury and the information procedures used? What are their comparative differences?

5. How many votes does it take to deliver a true bill of indictment in the reader's state if the grand jury is used? What effect does the number of votes have on the process?

6. Does the reader's state employ a sentencing grid system like that used in Middle State? Would the reader's state benefit from the comprehensive reform measures described in this chapter?

7. Is plea bargaining overused and abused in our system of justice? What are the alternatives to the characteristic plea bargaining process described in this chapter?

SOURCES AND SUGGESTED READING

Abadinsky, Howard. 1991. *Law and Justice: An Introduction to the American Legal System*. 2d ed. Chicago: Nelson–Hall Publishers.

Boland, Barbara, Catherine H. Conly, Lynn Warner, Ronald Sones, and William Martin. 1988. *The Prosection of Felony Arrests*. Washington, D.C.: U.S. Government Printing Office.

Carp, Robert A., and Ronald Stidham. 1990. *Judicial Process in America*. Washington, D.C.: Congressional Quarterly, Inc.

Cole, George F., ed. 1993, *Criminal Justice: Law and Politics*. 6th ed. Belmont, Calif.: Wadsworth Publishing Co.

Emerson, Deborah D. 1984. *The Role of the Grand Jury and the Preliminary Hearing in Pretrial Screening*. Washington, D.C.: U.S. Government Printing Office.

_____. 1983. *Grand Jury Reform: A Review of the Key Issues*. Washington, D.C.: U.S. Government Printing Office.

Feeley, Malcolm. 1984. "Legal Realism." In *The Guide to American Law: Everyone's Legal Encyclopedia*, 129–31. St. Paul: West Publishing Co.

_____. 1979. *The Process Is the Punishment: Handling Cases in a Lower Court*. New York: Russell Sage Foundation.

Senna, Joseph J., and Larry J. Siegel. 1987. *Introduction to Criminal Justice*. 4th ed. St. Paul: West Publishing Co.

Court Cases

Barker v. *Wingo*, 407 U.S. 514, 92 S.Ct. 2182, 33 L.Ed.2d 101 (1972)

Klopfer v. *North Carolina*, 386 U.S. 213, 87 S.Ct. 988, 18 L.Ed.2d 1 (1967)

CHAPTER ELEVEN

A MURDER TRIAL

> "A judge shall perform judicial duties without bias or prejudice. A judge shall not, in the performance of judicial duties, by words or conduct manifest bias or prejudice, including but not limited to bias or prejudice based upon race, sex, religion, national origin, disability, age, sexual orientation or socioeconomic status, and shall not permit staff, court officials and others subject to the judge's direction and control to do so."
>
> Canon Three (B-5): ABA Rules Code of Judicial Conduct

This chapter illustrates the basic elements of a criminal trial involving a potential capital offense. Note that citations for cases referred to by name and date in this chapter can be found in the Sources and Suggested Reading section at the end of this chapter.

The second suspect in the Jiffy Stop robbery, Robert Jackson, had been arrested just before Jesse Williams was scheduled for arraignment. Robert Jackson's arrest, initial appearance, and court appointment of private counsel is described in Chapter Ten. Attorney Alvin Sharp was appointed to represent Robert Jackson.

Jackson was being held without bail in the Capital City jail when Attorney Sharp visited him for an initial interview. This meeting revealed a frightened eighteen-year-old defendant who had a different story to tell about the robbery from that told by Jesse Williams. Robert Jackson said he had no knowledge of the robbery before the incident took place. He claimed he did not shoot the victim and was not in the store at the time of the shooting. He claimed that Jesse Williams shot the victim and robbed the store while he was putting gas into the car. He further claimed that he had no prior knowledge of Jesse Williams's intent to rob the store, or even that Jesse had a gun.

Attorney Sharp was impressed by the young man's story, but he was highly skeptical about his ability to defend his client based on such a story. He knew from the police charges that Robert had been charged with a class A felony—armed robbery, that he had resisted arrest, and that he was caught in possession of the illegal firearm used in the robbery and shooting of the store owner.

The attorney's preliminary investigation tended to verify the defendant's story, but there was no specific evidence available that would convince a judge to dismiss the charges against Robert Jackson. Attorney Sharp advised his client to waive his preliminary hearing set for September 30, and the judge bound the case over to the grand jury without a hearing.

Defense Investigation

Attorney Sharp investigated Robert's background. The police confirmed that they had no record on Robert. The lawyer was given a copy of the laboratory report that matched Robert's fingerprints with those obtained from the crime scene. That report also showed that the markings on the bullet recovered from the victim's head matched a sample fired from the handgun Robert was carrying when arrested.

Robert's mother was a hardworking, respected person in the neighborhood. She was shocked about her son's involvement in criminal activity. She described him as a good boy. She said he had a lot of trouble growing up without a father, but he made good grades in high school and had graduated in May 1992 in the upper half of his class. She was proud of him and had encouraged him to go to college and do something useful with his life. Robert's mother did not know Jesse Williams, but she had warned her son to stay away from drugs and to be independent.

The neighborhood friends and acquaintances confirmed Robert's mother's story. Robert had never been violent, or even in trouble, to their knowledge. All of them described him as a good kid. Robert and his mother lived in a poor neighborhood, and his mother worked as a housekeeper in a big hotel downtown. She put in long hours and was very dependable, according to her employer. She had never missed work in the fifteen years she had been employed there.

Robert's science teacher confirmed the background information gathered so far about Robert. She said Robert was a dependable student whom she had advised to go to college. She found it hard to believe that he would be involved in an armed robbery. "All these kids try drugs and get a little wild when they get out of high school, but Robert was just not the type to shoot somebody. He wanted to be an astronaut and was interested in science. He respected his teachers and even did extra work to keep his grades up," said the teacher.

Attorney Sharp was beginning to believe his client's story, but none of the information he had gathered could be used to prevent Robert from being convicted, at least as an accomplice in the crime. An **accomplice** is one who knowingly, voluntarily, and with common intent unites with the principal offender in the commission of the crime.

If Robert's story were acccepted as the truth, he still would be guilty as an "aider and abetter" of the crime. He took part of the proceeds of the crime and aided in concealing the weapon used in the crime. His presence at the scene and failure to do anything to alert the authorities or stop the crime from taking place would imply guilt. The defense attorney would have difficulty convincing a jury that Robert had no knowledge of the robbery before it took place. The prosecutor would have to prove intent on Robert's part, but the fact that Robert accepted the money and the gun were enough to imply intent.

accomplice: one who is in some way associated with the commission of a crime; one who aids or assists in or is an accessory to a crime.

Prosecutor's Decision

At the district attorney's office, Robert Jackson's case was processed in much the same manner as that described in Jesse Williams's case. Once the preliminary hearing was waived and the case was bound over to the grand jury, Criminal Court Judge L.B. Long was assigned to the case. The district attorney's office then assigned Glen Hawkins to the case, since he was the attorney in charge of cases in Judge Long's court. Rusty Kovaks would be consulted, but the two cases would be handled separately. Glen's office was close to Rusty's office, and they had briefly discussed the two cases. Like Rusty, Glen was an experienced assistant district attorney assigned to the special criminal unit.

On November 7, the district attorney called Glen Hawkins into his office and asked him to bring Robert Jackson's file. The morning newspaper carried a front-page story about the victim and the robbery of the convenience store. The district attorney showed Glen the headline to the article that read, "VICTIM DIES: ROBBER COULD GET OUT IN THREE YEARS."

"Do you have the file on this Robert Jackson they say has been arrested in connection with the robbery?" asked the district attorney.

"Yes, Rusty handled the Jesse Williams case," Glen replied. "I haven't had a chance to do anything on the second one charged, but Rusty thinks this Jackson guy did the shooting."

"Rusty had better be right, Glen," said the district attorney. "I'm getting phone calls on this already. I want this Jackson prosecuted for first-degree murder. We have to put a stop to this killing. I've got an election coming up next year."

"I'll do my best," said Glen.

Glen Hawkins went back to his office and read the file on Robert Jackson thoroughly. He noticed that Robert was only eighteen years old and had no prior record. But Robert had resisted arrest, and he had the gun used in the robbery to kill the victim, all of which tended to confirm Jesse's story that Robert did the shooting. Glen's next step was to go for a grand jury indictment. He noted that the eyewitness, Frank Builder, had said he got a good look at one of the robbers at the convenience store on the night of the robbery.

He called Detective Develon at the police station and had him set up an identification lineup to see if the witness could make a positive identification of Robert Jackson. "Does Jackson have a lawyer assigned to his case?" Glen asked Mike Develon.

"Yeah, Al Sharp's been in here to see Jackson," answered Mike.

"Give him a call and invite him to the lineup. I want to make sure we don't lose any evidence on this one," said Glen.

Right to Counsel at Lineup Identification

In *United States v. Wade*, 388 U.S. 218, 87 S.Ct. 1926, 18 L.Ed.2d 1149 (1967), the United States Supreme Court held that the accused has the right to have counsel present to witness a **pretrial lineup** if a complaint or indictment has been issued. The presence of counsel might not be necessary when a complaint has not yet been filed, but the assistant district attorney was taking no chances that might cause evidence to be suppressed. When the right to counsel is violated at a "critical stage," an identification may be excluded at trial.

pretrial lineup: a postindictment lineup is a "critical stage" in a criminal proceeding, so the accused has a constitutional right to counsel.

The Lineup Procedure

At the lineup, which took place on November 8, Frank Builder identified Robert Jackson in a line of seven inmates. "That's the one I saw running around the car and getting into the passenger side. He's the third one from the left," said Frank Builder.

The identification was witnessed by the assistant district attorney, Glen Hawkins; by Robert's lawyer, Alvin Sharp; and by Sgt. Develon. A supplemental statement was drafted, and it was signed by Frank Builder and the witnesses as a true and accurate copy of the identification. Al Sharp raised no objections to the procedure, during which the assistant district attorney informed the defense attorney that the victim, Samual Stone, had died. Al had already read the newspaper account and knew his client was in more trouble than he would have been in had the victim not died.

"My client admits he was there when the robbery took place," Al told the district attorney, "but he did not do the shooting. That was Jesse Williams's gun you caught him with. He's got a clean record, and I believe the kid."

"Come on, Counselor," Glen responded. "You can't be serious. We got this guy cold. You just saw the positive witness ID. We are going to charge your guy with first-degree murder."

THE DEATH PENALTY

capital punishment: punishment by the death penalty.

The most severe penalty for crime is also the most controversial. **Capital punishment** has been extensively applied throughout American history and usually has been reserved for the most serious offenses of murder and rape. Between 1930 and 1967, there were 3,859 convicted criminals executed in the United States. Blacks made up only about eleven percent of the population of the United States during that period, but fifty-three (53.5) percent of those executed were blacks (Bowers 1974).

During the twentieth century, the death penalty has been criticized as being racially discriminatory in application, lacking in provable deterrent qualities, and inhumane. Critics have pointed to the finality and brutality of the act and the possibility of executing innocent persons by mistake. Most modern industrial societies have abolished the death penalty, as have several American states. However, the death penalty is supported by a majority of American citizens, and public pressure to carry out this form of punishment is mounting.

Constitutional Status of the Death Penalty

cruel and unusual punishment: prohibited by the Eighth Amendment to the United States Constitution.

The constitutionality of the death penalty has been a major issue before the courts since the 1950s. The Eighth Amendment prohibits **cruel and unusual punishment**. This phrase was derived from the English Bill of Rights of 1689. The phrase was then understood to refer to such ancient practices as branding, drawing and quartering, burning alive, and crucifixion. But the English common law tradition has allowed the concept to be expanded to include "evolving standards of decency." As Chief Justice Earl Warren noted in *Trop v. Dulles*, 356 U.S. 86, 78 S.Ct. 590, 2 L.Ed.2d 630 (1958), the court must determine the meaning of the Eighth Amendment from the "evolving standards of decency that mark the progress of a maturing society."

Evidence was mounting, in a series of court cases, that the death penalty had been carried out in a racially biased manner and that no deterrent effect had been proven to result from imposition of it. Comparative analysis also revealed no real distinction between the few who were executed as opposed to the many convicted of the same crimes who were not executed.

In 1972, the Supreme Court finally confronted the issue in the famous case of *Furman v. Georgia*. A brief per curium (by the court) decision, supported by five justices, declared invalid every state death penalty statute then in existence. The five-member majority agreed that "the imposition and carrying out of the death penalty in these cases [several were considered] constituted cruel and unusual punishment in violation of the Eighth and Fourteenth Amendments." The justices, however, agreed on little else, since each member of the majority wrote a separate opinion in an attempt to explain why the death penalty constituted such a violation. Most of the arguments centered around the arbitrary nature of implementation of the death penalty, but two justices, Brennan and Marshall, held that the death penalty was unconstitutional per se (in itself).

Four years later, in *Gregg v. Georgia*, 428 U.S. 153, 96 S.Ct. 2909, 49 L.Ed.2d 859 (1976), the Supreme Court upheld a new Georgia death penalty statute that instituted a two-stage (bifurcated) trial process and state supreme court review comparing the application of the death penalty in similar cases. This new process required that first the defendant be convicted of first-degree murder, and then, that a second trial be held concerning the sentencing, at which statutorily defined aggravating and mitigating circumstances could be argued. Only if there were a finding of at least one aggravating factor using the standard of "beyond a reasonable doubt" could the death penalty be imposed.

The Supreme Court, in *Gregg*, held that the death penalty was constitutional if the procedure included adequate safeguards against it being inflicted in an arbitrary and capricious manner. The concerns expressed in *Furman* could be met by a carefully drafted statute that ensured that the sentencing authority would be given adequate information and guidance. Since *Gregg*, a solid majority of the Court has refused to reconsider the general constitutionality of capital punishment. Thirty-six states and the federal government have enacted new death penalty statutes, and the number of actual executions is increasing. By the end of 1989, one hundred and twenty individuals had been executed under these new statutes, and some 2,250 inmates remained on "death row." More whites are now being executed (59%) as opposed to blacks and other races (41%) (*United States Statistical Abstract* 1991).

In *Coker v. Georgia*, 433 U.S. 584, 97 S.Ct. 2861, 53 L.Ed.2d 982 (1977), the Court held the **death penalty for rape** of an adult woman unconstitutional as cruel and unusual punishment. The new death penalty statutes generally are imposed in connection with pre-meditated murder, but the Court in *Coker* left unanswered the issue of imposing the death penalty to prevent and deter other types of crime. The *Coker* decision has put a stop to executions for rape, in which the ratio under earlier laws demonstrated the most pronounced racial bias. Eight blacks to one white were executed for rape between 1930 and 1967 (*United States Statistical Abstract* 1991).

death penalty for rape: prohibited as cruel and unusual punishment by court decision.

In subsequent cases in 1983 and 1984, the Court indicated its growing impatience with endless stays of execution by expediting procedures to review habeas corpus petitions filed by death row inmates. In *Pulley v. Harris*, 465 U.S. 37, 104 S.Ct. 871, 79 L.Ed.2d 29 (1984), the Court resolved a major issue by holding that a state court need not review a death sentence to ensure its "proportionality" to the punishment imposed upon others for similar offenses.

CRIMINAL DISCOVERY PROCESS

criminal discovery: differs from civil discovery in that it is more restrictive; depositions are taken only under unusual circumstances; defendant does not have to testify.

The **criminal discovery** process differs considerably from that described in connection with the civil process in earlier chapters. In general, the criminal discovery process is more restrictive. Deposition taking is limited to prospective witnesses who will be unable to attend the trial. The prosecutor must give the defendant access to all material evidence and allow for independent testing of such evidence.

The defense can subpoena witnesses and require relevant evidence to be produced. Physical and mental examinations can be required if relevant. The names of witnesses against the accused may be required and produced, but the prosecution's witnesses are not subject to cross-examination prior to trial, and their statements may be withheld until the trial.

The defendant's right to remain silent ensures that the prosecution will not be able to cross-examine the witness before trial unless this right is waived. If the defendant takes the stand voluntarily in his or her own defense, the prosecutor may have a chance to cross-examine the defendant. In jury trials, the defendant's past criminal record can be suppressed—a motion *in limine* may prevent any mention of such a record. The United States Supreme Court has held that the prosecutor must share any **exculpatory evidence** (that which tends to relieve the accused of guilt) with the defense whether it is requested or not (see *United States v. Agurs*, 427 U.S. 97, 96 S.Ct. 2392, 49 L.Ed.2d 342 [1976]).

exculpatory evidence: evidence that tends to indicate defendant's innocence or mitigate defendant's criminality.

The Murder Indictment

The grand jury indicted Robert Jackson for first-degree murder on September 18. A front-page newspaper article heading read, "ACCUSED ROBBER INDICTED FOR FIRST-DEGREE MURDER." Al Sharp met with his client to explain what had happened.

"How could they do that? I didn't kill anybody. There's no way I'm going to plead guilty to that charge," declared Robert.

"I don't think a jury will convict you of first-degree murder either, Robert," replied the attorney. "The DA wants to score some points, but Middle State courts have held that when one enters into a scheme with another to commit the felony of armed robbery, a conviction for first-degree murder may result if the victim dies as a result of injuries sustained in the robbery. Both of the defendants are responsible for the death, regardless of who actually committed the murder and whether the killing was specifically contemplated by the other."

"You mean I could be convicted even if I didn't know about what Jesse had in mind?" asked Robert.

"No, but we will have a hard time proving you were not an accomplice, given the evidence," answered the attorney.

"I thought a person was innocent until proven guilty," Robert stated.

"That's true," confirmed Attorney Sharp. "The prosecutor will have to prove intent, but your actions imply intent unless you can produce some evidence to refute that implication. If we can produce enough evidence to raise a 'reasonable doubt' about your intent, we can beat this rap. That means you will have to testify and convince the jury you are telling the truth. Can you do that, Robert?"

Robert was not sure he would be able to convince a jury; it would be his word against Jesse's. Al was convinced that they would have to produce Jesse

Williams as a witness, and he reviewed the list of items he could obtain to prepare for trial. He told Robert they would not have prior access to any prosecution witness statements, but they could get a list of the witnesses the prosecution intended to call. Al thought he might be able to get a copy of Jesse's confession. The confession would be a matter of public record, and Al could have the court produce it.

Robert pleaded not guilty and demanded a jury trial at the arraignment. The trial was set for November 23, 1992. The attorney would have a little more than sixty days to prepare for trial. He was able to obtain a copy of Jesse's confession, and he showed it to Robert.

"It's a lie," said Robert. "The whole thing was his idea."

"Yeah, but why are they going to believe you?" asked the attorney. "The gun was found in your possession. Can we prove it was his gun?"

"I don't know; I didn't even know he had it," Robert replied.

"I could check to find out if any of his friends know where he got it," said Al. "Now let's go over everything that you can think of in connection with Jesse Williams and the crime. I want to know every detail about what happened that night and about how you were arrested."

Attorney Sharp took extensive notes as Robert explained the details. These notes were taken to the office where the attorney dictated a thorough set of notes for his file and had his secretary type them. The next day, Attorney Sharp called in his paralegal assistant, Mark Adler, and they reviewed the notes together. Mark was very interested in the case and thought Jesse Williams was lying to save himself from a murder charge. Al agreed, but noted, "We've got to prove that to a jury. We need to catch Jesse in some inconsistencies that will prove he's lying."

"We need to make a list of everything that appears inconsistent in the two defendants' statements," Al told Mark. "We have the lab reports. Go down and get the serial number on the gun and see if Sgt. Develon will give you a list of Jesse's known friends. You need to question them to find out if anybody can testify that the gun belonged to Jesse Williams. Also, we will need the death certificate that designates the cause of death of the victim. Let me know if you think of anything else we need to check out."

PRETRIAL PLANNING

Mark Adler and Attorney Alvin Sharp met later to discuss the results of their investigations and to plan the defense strategy in the case of *State v. Robert Jackson*, which was scheduled for trial on November 23.

Defense Strategy

The defense had discovered little in the way of new evidence during the preliminary investigation. A friend of Jesse Williams told Mark that Jesse had made a statement to him that Jesse had bought a gun from Jake Jones who lived in one of the four apartments where Jesse lived—467 Elm Street, apartment 3. But this person could not be found. He had moved out of the apartment, and there was no record of his whereabouts. This secondhand information would be useless in court, as it would be suppressed as hearsay. Serial number checks indicated that the gun was not registered with the police.

Mark said he would keep looking for Jake Jones, but he did not have much information on him. Al told Mark to check the jail and prison records for Jake Jones to see if he could be located in that manner.

"We've got one break," said Al. "I talked with Robert and asked him what he did with the $100 Jesse had given him from the robbery. He said he didn't want the money and had put it into an envelope and mailed it to Mrs. Stone, the victim's wife."

"Has she confirmed that?" asked Mark.

"Yes," Al replied. "She told me over the phone that she had received $100 in cash in an envelope with no return address. She thought it was from someone who felt sorry for her."

"When did she receive it?" asked Mark.

"She says it was about two weeks before her husband died, and therefore before Robert was arrested," answered Al. "She destroyed the envelope, unfortunately. We will want to call her as a witness. Her testimony will be a big advantage for Robert."

Mark continued the report of his preliminary work. "I've gone over the two statements we have and basically it's Robert's word against Jesse's. That means that Robert's character witnesses will give us an edge, but we'll just have to hope that we can catch Jesse in some inconsistencies."

Al agreed, then commented, "We will want to call Robert's science teacher, Alexanderia Poole, as a character witness."

Attorney Sharp told Mark he could find nothing in the record or the account Robert had given him that indicated the need for any pretrial motions. "We could ask for a **continuance** if we don't find this Jake Jones we're looking for, but other than that any delay is just going to work against our client," said Al.

Possible pretrial motions include:

1. a **suppression motion** requiring a pretrial hearing to exclude evidence illegally obtained;
2. a nolle prosequi motion made by the prosecutor;
3. a motion to disqualify the judge;
4. a motion to request a psychological examination of the accused; and
5. a request for a pretrial conference, change of venue (place of trial), to quash the indictment, or for a bill of particulars.

None of these motions seemed applicable in the case against Robert Jackson.

"We need to draft interrogatories to the prosecutor, Glen Hawkins," the defense attorney stated. "They usually give us permission to open their file, but this case indicates that they may want to keep us away from some of the witness statements. Let's try to make a specific request for everything we can think of that they may have. Sometimes they will give us open file permission and then leave out material they don't want us to find. This may lead us to believe they don't have anything else. I don't want that to happen in this case. If they refuse, we can go to the judge for a ruling."

continuance: postponement of a session, hearing, trial, or other proceeding to a subsequent day or time.

suppression motion: motion to the effect that evidence sought to be admitted should be excluded because it was illegally acquired.

Prosecution Strategy

Glen Hawkins received the interrogatories requesting the names of the witnesses the prosecution intended to call in the case, the specific times and places where alleged events took place, the names of witnesses to the alleged crime and of the arresting officers as well as those responding to the crime report, and the relevant police reports.

Glen pulled his file on Robert Jackson and reviewed the case again. He made a list of the witnesses and the laboratory evidence. After rereading the confession Jesse had given to Sgt. Develon and Rusty Kovaks, he asked Rusty to review the evidence with him.

"Al Sharp is the defense attorney for Robert Jackson," said Glen. "Al implied at the lineup, where Robert was identified, that Jesse Williams might by lying about Robert doing the shooting. We found the gun in Robert's possession, but do you think he can crack Jesse's story?"

Rusty said, "It's possible. Jesse made a pretty good deal with me. He lied first about his alibi, but he knows that we'll prosecute him for perjury if he's lying this time."

"I'll make sure he knows that he could get three more years for perjury," said Glen.

After the exchange of interrogatories and requests to produce documents and material evidence, the following list of witnesses and other forms of evidence was made available to both parties and the judge:

Witnesses

Prosecution:
1. Jesse Williams;
2. Frank Builder;
3. Sgt. Michael Develon; and
4. Kate Wissenschaftler (police laboratory director).

Defense:
1. Robert Jackson;
2. Alexanderia Poole;
3. Jake Jones; and
4. Mrs. Samuel Stone.

Documents

1. pictures of crime scene and victim's injuries;
2. laboratory report of fingerprints found at crime scene;
3. laboratory report of test firing of gun found in possession of the defendant;
4. bullet taken from victim's head;
5. gun found in possession of defendant; and
6. death certificate showing cause of victim's death.

THE TRIAL

On February 23, 1993, Robert Jackson's case was announced by the bailiff in Capital City's Criminal Court, presided over by Judge L.B. Long. Judge Long noted that a jury trial had been demanded and that there was a first-degree murder charge involving a potential death sentence. He explained that the *voir dire* process would involve the selection of a single jury whose members would serve as the deciders of facts in dispute in a **bifurcated trial process**.

bifurcated trial process: trial of issues, such as guilt and punishment, or guilt and sanity, separately in criminal trial.

Bifurcated Trial Procedure

In Middle State, the death penalty statute required that there first be a unanimous conviction for first-degree murder, which was defined as "[a]n intentional, premeditated and deliberate killing of another." Included in that definition was the reckless killing of another committed in the perpetration of any first-degree felony: arson, rape, robbery, burglary, theft, kidnapping, or aircraft piracy.

If the defendant was found guilty beyond a reasonable doubt of first-degree murder, the same jury would have to be reconvened to determine whether the accused would be punished by death or by life imprisonment. These two penalties were the only ones for a person convicted of first-degree murder, which did not include robbery as a lesser included offense. The jury had to find the existence of one or more of the statutory aggravating circumstances, beyond a reasonable doubt, to impose the death penalty. The following list gives twelve **aggravating circumstances** provided in Middle State's Criminal Code.

aggravating circumstances: circumstances attending the commission of a crime that increase defendant's guilt or add to injurious consequences of the crime.

State Code List of Aggravating Circumstances

Middle State Code provides that no death penalty shall be imposed by a jury but upon a unanimous finding of the existence of one or more of the statutory aggravating circumstances, which shall be limited to the following:

1. The murder was committed against a person less than twelve years of age, and the defendant was eighteen years of age or older.

2. The defendant was previously convicted of one or more felonies, other than the present charge, that involved the use or threat of violence to a person.

3. The defendant knowingly created a great risk of death to two or more persons, other than the victim murdered, during the act of murder.

4. The defendant committed the murder for remuneration or the promise of remuneration, or employed another to commit the murder for remuneration or the promise of remuneration.

5. The murder was especially heinous, atrocious, or cruel in that it involved torture or depravity of mind.

6. The murder was committed for the purpose of avoiding, interfering with, or preventing a lawful arrest or prosecution of the defendant or another.

7. The murder was committed while the defendant was engaged in committing, or was an acccomplice in the commission of, or was attempting to commit, or was fleeing after committing or attempting to commit, any first-degree murder, arson, rape, robbery, burglary, larceny, kidnapping, aircraft piracy, or unlawful throwing, placing, or discharging of a destructive device or bomb.

8. The murder was committed by the defendant while the defendant was in lawful custody or in a place of lawful confinement or during the defendant's escape from lawful custody or from a place of lawful confinement.

9. The murder was committed against any peace officer, corrections official, corrections employee, or fire fighter who was engaged in the performance of his or her duties, and the defendant knew or reasonably should have known that the victim was a peace officer, corrections official, corrections employee, or fire fighter engaged in the performance of his or her duties.

10. The murder was committed against any present or former judge, district or state attorney general, or assistant district or assistant state attorney general due to or because of that person's official duty or status, and the defendant knew that the victim occupies or occupied said office.

11. The murder was committed against a national, state, or local popularly elected official due to or because of the official's lawful duties or status, and the defendant knew that the victim was such an official.

12. The defendant committed "mass murder," which is defined as the murder of three or more persons within the state of Middle State within a period of forty-eight months, and perpetrated in a similar fashion in a common scheme or plan.

The state law also provided that in arriving at the punishment, the jury had to consider any **mitigating circumstances**. The mitigating circumstances included but were not limited to, the criteria given in the following list:

mitigating circumstances: circumstances that reduce the degree of moral culpability, but do not justify or excuse the offense in question.

State Code List of Mitigating Circumstances

Middle State Code provides that in arriving at the punishment, the jury shall consider any mitigating circumstances, which shall include, but not be limited to, the following:

1. The defendant has no significant history of prior criminal activity.

2. The murder was committed while the defendant was under the influence of extreme mental or emotional disturbance.

3. The victim was a participant in the defendant's conduct or consented to the act.

4. The murder was committed under circumstances that the defendant reasonably believed to provide a moral justification for his or her conduct.

5. The defendant was an accomplice in the murder committed by another person, and the defendant's participation was relatively minor.

6. The defendant acted under extreme duress or under the substantial domination of another person.

7. The defendant was very young or advanced in age at the time of the crime.

8. The capacity of the defendant to appreciate the wrongfulness of the conduct or to conform his or her conduct to the requirements of the law was substantially impaired as a result of mental disease or defect or intoxication that was insufficient to establish a defense to the crime but that substantially affected the defendant's judgment.

9. Any aspect of the defendant's character or record or any aspect of the circumstances of the offense favorable to the defendant that is supported by the evidence.

If the jury decided the death penalty was warranted, the jurors would be required to use a verdict form (see Form 11-1) on which they would list the aggravating circumstances that outweigh the mitigating circumstances. The jurors would have to sign their names to the appropriate sections of this document.

Criminal Voir Dire

Judge Long had received a request from the parties concerning the number of alternate jurors to be involved and decided that a jury of twelve would be impaneled, with four alternates chosen in case the lengthy process resulted in unforeseen circumstances that would require replacements.

The voir dire and trial process in criminal cases follow the same general outlines described earlier in the civil trial process. However, the detailed **rules of criminal procedure** are applied. In criminal trials, more peremptory challenges usually are allowed than in civil cases. The number of peremptory challenges varies with the severity of the potential punishment. In death penalty cases, Middle State allowed the defense fifteen peremptory challenges, and the prosecution eight. Each side would get one additional peremptory challenge for each alternate juror selected.

The voir dire process is quite lengthy and time-consuming in criminal trials; at least three days of the court's time is consumed with jury selection alone in such cases. The skills of the lawyers are severely tested in making the extensive number of decisions required. In many cases, if adequate resources are available, private research consultants are hired to advise the lawyers in their selections. Robert Jackson had no such resources, so Alvin Sharp had to rely upon his own judgment. His law firm would lose money on this case, and he had no interest in delaying the trial process.

rules of criminal procedure: detailed rules of procedure in criminal cases that govern the steps involved in that process; each jurisdiction has such rules.

Peremptory Challenge Issues

Until 1986, both sides could use any criteria whatsoever to exclude potential jurors with their peremptory challenges. But in 1986, the Supreme Court ruled, in *Batson v. Kentucky*, that the equal protection clause of the Fourteenth Amendment precludes prosecutors from striking blacks (and other minorities) from the jury simply because the prosecutor thinks blacks will be partial toward black defendants. This ruling was reaffirmed and broadened in *Powers v. Ohio* (1991) when the Court ruled that it is unconstitutional to exclude blacks on the basis of race even when defendants are white. Justice Kennedy said, in the majority opinion, "Race cannot be a proxy for determining juror bias or competence."

When prosecutors challenge racial minorities, they may be required to explain their grounds for objection apart from the matter of race. However, "[e]ven after the *Batson* decision, race [has] continued to be used as a basis for peremptory challenges because trial judges have yet to engage in searching probes of the reasons for such challenges" (Levine 1992, 51).

Form 11.1

JURY VERDICT FORM
FOR DEATH SENTENCING

PUNISHMENT OF DEATH

(1) We, the jury, unanimously find the following listed statutory aggravating circumstance or circumstances:

(Here list the statutory aggravating circumstance or circumstances so found, which shall be limited to those enumerated by the Court for your consideration.)

_____
_____
_____
_____
_____
_____

(2) We, the jury, unanimously find that the statutory aggravating circumstance or circumstances so listed above outweigh the mitigating circumstance or circumstances.

(3) Therefore, we, the jury, unanimously find that the punishment for the defendant, shall be death.

Jury Foreman	Juror
Juror	Juror
Juror	Juror
Juror	Juror
Juror	Juror
Juror	Juror

[A similar form would be provided for Punishment of Life Imprisonment, which was the only other alternative once the defendant was convicted of first-degree murder.]

Juror Opposition to the Death Penalty

For 18 years, 1968-1986, the Supreme Court held that trial judges may not exclude prospective jurors because they oppose the death penalty (*Witherspoon v. Illinois* [1968]). However, in 1986, the Court significantly altered this rule by allowing exclusions in presentence procedures when prospective jurors state that they could not under any circumstances vote to impose the death penalty. Chief Justice William Rehnquist noted that such "death-qualified" juries consist of people with "shared attitudes" who are "somewhat more conviction prone" than other juries. But he concluded, nonetheless, that such exclusions do not violate a defendant's constitutional right to an impartial jury (*Lockhart v. McCree* [1986]).

Opponents' Opening Statements

After what seemed to be endless questioning of prospective jurors, deliberations over the elimination of some of them for cause, and the use by both parties of their allotted peremptory challenges, the court arrived at a jury of twelve with four alternates.

Judge Long called for opening statements, first from the prosecutor and then from the defense.

Prosecutor's Opening Statement

"Ladies and gentlemen of the jury: the accused, Robert Jackson, killed Samuel P. Stone in the course of an armed robbery on the night of August 11, 1992.

"He is the person who entered the Jiffy Stop Market on that night with his accomplice, Jesse Williams. They both intended to rob that convenience market and had conspired to commit robbery before entering the store. Robert Jackson had the gun and threatened the store owner, Sam Stone. Mr. Stone tried to defend himself, and Robert shot him.

"Those are the simple facts that the state will prove to you are true beyond a reasonable doubt. The laws of Middle State do not require that the state prove that Robert intended to kill the store owner, but merely that he intended to rob, and did kill, the victim in the course of that robbery. Robert Jackson planned that robbery with Jesse Williams, and they carried it out together.

"Frank Builder, a local contractor, who will testify here today, saw Robert Jackson as he jumped into Jesse Williams's car, and the two robbers made their getaway from the scene of the crime. This alert and responsible citizen gave the police an accurate description of the vehicle used in the crime and later identified Robert Jackson in a police lineup witnessed by the defendant's own attorney.

"This eyewitness will tell you what he saw when he entered the Jiffy Stop Market minutes after the robbery—Sam Stone shot in the head with blood oozing out of his body, and the cash register empty.

"Police Detective Michael Develon will describe his investigation of the crime scene and the fingerprints that he found at the scene of the crime. He will also tell how he apprehended Jesse Williams and Robert Jackson. Jesse Williams has been sentenced to serve ten years in the state penitentiary for his crime as Robert Jackson's accomplice. In his confession, he told us where Robert Jackson could be found and where the gun was located that was used to kill Sam Stone.

Detective Develon will tell you how Robert Jackson ran out the back door of his house carrying the pistol used to kill his victim, Sam Stone.

"The police laboratory director, Kate Wissenschaftler, who is an acknowlgeded fingerprint and ballistics expert, will testify that the fingerprints found at the scene of the crime matched those of Robert Jackson. She also will explain how she matched the markings on the bullet removed from the victim with those test-fired from the gun Robert Jackson was carrying when he was apprehended.

"All this evidence corroborates the story Jesse Williams will tell you about his part in this senseless crime. He will tell you about how the two met in a bar that night. They became bored and they went out looking for excitement. They talked about how they could get some money to buy drugs and sex. And they looked for a likely place to get that money. They went into that store with the planned intent to commit robbery. Jesse distracted the store owner while Robert pulled the gun on him and demanded that he hand over the cash in his register. Sam Stone went for his gun from under the counter, and Robert shot him in the head. That gunshot wound to the head resulted in the massive brain damage that the attending physician describes as the cause of death on his death certificate. The robbers took the contents of the cash register and took off, leaving an innocent man mortally wounded behind the counter.

"Robert Jackson knew he was guilty of this crime. He conspired with Jesse Williams to commit it. He fled the scene of the crime that night, and he attempted to evade the police by fleeing from the arresting officers with the gun used to kill Samuel P. Stone.

"The people of this community are fed up with these reckless thieves who use deadly weapons to gun down innocent, hardworking citizens. Robert Jackson killed Sam Stone for $300 so he could buy drugs and sex. He did it for a thrill, and he should be convicted of first-degree murder because he's guilty."

Defense Opening Statement

"Ladies and Gentlemen of the jury: Robert Jackson stands before you accused of a crime he did not commit. The state has just listed all the evidence that they will present which appears to implicate Robert Jackson as the person who shot the store owner, Sam Stone, during the robbery that took place on August 11th at the Jiffy Stop Market.

"Robert Jackson did not shoot the victim, nor did he conspire to rob the Jiffy Stop Market. He unwittingly became involved with a vicious killer who robbed the market that night and shot the store owner. Jesse Williams owned the gun that killed Sam Stone, and he alone is guilty of this crime. Jesse Williams lied to the police officers and to the court in his confession in order to save his own neck.

"Robert Jackson will take the witness stand and tell you the truth about what happened that night. Sometimes the truth is stranger than fiction. And this is why his story is so compelling; he couldn't have made it up. Robert is a young man whose trusting and immature nature got him into bad trouble that night. He was looking for excitement, which is normal for a youth of eighteen who wants to experience life. But little did he know about the vicious character of the person he met, in a bar, on the night of August 11th.

"After he and Jesse Williams left that bar, where they had met for the first time, they talked about buying drugs. Jesse said he knew how they could get some money. But Robert had no idea that Jesse was willing to rob and kill to get it. When they pulled into the Jiffy Stop Market at about 11:30, Robert thought they were there to get gas. He filled Jesse's tank with gas while Jesse Williams went to pay for it. He had no idea that Jesse was going to rob the store and shoot the owner.

"When he heard the gunshot, he was pumping gas into Jesse Williams's car. Jesse came running out and told him to get into the car. Not fully realizing what had happened, Robert did as he was told. When Jesse told him what had happened, he got scared because Jesse told him he would be found guilty as an accomplice if they got caught. Robert told Jesse to take him home. Then Jesse began his plot to shift the blame to Robert. He told Robert the cops would be looking for him. They were both aware that someone had pulled in behind Jesse's car at the scene of the robbery and might be able to identify it. Jesse dumped the gun and $100 in cash in Robert's lap and told him to hide the gun for him.

"Robert did not argue with Jesse because he wanted to get out of that car and into his house as soon as possible. Only after that did he realize the seriousness of the trouble he was in. He heard from neighbors that the store had been robbed and the owner shot. The more he thought about the situation, the more frightened and irrational he became. He thought nobody would believe him.

"I ask you, ladies and gentlemen, what would you do in this situation? Robert thought he would be found guilty if he turned himself in to the police. He felt compassion when he found out the store owner was in critical condition. But the only thing he could think of to do was to return the money. He then decided to send the money from the robbery back to the store.

"Mrs. Samuel Stone will tell you she received the $100 in a plain envelope before Robert was arrested and before her husband died. This was an act of a decent young man who felt compassion and remorse for the victim of a crime, not a criminal who intentionally or recklessly committed armed robbery.

"Robert's science teacher, Alexandria Poole, will tell you that the defendant is a decent young man who had a bright future until this tragic event took place in his life. He respected his teachers and worked hard to learn. His teacher recommended that he go on to college, and he had been accepted at Middle State University.

"I know Robert's story is difficult to believe, but the defense does not rely upon Robert's testimony alone. We have located the person who sold the gun, used in the robbery, to Jesse Williams. His name is Jake Jones, and he will testify that he sold the gun to Jesse three months before the robbery took place.

"Ladies and gentlemen of the jury, the prosecutor must prove that Robert Jackson intended to commit this robbery, and you must believe that beyond a reasonable doubt. The defense evidence and testimony will provide that reasonable doubt. I know that you will listen carefully to this evidence and not act out of prejudice, fear, or hatred in making your decision. Robert Jackson is not guilty of this crime."

Prosecutor's Case in Chief

Glen Hawkins called his first witness, Frank Builder, who was placed under oath and seated in the witness box. The prosecutor asked a few questions about

Frank's identification and background, then moved into a line of questions that enabled the witness to relate his observations to the jury.

Direct Examination

Frank Builder told the jury that he had seen the defendant and another person, whom he could not identify, jump into a car parked in front of the Jiffy Stop Market that night. He was suspicious that something was wrong and noted the license number of the vehicle. He went into the store and found the victim, Sam Stone, shot in the head behind the counter. The store owner was unconscious, holding a gun in his right hand, and the cash register was empty.

Frank identified photographs of the crime scene and of the victim that were taken by law enforcement officers. These pictures were given to the jury for their consideration while Mr. Builder was testifying.

The prosecutor proceeded to discuss the lineup at which Frank had identified Robert Jackson as the person he had seen leaving Jiffy Stop Market just before he discovered the victim. Frank Builder said he was certain that this was the person he had seen leaving the crime scene. The prosecutor submitted the witness's statement from the lineup to the judge and noted that it was witnessed by the defendant's attorney.

Glen Hawkins indicated that he had no further questions of this witness, and the judge called upon the defense counsel to cross-examine him. Alvin Sharp asked the judge to call a recess while he examined the earlier statement made by the witness. Judge Long agreed and granted a two-hour lunch recess.

Cross-examination

After lunch, the defense attorney began his cross-examination by asking Frank Builder to think carefully about exactly what he had seen when he first pulled into the Jiffy Stop Market on the night of the robbery.

"I saw the defendant run across the back of the car parked there and jump into the car," said Frank.

"In which direction was he moving, toward the store entrance or away from it?" asked the attorney.

"He was moving away from the pumps and toward the entrance to the market," replied the witness.

"Would you say he was going from the gasoline pumps to the passenger side of the car?" asked the lawyer.

"Yes, that is correct," Frank answered.

There was no further questioning of this witness, and the trial moved on to the second witness for the prosecution, Detective Michael Develon.

Direct Examination

Sgt. Develon related the details of his investigation and apprehension of the two suspects identified by the first witness. He explained that his detective squad had been able to lift two sets of fingerprints from the scene of the crime that matched those of Robert Jackson. One set was taken from the gas cap that matched Jesse Williams's car, which was found in front of the pumps at the Jiffy Stop Market. The other set of prints was taken from the gasoline hose handle that was found lying on the concrete next to the pump.

The prosecutor followed several lines of questioning about the apprehension of Jesse Williams and his confession witnessed by Jesse's attorney, Jill Adams. Jesse Williams's confession was entered into evidence at this time. The prosecutor prompted his witness with questions that allowed the officer to tell the jury in his own words exactly how the officers arrested Robert Jackson.

Sgt. Develon explained that Robert ran out the back door of his home carrying the weapon used in the robbery. The officers apprehended the defendant after a chase that ended in a neighbor's house. An officer had seen the defendant drop the weapon into the neighbor's trash can just before he ran into the house.

The prosecutor introduced the gun into evidence and asked the witness to identify it. Sgt. Develon identified it as the weapon recovered from the trash can where it had been dropped by the defendant.

Cross-examination

The defense attorney had only a few questions for Mike Develon on cross-examination. "Did you find any fingerprints belonging to the defendant in the store where the victim was shot?" the defense attorney asked the officer.

"No," replied Sgt. Develon.

Direct Examination

The prosecutor called Kate Wissenschaftler to the witness stand. After establishing her credentials as an expert witness with a long history of court testimony, the prosecutor asked Kate to explain her analysis of the fingerprints lifted from the scene of the crime and how she concluded that they matched those taken from Robert Jackson when he was booked. She showed slides of the matched prints on a large screen set up in the courtroom. Her expert conclusion was that the prints were identical.

The prosecutor then asked Kate to describe how she examined the relationship between the bullet removed from the victim's head and the sample bullet fired from the gun that was previously introduced into evidence. Again Kate showed slides, this time of the two bullets, as she explained that one bullet was test-fired from the suspect's gun into a soft jell to preserve its markings. She pointed out the identical markings on the two bullets and concluded that in her expert opinion, there was no question that the two bullets were fired from the same gun.

The prosecutor had no further questions, and the defense attorney declined to cross-examine the witness.

Direct Examination

Glen Hawkins called Jesse Williams as his final witness. Jesse was escorted by a uniformed police officer who brought him into the courtroom after he was called by the judge. All witnesses had been excluded from the courtroom except while giving testimony to ensure that each witness would give testimony independently. All witnesses were sworn to "tell the truth, the whole truth, and nothing but the truth" before they gave their testimony.

Glen Hawkins reminded Jesse that he was under oath and could be prosecuted for perjury if he did not tell the truth, the whole truth, and nothing but the truth. The prosecutor then moved through a series of detailed questions, concentrating on the exact words that were used in conversations Jesse had with the defendant on the night of the robbery.

Jesse said, "We left the bar because we were bored—there was nothing going on there. We drove around and talked about doing drugs and girls. Robert wanted to know where we could get some money; he said he was broke. I told him we could look for an easy score, and he said, 'That sounds great.' Then he asked me if I had a gun, and I showed him my pistol. He asked me if he could use the gun to make the score that night, and I asked him if he thought he could handle it. He said he could, so I agreed."

The prosecutor asked Jesse why they selected the Jiffy Stop Market, and Jesse explained that there was nobody around. "Robert said he knew the place and that there were no cameras or security systems there. He only lived three blocks away."

Jesse said Robert had the gun "poked" down in his pants when they went into the market. Jesse went to get a six pack of beer while Robert looked around. When Jesse got to the counter where the victim, Sam Stone, was sitting, Robert pulled the gun and said, "Hand over the money in the cash register." Jesse said the store owner acted like he was reaching for the cash register, but he went for his gun instead, and Robert shot him. They then took the contents of the cash register, "just the bills, no checks or change."

"What did you do then?" asked the prosecutor.

"We left as fast as we could," Jesse replied. "Somebody pulled into the station just before we left, and we got scared that they would be able to identify the car. Then we divided up the money, and I took Robert home. I told him to hide the gun for me because I might get stopped."

Glen Hawkins asked a number of questions about Jesse's visit with his girlfriend that night. Jesse claimed he gave her most of his half of the cash from the robbery before he was arrested. The prosecutor ended his direct examination, and the judge called for the defense to cross-examine the witness.

Cross-examination

Al Sharp came to his feet slowly and took his place at the podium, obviously engrossed in thought and taking his time to select his first question.

"The prosecutor told you that we were going to call Jake Jones to the stand, didn't he?" asked the attorney, and quickly added, "Don't lie to me, Jesse, the prosecutor's right here and I can ask him."

"Yeah," answered Jesse.

"Who is Jake Jones?" asked the defense attorney.

"He's my neighbor who lived in the apartment next to mine," replied Jesse.

"Did he sell you this gun?" asked the attorney as he held up the prosecution's exhibit.

"Yeah," admitted Jesse.

The attorney asked the judge for permission to approach the witness with the document containing Jesse's confession that was previously introduced. "You swore to tell the whole truth when you gave your confession. Where does it state that you loaned your gun to Robert Jackson?" Al asked.

"Nobody asked me about it then," Jesse replied.

"You said Robert shot the store owner," Al continued. "How could he do that while he was pumping gas?"

"I didn't say he was pumping gas," Jesse stated.

"How did his fingerprints get on the gas pump and the gas cap, Jesse?" asked the defense attorney.

"I don't know," answered Jesse.

"You told the police that you were at your girlfriend's apartment at the time of the robbery, did you not?" asked the attorney.

"Yes," said Jesse.

"Did you lie to the police, Jesse?" asked the attorney.

"Yeah, I guess so." Jesse replied.

"Your witness, Counselor," Al Sharp told the prosecutor.

Redirect Examination

The prosecutor returned to the podium and attempted to recover his witness by asking, "Did Robert Jackson put gas in your car that night at the Jiffy Stop Market?"

"Yes, he did, but that was before we went into the store," said Jesse.

The defense attorney just smiled and declined to recross-examine the witness. Glen Hawkins said, "The prosecution rests, Your Honor." And Judge Long called a recess until the next day when the defense would present its case in chief.

Defense Case in Chief

Alvin Sharp called Robert Jackson as his first witness the next morning.

Direct Examination

Robert was nervous, but his attorney began by asking about his background, friends, and family. Robert began to relax as he described his affection for his mother who had worked hard to put him through school. He said he had been admitted to college at Middle State University before he got into all this trouble. He told the jury he had never been arrested and had never been in trouble with the law before this incident.

The defense attorney asked Robert to tell the court how he met Jesse Williams. Robert explained that he had met Jesse for the first time the night of the robbery in a bar on Fifteenth Street called the "Pub." He said he just went in to get a beer and see if anything was going on. He sat down beside Jesse at the counter, and they started talking. They talked about drugs and girls. Robert said he thought Jesse was "pretty cool, at first." The attorney asked him to explain what he meant by that, and Robert said, "You know, I thought he had been around and knew how to handle himself."

"What did you do after you left the bar, Robert?" asked the defense attorney.

"We drove around looking for another place where we might find some girls and maybe get a party started. That's what I thought we were doing," said Robert.

"What else did you talk about?" prompted the attorney.

"That's all we talked about. I didn't talk to him about robbing anybody, and I didn't even know he had a gun until after we left the market,' Robert replied.

"What happened next?" asked the attorney.

"We pulled into the Jiffy Stop Market to get some gas," said Robert. "Jesse asked me to fill up the tank for him. Then I heard a gunshot and Jesse came running out. He told me to get in the car. I pulled the hose out of the tank and threw it over on the platform next to the pump, then I ran around to the passenger's side of the car and jumped in."

"What did Jesse say had happened?" prompted the attorney.

"He said the owner pulled a gun on him and he had to shoot him," said Robert.

"And what did you say?" asked the attorney.

"I said, 'What the hell did you do that for?'" replied Robert. "Jesse looked wild and scared, and it began to dawn on me that he had held up that store and shot the owner. Jesse said the driver of the truck that pulled in behind us must have seen us."

"What happened then?" asked the lawyer.

"I told Jesse to take me home, I didn't want to get into trouble with the police," said Robert. "Jesse said that if we got caught, we would both be guilty, and that's when I really got scared."

"What happened when you got to your house?" continued the attorney.

"I started to get out, and Jesse shoved the gun in my lap and gave me a fist full of cash from the robbery. He said to hide the gun for him because the cops might stop him. I didn't argue with him; I just wanted to get away from him," Robert replied.

Robert explained how he went to his room and hid the gun and the money. He did not sleep at all that night thinking about the trouble he was in. The more he thought about it, the more frightened he became. He knew no one would believe his story. Robert got a little emotional at this point, and a few tears ran down his cheeks as he explained his frustration with the situation.

When Robert had regained his composure, Al asked him what he did with the money. Robert explained that he heard the next day that the Jiffy Stop Market had been robbed and the owner shot. His friend down the street told him. He stayed inside the house after that and was afraid to go outside. He felt sick and depressed. He waited for the police to come and get him for about a week, and when they didn't, he began to think it might be safe to go out. He went to see his friend, but he couldn't even talk to *her* about it. When he found out that Mr. Stone was in critical condition, he decided to send the money back to the store. He said, "It was the least I could do."

The defense attorney indicated that he had completed his direct examination. Glen Hawkins asked the judge for a recess to enable him to prepare for cross-examination of this important witness whose testimony he had heard for the first time. The judge granted a continuance until the next day, when the trial would resume.

Cross-examination

The prosecutor began his cross-examination of the defendant the next morning by asking, "Isn't it true that you drove around with Jesse looking for a way to get money to buy drugs and sex?"

"Yes, I guess so," answered Robert.

"Did you have any money that night before the robbery, Robert?" asked the prosecutor.

"No," said the defendant.

"You suggested the Jiffy Stop Market, didn't you?" asked the attorney.

"No, Jesse just pulled in there," said Robert.

"But you had been there before, hadn't you?" asked the prosecutor.

"Yes," said Robert.

"And you told Jesse there were no surveillance cameras and it would be an easy score, didn't you?" asked the attorney.

"No, I did not say that," answered the defendant.

"You felt guilty and that's why you sent the money back to the store, isn't that right, Robert?" asked the lawyer.

"Yes, I felt sorry for the owner, but I didn't kill him," answered Robert.

"You knew what you were doing that night, Robert," the prosecutor continued. "You are smart enough to know that drugs and sex cost money. Where were you going to get it, pick it up on the street?"

"Objection, argumentative. He's badgering the witness, Your Honor," said the defense attorney.

"Sustained, you don't have to answer that question," responded the judge.

"No further questions, your honor," said the prosecutor as he left the podium. The defense attorney felt no need for a redirect examination and called his next witness, Alexandria Poole. The high school teacher was placed under oath and took her seat in the witness box.

Direct Examination

After establishing Alexandria Poole's identity as a high school science teacher with fifteen years of teaching experience in Capital City, the attorney asked her to describe how well she knew Robert Jackson. She said she knew him better than she knew most of her students. He was very interested in science, particularly the space program, and had written a good paper for her on the subject.

Attorney Sharp asked the teacher to describe Robert's character from her observations. She said he was a good student who respected his teachers. She had never heard of him causing any trouble. He worked hard for his grades and even did extra work to raise his grades. She had written a recommendation for him and helped him with his college application.

"Has he ever lied to you?" asked the attorney.

"No, never. He was always honest and conscientious," replied the teacher.

The prosecutor declined to cross-examine the witness, and the defense attorney called the wife of the victim, Mrs. Samuel Stone, to the stand. Mrs. Stone was placed under oath and seated in the witness chair.

Direct Examination

Al Sharp asked her to identify herself and expressed his sympathy for her loss caused by the senseless crime that took her husband's life.

"I know this is difficult for you, but I will have to ask you a few questions," said Al. "Did you receive the sum of approximately $100, in cash, after the robbery?"

"Yes, I did," Mrs. Stone answered.

"When did you receive this money?" prompted the lawyer.

"About two weeks before my husband died. I did not save the envelope. I thought it was from someone who felt sorry for my husband. It had no return address," said the witness.

"Thank you, Mrs. Stone," said the attorney as he left the podium.

Cross-examination

The prosecutor asked Mrs. Stone to tell the court how much money was taken in the robbery. She said that it was about $300, and then she began to cry, saying that her husband had given more money than that to the children in the neighborhood for Christmas.

The prosecutor declined to ask any further questions. Al Sharp stated, "The defense rests, Your Honor." There was no need to call Jake Jones, since his testimony had been verified by the prosecution witness Jesse Williams. The judge declared a recess until the next day, when they would hear closing arguments.

Closing Arguments

Prosecutor's Closing Arguments

"Ladies and gentlemen of the jury: the state will not ask for the death penalty in this case. There are acknowledged mitigating circumstances which preclude that extreme punishment. However, Robert Jackson was an accomplice in this crime, and the law imposes the same penalty on one who aids and abets regardless of who did the actual killing.

"The judge will charge you with a clear understanding of your responsibilities under the law, but the evidence you have heard concerning intent in this case boils down to how much of the testimony of the two suspects you are willing to accept as the truth. There is no question that both of these culprits, who testified against each other, were involved in the crime. Who pulled the trigger is not relevant to your verdict if you find that both conspired to commit this robbery. They may even be lying to protect each other. The consistent fact remains that Jesse Williams and Robert Jackson went riding around that night looking for money to buy drugs and sex. They planned to commit that robbery, and Robert picked the Jiffy Stop Market because he knew that it was an easy score.

"The judge will charge you with a description of the lesser included offenses in this case. He will tell you that if you have "reasonable doubt" concerning first-degree murder, you will have to decide whether the defendant is guilty of second-degree murder or accessory after the fact. These crimes carry lesser punishments, but this criminal activity on Robert Jackson's part cannot be allowed to go unpunished.

"Robert Jackson knew, or should have known, what was about to happen that night. Regardless of whose story you believe, he was there at the Jiffy Stop Market while the robbery took place. He stood ready to, and did, lend assistance in the perpetration of armed robbery that resulted in the death of an innocent victim.

"This community cannot be made safe unless the good citizens, like you, make the hard choices that will ensure that criminals are punished."

Defense Closing Argument

"Ladies and gentlemen of the jury: Robert Jackson is not a criminal. He is a decent young man with a promising future. His youth and immaturity got him into trouble the night of the robbery and the senseless killing of Sam Stone; but Robert Jackson did not kill him—Jesse Williams did.

"Robert Jackson was outside the store pumping gas into the car when Sam Stone was shot. You have heard corroborated evidence by the defendant, by the eyewitness, Frank Builder, and by the fingerprint expert that Robert was at the gas pumps. He did not know what was taking place inside the store when Jesse Williams robbed and shot his victim.

"The defendant denies that he engaged in the planning of this robbery, and he had no intention of robbing that convenience store. He would not have been so foolish as to stand there flatfooted, pumping gas, if he had known what was going to happen inside the store.

"Jesse Williams is a liar and a convicted criminal. He lied to the police officers when he was arrested, he manufactured that alibi about being with his girlfriend at the time of the robbery, and he's lying now. In Jesse Williams's warped criminal mind, he may have thought Robert knew what he, alone, intended to do that night.

"Robert Jackson found himself helpless and in a dilemma after he realized what had happened. He showed his sense of moral responsibility when he returned the money. His science teacher has told you that he would never lie, and he is not lying now.

"He has told you the truth, ladies and gentlemen, and his future is in your hands."

Judge's Charge to the Jury

Judge Long declared a recess until the next day when he would present his charge to the jury. He would take the opposing attorneys' requests into consideration in drafting the charge that would be given to the jury for their deliberation. The next day, Judge L.B. Long addressed the jury, "Ladies and gentlemen of the jury: you have heard the evidence in this case and it is now my duty and responsibility to instruct you on what the laws of this state require."

First-Degree Murder

first-degree murder: premeditated homicide or, in most states, homicide committed in connection with arson, rape, robbery, or burglary.

Judge Long explained, "The defendant, Robert Jackson, is accused of **first-degree murder** in perpetration of a felony. A person commits murder in the first degree if that person kills someone during the perpetration of armed robbery.

"For you to find the defendant guilty of murder in the first degree, the state must have proven beyond a reasonable doubt the existence of the following essential elements:

1. that the defendant unlawfully killed the alleged victim;
2. that the killing was committed during the perpetration or attempt to perpetrate the alleged robbery; that is, that the killing was closely connected to the alleged robbery and was not a separate, distinct, and independent event; and
3. that the defendant specifically intended to commit the alleged robbery.

"If you find that the above three elements exist beyond a reasonable doubt, it is not necessary that the state prove an intention to kill or that the alleged killing was done willfully, deliberately, with premeditation, and with malice."

Aiding and Abetting

The judge then discussed the concept of aiding and abetting. He told the jury, "All persons **aiding and abetting**, or ready and consenting to aid and abet, in any criminal offense are guilty of a crime. An aider and abettor is one who advises, counsels, procures, or encourages another to commit a crime.

"The law does not require an actual eyewitness presence at the scene of the crime. Only a constructive presence is necessary to charge one as an aider and abettor. As a general rule, one is deemed to be constructively present if one is at the time performing any act in furtherance of the felony, or is in a position to give information that would aid the actual perpetrator or prevent others from discouraging and stopping the perpetrator. The distance of the alleged aider and abettor from the scene of the crime is immaterial. A common example of a constructive presence at a crime scene is where one "keeps watch" at a distance from the scene of the crime in order to warn of the approach of danger, or where one provides transportation to facilitate the escape of the actual perpetrator of the crime.

"Constructive or actual presence, however, is not sufficient to make one a principal of the crime. There must be some evidence, at least circumstantial, that the defendant knowingly participated in the crime. The defendant must have had knowledge of the crime being committed, and an intent to aid and abet. An aider and abettor who has knowledge of the principal's unlawful intent and assists the principal is guilty in the same degree as the principal. When the aider and abettor does not share in the principal's intent, however, but is controlled by his or her own intent, the degree of guilt of the aider and abettor is not necessarily that of the principal.

"In determining the degree of the defendant's guilt, you should consider his criminal intent, and not the intent and degree of guilt of the principal offender whom the defendant is accused of aiding and abetting. If you find from the proof that the defendant is guilty, beyond a reasonable doubt, of murder in the first degree, you will so report, and your verdict in that event shall be: 'We, the jury, find the defendant guilty of murder in the first degree.'"

aiding and abetting: to assist, facilitate, or advance the commission of a crime; to encourage, counsel, or incite the commission of a crime.

Second-Degree Murder

At this point, the judge gave the jury instructions regarding the lesser included offense of second-degree murder, saying, "If you find the defendant is not guilty of murder in the first degree, or if you have a reasonable doubt about his guilt, you must acquit him of this offense. You must then consider whether the defendant is guilty of **second-degree murder**, which is a lesser included offense.

"For you to find the defendant guilty of the lesser included offense of second-degree murder, you must find:

1. that the defendant unlawfully and willfully killed the alleged victim; and
2. that the killing was malicious.

second-degree murder: in most states, all forms of murder other than first degree. Most states have lesser degrees of killing such as manslaughter, criminally negligent homicide, and vehicular homicide.

"If one person, upon a sudden impulse of passion, without adequate provocation, and disconnected with any previously formed design to kill, kills another willfully and maliciously, such killing is unlawful and is murder in the second degree."

Accessory After the Fact

accessory after the fact: a person who, knowing a felony has been committed by another, receives, releaves, comforts, or assists the felon.

A person is an **accessory after the fact** who, after the commission of a felony, with knowledge or reasonable grounds to believe that the offender has committed the felony, and with the intent to hinder the arrest, trial, conviction, or punishment of the offender, engages in any of the following acts:

1. harbors or conceals the offender;
2. provides or aids in providing the offender with any means of avoiding arrest, trial, conviction, or punishment; or
3. warns the offender of impending apprehension or discovery.

The judge explained this offense to the jury, then continued with his instructions as follows.

"If you find from the proof that the defendant is guilty, beyond a reasonable doubt, of accessory after the fact, second-degree murder, or first-degree murder, you will so report your verdict on each charge. In the event you find the defendant guilty of any of these charges, your verdict shall be: 'We, the jury, find the defendant guilty of the specific charge.'

"If you find that the defendant is not guilty of any of these crimes, or if you have a reasonable doubt about his guilt, then you must acquit him of these offenses.

"The charge concerning aiding and abetting applies to both of the lesser included offenses of second-degree murder and accessory after the fact, as well as to the crime of first-degree murder. Your first task will be to appoint a foreperson who will be responsible for recording your decisions on each of the three crimes charged. Your decisions must be unanimous, and you are to continue to deliberate until this is accomplished."

Verdict and Sentencing

The judge instructed the bailiff to sequester the jury for its deliberations. The documentary and material evidence as well as the judge's charge to the jury were allowed in the jury room for use during the jury's deliberation.

After several hours of deliberation, the jury reached a verdict of not guilty of first-degree murder and not guilty of second-degree murder. The jury delivered a unanimous verdict, however, finding Robert Jackson guilty of accessory after the fact. Judge Long questioned the jury to make sure the decision was unanimous, then he pronounced the court's judgment, finding the defendant guilty of the crime of accessory after the fact.

Sentencing did not take place at this time. A background investigation and sentencing recommendation from the probation officer was conducted, and the judge pronounced sentence three weeks later.

Accessory after the fact was a class E felony under Middle State law and carried a sentence of one to six years that could be served in local jails. The sentencing grid allowed the judge to reduce the minimum sentence in cases in which there were mitigating circumstances. (See sentencing grid in Chapter Ten, Figure 10-1, for first time offender with mitigating circumstances.)

At the sentencing hearing, Judge Long arrived at the minimum sentence of less than one year (.9 years) in the local jail or workhouse. Robert could be released once thirty percent of that time (.2 years) was served. Judge Long used this opportunity to encourage Robert to go to college and get a good education. He hoped Robert had learned to be careful about association with persons of questionable character.

CHAPTER SUMMARY

1. This chapter describes a hypothetical situation that could lead to use of the full criminal trial process. Less than ten percent of criminal cases are actually tried, however. The overwhelming majority of convictions result from guilty pleas. Full trial cases are the exception, rather than the rule.

2. The United States Supreme Court has held that a person accused of any crime that carries a potential jail sentence has the right to counsel. In 1967, the Court held that a pretrial lineup after a complaint or indictment has been issued is a "critical stage" in the trial process and that the defendant, therefore, has the right to have counsel present as a witness.

3. In 1972, the Supreme Court held traditional death penalty statutes unconstitutional as violations of the Eighth and Fourteenth amendments prohibiting cruel and unusual punishment. However, four years later, in 1976, the Court upheld new death penalty statutes requiring a two-stage (bifurcated) trial process. The accused must be convicted of a death penalty crime, and then be sentenced in a second trial in which evidence of aggravating and mitigating circumstances are argued.

4. In 1977, the Supreme Court held that the imposition of the death penalty for rape of an adult woman is unconstitutional and constitutes cruel and unusual punishment.

5. The Supreme Court decisions regarding the death penalty have reduced the degree of racial bias in the implementation of the death penalty in the United States and have eliminated the practice of executing persons for the crime of rape, which was the area in which racial bias was most pronounced. All current death penalty statutes require convictions for first-degree murder, although the Court has left open the possibility of imposing the death penalty to prevent and deter other types of crime.

6. The criminal discovery process is more restrictive than the civil discovery process, but still requires that all material evidence be shared. Depositions are not taken, however, except in cases where the witness may be unable to appear in court. Both sides can demand the names of witnesses to be called, but the accused has a right to remain silent, and the prosecutor can withhold witness statements in some cases until the trial. The prosecutor must share any exculpatory evidence with the defense regardless of whether the defense requests it.

7. Both sides have the authority to subpoena witnesses, who are then required by law to appear and answer questions under oath at trial. Continuances and suppression motions for a pretrial hearing are the most frequently used pretrial motions during the discovery period, although there are many opportunities for delay and to request pretrial hearings regarding issues of discovery and trial conditions. Interrogatories and requests to produce evidence also are frequently used.

8. Lists of aggravating and mitigating circumstances are extensive in modern death penalty statutes, and the process of analyzing them is very complex. The lists provided in this chapter are typical of those used in the thirty-six states that currently impose the death penalty. Most modern societies and several American states have abolished the death penalty.

9. Criminal jury selection is marked by several exceptions that do not usually apply in the civil *voir dire* process. More extensive peremptory challenges are allowed in criminal cases than in civil cases, and lawyers and judges may not exclude minorities on the basis of race alone, although this rule is difficult to enforce.

10. The criminal trial process follows the general outline of the civil trial process, but the detailed rules of criminal procedure must be applied. These rules of procedure, like those regarding *voir dire*, are different in some of their specifics and exceptions.

11. An accomplice is one who aids and abets in the commission of a crime and is guilty of the same crime as the principal when the accomplice shares in the principal's intent. Lesser included offenses generally are required to be included in the judge's charge to the jury. The penalties for each lesser included offense are not given to the jury prior to an initial finding of guilt. A guilty verdict of first-degree murder requires a second trial to evaluate aggravating and mitigating circumstances in jurisdictions that impose the death penalty.

KEY TERMS

accomplice	exculpatory evidence	rules of criminal procedure
pretrial lineup	continuance	first-degree murder
capital punishment	suppression motion	aiding and abetting
cruel and unusual punishment	bifurcated trial process	second-degree murder
death penalty for rape	aggravating circumstances	accessory after the fact
criminal discovery	mitigating circumstances	

DISCUSSION QUESTIONS

1. Did the defense attorney properly advise the defendant to waive his preliminary hearing and try for a plea bargain as an accomplice? Why would such advice be given?

2. Should the death penalty be abolished? Is it still subject to abuse? Is there a general economic and racial bias in the use of the death penalty?

3. Why is the criminal discovery process more restrictive than the civil discovery process?

4. Why must exculpatory evidence be shared with the defense whether asked for or not? What does this rule reveal about the proper role of the prosecutor?

5. Why are suppression hearings frequently involved in the criminal trial process? Should any evidence have been suppressed in our illustrative case?

6. Are the aggravating circumstances listed in Middle State's statute likely to act as a deterrent to such crimes?

7. Should the prosecutor have charged Robert Jackson with first-degree murder in this case?

8. Would knowledge of the race of the defendant make any difference in the jury's verdict? Should it?

9. How important is it that the decider of facts in dispute be able to observe witnesses carefully during trial? How do a witness's demeanor, body language, and eye contact make one witness more believable than another?

10. If you had served on the jury in Robert Jackson's case, are there specific questions you would have wanted to ask? What questions, and of what witnesses?

11. How would you have decided the verdict in Robert Jackson's case? Was the decision of the jury fair?

SOURCES AND SUGGESTED READING

Bowers, William. 1974. *Executions in America*. Lexington, Mass.: Heath Company.

Carp, Robert A., and Ronald Stidham. 1990. *Judicial Process in America*. Washington, D.C.: Congressional Quarterly, Inc.

Kassin, Saul M., and Lawrence S. Wrightsman. 1988. *The American Jury on Trial: Psychological Perspectives*. New York: Hemisphere Publishing Corp.

Levine, James P. 1992. *Juries and Politics*. Pacific Grove, Calif.: Brooks/Cole Publishing Co.

Tennessee Code Annotated (See relevant sections of the criminal code in the reader's state to review differences in definitions and punishments.)

Tennessee Judicial Conference. 1988. *Tennessee Pattern Jury Instructions: Criminal* (T.P.I.-CRIM.). 2d ed. St. Paul: West Publishing Co. (See the practice volumes for the reader's state that contain model jury instructions.)

United States Statistical Abstract. U.S. Government Printing Office 1991.

COURT CASES

Batson v. *Kentucky*, 476 U.S. 79, 106 S.Ct. 1712, 90 L.Ed.2d 69 (1986)

Coker v. *Georgia*, 433 U.S. 584, 97 S.Ct. 2861, 53 L.Ed.2d 1982 (1977)

Furman v. *Georgia*, 408 U.S. 238, 92 S.Ct. 2726, 33 L.Ed.2d 346 (1972)

Gregg v. *Georgia*, 428 U.S. 153, 96 S.Ct. 2909, 49 L.Ed.2d 859 (1976)

Lockhart v. *McCree*, 476 U.S. 162, 106 S.Ct. 1758, 90 L.Ed.2d 137 (1986)

Powers v. *Ohio*, 111 S.Ct. 1364, 113 L.Ed.2d 411 (1991)

Pulley v. *Harris*, 465 U.S. 37, 104 S.Ct. 871, 79 L.Ed.2d 29 (1984)

Trop v. *Dulles*, 356 U.S. 86, 78 S.Ct. 590, 2 L.Ed.2d 630 (1958)

United States v. *Agurs*, 427 U.S. 97, 96 S.Ct. 2392, 49 L.Ed.2d 342 (1976)

United States v. *Wade*, 388 U.S. 218, 87 S.Ct. 1926, 18 L.Ed.2d 1149 (1967)

Witherspoon v. *Illinois*, 391 U.S. 510, 88 S.Ct. 1770, 20 L.Ed.2d 776 (1968)

CHAPTER TWELVE

EVALUATING THE CRIMINAL PROCESS

> "A judge shall be faithful to the law and maintain professional competence in it. A judge shall not be swayed by partisan interests, public clamor or fear of criticism."
>
> Canon Three (B-2): ABA Model Code of Judicial Conduct

This chapter concludes the discussion of the criminal justice process with an examination of the right of appellate review and an analysis of the most important issues concerning the criminal justice system. The first issue is the use of plea bargaining that is so prevalent in modern practice. This issue is examined from both the critics' and the supporters' points of view. The prison crisis in the United States is another major issue; most states are faced with a corrections dilemma because of their overcrowded prisons and inadequate resources to deal with the problem. Prisoners' rights issues also are discussed, and juvenile justice systems are described.

Finally, the differences between the criminal justice system of the United States and that of the Federal Republic of Germany are illustrated. Modern Germany has produced a unique criminal justice system that is comparable to our own in some respects but also is a reformed version of the European civil law systems that characterize continental European societies. The German system in many ways has incorporated the best elements of both legal systems.

APPELLATE REVIEW IN CRIMINAL CASES

The defendant's right of appeal in criminal cases is generally provided by state constitutional or statutory authority. The appeals process has the same function in criminal cases as it does in civil cases and is principally concerned with error correction and law development. However, in criminal cases, there are more federal constitutional guarantees and detailed interpretations of due process of law involved, which has increased the number of appellate review cases in the United States Supreme Court.

The Fifth Amendment prohibition against **double jeopardy** states, "[N]or shall any person be subject for the same offense to be twice put in jeopardy of life or limb. . . ." This statement means that the prosecutor cannot seek a new trial through the appeals process.

double jeopardy: Fifth Amendment prohibition against a second prosecution after a first trial for the same offense; prohibits prosecutor from seeking another trial through an appeal.

For the defendant, appeal is considered a critical stage in the criminal process. According to the Court in *Douglas v. California*, 372 U.S. 353, 83 S.Ct. 814, 9 L.Ed.2d 811 (1963), an indigent defendant is entitled to appointed counsel for the first appeal as a matter of right.

Previous chapters have discussed many of the major results of Supreme Court decisions in appeals cases that have involved the minimal federal constitutional guarantees related to issues covered in the Fourth, Fifth, Sixth, and Eighth amendments as applied by the Court through the Fourteenth Amendment due process and equal protection clauses. There are even more fundamental due process guarantees in the original Constitution. One guarantee is that the "privilege of the writ of habeas corpus shall not be suspended, unless when in Cases of Rebellion or Invasion the public Safety may require it." Two other guarantees prohibit bills of attainder and ex post facto laws—ancient injustices that are specifically prohibited to both state and national governments. (See article I, sections 9 and 10, of the Constitution in Appendix A.)

writ of habeas corpus (you have the body): presents the issue of whether a prisoner is restrained of liberty without due process.

The **writ of habeas corpus** is discussed in more detail later in this chapter in connection with prisoners' rights. However, this guarantee extends back to the Magna Carta (1215) in Anglo-American jurisprudence and is perhaps the most fundamental right of the accused, incarcerated person. The writ is a court order directing an official who has a person in custody to bring the prisoner to court and to show cause for the prisoner's detention. Congress may suspend this guarantee in cases of rebellion or invasion, although a number of state constitutions absolutely forbid its suspension. Habeas corpus is generally considered the most important guarantee of liberty in that it prevents arbitrary arrest and imprisonment.

ex post facto laws: laws passed after the commission of an act, retrospectively changing the legal definition or consequences of the act or deed.

Ex post facto laws are retroactive laws that seek to make into a crime an act that was not a crime when committed, or that increase the penalty for crime after its commission, or that change the rules of evidence to make conviction easier. The prohibition against such laws does not extend to civil laws or to laws that are favorable to an accused person. This concept is fundamental to the idea of rule of law.

A **bill of attainder** is a "legislative trial" of an individual that declares guilt and metes out punishment by legislative act. Impeachment trials, which are not considered bills of attainder, are permitted, but they are confined to removal of a person from office. Criminal trials must be held in court. The constitutional guarantee that forbids bills of attainder is a fundamental ingredient in the concept of separation of powers and of freedom itself.

bills of attainder: legislative acts that inflict punishment on a person without a judicial trial.

These constitutional guarantees in criminal cases have resulted in great expansion of the use of the appeals process, particularly since the 1960s when the Supreme Court extended these minimal guarantees to state as well as federal procedures. This chapter focuses on general criticisms of the criminal justice process rather than repeating the material regarding appeals that has been covered in Part II in the discussion of the civil process.

PLEA BARGAINING ISSUES

The prevalence of plea bargaining in the American criminal justice system is one of its most prominent features. In continental European courts, plea bargaining does not exist because a trial cannot be avoided with a plea of guilty. The American practice of plea bargaining dates back more than one hundred years and "appears to have become well entrenched in a number of United States jurisdictions by the 1880s" (Sanborn 1986, 134). Sanborn reports that guilty pleas comprised as much as eighty-five percent of the total number of convictions in New York City during the last two decades of the nineteenth century.

During the 1920s, plea bargaining began to be criticized as a device for enabling politically connected defendants to gain preferential treatment. Then in the 1950s, it was condemned because of the coercion involved in "forcing" a defendant to plead guilty (Nardulli 1978). In current debates, plea bargaining is criticized for providing criminals with excessive leniency and for coercing defendants to waive their constitutional rights to a trial (Abadinsky 1991, 297–98).

Arguments Against Plea Bargaining

The most common criticism of the extensive practice of plea bargaining is that it is symptomatic of a system that is operated to further the needs of the principal actors rather than the needs or interests of justice or the public. Expanding case loads and limited resources provide an excuse for handling cases through the truncated plea bargaining process. Judges, prosecutors, and defense attorneys gradually have accepted the path of least resistance and have become coopted into believing that plea bargaining is justified because it enables the system to function efficiently, that is, with a minimum amount of difficulty or disruption.

Abandonment of Adversarial Justice

Abraham Blumberg argues that plea bargaining has led to an abandonment of the adversarial idea, and the practice of criminal law has been reduced to a "con" (confidence) game: "All court personnel, including the accused's own lawyer, tend to be coopted to become agent-mediators who help the accused redefine his situation and restructure his perceptions concomitant with a plea of guilty" (Blumberg 1967, 20).

Manipulation of the Defendant

Overcharging by police and prosecutors is often cited by critics of plea bargaining as a means of manipulating the accused. The defense attorney frequently accepts this practice and becomes a part of the manipulation process. Albert Alschuler states that "overcharging and subsequent charge reduction are often the components of an elaborate sham, staged for the benefit of the defense attorneys. The process commonly has little or no effect on the defendant's sentence, and prosecutors may simply wish to give defense attorneys a 'selling point' in their efforts to induce defendants to plead guilty" (Alschuler 1968, 95).

Manpower Deficiencies

Public defenders "prefer a quick disposition because their manpower barely suffices to handle their case load" (Jacob and Eisenstein 1977, 26). Private attorneys who handle indigent cases have a disincentive to try cases because of the low fees paid by the state governments. A New York City Bar Association report in 1985 revealed that "barely [one-half of one] .5 percent of the cases handled by society [public defender] attorneys resulted in a trial and more complex cases were referred to court-appointed counsel, many of whom were incompetent, if not senile" (Margolick 1985, E4).

Undermines Respect for the System

The general atmosphere of the plea bargaining system promotes a socialization process that affects the typical defense counsel—whether private, public defender, or assigned. "In the process of handling their cases, new defense attorneys learn that the reality of the court differs from what they had expected; through rewards and sanctions, they are taught to proceed in a certain fashion" (Heumann 1978, 57). In particular, Heumann points out that defense attorneys learn to avoid legal challenges that can gain the enmity of prosecutors and judges. Conformity is rewarded, and attorneys can expect to build credit by avoiding time-consuming motions or engaging in actions perceived to be frivolous challenges. This credit then can be drawn upon in a case that the defense attorney deems important. As one public defender remarked, "You go to the judge and you say, 'Look, judge, I'm busting my buns every day in this dang court, and I need a break on this case.' It has nothing to do with justice, nothing to do with the law. I need a break" (quoted in Eisenstein et al. 1988, 30).

The widespread nature of the practice of plea bargaining has been illustrated by Malcolm Feeley, who studied the process intensively in misdemeanor courts in New Haven, Connecticut. He examined 1,600 cases in detail and followed them through the system—none of them went to trial. All of the cases involved petty offenses that carried less than one-year sentences, and all of them were either dismissed, settled by guilty pleas, "nolled" (kicked), or had the bail forfeited. At the misdemeanor level, the plea bargain includes a bid to have the case "nolled," which is a frequent occurrence, since the petty offense may not be worth the prosecutor's time (Feeley 1979, 185–92).

Frequency of Plea Bargaining

In felony cases, trials are held more frequently than in misdemeanor cases, but rates vary substantially across the country. Plea bargaining is not synonymous with guilty pleas; however, most studies demonstrate that a high percentage of guilty pleas are bargained in practice. The practice is considered to be more frequent in urban areas, but Zawitz found that even in Pueblo, Colorado, only one percent of cases went to trial. Of the twenty-seven cities studied, Seattle, Washington, had the highest percentage of trials (15%), and Pueblo, Colorado, had the lowest percentage (1%). The median was five percent (Zawitz 1988).

The typical outcome of one hundred felony arrests brought by the police for prosecution, illustrated in Figure 12-1, provides a visual overview of the types of statistics that characterize the current process. These are aggregate figures, however, and do not reveal the current practices in particular jurisdictions.

Threats of Harsher Sentences

The threat of a harsher sentence if the accused is convicted at trial is often cited as an objectionable practice in plea bargaining because it encourages a defendant to waive the constitutional right to a trial. In some cases, particularly in cases involving misdemeanor offenses, the accused may be given a choice of going to trial, with a chance to prove innocence, or pleading guilty and going free. If the accused is indigent or cannot make bail, the prisoner may serve more time awaiting court dates than that which constitutes the maximum punishment for the offense.

FIGURE 12.1 Typical Outcome of One Hundred Felony Arrests Brought by Police for Prosecution

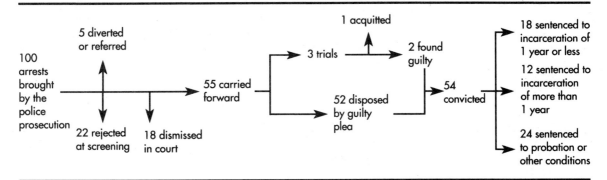

Source: Boland, Barbara and Brian Forst. Bureau of Justice Statistics. *The Prevelence of Guilty Pleas*. Washington D.C.: U.S. Government Printing Office, 1984.

Sentencing Disparity

Plea bargaining contributes to sentencing disparity and, in the eyes of both the accused and the general public, often allows defendants to beat the system. This practice undermines respect for the criminal justice process.

For these reasons, the National Advisory Commission on Criminal Justice Standards and Goals, in 1973, recommended that the practice of granting concessions in return for guilty pleas should be prohibited (National Advisory Commission 1973, 46).

Arguments for Plea Bargaining

The extensive practice of plea bargaining is justified on the basis of expediency and efficient utilization of resources. Most practitioners, and even informed observers, when asked to explain the existence of plea bargaining, point to the overwhelming case load that threatens the system. Most supporters of plea bargaining claim, "Nobody likes plea bargaining, but it's the only way the system can survive."

Reduces Court Overload

Chief Justice Warren Burger, writing for the majority of the Court in the case of *Santobello v. New York*, which upheld court enforcement of plea bargain agreements in 1971, stated the argument plainly:

> The disposition of criminal charges by agreement between the prosecutor and the accused, sometimes loosely called "plea bargaining," is an essential component of the administration of justice. Properly administered, it is to be encouraged. If every criminal charge were subjected to a full-scale trial, the States and the Federal Government would need to multiply by many times the number of judges and court facilities. (*Santobello v. New York*, 404 U.S. 257, 92 S.Ct. 495, 30 L.Ed.2d 427 [1971]).

Provides Rough Justice

Malcolm Feeley accepts plea bargaining in the misdemeanor courts because he finds that the informal practices are highly predictable and provide evidence of adversarial combat. However, Feeley does not describe the process of "bargaining" in the sense of haggling over the worth of a case. His investigation revealed that plea bargaining evidences relatively stable norms of behavior and expectations in an informal commitment to a sense of "rough justice." Feeley admits that the appearance of justice suffers from a court process "where the overwhelming majority of cases took just a few seconds" (Feeley 1979, 11).

In felony cases, prosecutors are likely to engage in careful investigation and make careful plea bargain decisions. A study conducted by Stephen Lagoy, Joseph Senna, and Larry Siegal found that certain information was weighed heavily in the prosecutorial decision to accept a plea bargain. Factors such as the nature of the offense; the defendant's prior record and age; and the type, strength, and admissibility of the evidence were important considerations in making the plea-bargaining decision.

The study mentioned above also found that prosecutors in low-population, rural areas not only employed more information while making their decisions, but also were more likely than their counterparts in high-population, urban areas to accept plea bargains. The authors state that "this finding tends to dispute the notion that plea bargaining is a response to overcrowding in large urban courts" (Lagoy et al. 1976, 462).

Overcrowding of the Courts

Conclusions similar to those reached by Lagoy et al. were reached by William McDonald in a study of plea bargaining in six court jurisdictions. The study found that plea negotiations were not conducted in a haphazard manner, nor were they used by prosecutors to engage in fraud or other deceptive practices. Prosecutors did not overcharge suspects with the idea of forcing them to plead to a more reasonable charge (McDonald 1975).

A federal study by Barbara Boland and Brian Frost involving fourteen jurisdictions across the country supports these findings. The jurisdictions with the highest number of plea bargains were not located exclusively in high-crime areas where case load pressure was a factor. Thus, case load pressure does not seem to play as important a role in plea negotiations as some critics have thought. The study also found that jurisdictions holding a large number of trials tended to be more selective in the cases they processed and were more likely to screen out weak cases before trial. Most plea bargains were for the top charge filed against the defendant. Those who pleaded guilty were more likely to do time but were less likely to go to state prison. Although punishment was more certain with a plea bargain, it was less severe than that meted out at trial (Boland and Frost 1984).

Saves Time and Effort

Prosecutors, defense counsel, and judges defend plea bargaining because it saves time and effort. The National Institute for Law Enforcement and Criminal Justice (1978) found that efforts to eliminate plea bargaining were met with resistance by assistant prosecutors and others in the system, namely, judges and defense attorneys. The police also defend the use of plea bargaining because they do not have to make court appearances; they claim that in most cases, their time is better used in preventing and solving crimes.

Admission of Guilt

Penologists argue that the first step toward rehabilitation is for a criminal to admit guilt. Some argue that a guilty plea is, at least nominally, the first step toward a successful return to society. However, if the defendant feels coerced or pressured into admitting guilt to a lesser offense that the defendant knows he or she did not commit, the guilty plea may have the opposite effect.

Development of Guidelines

Many supporters of plea bargaining argue that safeguards and guidelines have been developed to prevent violation of due process and to ensure that innocent defendants do not plead guilty under coercion. They point to the following measures as realistic efforts to deal with problems associated with plea bargaining:

1. the judge questions the defendant about the facts of the guilty plea before accepting the plea;
2. the defense counsel is present and able to advise the defendant of his or her rights;
3. open discussions about the plea occur between the prosecutor and the defense attorney; and
4. full and frank information regarding the offender and the offense is made available at the arraignment stage of the process.

Prohibition of Plea Bargaining Tried

Supporters argue that judicial supervision ensures that plea bargaining is done in a fair manner. Specific guidelines by the office of the chief prosecutor, prepleading investigations, prepleading reports, and pretrial settlement conferences are methods of improving the existing system without prohibiting plea bargaining.

Prohibition of plea bargaining has been tried in numerous jurisdictions throughout the United States. The most notable example is Alaska, which prohibited prosecutors from granting concessions to defendants in exchange for guilty pleas in 1975. The states of Iowa, Arizona, the District of Columbia, and Delaware have made efforts to abolish plea bargaining, as has the city of Honolulu, Hawaii.

Efforts at prohibition of plea bargaining have been disappointing because the system can adapt to the status quo by altering other factors. The number of trials may increase, the sentence severity may change, more questions regarding a speedy trial may arise, and discretion may be shifted to a higher level in the system (Senna and Siegel 1987, 318).

Constitutional Issues

Defendants who plead guilty as a result of a plea bargain forfeit several constitutional rights, including, among others, the Fifth Amendment right against self-incrimination and the Sixth Amendment rights to a public trial and to confront one's accusers, as well as the presumption of innocence. This issue has stimulated considerable debate about the acceptance of certain practices as meeting valid constitutional due process standards.

Voluntariness of the Plea

The United States Supreme Court has reviewed the constitutional issues of plea bargaining in a series of court decisions involving primarily the voluntariness of guilty pleas. In *Boykin v. Alabama*, 395 U.S. 238, 89 S.Ct. 1709, 23 L.Ed.2d 274 (1969), the Court held that an affirmative action, such as a verbal statement, indicating that the plea was made voluntarily must exist on the record before a trial judge may accept a guilty plea. In *Brady v. United States*, 397 U.S. 742, 90 S.Ct. 1463, 25 L.Ed.2d 747 (1970), the Court held that a guilty plea is not invalid merely because it is entered to avoid the possibility of the death penalty. Justice White, in his opinion for the Court, upheld the constitutionality of plea bargaining as having a "mutuality of advantage." He stated that the state "conserves scarce judicial and prosecutorial resources" and achieves "more promptly imposed punishment"; and at the same time, the defendant's "exposure is reduced, the correctional process can begin immediately, and the practical burdens of a trial are eliminated."

Prosecutor Responsibility to Honor the Bargain

Once a plea bargain has been agreed to by the prosecutor, it must be honored. This legal principle was clearly established in *Santobello v. New York*, 404 U.S. 257, 92 S.Ct. 495, 30 L.Ed.2d 427 (1971), in which the state prosecutor reneged on a bargain struck with the defendant. The bargain was not fulfilled because of a change in prosecutors, and the defendant was given a maximum sentence contrary to the plea agreement. The Supreme Court reversed the decision.

Prosecutor Threats

Critics of plea bargaining question the constitutionality of defendants' forfeiting of their rights no matter how thorough the bargaining process, and the Supreme Court has been willing to consider some of these complaints. In a highly controversial decision that split the Court five to four, the Supreme Court held that a defendant's due process rights are not violated when a prosecutor threatens to reindict the accused on more serious charges if the accused does not plead guilty to the original offense (*Bordenkircher v. Hayes*, 434 U.S. 357, 98 S.Ct. 663, 54 L.Ed.2d 604 [1978]).

The defendant, Paul Hayes, was indicted by a Kentucky grand jury for forging a check in the amount of $88.30, an offense then punishable by a term of two to ten years. The prosecutor offered to recommend a sentence of five years' imprisonment if Hayes pleaded guilty. The prosecutor also stated that if Hayes did not plead guilty, the prosecutor would return to the grand jury and seek an indictment under the Kentucky Habitual Criminal Act, which would subject Hayes to a mandatory life sentence because of his two prior felony convictions.

Hayes pleaded not guilty, and the prosecutor obtained an indictment charging him under the Habitual Criminal Act. At trial, the jury found Hayes guilty of the original charge; and under the Habitual Criminal Act, Hayes was sentenced to life imprisonment. The Kentucky Court of Appeals affirmed the sentence. On habeas corpus, the federal district court dismissed the petition, but the Court of Appeals for the Sixth Circuit reversed, holding that the prosecutor's conduct had violated Hayes's due process rights. The United States Supreme Court then granted certiorari to consider the constitutional question because of its importance to the administration of criminal justice.

On the Fourteenth Amendment issue, the circuit court had held that the substance of the plea offer itself violated the limitations imposed by the due process clause. However, the Supreme Court concluded that the appeals court was mistaken in its ruling. The majority stated that there is no element of punishment or retaliation as long as the accused is free to accept or reject the prosecution's offer. A rigid constitutional rule would prohibit a prosecutor from acting forthrightly in dealing with the defense, which would only invite unhealthy subterfuge that would drive the practice of plea bargaining back into the shadows from which it had so recently emerged. Thus, in *Bordenkircher v. Hayes*, 434 U.S. 357, 98 S.Ct. 663, 54 L.Ed.2d 604 (1978), the five-member majority held that a threat to indict on more serious charges was not a violation of the defendant's due process rights.

The *Bordenkircher* case illustrates the extent of prosecutorial discretion. Although the Court recognized the potential for individual and institutional abuse, it concluded that the prosecutor's conduct was not unlawful.

Effective Counsel

Another constitutional issue regarding plea bargains is whether defendants have a right to *effective* counsel. In *McMann v. Richardson*, 397 U.S. 759, 90 S.Ct. 1441, 25 L.Ed.2d 763 (1970), three defendants claimed that their confessions were coerced and that their court-appointed attorney had incompetently represented them. The Court, however, held that their attorney was "reasonably competent" and that defendants must assume the risk of "ordinary error" by their attorneys. However, in *Henderson v. Morgan*, 426 U.S. 637, 96 S.Ct. 2253, 49 L.Ed.2d 108 (1976), the Court set aside a conviction because the defendant pleaded guilty to second-degree murder without being informed of the consequences. The Court held that if a person of low mental ability has not been given an explanation of the difference between manslaughter and murder, the person's guilty plea is involuntary.

In *United States v. Cronic*, 466 U.S. 648, 104 S.Ct. 2039, 80 L.Ed.2d 657 (1984), Justice Stevens explained that the right to counsel includes the right to effective counsel because competent counsel is essential to the accusatory system and "the reliability of the trial process." Public defenders do not enjoy absolute immunity from being sued for incompetent representation. However, the Court has been reluctant to hold that defendants have been denied effective counsel.

In *Strickland v. Washington*, 466 U.S. 668, 104 S.Ct. 2052, 80 L.Ed.2d 674 (1984), Justice O'Connor set forth a difficult test for determining when the right to effective counsel has been denied. The defendant must first show that counsel's performance was deficient to the extent of making errors so serious that they constituted a denial of the counsel that is guaranteed in the Sixth Amendment. The defendant also must show that the deficient performance created prejudice against the defense to such an extent that it deprived the defendant of a fair trial.

Defendants have a right to effective counsel on their first appeal (*Evitts v. Lucey*, 469 U.S. 387, 105 S.Ct. 830, 83 L.Ed.2d 821 [1985]), although attorneys may withdraw from cases in which defendants tell their attorneys that they are going to lie on the witness stand, without denying the defendants' right to effective counsel. In 1989, the Court held that a judge may not compel a lawyer to serve as a defendant's court-appointed counsel.

PRISON CONDITIONS AND OVERCROWDING

The condition of the prisons throughout the United States in the past two decades has been severely criticized. More than thirty state prison systems have been the subject of federal lawsuits that have declared them in whole or in part unconstitutional. New prisons are being built throughout the country, and states gradually are making progress toward meeting the constitutional standards set by the courts.

The principal problem is overcrowding, which also has produced safety and security problems that courts have reacted to as violative of legal standards. The rise in prison populations can be explained in large part by the recent public demands to "get tough" with criminals and put them behind bars. State legislatures have enacted mandatory and fixed sentencing laws that have increased the number of people eligible for incarceration and that have limited the offender's chances for early release on parole. Mandatory incarceration for criminal offenses such as drunk driving, handgun use, and narcotics violations account for the soaring increases in prison and jail populations. (See Figure 12-2.)

FIGURE 12.2 Number of Sentenced State and Federal Prisoners, Year End, 1925–1990

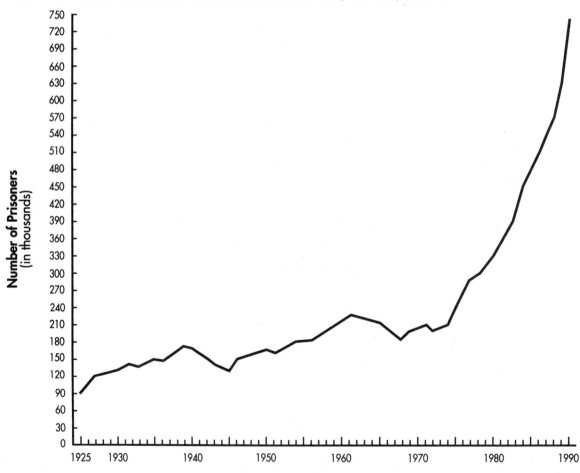

Source: Adapted from Bureau of Justice Statistics, *Prisoners 1925–1981*, updated.

Prison populations doubled in many states in the 1980s, and the overcrowding problem spilled over into local jails. By 1984, a federal survey of jail conditions found that the occupancy nationwide was 102% of stated capacity. Because of overflow conditions in the prisons, 24% of the jails were handling inmates from outside their jurisdictions. Of the 621 largest jails, 134 of them were under court order to reduce their populations, and 150 more were being ordered to improve conditions (Senna and Siegel 1987).

Prisoners' Rights

Prior to the 1960s, it was generally accepted that, upon conviction for a crime, an individual forfeited all rights not expressly granted by statutory law or correctional policy. State and federal courts had adopted a "hands off" doctrine of noninterference with corrections authorities unless the case clearly indicated a serious breach of the Eighth Amendment protection against cruel and unusual punishment.

The Federal Civil Rights Act (1963), 42 U.S.C. § 1983, contains a provision that makes:

> Every person who, under color of any statute, ordinance, regulation, custom, or usage of any State or Territory subjects, or causes to be subjected, any citizen of the United States or other person within the jurisdiction thereof to the deprivation of any rights, privileges, or immunities secured by the Constitution and laws shall be liable to the party injured in an action at law, suit in equity, or other proper proceeding for redress.

This language, often referred to as the **under color of law doctrine**, allows prisoners to sue for civil rights violations. In *Cooper v. Pate*, 378 U.S. 546, 84 S.Ct. 1733, 12 L.Ed.2d 1030 (1964), the Supreme Court ruled that inmates being denied the right to practice their religion are entitled to legal redress under 42 U.S.C. § 1983. An earlier decision in 1941, *Ex parte Hull*, declared that access to the courts for an inmate is a basic constitutional right. Subsequent decisions in the 1970s have expanded this concept to deal with the problems of lack of access to legal services in prisons and many other aspects of prison life. In the case of *Johnson v. Avery*, 393 U.S. 483, 89 S.Ct. 747, 21 L.Ed.2d 718 (1969), the Supreme Court held that unless the state could provide some reasonable alternative to inmates in the preparation of petitions for postconviction relief, a **jailhouse lawyer** must be permitted to aid illiterate inmates in filing habeas corpus petitions.

A habeas corpus petition involves a court order directing an official who has a person in custody to show cause for that person's detention. Illegal denial of rights can be brought before the courts in this manner. In *Haines v. Kerner*, 404 U.S. 519, 92 S.Ct. 594, 30 L.Ed.2d 652 (1972), the Court held that prisoners' petitions must be reviewed even if they have only a limited amount of legal merit. Ten years later, the expansion of a prisoner's access to the federal courts was somewhat limited by actions of the conservative Burger Court. In *Rose v. Lundy*, 455 U.S. 509, 102 S.Ct. 1198, 71 L.Ed.2d 379 (1982), the Court held that before a federal court can review an inmate's habeas corpus petition, the inmate must exhaust all legal avenues available in the state courts. The current Rehnquist Court has moved even further in the direction of limiting access to the federal courts through these petitions (see "The Death Penalty" in Chapter Eleven).

The substantive rights areas of current recognition by the courts include limited prisoners' rights in regard to freedom of the press, freedom of religion, the

under color of law doctrine: federal statute prohibiting denial of constitutional rights under a disguise or pretext of law.

"jailhouse lawyer": inmate of a penal institution who spends his or her time reading the law and giving legal assistance and advice to inmates.

habeas corpus petition: petition for the writ of habeas corpus as a postconviction remedy that extends to all constitutional challenges.

right to medical treatment, and the right to be free from cruel and unusual punishment.

Freedom of Communications

The courts have consistently held that only when a compelling state interest exists can prisoners' First Amendment rights be modified. Corrections authorities, therefore, must justify the limiting of freedom of speech by showing that granting such freedom would threaten institutional security. Recent decisions have upheld prisoners' rights to receive mail from one another, but prison officials can restrict mail to prisoners in temporary disciplinary detention as a means of increasing the deterrent value of the punishment. In 1980, the institutional policy of refusing to deliver mail in a language other than English was held unconstitutional.

The right to send and receive communications with the outside world is a fundamental right of prisoners recognized by the courts. In *Pocunier v. Martinez*, 416 U.S. 396, 94 S.Ct. 1800, 40 L.Ed.2d 224 (1974), the Supreme Court held that censorship is allowable only when justified by prison security needs and when the restrictions are not greater than those demanded by security precautions. Correspondence with the media, however, may be limited. In *Saxbe v. Washington Post Co.*, 417 U.S. 843, 94 S.Ct. 2811, 41 L.Ed.2d 514 (1974), the Court held that a federal prison rule forbidding individual press interviews with specific inmates was justified. The Federal Bureau of Prisons successfully argued that interviews enhance the reputation of particular inmates and jeopardize the possibility of achieving equal treatment of prisoners in prison.

Freedom of Religion

Religious freedom is a fundamental right and was the first area in which the courts lifted their hands off doctrine. Subsequent decisions have established that an inmate may hold any belief he or she chooses, but may be denied participation in some aspects of that religion.

Right to Medical Care

In 1976, after reviewing the legal principles established during the previous twenty years, the Supreme Court, in *Estelle v. Gamble*, clearly stated that the inmate's right to medical care is supported by the constitutional guarantee against cruel and unusual punishment. The Court stated, "Deliberate indifference to serious medical needs of prisoners constitutes the 'unnecessary and wonton infliction of pain' . . . proscribed by the Eighth Amendment."

Human Dignity

Treatment of prisoners that (1) degrades the dignity of human beings, (2) is more severe than the offense for which it is given, or (3) shocks the general conscience and is fundamentally unfair, has been held unconstitutional by the courts. Corporal punishment has been severely limited by court decisions, and even solitary confinement under prolonged and barbaric conditions has been held to be in violation of the Eighth Amendment. Prisoners have a right to adequate personal hygiene, exercise, mattresses, ventilation, and rules specifying how they can earn release from solitary confinement.

More than thirty state prison systems were placed under court orders in the 1980s as a result of the conditions of prisoners that were judged to violate the principles of cruel and unusual punishment. The Texas case of *Estelle v. Ruiz*, 503 F.Supp. 1265 (1980), however, illustrates some of the problems of achieving prison reform through court order. The Texas Department of Corrections was ordered to alleviate overcrowding, abolish the practice of inmate trustees who had previously controlled the prison, hire more staff, improve medical treatment and other services, institute progressive programming, and adhere to the principles of procedural due process in dealing with inmates.

James Marquart and Ben Crouch studied conditions in a Texas penitentiary, the Eastham Unit, both before and after the changes brought about by this legal intervention. The study concentrated primarily on the court's decision to eliminate "building tenders" (inmates who controlled many aspects of prison discipline) and found that the impact of that decision led to a crisis in the control of inmates. Prisoner expectations of fairness rose, but so did the number of infractions of prison rules. A period of tension and staff demoralization produced more violence than before the court orders (Marquart and Crouch 1985, 557–86).

Such short-term results may be offset by the long-term impact of the court-ordered changes. Prison systems other than that studied by Marquart and Crouch have witnessed beneficial changes as a result of the court orders.

Community-Based Programs

Community treatment in corrections has become prominent in the last twenty years. Today there are hundreds of private and state-administered community programs. Drug and alcohol treatment, community-based group therapy, and educational programs that employ exoffenders are used for lesser offenses and nonviolent crimes. Probationary release under some supervision and inducements to require utilization of these programs are being tried in many communities. The traditional **community-based programs** include juvenile justice systems that have been developed in all jurisdictions as well as pretrial diversion programs that were instituted in the 1960s.

Juvenile Justice Systems

Today's juvenile court systems embody both rehabilitative and legalistic orientations. The development of separate systems for handling juvenile offenders is a twentieth century reform that has been severely criticized by many people. Like the adult corrections systems, these systems have witnessed many changes since the 1960s.

The central concept of the juvenile justice systems is the principle of ***parens patriae***. This term refers to governmental authority to treat delinquents as the parent would be expected to treat them when they violate rules. The state is to act on behalf of the parent in the interests of the child.

Prior to the 1960s, juvenile court proceedings were informal and were subject to relaxed procedural rights. After the 1960s, however, the United States Supreme Court began to set a series of precedents making it clear that the most fundamental constitutional rights of children have to be respected. These legalistic reforms have produced a reaction consistent with the recent "get tough on criminals" attitude, brought on in part by increasingly serious violations of the law by children.

community-based programs: correctional programs that provide rehabilitation or punishment supervision at the community level rather than in prison.

parens patriae (parent of the country): refers traditionally to role of the state as sovereign and guardian of persons under legal disability.

juvenile justice systems: juvenile courts and corrections facilities having special jurisdiction, of a paternal nature, over delinquent, dependent, and neglected children.

Juvenile justice systems are still characterized by important differences in the procedures followed and the treatment of the accused, compared to adult justice systems; however, court decisions have blurred these differences. The primary purpose of juvenile procedures is protection and treatment of the child according to the principle of *parens patriae*. The aim is not primarily punishment of the guilty. Age determines the jurisdiction of juvenile courts, which is generally available to those under eighteen years of age. However, juvenile jurisdiction may be waived, and for serious crimes—even, in some states, those carrying the death penalty—the accused may be tried as an adult. Some states, however, prohibit the death penalty for those under eighteen. Status offenses still exist, allowing juveniles to be held responsible for acts that would not be criminal if they were committed by adults. However, some courts are looking more carefully at parents' and guardians' responsibilities in these matters.

Administrative Character of Juvenile Proceedings

Juvenile proceedings are not considered criminal proceedings, and they generally are conducted on an informal basis. Juvenile court records must be kept confidential, and parents are highly involved in the process. However, the standards for arrests of juveniles are less stringent than those for adults. Juveniles usually are released into parental custody, as opposed to being released on bail like adults. Since the proceedings technically are not criminal proceedings, juveniles have no rights to jury trials (unless they are being tried as adults).

Indeterminate terms in correctional facilities for juvenile and youthful offenders are the form of institutional dispositions. The juvenile's procedural rights are based on the concept of fundamental fairness, as opposed to the adult's rights to due process under the Bill of Rights and the Fourteenth Amendment. A juvenile has the right to rehabilitation treatment under the Fourteenth Amendment, but an adult has no such right. The juvenile's record is sealed when the age of majority is reached, while the adult's criminal record is permanent.

Protected Rights

Search and seizure rules, *Miranda* warnings, protection from prejudicial lineups, the right to counsel, and other safeguards to protect juveniles when they make confessions are similar to those that protect adults. Pretrial motions, rules concerning plea negotiations, and the right to a trial based on the "beyond a reasonable doubt" standard of proof also are similar to adult standards. Some of the leading cases that establish these legal safeguards and standards are: *Kent v. United States*, 383 U.S. 541, 86 S.Ct. 1045, 16 L.Ed.2d 84 (1966), *In re Gault*, 387 U.S. 1, 87 S.Ct. 1428, 18 L.Ed.2d 527 (1967), *In re Winship*, 397 U.S. 358, 90 S.Ct. 1068, 25 L.Ed.2d 368 (1970), and *Breed v. Jones*, 421 U.S. 519, 95 S.Ct. 1779, 44 L.Ed.2d 346 (1975).

CRIMINAL PROCEDURES IN OTHER COUNTRIES

The American criminal justice procedures have been subject to a number of criticisms. Issues of law and order and of criminal procedure are some of the most controversial subjects of political debate in the United States. Stories in the mass media constantly expose the public to the enormous problems of the criminal justice system, and many people consider it to have failed in the achievement of its most important objective, the deterrence of crime.

Modern western European democracies, on the other hand, have more highly respected criminal justice systems that have not stimulated such dissatisfaction and controversy. One of the leading American specialists in comparative criminal procedure, John Langbein (1977), concludes that in modern western European democracies: "Except for political cases, which no system handles well . . . the task of detecting and punishing crime is generally perceived to be handled effectively and fairly."

The modern European democracies—France, Germany, the Netherlands, the Scandinavian countries, and others—have in common the civil law heritage described in Chapter One. The differences between civil law countries and common law countries are in many ways less pronounced today than in earlier periods. Both systems have evolved in practice to institute important protections of fundamental human rights. There are significant differences, however, in administrative procedures and practices.

Historical connotations of the term *inquisitorial*, which refers to the characteristic feature in civil law systems of the judge's active role in the trial, has led to several misconceptions about civil law procedures. Many of these misunderstandings stem from contrasts between the earlier English and civil law systems during the Spanish Inquisition in the Middle Ages.

Mary Ann Glendon, Michael Gordon, and Christopher Osakwe explain that there are three common misconceptions about criminal procedures in civil law countries: "that the accused is presumed guilty until proved innocent, that there is no jury trial, and that the trial is conducted in an 'inquisitorial' fashion." These authors conclude that the first notion is simply false. The second notion is incorrect in regard to some systems, and as to others, it overlooks the fact that lay judges who participate on mixed courts with professional judges are a functional analog to the jury. The third notion they refute by explaining that the active role played by the judges in the conduct of the trial is better described by the connotations of the term *nonadversarial* (Glendon et al. 1982, 94).

Plea Bargaining Differences

One major difference between civil law and common law systems is that plea bargaining is effectively eliminated in the civil law systems. All criminal cases of a felony nature are tried before a judicial tribunal, where witnesses are called and facts are ascertained regardless of whether the accused has pleaded guilty. The prosecutors' role in civil law systems also differs significantly from that of American prosecutors. Prosecutors do not question the witnesses at trial; rather, the court conducts such questioning.

Victims' Rights

Victims play a more significant role in most civil law systems. "In some countries, if the same wrongful act gives rise to both criminal and civil liability, the injured person is permitted to intervene directly in the criminal action rather than bringing a separate civil suit" (Glendon et al. 1982, 96). The court may order civil damages to be paid to the victim as part of the disposition of the criminal case. These damages work like restitution in modern American practice, but the civil law system avoids the extra burden on the courts of separate civil suits filed to recover damages incurred by the victim.

Comparison of German and American Procedures

The European civil law systems differ substantially from each other today. Although they can be compared with the American system, most of them are unitary political systems. The German Federal Republic offers a federal system with interesting features of structure and process that provide useful contrast with our criminal procedures. Germany has incorporated many of the American concepts of criminal justice while preserving its basic civil law traditions.

The German practice recognizes the victim's interest, and the victim is allowed to intervene on the side of the prosecution. Pleadings are unnecessary, and therefore, there is no *nolo contendere* plea. In certain types of cases, if the prosecutor declines to bring charges, an injured person may be permitted to bring a criminal proceeding individually or seek court action to force the state's attorney to prosecute. In Germany and in most other civil law countries, however, the prosecutor has no discretion not to prosecute (*nolle prosequi*) when there is reasonable cause to believe the defendant has committed a serious offense. Therefore, there is no plea bargaining with the prosecutor. There are, however, informal methods of encouraging cooperation in open court.

Criminal Discovery and Rules of Evidence

Discovery rules in criminal cases in Germany give the defendant unlimited access to all the evidence assembled by the prosecution. Independent judicial authority to engage in electronic surveillance is required, and evidence obtained through unauthorized means is subject to exclusion.

The rules of evidence in Germany are considerably simplified in comparison to those in America because trained jurists are involved in the deliberations conducted after the witnesses and evidence have been heard in open court. Bench conferences and jury dismissals to allow argument on legal points are unnecessary, since all decision makers are allowed to ask questions of witnesses. The prosecutor is essentially a resource for fact discovery and investigation, not the accuser; the prosecutor's role is to assemble all the facts for the court—those that prove innocence as well as those that prove guilt.

Appellate Review

In Germany, both the prosecution and the defense have the right to appeal. In the United States, the prohibition against double jeopardy prohibits appeals by the prosecution. The intermediate German appeals court may involve a full retrial of the case, *de novo*, if the appeals court deems it warranted. The appeals court in such cases may question witnesses again, take new evidence into consideration, and send for expert opinions. The court designates expert witnesses who are chosen independently by the court upon request of the parties. As in the United States, the highest courts are appellate courts, that is, they consider only questions of law in dispute.

German Constitutional Court

Questions of constitutional law are decided by special courts that are independent of the regular courts in Germany. The Constitutional Court is composed of two chambers, or "Senates," with eight members serving in each chamber for twelve-year terms. Members are appointed by the two houses of the legislature. This court has sweeping powers of judicial review and is one of the most innovative features of the postwar German legal system. It borrows from our example of judicial review, but goes far beyond it. The two chambers handle questions of judicial review of legislation, disputes between the federal (national) government and the states (*Laender*), and direct petitions of individuals charging violation of constitutionally guaranteed basic rights.

The German legislature has provided that individuals who believe their rights have been violated by actions (such as acts of legislation) against which there is no alternative route of appeal may complain directly to the Constitutional Court. Such actions do not involve court costs or even the participation of legal counsel (Heidenheimer 1971, 235).

A new level of review of human rights violations now exists in the form of the European Court of Human Rights. This court has established new precedents, beginning in 1960, allowing individual access to the court and holding national courts responsible for violations of rights that are internationally protected among the member states of the Council of Europe, which now includes twenty-six European nations (Solmanson 1990, 300).

Thus, in Germany, there is constitutional and even supranational protection against arbitrary arrest and incarceration. Under the modern German criminal code, the accused has the right to remain silent, the right to the benefit of counsel, and the right to be represented by counsel during interrogation and critical stages. The accused individual's right to receive a fair trial is ensured through extensive appeal guarantees. The use of a panel of judges is required in all felony cases at the trial and appeals levels. Capital punishment no longer exists, and maximum sentences generally are lower than those in the United States.

Unified Criminal Code

In the Federal Republic of Germany, the West German criminal code, which now applies to former East Germany as well, provides uniform criminal procedures and standards even though the federal system is somewhat similar to our own. The major difference is that in the German system, criminal statutory law of a felony nature is the responsibility of the federal parliament and is limited by the national constitution. The ancient Roman law from which the German system has evolved has been modified by new enactments but retains many of the basic features that have proven valuable.

Federal Differences

The German federal system differs substantially from the American federal model in that it effectively prevents the vast inequities in sentences and punishments for the same crime that are prevalent in the United States. There is only one hierarchy of courts in felony criminal cases, compared to fifty-one hierarchies in the United States. There are no original federal trial courts; the federal courts function as appellate courts. All lower criminal courts are required to adhere to national standards. Constitutional issues may be taken directly to the separate Constitutional Court.

German Procedure Illustrated

In the modern German context, a person arrested by the police under the circumstances used in our illustrative criminal case would be handled differently. The state's attorney assigned to the case, and the police under the responsibility of the state's attorney, would be required to conduct an extensive pretrial investigation and prepare a written report for the court. There would be no question about whether Jesse Williams would go to trial. There would be no opportunity, nor incentive, for the state's attorney to engage in a plea bargain with the defendant. The defendant would be provided with a private defense attorney of his choice with whom he could consult before agreeing to be interrogated by the state's attorney. He would have the right to remain silent. At the trial, the court would call the witnesses based upon the state's attorney's report and the defense attorney's requests.

Trial Court Composition

The German trial court is composed of three trained professional jurists and two lay persons. Judges are not elected but are professionally trained civil servants. The five members of the court have the function of making an independent judgment, and all the members may participate in the questioning of witnesses. After the court has exhausted its questioning, the defense attorney is allowed to put questions to the witnesses. There is no contest between lawyers as is typical of the American adversarial system.

Role of the District Attorney (State's Attorney)

The state's attorney is called upon by the court members to answer questions about the investigation, or is ordered to conduct further investigations as deemed necessary, under the German criminal justice system. Expert witnesses are named by the court and paid at state expense. Any inducement to confess is provided in open court. The defense attorney will counsel the defendant that cooperation with the court will encourage leniency on the part of the members in making their sentencing decisions.

Even if the accused cooperates with the court and provides information about an accomplice, all admissible evidence is heard in the trial. The object is to give the court panel a complete understanding of the facts to enable them to arrive at an informed judgment. Therefore, all evidence is presented even if the defendant pleads guilty and offers a confession. The accused has a right to remain silent and cannot be forced to take the witness stand.

Disposition of Cases at Trial

In Germany, court decisions concerning both guilt and sentencing are made by a majority of the five members of the court. Decisions do not have to be unanimous, as in typical American practice. If new facts are discovered after the person is found not guilty, an appeal may be taken by the state's attorney to the state appeals court (*Oberlandesgericht*). If the five judges on this panel agree that a second trial is warranted, they may order another trial at the level of original jurisdiction (*Landgericht*).

If the defendant is found guilty and sentenced, the defendant may appeal for a new trial on the basis of either new facts or procedural or substantive error of the trial court. The right of appeal is not discretionary; the appeals court must hear the case. The defendant may petition the Constitutional Court for alleged violations of constitutional law, and may even petition the European Court of Human Rights concerning violations of international treaty obligations in the area of human rights. This new development exists in contrast to traditional concept of international law which recognizes only states as parties.

Sentencing

Armed robbery involving critical injury of the victim is subject to a sentence range in Germany of not less than five and not more than fifteen years in the penitentiary. Death of the victim is considered murder, and the accused is subject to a possible life sentence. A person sentenced to a life term may be released after serving fifteen years upon approval of the court. The death penalty is not permitted. The person sentenced must serve a minimum of two-thirds of the sentence imposed and will be released early only if the prisoner shows evidence of rehabilitation and poses no danger to the public in the eyes of the court of original jurisdiction.

Release Decisions

In the United States, the widespread practice of using parole boards appointed by the governor to decide if a prisoner is eligible for release is a questionable practice. In Germany, this decision is made by the court that sentenced the prisoner, which assumes responsibility for deciding whether that person is ready to be released before the entire sentence is served. The overcrowded conditions of American prisons place enormous pressure upon parole boards to release prisoners early. The average time served in the United States is from twenty to thirty percent of the sentence, as opposed to the rule in Germany that a minimum of two-thirds of the sentence must be served.

There are transitional programs to facilitate reintegration back into normal society, but Germany has no parole boards and no parole supervision bureaucracy. Inmates who have served less than full sentences are released in custody of responsible individuals, and a correctional officer is given oversight authority.

CHAPTER SUMMARY

1. In the United States the defendant's right of appeal is established in almost all jurisdictions, and the Supreme Court has recognized a right of indigents to appointed counsel for a first appeal as a matter of right. The appeals process in criminal cases is substantially the same as that in civil cases but involves more federal constitutional guarantees. In addition to the Fourth, Fifth, Sixth, and Eighth amendment provisions applied against state actions through the Fourteenth Amendment, there are fundamental rights involving the writ of *habeas corpus* and prohibitions against *ex post facto* laws and bills of attainder.

2. Plea bargaining is one of the most prominent features of the American criminal justice system. Although plea bargaining varies by jurisdiction, the use of this procedure has increased in modern times and has become an expected part of the process. A number of issues have been raised about how this practice affects the fairness of, and respect for, the criminal process.

3. Critics of plea bargaining argue that the practice undermines the fundamental premises of the adversarial system and serves to further the interests of the principal actors in the process rather than those of society or justice. Supporters argue that if plea bargaining is properly administered, it is an essential component of the administration of justice.

4. The Supreme Court has upheld plea bargaining as mutually advantageous, but the plea must be voluntarily and knowingly given. A guilty plea is not invalid merely because it is entered to avoid the possibility of the death penalty. Agreements must be honored by prosecutors, but the accused may withdraw the plea without prejudice if it is not accepted by the judge. The practice of prosecutors using threats to prosecute the defendant on more serious charges if the defendant does not plead guilty has been upheld.

5. Overcrowding in prisons, and consequently in jails, has become a major problem during the last decade. Prison populations are expanding at unprecedented rates because of public and legislative reaction to the crime problem and demands to "get tough" with criminals. The courts in more than thirty states have ordered measures to reduce overcrowding and to ensure compliance with constitutional standards.

6. The Federal Civil Rights Act (42 U.S.C. § 1983) prohibits deprivation of any person's civil rights under color of law. This statute has been used effectively to extend limited constitutional guarantees of prisoners' rights since 1963. Prisoners have the right to file petitions to the courts concerning violations of their constitutional rights, and they have a right of access to "jailhouse lawyers" to assist them in certain cases if reasonable alternatives are not available.

7. *Habeas corpus* petitions are methods of bringing issues of denial of fundamental rights before the courts. The federal courts have limited these petitions somewhat in the last ten years by requiring that inmates first exhaust all legal state remedies before the case may be heard in federal courts.

8. Juvenile justice systems are a traditional method of dealing with juvenile crime; however, the increasing seriousness of juvenile crimes and the urge to "get tough" on criminals have led to more juveniles being tried as adults. The juvenile justice systems are based on the concept of separate court administration employing the principle of *parens patriae*, under which the state acts as parents in the interests of the child.

9. Court decisions since the 1960s have injected more consideration of constitutional rights into the nation's juvenile justice systems, but significant differences continue to exist between treatment of juveniles and adults. Juvenile proceedings are informal, court records are sealed, parents are highly involved, and there is no right to a jury trial. In addition, status offenses exist for juveniles—that is, offenses that would not be crimes if they were committed by adults; procedural rights are based on the concept of fundamental fairness; and juveniles have a right to rehabilitation treatment.

10. Community-based corrections programs today include hundreds of private and state-administered programs. Probationary, drug and alcohol, group therapy, educational, and other types of programs are being employed more frequently to alleviate prison overcrowding.

11. Criminal procedures in modern European democracies generally are perceived as handling criminal detection and punishment efficiently and fairly. Plea bargaining does not exist because all cases are tried by a panel of judges. These nonadversarial systems offer recognition of the victim's interests, open discovery rules, and simplified rules of evidence. All members of the decision-making body are allowed to ask questions of witnesses.

12. The German criminal justice procedure features a federal system under which basic individual rights are protected, and there is a unified criminal code for the entire nation. The unified procedures and sentencing structures allow for greater consistency in sentences and punishment. Plea bargaining does not exist. All cases are tried before a panel of judges that includes two lay persons and three professional judges. Maximum sentences generally are less severe than those given in American jurisdictions, but the sentences and the manner in which they are carried out are more consistent.

KEY TERMS

double jeopardy

writ of *habeas corpus*

ex post facto laws

bills of attainder

under color of law doctrine

"jailhouse lawyer"

habeas corpus petition

community-based programs

parens patriae

juvenile justice systems

DISCUSSION QUESTIONS

1. Does the extensive practice of plea bargaining undermine respect for the court system?

2. What costs would be involved if all felony cases had to be tried?

3. Would the elaborate nature of the American jury trial system have to be abandoned if all felony cases had to go to trial?

4. What are the major causes and effects of prison overcrowding?

5. Should prisoners have rights that are protected by the courts?

6. What types of corrections programs are the most effective in achieving the goals of protection of society and rehabilitation of prisoners?

7. Do the procedures that are typical of civil law systems in western European democracies offer any possible solutions to problems of the criminal justice system in the United States?

SOURCES AND SUGGESTED READING

Abadinsky, Howard. 1991. *Law and Justice: An Introduction to the American Legal System*. Chicago: Nelson-Hall Publishers.

Abraham, Henry J. 1986. *The Judicial Process*. 5th ed. New York: Oxford University Press.

Alschuler, Albert. 1968. "The Prosecutor's Role in Plea Bargaining." *Yale Law Review* 84:1175.

Blumberg, Abraham S. 1967. "The Practice of Law as a Confidence Game: Organizational Cooptation of a Profession." *Law and Society Review* 1:15–39.

Boland, Barbara, Catherine H. Conly, Lynn Warner, Ronald Sones, and William Martin. 1988. *The Prosecution of Felony Arrests, 1986*. Washington, D.C.: U.S. Government Printing Office.

_____, and Brian Frost. 1984. *Bureau of Justice Statistics. The Prevelence of Guilty Pleas*. Washington, D.C.: U.S. Government Printing Office.

Cole, George F., ed. 1988. *Criminal Justice: Law and Politics.* 5th ed. Pacific Grove: Brooks/Cole Publishing Co.

Eisenstein, James, Roy B. Fleming, and Peter F. Nardulli. 1988. *The Contours of Justice: Communities and Their Courts.* Boston: Little, Brown.

Feeley, Malcolm M. 1979. *The Process Is the Punishment.* New York: Russell Sage Foundation.

———. 1982. "Plea Bargaining and the Structure of the Criminal Process." *Justice System Journal* 7 (Winter):338–55. (Reprinted in Cole 1988, 467.)

Glendon, Mary Ann, Michael W. Gordon, and Christopher Osakwe. 1982. *Comparative Legal Traditions.* St. Paul: West Publishing Co.

Heidenheimer, Arnold J. 1971. *The Governments of Germany* 3d ed. New York: Crowell Co.

Heumann, Milton. 1978. *Plea Bargaining.* Chicago: University of Chicago Press.

Jacob, Herbert, and James Eisenstein. 1977. *Felony Justice.* Boston: Little, Brown.

Lagoy, Stephen P., Joseph J. Senna, and Larry J. Siegel. 1976. "An Empirical Study on Information Usage for Prosecutorial Decision Making in Plea Negotiations." *American Criminal Law Review* 13:435.

Langbein, John. 1977. *Comparative Criminal Procedures: Germany.* St. Paul: West Publishing Co.

Margolick, David. 1985. "The Legal Aid Society on the Defensive." *New York Times* (Aug. 4):E4.

Marquart, James W., and Ben M. Crouch. 1985. "Judicial Reform and Prisoner Control: The Impact of *Ruiz v. Estelle* on a Texas Penitentiary." *Law and Society Review* 19:557–86. (Reprinted in Cole 1988, 416–41.)

McDonald, William. 1985. *Plea Bargaining: Critical Issues and Common Practices.* Washington, D.C.: U.S. Government Printing Office.

Meador, Daniel J. 1983. "German Appellate Judges: Career Patterns and American-English Comparisons." *Judicature* 1(June–July):16–27.

Nardulli, Peter F. 1978. "Plea Bargaining: An Organizational Perspective." *Journal of Criminal Justice* 6(Fall):217–31.

National Advisory Commission on Criminal Justice Standards and Goals. 1973. *Task Force Report on Courts.* Washington, D.C.: U.S. Government Printing Office.

Sanborn, Joseph B., Jr. 1986. "A Historical Sketch of Plea Bargaining." *Justice Quarterly* 3(June):111–38.

Senna, Joseph J., and Larry J. Siegel. 1987. *Introduction to Criminal Justice.* 4th ed. St. Paul: West Publishing Co.

Solmonson, William R. 1990. *Fundamental Perspectives on International Law.* St. Paul: West Publishing Co.

United States Department of Justice. 1978. *The Nation's Toughest Drug Law: Evaluating the New York Experience.* Washington, D.C.: Bureau of the Census.

United States Statistical Abstract, 1992.

Zawitz, Marianne W. 1988. *Report to the Nation on Crime and Justice.* 2d ed. Washington, D.C.: U.S. Government Printing Office.

Court Cases

Bordenkircher v. *Hayes*, 434 U.S. 357, 98 S.Ct. 663, 54 L.Ed.2d 604 (1978)

Boykin v. *Alabama*, 395 U.S. 238, 89 S.Ct. 1709, 23 L.Ed.2d 274 (1969)

Brady v. *United States*, 397 U.S. 742, 90 S.Ct. 1463, 25 L.Ed.2d 747 (1970)

Breed v. *Jones*, 421 U.S. 519, 95 S.Ct. 1779, 44 L.Ed.2d 346 (1975)

Cooper v. *Pate*, 378 U.S. 546, 84 S.Ct. 1733, 12 L.Ed.2d 1030 (1964)

Douglas v. *California*, 372 U.S. 353, 83 S.Ct. 814, 9 L.Ed.2d 811 (1963)

Estelle v. *Gamble*, 429 U.S. 97, 97 S.Ct. 285, 50 L.Ed.2d 25 (1976)

Estelle v. *Ruiz*, 503 F.Supp. 1265 (S.D. Tex. 1980)

Evitts v. *Lucey*, 469 U.S. 387, 105 S.Ct. 830, 83 L.Ed.2d 821 (1985)

Gault, In re, 387 U.S. 1, 87 S.Ct. 1428, 18 L.Ed.2d 527 (1967)

Henderson v. *Morgan*, 426 U.S. 637, 96 S.Ct. 2253, 49 L.Ed.2d 108 (1976)

Hull, Ex parte, 312 U.S. 546, 61 S.Ct. 640, 85 L.Ed. 1034 (1941)

Johnson v. *Avery*, 393 U.S. 483, 89 S.Ct. 747, 21 L.Ed.2d 718 (1971)

Kent v. *United States*, 383 U.S. 541, 86 S.Ct. 1045, 16 L.Ed.2d 84 (1966)

Lawless v. *Ireland*, 31 International Law Reports 290 (1960)

McMann v. *Richardson*, 397 U.S. 759, 90 S.Ct. 1441, 25 L.Ed.2d 763 (1970)

Morrissey v. *Brewer*, 408 U.S. 471, 92 S.Ct. 2593, 33 L.Ed.2d 484 (1972)

Procunier v. *Martinez*, 416 U.S. 396, 94 S.Ct. 1800, 40 L.Ed.2d 224 (1974)

Rose v. *Lundy*, 455 U.S. 509, 102 S.Ct. 1198, 71 L.Ed.2d 379 (1982)

Santobello v. *New York*, 404 U.S. 257, 92 S.Ct. 495, 30 L.Ed.2d 427 (1971)

Saxbe v. *Washington Post Co.*, 417 U.S. 843, 94 S.Ct. 2811, 41 L.Ed.2d 514 (1974)

Strickland v. *Washington*, 466 U.S. 668, 104 S.Ct. 2052, 80 L.Ed.2d 674 (1984)

United States v. *Cronic*, 466 U.S. 648, 104 S.Ct. 2039, 80 L.Ed.2d 657 (1984)

Winship, In re, 397 U.S. 358, 90 S.Ct. 1068, 25 L.Ed.2d 368 (1970)

CHAPTER THIRTEEN

UNDERSTANDING ADMINISTRATIVE DUE PROCESS

> "[A]dministrative law includes the entire range of action by government with respect to the citizen and by the citizen with respect to the government, except for those matters dealt with by the criminal law, and those left to private litigation. . . ."
>
> —Federal District Court Judge Henry Friendly

The third grand division of legal procedures is generally referred to as administrative law. It is one of the least understood and most controversial areas of law. Nonetheless, it is also the most dynamic and expanding area of legal activity in our increasingly regulated society.

Although the field of administrative law is exceptionally broad, as indicated by Judge Friendly above, administrative legal actions are another form of due process of law. Administrative due process is the subject of this chapter. This overview of the basic areas of administrative legal procedure is not intended to explain thoroughly the vast field of administrative law; that would require a separate course. The objective of this chapter is to provide a description of the basic concepts of administrative due process.

Modern governments, including both the federal and state governments in the United States, exercise extensive regulatory authority. This authority includes "rule making" powers to determine the detailed rules and regulations that implement specific legislation. It also includes authority to investigate and impose penalties for noncompliance with administrative regulations. The rule-making, investigative, and adjudicative functions of administrative agencies are discussed in this chapter, as well as the oversight function of the courts and the power of judicial review.

Other countries, particularly those on the continent of Europe, have had more experience with the problems of modern bureaucracies that administer the welfare state. The procedures of some of these countries are discussed in this chapter, since they illustrate interesting institutional developments that address such problems. The office of *ombudsman*, for example, which originated in Sweden, provides assistance to individuals who must defend their interests and rights against powerful bureaucracies. In France and Germany, separate and independent administrative law courts provide the average person with access to the courts to address the problems of powerful bureaucracies.

STATE AND FEDERAL REGULATORY AGENCIES

Government has always been associated with regulatory activity and the development of common standards of behavior that promote the health, safety, and morals of the people. When our federal system was established, the states generally were thought to have this basic authority, and only limited powers of regulation were given to the national government. The increasingly interdependent nature of modern society has led to the recognition that national standards are required in many areas of activity.

Federal Regulation

The United States Constitution provides a limited role for the national government in the area of regulatory activity, but constitutional amendments and court interpretations have significantly altered this role. The vagueness of the Constitution leaves considerable room for interpretation regarding what powers are to be surrendered to the national government.

Regulation of money, patents and copyrights, weights and measures, Indian affairs, and foreign policy were clearly recognized in the earliest days of the republic as areas subject to federal regulation. Congress created administrative agencies to issue patents in 1790 and to manage Native American affairs in 1796; however, the primary growth in federal regulatory agencies has occurred since 1900.

The antitrust movement of the Progressive Era met with strong court opposition to the expansion of federal regulatory authority, which did not occur until the New Deal period in the late 1930s. Prior to the Supreme Court's dramatic reversal of its "dual federalist" interpretation of the commerce clause, regulation of the nation's economic and social affairs was left to the state and local governments.

We now have some forty-two federal regulatory agencies, the overwhelming majority of which were created during and after the decade of the 1930s when the Supreme Court began to broaden its view of the original constitutional grant of national authority to regulate commerce "among the several states. . . ." Thus, federal regulatory agencies are relatively new, but they have become extensive and important in many areas of business, economic, and social policy. The supremacy clause of the Constitution gives the national government power to preempt state authority, if that is the intent of Congress.

State Regulation

Many regulatory bodies exist at the state and local levels of government. State administrative agencies monitor environmental pollution; license drivers; determine automobile insurance rates; oversee public utilities; and regulate a wide range of professions and occupations including hairdressers, barbers, teachers, doctors, lawyers, and psychologists. Local administrative agencies operate zoning boards, housing authorities, water and sewer commissions, and historical commissions.

The extent of modern governmental regulatory activity is so pervasive that hardly any area of human endeavor is spared some form of regulatory restriction. The First Amendment areas of clearly protected fundamental rights—speech, press, organization, and religion—are the most obvious areas that are relatively free from governmental regulations. But even in these areas, when a "compelling state interest" has been demonstrated, the courts have allowed exceptions. Today, it is easier to construct a list of those areas that are not regulated than of those which are regulated. Both Congress and the states have responded to increasing demands that the government use its authority to regulate abusive business practices and to protect the health and safety of the people.

The corresponding increase in governmental bureaucracies at both the federal and state levels has resulted in the development of numerous departments of government. These departments represent the major divisions of governmental activity, but they are complex organizations that have been divided into specialized agencies. Relatively few of these agencies are regulatory in character.

The states have less clearly defined specialization of agencies within departments than does the federal government. A simple classification of federal agencies according to the mission of each agency, as defined by law, includes: (1) clientele agencies, (2) agencies for maintenance of the Union, (3) regulatory agencies, and (4) redistributive agencies (Lowi and Ginsberg 1992, 319–21). These types of agencies, other than regulatory agencies, are essentially service functions that do not have the authority to impose regulatory rules.

Regulatory Agencies

A **regulatory agency** is defined as an agency or commission that has been delegated relatively broad powers and is authorized by the legislative body to make detailed rules governing the conduct of individuals and business activity within broad legislative guidelines. Some regulatory agencies, such as the Environmental Protection Agency (EPA), have departmental status; most of these agencies, however, are bureaus within departments, such as the Food and Drug Administration (FDA) in the Department of Health and Human Services, the Occupational Safety and Health Administration (OSHA) in the Department of Labor, and the Agricultural Stabilization and Conservation Service (ASCS) in the Department of Agriculture.

regulatory agency: an agency or commission that has been delegated rule-making authority by the legislative body.

Other regulatory agencies are independent regulatory commissions that are somewhat isolated from presidential control. Examples of these independent commissions include the Interstate Commerce Commission (ICC), which dates back to 1883, and the Federal Trade Commission (FTC) created in 1914. As Lowi and Ginsberg explain, "whether departmental or independent, an agency is regulatory if Congress delegates relatively broad powers over a sector of the economy or a type of commercial activity and authorizes it to make rules governing the conduct of people and businesses within that jurisdiction" (Lowi and Ginsberg 1992, 337–38).

Rules made by regulatory agencies have the effect of legislation as long as they are made within the bounds of the authorizing, or enabling, act and meet constitutional standards. This delegation of governmental authority generally has been upheld by the courts and allows specific agencies to exercise quasi-legislative and quasi-judicial powers, in addition to their obvious executive function.

The Rule-making Function

Regulatory agencies came into existence because legislative bodies recognized that they could not achieve desired regulatory goals within the existing governmental structure. Although legislative bodies could provide general policy direction, they possessed limited subject matter expertise and could not devote attention to the multitude of problems that are involved in the development of detailed regulatory rules and their enforcement. Regulatory agencies placed within existing governmental departments or created expressly for this purpose can assemble the necessary factual data and expertise to draft detailed rules and work toward achieving the objectives stipulated in the legislation.

Enabling Acts

enabling acts: statutory authority defining the functions and powers of governmental agencies.

Regulatory agencies are created by legislative enactments referred to as **enabling acts**. These acts create agencies or authorize the chief executive to create agencies. The enabling act determines the agency's organizational structure, defines its functions and powers, and establishes basic operational standards and guidelines. These standards and guidelines help reviewing courts control the abuse of discretion. Courts also use the agency's own written directives (rules) to assess whether an agency is operating according to the legislature's intent.

Regulatory Functions

Governmental agencies perform a variety of functions. For example, they monitor businesses and professions in order to prevent the use of unfair methods of competition and the use of fraud and deceptive practices; they help ensure that manufacturers produce pure medications and that food products are safe to consume; and they function to protect society from environmental pollution and insider stock trading practices. The regulatory agencies are those units specifically authorized to draft the detailed rules necessary to carry out the will of the legislative act that grants them authority.

Rule making

rule making: the process of developing detailed rules or regulations having the force of law and issued by executive authority.

quasi-legislative powers: delegated rule-making authority.

The term **rule making** is often used to describe the **quasi-legislative powers** of regulatory agencies. Agencies that have been granted rule-making functions are authorized to make, alter, or repeal rules and regulations to the extent permitted by the terms of their enabling statutes. These statutes set the general standards, authorize the agencies to determine the content of the regulations, and provide general sanctions for noncompliance with administrative directives.

Federal Sources

The body of substantive federal administrative law can be found in the extensive volumes of the *Code of Federal Regulations* (CFR) described in Chapter Eight. These volumes of detailed rules now exceed the volumes of legislation found in the *United States Code* (USC). For example, four pages in USC explaining an act of Congress amending the Clean Air Act may eventually turn into over four hundred pages in CFR of rules and regulations that have the force of law for the regulated industry.

State Sources

The states' bodies of substantive administrative law are somewhat less well-defined than those of federal law. Many states publish separate administrative codes similar to the CFR. The entire body of substantive administrative law may be more difficult to find in states that do not publish such indexed codes, but administrative rules in these states can be found in separate administrative publications.

Administrative Procedures Acts

At the federal level, the **Administrative Procedures Act** of 1946 and its amendments provide detailed procedural rules for drafting and promulgating administrative regulations and define the rights of persons and corporations affected by these regulations. This legislation has become the major source of law governing the procedures of regulatory agencies and provides for judicial review of administrative determinations. The states have enacted legislation in recent years that closely resembles the federal requirements in the area of administrative procedure.

administrative procedures acts: laws enacted by federal and many state jurisdictions governing practices and procedures before administrative agencies.

The Investigative Function

Governmental administrative agencies cannot develop the necessary facts and knowledge to perform their regulatory functions without extensive investigative powers. Thus, as regulation has expanded and intensified, legislative and judicial authorities have conferred broad investigative powers to practically all administrative agencies.

Statutes usually grant an agency the power to use a variety of methods in carrying out its fact-finding functions. These methods include requirements of reports from regulated businesses, the conducting of inspections, and the use of judicially enforced subpoenas. Failure to comply with agency requests for information is usually dealt with swiftly by easily obtained court orders requiring compliance.

Investigative Power

The power to investigate is one of the functions that distinguishes the administrative law process from the traditional civil law process. The administrative law process is more like the criminal law process in that the investigative power gives governmental agencies a standing right to monitor and detect violations of rules.

In regard to administrative agencies, this power extends to the development of information necessary to create or alter existing rules. Modern administrative agencies have become specialized, and attempts have been made to employ the idea of "separation of powers" within particular departments or bureaus. Hence, some agencies have been created primarily to perform the fact-finding or investigative function.

Administrative agencies are limited by constitutionally protected rights. Corporations are vested with a certain element of public interest in that they are licensed by governmental authority, so the extent of the administrative agencies' authority to investigate them is considerably greater than that which is granted to agencies in their investigation of individuals. Warrants are usually required, particularly in detailed administrative investigations.

The Adjudicative Function

When a regulatory agency's actions involve enforcement of the rule-making function, the agency does not have to make use of the ordinary courts used in civil and criminal cases. The **quasi-judicial powers** of administrative agencies are extensive. The internal procedures that have been developed through statutory enactment and court interpretation to prevent abuse of authority involve the determination of legal rights, duties, and obligations, as well as fact-finding procedures involving adjudicatory hearings that resemble a court's decision-making process.

quasi-judicial powers: internal agency procedures involving fact-finding hearings that resemble court decision-making process.

Judicial Oversight

In cases involving the rule-making function and the imposition of regulatory fines, the affected individual or corporation must pursue all administrative remedies before seeking court action to overturn an administrative ruling. After the agency has made its final judgment in such disputed cases, the affected party must file an appeal at the appellate court level and successfully argue that the agency exceeded the limitations of its legislative authority, or that the legislative enabling act violates some constitutional provision. This appeal action to the regular courts which have appellate jurisdiction is referred to as judicial review. The term *judicial review* is used in the same sense here as in Chapter One—the power of the courts to hold acts of all governmental agencies unconstitutional and, therefore, unenforceable.

Thus, administrative regulatory agencies have internal functions that resemble the trial level courts in civil and criminal cases. Judicial review by appellate courts acts as a check on potential abuse, but the agency performs the fact-finding function. Even in cases in which the courts find administrative abuse, the issue is remanded back to the administrative agency with instructions for proper procedure.

Actions of governmental administrative agencies may involve the filing of both civil and criminal suits against alleged violators of the law. Such suits are subject to the same procedures previously described in the chapters on civil and criminal process. The administrative due process, however, which is the focus of this chapter, is distinctively different from civil and criminal due process.

due notification: to be informed of the action taken against an individual, corporation, or agency.

fair hearing: one in which authority is fairly exercised; consistent with fundamental principles of justice; to present evidence, cross-examine, and have findings supported by evidence.

Quasi-judicial Procedure

Before administrative sanctions can be imposed, an alleged violator is entitled to (1) **due notification** of the actions of the agency adversely affecting the legal interests of the individual or corporation, and (2) a **fair hearing** before an impartial and competent tribunal that affords the affected party the opportunity to be heard and allows confrontation of witnesses. These basic rules are explained in detail in the federal Administrative Procedures Act and various state administrative procedures acts. Such procedural rules are supplemented by the enabling acts that create the administrative agencies involved. The type of procedure required varies from agency to agency.

Fundamental Due Process

The United States Supreme Court has held that the fundamental constitutional guarantee of due process of law applies to both state and federal actions. The principles of due process require at least rudimentary procedural fairness. Even the actions of local school boards in suspending students for disciplinary infractions of school rules require some degree of procedural fairness, as the case of *Goss v. Lopez*, 419 U.S. 565, 95 S.Ct. 729, 42 L.Ed.2d 725 (1975) illustrates.

Goss v. Lopez

419 U.S. 565
U.S. Supreme Court
January 22, 1975
Justice White

This appeal by various administrators of the Columbus, Ohio, Public School System (CPSS) challenges the judgment of a three-judge federal court, declaring that appellees—various high school students in the CPSS—were denied due process of law contrary to the command of the Fourteenth Amendment in that they were temporarily suspended from their high schools without a hearing either prior to suspension or within a reasonable time thereafter, and enjoining the administrators to remove all references to such suspensions from the students' records.

Ohio law, Rev. Code Ann. §3313.64 (1972), provides for free education to all children between the ages of 6 and 21. Section §3313.66 of the Code empowers the principal of an Ohio public school to suspend a pupil for misconduct for up to 10 days or to expel him. In either case, he must notify the student's parents within 24 hours and state the reasons for his action. A pupil who is expelled, or his parents, may appeal the decision to the Board of Education and in connection therewith shall be permitted to be heard at the board meeting. The Board may reinstate the pupil following the hearing. No similar procedure is provided in §3313.66 or any other provision of state law for a suspended student. Aside from a regulation tracking the statute, at the time of the imposition of the suspensions in this case the CPSS itself had not issued any written procedure applicable to suspensions. Nor, so far as the record reflects, had any of the individual high schools involved in this case. Each, however, had formally or informally described the conduct for which suspension could be imposed.

The nine named appellees, each of whom alleged that he or she had been suspended from public high school in Columbus for up to 10 days without a hearing pursuant to Section 3316.66, filed an action under 42 U.S.C. § 1983 against the Columbus Board of Education and various administrators of the CPSS. The complaint sought a declaration that Section 3313.66 was unconstitutional in that it permitted public school administrators to deprive plaintiffs of their rights to an education without a hearing of any kind, in violation of the procedural due process component of the Fourteenth Amendment. It also sought to enjoin the public school officials from issuing future suspensions pursuant to Section 3313.66 and to require them to remove references to the past suspensions from the records of the students in question.

The proof below established that the suspensions arose out of a period of widespread student unrest in the CPSS during February and March 1971.... Two named plaintiffs, Dwight Lopez and Betty Crome, were students at the Central High School and McGuffey Junior High School, respectively. The former was suspended in connection with a disturbance in the lunchroom which involved some physical damage to school property. Lopez testified that at least 75 other students were suspended from his school on the same day. He also testified below that he was not a party to the destructive conduct but was instead an innocent bystander. Because no one from the school testified with regard to this incident, there is no evidence in the record indicating the official basis for concluding otherwise. Lopez never had a hearing.

Betty Crome was present at a demonstration at a high school other than the one she was attending. There she was arrested together with others, taken to the police station, and released without being formally charged. Before she went to school on the following day, she was notified that she had been suspended for a 10-day period. Because no one from the school testified with respect to this incident, the record does not disclose how the McGuffey Junior High School principal went about making the decision to suspend Crome, nor does it disclose on what information the decision was based. It is clear from the record that no hearing was ever held....

At the outset, appellants contend that because there is no constitutional right to an education at public expense, the Due Process Clause does not protect against expulsions from the public school system. This position misconceives the nature of the issue and is refuted by prior decisions. The Fourteenth Amendment forbids the State to deprive any person of life, liberty, or property without due process of law. Protected interests in property are normally "not created by the Constitution. Rather, they are created and their dimensions are defined" by an independent source such as state statutes or rules entitling the citizen to certain benefits....

Although Ohio may not be constitutionally obligated to establish and maintain a public school system, it has nevertheless done so and has required its children to attend. Those young people do not "shed their constitutional rights" at the schoolhouse door.... "The Fourteenth Amendment, as now applied to the States, protects the citizen against the State itself and all of its creatures—Boards of Education not excepted." The authority possessed by the State to prescribe and enforce standards of conduct in its schools, although concededly very broad, must be exercised consistently with constitutional safeguards. Among other things, the State is constrained to recognize a student's legitimate entitlement to a public education as a property interest which is protected by the Due Process Clause and which may not be taken away for misconduct without adherence to the minimum procedures required by that clause.

The Due Process Clause also forbids arbitrary deprivations of liberty. "Where a person's good name, reputation, honor, or integrity is at stake because of what the government is doing to him," the minimal requirements of the Clause must be satisfied. School authorities here suspended appellees from school for periods of up to 10 days based on charges of misconduct. If sustained and recorded, those charges could seriously damage the students' standing with their fellow pupils and their teachers as well as interfere with later opportunities for higher education and employment. It is apparent that the claimed right of the State to determine unilaterally and without due process whether that misconduct has occurred immediately collides with the requirements of the Constitution....

A short suspension is, of course, a far milder deprivation than expulsion. But "education is perhaps the most important function of state and local governments,"... and the total exclusion from the educational process for more than a trivial period, and certainly if the suspension is for 10 days, is a serious event in the life of the suspended child. Neither the property interest in educational benefits temporarily denied nor the liberty interest in reputation, which is also implicated, is so insubstantial that suspensions may constitutionally be imposed by any procedure the school chooses, no matter how arbitrary....

At the very minimum, therefore, students facing suspension and the consequent interference with a protected property interest must be given *some* kind of notice and afforded *some* kind of hearing. "Parties whose rights are to be affected are entitled to be heard; and in order that they may enjoy that right, they must first be notified."...

The prospect of imposing elaborate hearing requirements in every suspension case is viewed with great concern, and many school authorities may well prefer the untrammeled power to act unilaterally, unhampered by rules about notice and hearing. But it would be a strange disciplinary system in an educational institution if no communication was sought by the disciplinarian with the student in an effort to inform him of his dereliction and to let him tell his side of the story in order to make sure that an injustice is not done. "Fairness can rarely be obtained by secret, one-sided determination of facts decisive of rights...." "Secrecy is not congenial to truth-seeking and self-righteousness gives too slender an assurance of rightness. No better instrument has been devised for arriving at truth than to give a person in jeopardy of serious loss notice of the case against him and opportunity to meet it."...

Students facing temporary suspension have interests qualifying for protection of the Due Process Clause, and due process requires, in connection with a suspension of 10 days or less, that the student be given oral or written notice of the charges against him and, if he denies them, an explanation of the evidence the authorities have and an opportunity to present his side of the story. The Clause requires at least these rudimentary precautions against unfair or mistaken findings of misconduct and arbitrary exclusion from school....

We stop short of construing the Due Process Clause to require, countrywide, that hearings in connection with short suspensions must afford the student the opportunity to secure counsel, to confront and cross-examine witnesses supporting the charge, or to call his own witnesses to verify his version of the incident. Brief disciplinary suspensions are almost countless. To impose in each such case even truncated trial-type procedures might well overwhelm administrative facilities in many places and, by diverting resources, cost more than it would save in educational effectiveness. Moreover, further formalizing the suspension process and escalating its formality and adversary nature may not only make it too costly as a regular disciplinary tool but also destroy its effectiveness as part of the teaching process.

On the other hand, requiring effective notice and informal hearing permitting the student to give his version of the events will provide a meaningful hedge against erroneous action. At least the disciplinarian will be alerted to the existence of disputes about facts and arguments about cause and effect. He may then determine himself to summon the accuser, permit cross-examination, and allow the student to present his own witnesses. In more difficult cases, he may permit counsel. In any event, his discretion will be more informed and we think the risk of error substantially reduced. . . .

We should also make it clear that we have addressed ourselves solely to the short suspension, not exceeding 10 days. Longer suspensions or expulsions for the remainder of the school term, or permanently, may require more formal procedures. Nor do we put aside the possibility that in unusual situations, although involving only a short suspension, something more than the rudimentary procedures will be required.

The District Court found each of the suspensions involved here to have occurred without a hearing, either before or after the suspension, and that each suspension was therefore invalid and the statute unconstitutional insofar as it permits such suspensions without notice or hearing. Accordingly, the judgment is
Affirmed.

Justice Powell, with whom the Chief Justice, Justice Blackmun, and Justice Rehnquist join, dissenting.

The Court today invalidates an Ohio statute that permits student suspensions from school without a hearing "for not more than ten days." . . .

The Court's decision rests on the premise that, under Ohio law, education is a property interest protected by the Fourteenth Amendment's Due Process Clause and therefore that any suspension requires notice and a hearing. In my view, a student's interest in education is not infringed by a suspension within the limited period prescribed by Ohio law. Moreover, to the extent that there may be some arguable infringement, it is too speculative, transitory, and insubstantial to justify imposition of a *constitutional* rule. . . .

The Court thus disregards the basic structure of Ohio law in posturing this case as if Ohio had conferred an unqualified right to education, thereby compelling the school authorities to conform to due process procedures in imposing the most routine discipline. . . .

The Ohio suspension statute allows no serious or significant infringement of education. It authorizes only a maximum suspension of eight school days, less than 5% of the normal 180-day school year. Absences of such limited duration will rarely affect a pupil's opportunity to learn or his scholastic performance. Indeed, the record in this case reflects no educational injury to appellees. Each completed the semester in which the suspension occurred and performed at least as well as he or she had in previous years. Despite the Court's unsupported speculation that a suspended student could be "seriously damaged," there is no factual showing of any such damage to appellees. . . .

Today's opinion . . . holds in effect that government infringement of any interest to which a person is entitled, no matter what the interest or how inconsequential the infringement, requires *constitutional* protection. As it is difficult to think of any less consequential infringement than suspension of a junior high school student for a single day, it is equally difficult to perceive any principled limit to the new reach of procedural due process.

The majority opinion in this case illustrates the minimal requirements of **administrative due process**; however, the extent of procedural rights that must be complied with by governmental agencies is by no means uniform. These rights, beyond the minimal requirements, depend on the specific provisions of the statutory enabling act and the agency's own procedural rules. Various boards or commissions may conduct the required fair hearings, but many agencies now require that administrative law judges conduct these hearings.

administrative due process: notice, fair hearing, and conformity with established rules are minimal requirements of due process.

Administrative Law Judges

The **administrative law judge** (ALJ) is an official who conducts hearings for a regulatory agency and makes recommendations to the heads of the agency on issuance of administrative orders. These individuals were called "hearing examiners" before the 1978 amendments to the Administrative Procedures Act, which renamed them administrative law judges and strengthened their independence. Federal administrative law judges are appointed under civil service rules and are protected against arbitrary dismissal and loss of salary. There are approximately twelve hundred of these judges who serve in thirty federal departments and agencies.

administrative law judge: one who presides at an administrative hearing with power to make agency determinations of fact; federal ALJs were formerly called "hearing examiners."

The OSHA Procedure Illustrated

A typical example of the quasi-judicial fact-finding process involving administrative fines imposed by the Occupational Safety and Health Administration (OSHA) is the use of administrative law judges who conduct hearings in disputed cases.

An employee who suspects that there are safety violations in the workplace can contact the local OSHA office and file a complaint. The OSHA agency is authorized to make an unannounced inspection of the premises and has broad powers to investigate alleged violations of agency standards. If the inspection reveals violations, the government inspector may issue either civil or criminal citations.

For civil citations, OSHA may impose fines of up to seventy thousand dollars for each willful and repeated violation and seven thousand dollars for less serious violations. These limits are subject to change by legislative enactment to provide reasonable inducement to enforce the agency's policies.

An employer against whom a fine is levied may contest the citation by filing an appeal with the OSHA agency within a limited period of time. The employer is then given a hearing at a specified date before an administrative law judge. The judge allows both the inspector and the employer to present evidence regarding the factual nature of the findings alleged by the agency. If the agency citation is found to be in error, the judge may dismiss or alter the citation in much the same way that local courts of limited jurisdiction handle traffic citations. However, administrative fines and actions frequently are much more costly to the industry involved than traffic fines.

The judge's decision is not the final decision of the agency, and even if the judge finds against the employer, the adversely affected party has another opportunity to appeal to the three-member Occupational Health Review Commission. This commission is appointed by the president and has final administrative authority to overrule the judge's decision. If no member of the commission is willing to place the matter on the commission's agenda, the administrative law judge's decision becomes the final action of the agency after thirty days.

Administrative agencies are authorized to issue criminal citations in certain cases, although they do so infrequently. When a criminal citation is warranted, the case is handed over to the Justice Department for criminal prosecution.

Judicial Review

In the area of enforcement of administrative rules and regulations, where governmental agencies have the authority to impose civil penalties and fines and withhold licenses, the courts have regarded these agencies as collaborators in the task of safeguarding the public interest. Unless exceptional circumstances exist, therefore, the courts are reluctant to interfere with the operation of a program administered by a governmental agency. This policy of judicial self-restraint usually results in the court's deference to the governmental agency in the performance of its constitutionally recognized functions.

Ripeness for Court Action

Parties against whom administrative actions are taken must first seek administrative remedies for their complaints. They must **exhaust administrative remedies** before the courts consider the issue "ripe" for judicial intervention. There are exceptions to this rule, but the complaining party must meet the heavy burden of providing proof that the court's failure to interrupt the administrative process would be unfair. To determine this standard of fairness, the court considers: (1) the possibility of injury if the case is not heard, (2) the degree of doubt of the agency's jurisdiction, and (3) the requirement of the agency's specialized knowledge (Grilliot and Schubert 1992, 490).

exhaust administrative remedies: courts must be satisfied that an individual seeking court action has first pursued all available administrative remedies.

Deference to Agency Expertise

Reviewing courts often acknowledge that the fact situations and agency standards are complex and technical, and the courts rely on the agency's expertise. The courts uphold the administrative findings if they are satisfied that the agency examined the issues, reached its decision within appropriate standards, and followed the required procedures. Since the court action is essentially a review function, the complaint before the court must be filed at the appeals court level. As in other appellate jurisdiction cases, the court hears only questions of law in dispute. Questions of fact are left to the agency's procedures and are given the same deference given to jury decisions when all applicable due process procedures are followed. Even when the court rules against the agency on legal issues, the matter is usually remanded to the administrative agency for further fact finding.

The regulatory authority of the federal government appears to be extensive, but the states share this authority. The state powers may be even more pervasive in their impact on individuals. In areas in which the federal government has not precluded state regulation, the state courts are the final authority.

OTHER SPECIALIZED COURTS

State and federal governments have created many specialized courts with limited jurisdiction to handle various types of cases. Among those at the federal level are the United States Tax Court, and the United States Court of Claims. These **specialized federal courts** were created by Congress under the authority granted in article I of the Constitution for the express purpose of helping to administer specific congressional statutes. They often possess administrative and quasi-legislative as well as judicial duties.

State legislatures have created many similar quasi-judicial bodies, often called **commissions**. State public service commissions and workers' compensation commissions (or boards) are some of the more prominent administrative bodies that perform many court functions. These bodies are administrative in character and are not properly said to have the inherent powers of a court, but nontheless, they perform significant judicial functions. Increasingly, states have attempted to relieve the overloaded civil courts and reduce costs by the institution of such quasi-judicial administrative agencies.

In direct contrast to the rather vague and disorganized system of administrative law procedures found in the United States, several European countries have separate, well-defined administrative court systems. According to Henry J. Abraham, the explanation for this major distinction goes back to the ancient Anglo-Saxon principle that "the king can do no wrong." (Abraham 1986, 273). This principle forms a fundamental rule of law known as **sovereign immunity**. The basic principle of sovereign immunity in Anglo-American law is that the state cannot be sued without its express consent.

Because of sovereign immunity, the practice of initiating civil liability suits against the individual government official in regular court jurisdiction, and not against the state or federal government, has become the normal practice of redressing civil wrongs in Anglo-American law. This system has important implications for the overloaded court dockets in the United States and the extensive number of civil suits filed against public officials.

Many law enforcement officers are weighted down with heavy burdens of civil cases filed against them personally for alleged civil wrongs. Corrections officials, school administrators, teachers, and other civil servants question why, in performing a governmental duty, a civil servant should be personally responsible for civil liability. Modern governments in the United Kingdom and the United States require many of these public officials to be bonded (insured) against such liability suits, and state agencies assist in their defense. But the time, inconvenience, and expense of such a system is a major problem that demoralizes many civil servants.

Both Britain and the United States have enacted modern statutes to allow civil suits (claims) against the government itself. These laws make the government responsible for the actions of their servants under certain circumstances. Most of these statutes have loopholes and exceptions and generally exclude law enforcement agencies such as the police, military services, and foreign affairs.

United States Claims Court

In the United States, the Tort Claims Act of 1946 allows injured parties or aggrieved employees of the federal government to bring suit in federal district court or the United States claims court. The claims court is located in Washington, D.C., and may hear a broad range of contractual and tort claims.

---

specialized federal courts: courts created by Congress under authority granted in article I, as opposed to article III, of the Constitution. They often possess administrative and quasi-legislative as well as judicial duties.

commissions: term often used in regard to state quasi-judicial bodies, also called "boards."

sovereign immunity: doctrine precludes litigant from asserting an otherwise meritorious cause of action against a sovereign or a party with sovereign attributes unless the sovereign consents to suit.

United States Tax Court

The United States Tax Court has jurisdiction over those matters where the federal government has given its consent in advance to be sued. The Tax Court was transformed into a legislative court in 1969. This court still has some characteristics of a quasi-administrative agency, but it is independent of the Internal Revenue Service in many respects and, thus, is the closest relative of the independent continental European administrative courts. Its jurisdiction includes disputes over tax assessments made by the Internal Revenue Service (IRS). The Commissioner of the IRS is always the defendant party and a "repeat player" with certain advantages. The Tax Court may conduct trials anywhere in the United States, and its case load is quite large, reaching over 42,000 cases in 1985.

Thus, some movement has been made toward the creation of truly independent courts that allow individuals to sue the government per se. The United States Supreme Court also has made significant case law decisions that have liberalized access to the courts.

In *Butz v. Economou*, 438 U.S. 478, 98 S.Ct. 2894, 57 L.Ed.2d 895 (1978), the Court permitted suits against federal officials who were or should have been aware that they were violating constitutional rights except when it has been demonstrated that absolute immunity is essential for conducting the public business. In subsequent Court decisions, local governments have been made subject to damage suits for civil rights violations (*Monell v. New York City Department of Social Services*, 436 U.S. 658, 98 S.Ct. 2018, 56 L.Ed.2d 611 [1978]); municipalities have not been allowed to assert the good faith of their officials as a defense (*Owen v. City of Independence Missouri*, 445 U.S. 622, 100 S.Ct. 1398, 63 L.Ed.2d 673 [1980]); and private parties have been held entitled to sue their own states whenever state policy allegedly violates any federal law (*Maine v. Thiboutot*, 448 U.S. 1, 100 S.Ct. 2502, 65 L.Ed.2d 555 [1980]).

In spite of these significant decisions, the principle of sovereign immunity still leaves many areas of governmental responsibility immune from ordinary liability that would have allowed recovery of damages if the acts had been done by private parties. (Abraham 1986, 277).

ADMINISTRATIVE PROCEDURE IN OTHER COUNTRIES

The modern industrial societies of western Europe have been engaged in extensive governmental regulation for a longer period of time than has the United States. Consequently, criticism of bureaucratic power with its potential for abuse has been instrumental in developing institutional responses to such problems.

The Scandinavian Ombudsman

ombudsman: an official or semiofficial office to which people may come with grievances connected with government; stands between, and represents, the citizen before the government.

In the Scandinavian countries, an institution known as the **ombudsman** originated in Sweden in the nineteenth century. It started in the legislative body as a means of controlling the observance of laws by judges, civil servants, and military officers. In recent times, it has become an investigative and oversight agency that processes complaints about bureaucratic agencies and assists individuals and groups to resolve disputes with governmental agencies.

Originally the office of the *ombudsman* was not empowered to make any direct corrections or adjustments of improprieties, but rather to investigate and report complaints of improprieties to a special committee of the parliamentary body in Sweden. This function, which began as early as 1809, was extended to a separate office of Military Ombudsman in 1915 that was designed to investigate military affairs exclusively. In 1968, the separate military office was merged with the Parliamentary Ombudsman.

The role of *ombudsman* in Sweden today has been extended to include the Parliamentary Ombudsman, Antitrust Ombudsman, Consumer Ombudsman, Press Ombudsman, and Equal Opportunities Ombudsman. These offices provide extensive coverage of many bureaucratic functions and solutions to problems resulting from abuse of authority.

The Parliamentary Ombudsman's office has responsibility for oversight functions related to all state and municipal agencies and bodies, as well as their personnel, exclusive of Cabinet Ministers or members of the Parliament or of municipal councils.

The Antitrust Ombudsman was created in 1954 and is appointed by the government. This office is responsible for overseeing the application of the Restrictive Trade Practices Act (Swedish antitrust law) for the purpose of promoting economic competition in the public interest. This purpose essentially is accomplished through negotiations to eliminate harmful effects of restraints on competition. Failure of resolution through negotiation with the other party may invite the *ombudsman* to bring the case to the Market Court, which is a special tribunal comprising two jurists and representatives of the business community and consumers.

The Consumer Ombudsman was created in 1971. This official is appointed to supervise laws for the protection of consumers relative to perceived improper commercial marketing practices.

The Press Ombudsman was established in 1969 and is appointed by a special committee comprised of the principal Parliamentary Ombudsman and the chairs for both the Swedish Bar Association and the Swedish Press Council. This office is responsible for investigating complaints of alleged violations of press ethics and reporting substantiated violations to the Swedish Press Council or directly censuring the newspaper involved.

The Equal Opportunities Ombudsman was established in 1980 and provides for the adoption of active measures promoting equality. This office has the responsibility of persuading employers voluntarily to follow the law by participating in efforts to promote equality at work. It has ultimate responsibility for pleading the cause in the Labor Court for those employees who allege employment discrimination.

Denmark and Norway have adopted *ombudsman* arrangements similar to those used in Sweden. Other European countries have established limited adaptations of the *ombudsman* offices.

French and German Administrative Courts

The separate French and German **administrative courts** have a long tradition dating back to the nineteenth century. These courts provide separate, independent court hierarchies designed to provide easy access for individuals to address their grievances in a specialized court system.

French Administrative Courts

The French administrative courts are linked more to the executive branch of government than the regular judiciary, but this court system operates a truly in-

administrative courts: in Germany, France, and some other countries, separate and independent administrative courts provide simplified access to courts for adjudication of disputes with governmental agencies.

dependent court structure. It is more simply organized than the regular court structure and features two basic hierarchical levels—the Regional Councils or Administrative Tribunals, and the multipurpose Council of State that serves as the ultimate appeals court. There also are a number of special collateral administrative tribunals, but the system is known for its simplicity and unusually rapid and efficient adjudicatory process.

This court system has the jurisdiction to hear and investigate complaints concerning abuse of governmental authority, to annul an illegal decision or agency action, and to award payment for damages.

Injured parties, or plaintiffs, may file a complaint against a governmental official or agency by filling out an official complaint form. Private legal counsel need not be retained in order to file a complaint. The court usually conducts the investigation itself, saving the plaintiff the cost of legal action. Sometimes an oral hearing is held, at which time litigants may present arguments either personally or through legal counsel. The administrative courts may nullify administrative actions as well as award damages to the plaintiff.

The powers of the French administrative courts are similar to those of judicial review in American courts, but the system lacks the authority to declare a law unconstitutional. A French constitutional court of preview may rule on the constitutionality of acts before they are promulgated.

Henry Abraham concludes that the French system provides a more complete review of administrative action than do the systems in Britain and the United States. He asserts that "the cost of litigation is smaller, accessibility to the courts is greater, review is more easily available, scope of review is larger, state liability for damages is less circumscribed, and settlement is far more prompt and efficient" (Abraham 1986, 281).

The French government considers itself totally liable for service-connected faults of public officers and state agencies, including damage caused by personal fault of public officials. In such cases, the government promptly pays for damages to the injured party, and the officer at fault becomes personally liable to the state.

German Administrative Courts

The modern federal structure of Germany, created after World War II, witnessed a revival of the concept of a highly independent administrative court system to oversee the potential abuses of bureaucratic power and to protect citizens against unauthorized use of governmental authority.

The German and French Models

The most important differences between the French and German administrative court systems relate to the degree of specialization of the German courts and the federal character of the German system, as opposed to the unitary character of the French system. The modern German governmental structure was created in the years after World War II (1945–1953) when conditions were most conducive to the incorporation of the best ideas of modern governmental experience. In particular, with regard to the organizational structure of the court system, the framers of the German constitution sought assurance that the future German state would adhere to the rule of law.

Unique Features of the German Court System

The German court system (see Figure 13-1) is unique in that it is both decentralized and unified at the same time. The system contains five separate and distinct court hierarchies, divided by subject matter jurisdiction. Each hierarchy has lower courts and judges administered by the state governments.

Each state has a ministry of justice and is responsible for the administration of the lower trial courts and intermediate appellate courts in that district. The federal government has responsibility for the administration of the highest appeals courts in all five subject matter court hierarchies.

As Daniel J. Meador explains, "Although Germany is a federal structure, unlike the United States it has no dual, parallel set of state and federal courts; at any given level in the judiciary, whether trial or appellate, there is only one court" (Meador 1983, 17–18).

Ordinary Courts

The ordinary court jurisdiction in Germany handles all civil and criminal cases (as described in Chapters Seven and Twelve). The German government accepts the concept of modern French law that all governmental agencies can be sued for service-connected faults of public officials and state agencies. Local, state, and national governments can be held responsible for civil liabilities (such as negligence and breach of contract). These matters are handled by the ordinary courts as a part of private law. The ordinary courts also handle matters dealing with "fair compensation" for payment of property taken by the government for public use.

Separate Administrative Courts

The German administrative court jurisdiction includes all alleged abuses of administrative authority in its rule-making and rule application functions. This highly independent court structure rules on disputes arising out of the acts of administrative agencies. These matters include all acts of agencies, including the specialized courts, in matters of finance and taxation as well as the issues arising out of decisions in the area of social services. Hence, the administrative courts have a basic oversight function, and for this reason, the judges at all levels of the administrative court hierarchy are appointed for life terms and cannot be removed.

Administrative Court Jurisdiction

The administrative court jurisdiction in Germany does not include constitutional questions. These questions are handled by the independent Federal Constitutional Court, which has been given the authority to rule on questions concerning the constitutional structure and disputes arising from the provisions of the constitution. The administrative courts, on the other hand, rule on issues of abuse of authority through administrative acts. An administrative act is defined as any disposition, order, decree, decision, or other authoritative action that an administrative agency has taken in the area of administrative practice.

Special Expert Panels of Judges

The German system combines the beneficial coordinating functions of the French administrative law court system with a decentralized federal administra-

FIGURE 13.1 The German Court System

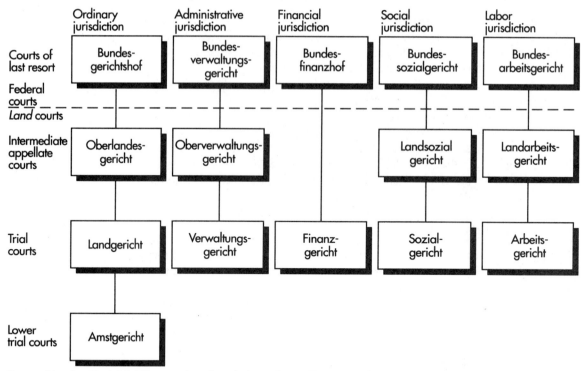

Source: Meador, Daniel J. "German Appellate Judges: Career Patterns and American-English Comparison." *Judicature*, Vol. 67, 1983.

tion and allows for extensive specialization of court expertise. Even within the hierarchy of the specialized courts, there is opportunity for further development of court expertise in complicated areas of technical administration by the use of specialized panels that hear particular types of cases on a regular basis.

The judges are required to have the same basic qualifications in all of these specialized courts. The training of lawyers, judges, and prosecutors is extensive, and all judges must meet the same minimal requirements. Judges with special backgrounds are used in the specialized court areas; for example, all financial court judges are required to have backgrounds in accounting. The independence of the administrative court hierarchy is especially emphasized, and judges cannot be transferred against their will.

The separate French and German administrative courts indicate the logical extension of many of the developments that have occurred in the United States in recent years. Our federal Tax Court has made some of these changes by creating an independent set of courts to oversee bureaucratic power and monitor for potential abuse.

CHAPTER SUMMARY

1. Administrative law is the most dynamic and expanding area of law today. It includes both state and federal regulatory authority, the rules of which have the force of law. Administrative agencies exercise legislative, quasi-judicial, and executive functions.

2. Federal regulatory agencies have become extensive and important in many areas of business, economic, and social policy since the decade of the 1930s, but state regulatory activity also has expanded in modern times. State and federal authorities now regulate almost all areas of human activity.

3. Regulatory agencies have broad powers to make detailed rules and regulations governing the conduct of individuals and business activity. These agencies are given rule-making and enforcement powers by legislative enabling acts that are upheld by the courts as long as they do not violate constitutional limitations.

4. The powers of administrative agencies are defined as quasi-legislative and quasi-judicial functions. The decisions of these agencies have the force of law. The detailed administrative rules and regulations are found in the *Code of Federal Regulations* and similar publications by state agencies.

5. The Federal Administrative Procedures Act of 1946 and similar state statutory authority provide detailed procedures and rights of persons and corporations affected by administrative regulations. Agencies have broad investigative powers that enable them to perform their governmental functions.

6. Regulatory agencies may take enforcement actions without using the ordinary courts regularly used for civil and criminal cases. They may impose civil fines and penalties, which can be appealed through the agency's own internal procedures for a fair hearing and review of lower agency decisions.

7. A party affected by administrative actions has a right to due notification, to a fair hearing, and to an opportunity to challenge the decision in appeals court after all administrative remedies have been exhausted. These are the minimal requirements of administrative due process.

8. Administrative law judges, who conduct fair hearings, have been strengthened in their independence from agency influence at the federal level, but generally their decisions can be overruled by the highest administrative authority in the agency.

9. Judicial review of agency decisions usually must be filed at the appeals court level. The basic criteria for overruling an administrative decision is an agency's failure to provide the required constitutional administrative due process. Agency rules may not exceed legislative authority, and the underlying legislative authority may be challenged. Fact-finding procedures usually are left to the administrative agency.

10. Specialized courts have been established at the federal level, but internal agency fact-finding procedures are used extensively to deal with administrative disputes. Continental European countries have developed separate, well-defined administrative court systems to deal with these matters.

11. The Anglo-American concept of sovereign immunity makes it difficult to hold governmental agencies responsible for their actions. Governments in the United States and the United Kingdom have passed legislation making it possible to sue the government for claims in ordinary civil liability, but the process often is cumbersome and costly to the injured party.

12. The Scandinavian *ombudsman* offices have become investigative oversight agencies that process complaints about bureaucratic agencies and assist individuals to resolve disputes with governmental agencies. Other countries have adopted similar *ombudsman* arrangements or have established limited adaptations of the *ombudsman* offices.

13. Modern French and German court systems illustrate fully developed court structures that provide parties with access to the courts to address grievances concerning abuse of administrative powers. These administrative courts are efficient, provide access to the courts as fact-finding agents, and effectively extend the rule of law to the administrative process.

KEY TERMS

regulatory agency
enabling acts
rule making
quasi-legislative powers
administrative procedures acts
quasi-judicial powers

due notification
fair hearing
administrative due process
administrative law judge
exhaust administrative remedies

specialized federal courts
commissions
sovereign immunity
ombudsman
administrative courts

DISCUSSION QUESTIONS

1. What is administrative law, and how important is this area of the law in modern society?

2. How extensive is federal and state regulatory activity in the United States today?

3. What are the basic investigative, rule-making, and enforcement powers given to regulatory agencies by the enabling acts of legislative authority?

4. Where can the detailed rules and regulations of administrative agencies that have the force of law be found?

5. What is meant by fundamental due process of law, and how have modern state and federal administrative procedures acts attempted to codify and extend procedural rules?

6. What basic procedural rights are involved in the minimal requirements of administrative due process?

7. What is involved in the process of administrative hearings and judicial review by the courts?

8. How have the criticisms of sovereign immunity and the lack of independent administrative courts resulted in changes in the United States?

9. Would extension of the Scandinavian *ombudsman* system in the United States strengthen the citizen's ability to prevent administrative abuse of authority?

10. Should the United States consider adoption of some version of the administrative law courts of continental European countries?

SOURCES AND SUGGESTED READING

Abraham, Henry J. 1986. *The Judicial Process*. 5th ed. New York: Oxford University Press.

Grilliot, Harold J., and Frank A. Schubert. 1992. *Introduction to Law and the Legal System*. 5th ed. Boston: Houghton Mifflin Co.

Lowi, Theodore J., and Benjamin Ginsberg. 1992. *American Government: Freedom and Power*. 2d ed. New York: W.W. Norton & Co.

Meador, Daniel J. 1983. "German Appellate Judges: Career Patterns and American-English Comparisons." *Judicature* 67.

_____. 1981. "Appellate Subject Matter Organization: The German Design from an American Perspective." *International and Comparative Law Review* 27.

Neubauer, David W. 1991. *Judicial Process: Law, Courts and Politics in the United States*. Pacific Grove, Calif.: Brooks/Cole Publishing Co.

Wilson, James Q. 1989. *Bureaucracy: What Government Agents Do and Why They Do It*. New York: Basic Books.

COURT CASES

Arndt v. Department of Licensing, 147 Mich. App. 97, 383 N.W.2d 136 (1986)

Butz v. Economou, 438 U.S. 478, 98 S.Ct. 2894, 57 L.Ed.2d 895 (1978)

Dow Chemical Co. v. United States, 476 U.S. 227 (1986)

Goss v. Lopez, 419 U.S. 565, 106 S.Ct. 1819, 90 L.Ed.2d 226 (1975)

Maine v. Thiboutot, 448 U.S. 1, 100 S.Ct. 2502, 65 L.Ed.2d 555 (1980)

Monell v. Department of Social Services of New York City, 436 U.S. 658, 98 S.Ct. 2018, 56 L.Ed.2d 611 (1978)

Owen v. City of Independence, Missouri, 445 U.S. 622, 100 S.Ct. 1398, 63 L.Ed.2d 673 (1980)

CONCLUSION

Equal justice under the law has not been fully realized in the United States, or in any society. It remains, however, the essential goal to which we aspire and represents the most fundamental spirit of the law. Since the Norman kings sent judges of the *Curia Regis* out to do justice and equity in the 12th Century, this goal has remained alive in Anglo-American jurisprudence. The quest to perfect the rule of law has led to elaborate procedural due process guarantees that have been described in this introduction to American law.

Some would contend that our system has placed greater emphasis upon control of governmental abuse than control of individual abuses against others in society. Our society is increasingly becoming aware of these criticisms. Many victims of crime argue that they are also victims of the criminal justice system. The enormous problem of securing public safety and the increasing degree of violence in our society is evident. What is not so clear is whether or not the government alone can effectively deal with this crisis. Many assert that this crisis is the result of a moral decay in society and must be dealt with by more emphasis on moral education.

This introduction to American law has attempted to acknowledge the important criticisms of our system in its civil, criminal, and administrative legal processes. Our legal system is cumbersome and perhaps excessively detailed. It may place too much emphasis on adversarial relationships and is confused by the federal structure which creates fifty-one legal systems in our society. The criminal justice system, even within particular jurisdictions, often lacks coordination. Tort litigation in our society is too costly and does not always adequately compensate the appropriate individuals for their personal losses. All aspects of society share in providing much needed solutions to these problems.

The intended purpose of this introduction to American law and the legal system has not been primarily directed toward problem identification or problem solutions regarding the legal system. Rather the focus of this text has been to provide an understanding of the basic terms and concepts used in modern Anglo-American jurisprudence. It is hoped that this introduction has served to assist the reader in achieving a clearer understanding of the language and procedures of law in the United States.

Law is too important to society to be left to professionals alone. Every citizen needs to become more informed about the law; and law-related education needs to be promoted throughout the educational system. Understanding how to find the law and the ability to read it with some degree of competence is essential to effective citizen participation. We cannot participate as informed citizens in the process of changing our laws if we cannot find them and first understand the standards we intend to change.

It is hoped that the reader will be better prepared for more advanced courses in law-related subjects after completing this text. The fundamental principles of the law have been explained and illustrated. However, as the library assignment should have made clear, there are many aspects of the law that have to be omitted from this introduction.

The comparative law features of this textbook have been offered to provide contrast with the characteristic features of American law so that the reader may begin to see alternatives that may have promise in exploring solutions to our particular problems. Americans generally are not exposed to the legal characteristics of other countries, perhaps because we think of our legal system as a superior system that protects our basic democratic rights and preserves a free society. This is true, at least in part; but we are also increasingly realizing that our system has many inherent defects that affect our safety and happiness.

The law is not just a set of rules that restrict our liberties. It is a dynamic and ever-changing process that requires the development of standards for dispute settlement that will preserve and protect our most cherished values of life, liberty, and pursuit of happiness.

APPENDIX A

THE CONSTITUTION OF THE UNITED STATES OF AMERICA

We the People of the United States, in Order to form a more perfect Union, establish Justice, insure domestic Tranquility, provide for the common defence, promote the general Welfare, and secure the Blessings of Liberty to ourselves and our Posterity, do ordain and establish this CONSTITUTION for the United States of America.

ARTICLE I

Section 1. All legislative Powers herein granted shall be vested in a Congress of the United States, which shall consist of a Senate and House of Representatives.

Section 2. [1] The House of Representatives shall be composed of Members chosen every second Year by the People of the several States, and the Electors in each State shall have the Qualifications requisite for Electors of the most numerous Branch of the State Legislature.

[2] No person shall be a Representative who shall not have attained to the Age of twenty-five Years, and been seven Years a Citizen of the United States, and who shall not, when elected, be an Inhabitant of that State in which he shall be chosen.

[3] Representatives and direct Taxes shall be apportioned among the several States which may be included within this Union, according to their respective Numbers, which shall be determined by adding to the whole Number of free Persons, including those bound to Service for a Term of Years, and excluding Indians not taxed, three fifths of all other Persons. The actual Enumeration shall be made within three Years after the first Meeting of the Congress of the United States, and within every subsequent Term of ten Years, in such Manner as they shall by Law direct. The Number of Representatives shall not exceed one for every thirty Thousand, but each State shall have at Least one Representative; and until such enumeration shall be made, the State of New Hampshire shall be entitled to chuse three, Massachusetts eight, Rhode-Island and Providence Plantations one, Connecticut five, New York six, New Jersey four, Pennsylvania eight, Delaware one, Maryland six, Virginia ten, North Carolina five, South Carolina five, and Georgia three.

[4] When vacancies happen in the Representation from any State, the Executive Authority thereof shall issue Writs of Election to fill such Vacancies.

[5] The House of Representatives shall chuse their Speaker and other Officers; and shall have the sole Power of Impeachment.

Section 3. [1] The Senate of the United States shall be composed of two Senators from each State, chosen by the Legislature thereof, for six Years; and each Senator shall have one Vote.

[2] Immediately after they shall be assembled in Consequence of the first Election, they shall be divided as equally as may be into three Classes. The Seats of the Senators of the first Class shall be vacated at the Expiration of the Second Year, of the second Class at the Expiration of the fourth Year, and of the third Class at the Expiration of the sixth Year, so that one-third may be chosen every second Year; and if Vacancies happen by Resignation, or otherwise, during the Recess of the Legislature of any State, the Executive thereof may make temporary Appointments until the next Meeting of the Legislature, which shall then fill such Vacancies.

[3] No person shall be a Senator who shall not have attained to the Age of thirty Years, and been nine Years a Citizen of the United States, and who shall not, when elected, be an Inhabitant of that State for which he shall be chosen.

[4] The Vice President of the United States shall be President of the Senate, but shall have no Vote, unless they be equally divided.

[5] The Senate shall chuse their Officers, and also a President pro tempore, in the absence of the Vice President, or when he shall exercise the Office of President of the United States.

[6] The Senate shall have the sole Power to try all Impeachments. When sitting for that Purpose, they shall be on Oath or Affirmation. When the President of the United States is tried, the Chief Justice shall preside: And no Person shall be convicted without the Concurrence of two-thirds of the Members present.

[7] Judgment in Cases of Impeachment shall not extend further than to removal from Office, and disqualification to hold and enjoy any Office of honor, Trust, or Profit under the United States: but the Party convicted shall nevertheless be liable and subject to Indictment, Trial, Judgment, and Punishment, according to Law.

Section 4. [1] The Times, Places and Manner of holding Elections for Senators and Representatives, shall be prescribed in each State by the Legislature thereof; but the Congress may at any time by Law make or alter such Regulations, except as to the Places of chusing Senators.

[2] The Congress shall assemble at least once in every Year, and such Meeting shall be on the first Monday in December, unless they shall by Law appoint a different Day.

Section 5. [1] Each House shall be the Judge of the Elections, Returns, and Qualifications of its own Members, and a Majority of each shall constitute a Quorum to do Business; but a smaller Number may adjourn from day to day, and may be authorized to compel the Attendance of absent Members, in such Manner, and under such Penalties as each House may provide.

[2] Each House may determine the Rules of its Proceedings, punish its Members for disorderly Behavior, and with the Concurrence of two thirds, expel a Member.

[3] Each House shall keep a Journal of its Proceedings, and from time to time publish the same, excepting such Parts as may in their Judgment require Secrecy; and the Yeas and Nays of the Members of either House on any question shall, at the Desire of one fifth of those Present, be entered on the Journal.

[4] Neither House, during the Session of Congress, shall, without the Consent of the other, adjourn for more than three days, nor to any other Place than that in which the Two Houses shall be sitting.

Section 6. [1] The Senators and Representatives shall receive a Compensation for their Services, to be ascertained by Law, and paid out of the Treasury of the United States. They shall in all Cases, except Treason, Felony and Breach of the Peace, be privileged from Arrest during their Attendance at the Session of their respective Houses, and in going to and returning from the same; and for any Speech or Debate in either House, they shall not be questioned in any other Place.

[2] No Senator or Representative shall, during the Time for which he was elected, be appointed to any civil Office under the Authority of the United States, which shall have been created, or the Emoluments whereof shall have been encreased during such time; and no Person holding any Office under the United States, shall be a Member of either House during his Continuance in Office.

Section 7. [1] All Bills for raising Revenue shall originate in the House of Representatives; but the Senate may propose or concur with Amendments as on other Bills.

[2] Every Bill shall have passed the House of Representatives and the Senate, shall, before it become a Law, be presented to the President of the United States; if he approve he shall sign it, but if not he shall return it, with his Objections to that House in which it shall have originated, who shall enter the Objections at large on their Journal, and proceed to reconsider it. If after such Reconsideration two thirds of that House shall agree to pass the Bill, it shall be sent, together with the Objections, to the other House, by which it shall likewise be reconsidered, and if approved by two thirds of that House, it shall become a Law. But in all such Cases, the Votes of both Houses shall be determined by Yeas and Nays, and the Names of the Persons voting for and against the Bill shall be entered on the Journal of each House respectively. If any Bill shall not be returned by the President within ten Days (Sundays excepted) after it shall have been presented to him, the Same shall be a Law, in like Manner as if he had signed it, unless the Congress by their Adjournment prevent its Return, in which Case it shall not be a Law.

[3] Every Order, Resolution, or Vote to which the Concurrence of the Senate and House of Representatives may be necessary (except on a question of Adjournment) shall be presented to the President of the United States; and before the Same shall take Effect, shall be approved by him, or being disapproved by him shall be repassed by two thirds of the Senate and House of Representatives, according to the Rules and Limitations prescribed in the Case of a Bill.

Section 8. The Congress shall have Power

[1] To lay and collect Taxes, Duties, Imposts and Excises, to pay the Debts and provide for the common Defence and general Welfare of the United States; but all Duties, Imposts and Excises shall be uniform throughout the United States;

[2] To borrow money on the credit of the United States;

[3] To regulate Commerce with foreign Nations, and among the several States, and with the Indian Tribes;

[4] To establish an uniform Rule of Naturalization, and uniform Laws on the subject of Bankruptcies throughout the United States;

[5] To coin Money, regulate the Value thereof, and of foreign Coin, and fix the Standard of Weights and Measures;

[6] To provide for the Punishment of counterfeiting the Securities and current Coin of the United States;

[7] To Establish Post Offices and post Roads;

[8] To promote the Progress of Science and useful Arts, by securing for limited Times to Authors and Inventors the exclusive Right to their respective Writings and Discoveries;

[9] To constitute Tribunals inferior to the Supreme Court;

[10] To define and punish Piracies and Felonies committed on the high Seas, and Offenses against the Law of Nations;

[11] To declare War, grant Letters of Marque and Reprisal, and make Rules concerning Captures on Land and Water;

[12] To raise and support Armies, but no Appropriation of Money to that Use shall be for a longer Term than two Years;

[13] To provide and maintain a Navy;

[14] To make Rules for the Government and Regulation of the land and naval Forces;

[15] To provide for calling forth the Militia to execute the Laws of the Union, suppress Insurrections and repel Invasions;

[16] To provide for organizing, arming, and disciplining the Militia, and for governing such Part of them as may be employed in the Service of the United States, reserving to the States respectively, the Appointment of the Officers, and the Authority of training the Militia according to the discipline prescribed by Congress;

[17] To exercise exclusive Legislation in all Cases whatsoever, over such District (not exceeding ten Miles square) as may, by Cession of particular States, and the acceptance of Congress, become the Seat of the Government of the United States, and to exercise like Authority over all Places purchased by the Consent of the Legislature of the State in which the Same shall be, for the Erection of Forts, Magazines, Arsenals, dock-Yards, and other needful Buildings;—And

[18] To make all Laws which shall be necessary and proper for carrying into Execution the foregoing Powers, and all other Powers vested by this Constitution in the Government of the United States, or in any Department or Officer thereof.

Section 9. [1] The Migration or Importation of Such Persons as any of the States now existing shall think proper to admit, shall not be prohibited by the Congress prior to the Year one thousand eight hundred and eight, but a tax or duty may be imposed on such Importation, not exceeding ten dollars for each Person.

[2] The privilege of the Writ of Habeas Corpus shall not be suspended, unless when in Cases of Rebellion or Invasion the public Safety may require it.

[3] No Bill of Attainder or ex post facto Law shall be passed.

[4] No capitation, or other direct, Tax shall be laid, unless in Proportion to the Census or Enumeration herein before directed to be taken.

[5] No Tax or Duty shall be laid on Articles exported from any State.

[6] No preference shall be given by any Regulation of Commerce or Revenue to the Ports of one State over those of another; nor shall Vessels bound to, or from, one State be obliged to enter, clear, or pay Duties in another.

[7] No money shall be drawn from the Treasury, but in Consequence of Appropriations made by Law; and a regular Statement and Account of the Receipts and Expenditures of all public Money shall be published from time to time.

[8] No Title of Nobility shall be granted by the United States: And no Person holding any Office of Profit or Trust under them, shall, without the Consent of the Congress, accept of any present, Emolument, Office, or Title, of any kind whatever, from any King, Prince, or foreign State.

Section 10. [1] No State shall enter into any Treaty, Alliance, or Confederation; grant Letters of Marque and Reprisal; coin Money; emit Bills of Credit; make any Thing but gold and silver Coin a Tender in Payment of Debts; pass any bill of Attainder, ex post factor Law, or Law impairing the Obligation of Contracts, or grant any Title of Nobility.

[2] No State shall, without the Consent of the Congress, lay any Imposts or Duties on Imports or Exports, except what may be absolutely necessary for executing its inspection Laws: and the net Produce of all Duties and Imposts, laid by any State on Imports or Exports, shall be for the Use of the Treasury of the United States; and all such Laws shall be subject to the Revision and Control of the Congress.

[3] No State shall, without the Consent of Congress, lay any duty of Tonnage, keep Troops, or Ships of War in time of Peace, enter into any Agreement or Compact with another State, or with a foreign Power, or engage in War, unless actually invaded, or in such imminent Danger as will not admit of delay.

ARTICLE II

Section 1. [1] The executive Power shall be vested in a President of the United States of America. He shall hold his Office during the Term of four Years, and together with the Vice President, chosen for the same Term, be elected, as follows:

[2] Each State shall appoint, in such Manner as the Legislature thereof may direct, a Number of Electors, equal to the whole Number of Senators and Representatives to which the State may be entitled in the Congress: but no Senator or Representative, or Person holding an Office of Trust or Profit under the United States, shall be appointed an Elector.

[3] The Electors shall meet in their respective States, and vote by Ballot for two persons, of whom one at least shall not be an Inhabitant of the same State with themselves. And they shall make a List of all the Persons voted for, and of the Number of Votes for each; which List they shall sign and certify, and transmit sealed to the Seat of the Government of the United States, directed to the President of the Senate. The President of the Senate shall, in the Presence of the Senate and House of Representatives, open all the Certificates, and the Votes shall then be counted. The Person having the greatest Number of Votes shall be the President, if such Number be a Majority of the whole Number of Electors appointed; and if there by more than one who have such Majority, and have an equal Number of Votes, then the House of Representatives shall immediately chuse by Ballot one of them for President; and if no Person have a Majority, then from the five highest on the List the said House shall in like Manner chuse the President. But in chusing the President, the Votes shall be taken by States, the Representation from each State having one Vote; A quorum for this Purpose shall consist of a Member or Members from two-thirds of the States, and a Majority of all the States shall be necessary to a Choice. In every Case, after the Choice of the President, the Person having the greatest Number of Votes of the Electors shall be the Vice President. But if there should remain two or more who have equal Votes, the Senate shall chuse from them by Ballot the Vice President.

[4] The Congress may determine the Time of chusing the Electors, and the Day on which they shall give their Votes; which Day shall be the same throughout the United States.

[5] No person except a natural born Citizen, or a Citizen of the United States, at the time of the Adoption of this Constitution, shall be eligible to the Office of President; neither shall any Person be eligible to that Office who shall not have attained to the Age of thirty-five Years, and been fourteen Years a Resident within the United States.

[6] In case of the removal of the President from Office, or of his Death, Resignation, or Inability to discharge the Powers and Duties of the said Office, the same shall devolve on the Vice President, and the Congress may by Law provide for the Case of Removal, Death, Resignation or Inability, both of the President and Vice President, declaring what Officer shall then act as President, and such Officer shall act accordingly, until the Disability be removed, or a President shall be elected.

[7] The President shall, at stated Times, receive for his Services, a Compensation, which shall neither be encreased nor diminished during the Period for which he shall have been elected, and he shall not receive within that Period any other Emolument from the United States, or any of them.

[8] Before he enter on the Execution of his Office, he shall take the following Oath or Affirmation:—"I do solemnly swear (or affirm) that I will faithfully execute the Office of President of the United States, and will to the best of my Ability, preserve, protect and defend the Constitution of the United States."

Section 2. [1] The President shall be Commander in Chief of the Army and Navy of the United States, and of the Militia of the several States, when called into the actual Service of the United States; he may require the Opinion, in writing, of the principal Officer in each of the executive Departments, upon any subject relating to the Duties of their respective Offices, and he shall have Power to grant Reprieves and Pardons for Offenses against the United States, except in Cases of Impeachment.

[2] He shall have Power, by and with the Advice and Consent of the Senate, to make Treaties, provided two-thirds of the Senators present concur; and he shall nominate, and by and with the Advice and Consent of the Senate, shall appoint Ambassadors, other public Ministers and Consuls, Judges of the Supreme Court, and all other Officers of the United States, whose Appointments are not herein otherwise provided for, and shall be established by Law; but the Congress may by Law vest the Appointment of such inferior Officers, as they think proper, in the President alone, in the Courts of Law, or in the Heads of Departments.

[3] The President shall have Power to fill up all Vacancies that may happen during the Recess of the Senate, by granting Commissions which shall expire at the End of their next Session.

Section 3. He shall from time to time give to the Congress Information of the State of the Union, and recommend to their Consideration such Measures as he shall judge necessary and expedient; he may, on extraordinary Occasions, convene both Houses, or either of them, and in Case of Disagreement between them, with Respect to the Time of Adjournment, he may adjourn them to such Time as he shall think proper; he shall receive Ambassadors and other public Ministers; he shall take Care that the Laws be faithfully executed, and shall Commission all the Officers of the United States.

Section 4. The President, Vice President and all civil Officers of the United States, shall be removed from Office on Impeachment for, and Conviction of, Treason, Bribery, or other high Crimes and Misdemeanors.

ARTICLE III

Section 1. The judicial Power of the United States, shall be vested in one supreme Court, and in such inferior Courts as the Congress may from time to time ordain and establish. The Judges, both of the supreme and inferior Courts, shall hold their Offices during good Behaviour, and shall, at stated Times, receive for their Services a Compensation which shall not be diminished during their Continuance in Office.

Section 2. [1] The judicial Power shall extend to all Cases, in Law and Equity, arising under this Constitution, the Laws of the United States, and Treaties made, or which shall be made under their Authority;—to all Cases affecting Ambassadors, other public Ministers and Consuls;—to all Cases of admiralty and maritime Jurisdiction;—to Controversies to which the United States shall be a Party;—to Controversies between two or more States;—between a State and Citizens of another State;—between a State and Citizens of different States;—between Citizens of the same State claiming Lands under Grants of different States, and between a State, or the Citizens thereof, and foreign States, Citizens or Subjects.

[2] In all Cases affecting Ambassadors, other public Ministers and Consuls, and those in which a State shall be Party, the supreme Court shall have original Jurisdiction. In all the other Cases before mentioned, the supreme Court shall have appellate Jurisdiction, both as to Law and Fact, with such Exceptions, and under such Regulations as the Congress shall make.

[3] The trial of all Crimes, except in Cases of Impeachment, shall be by Jury; and such Trial shall be held in the State where the same Crimes shall have been committed; but when not committed within any State, the Trial ;shall be at such Place or Places as the Congress may by Law have directed.

Section 3. [1] Treason against the United States, shall consist only in levying War against them, or, in adhering to their Enemies, giving them Aid and Comfort. No Person shall be convicted of Treason unless on the Testimony of two Witnesses to the same overt Act, or on Confession in open Court.

[2] The Congress shall have power to declare the Punishment of Treason, but no Attainder of Treason shall work Corruption of Blood, or Forfeiture except during the Life of the Person attainted.

ARTICLE IV

Section 1. Full Faith and Credit shall be given in each State to the public Acts, Records, and judicial Proceedings of every other State. And the Congress may by general Laws prescribe the Manner in which such Acts, Records and Proceedings shall be proved, and the Effect thereof.

Section 2. [1] The Citizens of each State shall be entitled to all Privileges and Immunities of Citizens in the several States.

[2] A Person charged in any State with Treason, Felony, or other Crime, who shall flee from Justice, and be found in another State, shall on demand of the executive Authority of the State from which he fled, be delivered up, to be removed to the State having Jurisdiction of the Crime.

[3] No Person held to Service or Labour in one State, under the Laws thereof, escaping into another, shall, in Consequence of any Law or Regulation therein, be discharged from such Service or Labour, but shall be delivered up on Claim of the Party to whom such Service or Labour may be due.

Section 3. [1] New States may be admitted by the Congress into this Union; but no new State shall be formed or erected within the Jurisdiction of any other State; nor any State be formed by the Junction of two or more States, or parts of States, without the Consent of the Legislatures of the States concerned as well as of the Congress.

[2] The Congress shall have Power to dispose of and make all needful Rules and Regulations respecting the Territory or other Property belonging to the United States; and nothing in this Constitution shall be so construed as to Prejudice any Claims of the United States, or of any particular State.

Section 4. The United States shall guarantee to every State in this Union a Republican Form of Government, and shall protect each of them against Invasion; and on Application of the Legislature, or of the Executive (when the Legislature cannot be convened) against domestic Violence.

ARTICLE V

The Congress, whenever two-thirds of both Houses shall deem it necessary, shall propose Amendments to this Constitution, or, on the Application of the Legislatures of two-thirds of the several States, shall call a Convention for proposing Amendments, which, in either Case, shall be valid to all Intents and Purposes, as part of this Constitution, when ratified by the Legislatures of three-fourths of the several States, or by Conventions in three-fourths thereof, as the one or the other Mode of Ratification may be proposed by the Congress; Provided that no Amendment which may be made prior to the Year One thousand eight hundred and eight shall in any Manner affect the first and fourth Clauses in the Ninth

Section of the first Article; and that no State, without its Consent, shall be deprived of its equal Suffrage in the Senate.

ARTICLE VI

[1] All Debts contracted and Engagements entered into, before the Adoption of this Constituion shall be valid against the United States under this Constitution, as under the Confederation.

[2] This Constitution, and the Laws of the United States which shall be made in Pursuance thereof; and all Treaties made, or which shall be made, under the Authority of the United States, shall be the supreme Law of the Land; and the Judges in every State shall be bound thereby, any Thing in the Constitution or Laws of any State to the Contrary notwithstanding.

[3] The Senators and Representatives before mentioned, and the Members of the several State Legislatures, and all executive and judicial Officers, both of the United States and of the several States, shall be bound by Oath or Affirmation, to support this Constitution; but no religious Test shall ever be required as a Qualification to any Office or public Trust under the United States.

ARTICLE VII

The Ratification of the Conventions of nine States shall be sufficient for the Establishment of this Constitution between the States so ratifying the Same.

Articles in addition to, and amendment of, the constitution of the United States of America, proposed by Congress, and ratified by the legislatures of the several states, pursuant to the fifth article of the original constitution

AMENDMENT I [1791]

Congress shall make no law respecting an establishment of religion, or prohibiting the free exercise thereof; or abridging the freedom of speech, or of the press; or the right of the people peaceably to assemble and to petition the Government for a redress of grievances.

AMENDMENT II [1791]

A well regulated Militia, being necessary to the security of a free State, the right of the people to keep and bear Arms, shall not be infringed.

AMENDMENT III [1791]

No Soldier shall, in time of peace be quartered in any house, without the consent of the Owner, nor in time of war, but in a manner to be prescribed by Law.

AMENDMENT IV [1791]

The right of the people to be secure in their persons, houses, papers, and effects, against unreasonable searches and seizures, shall not be violated, and no Warrants shall issue, but upon probable cause, supported by Oath or affirmation, and particularly describing the place to be searched, and the persons or things to be seized.

AMENDMENT V [1791]

No person shall be held to answer for a capital, or otherwise infamous crime, unless on a presentment or indictment of a Grand Jury, except in cases arising in the land or naval forces, or in the Militia, when in actual service in time of War or public danger; nor shall any person be subject for the same offence to be twice put in jeopardy of life or limb; nor shall be compelled in any criminal case to be a witness against himself, nor be deprived of life, liberty, or property, without due process of law; nor shall private property be taken for public use, without just compensation.

AMENDMENT VI [1791]

In all criminal prosecutions, the accused shall enjoy the right to a speedy and public trial, by an impartial jury of the State and district wherein the crime shall have been committed, which district shall have been previously ascertained by law, and to be informed of the nature and cause of the accusation; to be confronted with the witnesses against him; to have compulsory process for obtaining witnesses in his favor, and to have the Assistance of Counsel for his defence.

AMENDMENT VII [1791]

In suits at common law, where the value in controversy shall exceed twenty dollars, the right of trial by jury shall be preserved, and no fact tried by jury, shall be otherwise reexamined in any Court of the United States, than according to the rules of the common law.

AMENDMENT VIII [1791]

Excessive bail shall not be required, nor excessive fines imposed, nor cruel and unusual punishments inflicted.

AMENDMENT IX [1791]

The enumeration in the Constitution, of certain rights, shall not be construed to deny or disparage others retained by the people.

AMENDMENT X [1791]

The powers not delegated to the United States by the Constitution, nor prohibited by it to the States, are reserved to the States respectively, or to the people.

AMENDMENT XI [1798]

The Judicial power of the United States shall not be construed to extend to any suit in law or equity, commenced or prosecuted against one of the United States by Citizens of another State, or by Citizens or Subjects of any Foreign State.

AMENDMENT XII [1804]

The electors shall meet in their respective states and vote by ballot for President and Vice-President, one of whom, at least, shall not be an inhabitant of the same state with themselves; they shall name in their ballots the person voted for as President, and in distinct ballots the person voted for as Vice-President, and they shall make distinct lists of all persons voted for as President, and of all persons voted for as Vice-President, and of the number of votes for each, which lists they shall sign and certify, and transmit sealed to the seat of the government of the United States, directed to the President of the Senate;—The President of the Senate shall, in presence of the Senate and House of Representatives, open all the certificates and the votes shall then be counted;—The person having the greatest number of votes for President, shall be the President, if such number be a majority of the whole number of Electors appointed; and if no person have such majority, then from the persons having the highest numbers not exceeding three on the list of those voted for as President, the House of Representatives shall choose immediately, by ballot, the President. But in choosing the President, the votes shall be taken by states, the representation from each state having one vote; a quorum for this purpose shall consist of a member or members from two-thirds of the states, and a majority of all the states shall be necessary to a choice. And if the House of Representatives shall not choose a President whenever the right of choice shall devolve upon them, before the fourth day of March next following, then the Vice-President shall act as President, as in the case of the death or other constitutional disability of the President.—The person having the greatest number of votes as Vice-President, shall be the Vice-President, if such number be a majority of the whole number of Electors appointed, and if no person have a majority, then from the two highest numbers on the list, the Senate shall choose the Vice-President; a quorum for the purpose shall consist of two-thirds of the whole number of Senators, and a majority of the whole number shall be necessary to a choice. But no person constitutionally ineligible to the office of President shall be eligible to that of Vice-President of the United States.

AMENDMENT XIII [1865]

Section 1. Neither slavery nor involuntary servitude, except as a punishment for crime whereof the party shall have been duly convicted, shall exist within the United States, or any place subject to their jurisdiction.

Section 2. Congress shall have power to enforce this article by appropriate legislation.

AMENDMENT XIV [1868]

Section 1. All persons born or naturalized in the United States, and subject to the jurisdiction thereof, are citizens of the United States and of the State wherein they reside. No State shall make or enforce any law which shall abridge the privileges or immunities of citizens of the United States; nor shall any State deprive any person of life, liberty, or property, without due process of law; nor deny to any person within its jurisdiction the equal protection of the laws.

Section 2. Representatives shall be apportioned among the several States according to their respective numbers, counting the whole number of persons in each State, excluding Indians not taxed. But when the right to vote at any election for the choice of electors for President and Vice-President of the United States, Representatives in Congress, the Executive and Judicial officers of a State, or the members of the Legislature thereof, is denied to any of the male inhabitants of such State, being twenty-one years of age, and citizens of the United States, or in any way abridged, except for participation in rebellion, or other crime, the basis of representation therein shall be reduced in the proportion which the number of such male citizens shall bear to the whole number of male citizens twenty-one years of age in such State.

Section 3. No person shall be a Senator or Representative in Congress, or elector of President and Vice-President, or hold any office, civil or military, under the United States, or under any State, who, having previously taken an oath, as a member of Congress, or as an officer of the United States, or as a member of any State legislature, or as an executive or judicial officer of any State, to support the Constitution of the United States, shall have engaged in insurrection or rebellion against the same, or given aid or comfort to the enemies thereof. But Congress may by a vote of two-thirds of each House, remove such disability.

Section 4. The validity of the public debt of the United States, authorized by law, including debts incurred for payment of pensions and bounties for services in suppressing insurrection or rebellion, shall not be questioned. But neither the United States nor any State shall assume or pay any debt or obligation incurred in aid of insurrection or rebellion against the United States, or any claim for the loss or emancipation of any slave; but all such debts, obligations and claims shall be held illegal and void.

Section 5. The Congress shall have power to enforce, by appropriate legislation, the provisions of this article.

AMENDMENT XV [1870]

Section 1. The right of citizens of the United States to vote shall not be denied or abridged by the United States or by any State on account of race, color, or previous condition of servitude.

Section 2. The Congress shall have power to enforce this article by appropriate legislation.

AMENDMENT XVI [1913]

The Congress shall have power to lay and collect taxes on incomes, from whatever source derived, without apportionment among the several States, and without regard to any census or enumeration.

AMENDMENT XVII [1913]

The Senate of the United States shall be composed of two Senators from each State, elected by the people thereof, for six years; and each Senator shall have one vote. The electors in each State shall have the qualifications requisite for electors of the most numerous branch of the State legislatures.

When vacancies happen in the representation of any State in the Senate, the executive authority of such State shall issue writs of election to fill such vacancies: *Provided*, That the legislature of any State may empower the executive thereof to make temporary appointments until the people fill the vacancies by election as the legislature may direct.

This amendment shall not be so construed as to affect the election or term of any Senator chosen before it becomes valid as part of the Constitution.

AMENDMENT XVIII [1919]

Section 1. After one year from the ratification of this article the manufacture, sale, or transportation of intoxicating liquors within, the importation thereof into, or the exportation thereof from the United States and all territory subject to the jurisdiction thereof for beverage purposes is hereby prohibited.

Section 2. The Congress and the several States shall have concurrent power to enforce this article by appropriate legislation.

Section 3. This article shall be inoperative unless it shall have been ratified as an amendment to the Constitution by the legislatures of the several States, as provided in the Constitution, within seven years from the date of submission hereof to the States by the Congress.

AMENDMENT XIX [1920]

The right of citizens of the United States to vote shall not be denied or abridged by the United States or by any State on account of sex.

Congress shall have the power to enforce this article by appropriate legislation.

AMENDMENT XX [1933]

Section 1. The terms of the President and Vice President shall end at noon on the 20th day of January, and the terms of Senators and Representatives at noon on the 3d day of January, of the years in which such terms would have ended if this article had not been ratified; and the terms of their successors shall then begin.

Section 2. The Congress shall assemble at least once in every year, and such meeting shall begin at noon on the 3d day of January, unless they shall by law appoint a different day.

Section 3. If, at the time fixed for the beginning of the term of the President, the President elect shall have died, the Vice President elect shall become President. If a President shall not have been chosen before the time fixed for the beginning of his term, or if the President elect shall have failed to qualify, then the Vice President elect shall act as President until a President shall have qualified; and the Congress may by law provide for the case wherein neither a President elect nor a Vice President elect shall have qualified, declaring who shall then act as President, or the manner in which one who is to act shall be selected, and such person shall act accordingly until a President or Vice President shall have qualified.

Section 4. The Congress may by law provide for the case of the death of any of the persons from whom the House of Representative may choose a President whenever the right of choice shall have devolved upon them, and for the case of the death of any of the persons from whom the Senate may choose a Vice President whenever the right of choice shall have devolved upon them.

Section 5. Sections 1 and 2 shall take effect on the 15th day of October following the ratification of this article.

Section 6. This article shall be inoperative unless it shall have been ratified as an amendment to the Constitution by the legislatures of three-fourths of the several States within seven years from the date of its submission.

AMENDMENT XXI [1933]

Section 1. The eighteenth article of amendment to the Constitution of the United States is hereby repealed.

Section 2. The transportation or importation into any State, Territory, or possession of the United States for delivery or use therein of intoxicating liquors, in violation of the laws thereof, is hereby prohibited.

Section 3. This article shall be inoperative unless it shall have been ratified as an amendment to the Constitution by conventions in the several States, as provided in the Constitution, within seven years from the date of the submission hereof to the States by the Congress.

AMENDMENT XXII [1951]

Section 1. No person shall be elected to the office of the President more than twice, and no person who has held the office of President, or acted as President, for more than two years of a term to which some other person was elected President shall be elected to the office of the President more than once. But this Article shall not apply to any person holding the office of President when this Article was proposed by the Congress, and shall not prevent any person who may be holding the office of President, or acting as President, during the term within which the Article becomes operative from holding the office of President or acting as President during the remainder of such term.

Section 2. This article shall be inoperative unless it shall have been ratified as an amendment to the Constitution by the legislatures of three-fourths of the several States within seven years from the date of its submission to the States by the Congress.

AMENDMENT XXIII [1961]

Section 1. The District constituting the seat of Government of the United States shall appoint in such manner as the Congress may direct:

A number of electors of President and Vice President equal to the whole number of Senators and Representatives in Congress to which the District would be entitled if it were a State, but in no event more than the least populous State; they shall be in addition to those appointed by the States, but they shall be considered, for the purposes of the election of President and Vice President, to be electors appointed by a State; and they shall meet in the District and perform such duties as provided by the twelfth article of amendment.

Section 2. The Congress shall have power to enforce this article by appropriate legislation.

AMENDMENT XXIV [1964]

Section 1. The right of citizens of the United States to vote in any primary or other election for President or Vice President, for electors for President or Vice President, or for Senator or Representative in Congress, shall not be denied or abridged by the United States or any State by reason of failure to pay any poll tax or other tax.

Section 2. The Congress shall have power to enforce this article by appropriate legislation.

AMENDMENT XXV [1967]

Section 1. In case of the removal of the President from office or his death or resignation, the Vice President shall become President.

Section 2. Whenever there is a vacancy in the office of the Vice President, the President shall nominate a Vice President who shall take the Office upon confirmation by a majority vote of both houses of Congress.

Section 3. Whenever the President transmits to the President pro tempore of the Senate and the Speaker of the House of Representatives his written declaration that he is unable to discharge the powers and duties of his office, and until he transmits to them a written declaration to the contrary, such powers and duties shall be discharged by the Vice President as Acting President.

Section 4. Whenever the Vice President and a majority of either the principal officers of the executive departments, or of such other body as Congress may by law provide, transmit to the President pro tempore of the Senate and the Speaker of the House of Representatives their written declaration that the President is unable to discharge the powers and duties of his office, the Vice President shall immediately assume the powers and duties of the office as Acting President.

Thereafter, when the President transmits to the President pro tempore of the Senate and the Speaker of the House of Representatives his written declaration that no inability exists, he shall resume the powers and duties of his office unless the Vice President and a majority of either the principal officers of the executive department, or of such other body as Congress may by law provide, transmit within four days to the President pro tempore of the Senate and the Speaker of the House of Representatives their written declaration that the President is unable to discharge the powers and duties of his office. Thereupon Congress shall decide the issue, assembling within 48 hours for that purpose if not in session. If the Congress, within 21 days after receipt of the latter written declaration, or, if Congress is not in session, within 21 days after Congress is required to assemble, determines by two-thirds vote of both houses that the President is unable to discharge the powers and duties of his office, the Vice President shall continue to discharge the same as Acting President; otherwise, the President shall resume the powers and duties of his office.

AMENDMENT XXVI [1971]

Section 1. The right of citizens of the United States, who are eighteen years of age, or older, to vote shall not be denied or abridged by the United States or by any state on account of age.

Section 2. The Congress shall have the power to enforce this article by appropriate legislation.

AMENDMENT XXVII [1992]

No law, varying the compensation for the services of the Senators and Representatives, shall take effect, until an election of Representatives shall have intervened.

APPENDIX B

ILLUSTRATIVE CASES IN LAW

The following cases will give beginning students practice in reading and briefing cases of general interest. These cases illustrate many of the fundamental concepts introduced in Part I of this textbook and demonstrate the use of these concepts in practice.

Common Law Development

The *Du Pont* case illustrates the manner in which judges decide questions concerning justiciability of disputes and ways in which the common law remains alive today. This civil case involves diversity of citizenship of the two parties and, therefore, illustrates an area of overlapping jurisdiction between state and federal courts. Since Du Pont had the initial choice of trial courts, the Christophers have the same choice on appeal. The federal court, however, is bound by the *Erie* doctrine to decide the issue using Texas substantive law.

The *Restatement of Torts* is a general formulation of the principles of common law that have evolved from case law development. These principles have been reformulated by the American Law Institute to resemble the form of statutory law. The *Restatement* does not have the specific force of law until recognized by the courts of appropriate jurisdiction.

An **interlocutory appeal** is an appeal to review a preliminary trial court judgment prior to trial on the merits of the case. The Federal Interlocutory Appeals Act grants discretion to the courts of appeals to review any interlocutory order whatever in a civil case if the trial judge, in making the order, has stated in writing that the order involves a controlling question of law regarding which there is substantial ground for difference of opinion and that an immediate appeal from the order may materially advance the ultimate termination of litigation (28 U.S.C.A. § 1292[b]).

The abbreviation "F.2d" in the citation for this case denotes the case reporter series entitled *Federal Reporter* (2nd edition). All federal appeals court cases are found in this series of volumes.

E. I. Du Pont de Nemours & Company, Inc. v. Christopher

431 F.2d 1012
United States Court of Appeals, Fifth Circuit
August 25, 1970

GOLDBERG, JUSTICE. This is a case of industrial espionage in which an airplane is the cloak and a camera the dagger. The defendants-appellants, Rolfe and Gary Christopher, are photographers in Beaumont, Texas. The Christophers were hired by an unknown third party to take aerial photographs of new construction at the Beaumont plant of E. I. du Pont de Nemours & Company, Inc. Sixteen photographs of the Du Pont facility were taken from the air on March 19, 1969, and these photographs were later developed and delivered to the third party.

Du Pont employees apparently noticed the airplane on March 19 and immediately began an investigation to determine why the craft was circling over the plant. By that afternoon the investigation had disclosed that the craft was involved in a photographic expedition and that the Christophers were the photographers. Du Pont contacted the Christophers that same afternoon and asked them to reveal the name of the person or corporation requesting the photographs. The Christophers refused to disclose this information, giving as their reason the client's desire to remain anonymous.

Having reached a dead end in the investigation, Du Pont subsequently filed suit against the Christophers, alleging that the Christophers had wrongfully obtained photographs revealing Du Pont's trade secrets which they then sold to the undisclosed third party. Du Pont contended that it had developed a highly secret but unpatented process for producing methanol, a process which gave Du Pont a competitive advantage over other producers. This process, Du Pont alleged, was a trade secret developed after much expensive and time-consuming research, and a secret which the company had taken special precautions to safeguard. The area photographed by the Christophers was the plant designed to produce methanol by this secret process, and because the plant was still under construction parts of the process were exposed to view from directly above the construction area. Photographs of that area, Du Pont alleged, would enable a skilled person to deduce the secret process for making methanol. Du Pont thus contended that the Christophers had wrongfully appropriated Du Pont trade secrets by taking the photographs and delivering them to the undisclosed third party. In its suit Du Pont asked for damages to cover the loss it had already sustained as a result of the wrongful disclosure of the trade secret and sought temporary and permanent injunctions prohibiting any further circulation of the photographs already taken and prohibiting any additional photographing of the methanol plant.

The Christophers answered with motions to dismiss for lack of jurisdiction and failure to state a claim upon which relief could be granted. Depositions were taken during which the Christophers again refused to disclose the name of the person to whom they had delivered the photographs. Du Pont then filed a motion to compel an answer to this question and all related questions.

On June 5, 1969, the trial court held a hearing on the pending motions. The court denied the Christophers' motions to dismiss for want of jurisdiction and failure to state a claim. The court granted Du Pont's motion to compel the Christophers to divulge the name of their client. Agreeing with the trial court's determination that Du Pont had stated a valid claim, we affirm the decision of that court.

This is a case of first impression, for the Texas courts have not faced this precise factual issue, and sitting as a diversity court we must sensitize our *Erie* antennae to decide what the Texas courts would do if such a situation were presented to them. The only question involved in this interlocutory appeal is whether Du Pont has asserted a claim upon which relief can be granted. The Christophers argued both at trial and before this court that they committed no "actionable wrong" in photographing the Du Pont facility and passing these photographs on to their client because they conducted all of their activities in public airspace, violated no government aviation standard, did not breach any confidential relation, and did not engage in any fraudulent or illegal conduct. In short, the Christophers argue that for an appropriation of trade secrets to be wrong there must be a trespass, other illegal conduct, or breach of a confidential relationship. We disagree.

It is true, as the Christophers assert, that the previous trade secret cases have contained one or more of these elements. However, we do not think that the Texas courts would limit the trade secret protection exclusively to these elements. On the contrary, in Hyde Corporation v. Huffines, 1958, 158 Tex. 566, 314 S.W.2d 763, the Texas Supreme Court specifically adopted the rule found in the Restatement of Torts which provides:

> One who discloses or uses another's trade secret, without a privilege to do so, is liable to the other if
> (a) he discovered the secret by improper means, or
> (b) his disclosure or use constitutes a breach of confidence reposed in him by the other in disclosing the secret to him. . . .

Thus, although the previous cases have dealt with a breach of a confidential relationship, a trespass, or other illegal conduct, the rule is much broader than the cases heretofore encountered. Not limiting itself to specific wrongs, Texas adopted subsection (a) of the Restatement which recognizes a cause of action for the discovery of a trade secret by any "improper" means.

The question remaining, therefore, is whether aerial photography of plant construction is an improper means of obtaining another's trade secret. We conclude that it is and that the Texas courts would so hold. The supreme court of that state has declared that "the undoubted tendency of the law has been to recognize and enforce higher standards of commercial morality in the business world." Hyde Corporation v. Huffines, *supra* 314 S.W.2nd at 773. That court has quoted with approval articles indicating that the *proper* means of gaining possession of a competitor's secret process is "through inspection and analysis" of the product in order to create a duplicate. Later another Texas court explained:

> The means by which the discovery is made may be obvious, and the experimentation leading from known factors to presently unknown results may be simple and lying in the public domain. But these facts do not destroy the value of the discovery and will not advantage a competitor who by unfair means obtains the knowledge *without paying the price expended by the discoverer*. (Brown v. Fowler, Tex. Civ. App. 1958, 316 S.W.2d 111.)

We think, therefore, that the Texas rule is clear. One may use his competitor's secret process if he discovers the process by reverse engineering applied to the finished product; one may use a competitor's process if he discovers it by his own independent research; but one may not avoid these labors by taking the process from the discoverer without his permission at a time when he is taking reasonable precautions to maintain its secrecy. To obtain knowledge of a process without spending the time and money to discover it independently is *improper* unless the holder voluntarily discloses it or fails to take reasonable precautions to ensure its secrecy.

In the instant case the Christophers deliberately flew over the Du Pont plant to get pictures of a process which Du Pont had attempted to keep secret. The Christophers delivered their pictures to a third party who was certainly aware of the means by which they had been acquired and who may be planning to use the information contained therein to manufacture methanol by the Du Pont process. The third party has a right to use this process only if he obtains this knowledge through his own research efforts, but thus far all information indicates that the third party has gained this knowledge solely by taking it from Du Pont at a time when Du Pont was making reasonable efforts to preserve its secrecy. In such a situation Du Pont has a valid cause of action to prohibit the Christophers from improperly discovering its trade secret and to prohibit the undisclosed third party from using the improperly obtained information.

We note that this view is in perfect accord with the position taken by the authors of the restatement. In commenting on improper means of discovery the savants of the Restatement of Torts said:

f. *Improper Means of Discovery*. The discovery of another's trade secret by improper means subjects the actor to liability independently of the harm to the interest in the secret. Thus, if one uses physical force to take a secret formula from another's pocket, or breaks into another's office to steal the formula, his conduct is wrongful and subjects him to liability apart from the rule stated in this section. Such conduct is also an improper means of procuring the secret under this rule. But means may be improper under this rule even though they do not cause any other harm than that to the interest in the trade secret. Examples of such means are fraudulent misrepresentations to induce disclosure, tapping of telephone wires, eavesdropping or other espionage. A complete catalogue of improper means is not possible. In general they are means which fall below the generally accepted standards of commercial morality and reasonable conduct.

In taking this position we realize that industrial espionage of the sort here perpetrated has become a popular sport in some segments of our industrial community. However, our devotion to freewheeling industrial competition must not force us into accepting the law of the jungle as the standard of morality expected in our commercial relations. Our tolerance of the espionage game must cease when the protections required to prevent another's spying cost so much that the spirit of inventiveness is dampened. Commercial privacy must be protected from espionage which could not have been reasonably anticipated or prevented. We do not mean to imply, however, that everything not in the plain view is within the protected vale, nor that all information obtained through every extra optical extension is forbidden. Indeed, for our industrial competition to remain healthy there must be breathing room for observing a competing industrialist. A competitor can and must shop his competition for pricing and examine his products for quality, components, and methods of manufacture. Perhaps ordinary fences and roofs must be built to shut out incursive eyes, but we need not require the discoverer of a trade secret to guard against the unanticipated, the undetectable, or the unpreventable methods of espionage now available.

In the instant case Du Pont was in the midst of constructing a plant. Although after construction the finished plant would have protected much of the process from view, during the period of construction the trade secret was exposed to view from the air. To require Du Pont to put a roof over the unfinished plant to guard its secret would impose an enormous expense to prevent nothing more than a school boy's trick. We introduce here no new or radical ethic since our ethos has never given moral sanction to piracy. The market place must not deviate far from our mores. We should not require a person or corporation to take unreasonable precautions to prevent another from doing that which he ought not to do in the first place. Reasonable precautions against predatory eyes we may require, but an impenetrable fortress is an unreasonable requirement, and we are not disposed to burden industrial inventors with such a duty in order to protect the fruits of their efforts. "Improper" will always be a word of many nuances, determined by time, place, and circumstances. We therefore need not proclaim a catalogue of commercial improprieties. Clearly however, one of its commandments does say "thou shall not appropriate a trade secret through deviousness under circumstances in which countervailing defenses are not reasonably available."

Having concluded that aerial photography, from whatever altitude, is an improper method of discovering the trade secrets exposed during construction of the Du Pont plant, we need not worry about whether the flight pattern chosen by the Christophers violated any federal aviation regulations. Regardless of whether the flight was legal or illegal in that sense, the espionage was an improper means of discovering Du Pont's trade secret.

The decision of the trial courts is affirmed and the case remanded to that court for proceedings on the merits.

CASE QUESTIONS

1. Can you state the holding of this case in clear, concise terms, including the important facts that would be required to be similar if this decision is used as precedent in like cases in the future?

2. What methods of legal reasoning are used to arrive at the court's conclusion?

3. Was Du Pont really interested in suing the Christophers or somebody else for damages?

4. When does a rule of social morality become law?

5. Would a lawyer have been able to predict the result of the *Du Pont* case with a high degree of certainty?

6. Has the spirit of the law or the letter of the law been applied in this case?

7. If the court had ruled in favor of the Christophers, how would the functioning of the law have been affected by changing technology?

Fundamental Due Process

The *Ryan* case illustrates a form of procedural due process that courts have applied even against private universities. This case is a civil action, but contains many of the fundamental ideas of fairness used in administrative actions regarding governmental agencies. The common law method of accretion of law is illustrated in this case. The question of whether the facts in this case are on point (alike) or whether there are important differences in regard to the precedent cited should be examined.

Ryan v. Hofstra University

67 Misc. 2d 651, 324 N.Y.S.2d 964
Supreme Court, Nassau County
October 14, 1971

HARNETT, JUSTICE. Hofstra University, though termed a "private" university, cannot expel, bar and fine a student wtihout following fair and reasonable procedures. It cannot be arbitrary. It must abide by constitutional principles of fair conduct implicit in our society.

Issues surrouding the conduct of college students and their treatment by college officials tend to be emotionally charged. When campus unrest marches apace with an older generation's discontentment with it, difficulties arise in sifting out legal substance and retaining the long view necessary for social continuance. Many changes have come in legal implication as society has grown and institutions altered, producing overlaps and perspectives unimagined earlier. More narrowly to the point, university character has changed over the years, as have the relationships of people of all ages and kinds to the state and the numerous activities of mixed public and private nature which continually insinuate themselves into our lives.

Here we have Robert Ryan, Jr., accused of throwing rocks through the book store window at Hofstra. It is the case of a young man accused of vandalism of college property. If he is guilty, he should be punished and the university should have broad discretion to punish him. It would be the university's duty for the protection of its people and facilities to address itself firmly to his discipline. However, the university too is a creature of the law. The university must abide by legal procedures and respect private rights. If the university is to break the law by violating private rights, it has no superior legal or moral position to one whose law breaking consists of breaking windows.

Nineteen-year-old Robert Ryan, Jr., was a Hofstra freshman last semester, and a mover in student protests against tuition increases. He was suspected by the administration of previous violent conduct, although no charges were made and no disciplinary proceedings were had.

On June 10, 1971, Robert was apprehended on campus by security police and accused of throwing a rock through the plate glass display window of the university bookstore that evening. He was taken to the campus security office where, under disputed circumstances, in the sole presence of the campus security chief and the dean of students, he wrote out a confession in which he admitted guilt to three separate rock-throwing incidents.

On June 11, 1971, he was called to face a disciplinary committee of three staff members appointed by the dean. According to the testimony of a committee member, he repeated there his guilt to the rock-throwing incidents, although later in court he recanted his admissions. The committee later also spoke with a school psychologist, and the chief security officer, and apparently considered the statement of a security policeman who claimed to be an eyewitness. It then reported to the dean.

On June 22, 1971, the dean expelled Robert from Hofstra, severing him from the University "completely and permanently." He barred Robert from any part of the campus without his express prior permission under pain of arrest as a trespasser. Finally, he fined Robert and his family $1,011.61 for the ostensible cost of replacing the windows.

At no time prior to his expulsion, barring and fining, was Robert given a choice of procedure, was he represented by any counsel, nor did he have an opportunity to confront any witnesses, nor was he interviewed by any school psychologist or medical personnel.

The dean claims that Robert was guilty of the rock-throwing charges, and that in light of these and the other uncharged incidents he was troublesome and emotionally disturbed. Robert claims he is innocent, that his confession was pressured from him, and that the university is and has been harassing him because of his tuition protest activities.

The Hofstra Disciplinary Regulations for Nonacademic Conduct provide that when the dean of students is advised of an incident possibly requiring disciplinary action he may either interview the student himself or refer the matter to a member of his staff. Upon determining that disciplinary hearing is appropriate, the student is given a choice of appearing before either a student judiciary board or members of the dean of student's staff.

The dean specified in his testimony that Robert was not given a choice of the student judiciary board, based on that portion of the Hofstra rules which provide that a student "whose records suggest significant emotional or psychological disturbances which may be relevant" will be heard only by the dean's staff. The dean did not consult any psychologist or psychiatrist before making the disciplinary reference to his staff committee. The testimony was that the staff committee concerned itself with emotional disturbance upon talking with a university psychologist.

There are no rules as to the procedures of the dean's staff committee except that its members present their recommendations to the dean. The dean must then interview the student and give his decision. Hofstra's rules do provide an "appeal" procedure for non-academic disciplinary situations. If the student believes that the dean's punishment is inappropriate, he may have a hearing by a review committee of five university staff and faculty members and two students upon his petition submitted to the vice president for student affairs within ten days after penalty. The vice president is then supposed to advise the student of his right to call witnesses on his behalf and to confront and cross-examine those who appear against him and of his right to seek counsel, which counsel is limited, however, only to a university staff or faculty member.

The review committee is charged with examining the evidence, hearing witnesses as to the facts and the student's character, and weighing extenuating circumstances. The administration, but not the student, has a further right of appeal to the university board of trustees.

During June, Robert orally requested of the dean and the Hofstra vice president of student affairs a hearing, but was told that he had to petition in writing. A lawyer representing Robert requested an appeal hearing by letter dated July 9, 1971, to the dean. This letter was returned to the lawyer suggesting that the request be directed to the university vice president for student affairs. Thereupon, the attorney mailed a similar letter to that official on July 23, 1971, requesting that the review be held prior to the fall semester, but the administration took no action on this.

On August 4, 1971, Robert requested that because of family illness the hearing be delayed until the fall and that he be permitted to attend classes pending the completion of the appeal. This request was turned down by the vice president for student affairs on August 9, 1971, who volunteered that Robert's right to petition for a hearing was extended to September 1, 1971. On August 26, 1971, Robert wrote personally to the vice president for student affairs requesting an appeal. On September 9, 1971, Robert received a letter (dated September 1st) from an assistant president stating that there was no more vice president for student affairs, advising Robert that he would be notified of a hearing date "as soon as practicable," and directing communication to him.

On September 14, 1971, without any further word from the administration as to review, Robert commenced this proceeding to compel Hofstra to readmit him to classes. On September 16, 1971, classes reopened at Hofstra for the fall season. Sometime after the hearing of this judicial proceeding on September 23, 1971, a review proceeding was first scheduled for October 5, 1971.

Essentially, Robert's contention is that the university's action was improper and arbitrary and that the proceedings deprived him of due process of law. In reply, Hofstra asserts that the university acted properly and that Hofstra, as a private institution, was not legally obliged to afford fair process to its students. Hofstra argues that since it is a private university it suffers no restriction at all in its disciplining of its students. However one gauges the contemporaneous sensitivity of this attitude, it is plainly not the law. Whatever the application to this case, there are some limits.

The dean testified that he gave Robert no choice of appearing before the student judiciary board because of that provision of the rules requiring staff referral only for "students whose records suggest significant emotional or psychological disturbance." Even though Robert was sent to the staff committee and given no student judiciary board choice because of an assumed record of emotional or psychological disturbance, Robert was at no time interviewed by any medical or psychological personnel, nor were any records produced suggesting the offending disturbance.

Under the adopted rules, Robert was entitled to a student judiciary board choice unless the record suggested significant emotional disturbance on his part. There was no proof of any such record prior to his referral to the dean's committee. It was indeed the reverse. It was the staff committee which raised the emotional concern after the student judiciary board choice had already been withheld.

Accordingly, in the absence of a foundation for his conduct, the dean acted arbitrarily and in abuse of discretion in not giving Robert the choice of appearing before a student judiciary board as required by the Hofstra rules.

Implicit in the rules must be a requirement for the university to act with reasonable promptness on review applications. The testimony reflects without doubt that the Hofstra administration delayed materially in scheduling a review hearing. Where after oral notification, it had a written notice on July 9, 1971, and subsequent written requests on July 23rd and August 26th, it first scheduled an appeal hearing on October 5, 1971, three weeks after school reopened. And this scheduling came only after the court hearing in this proceeding.

Given the time necessary to conduct an appeal and reach a reasoned decision, it is apparent that the procedure adopted will necessarily deprive Robert of a semester's attendance in class, or at best put him under an onerous make-up schedule, if possible, even if he is totally successful on appeal.

This delay works the imposition of a significant penalty which entirely bypasses the review procedure, and must be termed arbitrary and capricious, and abusive of discretion, on the part of the Hofstra administration.

The university's insistence on a written petition in Robert's personal hand to the vice president for student affairs as an excuse for delay is hypertechnical and not legitimate justification. After oral notice from Robert, it rejected the first written communication from his lawyer because it was addressed to the moving and visible dean and not to a certain vice president, and then rejected the lawyer's written request to the officer to which it directed him on the ground that Robert personally, not a lawyer, had to write out the request. The administration was fully and fairly informed by the lawyer's letters of July 9, 1971, to the dean of students and of July 23, 1971, to the vice president of student affairs. A lawyer acts as a personal representative of his client and for him. The administration's treatment of this simple request for review smacks of a "runaround." Moreover, if technicality is the order of the day, nothing in the rules precludes petition by a lawyer writing on behalf of a student, unlike the review procedures which specifically limit right to counsel. Amusingly enough, even the administration departed from its insistence on communication with one indispensable officer as the touchstone for its procedure, for in August Hofstra dispensed with its position of vice president for student affairs altogether. After Robert had personally petitioned that requisite officer, it turned out the office no longer existed, and the university itself requested Robert to communicate with some assistant president. Even then it delayed for six more weeks until October 5, 1971.

Finally, the hasty imposition on Robert and his family of a money fine in excess of $1000 for three separate incidents, of which only one had a claimed eyewitness, without even submitted proof of damage, was precipitous. The family was not heard at all and in no way signed for any responsibility. A particularly unreasonable part of the skimpy procedure here is that the expelled student cannot get a transcript to enable transfer admission to another school until he pays the fine to the university. Accordingly, a student is put into the position of being required to pay or prosecute a successful appeal, no matter the time delay, before he can transfer to another school. This financial obligation springs into existence without benefit of counsel or fair hearing.

In Dixon v. Alabama Board of Education, 294 F.2d 150, the court held a student could not be expelled from a tax supported university without notice and some opportunity to be heard. In defining "due process," the court emphasized that the nature of the hearing depended on the circumstances of the particular case. It said that "full dress judicial hearings" are not required, because they are not appropriate to college context, but that the requirements of due process are fulfilled by having "the rudimentary elements of fair play." There must be "every semblance of fairness" in school disciplinary procedure. Due process is then a variable thing. Something different is called for by a criminal trial than a college disciplinary proceeding. But, the constant factor is that the procedure afforded must be traditionally fair and conscionable in the context taken.

Bearing in mind that this is a college disciplinary matter, and not a criminal trial (although the acts charged are crimes and admissions taken damaging), it must be observed that Robert's treatment fell short of the rudimentary requirements of fair play.

In the collegiate context, the initial nonacademic discipline procedure at Hofstra is not unreasonable, provided it is followed. Since the subsequent appeal or review procedure contemplates an open hearing with witnesses and confrontation, the juxtaposition is not inconsistent with the need to keep order. But when the prescribed procedure is not followed, when punitive delay is set in, and when excessive punishment is summarily dealt, the administration violates the necessary rudiments of fair play.

Based on the findings and principles set forth above, the action of the Hofstra University dean in expelling Robert Ryan, Jr., barring him from the campus, and fining him and his family will be nullified.

CASE QUESTIONS

1. Do you agree with the court's ruling in this case, and why or why not?

2. If you were the lawyer for Hofstra University, would you appeal this decision? Why or why not?

3. Would the judge have ruled the same way if Hofstra had merely expelled the student? Why or why not?

4. What is meant by a fair hearing?

5. What procedural rules exist on the reader's campus?

6. Is the court creating law in this case, or merely following stare decisis?

Vagueness and Substantive Due Process

The *Moore* case involves use of the basic principle of conflict of laws to render part of a statutory law unconstitutional. The concepts of vagueness and substantive due process are illustrated in this case. Substantive due process limits the legislative authority and requires that the enactment provide a standard that can be applied by the court. Note that this is a trial level court making a decision in a criminal case about the applicability of a state statute. Judges at all levels take an oath to uphold the Constitution. Intent is a significant element in criminal cases where guilt must be established beyond a reasonable doubt.

People v. Moore
377 N.Y.S.2d 1005
Fulton County Court
December 12, 1975

MARIO M. ALBANESE, JUDGE. These defendants, all municipal officials of the City of Gloversville, New York, were indicted, charging them with violating Article 18, Section 805-a subdivision (1) of the General Municipal Law of the State of New York.

All three defendants move for the dismissal of this particular charge on the grounds the same is unconstitutional claiming it fails to adequately and sufficiently set a standard by which reasonable men could reach a determination as to what are "circumstances in which it could reasonably be inferred that the gift was intended to influence the defendants or could reasonably be expected to influence them in the performance of their respective official duties"; the statute, so it is further claimed, is so vague and unspecific that a reasonable man would be compelled to speculate at his peril whether the statute permits or prohibits the act he contemplates committing and as such, is repugnant to the due process clause of the Constitutions of the United States and New York, as well as violative of the protection afforded an individual thereunder.

The District Attorney, on the other hand, directly opposes the contentions of the three defendants, claiming instead that the entire act is constitutional without any vagueness, uncertainty or ambiguity and all that is required to identify the nature of the conduct prohibited is the exercise of common sense.

The pertinent portion of Section 805-a of the General Municipal Law reads as follows:

No municipal officer or employee shall: a. directly or indirectly, solicit any gift, or accept or receive any gift having a value of twenty-five dollars or more, whether in the form of money, service, loan, travel, entertainment, hospitality, thing or promise, or in any other form, under circumstances in which it could reasonably be inferred that the gift was intended to influence him, or could reasonably be expected to influence him, in the performance of his official duties or was intended as a reward for any official action on his part.

To ascertain the legislative background, its intents and purposes the Court referred to the "Report of the Governor's Special Commission on Ethical Standards in Public Service," dated December 12, 1969, with Malcolm Wilson, then Lieutenant Governor, as its Chairman. This report sets forth the intended and express proscription of two distinct and separate types of conduct, the first of which forbids the *solicitation*, directly or indirectly, *of any gift of any value* (italics added for emphasis) under all circumstances; the second forbids the *acceptance* or *receipt* (italics added for emphasis) of any gift of Twenty-Five Dollars ($25.00) or more, even if unsolicited, whether in the form of money or in any other form, under circumstances intended or expected to influence the official in his official duties.

A municipal officer or employee, under the first prohibition, is forbidden to: "directly or indirectly, solicit any gift." This particular prohibition and language is clear, definite and unequivocal, so much so that no rational argument can be levied against its intent and meaning. This being so, the Court will dispose of this portion of the statute before us without further discussion thereon by declaring the first prohibition to be constitutional.

With respect to the second prohibition, a municipal officer or employee is forbidden to:

accept or receive any gift having a value of twenty-five dollars or more, whether in the form of money, service, loan, travel, entertainment, hospitality, thing or promise, or in any other form, under circumstances in which it could reasonably be inferred that the gift was intended to influence him, or could reasonably be expected to influence him, in the performance of his official duties or was intended as a reward for any official action on his part.

The wording and language of this second proscription presents a different and difficult situation more specifically that portion thereof which reads: "*under circumstances in which it could reasonably be inferred that the gift was intended to influence him, or could reasonably be expected to influence him.*" (Italics added for emphasis.) The Court holds such language to be vague and without any standard or guidelines whatsoever; accordingly, is unconstitutional as violative of the due process and equal protection clauses of the Constitutions of the State of New York and the United States.

The wording being examined hereunder is lacking in specificity. It should clearly indicate what it is a man's duty to avoid. It must be so "clear and positive" as to give "unequivocal warning" to citizens of the rule to be obeyed. Furthermore, it has no well-defined or agreed upon meaning. Tozer v. United States, 8 Cir., 52 F. 917, states in part that a person should be "able to know in advance whether his act is criminal or not." In short, this language also suffers from vagueness. The test of due process is met by a statute whose language is sufficiently definite to establish a standard of conduct ascertainable by persons familiar with the field in which the statute is operative.

In the opinion of this Court, these are serious deficiencies that result in a denial of due process. Connally v. General Construction Co., 269 U.S. 385, 46 S.Ct. 126, 70 L.Ed. 322 holds: "A statute which either forbids or requires the doing of an act in terms so vague that men of common intelligence must necessarily guess at its meaning and differ as to its application violates the first essential of due process of law." The test in matters of this kind as to whether or not a statute may be upheld as constitutional seems to be whether the phrases used have "a technical or other special meaning . . . or a well-settled common law meaning" or whether the text of the statute involved or the subject with which it dealt sets up some kind of standard.

The additional language ("under circumstances, etc.") in our particular case does not condemn any act, omission or clearly defined set of circumstances but, in fact leaves it to the discretion if not the whim of the police or enforcement official to determine or ascribe criminality or wrongdoing. More disturbing still, it is the intent of the donor and not that of the municipal official that controls—a contention with which the District Attorney fully concurs. Admittedly, then, one intending no wrong can nevertheless be victimized by accepting or receiving a gift by the malintent of the giver alone. That this is unfair and repugnant is self-evident. These are serious deficiencies which also deny to one the equal protection of the law as guaranteed by the Constitution.

In conclusion, the Court interprets the statute to be read in the disjunctive delineating as aforementioned, the distinction between the two conducts so prohibited and as such, is severable. Also: "A statute may be constitutional in part and unconstitutional in part, and the invalid part may be severed from the remainder, if after the severance the remaining portions are sufficient to effect the legislative purposes deducible from the entire act, construed in the light of contemporary events." The first prohibition, being constitutional, is retained, while the second prohibition, being unconstitutional, is to be severed from Section 805-a of the General Municipal Law of the State of New York, and of no force and effect.

CASE QUESTIONS

1. How does the court define vagueness in this decision?

2. Is it clear whether the defendants were charged with the first or second part of the state statutory provision in question?

3. Could the defendants be tried on the basis of the first part of the statute? Why or why not?

4. How could the legislature change the statute to make it enforceable through the courts?

Criminal Standards of Due Process

In the *Braly* case, the exacting standards of due process in criminal cases are illustrated. A crime is a very serious offense, and this case involves two convictions for felonies (serious crimes) as opposed to misdemeanors (minor criminal offenses). Conviction for a serious crime requires proof of culpability (guilt), which includes mental intent (mens rea). This element of crime is usually specified in the statute defining the crime. Conspiracy is an inchoate (or vague) crime requiring proof of deliberate planning to commit a crime. Sufficiency of evidence refers to at least some admissible evidence. The rules of evidence are extensive, but all courts are required to prohibit the use of hearsay (secondhand) evidence in criminal and civil trials. The standard of proof in criminal cases is beyond a reasonable doubt.

People vs. Braly
532 P.2d 325
Supreme Court of Colorado
January 20, 1975

GROVES, JUSTICE. Defendant Terrell Braly was tried by a jury and convicted of conspiracy to sell narcotic drugs and assault with a deadly weapon. On appeal, defendant challenges the sufficiency of the evidence on both counts and assigns further prejudicial errors at trial. We reverse both convictions.

The circumstances surrounding the charges against the defendant are as follows. Two undercover police officers, agent Carter and O'Dell, attempted to arrange a purchase of fifty pounds of marijuana from one Stahl. Carter contacted Stahl by telephone. Stahl told him that he could sell fifty pounds of marijuana, and that the price would be $4,200. Stahl told Carter to come to his house in Boulder at about 5:30 or 6 that afternoon. Upon the arrival of agents Carter and O'Dell, Mr. Stahl asked to see the money and officer O'Dell showed it to him. Stahl told the officers to return in about a half hour; they then left, and did return at about 6:30.

On their return, the agents went into the Stahl residence. Stahl made a phone call and then told them that he wanted to talk further about the purchase, but not in the house, suggesting the use of the agents' vehicle. There the three talked further about the proposed buy and at about 7 p.m. the agents dropped Stahl off at the hill area in Boulder. They picked him up again at about 8 and returned to Stahl's house. That evening, at about 8:30, there was a knock at the door. Stahl asked the agents to go to the basement bedroom and to wait for him. The agents heard voices upstairs, and then Stahl returned to the basement and gave them a Winston cigarette pack containing two marijuana cigarettes, explaining that this was a sample of the marijuana that was the subject of the purchase. Stahl told the agents that he had the marijuana but wanted to have the money before they could see the narcotics. Stahl made several trips up and down the stairs. Finally, he took the agents up with him and asked them to remain inside a bedroom upstairs. Stahl, acting as a go-between for the agents and the people in the other bedroom, was given the money which he showed to the others, who questioned whether it was marked. Agent Carter asked if he could see the marijuana. Shortly thereafter, the deal fell through. Except for an earlier visit, when the agents saw Stahl's mother and sister, no one was seen by the agents in the Stahl house. There was testimony by a surveillant officer that the defendant was in the house while the agents were last there; and the defendant's counsel stipulated that he was there at the time in question.

The events that followed are confusing. When the defendant and his companion left the Stahl house that night, surveillance cars attempted to follow the car that defendant was driving and a car of a companion of Braly. It becomes unclear who was following—or who was trying to elude—whom but the record reflects a classic "cops and robbers" chase through the streets of Boulder, complete with squealing tires and U-turns. Six cars were involved, four of which were police vehicles. At one point, however, the car which defendant was driving came alongside a surveillance car and swerved toward it about three times, and the surveillance car took evasive action, swerving toward the right curb. The testimony of the defendant, and of the police, indicates that there were two lanes of travel in that direction, and that defendant's car never left his lane of traffic, nor did it hit the agents' car. Further the testimony indicates that the defendant could have hit the agents' car if he had so desired, and that the agents' car never left the roadway, though its tires squealed and at one point bumped the curb.

Shortly thereafter, defendant was stopped and arrested. The assault charge stems from the interlude in the automobiles. No marijuana, other than the two cigarettes, was recovered. The prosecution's case was established through the testimony of the narcotics and surveillance officers, and through the testimony of Stahl's mother as to what she had overheard and what her son had told her. Stahl never testified, though his statements composed a major portion of the prosecution's evidence.

The defendant, testifying in his own behalf, stated that he had gone to the Stahl house in an attempt to take the agents' money and leave, after having been told that the men at Stahl's house were narcotics agents. A Dan Conley testified that he had contacted the defendant on the afternoon of the 6th, and had told him not to go to the Stahl house that night because the people there would be narcotics agents.

[The court reversed the conspiracy to sell narcotics conviction because of insufficient evidence.] Defendant was charged with assault under C.R.S. 1963, 40-2-34 which reads in pertinent part:

> An assault with a deadly weapon, instrument or other thing, with an intent to commit upon the person of another a bodily injury where no considerable provocation appears or where the circumstances of the assault show an abandoned or malignant heart, shall be adjudged to be a felony. . . .

Assault is defined under C.R.S. 1963, 40-2-33 to be an "unlawful attempt coupled with a present ability to commit a violent injury on the person of another."

The intent with which the act is committed is the gist of the offense.

Where a crime consists of an act combined with a specific intent, the intent is just as much an element of the crime as is the act. In such cases, mere general malice or criminal intent is insufficient, and the requisite specific intent must be shown as a matter of fact, either by direct or circumstantial evidence. The rule is especially applicable where a statutory offense, consisting of an act and a specific intent, constitutes substantially an attempt to commit some higher offense than that which the accused succeeded in accomplishing. The general rule that a criminal intention will be presumed from the commission of the unlawful act does not apply; and proof of the commission of the act does not warrant the presumption that accused had the requisite specific intent. Although it is settled that even specific intent may be inferred from the circumstances, it is argued that the circumstances in this case seem to negate such specific intent. We agree. The testimony of the officers, and of the defendant, showed that the car defendant was driving never left his lane of traffic; that there were two lanes traveling in the direction of the two cars; that there was adequate room in both lanes; and that although defendant could have made contact if he had wanted to, no contact was made.

The court in Shreeves v. People, 126 Colo. 413, 249 P.2d 1020 (1952), stated:

> The term "abandoned and malignant heart" as the same is used in the statute here under consideration, is evidenced by the use of some instrumentality likely to produce great bodily harm, and by the brutal and unrestrained use of such instrumentality in the commission of the crime charged.

In viewing the facts in the light most favorable to the prosecution, we think that there was not sufficient evidence to establish criminal assault.

Judgment reversed and cause remanded with directions to grant defendant's motion for acquittal as to both counts.

LEE, JUSTICE (concurring in part and dissenting in part). The evidence presented by the People, together with the reasonable inferences therefrom, concerning the manner in which the defendant drove his vehicle during the "cops and robbers" chase, in my view, was sufficient to sustain the verdict of guilty of assault with a deadly weapon.

Viewing the chase in the context of the events of the evening, as described in the majority opinion, it becomes clear that the swerving of defendant's vehicle was not the innocent act of one who was lawfully operating his vehicle on the streets of Boulder and who unfortunately became the victim of a mechanical brake or steering malfunction, as the defendant suggested in his testimony. The swerving was not an isolated occurrence but happened, according to the police officers, three times during the high-speed chase which lasted for a period of approximately twenty minutes.

The jury could reasonably conclude under all the circumstances that the defendant three times deliberately swerved his car toward the surveillance car during the chase, thus forcing the surveillance car to take evasive action to avoid a collision and potentially grievous personal injuries; that the defendant's conduct in driving his car toward the police car was motivated by an abandoned and malignant heart, as evidenced by the unrestrained manner in which the car was being driven at the time; and that defendant's intention was to cause bodily injury upon the officers in the other car.

That the defendant's car did not cross the lane dividing the two driving lanes or make actual contact with the police car would not, in my view, lessen the criminal culpability demonstrated by the defendant in the operation of his car under the circumstances then existing.

I would affirm the judgment of conviction of assault with a deadly weapon.

CASE QUESTIONS

1. Was Braly found to be innocent of these crimes?

2. Do you agree with the majority of the court or with the dissenter?

3. What would have been the most appropriate criminal charge in this case, given the facts presented?

4. Should the court be able to override the jury in cases like this one? Why or why not?

Civil Due Process

The *Katko* case illustrates that criminal and civil actions are completely independent of each other. They are separate forms of legal action. In criminal cases, only the prosecutor can file suit, but in a civil action, the injured party is allowed to initiate legal process to recover damages. This case also illustrates the distinctive functions of the trial courts and the appeals courts. Appeals courts do not include juries and do not conduct fact-finding procedures. They must rely upon trial courts to develop the facts and to decide upon issues of fact in dispute. Juries often are used in both civil and criminal cases to decide questions of fact in dispute. Appeals courts decide questions of law in dispute, and these issues must be raised at the trial court level in order to be reviewed by appeals courts.

Katko v. Briney

183 N.W.2d 657
Supreme Court of Iowa
February 9, 1971

MOORE, CHIEF JUSTICE. The primary issue presented here is whether an owner may protect personal property in an unoccupied boarded-up farm house against trespassers and thieves by a spring gun capable of inflicting death or serious injury.

We are not here concerned with a man's right to protect his home and members of his family. Defendants' home was several miles from the scene of the incident to which we refer infra.

Plaintiff's action is for damages resulting from serious injury caused by a shot from a 20-gauge spring shotgun set by defendants in a bedroom of an old farm house which had been uninhabited for several years. Plaintiff and his companion, Marvin McDonough, had broken and entered the house to find and steal old bottles and dated fruit jars which they considered antiques.

At defendants' request plaintiff's action was tried to a jury consisting of residents of the community where defendants' property was located. The jury returned a verdict for plaintiff and against defendants for $20,000 actual and $10,000 punitive damages.

After careful consideration of defendants' motions for judgment notwithstanding the verdict and for new trial, the experienced and capable trial judge overruled them and entered judgment on the verdict. Thus we have this appeal by defendants.

Most of the facts are not disputed. In 1957 defendant Bertha L. Briney inherited her parents' farm land in Mahaska and Monroe Counties. Included was an eighty-acre tract in southwest Mahaska County where her grandparents and parents had lived. No one occupied the house thereafter. Her husband, Edward, attempted to care for the land. He kept no farm machinery thereon. The outbuildings became delapidated.

For about ten years, 1957 to 1967, there occurred a series of trespassing and housebreaking events with loss of some household items, the breaking of windows and "messing up of the property in general." The latest occurred June 8, 1967, prior to the event on July 16, 1967, herein involved.

Defendants through the years boarded up the windows and doors in an attempt to stop the intrusions. They had posted "no trespass" signs on the land several years before 1967. The nearest one was thirty-five feet from the house. On June 11, 1967, defendants set a "shotgun trap" in the north bedroom. After Mr. Briney cleaned and oiled his 20-gauge shotgun, the power of which he was well aware, defendants took it to the old house where they secured it to an iron bed with the barrel pointed at the bedroom door. It was rigged with wire from the doorknob to the gun's trigger so it would fire when the door was opened. Briney first pointed the gun so an intruder would be hit in the stomach but at Mrs. Briney's suggestion it was lowered to hit the legs. He admitted he did so "because I was mad and tired of being tormented" but "he did not intend to injure anyone." He gave no explanation of why he used a loaded shell and set it to hit a person already in the house. Tin was nailed over the bedroom window. The spring gun could not be seen from the outside. No warning of its presence was posted.

Plaintiff lived with his wife and worked regularly as a gasoline station attendant in Eddyville, seven miles from the old house. He had observed it for several years while hunting in the area and considered it as being abandoned. He knew it had long been uninhabited. In 1967 the area around the house was covered with high weeds. Prior to July 16, 1967, plaintiff and McDonough had been to the premises and found several old bottles and fruit jars which they took and added to their collection of antiques. On the latter day about 9:30 P.M. they made a second trip to the Briney property. They entered the old house by removing a board from a porch window which was without glass. While McDonough was looking around the kitchen area plaintiff went to another part of the house. As he started to open the north bedroom door the shotgun went off striking him in the right leg above the ankle bone. Much of his leg, including part of the tibia, was blown away. Only by McDonough's assistance was plaintiff able to get out of the house and after crawling some distance was put in his vehicle and rushed to a doctor and then to a hospital. He remained in the hospital forty days.

Plaintiff's doctor testified he seriously considered amputation but eventually the healing process was successful. Some weeks after his release from the hospital plaintiff returned to work on crutches. He was required to keep the injured leg in a cast for approximately a year and wear a special brace for another year. He continued to suffer pain during this period.

There was undenied medical testimony plaintiff had a permanent deformity, a loss of tissue, and a shortening of the leg.

The record discloses plaintiff to trial time had incurred $710 medical expense, $2056.85 for hospital service, $61.80 for orthopedic service and $750 as a loss of earnings. In addition thereto the trial court submitted to the jury the question of damages for pain and suffering and for future disability.

Plaintiff testified he knew he had no right to break and enter the house with intent to steal bottles and fruit jars therefrom. He further testified he had entered a plea of guilty to larceny in the nighttime of property of less than $20 value from a private building. He stated he had been fined $50 and costs and paroled during good behavior from a sixty-day jail sentence. Other than minor traffic charges this was plaintiff's first brush with the law. On this civil case appeal it is not our prerogative to review the disposition made of the criminal charge against him.

The main thrust of defendants' defense in the trial court and on this appeal is that "the law permits use of a spring gun in a dwelling or warehouse for the purpose of preventing the unlawful entry of a burglar or thief." They repeated this contention in their exceptions to the trial court's instructions 2, 5, and 6. They took no exception to the trial court's statement of the issues or to other instructions.

In the statement of issues the trial court stated plaintiff and his companion committed a felony when they broke and entered defendants' house. In instruction 2 the court referred to the early case history of the use of spring guns and stated under the law their use was prohibited except to prevent the commission of felonies of violence and where human life is in danger. The instruction included a statement breaking and entering is not a felony of violence.

Instruction 5 stated: "You are hereby instructed that one may use reasonable force in the protection of his property, but such right is subject to the qualification that one may not use such means of force as will take human life or inflict great bodily injury. Such is the rule even though the injured party is a trespasser and is in violation of the law himself."

Instruction 6 stated: "An owner of premises is prohibited from willfully or intentionally injuring a trespasser by means of force that either takes life or inflects great bodily injury; and therefore a person owning a premise is prohibited from setting out 'spring guns' and like dangerous devices which will likely take life or inflict great bodily injury, for the purpose of harming trespassers. The fact that the trespasser may be acting in violation of the law does not change the rule. The only time when such conduct of setting a 'spring gun' or like dangerous device is justified would be when the trespasser was committing a felony of violence or a felony punishable by death, or where the trespasser was endangering human life by his act."

Instruction 7, to which defendants made no objection or exception, stated: "To entitle the plaintiff to recover for compensatory damages, the burden of proof is upon him to establish by a preponderance of the evidence each and all of the following propositions:

"1. That defendants erected a shotgun trap in a vacant house on land owned by defendant, Bertha L. Briney, on or about June 11, 1967, which fact was known only by them, to protect household goods from trespassers and thieves.

"2. That the force used by defendants was in excess of that force reasonably necessary and which persons are entitled to use in the protection of their property.

"3. That plaintiff was injured and damaged and the amount thereof.

"4. That plaintiff's injuries and damages resulted directly from the discharge of the shotgun trap which was set and used by defendants."

The overwhelming weight of authority, both textbook and case law, supports the trial court's statement of the applicable principles of law.

Prosser on Torts, third edition, pages 116–18, states: the law has always placed a higher value upon human safety than upon mere rights in property, it is the accepted rule that there is no privilege to use any force calculated to cause death or serious bodily injury to repel the threat to land or chattels, unless there is also such a threat to the defendant's personal safety as to justify a self-defense. ... Spring guns and other man-killing devices are not justifiable against a mere trespasser, or even a petty thief. They are privileged only against those upon whom the landowner, if he were present in person would be free to inflict injury of the same kind.

Restatement of Torts, section 85, page 180, states:
The value of human life and limbs, not only to the individual concerned but also to society, so outweighs the interest of a possessor of land in excluding from it those whom he is not willing to admit thereto that a possessor of land has, as is stated in § 79, no privilege to use force intended or likely to cause death or serious harm against another whom the possessor sees about to enter his premises or meddle with his chattel, unless the intrusion threatens death or serious bodily harm to the occupiers or users of the premises. ... A possessor of land cannot do indirectly and by a mechanical device that which, were he present, he could not do immediately and in person. Therefore, he cannot gain a privilege to install, for the purpose of protecting his land from intrusions harmless to the lives and limbs of the occupiers or users of it, a mechanical device whose only purpose is to inflict death or serious harm upon such as may intrude, by giving notice of his intention to inflict, by mechanical means and indirectly, harm which he could not, even after request, inflict directly were he present.

In Hooker v. Miller, 37 Iowa 613, we held defendant vineyard owner liable for damages resulting from a spring gun shot although plaintiff was a trespasser and there to steal grapes. At pages 614, 615, this statement is made: "This court has held that a mere trespass against property other than a dwelling is not a sufficient justification to authorize the use of a deadly weapon by the owner in its defense; and that if death results in such a case it will be murder, though the killing be actually necessary to prevent the trespass. State v. Vance, 17 Iowa 138." At page 617 this court said: "[T]respassers and other inconsiderable violators of the law are not to be visited by barbarous punishments or prevented by inhuman inflictions of bodily injuries."

The facts in Allison v. Fiscus, 156 Ohio 120, 100 N.E.2d 237, 44 A.L.R.2d 369, decided in 1951, are very similar to the casé at bar. There plaintiff's right to damages was recognized for injuries received when he feloniously broke a door latch and started to enter defendant's warehouse with intent to steal. As he entered a trap of two sticks of dynamite buried under the doorway by defendant owner was set off and plaintiff seriously injured. The court held the question whether a particular trap was justified as a use of reasonable and necessary force against a trespasser engaged in the commission of a felony should have been submitted to the jury. The Ohio Supreme Court recognized plaintiff's right to recover punitive or exemplar damages in addition to compensatory damages.

In United Zinc & Chemical Co. v. Britt. 258 U.S. 268, 275, 42 S.Ct. 299, page 299, 66 L.Ed. 615, 617, the Court states: "The liability for spring guns and mantraps arises from the fact that the defendant has ... expected the trespasser and prepared an injury that is no more justified than if he had held the gun and fired it."

In addition to civil liability many jurisdictions hold a land owner criminally liable for serious injuries or homicide caused by spring guns or other set devices. See State v. Childers, 133 Ohio 508, 14 N.E.2d 767 (melon thief shot by spring gun); Pierce v. Commonwealth, 135 Va. 635, 115 S.E. 686 (policeman killed by spring gun when he opened unlocked front door of defendant's shoe repair shop); State v. Marfaudille, 48 Wash. 117, 92 P. 939 (murder conviction for death from spring gun set in a trunk); State v. Beckham, 306 Mo. 566, 267 S.W. 817 (boy killed by spring gun attached to window of defendant's chili stand); State v. Green, 118 S.C. 279, 110 S.E. 145, 19 A.L.R. 1431 (intruder shot by spring gun when he broke and entered vacant house).

In Wisconsin, Oregon, and England the use of spring guns and similar devices is specifically made unlawful by statute. 44 A.L.R., section 3, pages 386, 388.

The legal principles stated by the trial court in instructions 2, 5, and 6 are well established and supported by the authorities cited and quoted supra. There is no merit in defendants' objections and exceptions thereto. Defendants' various motions based on the same reasons stated in exceptions to instructions were properly overruled.

Plaintiff's claim and the jury's allowance of punitive damages, under the trial court's instructions relating thereto, were not at any time or in any manner challenged by defendants in the trial court as not allowable. We therefore are not presented with the problem of whether the $10,000 award should be allowed to stand.

We express no opinion as to whether punitive damages are allowable in this type of case. If defendants' attorneys wanted that issue decided it was their duty to raise it in the trial court.

The rule is well established that we will not consider a contention not raised in the trial court. In other words we are a court of review and will not consider a contention raised for the first time in this court.

Under our law punitive damages are not allowed as a matter of right. When malice is shown or when a defendant acted with wanton and reckless disregard of the rights of others, punitive damages may be allowed as punishment to the defendant and as a deterrent to others. Although not meant to compensate a plaintiff, the result is to increase his recovery. He is the fortuitous beneficiary of such an award simply because there is no one else to receive it.

The jury's findings of fact including a finding defendants acted with malice and with wanton and reckless disregard, as required for an allowance of punitive or exemplary damages, are supported by substantial evidence. We are bound thereby.

This opinion is not to be taken or construed as authority that the allowance of punitive damages is or is not proper under circumstances such as exist here. We hold only that question of law not having been properly raised cannot in this case be resolved.

Study and careful consideration of defendants' contentions on appeal reveal no reversible error.

Affirmed.

Larson, Justice (dissenting). I respectfully dissent, first, because the majority wrongfully assumes that by installing a spring gun in the bedroom of their unoccupied house the defendants intended to shoot any intruder who attempted to enter the room. Under the record presented here, that was a fact question. Unless it is held that these property owners are liable for injury to an intruder from such a device regardless of the intent with which it is installed, liability under these pleadings must rest upon two definite issues of fact, i.e., did the defendants intend to shoot the invader, and if so, did they employ unnecessary and unreasonable force against him?

It is my feeling that the majority oversimplifies the impact of this case on the law, not only in this but other jurisdictions, and that it has not thought through all the ramifications of this holding.

There being no statutory provisions governing the right of an owner to defend his property by the use of a spring gun or other like device, or of a criminal invader to recover punitive damages when injured by such an instrumentality while breaking into the building of another, our interest and attention are directed to what should be the court determination of public policy in these matters. On both issues we are faced with a case of first impression. We should accept the task and clearly establish the law in this jurisdiction hereafter. I would hold there is no absolute liability for injury to a criminal intruder by setting up such a device on his property, and unless done with an intent to kill or seriously injure the intruder, I would absolve the owner from liability other than for negligence. I would also hold the court had no jurisdiction to allow punitive damages when the intruder was engaged in a serious criminal offense such as breaking and entering with intent to steal.

CASE QUESTIONS

1. Do you agree with the majority opinion of the court or with the dissenter?
2. Should this case have been treated as one of first impression considering the public policy issues involved?
3. Could the state legislature overrule the supreme court and change the law?
4. Is there a conflict of law involved in this case?

Contracts

In the *Marvin* case, the court's decision illustrates that even oral promises may create legal obligations for the parties involved. The plaintiff in this case filed the suit in contract and did not attempt to rely on the concept of common law marriage that is recognized in some states. Contracts must be made under conditions required by law in order to be enforced by the courts: the contracting parties must be of legal age, there must be an exchange of some consideration of value between the two parties, and the contract cannot involve a promise to do an illegal act.

Marvin v. Marvin
134 Cal. Rptr. 815, 557 P.2d 106
Supreme Court of California
December 27, 1976

TOBRINER, JUSTICE. During the past 15 years, there has been a substantial increase in the number of couples living together without marrying. Such nonmarital relationships lead to legal controversy when one partner dies or the couple separates. We take this opportunity to declare the principles which should govern distribution of property acquired in a nonmarital relationship.

We conclude that the courts should enforce express contracts between nonmarital partners except to the extent that the contract is explicity founded on the consideration of meretricious sexual services.

In the instant case plaintiff, Michelle Marvin, and defendant, Lee Marvin, lived together for seven years without marrying; all property acquired during this period was taken in defendant's name. When plaintiff sued to enforce a contract under which she was entitled to half the property and to support payments, the trial court granted judgment on the pleadings for defendant, thus leaving him with all property accumulated by the couple during their relationship.

Plaintiff avers that in October of 1964 she and defendant "entered into an oral agreement" that while "the parties lived together they would combine their efforts and earnings and would share equally any and all property accumulated as a result of their efforts whether individual or combined." Furthermore, they agreed to "hold themselves out to the general public as husband and wife" and that "plaintiff would further render her services as a companion, homemaker, housekeeper and cook to . . . defendant."

Shortly thereafter plaintiff agreed to "give up her lucrative career as an entertainer and singer" in order to "devote her full time to defendant as a companion, homemaker, housekeeper and cook;" in return defendant agreed to "provide for all of plaintiff's financial support and needs for the rest of her life."

Plaintiff alleges that she lived with defendant from October of 1964 through May of 1970 and fulfilled her obligations under the agreement. During this period the parties as a result of their efforts and earnings acquired in defendant's name substantial real and personal property, including motion picture rights worth over $1 million. In May of 1970, however, defendant compelled plaintiff to leave his household. He continued to support plaintiff until November of 1971, but thereafter refused to provide further support.

On the basis of these allegations plaintiff asserts two causes of action. The first, for declaratory relief, asks the court to determine her contract and property rights; the second seeks to impose a constructive trust upon one half of the property acquired during the course of the relationship.

In Trutalli v. Meraviglia (1932) 215 Cal. 698, 12 P.2d 430 we established the principle that nonmarital partners may lawfully contract concerning the ownership of property acquired during the relationship. We reaffirmed this principle in Vallera v. Vallera (1943) 21 Cal.2d 681, 685, 134 P.2d 761, 763, stating that "If a man and woman [who are not married] live together as husband and wife under an agreement to pool their earnings and share equally in their joint accumulations, equity will protect the interests of each in such property."

In the case before us plaintiff, basing her cause of action in contract upon these precedents, maintains that the trial court erred in denying her a trial on the merits of her contention. Although that court did not specify the ground for its conclusion that plaintiff's contractual allegations stated no cause of action, defendant offers some four theories to sustain the ruling; we proceed to examine them.

Defendant first and principally relies on the contention that the alleged contract is so closely related to the supposed "immoral" character of the relationship between plaintiff and himself that the enforcement of the contract would violate public policy. He points to cases asserting that a contract between nonmarital partners is unenforceable if it is "involved in" an illicit relationship. A review of the numerous California decisions concerning contracts between nonmarital partners, however, reveals that the courts have not employed such broad and uncertain standards to strike down contracts. The decisions instead disclose a narrower and more precise standard: a contract between nonmarital partners is unenforceable only to the extent that it explicitly rests upon the immoral and illicit consideration of meretricious sexual services.

Although the past decisions hover over the issue in the somewhat wispy form of the figures of a Chagall painting, we can abstract from those decisions a clear and simple rule. The fact that a man and woman live together without marriage, and engage in a sexual relationship, does not in itself invalidate agreements between them relating to their earnings, property, or expenses. Neither is such an agreement invalid merely because the parties may have contemplated the creation or continuation of a nonmarital relationship when they entered into it. Agreements between nonmarital partners fail only to the extent that they rest upon a consideration of meretricious sexual services. Thus the rule asserted by defendant, that a contract fails if it is "involved in" or made "in contemplation" of a nonmarital relationship, cannot be reconciled with the decisions.

Defendant secondly relies upon the ground suggested by the trial court: that the 1964 contract violated public policy because it impaired the community property rights of Betty Marvin, defendant's lawful wife. Defendant points out that his earnings while living apart from his wife before rendition of the interlocutory decree were community property under 1964 statutory law and that defendant's agreement with plaintiff purported to transfer to her a half interest in that community property. But whether or not defendant's contract with plaintiff exceeded his authority as manager of the community property defendant's argument fails for the reason that an improper transfer of community property is not void *ab initio*, but merely voidable at the instance of the aggrieved spouse.

In the present case Betty Marvin, the aggrieved spouse, had the opportunity to assert her community property rights in the divorce action. The interlocutory and final decrees in that action fix and limit her interest. Enforcement of the contract between plaintiff and defendant against property awarded to defendant by the divorce decree will not impair any right of Betty's, and thus is not on that account violative of public policy.

Defendant's third contention is noteworthy for the lack of authority advanced in its support. He contends that enforcement of the oral agreement between plaintiff and himself is barred by Civil Code section 5134, which provides that "All contracts for marriage settlements must be in writing. . . ." A marriage settlement, however, is an agreement in contemplation of marriage in which each party agrees to release or modify the property rights which would otherwise arise from the marriage. The contract at issue here does not conceivably fall within that definition, and thus is beyond the compass of section 5134.

Defendant finally argues that enforcement of the contract is barred by Civil Code section 43.5, subdivision (d), which provides that "No cause of action arises for . . . [b]reach of a promise of marriage." This rather strained contention proceeds from the premise that a promise of marriage impliedly includes a promise to support and to pool property acquired after marriage to the conclusion that pooling and support agreements not part of or accompanied by promise of marriage are barred by the section. We conclude that section 43.5 is not reasonably susceptible to the interpretation advanced by defendant, a conclusion demonstrated by the fact that since section 43.5 was enacted in 1939, numerous cases have enforced pooling agreements between nonmarital partners, and in none did court or counsel refer to section 43.5

In summary, we base our opinion on the principle that adults who voluntarily live together and engage in sexual relations are nonetheless as competent as any other persons to contract respecting their earnings and property rights. Of course, they cannot lawfully contract to pay for the performance of sexual services, for such a contract is, in essence, an agreement for prostitution and unlawful for that reason. But they may agree to pool their earnings and to hold all property acquired during the relationship in accord with the law governing community property; conversely they may agree that each partner's earnings and the property acquired from those earnings remain the separate property of the earning partner. So long as the agreement does not rest upon illicit meretricious consideration, the parties may order their economic affairs as they choose, and no policy precludes the courts from enforcing such agreements.

In the present instance, plaintiff alleges that the parties agreed to pool their earnings, that they contracted to share equally in all property acquired, and that defendant agreed to support plaintiff. The terms of the contract as alleged do not rest upon any unlawful consideration. We therefore conclude that the complaint furnishes a suitable basis upon which the trial court can render declaratory relief. The trial court consequently erred in granting defendant's motion for judgment on the pleadings.

CASE QUESTIONS

1. Has the court decided that the plaintiff has a valid contract in this case? Why or why not?

2. Is the court making new law in the case, or merely relying on stare decisis?

3. What considerations of morality are involved in the *Marvin* case?

4. How is the concept of equity illustrated in the case?

APPENDIX C
WITNESS STATEMENTS

Witness Statement 1
JANE CONSUMER

This statement was given by Jane Consumer on September 10, 1992, during deposition attended by Bill Green and Maria Farmer, and before a notary public.

1 My name is Jane Consumer. I am forty-six years old and am the wife of the deceased,
2 William P. Consumer. I am a housewife, married to the deceased for the past twenty years,
3 and mother of three children, ages 19, 15, and 7, at the time of the accident that killed my
4 husband.
5 On the evening of the accident, my husband and I were returning home from shop-
6 ping and dinner in Capital City, thirty miles from our home. My husband, Bill, was driving
7 our family car, a 1990 Supreme Brougham Executive. We were nearly home when a rain
8 shower began to fall. I noticed that Bill was going about 65, and he slowed down to about
9 60 as he turned the windshield wipers on. We came upon a van traveling in the right lane
10 of the interstate highway at a slower speed. Bill turned the wheel to pass the van and I
11 heard a loud noise, like something popped under the car. Bill screamed in panic, as he
12 tried to get back into the left traffic lane. "My God, the wheel won't turn!" he shouted. By
13 this time the car was going across the grassy part of the median and seemed to speed up.
14 I could see a truck in front of us on the opposite side of the interstate and I closed my eyes
15 and tried to brace myself. That's all I remember about the crash.
16 I remember an officer asking me if I could move my limbs. He may have prevented me
17 from injuring my spinal cord by keeping me calm until the ambulance arrived. They put a
18 brace on me and lifted me into the ambulance. Bill was unconscious and bleeding on the
19 driver's side. The emergency crew went back to help him. It seemed like forever before they
20 brought him back in a stretcher into the ambulance with me. He never regained conscious-
21 ness while the ambulance attendant worked over him trying to give him blood. They did
22 their best to save him.
23 They kept me in the hospital for two weeks. The doctors put me under sedation and
24 reset my back. When I regained consciousness, I was in traction and was kept that way for
25 a week and a half. Even after they released me from the hospital, I had to go back for
26 therapy three times a week. Luckily everything has healed.
27 The car we were driving at the time of the accident was purchased from the City Auto
28 Company on October 20, 1989. It was a 1990 model, and we took it in for regular mainte-
29 nance. Last winter we had some trouble with it on snow and ice. It was always getting
30 stuck, even on a slight hill, and Bill got mad when we had to get someone to help us. He
31 also noticed that the car leaned to the left when it was standing on the flat surface of our
32 driveway. He told me he had complained to the service department at the City Auto Com-
33 pany, but they indicated that there was nothing wrong with it.
34 We had driven the car for two years, and it only had 22,000 miles on it when the acci-
35 dent occurred. Bill had received a recall letter from the factory just before the accident. He
36 planned to take it into the garage to get the needed repairs when the accident took place.
37 He received the letter on Thursday and the accident occurred the next day, on September
38 8, 1991.

                                                                              Jane Consumer

SEAL OF NOTARY PUBLIC

Witness Statement 2
JIM TRUCKER

This statement was given by Jim Trucker on September 11, 1992, at a deposition attended by Bill Green and Maria Farmer, and before a notary public.

1 My name is Jim Trucker. I am thirty-six years old and have been employed by Big City
2 Haulers, Inc., for the last five years. I live in Capital City, Middle State. I was driving an
3 eighteen-wheel, tractor-trailer rig from River City to Capital City on the night of September
4 8, 1991, when an automobile driven by the deceased, William P. Consumer, collided with
5 the rear corner of my trailer.
6 I was going about 65 on Interstate 24, traveling north toward Capital City. A rainstorm
7 set in just before the accident. It was dark, about 10:30 at night, and I had just come un-
8 der an overpass when I saw lights coming at me from the opposite side of the interstate.
9 They were coming right at me, so I "put the pedal to the metal" and sped up as much as
10 possible to try to get past before the other vehicle collided with my truck. It was the only
11 thing I could think of to do at the time. I could see the car missed by tractor, but I felt the
12 crash that caused the rig to begin to sway. I knew it had hit my trailer, so I pulled over as
13 soon as possible. I put out my hazard lights and went back to check on the wreck. I could
14 see it was bad and that the passengers needed help right away. So I got back in the cab
15 and used my CB radio to call for help.
16 Then I went to the wreck. I could see that the driver's side was collapsed, and I didn't
17 even try to open it. The passenger side was free, and I opened the door. Jane Consumer
18 was unconscious in the passenger seat. She had taken a bad crash, and I didn't think I
19 should try to move her. The highway patrol car arrived in a few minutes, and I was glad to
20 let the officer take over.
21 The police officer and I helped the ambulance emergency crew to free the driver, and
22 they took the two passengers off to the hospital. By this time it had stopped raining, and I
23 went back to check on my rig. The left rear corner of my trailer was smashed and the tail-
24 gate was bent back toward the right side, but I was able to move it. I recorded the license
25 number of the vehicle that hit me, and talked with the patrolman while he filled out the ac-
26 cident report.

Jim Trucker

SEAL OF NOTARY PUBLIC

Witness Statement 3
GEORGE GOODCOP

This statement was given by Patrolman George Goodcop on September 14, 1992, at a deposition attended by Bill Green and Maria Farmer, and before a notary public.

1 My name is Patrolman George Goodcop. I am thirty years old and have been a high-
2 way patrolman for the past four years. I was on duty driving patrol on Interstate 24 when
3 the accident involving the death of William P. Consumer took place on September 8, 1991.
4 I received a call from the dispatcher at about 10:40 p.m. informing me of an accident
5 about three miles from Centerville on I-24 north. Since I was very close to this location, it
6 only took me about five minutes to arrive on the scene. Jim Trucker was already on the
7 scene, and there was no immediate danger to other vehicles. The wrecked passenger car
8 was off of the highway on the right side of the northbound portion of the interstate, and
9 the trucker assured me that his vehicle was well off the highway and marked with hazard
10 lights.
11 The trucker had opened the passenger door of the crashed automobile and a female
12 passenger was strapped in a forward position, her head leaning against the dash. She
13 was regaining consciousness, and I asked her to see if she could move her legs and arms.
14 She indicated that she could and attempted to right herself in the seat. This obviously
15 caused her pain, and I cautioned her to stay in her original position. Her back was more
16 than likely injured, and I wanted the medics to remove her with their equipment.
17 I used my flashlight to try to examine the driver, but could conclude very little about his
18 condition. His face was smashed up against the window and he was wrapped around the
19 steering wheel. Blood was everywhere, and I knew he was in very bad condition. The driv-
20 er's side of the vehicle was crushed, and the driver could not be accessed through the
21 driver's door.
22 The ambulance arrived in about ten minutes, by this time it was nearly 11:00. The
23 emergency crew removed the passenger, and then we all helped to pry the driver's door
24 open to remove the driver. As I stated in my accident report, the passenger was wearing
25 her seat belt, but the driver was not wearing a seat belt. The automobile involved was rest-
26 ing with the front facing west and was located on the right far side of the interstate north-
27 bound lanes. From the condition of the vehicle, it had obviously taken the impact of the
28 crash on the driver's side.
29 After inspecting the condition of the tractor-trailer rig and the skid marks across the
30 median, it was clear that the driver of the passenger car had lost control while driving
31 south on the interstate and had proceeded across the median, colliding with the trailer of
32 the trucker's rig on the rear corner. The motor and hood of the passenger car had hit the
33 trucker's tailgate, and the driver's side had received the full impact of the corner of the
34 trailer. I made the following sketch of the collision in my report.

_____
George Goodcop

SEAL OF NOTARY PUBLIC

Witness Statement 4
MACK RACER

This statement was given by Mack Racer on September 15, 1992, at a deposition attended by Bill Green and Maria Farmer, and before a notary public.

1   My name is Mack Racer. I'm forty years old and am self-employed as the owner of
2   Speed Shop in Centerville, Middle State. I trained as a mechanic, obtaining a certificate of
3   qualification from the Factory Motor Company in 1982. I also have twenty years of experi-
4   ence working on Factory Motor Company vehicles as well as those of other manufacturers.
5   I have worked for several nationally famous race car drivers as a mechanic and engineer-
6   ing consultant regarding safety features of racing stock cars.
7   I was asked to inspect the 1990 Supreme Brougham Executive owned by William P.
8   Consumer. It had been towed to a garage in Centerville where I examined the wreckage
9   carefully. I jacked up the vehicle and removed the suspension coils from both sides of the
10 undercarriage. The left coil spring was broken in half and was obviously made of thinner
11 metal than the coil spring removed from the right side. These springs hold the passenger
12 vehicle about six inches above the axle to ensure a smooth ride. If one of them breaks at
13 the base, as in this case, the car would drop about six inches to the left. This would ac-
14 count for the driver's inability to right the vehicle in a turn.
15   The coils that I removed are in the possession of the plaintiff, and I can attest to the
16 fact that they do not belong on the same vehicle. They were obviously made for two differ-
17 ent vehicles having different weights and suspension requirements. I don't know how they
18 got on this vehicle, but they should not have been used together. Both of these coils should
19 have been identical. Their differences would account for the leaning to the left complained
20 of by the plaintiff. I measured them, and the left coil (complete) is about one inch shorter
21 than the right coil.
22   A reasonably alert mechanic trained by the Factory Motor Company should have de-
23 tected the difference from a visual inspection and the vehicle's appearance, since the com-
24 plaint noted the leaning to the left. An inspection of the vehicle after the accident indicates
25 that it was unlikely that the left coil was damaged by the impact of the collision. The stress
26 from the impact would have been on the right coil, since it would have had to absorb the
27 impact to the left driver's side. At any rate, I don't think the collision broke the coil. It must
28 have happened before the accident.

                                          Mack Racer

SEAL OF NOTARY PUBLIC

Witness Statement 5
SUPERIOR TESTER

This statement was given by Superior Tester on August 6, 1992, at a deposition attended by John Gaither and Cora Smith, and before a notary public.

1 My name is Superior Tester. I am forty-six years old and have been employed by the
2 Factory Motor Company for the past eight years as a laboratory technician and safety en-
3 gineer. I was promoted two years ago to director of testing for the company. I have a mas-
4 ters degree in mechanical engineering from the Massachusetts Institute of Technology.
5   In January of 1991, my lab was asked to test coils manufactured by our supplier, Ace
6 Suppliers, Inc. The Factory Motor Company production director indicated on the work or-
7 der that there had been a mix-up and these coils were mounted on 250 of our 1990 Su-
8 preme Brougham Executive model autos by mistake. The order required that we test the
9 coils that were mistakenly mounted on these passenger cars. We have three simulation ma-
10 chines that replicate the wear and stress on such coils; so we set up the test on all three
11 machines with a mistaken coil and a normal coil mounted on each machine.
12   After the machines had been running for a simulation equivalent of more than 200,000
13 miles, the coils we were testing began to break. The first coil to break was one of the mis-
14 takenly mounted coils. It broke at 1726 hours, or the equivalent of 207,120 miles. The sec-
15 ond coil to break was one of the normal coils that broke at 1824 hours. Another mistaken
16 coil broke at 1891 hours, when we stopped our testing. Our normal wear standard is 1700,
17 or the equivalent of 204,400 miles. Since the mistaken coils met this standard, we con-
18 cluded that the coils were safe under normal driving conditions for the expected life of the
19 vehicle.
20   The coils in question were about one inch shorter than the normal coil and would have
21 caused some tilting of the vehicle. The suspension coils are primarily to ensure a smooth
22 ride, and even if one broke, it would not cause the vehicle to go out of control. The vehicle
23 would be supported by the shock absorbers and would not drop more than three inches. It
24 would cause some noise and discomfort, but would not cause an accident under normal
25 driving conditions.
26   At a conference with the production director in May of 1991, we discussed this prob-
27 lem, and he concluded that it would not be necessary to recall the vehicles in question
28 based on our lab report. Later in August of 1991, we had a second conference on this
29 subject. He told me they had been getting a number of complaints about the appearance
30 of the automobiles while standing on a flat surface. At this time, we decided to recall them
31 and have the coils replaced, primarily to satisfy customer complaints. We did not believe
32 these coils posed a safety hazard. We have no reports of accidents in our records concern-
33 ing this problem, with the exception of the case in question here.

                                                                                       Superior Tester

SEAL OF NOTARY PUBLIC

Witness Statement 6
JACKIE LIFESAVER

This statement was given by Jackie Lifesaver on September 18, 1992, at a deposition attended by John Gaither and Cora Smith, and before a notary public.

1   My name is Jackie Lifesaver. I am thirty-five years old and have been employed by the
2   Rural County Emergency Squad for the past six years. I am a licensed emergency medical
3   attendant and was in charge of the emergency team that assisted Mrs. Consumer and her
4   husband on the night of the accident.
5   My assistant, Ron Helper, and I received an emergency call to a location about three
6   miles from Centerville on I-24 north at about 10:40 p.m. on September 8, 1991. When we
7   arrived on the scene, the highway patrol officer was already there. We were able to re-
8   move the female passenger after applying a back brace and carefully placing her on the
9   stretcher. The driver was in worse shape. His side of the vehicle was crushed, and we had
10 to use special prying equipment we carry to open the door on his side. I crawled in from
11 the opposite side across the passenger's seat and tried to stop the bleeding. I got a faint
12 pulse, but there was no way to stop the bleeding. His head was smashed partly through
13 the windshield, but his more serious injuries were in the chest area.
14 He was not wearing a seat belt, and the impact of the crash had thrust him against
15 the steering column. I knew this meant internal bleeding and chest wounds. An air bag or
16 seat belts could have saved him, but neither were employed. I smelled alcohol on his
17 breath and observed an empty beer can on the floorboard next to the driver's seat.
18 By this time, my assistant and the patrol officer had managed to free the driver's door,
19 and we were able to remove him from the vehicle. We set up a blood transfusion before
20 leaving for the hospital. I was driving and my assistant was attending the victims in the rear
21 of the emergency vehicle. When we arrived at the hospital, the emergency doctor on duty
22 checked the driver's vital signs and could get no pulse.

Jackie Lifesaver

SEAL OF NOTARY PUBLIC

Witness Statement 7
PROFESSOR DRIVESAFE

This statement was given by Professor Drivesafe on August 8, 1992, at a deposition attended by John Gaither and Cora Smith, and before a notary public.

1 My name is Professor Drivesafe. I am fifty-two years old and am employed as profes-
2 sor of safety engineering at Lake State University. I have a master's degree from Lake State
3 University in engineering and a Ph.D. from the California Institute of Technology. My partic-
4 ular field of expertise is in automobile safety, and I have served as a consultant in numer-
5 ous automobile accidents where I have been called upon to assess the causes of these
6 accidents. I have also authored several professional papers on the causes of automobile
7 accidents and safety engineering.
8   I was asked to examine the automobile involved in the accident that took place on
9 I-24 on September 8, 1991, and to assess the causes of this accident. After thorough in-
10 vestigation of the automobile, the two coils removed from the vehicle, and the scene of the
11 crash, it is my scientific judgment that the accident was caused by hydroplaning due to the
12 rain storm that was occurring at the time of the accident.
13   The scene of the accident presents a classic example of the type of gentle slope that
14 produces the conditions for vehicle hydroplaning when there is a heavy rain. That area re-
15 corded one inch of rain in less than half an hour on the night of the accident. This amount
16 of rainfall would produce enough water flowing down the slope in question to raise the
17 front wheels above the surface of the pavement. This would account for the driver's inability
18 to steer the vehicle.
19   The broken coil was most likely a result of the impact and spinning of the vehicle after
20 the crash. The vehicle struck the rear corner of the truck and was pulled around by the
21 tractor-trailer's forward motion, so that it made a complete turn, ending up facing in the
22 opposite direction from that of initial impact.
23   The Department of Transportation safety standards were not violated by the coils used
24 in the production of the vehicle in question. There are no suspension coil standards im-
25 posed by federal authority. The coil suspension on this vehicle is a comfort feature and not
26 a vital engineering component. Even if the coil did break at a crucial moment, the shock
27 absorbers would have prevented it from affecting the steering capabilities of the vehicle. I
28 cannot conclude from these facts that the suspension coil in question was the cause of the
29 accident.

_____
Professor Drivesafe

SEAL OF NOTARY PUBLIC

Witness Statement 8
JAN INTERN

This statement was given by Dr. Jan Intern on September 18, 1992, at a deposition attended by John Gaither and Cora Smith, and before a notary public.

1 My name is Jan Intern. I am forty-two years old and I am presently self-employed in
2 my own private practice as a physician specializing in internal medicine. I graduated from
3 Vanderbilt Medical School in 1989 and was employed as emergency intern at Mid-State
4 Hospital in Centerville from October 1, 1989, to November 10, 1991.
5 On the evening of September 8, 1991, I was serving as emergency medical physician
6 at Mid-State Hospital. We received a call from the medics at about 11:15 p.m. indicating
7 that two severely injured patients were in route to the hospital. When they arrived at about
8 11:25 p.m., I examined the two patients as quickly as possible. The male patient was the
9 most severely injured and was suffering from internal bleeding caused by severe chest
10 wounds. We could not get a pulse and attempted to revive his heart function. This proce-
11 dure was unsuccessful, and I concluded that any further attempt to revive him would be
12 futile. The female patient suffered severe back injury but had been carefully handled by the
13 medics and was properly transported, preventing further injury. We stabilized her condition
14 and x-rayed the extent of the damage to the spine.
15 Later I reexamined the body of the male patient to determine the cause of death and
16 to file a death certificate. X-rays revealed that the impact to his chest had crushed his heart
17 and severed internal arteries, causing massive bleeding that filled the chest cavity. We
18 could have saved him if he had been wearing a seat belt or if the car had been equipped
19 with a driver's side air bag. This kind of injury could only have been caused by impact
20 against the steering wheel. His head injuries were minor and would not have caused
21 death.
22 I did smell alcohol on his breath so I took some blood samples, but because he had
23 been given two pints of whole blood by the medics, the sample would be of no value in
24 determining how much alcohol he had consumed.

                                                                             Jan Intern

SEAL OF NOTARY PUBLIC

GLOSSARY OF KEY TERMS

Accessory after the fact. A person who, knowing a felony to have been committed by another, receives, relieves, comforts, or assists the felon.

Accomplice. One who knowingly, voluntarily, and with common intent unites with the principal offender in the commission of a crime; one who is in some way concerned or associated in commission of a crime; partaker of guilt; one who aids or assists or is an accessory.

Actus reus. A wrongful act or deed that renders the actor criminally liable if combined with mens rea.

Administrative courts. Separate and independent courts in Germany, France, and other countries that provide individuals with simplified access to courts to adjudicate disputes with governmental agencies.

Administrative due process. The minimal requirements of administrative legal procedure, which are notice, fair hearing, and conformity with the established rules of the administrative agency.

Administrative law. The branch of law that includes the entire range of action by government with respect to the citizen and by the citizen with respect to government. All legal matters not classified as civil or criminal legal actions are administrative in character.

More specifically, the area of law that creates administrative agencies, establishes their authority to make rules and their methods of procedures, determines their scope of judicial review of agency practices and actions, and sets forth the rights of persons and companies regulated by these agencies. The term also describes the rules and regulations made by administrative agencies.

Administrative law judge (ALJ). One who presides at an administrative hearing with power to make agency determinations of fact. Federal ALJs were formerly called "hearing examiners." The Administrative Procedures Act has provided these federal officers with greater independence than that which they had in the past.

Administrative legal action. A legal action brought against the administrative agency involving an administrative process of appeal through internal fact-finding procedures that resemble the judicial process. (See Administrative due process.)

Administrative procedures acts. Laws enacted by federal and many state jurisdictions governing practices and proceedings before administrative agencies; these acts also regulate the rule-making process of agencies. The federal law enacted by Congress in 1946 can be found at 60 Stat. 237, 5 U.S.C.A.

Adversarial process. Common law trial procedures in contested cases in which lawyers play the dominant role, in a contest of lawyers, in questioning witnesses at trial and in persuading the jury or judge.

The fundamental assumption of this process is that the contest between lawyers and witnesses before an impartial judge and jury will make the truth known.

Affidavit. A written statement of facts, made voluntarily, and confirmed by oath or affirmation.

Affirmative defense. A matter constituting a defense that relieves the defendant of legal liability. Disproving one of the elements required by tort or contract law is also an affirmative defense. (See Comparative negligence; Contributory negligence; Voluntary assumption of known risk.)

Aggravating circumstances. Any circumstance attending the commission of a crime or tort that increases the defendant's guilt or the enormity of the crime or that adds to its injurious consequences, but which is above and beyond the essential constituents of the crime or tort itself. (See contrasting term "mitigating circumstances")

Aiding and abetting. The act of advising, counseling, procuring, or encouraging another to commit a crime. One who assists another to commit a crime may be a principal, if present, or an accessory before or after the fact of the crime.

Alternative dispute resolution (ADR). A modern movement to encourage use of alternative methods of dispute resolution to relieve the congestion in the courts. The basic alternative methods are conciliation, mediation, and arbitration.

American Bar Association (ABA). A voluntary national association that represents the legal profession in the United States. The association is influential in developing model ethical standards and issuing opinions interpreting these rules that have been adopted by most state and local bar associations.

Analogistic reasoning. That form of legal reasoning by analogy, or analysis of likeness. Stare decisis requires classification of fact situations as being included or excluded from the precedent in question. Like situations must be treated in like manner.

Answer. The response to a civil complaint filed against the defendant. The answer is one of the basic pleadings; failure to respond to a complaint may result in judgment by default to the plaintiff.

Appeals court. Courts above the trial court in the hierarchy of courts (generally called courts of appeal and supreme courts). These courts function as courts of review regarding decisions and fact-finding processes that have taken place in lower level courts. At least three judges consider questions of law in dispute.

Appellant. Party bringing the appeal, who also has the burden of proof on appeal. Either party may appeal.

Appellate brief. Written argument that must be filed on appeal by the appellant (party bringing the appeal).

Appellate courts. (See Appeals courts.)

Appellee. Party against whom the appeal is filed. This party may have been either the plaintiff or defendant at trial.

Arbitration. Settlement of disputes by prior agreement to accept the decision of a third party as authoritative. Arbitration agreements in areas such as labor-management disputes traditionally are part of the contracts negotiated between the parties. Arbitrators are drawn from a mutually acceptable list of professionals. (See also Conciliation; Mediation.)

Court-annexed arbitration is a new development imposed by many courts at both the state and federal levels. In this situation, the arbitrator's decision can be appealed in the regular courts.

Arraignment. Procedure whereby the accused is brought before the court to plead to the criminal charges in the indictment or information.

Arrest. To deprive a person of liberty by legal authority.

Arrest warrant. A written order, made on behalf of the state based on a complaint issued pursuant to a statute or court rule, that commands a law enforcement officer to arrest and bring a person before a magistrate.

Attorneys' conference. A conference between the opposing attorneys in a lawsuit. The most important conference takes place after the discovery period and prior to the judge's conference with the attorneys; the purpose of the meeting is to clarify issues in dispute and provide an opportunity for out-of-court settlement.

Axiom. A maxim widely accepted on its intrinsic merit; a proposition regarded as a self-evident truth.

Bail. A monetary amount that will procure the release of one charged with an offense and will ensure that person's future attendance in court and compel that person to remain within the jurisdiction of the court.

Bar Examination. A test administered by state bar associations and required as a condition for acquiring a license to practice law in that state. There is a federal bar examination process that is necessary to obtain a license to practice law before the United States Supreme Court. Most states and the federal courts have reciprocal agreements to honor the licenses of other states after a lawyer has practiced law for more than five years.

Barrister. A member of an elite core of lawyers in England who is authorized to argue most serious cases for litigants at trial. The preliminary work on the cases is done by a solicitor, and the solicitor is obliged to seek a barrister to provide adequate counsel at trial.

Bench trial. A trial conducted without a jury. The judge performs the functions of both trier of fact (the jury's role) and decider of questions of law in dispute. These trials, like jury trials, are adversarial in nature. This is the trial procedure used in most civil cases.

Best evidence rule (or primary evidence rule). A rule of evidence that asserts that the best evidence available to a party is the most original evidence that can be procured in the existing situation. Secondary evidence is evidence that falls short of this standard and generally is to be excluded. (Federal Rules of Evidence 1002.)

Bifurcated trial process. Trial of issues separately, such as guilt and punishment in death penalty cases and guilt and sanity in criminal cases.

Bills of attainder. Special acts of the legislature inflicting punishment upon persons without any conviction in the ordinary course of judicial proceedings; prohibited by the United States Constitution to both state and federal legislative authorities.

Black letter law. Written law in statutory or constitutional form. Annotated codes contain black letter law and commentary.

Breach of contract. Failure, without legal excuse, to perform any promise that forms the whole or part of a contract.

Burden of proof. In the law of evidence, the necessity of affirmatively providing a fact or facts in dispute on an issue raised between the parties in a cause.

Canon law. That body of law developed by the Roman Catholic Church in Medieval Europe in an attempt to replace the void left by the decline of Roman authority.

Canons of ethics. The major standards of ethics for lawyers and judges that are published by the American Bar Association in their Model Code of Judicial Conduct and Model Rules of Professional Conduct (formerly the Model Code of Professional Responsibility).

Capital punishment. The death penalty.

Case law. That body of law created by judicial precedent. Common law is developed entirely from this source. The body of case law that interprets constitutional or statutory provisions is case law, but is not considered part of the common law proper and has a higher status in the hierarchy of laws.

Case of first impression. A dispute involving factual situations that have never been decided upon by a court of law. The decision of the court will establish new precedent. This is the basic method of creation of law in the common law tradition.

Cause of action. A recognized legal cause of action based on established principles of the law that must exist in order for a court to have jurisdiction over a particular dispute. A case may be dismissed at any time upon a ruling of failure to present a cause of action based upon a right in law.

Certiorari. (See Writ of certiorari.)

Challenges for cause. Challenges to the inclusion of a particular juror in which some cause or reason for that person's elimination from the jury is alleged. The judge must decide if there is sufficient reason to eliminate the juror from the trial. There is no limit to the number of these challenges, and even during trial, a juror may be challenged for cause and excluded from the jury. (See also Peremptory challenges.)

Chancery Court. A court of equity originating in Medieval England in which the practice of granting exceptions to the strict application of law under certain conditions developed. Some American states use this name for courts, but all courts, in both England and the United States, use the concepts of law and equity that were developed in the Chancery Court.

Charge to the jury. The final address by the judge to the jury that instructs the jurors about their responsibilities. In modern practice, preliminary instructions are allowed, but the important charge is given after both parties have rested their cases. The charge summarizes the case and instructs the jury about the rules of law that apply to the issues in the case. The charge usually is committed to writing and given to the jury to use in their deliberations. Further requested instructions may be given at the judge's discretion. The charge is one of the most important objects of appeal review.

Civil law. The system of jurisprudence derived from the Roman Empire, as distinguished from the common law of England. (See also Civil law countries; Codes.)

Laws concerned with civil or private rights and remedies, as contrasted with criminal laws, in American jurisprudence.

Civil law countries. Countries such as France, Italy, Germany, Spain, and most other continental European countries that practice civil law jurisprudence, which is a particular philosophy of law that originated in ancient Rome. Most legal systems are based on civil law jurisprudence in which, unlike common law jurisprudence, there is no official recognition of a body of judge-made law.

Civil legal action. A legal action taken for the purpose of resolving a noncriminal dispute. Private individuals or corporations may initiate such actions to resolve many forms of disputes, including those involving governmental agents. Remedies may include compensatory and punitive damages or specific performance orders of compliance.

Class action suit. An action brought on behalf of other persons similarly situated. This practice has led to modern "mass litigation" involving hundreds and thousands of plaintiffs and defendants in lawsuits.

Closing arguments. The final address of counsel for the two opposing parties in a trial; often referred to as the "summation."

Code. (See Codes.)

Codes. A series of volumes that organize state and federal statutory and constitutional law by topic for ease of reference. These volumes include notations to case law interpretations of the black letter law. Common law may be codified by statutory enactment, but the common law proper is referenced in a different manner (see Reporters).

Commission. A board or committee officially appointed and empowered to perform certain acts or exercise certain jurisdiction of a public nature (e.g., "Public Service Commission)."

Common law. A body of judge-made law that has no source other than judicial precedent. It is derived from case law, but not all case law is common law. Statutory and constitutional interpretations are not part of the common law proper. (See Case law, Hierarchy of laws.)

Common law countries. Countries, including England, Canada, Australia, New Zealand, India, Pakistan, Israel, and the United States, that have the common characteristics of former British colonial rule and recognition of a body of judge-made law. Although it is part of the United Kingdom today, Scotland still has a legal system derived from Roman law heavily influenced by English common law.

Community-based programs. Corrections programs under local jurisdiction such as drug rehabilitation and pretrial diversion.

Comparative negligence. A modern form of affirmative defense in negligence cases. Most jurisdictions allow a percentage of the negligence to be attributed to the plaintiff and still allow recovery for damages. The percentage of plaintiff negligence is discounted from the total claim if the plaintiff wins. This percentage cannot exceed fifty percent of the fault. (See also Contributory negligence; Voluntary assumption of known risk.)

Complaint. The initial pleading in a lawsuit. The complaint must be filed in the proper court that has jurisdiction to hear the case. It must name the parties, show a legal cause of action, and be filed within the proper time limitations.

Conciliation. The adjustment and settlement of a dispute in a friendly, unantagonistic manner. Used in courts in attempts to avoid trial and in labor disputes before arbitration. (See also Arbitration; Mediation.)

Confession. Voluntary statement made by a person acknowledging that he or she is guilty of an offense and disclosing the circumstances of the act.

Conflict of interest. Ethical conflict involving violation of trust in matters of private interest and gain; for example, a lawyer serving two clients with opposing interests.

Conflict of law. That area of common law dealing with the resolution of disputes involving two or more laws in conflict with each other. The rules governing these conflicts generally assert that the law which is more fundamental will prevail. However, there are many other principles that may influence the outcome of such conflicts. [See *Restatements of the Law: Conflict of Law.*]

Constitutional law. That body of law that has been ratified by the people. The United States Constitution was originally ratified by each of the former colonies. Amendments and other changes to the Constitution now require ratification by three-fourths of the states through their legislatures or state conventions. State constitutional change usually requires ratification by popular referendum (vote). Constitutional law, which includes case law based upon the Constitution, is the highest form of law in the hierarchy of laws.

Contingency fee contract. A typical method of contracting for legal services in tort cases in the United States, by which the lawyer is paid for services only if a favorable award is achieved. If unsuccessful, the client is obligated to pay only court costs and expenses. This form of contract is powerful incentive to lawyers and plaintiffs to seek damages and vigorously pursue the case. The rationale for the large percentages in the typical contract is that the lawyer must take a high risk and, since many cases are lost, make up for cases that are lost in those that win.

Continuance. Postponement of a session, hearing, trial, or other proceeding to a subsequent day or time.

Contracts. That body of law governing enforcement of private agreements made within the limits of constitutional, statutory, and common law. Contracts are binding to the parties to the agreements and may be enforced in the courts of proper jurisdiction. The United States Constitution prohibits abrogation of contracts.

Contributory negligence. An act or omission amounting to want of ordinary care on the part of the complaining party which, concurring with the defendant's negligence, is the proximate cause of injury. Contributory negligence may be an absolute defense against negligence liability in some jurisdictions; however, other jurisdictions use comparative negligence to enable the plaintiff to recover for a percentage of the injuries, once his or her part in contributory negligence is deducted, as long as the defendant's negligence is greater. (See also Comparative negligence; Voluntary assumption of known risk.)

Control subsystem. The police function of maintaining order, which is shared with the general public. Control, court, and corrections are subsystems of the overall criminal justice system.

Corpus delicti. The body or substance of the crime, which ordinarily includes two basic elements: actus reus and mens rea.

Court costs. The costs assessed by the court for handling the legal action. The party bringing the legal action is responsible for initial payment of the court costs, but the judgment adds court costs to the award, generally requiring the losing party to pay this expense.

Court subsystem. That part of the criminal process involving the courts directly. When a case leaves the control subsystem under the discretion of the police and is transferred to the prosecutor, it moves into the court subsystem.

Crimes. That body of laws governing individual behavior that have been established, generally by legislative authority, as offenses against society. Although citizens may file criminal complaints, the authorized agent of the government known as the prosecutor must bring legal action. Punishments include fines, incarceration, and even the death penalty in extreme cases.

Criminal discovery. Discovery in the criminal process, which differs from that in the civil process in that it is more restrictive, and depositions are taken only under unusual circumstances. A defendant does not have to testify.

Criminal legal action. A legal action brought by a designated agent of the government known as a prosecutor for the purpose of sanctioning criminal behavior.

Cross-examination. Procedure used in examination of witnesses called by the opposing party. The lawyer may use leading questions during the cross-examination and often begins, "Isn't it true that..." The purpose of cross-examination is to challenge the credibility of the witness; the subject matter is usually confined to that brought out on direct examination by the lawyer who called the witness.

Cruel and unusual punishment. Punishment that is prohibited by the Eighth Amendment to the United States Constitution. The prohibition is applied to the states through the Fourteenth Amendment.

Death penalty for rape (of adult). Prohibited as cruel and unusual punishment by court decision.

Deductive logic. Consistent reasoning. (See Syllogism.)

Defendant. The party against which a civil or criminal legal action is taken. The case name lists the name of the defendant last, and this case name remains with the case through appeal. However, in some criminal cases, the defendant may file a separate civil action to effect appeal, as in *Mapp v. Ohio*, in which case the former defendant becomes the plaintiff in the appeal case.

Demurrer. (See Judgment on the pleadings.)

Deposition. The testimony of a witness given not in open court, but where opposing lawyers may be present and may cross-examine the witness. This testimony is recorded by a court reporter, written, and attested to under oath. Deposition sessions are often arranged through the cooperation of opposing lawyers to save costs. Depositions are frequently used in court to impeach witnesses who give inconsistent testimony or when personal testimony is not possible at trial.

Dicta (or obiter dicta). Statements and opinions given by the court in a particular case that are not "on point" (that is, relevant to the particular facts of the case) and cannot be considered as part of the precedent created by the case.

Directed verdict. An order from a judge to decide the case in favor of one of the parties due to failure on the part of the opposing party to present enough evidence to support a contested issue of fact. The plaintiff must show at least some evidence to support the claim; and the defendant must show at least some evidence that there are facts in dispute about which reasonable persons could differ.

Direct examination. Examination of a witness by the legal counsel who calls that witness. Leading questions are not allowed—the lawyer must avoid asking questions that put words in the witness's mouth.

Discovery. The pretrial devices that can be used by a party during preparation for trial to obtain facts and information about the case from the other party. These devices include depositions upon oral and written questions; interrogatories; and requests for production of documents or other types of evidence, for permission to enter upon land or other property, for physical and mental examinations, and for admission or exclusion of evidence.

Diversity jurisdiction. Jurisdiction in civil legal actions that is shared by the state and federal courts. The federal diversity of citizenshnip jurisdiction may be chosen by the party bringing the legal action in a case involving a claim greater than $50,000 where no federal question is involved.

Docket. A formal record of the proceedings in a court of justice that contains an entry in brief of all the important acts done in court in the conduct of each case.

A ***trial docket*** is a calendar of causes set to be tried during a specific term.

Double jeopardy. A second prosecution after a trial has been had for the same offense. Prohibited by the Fifth Amendment of the United States Constitution. An individual who has been acquitted at trial may not be tried again for the same offense; thus, a prosecutor is prohibited from appealing a case for the purpose of seeking another trial.

Due notification. Notice to the party—individual, corporation, or agency—against whom an action is taken.

Due process of law. The essential concept of limitation on governmental authority, including basic constitutional principles and rights. (See also Rule of law.)

Eminent domain. The power to take private property for public use by the state or federal government. The Fifth Amendment recognizes this power but requires adequate compensation.

Enabling acts. Statutory authority defining the functions and powers of governmental agencies.

Equity. Rules or principles of fairness that evolved from precedents developed in the English Chancery Court and extended by judicial practice in the United States. Equity is distinguished from the body of law proper. It is a supplement to the common law and represents the "conscience" or "spirit" of the law, which strives for justice (fairness). Enforcement actions take the form of judicial decrees (as opposed to judgments), such as injunctions and orders for specific performance, and may include penalties for contempt of court.

Erie doctrine. The doctrine under which the federal courts, in a diversity case of a civil nature in which no federal question or constitutional issue is involved, will apply the substantive law of the state in which the court sits (in which the case was filed), but will use the federal procedural rules. The holding in *Erie v. Thompkins* (1938) established this principle.

Estate. That body of law pertaining to wills, inheritances, probate matters, interests in land, and any other subjects in which property is involved.

Estoppel. A legal procedure barring evidence, testimony, or legal actions; a bar or impediment that precludes allegation or denial of a certain fact or state of facts. Estoppel may be invoked because of previous allegations, denials, conduct, or admissions, or as a result of a final adjudication of the matter in a court of law (***estoppel by judgment***).

Equitable estoppel refers to the doctrine by which a person may be precluded by his or her act or conduct, or by his or her silence when there is a duty to speak, from asserting a right that the person otherwise would have had.

Ethical standards. Standards in the legal profession that are not merely desirable virtues or expectations, but many of which have been elevated to the status of legally binding rules. Model statements of these standards for lawyers and judges are developed by the American Bar Association.

Exculpatory evidence. Evidence that tends to indicate the defendant's innocence or tends to mitigate the defendant's criminality.

Exhaust administrative remedies. To pursue all administrative remedies available before seeking court action.

Expert witness. Witnesses who are qualified by reason of special knowledge, education, training, or experience to answer hypothetical questions and give opinions that would not be allowed for unqualified witnesses. An adequate foundation must be presented in the direct examination regarding the witness's possession of special knowledge. Broad discretion is given to trial judges to rule on the expertise of witnesses.

Ex post facto laws. Laws passed after the occurrence of a fact or commission of an act that retrospectively change the legal consequences or relations of that fact or deed; such laws usually apply only to criminal acts and are prohibited by the United States Constitution.

Expropriation. A taking, as under eminent domain; also used in the context of a foreign government taking an American industry located in the foreign country.

Fact pleading. The old English form of pleadings in which proof of factual evidence was required in order to initiate a lawsuit.

Fair hearing. A hearing in which authority is exercised fairly and in a manner consistent with fundamental principles of justice; includes presentation of evidence, cross-examination, and findings that are supported by evidence.

Federal district courts. The basic trial level courts in the federal hierarchy of courts.

Federalism. A unique form of government first created by the United States Constitution. The term refers to the division of sovereignty between national and state government that defines the constitutional authority and governmental jurisdiction of each. Our Constitution accepts the existence of fifty-one separate, independent court systems and prescribes that disputes arising over this division are to be settled by the United States Supreme Court.

Federal question (jurisdiction). All questions pertaining to the United States Constitution, valid acts of Congress, or treaties are subject to federal jurisdiction.

Felonies. Crimes of a more grave or serious nature than misdemeanors. Modern statutes designate each individual crime as a misdemeanor or felony.

Final judgment. The final judgment of the trial court, which is not necessarily the final judgment in a case, since the case may be appealed to a court of appellate jurisdiction.

First-degree murder. Premeditated homicide or, in many states, homicide committed in connection with arson, rape, robbery, or burglary.

Grand jury. Body of citizens whose duty consists of determining whether probable cause exists in a criminal case to warrant an indictment. Distinguished from a petit (or trial) jury.

Guilty plea. Formal admission in court regarding the defendant's guilt that the defendant may make if he or she does so intelligently and voluntarily.

Habeas corpus petition. (See also Writ of habeas corpus.) Petition for writ of habeas corpus. As a postconviction remedy, it extends to all constitutional challenges.

Harmless error. Error at trial that would not have changed the outcome. (See Prejudicial error.)

Hearsay rule. Testimony in court of a statement made out of the court and offered to show the truth of matters asserted is not permitted under Federal Rules of Evidence 801(c), and similar rules of evidence applied in state courts. Such testimony is secondhand evidence, as distinguished from original evidence, that does not derive its value solely from the credibility of the witness but rests mainly on the veracity and competency of other persons.

Hierarchy of courts. The general ranking of courts in their order of superiority. Courts of limited jurisdiction are subordinate to courts of general jurisdiction (trial courts). Both types of lower courts are answerable to the intermediate appellate courts and the supreme court, usually in that order.

Hierarchy of laws. The general ranking of types of laws in order of their priority based upon the principle that a more fundamental law prevails over a less fundamental law. Hence, constitutional law, statutory law, common law, and contracts are listed in order of their priority.

Holding. The court's statement, in case law, of the specific principle of law used to decide the particular factual dispute before the court. It is the answer to the legal issue involved and must be stated in terms precise enough to be used as precedent in future cases.

Indictment. An accusation in writing found and presented by a grand jury to a court in which it is impaneled, charging a person with a crime.

Information. (See Information process.)

Information process. A process in which an accusation in writing is made by a public prosecutor, without the intervention of a grand jury, and the accused may demand a preliminary hearing.

Initial appearance. A court proceeding, in felony cases and misdemeanors in which arrests have been made, at which the judge advises the defendant of the charges against the defendant and of his or her rights, decides upon bail, and sets the date for a preliminary hearing.

Interlocutory appeal. An appeal of a legal issue from a preliminary judgment by a lower court to be decided by a court of appellate jurisdiction prior to the trial.

Interrogatories. Written questions sent to the opposing party who must serve written answers in reply. The answers are sworn to under oath, and the court has the authority to require answers as long as the questions are relevant to the legal action.

Jail. A place of confinement that is more than a police station lockup and less than a prison.

Jailhouse lawyer. Inmate of a penal institution who spends his or her time reading the law and giving legal assistance and advice to inmates.

Judge's role. One of impartiality and neutrality toward the parties. When a jury is used, the judge determines issues of law in dispute and the jury determines issues of fact in dispute. When a jury is not used, the judge determines issues of both law and fact in dispute.

Judgment. The official and authentic decision of a court of justice upon the respective rights and claims of the parties to an action or suit litigated and submitted to its determination.

Judgment as a matter of law (or judgment *non obstante veredicto* or n.o.v.—judgment notwithstanding the verdict). The term originally referred to a judgment entered for the plaintiff by order of the court even though there had been a jury verdict for the defendant. In modern practice, judges may reverse judgment in favor of either party. There must be sufficient cause in law for the judge's action, which would be the subject of close review by an appeals court. The most recent version of the Federal Rules of Civil Procedure uses the term *judgment as a matter of law* rather than the older term *judgment notwithstanding the verdict*.

Judgment on the pleadings. A decision by proper judicial authority concerning the adequacy of the original complaint considering questions of justiciability of the dispute. Some common issues are those concerning proper parties, court jurisdiction, legal basis for claim, and statutes of limitations. A demurrer is a form of motion on the pleadings that asks, "So what? Even if the complaint is true, there is no legal liability."

Judicial precedent. A previous judicial decision that has established a rule in case law to regulate the particular legal issue in question. The doctrine of following precedent is of great importance to the stability of the law, but precedent can be overruled when there is good reason.

Judicial review. The power of the courts to declare acts of governmental agencies deemed contrary to the Constitution void and nonenforceable. This power of the independent courts in the United States is widely accepted and extends to all courts and affects all governmental agencies, national and state. The highest appeals courts frequently review such actions because of their importance.

Jurisdiction. Areas of authority; the geographic area in which a court has power or the types of cases the court has power to hear.

Jurisprudence (or philosophy of law). The basic principles and theories of a particular school of thought about the origin, development, and logical extension and application of the law. Four schools of jurisprudence are: analytical, historical, philosophical, and sociological.

Jurisprudence is the science of the law, the function of which is to ascertain the principles on which legal rules are based, the classification of legal rules, and their logical extension.

Jury trial. Trial of matter or cause before a jury as opposed to trial before the judge alone. The defendant has a right to demand a jury trial in criminal cases in both state and federal jurisdictions. In civil cases, no general constitutional standard grants defendants the right to a jury trial.

In federal courts, the Seventh Amendment grants the right to jury trials in civil cases, but the United States Supreme Court has never considered it fundamental enough to be incorporated under the Fourteenth Amendment due process clause and applied to the states. Many state constitutions and statutes grant a right to trial by jury in civil cases. Almost all states refuse to grant such a right in equity cases and divorce decrees. In Federal equity cases a jury trial is not granted as a matter of right.

The right to a jury trial implies a trial by an impartial and qualified jury.

Juvenile justice systems. Juvenile courts and corrections facilities that have special jurisdiction of a paternal nature over delinquent, dependent, and neglected children.

Law. The set of rules and procedures recognized by governmental authority as legally binding that are used to resolve disputes between parties.

Law-related education. Educational programs developed by educators, bar associations, and concerned organizations to promote the integration of legal concepts into the modern curriculum. Organizations involved with law-related education include the American Bar Association, The Constitutional Rights Foundation, Law in a Free Society, and the National Street Law Institute.

Law School Admission Test (LSAT). An aptitude test provided by Law School Admissions Services that is nearly universally used in the United States and is generally given about equal weight with grade point averages in determining qualifications for law school admission.

Lawyer fees. Payments to lawyers for their services that are assessed through a variety of methods. Corporations usually keep lawyers on retainer, which is payment for representing the firm and refusing to represent potential opponents, and the fees for actual services are generally paid on an hourly basis. Contingency fees are typically used in tort cases in the United States. (See Contingency fee contract.)

Lawyer's role. That of advocate for the client. The lawyer is ethically obligated to represent the client to the best of his or her ability without violating the law or the lawyers' code of ethics.

Leading questions (rule). This basic rule of evidence generally prohibits the party calling the witness from asking questions that instruct the witness how to answer or put words into the witness's mouth to be echoed back. Questions that call for a yes or no answer usually are leading, but not always. "When did you stop beating your wife?" is a leading question.

Legal executives. The term used to describe paralegals in the British legal profession.

Lesser included offense. An offense composed of some, but not all, of the elements of the greater crime, and which does not have any element not included in the greater crime.

Liability. A general term for legal liability, or a duty owed to another because of a legal obligation.

Magistrates. Judicial officers usually used in connection with the courts of limited jurisdiction, such as justices of the peace.

Mala in se. Acts morally wrong in themselves; offenses against conscience.

Mala prohibita. Prohibited wrongs or offenses; acts that are made offenses by positive law.

Mandamus. (See Writ of mandamus.)

Mediation. The act of a third person who intervenes between two contending parties and attempts to aid them in arriving at their own conclusions in the settlement of the dispute. Mediation is distinguished from arbitration, in which the parties agree to abide by the decision of a mutually agreed-on third party. (See also Arbitration; Conciliation.)

Mens rea. A guilty mind or criminal intent; guilty knowledge and willfulness. (See also Actus reus.)

Misdemeanors. Offenses lower than felonies, generally those punishable by fine or imprisonment other than in a penitentiary (prison). Modern statutes designate each individual crime as a misdemeanor or felony.

Missouri Plan (or merit plan). A progressive plan for the selection of judges involving appointment by the governor from a short list of persons certified by an independent commission to be qualified for the position. The governor's appointee usually must stand for approval at the next general election.

Mitigating circumstances. Circumstances that may reduce the degree of moral culpability, but do not justify or excuse the offense in question.

Natural law. The concept of ideal law, or law that is in conformity with the nature of man and society, based on ancient principles of justice that have demonstrated their utility throughout history. Common law is based on natural law principles, as distinguished from positive law that is made by governments.

Negligence. Failure to exercise due care that results in an act or omission that causes injury to another. The standard of ordinary care is usually applied, that is, what a prudent person would consider a duty of care. There are degrees of failure to exercise due care, which result in slight, ordinary, or gross negligence. Criminal negligence, which is deemed by statute to be flagrant and reckless disregard of the safety of others, is punishable as a crime.

Negotiation. The act of conferring with the contending party in a dispute and attempting to arrive at a settlement of the matter without reference to a third party or the court; sometimes referred to as direct negotiations. Most civil complaints are settled out of court, and many settlements are accomplished through direct negotiations between the parties and their counsel.

Nolle prosequi (or nol-pros). A formal entry on the record by the prosecutor declaring that the case will not be prosecuted further. Illustrates the important discretionary power of the prosecutor.

Nolo contendere ("I will not contest it"). A plea in a criminal case that has a legal effect similar to a plea of guilty. Such a plea may not be used in a civil action against the defendant.

Nonadversarial process. The legal procedures used in civil law countries that substantially differ from the adversarial procedures that characterize the Anglo-American civil and criminal process. This term is used instead of the more traditional term *inquisitorial process* because of the erroneous connotations attached to that phrase.

Not guilty by reason of insanity. A defense at trial; or a plea at arraignment, upon which the judge sets a trial date. The defendant is required to notify the prosecutor of an intent to use this defense, and the prosecutor generally is required to prove sanity and, hence, guilt or culpability.

Not guilty plea. Plea entered by the accused at arraignment that indicates a desire to contest the charge at trial.

Notice pleading. The form of pleadings used in modern practice in the United States that do not have to prove allegations but do have to provide notification and an opportunity to be heard regarding the stated claim.

Ombudsman. An official or semiofficial office to which people may come with grievances connected with the government. The ombudsman stands between, and represents, the citizen before the government. Ombudsman offices, which originated in Sweden, have been diversely adopted in other countries in Europe.

"On Point." In citing precedents and stating holdings, one must be careful to stay "on point"—that is, relevant factual circumstances must be substantially the same as those in the case that established the precedent.

Opening statements. In American practice, the statements of the opposing sides at the beginning of a trial that consist of outlines of anticipated proof and that serve to explain the issues in contention. The purpose of these statements is to advise the jury of the facts relied upon and the issues involved so that the jury will be able to understand the evidence; however, these statements are not considered evidence.

Pain and suffering. A term used to describe not only physical discomfort and distress but also mental and emotional trauma which is recoverable as elements of damage in torts. Modern statutes may exclude such recovery; and generally, European countries do not allow such damages.

Paralegal (or legal assistant). A person with legal skills who works under the supervision of a lawyer or is otherwise authorized by law to use these skills.

The paralegal profession is one of the most rapidly growing legal professions in the United States today.

Parens patriae ("parent of the country"). Refers to the role of the state as sovereign and guardian of persons under legal disability.

Parole. Release from jail, prison, or other confinement after part of the sentence has been served. Parole boards of the state and federal government decide whether inmates shall be conditionally released from prison before completion of their sentences. In Germany, sentencing courts exercise this responsibility.

Peremptory challenges. Challenges by which counsel can eliminate potential jurors without showing cause. A limited number of these challenges, which are arbitrary and absolute, are given to each party in the typical jury selection process; the number allowed is specified in the law of the particular jurisdiction. Recent court decisions in criminal cases have established limitations to challenges based on the race of the potential juror. (See also Challenges for cause.)

Petit jury. The trial jury. (See also Grand jury.)

Plaintiff. The party bringing a civil legal action. The case name lists the name of the party bringing the action first, and this case name remains with the case through appeal, even if defendant brings the appeal. (See Defendant.)

Plea bargaining. Process whereby the accused and the prosecutor in a criminal case work out a mutually satisfactory disposition of the case subject to court approval.

Pleadings. The formal allegations by the parties of their respective claims and defenses, for the judgment of the court.

Political questions. Questions of which courts will refuse to take cognizance, or to decide, on account of their purely political character or because their determination by the courts would involve an encroachment upon the executive or legislative powers.

Matters of dispute that can be handled more appropriately by other branches of the government are not "justiciable." A state apportionment statute, however, is not a political question (*Baker v. Carr,* 369 U.S. 186 [1962]).

Positive law. Secular law made by governmental institutions or legislative authority. Positive law is distinguished from natural law principles, which are the basis of the common law.

Prejudicial error. Error substantially affecting appellant's legal rights and obligations; distinguished from harmless error, which does not affect the outcome of the trial.

Preliminary hearing. A hearing by a judge to determine whether a person charged with a crime should be held for trial or bound over to the grand jury. Evidence may be presented at this hearing, and the defendant has a right to counsel.

Present value. Adjustment to account for investment earnings of a specific sum of money over time.

Pretrial diversion. A system of recent origin by which certain defendants in criminal cases are referred to community agencies before trial, and their criminal complaints or indictments are held in abeyance while the defendant is given job training, counseling, or education. If the defendant responds successfully within a specified period, the charges against the defendant are dismissed.

Pretrial lineup. Police identification procedure. Postindictment lineups are considered a critical stage of criminal proceedings and the accused, therefore, has a constitutional right to have counsel present.

Prima facie case. A case that has proceeded upon sufficient proof to that stage where the finding will be supported unless overcome by evidence to the contrary. The Latin term *prima facie* means "on the face of it" and refers to a fact presumed to be true unless disproven by evidence to the contrary.

Primary evidence rule. (See Best evidence rule.)

Private law. That part of the law that is administered between private individuals or legal entities.

Probable cause. Reasonable cause that is more than mere suspicion; some evidence and reasonable grounds for belief in the existence of facts warranting the proceedings complained of. The degree of evidence required to meet the probable cause standard may increase as the case progresses through the pretrial stages.

Probate. The act or process of providing a will; all matters of which the probate courts have jurisdiction.

Procedural law. That body of rules governing administrative procedures and methods used to enforce the substantive law. The rules of civil and criminal procedure are extensive and include our most fundamental rights.

Products liability. Legal liability of manufacturers and sellers to compensate buyers, users, and even bystanders for damages or injuries suffered because of defects in goods purchased. (See also Strict liability.)

Prosecutor. That governmental agent designated by the state or federal government to represent the people in criminal legal actions. State and federal district attorneys usually are responsible for such actions, although special prosecutors may be appointed in some cases.

Public defender. An attorney appointed by a court or employed by a governmental agency whose work consists primarily of representing indigent defendants in criminal cases.

Public law. That branch of law that is concerned with the state in its political or sovereign capacity, including constitutional and administrative law. Both substantive and procedural aspects of criminal law are included.

Quasi-judicial powers. Internal agency procedures involving fact-finding hearings that resemble the decision-making process of the courts.

Quasi-legislative powers. The rule-making powers of governmental agencies that are similar to, but more limited than, those of law-making authorities.

Ratio decedendi. The legal principle on which a case law decision is based; the underlying rationale or spirit of the law on a particular issue. The legal reasoning of the court offers elaboration on the issue to facilitate greater understanding of the principle on which the decision is based.

Regulatory agency. An agency or commission (board) that has been delegated rule-making authority by the legislative body.

Reporters. A series of volumes for state court systems, regional districts, and federal courts in which case opinions are collected.

Request to produce. A formal request to gain access to material or documentary evidence relevant to the legal dispute during the discovery process; one of the instruments of discovery. A request to produce will be enforced by court order as long as the evidence requested is deemed relevant.

Res judicata. A ruling on the merits by a court of competent jurisdiction that is conclusive of the rights of the parties or their privies in all later suits on points and matters determined in the former suit. A matter that is res judicata is finally decided; any further legal action is barred, and the matter is finally put to rest.

Restatements (of the law). A series of authoritative volumes defining the general principles of common law written by scholars of the prestigious American Law Institute; description of hornbooks written by individual professors, such as *Prosser on Torts.*

Rule making. Creation of rules and regulations by administrative agencies delegated by legislative authority and limited by that authority in enabling acts. (See also Enabling acts.)

Rule of law. Limitation of governmental authority by reference to established legal principle and the impartial application of the spirit of the law. Separation of governmental powers and judicial independence are considered essential to this goal. (See also Due process of law.)

Rules of civil procedure. The rules of procedure, whether common law or statutory in nature, that govern civil legal actions. These rules are somewhat different in each state and for the federal courts. Most states have adopted modern statutory rules, but peculiarities exist for each jurisdiction, and procedures may vary according to the type of legal proceeding involved. The Federal Rules of Civil Procedure are referred to by the abbreviation Fed. R. Civ. P.

Rules of criminal procedure. Detailed rules of procedure in criminal cases that govern the steps involved in that process. Each jurisdiction has such rules; the Federal Rules of Criminal Procedure are referred to by the abbreviation Fed. R. Crim. P.

Rules of evidence. The aggregate of rules and principles regulating the admissibility, relevancy, and weight and sufficiency of evidence in legal proceedings. Each state has its own rules; the Federal Rules of Evidence are referred to by the abbreviation Fed. R. Evid.

Satisfaction of judgment. Payment of the court award for damages.

Search warrant. Written order issued by judicial authority directing a law enforcement officer to search and seize any property that constitutes evidence of a crime.

Second-degree murder. In most states, all forms of murder other than that in the first degree. Most states have lesser degrees of killing known as manslaughter, criminally negligent homicide, or vehicular homicide.

Selective incorporation (doctrine). This United States Supreme Court doctrine combines the fundamental rights concept with selected provisions of the federal Bill of Rights to define criminal due process and the Fourteenth Amendment prohibition against state denial of due process.

Sentencing grid. Modern sentencing plan that restricts judicial sentencing by classification of offenses and provides a narrow range of sentencing guidelines.

Service of process. The delivery of writs, summonses, and so on to the party to whom they are addressed or other acceptable party. Once these documents have been so delivered, they are said to have been served.

Solicitor. A trained and licensed lawyer in England who handles most legal matters until they go to trial in contested cases. The solicitor is authorized to give legal advice and oversee legal executives, but must employ a barrister to handle arguments at trial in most serious cases.

Sovereign immunity. Doctrine that precludes litigant from asserting an otherwise meritorious cause of action against a sovereign or party with sovereign attributes unless the sovereign consents to suit. Legislative authority to sue has been granted in many jurisdictions and for specific purposes. Immunity from lawsuits for acts of state, however, which only the sovereign can perform (such as the taxing power), has been faithfully guarded by legislatures and the courts.

Sovereignty. Supreme or ultimate authority, which is the basic premise of the modern nation-state. Jean Bodin asserted in the sixteenth century that in order to have a nation-state, some ultimate authority must have power to settle disputes.

The United States Constitution divides sovereignty between the national government and the states and is interpreted to protect the independence of each. (See *McCulloch v. Maryland*, 17 U.S. 316 [1819].)

Other meanings of sovereignty are: the self-sufficient source of political power from which all specific political powers are derived; the international independence of a state, combined with the right and power of regulating its internal affairs without foreign dictation; and a political society or state that is sovereign and independent.

Specialized federal courts. Courts created by Congress under authority granted in article I, as opposed to article III, of the Constitution. They often possess administrative and quasi-legislative as well as judicial duties.

Speedy trial. A right guaranteed by the Sixth Amendment and interpreted to mean that trial is to be provided without unnecessary or unreasonable delay. As applied to the states, the principle does not necessarily involve fixed time elements.

Speedy Trial Act. Federal Speedy Trial Act of 1974 added the statutory requirement of a "fixed time rule" to the guarantee of the right to a speedy trial in federal criminal cases. Some states have similar statutes.

Standing to sue. A concept utilized to determine if a party is sufficiently affected so as to ensure that a justiciable controversy is presented in court.

Stand mute before the court. A refusal on the part of the defendant to make a plea at arraignment, which must be considered as a plea of not guilty.

Stare decisis (*et non quieta movere*, or "stand by the decision and do not disturb what is settled"). The doctrine that is the basis for adhering to common law precedent in case law adjudication. This doctrine was established to preserve consistency, but it is not an absolutely binding rule—past precedents can be overruled, although such decisions are rare and must be based on good reason.

Statutes of limitations. Statutes prescribing limitations to the right of action on certain causes of action; that is, statutes declaring that no suit shall be maintained on such causes of action unless brought within a specified period of time after the right to such a suit has accrued.

Statutory law. The body of law that has been enacted by legislative authority, including relevant case law that provides specific interpretation of statutory law. Statutory law may codify and change the common law if that is the intent of the legislation.

Stipulation. An agreement by the opposing parties regarding any matter incidental to the proceedings or trial; a statement that the matter is not at issue and is agreed to by both parties.

Stop and frisk. The temporary seizure and "patting down" of a person who behaves suspiciously and appears to be armed.

Strict liability. Term commonly used to describe the special tort liability, defined in section 402A of the *Restatement (Second) of Torts*, that makes a seller or manufacturer liable for injuries caused by defective products. (See also Products liability.)

Subpoena (Latin, under penalty). A process by which a witness is commanded to appear before the court or in other legal proceedings to give testimony. The witness is ordered to lay aside pretenses and excuses. Other types of evidence can be ordered by subpoena.

Substantive law. That body of rules governing individual behavior in society in regard to crimes, torts (civil wrongs), and contracts.

Summary judgment. A short, concise, and immediate judgment that precludes jury action. If the judge determines that there are no issues of fact—but only questions of law—in dispute, the judge may issue a summary judgment.

Summons. A writ directed to a sheriff or other proper officer, requiring the officer to notify the person named that an action has been taken against that person in the court and that the person is required to appear, on the day named, and to answer the complaint in the action. (See Service of process.)

Suppression motion. Motion to the effect that evidence sought to be admitted should be excluded because it was illegally acquired. (Federal Rules of Criminal Procedure 12b and 41f.)

Survival action. One of two theories for recovery of damages by the estate of a person who is deceased. (See also Wrongful death action.) The survival theory assumes that the damages recoverable are what the deceased could have recovered had the deceased lived. Some states use both theories of recovery, while others use only one, to allow recovery to the estate of a deceased person by statute where the common law would not have allowed recovery.

Syllogism. The full logical form of a single argument that includes at least two premises and a conclusion that must of necessity follow if the premises are true; the reasoning involved in deductive logic; reasoning that is consistent.

Tort. A private or civil wrong or injury, other than breach of contract, for which the court will provide a remedy in the form of an action for damages.

Tort reform. The modern movement supported by insurance, business, and governmental interests to reduce tort costs by a variety of proposals that would generally limit the liability of those interests in products liability and other tort cases.

Torts. That body of law dealing with civil wrongs committed upon the person or property of another independent of contract.

Treason. Defined by the United States Constitution, article III, section 3, as "levying War against the United States"—adhering to their enemies or giving them aid and comfort. A conviction of treason requires two witnesses or confession in open court.

Trial courts. Courts of general jurisdiction in the states, and the federal district courts in the national system, that are the courts in which contested cases are tried and in which adversarial procedures are used.

Under color of law doctrine. Reference to provision of the Federal Civil Rights Act of 1963 that prohibits denial of constitutional rights under color of law. (42 U.S.C. § 1983) "Color" refers to an appearance or semblance—a disguise or pretext—as distinguished from that which is real.

Verdict (Latin "veredictum," a true declaration). The formal decision of a jury regarding the charge against the defendant, made after the judge has instructed the jurors about their responsibilities.

Voir dire (Law French, to speak the truth). The examination the court and counsel make of prospective jurors in regard to their competency, interests, prejudices, and so on. To voir dire a witness refers to the examination of that individual's credentials in court.

Voluntary assumption of known risk. One of the more significant legal defenses in products liability (or strict liability) cases. If the risk of use of a product is known and the person in question assumed that risk voluntarily, that person can be said to have assumed voluntarily a known risk. (See also Comparative negligence; Contributory negligence.)

Workers' compensation laws. Modern legislation that provides "no fault" and "limited liability" protection for workers who are injured on the job, making employers liable for compensation to these employees. About half of the states have established administrative claims boards to handle preliminary disputes regarding these claims.

Writ of certiorari. An order, dependent upon the discretion of the Court, to have the lower court records sent to the higher court for review. The term refers to the discretionary authority of the United States Supreme Court to decide, in most cases, whether it will hear an appeal. Four of the nine justices must grant the writ to indicate that the court will hear the case.

Writ of habeas corpus (you have the body). A variety of writs that is for the purpose of bringing a party before a court or judge. *Habeas corpus ad subjiciendum* refers to the presentation of the issue of whether a prisoner has been restrained of liberty in violation of due process of law.

Writ of mandamus. An order issuing from a court of competent jurisdiction commanding a public official to perform a purely ministerial duty imposed by law.

Wrongful death action. Type of lawsuit brought on behalf of a deceased person's beneficiaries that alleges that death was attributable to the willful or negligent act of another. Such action allows the estate to recover damages when the person injured is deceased. Wrongful death statutes specify the particular damages that are recoverable. Some states use two theories of recovery to specify different types of damages recoverable under each. (See also Survival action.) Other states use only abatement and survival actions.

Wrongful death and survival statutes. Statutes that define the rights of beneficiaries to sue and recover damages when the person who was wronged is deceased. (See also Wrongful death action; Survival action.)

INDEX

Key terms that have marginal definitions in the text and the Glossary are in boldface type, as are the pages on which the definitions appear.

Abbott v. American Honda Motor Co., 149, 152, 153, 154–58, 159, 163
Abraham, Henry J., 317, 320
Accessory after the fact, 278, 365
Accomplice, 254, 365
Act of Settlement of 1701 (England), 18
Actus reus, 207, 365
Adams, John, 23, 61
Administrative courts, 319, 365
French, 319–20, 321–22
German, 320, 321–22
Administrative due process, 305, 310–**15**, **365**
Administrative law, 305, 310, **365.** *See also* Regulatory agencies
codes, 185–86
due process in, 311–15
judicial review, 316
in other countries, 168, 318–22
sources of, 308–9
Administrative law judge (ALJ), 315, 365
in France and Germany, 321, 322
Administrative legal action, 70, **71, 365.** *See also* Administrative law
Administrative Procedures Act of 1946, 309, 310, 315

Administrative procedures acts, 309, 310, **365**
Admiralty cases, 56
Adversarial process, 169, 365
plea bargaining and, 285
Affidavit, 83, 365
example of, 84
Affirmative defense, 82, 365
in products liability vs. negligence, 88–89
Agencies, 342. *See also* Regulatory agencies
ombudsman and, 318–19
types of, 307
Aggravating circumstances, 262–63, 365
Aiding and abetting, 242, 254, **277, 366**
Alfini, James J., 162
Alternative dispute resolution (ADR), 162, 169, 171, **366**
American Bar Association (ABA), 30, 32, 35, 36, **43,** 239, **366**
ethical standards, 43, 44
American Digest System (West Publishing), 188
American Jurisprudence 2d (Am. Jur. 2d), 180, 182
American Law Institute (ALI), 187, 339
American Law Reports (A.L.R.), 180, 182

Analogistical reasoning, 58, 366
Annotated codes, 176, 190
administrative, 185–86
federal, 180–85
state, 177–80
Answer, 96, 103–4, **366**
example of, 105
Appeals court, 366. *See also* Appellate court
Appelant, 150, 366
Appellate brief, 151, 152, **366**
Appellate court(s), 51, 149, 339, 347, **366**
access to, 160
actions and functions, 150–52
example of case in, 152–59
federal, 53–55, 150, 151
in Germany, 171, 298
oral arguments in, 152
review of agency action, 310, 316
right of appeal to, 150, 151
role in criminal cases, 283–84
state 51–52, 150, 151
Appellee, 151, 366
brief of, 152
Aquinas, St. Thomas, 7
Arbitration, 162, 163, 171, **366**
Argersinger v. Hamlin, 213
Aristotle, 5, 7, 10, 23
Arraignment, 215, 239, **246, 366**

example of, 247–48
Arrest, 204–5, **214**–15, 244-45, 366
Arrest warrant, 215, 244, **366**
Articles of Confederation, 22
Asbestos cases, 164
Assizes of Clarendon and Northampton, 16
Attorneys' conference, 112, 366
Axiom, 67, 366

Bail, 217, 366
Baker v. Carr, 80
Ballentine's Law Dictionary, 187
Bar Examination, 37, 366
Barker v. Wingo, 237
Barrister, 35, 40, 169, **366**
Batson v. Kentucky, 264
Baum, Lawrence, 42
Bench trial, 97, 366
  in civil cases, number of, 161
Bendectin cases, 164
Benton v. Maryland, 210
Best evidence rule, 124, 366
Betts v. Brady, 213
Beyond a reasonable doubt standard, 71, 232, 257, 296, 345, 346
Bifurcated trial process, 257, 261–62, 366
Bill of Rights (English), 18, 256
Bill of Rights (U.S.), 23, 25, 208–9. *See also* specific amendments
  application to the states, 209–10
  text, 334–35
Bills of attainder, 284, 366–67
Binding arbitration contracts, 163
Bivens v. Six-Unknown Named Agents, 212
Black, Hugo L., 213
Black letter law, 56, 367
Blacks
  death penalty and, 256, 257
  exclusion from juries, 264
Black's Law Dictionary, 187
Blackstone, Sir William, 7, 18, 21
Bluebook (The): A Uniform System of Citation, 180, 189
Blumberg, Abraham, 285

Boland, Barbara, 288
Booking (of criminal suspect), 205
Bordenkircher v. Hayes, 209–91
Boykin v. Alabama, 290
Bracton, Henry, 16
Brady v. United States, 290
Breach of contract, 82, 367
Breed v. Jones, 296
Brown v. Board of Education of Topeka, 80
Brown v. Mississippi, 213
Burden of proof, 133, 143, **367**
Burger, Warren, 32, 212, 287, 293
Burr, Aaron, 68
Burton, Steven J., 58
Butz v. Economou, 318

Canon law, 13, 367
Canons of ethics, 43, 367
Capital punishment, 256–57, 301, **367**
  bifurcated trial process and, 257, 261–62
  counsel, right to, and, 212
  exclusion of prospective jurors and, 266
Cardozo, Benjamin, 209
Case law, 49–50, **55, 367**
  base elements of a case, 60, 65–66
  case method of training, 58–66
  and common law distinguished, 68
  finding, 186–92
  illustrative cases, 339–54
  updating, 192–96
Case of first impression, 18, 367
Cause of action, 81, 367
Certiorari. *See* Writ of certiorari
Challenges for cause, 118, 367
Chancery Court (England), **17,** 19, 25, **367**
Chapin, Bradley, 20
Charge to the jury, 142, 367
  example (civil trial), 142–45
  example (criminal trial), 276–78
Charles the Great (medieval emperor), 12

Cicero, Marcus Tullius, 7
  on natural law, 11–12
Citation
  of cases, 189–90
  of statutes, 178, 180
Civil Code des Frances, 13
Civil law, 9, 367
  civil legal action and, 13, 70
  U.S. Constitution and, 25
Civil law countries, 8, 9, 13, 14, 19, **367**
  criminal procedure in, 298
  judges in, 40
  jury trials, absence in civil cases, 169
  strict liability, absence in, 168
Civil legal action, 13, **51,** 70–71, 149, 348, **367**
  alternative dispute resolution methods, 162
  appeals process, 149–59
  cases filed, types of, 163
  ending, 159
  in Germany, 169–71
  initiating, steps involved, 77–92
  in other countries, 165-71
  pretrial process, 95–113
  problems of civil litigation, 169–65. *See also* Litigation
  trial, 117–45
  types of, 80–82
Civil procedure. *See* Civil legal action
Civil Rights Act of 1963, 292
Clark, Tom C., 211
Class action suit(s), 160, 367
  increase in, 164
Closing arguments, 120, 140, **367**
  examples (civil trial), 140–42
  examples (criminal trial), 275–76
Code(s), 9, 176, **367**
  administrative, 185–86
  federal, 180–85
  of Hammurabi, 9
  of Justinian, 11, 12, 13
  state annotated, 177–80
  unified criminal code in Germany, 299
Code law, 9. *See also* Civil law

Code of Federal Regulations (C.F.R.), 185–86, 308
Code pleadings, 96
Coke, Edward, 18
Coker v. Georgia, 257
Cole v. Arkansas, 210
Commentaries (Blackstone), 18
Commission, 317, 368
Common law, 9, 68, 368
 in American colonies, 19–20, 21–22
 after the American Revolution, 21–22, 24–25
 and case law distinguished, 68
 crime in, 207
 finding, 186–92
 in medieval England, 16
 merger with civil law in U.S. Constitution, 68
 pleadings under, 95
Common law countires, 8, 9, 19, 168 **368.** *See also* England
 strict liability in, 168
Community-based programs, 295, 368
Comparative negligence, 88, 368
Complaint, 96–97, 100, 368
 criminal, 217, 218
 example of, 98–99
 response to, 103–4, 105
Computer research, 188, 199
Conciliation, 162, 171, 368
Confession, 246, 368
 example of 243–44
Conflict model of crime, 207
Conflict of interest, 102, 118, 245, **368**
Conflict of laws, 67, **368**
Consensus model of crime, 207
Conspiracy, 346
Constitution (U.S.), 5, 8, 20, 31, 68, 69, 182, 306. *See also* Constitutional law; Due process of law; specific clauses and amendments
 civil and common law traditions merged in, 25
 criminal due process, 208–14
 federalism in, 22–23

 federal judiciary and, 52, 54–55, 65–66
 judicial review and, 23–24, 60-66
 separation of powers in, 23
 text, 329–38
Constitutional law, 67, 368
 in Germany, 298–99
Constitutional Rights Foundation, 32
Contempt of court, 104, 118
Contingency fee contract, 85, 170, **368**
 example of, 86
 litigation explosion and, 160, 167
Continuance, 260, 368
Contract(s), 68, 71, 85, **368**
 breach of, 82
 contingency fee, 85, 86, 160, 167, 170
 number of cases involving, 163
 oral promises and, 352
Contract law, 82
Contributory negligence, 88, 368
Control subsystem, 214, 368
Cooper v. Pate, 292
Corpus delicti, 207, 368
Corpus Juris Civilis, 11, 12, 13
Corpus Juris Secundum (C.J.S.), 180, 182
Counsel, 217, 224–25. *See also* Public defender
 application for, example of, 219–20
 effective, right to, 291
 at pretrial lineup, right to, 255
 right to, 212–13, 296
Court(s), 50–56. *See also* Administrative courts; Appellate courts; Federal courts; State courts; Trial courts; specific courts
 access to, 167
 administrators, 36
 case load problem (civil), 160, 161–62
 case load problem (criminal) and plea bargaining, 287, 288
 choice of, 90

 docket, 97
 federal, 52–56, 85, 87, 317–18
 German, 298–99, 300
 juvenile, 295–96
 as legal and political institutions, 6
 legitimacy of, 58
 number of cases in, 30
 settlement out of, 90–92
 state, 50–52
 state and federal in United States, 24–25
 subsystem phase of pretrial criminal process, 231–49
Court-annexed arbitration, 162, **366**
Court costs, 170, 368–69
Court hierarchy, 52, 371
 in Germany, 299
 state vs. federal, 53
Court subsystem, 232, 369
 pretrial phase of criminal case, 231-49
Crime(s), 71, 206, 346, **377**
 elements of, 207
 types of, 207–8
Criminal complaint, 217
 example of, 218
Criminal discovery, 258, 369
 in Germany, 298
Criminal justice process. *See* Criminal legal action
Criminal legal action, 51, 70, 71, **369**
 appellate review, 283–84
 arraignment, 246–48
 basic concepts, 206–8
 defense considerations, 239–45
 defense investigation, 254
 discovery process, 258
 due process, 208–14
 evaluating the criminal process, 283–301
 in federal courts, 56
 in Germany, 298–301
 grand jury, 234–37
 juvenile justice systems, 295–96
 lineup identification, 255–56
 in other countries, 296–97
 plea bargaining, 232, 242–43, 247, 284–91

pretrial planning, 259–61
pretrial process (court subsystem phase), 231–49
pretrial process (police subsystem phase), 203–66, 214–28
prison conditions and, 292–95
prosecutor's role, 231–34
sentencing, 248–49
speedy trial, right to, 237–39
trial, 261–62, 264–79
Criminal procedure. *See* Criminal legal action
Cross-examination, 123, 369
  example (civil trial), 125, 127, 128, 131, 133, 135, 136–37, 138
  example (criminal trial), 269, 270, 271–72, 273–74, 275
  leading questions during, 124
Crouch, Ben, 295
Cruel and unusual punishment, 256, 369
  prisoners' rights and, 292–95
Curia Regis, 14–15, 17, 327
Custodial interrogation, 205
  privilege vs. self-incrimination during, 213–14

Dalkon shield cases, 164
Damages (money), 80, 81, 82
  in civil law countries, 170, 297
  estimating, 90, 132, 138, 139
  limits to, for an estate, 89–90
  payment stayed by appeal, 151
  satisfaction of judgment and, 159
Death penalty. *See* Capital punishment
Death penalty for rape, 257, 369
Declaration of Independence, 20–21, 31
Deductive reasoning/logic, 57, 369
Defendant, 71, 369
  plea bargaining as manipulation of, 285
Demurrer. *See* Judgment on the pleadings

Deposition, 104, **106,** 109, 258, **369**
  examples of statements at, 356–63
Dicta, 59, 369
Dictionaries (legal), 187
Digests, 188–89, 190–92
Direct examination, 123, 369
  example (civil trial), 124–25, 127, 128, 129–31, 133-35, 136, 137–38
  example (criminal trial), 268–69, 270–71, 272–73, 274–75
  leading questions during, 123–24
Directed verdict, 133, 138, 140, **369**
Discovery, 104, 161, **369**
  criminal, 258
  depositions, 106, 109
  interrogatories, 106, 107–8
  production of documents, 109–10
District attorney. *See* Prosecutor
Diversity jurisdiction, 50, 55, 56, **85,** 87, 339, **369**
  case involving, 339–42
Docket, 97, 369
Documents
  introduced as evidence, 125, 126
  request to produce, 109–10, 111
Double jeopardy, 283, 369
Douglas v. California, 284
Drug Enforcement Administration, 34
Due notification 310, 370
Due process clause
  Fifth Amendment, 69
  Fourteenth Amendment, 55, 69, 209–10, 211, 212, 213, 237
Due process of law, 5, **69, 370**
  administrative, 305, 310–15
  arrest and, 214–15
  court decisions on, 210–14, 234, 237
  criminal, 208–14, 284, 346
  juveniles and, 296
  plea bargaining and, 289–91

procedural, 69–71, 327, 342
substantive, 245
Duncan v. Louisiana, 210
Du Pont de Nemours (E. I.) & Company, Inc. v. Christopher, 339–42

Education
  law-related, 32-33
  for lawyers, 37–39, 56–57. *See also* Legal reasoning
  legal research in, 175–76. *See also* Legal research
  for paralegals, 35
Eighth Amendment, 209, 210, 256, 257, 284
  prisoners' rights and, 292, 294
Eminent domain, 370
Enabling acts, 308, 370
Encyclopedias (legal), 180
England/English legal tradition, 9, 14–19, 169
  American law and, 19–20, 21
  Bill of Rights, 18
  common law, 16, 18–19
  early developments, 14–16, 207
  equity and Chancery, 17–18
  fact pleadings in, 95
  judge-made law, 14–15
  judges in, 40
  juries in, 234
  lawyers and paralegals in, 35–36
  sovereign immunity, principle of, 317
  strict liability in, 168
Equal protection clause (Fourteenth Amendment), 55
Equitable estoppel, 370
Equity, 17–18, 19, **68,** 71, **370**
  civil actions in, 80
  merging with law in United States, 25
***Erie* doctrine, 87,** 90, 339, **370**
Erie Railroad Co. v. Thompkins, 87
Estate, 79, 370
  damages recoverable by, 89–90
  standing to sue, 89
Estelle v. Gamble, 293–94

Estelle v. Ruiz, 295
Estoppel, 159, 370
Estoppel by judgment, 370
Ethical standards, 42, **43,** 370
   conflict of interest, 102
   for judges, 43–44
   for law enforcement officers, 45
   for lawyers, 44, 78
   for paralegals, 44-45
European Community, strict liability in, 168
European Court of Human Rights, 299, 301
Evarts Act, 150
Evidence, 232
   during criminal discovery, 258
   documents introduced as, 125, 126
   exclusionary rule and, 210–12
   rules of, 123–24
   rules of, in Germany, 298
Evitts v. Lucey, 291
Exclusionary rule, 210–12
   exceptions to, 212
Exculpatory evidence, 258, 370
Exhaust administrative remedies, 316, 370
Ex parte Hull, 292
Expert witness, 130, 131, 136, 138, 270, **370**
   in German civil cases, 170
Ex post facto laws, 284, 370
Expropriation, 370

Fact pleading, 95, 370
Fair hearing, 310, 370
Federal Bureau of Investigation, 30, 33, 34
Federal Bureau of Prisons, 34
Federal codes, 178, 180, 182–85
Federal courts, 50, 52–56. *See also* Federal district courts; United States Supreme Court
   appellate, 53–55, 150, 151, 152
   assignment of judges in, 100
   civil law case load, 160
   district, 52–53, 150
   habeas corpus access to, 293

jurisdiction, 55-56, 85, 87
jurors, number of, 119
reporting systems for cases, 188, 189–90, 192
specialized, 317–18
Federal district courts, 52–53, 90, **370**
   case load vs. that of appeals courts, 150
Federal government, 306. *See also* Regulatory agencies
   administrative codes, 185–86
   judges in, 41, 42
   law enforcement, careers in, 33–34
Federal grand juries, 235. *See also* Grand jury
Federal Interlocutory Appeals Act, 339
Federalism, 22–23, **370**
Federal question, 370
Federal Register, 185, 186
Federal Register Act of 1935, 185
Federal Reporter, 190, 339
Federal Rules of Appellate Procedure, 151, 182
Federal Rules of Civil Procedure, 95, 96, 182
Federal Rules of Criminal Procedure, 182, 215
Federal Rules of Evidence, 124, 182
Federal Supplement, 190
Feeley, Malcolm, 286, 287–88
Felony(ies), 208, 231, 346, **370**
   plea bargaining and, 286, 287, 288
   right to counsel and, 213
   warrantless arrests and, 214
Feudal law, 12–13, 14–15, 16
Field, David Dudley, 95
Fifth Amendment, 69, 209, 210, 213, 227, 283, 284, 289
Final judgment, 150, 370–71
First Amendment, 8, 307
   prisoners' rights and, 293
First-degree murder, 258, 262, **276**–77, **371**
Fourteenth Amendment, 257, 291
   due process clause, 55, 69, 209, 211, 212, 213, 237

   equal protection clause, 55
   incorporation of Bill of Rights and, 209–10, 211, 234
Fourth Amendment, 209, 210, 284
   exclusionary rule and, 211
France, 168, 305
   administrative courts, 319–20, 321–22
   Anglo-French in English courts, 14
   influence on U.S. law, 21–22
   Revolution, influence of, 13
Franklin, Benjamin, 22
Friendly, Henry, 305
Forst, Brian, 288
Furman v. Georgia, 257

General verdict, 143
Germany, 305
   administrative courts, 319, 320, 321–22
   civil procedures in, 169–71
   criminal procedures in, 298–301
   strict liability in, 168
Gideon v. Wainwright, 80, 210, 213
Glendon, Mary Ann, 297
Good faith exception (to exclusionary rule), 212
Gordon, Michael, 297
Goss v. Lopez, 311–15
Government(s). *See also* Federal government; Regulatory agencies; States
   agencies, 71, 306–16
   defined, 4
   local, and state law, 177
   ombudsman and, 318–19
Grand jury(ies), 31, 215, 225, **234,** 254, **371**
   example of procedure, 235–37
   federal and state, 235
   Fifth Amendment on, 210, 227
Great Britain. *See* England
Greeks (ancient), 57
   and roman law, 10–11
Gregg v. Georgia, 257
Guilty plea, 248, 289, 371
   example of, 247–48

Habeas corpus petition, 257, **293, 371.** *See also* Writ of habeas corpus
Habitual Criminal Act (Kentucky), 290
Haines v. Kerner, 293
Hamilton, Alexander, 23, 24
Hammurabi, Code of, 9
Harmless error, 371
Harris v. New York, 214
Hayes, Paul, 290
Health care costs, and costs of tort system, 167–68
Hearsay rule, 124, 259, 346, **371**
Henderson v. Morgan, 291
Henry I (English king), 14
Henry II (English king), 14, 16
Hierarchy of courts. *See* Court hierarchy
Hierarchy of laws, 67, 371
Hobbes, Thomas, 5
Holding, 59, 371
Holmes, Oliver, Wendell, Jr., 5, 49, 57, 58
Hornbooks, 188
Hurtado v. California, 210

Illinois v. Krull, 212
Immigration and Naturalization Service, 34
Indictment, 216, **234,** 237, 239, 258–59, **371**
bill of, example of, 238
Inductive reasoning, 57–58
Inevitable discovery exception (to exclusionary rule), 212
Information, 234
Information process, 227, 231, **371**
Initial appearance, 216–24, **371**
Injunction, 68, 80, 82
In re Gault, 296
In re Oliver, 210
In re Winship, 296
Insanity defense, 248
Institute for Court Management, 36
Institute of Legal Executives, 36
Interlocutory appeal, 339, **371**

Internal Revenue Code, 182
Internal Revenue Service, 318
Interrogatories, 104, **106,** 260, **371**
example of, 107–8
Intestate, 79

Jackson, Robert, 38
Jail, 371
Jailhouse lawyer, 293, 371
Japan, 165, 171
Jefferson, Thomas, 7, 20, 21, 60, 61, 68
Johnson, Earl W., 30
Johnson v. Avery, 292-93
Johnson v. Zerbst, 213
Judge(s), 345. *See also*
Administrative law judge
assignment of, 100
in bench trials, 97
characteristics, 42
charge to the jury (civil trial), 142–45
charge to the jury (criminal trial), 276–78
in civil law countries, 14, 40, 169, 297
in early English courts, 14–15
in England, 40
ethical standards, 43–44
federal judiciary, 53, 54, 55
in German civil cases, 169–70
in German criminal cases, 300
pretrial conference, 112–13
selection of, 40–42
in state appellate courts, 51–52
Judge's role, 43, 371
Judgment, 145, 371
Judgment as a matter of law, 145, 371
Judgment on the pleadings, 103, 371
Judicature Act of 1873 (Great Britain), 18
Judicial Conference of the United States, 96
Judicial precedent, 14, 18, 49, 58, **372**
Judicial review, 23–24, 67, **372**
of agency action, 310, 316

Marbury v. Madison, 60–66
Judiciary Act of 1789, 52, 61, 65, 85
Juris consultants (Roman), 11
Jurisdiction, 50, 372. *See also*
Diversity jurisdiction
of federal courts, 55–56, 85, 87
general vs. limited, courts of, 51
original, 51, 61, 65–66
of U.S. Court of Appeals for the Federal Circuit, 54
of U.S. Supreme Court, 55, 65–66
Jurisprudence, 3, 372
Jury(ies), 19, 31, 43, 51, 69, 297, 348. *See also* Grand jury; Petit jury
in bifurcated trial process, 261–62, 264
civil voir dire, 117–20
in civil vs. criminal actions, 71
criminal voir dire, 264, 266
judge's charge to (civil trial), 142–45
judge's charge to (criminal trial), 276–78
in medieval England, 15–16
number of jurors on, 119, 264
preliminary instructions to, 120
Jury trial, 97, 372
absence of in civil cases in civil law countries, 169
appeals from, 152
in civil cases, number of, 161
right to, 248
suppression of defendant's past record during, 258
Justice, Department of, 34
Justinian, 7
Code of, 11, 12, 13
Juvenile justice system, 295–**96, 372**

Katko v. Briney, 349–52
Kennedy, Anthony, 264
Kent v. United States, 296
King, Martin Luther, 7
Klopfer v. North Carolina, 210, 237

Kohlberg, Lawrence, 32
Kramer, Jerome, 38

Lagoy, Stephen, 288
Langbein, John, 297
Langdell, Christopher Columbus, 38
Law, 3, 4, 327–28, **372.** *See also* Administrative law; Black letter law; Case law; Civil law; Common law; Natural law; Positive law; Roman law
   black letter and case distinguished, 56
   choice of, 88–90
   civil actions in, vs. equity, 80
   citizen attitudes toward, 30–32
   English heritage, 14–19
   function, 4–5
   hierarchy of, 67–68
   methods of changing, 6–7
   politics and, 5–6
   pre-historical developments, 8
   Roman heritage, 9–14
   rule of, 5
   study of, 29. *See also* Education; Legal reasoning
   substantive vs. procedural, 68–69
   U.S. constitutional, 19–25, 67. *See also* Constitution (U.S.)
Law enforcement/police
   arrests by, 214–16
   employment opportunities in, 33–34
   ethical standards, 45
   example of work, 204–6
   exclusionary rule and, 210–12
   Miranda warning and, 213–14
Law in a Free Society, 32
Law office administration, 36
Law-related education, 32–33, **372**
Law reviews, 180, 182
Law School Admission Test (LSAT), 36, **37, 372**
Lawyer(s), 35. *See also* Counsel; Prosecutor; Public defender
   in civil law countries, 169
   demand for, 36–37
   education, 37–39
   ethical standards, 44
   finding, 78–80
   main activities, 175
   number of and liability/litigation problem, 159–60, 165–67
   profile, 40
   specialization by, 39–40
Lawyer-client privilege, 104, 224
Lawyer fees, 78, 79, **372.** *See also* Contingency fee contract
   differences between United States and other countries, 167
   in German civil cases, 170
Lawyers Co-operative/Bancroft Whitney Publishing Companies, 182, 189
Lawyer's role, 44, 372
Leading questions, 123–24, **372**
Lee, Charles, 61
Legal actions. *See* Administrative legal action; Civil legal action; Criminal legal action
Legal assistant, 34. *See also* Paralegal
Legal executives, 36, 372
Legal profession(s), 29–45
   education and, 32–33
   ethical standards, 42–45
   judges, 40–42
   law enforcement, 33–34
   lawyers, 36–40
   paralegals and law office managers, 34–36
   size of and litigation/liability problems, 159–60
Legal research, 175–99
   administrative codes, 185–86
   common law, 186–92
   digests, 190–92
   federal codes, 180–85
   other resources, 196–99
   primary sources, 188–89
   reporters, 189–90
   secondary sources, 187–88
   shepardizing, 192–96
   state annotated codes, 177–80
   statutory law, 176–86

Legal reasoning, 56
   case method of legal training and, 58–66
   forms of, 57–58
Lesser included offense, 246, 372
Lewis, Alfred J., 176
LEXIS, 188, 199
Liability, 372
   problem, 159, 163–65
   suits vs. government officials, 317, 318
Lineup. *See* Pretrial lineup
Litigation (civil), 327
   amount in United States, 30, 159–60
   case load problem, 160–63
   in Germany, 169–71
   liability problem, 159, 163–65
   number of lawyers and, 159–60, 165–67
   torts in other countries, 165–69
Littleton, Thomas, 18
Locke, John, 23
Lockhart v. McCree, 266
Long arm statutes, 100

McDonald, William, 288
McMann v. Richardson, 291
Madison, James, 5, 22, 23, 61
Magistrates, 42, 372
Magna Carta, 16, 284
Maine v. Thiboutet, 318
Mala in se, 207, 208, **372**
Mala probibita, 207, 208, **372**
Mallory v. Hogan, 210, 213
Mandamus. *See* Writ of mandamus
Mapp v. Ohio, 210, 211, 212
Marbury, William, 61, 66
Marbury v. Madison, 60–66, 67
Marquart, James, 295
Marshall, John, 68
   decision in *Marbury v. Madison,* 60, 61, 62–65, 66, 67
Marvin v. Marvin, 352–54
Massachusetts v. Sheppard, 212
Meador, Daniel J., 51, 321
Mediation, 162, 171, **373**
Mens rea, 207, 248, 346, **373**

Merit plan, 41. *See also* Missouri Plan
Military Court of Appeals, 54–55
Military Justice Act of 1983, 54
Minimum contacts requirement for diversity jurisdiction, 87
Miranda v. Arizona, 213–14
Miranda warning, 214, 296
Misdemeanors, 51, 207, **208,** 231, 346, **373**
  plea bargaining and, 286, 287–88
Missouri Plan, 41, 373
Mitigating circumstances, 263–64, **373**
Model Code of Judicial Conduct, 43, 44
Model Rules of Professional Conduct, 44, 78
Monell v. New York City Department of Social Services, 318
Montesquieu, Baron de, 23
Motion *in limine,* 258
Murder, *See* First-degree murder; second-degree murder

Napoleon (Bonaparte), 13
National Advisory Commission on Criminal Justice Standards and Goals, 287
National Association of Legal Assistants (NALA), 35
National Center for State Courts, 30, 160, 161, 163
National Federation of Paralegal Associations (NFPA), 35
National Institute for Law Enforcement and Criminal Justice, 288
National Street Law Institute, 32
Natural law, 7, 8, 13, 23, 25, **373**
  influence on Roman law, 11–12
Negligence, 85, **88, 373.** *See also* Comparative negligence; Contributory negligence
  general elements, 81–82
  vs. products liability, 88, 89
Negotiation, 161, 162, **373**
New Jersey v. T.L.O., 212

Nix v. Williams, 212
Nolle prosequi (nol-pros), 232, 260, 298, **373**
Nolo contendere, 248, 298, **373**
Nonadversarial process, 169, 373
Not guilty by reason of insanity, 248, **373**
Not guilty plea, 248, **373**
Notice pleading, 96, 373

Obiter dicta, 59, 369
Occupational Safety and Health Administration (OSHA), 307
  example of procedure, 315–16
O'Connor, Sandra Day, 291
Office of Juvenile Justice and Delinquency Prevention, 32
Ombudsman, 305, 318–19, **373**
On point, 59, 373
Opening statements, 120, 373
  example (civil trial), 120–23
  example (criminal trial), 266-68
Ordeal, trial by, 15
Osakwe, Christopher, 297
Out-of-court settlement, 160–61, 164
Owen v. City of Independence Missouri, 318
Own recognizance, release on (ROR/OR), 217

Pain and suffering, 167, 373
Palko v. Connecticut, 209
Panama Refining Co. v. Ryan, 185
Paralegal(s), 34–36, 97, **373–74**
  ethical standards, 44–45
  in other countries, 35–36
Parens patriae, **295,** 296, **374**
Parker v. Gladden, 210
Parliament, 16, 18, 20
Parole, 301, 374
Pashigian, Peter, 36
People v. Braly, 374–48
People v. Moore, 345–46
Peremptory challenges, 118–**19, 374**

  in criminal cases, 264
  death penalty and, 266
Petit, jury(ies), 31, 234, **374**
Plaintiff, 71, 374
Plato, 10
Plea bargaining, 232, 284–91, **374**
  absence in civil law countries, 297, 298
  arguments against, 285–87
  arguments for, 287–89
  constitutional issues, 289–91
  example of, 242–43, 247
  frequency of, 286
Pleadings, 95–104, **374**
  complaint, 96–97, 98–99
  defendant's response, 102–4
  fact and notice distinguished, 95–96
  judgment on the, 103–4
  service of process, 97, 100-102
Pocunier v. Martinez, 293
Pointer v. Texas, 210
Poisoned tree doctrine, 211
Police. *See* Law enforcement
Political questions, 5, 374
Ponzanelli, Giulio, 168
Positive law, 7–8, 207, **374**
Posner, Richard A., 150
Pound, Roscoe, 19
Powell v. Alabama, 212
Powers v. Ohio, 264
Prejudicial error, 150, 153, **374**
Preliminary hearing, 225–27, 254, **374**
Preponderance of evidence standard, 71, 143
Present value, 90, 133, 138, **374**
Pretrial conferences, 110, 112–13
  settlements in, 161
pretrial diversion, 374
Pretrial lineup, 255–56, 296, **374**
Pretrial process (civil case), 95–113
  discovery, 104–10
  pleadings, 95–104
  pretrial conferences, 110, 112–13
Pretrial process (criminal case)
  court subsystem phase, 231–49

police subsystem phase, 203–6, 214-28
Prima facie case, 133, 374
Primary evidence rule. *See* Best evidence rule
Primary sources (of common law), 188–92
Prisons
  community-based programs, 295
  overcrowding, 292, 294, 295, 301
  prisoners' rights, 292–95
Private law, 374
Probable cause, 215, 227, **374**
Probate, 79, 374
Probate courts, 51
Procedural law, 53, 56, **68**–**69, 374**
  civil procedure. *See* Civil legal action
  criminal procedure. *See* Criminal legal action
  due process, 69–71
  initiating a civil action, steps in, 77–92
Products liability, 85, **88,** 163, 164, **374**
  appellate case involving, 149, 152–59
  differences between the United States and other countries, 168
  hypothetical case involving, 95–113, 117–45
  vs. negligence, 88, 89
Products Liability Act of 1978 (Tennessee), 153
Prosecution, 51. *See also* Criminal legal action
Prosecutor, 71, 215, **231, 374–75**
  during criminal trial, 266–67, 268–72, 275–76
  in Germany, 298, 300
  plea bargaining and, 285, 290–91
  role in pretrial phase of criminal case, 231–34, 235
Prosser on Torts, 188
Public defender, 224–25, 245, 285, 291, **375**

Public law, 375
Public safety exception (to exclusionary rule), 212
Pulley v. Harris, 257

Quasi-judicial powers, 310, 375
Quasi-legislative powers, 308, 375

Rape, death penalty and, 256, 257
***Ratio decedendi,* 60, 375**
Reasonable doubt. *See* Beyond a reasonable doubt standard
Recross-examination, 123
Redirect examination, 123
  example (civil trial), 127, 128–29, 131, 138
  example (criminal trial), 272
Reeve, Tapping, 38
Regulations. *See* Administrative law
Regulatory agency(ies), 307, 375
  adjudicative function, 310–16
  administrative codes, 185–86
  federal regulation, 306
  investigative function, 309–10
  judicial review of, 310, 316
  rule-making function, 305, 308–9
  state regulation, 306–7
Rehnquist, William H., 212, 266, 293
Religion, freedom of, 293, 307
Reporters, 180, 188, 189–90, 191, **375**
Request to produce, 104, **109**–**10, 375**
Res judicata, 159, 375
Restatement (Second) of Torts, 88, 149, 153, 168, 187, 188, 339
***Restatements of the Law* (ALI),** 187–88, **375**
Restrictive Trades Practice Act (Sweden), 319
Robbery, 216, 246
Robinson v. California, 210
Roman Catholic church (during Middle Ages), 13

Roman law, 8, 9–14, 299
  absorption of Greek ideas, 10–11
  early, 9–10
  during the Middle Ages, 12–13
  modern French code and, 13–14
  natural law and, 11-12
Rose v. Lundy, 293
Rule making, 308, 375
Rule of law, 5, 6, **375**
Rules of civil procedure, 375. *See also* Federal Rules of Civil Procedure
Rules of criminal procedure, 264, 375
Rules of evidence, 123–24, **375**
  in Germany, 298
Ryan v. Hofstra University, 342–45

Santobello v. New York, 287, 290
Satisfaction of judgment, 159, 375
Saxbe v. Washington Post Co., 293
Shuck, Peter H., 159, 163, 164
Search and seizure, 296. *See also* Exclusionary rule; Fourth Amendment
  exclusionary rule and, 210–12
Search warrant, 217, 375
  application for, example of, 221–22
  example of, 223
Second-degree murder, 277–78, 375
Secondary sources (of common law), 187–88, 196–97
Selective incorporation, 209–10, 375
Self-incrimination, privilege against, 104, 289
  Miranda warning and, 213–14
Senna, Joseph, 288
Sentencing/sentences
  determinate, 240, 248
  example, 239–42, 247, 248–49, 278–79
  in Germany, 300–301
  mandatory, and prison overcrowding, 292

plea bargaining and, 286–87
Sentencing grid, 240–42, 248–49, **375**
Separation of powers, 5, 6, 309
  in U.S. Constitution, 23
Service of process, 100, 102, **375**
Session laws, 176, 183, 185
Seventh Amendment, 97
Shepard's Citations, 192, 194–96, 197, 198
Siegal, Larry, 288
Sixth Amendment, 209, 210, 212–13, 237, 291
Socrates, 10
Solicitor, 35, 376
Sovereign immunity, 317, 318, **376**
Sovereignty, 22, 23, 50, **376**
Specialized federal courts, 317–18, **376**
Special verdict, 143
Specific performance, 68, 80, 82
Speech, freedom of, 293, 307
Speedy trial, 237, 376
  federal and state statutes on, 239
Speedy Trial Act, 239, 374
Stamp Act, 234
Standing to sue, 89, 376
Stand mute before the court, 248, 376
Stare decisis, 14, 58, **376**
State(s)
  agencies, 185, 306–7, 309, 316. *See also* Regulatory agencies
  annotated codes, 177–80, 181
  digests, 188, 192
  grand juries, 235
  incorporation of Bill of Rights and, 209–10
  law enforcement, careers in, 33
  reporters, 188, 189
  speedy trial statutes, 239
State courts, 50–52
  appellate, 150, 151, 152–53
  civil law case load, 160
  judges in, 40–42, 100
  jurisdiction, 85, 87–88
  number of jurors, 119
  quasi-judicial bodies, 317

right of appeal in, 150
  U.S. Supreme Court and, 55
Statutes of limitations, 89, 376
Statutory law, 67, 176, **376**
  administrative codes, 185–86
  crime in, 207–8
  federal codes, 180–85
  state annotated codes, 177–80
Stevens, John Paul, 291
Stevens, Robert, 38
Stipulation, 112, 376
Stop and frisk, 214, 376
Strickland v. Washington, 291
Strict liability, 88, 153, 168, **376**
  differences between United States and other countries, 168
Subpoena, 109, 235, **376**
Substantive law, 53, 56, **69,** 345, **376**
Summary judgment, 113, 376
Summons, 100, 376
  example of, 101
Suppression motion, 260, 376–77
Supremacy clause (U.S. Constitution), 22, 24, 67
Supreme Court Reporter (S.Ct.), 189
Survival action, 377
Sweden, ombudsman in, 305, 318-19
Syllogism, 57, 61, **377**

Terry v. Ohio, 214
Theocracy, 8
Tort(s), 69, 71, 159, **377.** *See also* Negligence; Products liability
  common, 81
  costs of system, 164–65, 167–68
  differences between United States and other countries, 165–68
  high visibility actions, 164
  as percentage of all civil suits, 163
  suggested as replacement for exclusionary rule, 211–12
Tort Claims Act of 1946, 317

Tort law, 81–82
  politicization of, 163
Tort reform, 163–64, 165, **377**
Torts, 377
Treason, 208, 377
Treatises, 188
Trial, 51
  jury and bench distinguished, 97
  speedy, 237, 239, 289
Trial (civil legal action), 117–20, 169
  closing arguments, 140–42
  examination of witnesses, 123–40
  in Germany, 169–70
  judge's charge to jury, 142–45
  jury selection, 117–20
  opening statements, 120–23
  preliminary jury instructions, 120
  rarity of, 161
  verdict and judgment of the court, 145
Trial (criminal legal action), 253, 261–79, 289
  bifurcated procedure, 257, 262
  charge to the jury, 276–78
  closing arguments, 275–78
  defense case in chief, 272–75
  opening statements, 266–68
  pretrial planning, 259–61
  prosecutor's case in chief, 268–72
  verdict and sentencing, 278–79
  voir dire, 264–66
Trial courts, 50, 345, **377**
  appellate courts and, 150, 151, 152–53, 348
  federal, 52–53
  in German criminal cases, 300
  state, 50–51
Trial docket, 369
Trop v. Dullas, 256
Turow, Scott, 38
Twelve Tables (Roman law), 9

Under color of law doctrine, 292, 377
Uniform Arbitration Act of 1955, 162

Index **389**

United Kingdom. *See* England
United States. *See also*
    Constitution (U.S.); Federal
    government
  attitudes of citizens toward law,
    30–32
  colonial period, 19–20
  common law in, 19–20, 21–22
  distinctive legal concepts, 20–21
  federalism, 22–23
  judicial review, 23–24
  litigation, amount of, 30
  separation of powers, 23
  state and federal institutions,
    24–25
United States Claims Court, 317
United States Code (U.S.C.), 182,
  308
*U.S. Code: Congressional and
  Administrative News,* 185
United States Code Annotated
  (U.S.C.A.), 182, 183, 185
United States Code Service
  (U.S.C.S.), 182, 183, 185
United States Law Week (U.S.L.W.),
  199
United States Marshal's Service, 34
United States Reports (U.S.), 189
United States Supreme Court, 52,
  54, 55, 185, 255, 306
  on administrative due process,
    311–15
  on appellate review, right to, 150
  on capital punishment, 256–57
  on criminal due process, 209,
    210–14, 234, 237, 284
  on diversity jurisdiction, 87
  Marbury v. Madison, decision
    in, 60–66
  on peremptory challenges, 264,
    266
  on plea bargaining, 289–91
  on prisoners' rights, 292–95
  reporting decisions of, 189–90,
    199
  on suits vs. government, 318

*United States Supreme Court
  Reports—Lawyers' Edition,*
  189
United States Tax Court, 317, 318,
  322
United States v. Agurs, 258
United States v. Cronic, 291
United States v. Leon, 212
United States v. Wade, 255

Vagueness, 345
Venire, 118
Venue, 260
Verdict, 143, 145, **377**
  in criminal trial, example of,
    278–79
  death sentence, example of
    form, 264, 265
  directed, 133, 138, 140
  general and special
    distinguished, 143
  unanimous vs. majority, 143, 145
Victimless crimes, 208
Victims' rights, 217, 246–47
  in civil law systems, 297
  in German criminal process,
    298
Voir dire, 117–18, **377**
  challenges, 118–20
  criminal, 262, 264, 266
**Voluntary assumption of
  known risk, 88**–89, 142, **377**

Warrant. *See* Arrest warrant;
  Search warrant
Warren, Earl, 209, 256
Washington v. Texas, 210
Weeks v. United States, 211
Western legal tradition, 8–25
  English heritage, 14–19
  Roman heritage, 9–14
  U.S. constitutional
    developments, 19–25
WESTLAW, 188, 199
West Publishing Company, 182

key number system, 188, 189,
  190, 192
West's Federal Practice Digest, 192
White, Byron, 290
Wice, Paul, 38, 42
William the Conqueror (English
  king), 14
William III (English king), 18
Witherspoon vs. Illinois, 266
Witnesses
  agencies and, 310
  during criminal discovery, 258
  direct and cross-examination
    distinguished, 123
  examination of (civil trial),
    123–40
  examination of (criminal trial),
    268–75
  expert, 130, 131, 133, 136, 138,
    270
  in German criminal cases, 300
  grand jury, 235, 236
  impeaching of, 109
  questioning of, in civil law
    countries, 169, 170
  statements, examples of, 356–
    63
Wolf v. Colorado, 210, 211
Words and Phrases, 187
**Workers' compensation laws,
  81,** 163, **377**
*World-Wide Volkswagon Corp. v.
  Woodson,* 87
Writ of certiorari, 35, 377
Writ of error, 150
**Writ of habeas corpus, 284,
  377.** *See also* Habeas corpus
  petition
Writ of mandamus, 61, 65, 66,
  68, **377**
Wrongful death action, 377
Wrongful death and survival
  statutes, 89, 377

Zeno of Citium, 7